Conte

D0497379

Introduction to

Berlin

Seemingly in a perpetual state of transformation, Berlin is an extraordinary city. For over a century, events here have either mirrored or determined what has happened in the rest of Europe, and, fifteen years after the fall of the Berlin Wall, the city is on the move again, working furiously to re-create itself as the capital of Europe's most powerful country and as an international metropolis on a level with London, Paris or New York.

No one would come to Berlin for light-hearted sightseeing: this is a profoundly scarred city. Even in its flashiest sections it can still seem half-built, many of its modern buildings – on both sides of the former divide – somehow making it look less finished and more ugly. Unlike Paris, Amsterdam or Munich, Berlin isn't a city where you can simply stroll and absorb the atmosphere. You need to plan your trips and target your points of interest, using the city's excellent transport system to cover what can be longish distances. Those points of interest are, almost without exception, sombre: the Reichstag, looming symbol of the war years; the remains of the Wall; and several museums that openly and intelligently try to make sense of twentieth-century German history.

Given the range and severity of the events Berlin endured, it's no wonder it emerged far differently from anywhere else in Germany. West Berlin's unorthodox character made it a magnet for those seeking alternative life-styles – hippies and punks, gays and lesbians, artists and musicians all flocked there. Vital to this migration were the huge subsidies pouring in from the West German government to keep that portion of the city alive, and with money available for just about everything, Berlin developed a cutting-edge arts scene and a vibrant **nightlife** that continue to this day, long after the grants have dried up. Non-Germans came too, attracted by the city's tolerance. The large numbers of Turks, Greeks and Italians, who originally came as "guest workers" in the 1960s, make Berlin Germany's most cosmopolitan city by far – a fact reflected in the excellent variety of cuisine on offer in the city's **restaurants**.

Though cut off by the Wall for thirty years, the eastern part of the city has always been Berlin's real centre, and it took only a decade or so for it to reassert itself in this role. The area east of the

▲ Route of the Wall

Brandenburg Gate, focused around Unter den Linden and the adjoining eastern district of Prenzlauer Berg, has emerged as the city's prime magnet for shopping and entertainment. Sleek chrome and glass have replaced crumbling brick, yanking these districts out of a fifty-year slumber, while Potsdamer Platz, nothing but a barren field until a few years ago, is now a bustling entertainment quarter. It's an exciting, infectious scene and, for anyone familiar with the forlorn and unkempt eastern streets of the GDR, a slightly unbelievable one. Here especially, the rapid transformation of Berlin into capital city and economic and cultural powerhouse is evident.

Nowhere in the city is more than a stone's throw from a bar, be it a corner *Kneipe* or a slick upscale café – indeed, the variety of bars and restaurants is one of the city's great strengths. Its legendary, pretty much nonstop, nightlife is another: Berlin really is a twenty-four-hour city, and you'll never be short of something to do. But beware, the **pace of change** in Berlin, particularly in the eastern part of the city, is such that new cafés and restaurants open (and close) daily and traffic is frequently re-routed around building sites; one of the upsides, however, is that the city's state museums are undergoing radical revamping.

▲ Berliner Dom

5

What to see

▼ Tiergarten

Berlin is a remarkably difficult place to get a handle on, with several main drags and no clear centre. Most visitors begin their exploration on the city's premier boulevard **Unter den Linden**, starting at the most famous landmark, the **Brandenburg Gate**, then moving over to the adjacent seat of Germany's parliament, the **Reichstag**. Unter den Linden's most important intersection is with **Friedrichstrasse**, which cuts north–south; heading south takes you down a luxury shopping avenue to what used to be **Checkpoint Charlie**. At

Berlin nicknames

Change is part of the landscape in Berlin, but one thing that doesn't seem to wane is the enthusiasm of characteristically sharp-tongued Berliners for giving **nicknames** to their architectural gems. To tour these you're best starting at the top of the tele-asparagus (*Tele-Spargel*; Fehrnsehturm), before heading west to Eric's lamp shop (*Erich's Lampenladen*; Volkspalast) prior to crossing the puppet-bridge (*Puppenbrücke*; Schloss-brücke) to pass the commode (*Die Kommode*, Alte Bibliotek) and

the statue of Old Fritz (*Der Alte Fritz*; Frederick the Great). Following Unter den Linden west you travel through the Brandenburg Gate as the French horse thief (*Französische Pferde Dieb*; Napoleon) once did before he pinched the quadriga off the top. Here on the edge of the Tiergarten park you're spoilt for choice of which way to go: south to Karajan's circus (*Karajan's Zirkus*; Philharmonic); west to the pregnant oyster (*Schwangere Auster*; Haus der Kulturen der Welt) and the gold Else (*Goldene Else*; Siegesaüle); or north to the washing machine (*Washmaschine*; Bundeskanzleramt). Perhaps it's best to simply head up Reichstag's cupola to spot all of them, along with easily recogniz-able shapes of the hollow tooth with lipstick and powder pot (*Hohler Zahn mit Lippenstift und Puderdose*; Kaiserwilhelmgedächtniskirche) and the lanky fellow (*Langer Lulatsch*; Funkturm) in the distance.

its eastern end Unter den Linden is lined by stately Neoclassical buildings and terminates on the shores of **Museum Island**, home to eastern Berlin's leading museums, but its natural extension on the other side of the island is **Karl-Liebknecht-Strasse**, which leads to a distinctively GDR-era part of the city around **Alexanderplatz**, the eastern city's main commercial and transport hub. North from here, the swathe of land of the **Scheunenviertel** was once

▲ Detail, Victory Column statue

the heart of the city's Jewish community, and has some fascinating reminders of those days, though today it's best known for the bars and nightlife centred around Oranienburger Strasse.

Back at the Brandenburg Gate a walk south along the fringes of the gigantic **Tiergarten** park takes you to the swish modern Potsdamer Platz, which is slowly reasserting its role as Berlin's Picadilly Circus or Time Square, as it was in the 1930s. Huddled beside Potsdamer Platz is the **Kulturforum**, an agglomeration of cultural institutions that includes several high-profile art museums. The western fringes of the Tiergarten park are given over to a zoo, which is also the name of the main transport hub at this end of town, on the doorstep of **Charlottenburg** and **Wilmersdorf**. A stone's throw from here is the district's most notable landmark, the rotting tusk of the **Kaiser-Wilhelm-Gedächtniskirche** (Kaiser Wilhelm Memorial Church). The **Kurfürstendamm**, an upmarket shopping boulevard,

▲ Berlin bar

The Love Parade

Drawn in by fifteen million sound systems belting out techno and lurid outdoor debauchery, well over one million loved-up ravers descend on Berlin for the annual Love Parade on the second or third Saturday of every July. The event has spawned copycat parades around the globe – including Vienna, Tel Aviv, Cape Town and Leeds – but began modestly enough in 1989 as an extravagant birthday party for local DJ Dr Motte. He played his records from a float followed down Berlin's streets by a hundred or so of his friends who chanted "Friede, Freude, Eierkuchen" ("peace, joy and pancakes"), bemusing onlookers. Later that year, the Berlin Wall fell and somehow the event captured the mood of the time, gathering unbelievable momentum in subsequent years. By 1995 attendance was up to 300,000, grid-locking city-centre streets for the entire weekend. The following year the crowd doubled and the parade around town was rerouted to end in the Tiergarten park where gyrating, pill-popping and generous amounts of no-holes-barred sexual activity of all types found a natural home. This has been the pattern ever since, with the event culminating in a four-hour set around the Sigessäule traditionally played by Dr Motte himself and finishing around midnight. From here the floats head back to a dozen or so of Berlin's clubs, where as many will dance outside as inside until dawn. The annual cancellation rumours were no more than that until 2004 when the organizers couldn't stump up the money demanded by the city for the immense clean-up operation, but, given the growing commercialism of the event, it seems likely that sponsors will step forward to foot the bill in the future: check out the latest at ⓦwww.loveparade.de.

radiates southwest from the church, while in its northwestern reaches the districts contain the museums and gardens around the baroque **Schloss Charlottenburg**, the impressive 1930s **Olympic Stadium** and **Plötzensee prison** where the Nazis executed opponents to their regime.

Schöneberg and **Kreuzberg** are the two residential districts immediately south of the centre and are home to the most vibrant nightlife in the western half of the city. The former is the smarter of the two and popular as a gay area, while Kreuzberg is grungier and traditionally a non-conformist district.

Beyond Kreuzberg's eastern fringes, and back in what used to be East Berlin, **Friedrichshain** and **Prenzlauer Berg** flank the eastern side of the city centre. Friedrichshain offers some unusual architectural leftovers from the 1950s, while the cobbled streets of Prenzlauer Berg are one of the few places in which the atmosphere of prewar Berlin has been preserved.

▲ Pergamon Museum

The Berlin week

Berlin's a twenty-four-hour city, there's no doubt about that, but some things are best done on certain days – check the calendar below to make sure you don't miss a beat.

Tuesdays *Kinotag* in many of Berlin's cinemas means cheap cinema tickets – including at the Sony Center, the main English-language cinema.

Thursdays Berlin's exceptional state museums waive admission for the last four opening hours of the day. Most museums are open until 6pm, a few until 10pm.

Fridays Join the locals as the city takes all night to unwind from the working week – until dawn in many bars and clubs.

Saturdays Forage for cult objects in the city's flea markets and get tickets to watch Hertha BSC – the city's most successful football team – play in the gloriously revamped 1936 Olympic stadium.

Sundays Hit a café for the tremendous buffet brunches that have become so popular in Berlin. Then recuperate before joining thousands of inline skaters on the city streets.

Surrounding these two districts are the city's **eastern suburbs**, typified by an endless sprawl of prewar tenements punctuated by high-rise developments and heavy industry. The airy suburbs of **Pankow** at the northern end of this belt are the most attractive, and a district you can visit en route to the former concentration camp of **Sachsenhausen**, just to the north of the city in Oranienburg. Back in town, the industrial grime and high-density living reassert themselves in **Lichtenberg** and **Marzahn**, while the area around **Köpenick** at the city's southeastern edge, with its lakes and woodland dotted with small suburban towns and villages,

offers the truest break from the city, to the extent that it's easy to forget that this area still belongs to Greater Berlin.

Though generally overlooked by visitors, the **western suburbs** encompass some of Berlin's most attractive areas. Much of the area comprises

9

woodland (the Grunewald) and lakes (the Havel), a reminder that about a third of the western part of Berlin is either forest or park. It's also where you'll find the **Dahlem museum complex** (displaying everything from German folk art to Polynesian

▼ Brandenburg Gate

huts) and the medieval town of **Spandau**. Just west of Berlin's city limits is the town of **Potsdam**, where Frederick the Great's palace and gardens of **Sanssouci** have long been a major – and deserved – tourist draw.

When to go

Lying in the heart of Europe, Berlin's climate is continental: winters are bitingly cold, summers hot. If you're hanging on for decent weather, April is the soonest you should go: any earlier and you'll need to don winter clothing, earmuffs and a decent pair of waterproof shoes; this said, the city (especially the eastern part) does have a particular poignancy when it snows. Ideally, the best time to arrive is in May; June and July can be wearingly hot, though the famed Berlin air (*Berliner Luft* – there's a song about its vitality) keeps things bearable. The weather stays good (if unpredictable) right up until October.

Climatic conditions

	Jan	Feb	Mar	Apr	May	Jun	Jul	Aug	Sep	Oct	Nov	Dec
Temperature												
Max (°F)	48	52	63	72	82	86	90	88	82	70	55	50
(°C)	9	11	17	22	28	30	32	31	28	21	13	10
Min (°F)	10	10	19	28	36	43	48	46	39	30	25	16
(°C)	-12	-12	-7	-2	2	6	9	8	4	-1	-4	-9
Precipitation												
mm	43	38	38	43	56	71	53	66	46	36	51	56
Sunshine hours	2	3	5	6	8	8	8	7	6	4	2	1

things not to miss

It's not possible to see everything that Berlin has to offer on a short trip – and we don't suggest you try. What follows is a subjective selection of the city's highlights, ranging from vibrant nightlife to local cuisine and outstanding architecture, all arranged in colour-coded categories to help you find the very best things to see, do and experience. All entries have a page reference to take you straight to the guide, where you can find out more.

01 **Sanssouci** Page **206** • An easy day out to Potsdam brings you to a series of fine palaces.

02 The Reichstag Page **56** • Perhaps Germany's most famous landmark, this muscular Neoclassical building now has a magnificent glass cupola in which you can walk for free.

03 Jewish Museum Page **147** • Visitors throng here just to see the Libeskind-designed building, but the excellent museum is worthy of its home.

05 Berliner Weisse Page **239** • Few would argue this brew is one of the world's best, but since you order it in either green or red it must be one of the most unusual.

04 Tiergarten Page **114** • The city's green lung is full of attractive lakes and wooded nooks.

06 **Clubbing** Page **249** • You can party all night every night in Berlin's bewildering array of clubs.

07 **East Side Gallery** Page **154** • The Berlin Wall was always famous for its graffiti, and now, on the longest remaining stretch, murals record its demise.

09 **Tacheles** Page **106** • A taste of Berlin artists' squatter culture is offered in this multistorey countercultural workshop.

08 **Berlinomat** Page **281** • Sample local cutting-edge fashion from several designers in this large store.

10 **The Pergamon Museum** Page **84** • You'll find the Greek Pergamon Altar, the Ishtar Gate from Babylon and a bevy of Middle Eastern antiquities in this world-class museum.

11 **Schloss Charlottenburg** Page **134** • A huge eighteenth-century royal palace with pleasant gardens sprawling behind it.

13 **Kaiser-Wilhelm Gedächtniskirche** Page **132** • The most poignant reminder of Berlin's destruction in World War II is now a major landmark.

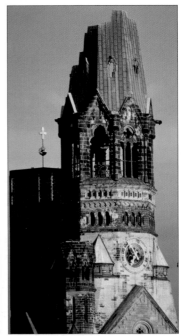

12 **Sony Center** Page **77** • Corporate architecture let loose along the former death strip of the Berlin Wall with spectacular results.

14 Hackescher Höfe Page 111 •

A series of elegant early-twentieth-century courtyards with stylish cafés and boutiques.

15 KaDeWe Page 283 • A

gigantic department store that's all class and has an excellent food court.

17 Fernsehturm Page 90

• Love or loathe its concrete curves, this Eastern-bloc relic has the best views over the city.

19 Berlin Wall Memorial

Page 104 • See the Wall as it once was in the only remaining completely preserved section.

16 The Love Parade Page 43

• The city's biggest annual event is a hedonistic worship of techno music, drugs and free-and-easy sexuality.

18 Sausages Page 230 • Berlin

snack bars serve every type of German sausage, but be sure to try currywurst, their speciality.

20 **Bars** Page **231** • Berlin's city-centre district throngs with countless hip bars.

22 **Brandenburg Gate** Page **58** • Portal to Berlin's most impressive street and witness to several historical episodes: Napoleon stole the quadriga; the Soviets placed the gate within the Berlin Wall and then the world watched as the Wall came down.

24 **Sachsenhausen** Page **173** • The former concentration camp for both the Nazis and Soviets makes for a grim but rewarding day-trip from the city.

21 **Sunday brunch** Page **233** • As hedonistic as the nightlife the night before, Sunday brunch buffets are Berlin's best hangover cure.

23 **Markets** Page **285** • Berlin loves its markets, with numerous food markets in each district and several weekly flea markets.

25 **Café Sibylle** Page **237** • A fine café on the Karl-Marx-Allee, with an interesting exhibition on the boulevard to boot.

Basics

Basics

Getting there

The quickest and generally cheapest way of reaching Berlin from most of the United Kingdom and Ireland is by air, and you would only choose another means of getting there if you had other places in between on your itinerary or needed your car there. No direct flights go to Berlin from the US and Canada or Australia and New Zealand; from all four countries you'll need to change flights at a major European hub like London or Amsterdam – in themselves both tempting stopovers.

Within a broad range of prices airfares also vary according to the **season**, with the highest being around June to August; fares drop during the "shoulder" seasons – September through October and April and May – and you'll get the best prices during the low season, November to March (excluding Christmas and New Year when prices are hiked up and seats are at a premium). Note also that flying at **weekends** ordinarily raises the price of a round-trip fare.

Apart from booking direct online (see below) you can sometimes also cut costs by going through a **specialist flight agent** – either a consolidator, who buys up blocks of tickets from the airlines and sells them at a discount, or a **discount agent**, who in addition to dealing with discounted flights may also offer special student and youth fares and a range of other travel-related services such as travel insurance, rail passes, car rentals, tours and the like. Another possibility is to see if you can arrange a **courier flight**, although you'll need a flexible schedule, and preferably be travelling alone with very little luggage. In return for shepherding a parcel through customs, you can expect to get a deeply discounted ticket. You'll probably also be restricted in the duration of your stay. If you travel a lot, discount travel clubs are another option – the annual membership fee may be worth it for benefits such as cut-price air tickets and car rental.

If Berlin is only one stop on a longer journey, you might want to consider buying a **Round-the-World** (RTW) ticket. Some travel agents can sell you an RTW ticket that will have you touching down in about a dozen cities. But since Berlin is rarely on the standard itineraries, you may find yourself travelling there from elsewhere in Europe overland. In this case, or if you are visiting Berlin as part of a longer European trip, **trains** are the most economical way to get to Berlin. You should look into an **Inter-Rail** or Eurail pass which covers train travel around most parts of Europe (see p.22).

Booking flights online

Many airlines and discount travel websites offer you the opportunity to book your tickets, hotels and holiday packages online, cutting out the costs of agents and middlemen; these are worth going for, as long as you don't mind the inflexibility of non-refundable, non-changeable deals. There are some bargains to be had on auction sites too, if you're prepared to bid keenly. Almost all airlines have their own websites, offering flight tickets that can sometimes be just as cheap, and are often more flexible.

Online booking agents and general travel sites

ⓦ **www.cheapflights.co.uk** (in UK & Ireland), ⓦ **www.cheapflights.com** (in US), ⓦ **www .cheapflights.ca** (in Canada), ⓦ **www .cheapflights.com.au** (in Australia). Flight deals, travel agents, plus links to other travel sites.
ⓦ **www.cheaptickets.com** Discount flight specialists (US only). Also at ☎ 1-888/922-8849.
ⓦ **www.ebookers.com** Efficient, easy to use flight finder, with competitive fares.
ⓦ **www.etn.nl/discount** A hub of consolidator and discount agent links, maintained by the non-profit European Travel Network.

Ⓦ **www.expedia.co.uk** (in UK), Ⓦ **www.expedia .com** (in US), Ⓦ **www.expedia.ca** (in Canada). Discount airfares, all-airline search engine and daily deals.

Ⓦ **www.flyaow.com** "Airlines of the Web" – online air travel info and reservations.

Ⓦ **www.gaytravel.com** US gay travel agent, offering accommodation, cruises, tours and more.

Ⓦ **www.geocities.com/thavery2000** An extensive list of airline websites and US toll-free numbers.

Ⓦ **www.hotwire.com** Bookings from the US only. Last-minute savings of up to forty percent on regular published fares. Travellers must be at least 18 and there are no refunds, transfers or changes allowed. Log-in required.

Ⓦ **www.kelkoo.co.uk** Useful UK-only price-comparison site, checking several sources of low-cost flights (and other goods & services) according to specific criteria.

Ⓦ **www.lastminute.com** (in UK), Ⓦ **www .lastminute.com.au** (in Australia), Ⓦ **www .lastminute.co.nz** (in New Zealand), Ⓦ **www .site59.com** (in US). Good last-minute holiday package and flight-only deals.

Ⓦ **www.opodo.co.uk** Popular and reliable source of low UK airfares. Owned by, and run in conjunction with, nine major European airlines.

Ⓦ **www.orbitz.com** Comprehensive web travel source, with the usual flight, car hire and hotel deals but also great follow-up customer service.

Ⓦ **www.priceline.co.uk** (in UK), Ⓦ **www .priceline.com** (in US). Name-your-own-price website that has deals at around forty percent off standard fares.

Ⓦ **www.skyauction.com** Bookings from the US only. Auctions tickets and travel packages to destinations worldwide.

Ⓦ **www.travelocity.co.uk** (in UK), Ⓦ **www .travelocity.com** (in US), Ⓦ **www.travelocity.ca** (in Canada), Ⓦ **www.zuji.com.au** (in Australia). Destination guides, hot fares and great deals for car rental, accommodation and lodging.

Ⓦ **www.travelshop.com.au** Australian site offering discounted flights, packages, insurance, and online bookings. Also on ☎ 1800/108 108.

From Britain and Ireland

The most convenient and usually cheapest way to get to Berlin from the UK is to fly – a journey of around ninety minutes. However, travelling by train through the Channel Tunnel is a reasonable alternative: the journey time from London to Berlin via Brussels is around twelve hours. Similarly, if travelling by car you can use the Eurotunnel services. There are also ferries to the Hook of Holland and Hamburg from Harwich, which cost significantly less but are often uncomfortable and tiring. There are no direct flights from Ireland to Berlin so your best bet is to fly via London.

By plane

Direct **scheduled flights** to Berlin are available **from London** on British Airways, easyJet, Air Berlin and Ryan Air. There are five daily BA flights from London Heathrow to Berlin Tegel; Air Berlin flies two to three times daily from London Stansted, also to Berlin Tegel; while Ryan Air flies twice a day from Stansted to Schönefeld. easyJet also flies to Schönefeld three times daily, but from Luton. The other UK airports with direct flights to Berlin include Newcastle and Bristol, with easyJet, and Manchester with both Air Berlin and BA. If you wish to fly to Berlin from other UK airports or from Ireland, using a connecting flight through London is the obvious choice, though you might consider flying via a major European hub like Frankfurt (for Lufthansa) Copenhagen (SAS) or Amsterdam (for KLM), which between them should give you a choice of around six or seven daily flights.

The published return **fare** of the national airlines can cost as much as £300, but in reality booking a week or so in advance and via online booking systems can easily halve this amount. Prices with the budget airlines – Air Berlin, easyJet and Ryanair – can start as low as £50 for a return fare, but you'll need to book at least a couple of months ahead at most times of year to secure this.

Airlines

Aer Lingus UK ☎ 0845/084 4444, Republic of Ireland ☎ 0818/365 000, Ⓦ www.aerlingus.ie.
Air Berlin UK ☎ 0870/738 8880, Ⓦ www.airberlin .com.
British Airways UK ☎ 0870/850 9850, Republic of Ireland ☎ 1800/626 747, Ⓦ www.ba.com.
easyJet UK ☎ 0871/750 0100, Ⓦ www.easyjet .com.
KLM (Royal Dutch Airlines) UK ☎ 0870/507 4074, Ⓦ www.klm.com.
Lufthansa UK ☎ 0845/773 7747, Republic of Ireland ☎ 01/844 5544, Ⓦ www.lufthansa.com.

Ryanair UK ☎0871/246 0000, Republic of Ireland ☎0818/30 30 30, ⓦwww.ryanair.com.
SAS (Scandinavian Airlines) UK ☎0845/607 2772, Republic of Ireland ☎01/844 5440, ⓦwww.scandinavian.net.

Discount travel agents

Co-op Travel Care UK ☎0870/112 0085, ⓦwww.travelcareonline.com. Flights and holidays around the world from the UK's largest independent travel agent. Non-partisan and informed advice.
Flightbookers UK ☎0870/010 7000, ⓦwww.ebookers.com, Republic of Ireland ☎01/241 5689, ⓦwww.ebookers.ie. Low fares on an extensive selection of scheduled flights and package deals.
German Travel Centre ☎020/8429 2900, ⓦwww.german-travel-uk.com. Discount flight specialist for Germany.
Go Holidays Republic of Ireland ☎01/874 4126, ⓦwww.goholidays.ie. City breaks and package tours.
Joe Walsh Tours Republic of Ireland ☎01/676 0991, ⓦwww.joewalshtours.ie. Long-established general budget fares and holidays agent.
Neenan Travel Republic of Ireland ☎01/607 9900, ⓦwww.neenantrav.ie. Specialists in European city breaks.
North South Travel ☎01245/608 291, ⓦwww.northsouthtravel.co.uk. Friendly, competitive travel agency, offering discounted fares worldwide. Profits are used to support projects in the developing world, especially the promotion of sustainable tourism.
Premier Travel UK ☎028/7126 3333, ⓦwww.premiertravel.uk.com. Discount flight specialists.
Rosetta Travel UK ☎028/9064 4996, ⓦwww.rosettatravel.com. Flight and holiday agent, specializing in deals direct from Belfast.
STA Travel UK ☎0870/160 0599, ⓦwww.statravel.co.uk. Worldwide specialists in low-cost flights, overland and holiday deals. Good discounts for students and under-26s.
Top Deck UK ☎020/7244 8000, ⓦwww.topdecktravel.co.uk. Long-established agent dealing in discount flights and tours.
Trailfinders UK ☎020/7938 3939, ⓦwww.trailfinders.com, Republic of Ireland ☎01/677 7888, ⓦwww.trailfinders.ie. One of the best-informed agents for travellers.
USIT Northern Ireland ☎028/9032 7111, ⓦwww.usitnow.com, Republic of Ireland ☎0818/200 020, ⓦwww.usit.ie. Specialists in student, youth and independent travel – flights, trains, study tours, TEFL, visas and more.
World Travel Centre Republic of Ireland ☎01/416 7007, ⓦwww.worldtravel.ie. Excellent fares to Europe and worldwide.

Package tours and specialist operators

Since the fall of the Wall, Berlin has featured as a destination for the major **package operators**, and an all-inclusive holiday can prove convenient, if a little pricey, especially for a short break. Prices start from around £200 for a two-night stay, including flights and accommodation in a centrally located hotel. Any high-street travel agent will have details of packages; those offered by the DER Travel Service (see below) are usually reasonable value.

British Airways Holidays ☎0870/240 0747, ⓦwww.baholidays.co.uk. Berlin City breaks starting at £240 (Jan–March) for two nights in a three-star hotel.
CIE Tours International Republic of Ireland ☎01/703 1888, ⓦwww.cietours.ie. Wide range of escorted tours. A ten-day visit to Berlin, Dresden and Prague costs around €1400.
Contiki UK ☎020/8290 6777, ⓦwww.contiki.co.uk. Tours and trips for 18–35-year-old party animals, with Berlin on some itineraries.
DER Travel Service ☎020/7290 1111; ⓦwww.dertravel.co.uk. The national German travel agency, offering a full range of tours, including city breaks in Berlin from £199.
Martin Randall Travel UK ☎020/8742 3355, ⓦwww.martinrandall.com. Small-group cultural tours, usually accompanied by lecturers: a four-day look at Berlin's new architecture costs around £900 including flights and accommodation; an eight-day Berlin, Potsdam, Dresden package around £1500.
Thomas Cook ☎0870/7500 512, ⓦwww.thomascook.co.uk. Long-established 24-hour travel agency for package holidays or scheduled flights.
Time Off ☎0845/733 6622. Flexible city breaks in various price ranges.
Travelscene ☎0870/7779 987, ⓦwww.travelscene.co.uk. Short breaks in all grades of accommodation.

By train

Travelling to Berlin **by train** will rarely save you any money and takes far longer than flying. By far the **fastest** and most popular train route to Berlin begins with **Eurostar** from London Waterloo to Brussels (2hr 40min), and then onto another train direct to Berlin or via Cologne, a total journey of around twelve hours. Return tickets for the complete journey begin at around £150, depending on your fare flexibility. You can get through ticketing – including the tube journey to Waterloo – from mainline stations in Britain; typical add-on prices are £30 from Edinburgh or Glasgow, £20 from Manchester and £15 from Birmingham.

Rail passes

If you plan to use the rail network to visit other regions of Germany, you might consider buying a **rail pass**. Specific **passes for travel in Germany only** can be bought before you go from the DER Travel Service and other agents – for a full list of national passes contact **German Rail**. The broadest-ranging pass for travel in Germany is the **EuroDomino Freedom pass**, which offers unlimited travel on the whole train network. Passes are valid for travel for between three and eight days within any one-month period (they do not have to be used on consecutive days). Prices range from €185 for three days to €280 for eight days (not necessarily consecutive) within a month.

InterRail passes cover eight European "zones" and are available for either 12- or 22-day or one-month periods; you must have been resident in Europe for at least six months before you can buy the pass. Two types of passes are available – one for people under 26 and a more expensive one for the over-26s. Germany is in the zone with Austria, Switzerland and Denmark. A 12-day Pass to travel in this area is £130/190 (under/over 26), a 22-day pass is £142/207; a two-zone pass valid for a month is £204/288; a three-zone pass £235/335; and an all-zone pass £265/379. The pass is available from Iarnród Éireann, International Rail and Rail Europe. InterRail passes do not include travel between Britain and the Continent, although pass holders are eligible for discounts on rail travel in Britain and Northern Ireland. The InterRail pass and the EuroDomino Freedom pass both give a discount on the cross-channel Eurostar service.

Rail contacts

Eurostar UK ☎0870/160 6600, ⓦwww.eurostar .com.
German Rail UK ☎0870/243 5363, ⓦwww .deutsche-bahn.co.uk.
Iarnród Éireann Republic of Ireland ☎01/703 1885, ⓦwww.irishrail.ie.

International Rail UK ☎0870/751 5000, ⓦwww.international-rail.com.
Rail Europe UK ☎0870/584 8848, ⓦwww .raileurope.co.uk.

By bus

Travelling to Berlin by **bus** won't bring any major savings over the cheapest air fares, and the journey will be long and uncomfortable, interrupted every three to four hours by stops at motorway service stations. The one advantage is that you can buy an open return at no extra cost.

Services are run by **Eurolines** from Victoria Coach Station in London, and are bookable through most travel agents and through any National Express agent. There are two buses daily to Berlin; the journey takes around 17 hours and costs £90 return. It's also worth looking out for special promotions, usually requiring reservation two weeks in advance, which can bring the price down to as little as £70. Starting your journey outside London can considerably add to the time, but adds little to the cost – the complete journey time from Edinburgh is 35 hours, but tickets start from £84. A **Europass** is available for Europe-wide travel for either fifteen days (£149/195 low/high season) thirty days (£209/290) and sixty days (£265/333) between London and 48 other European cities including Berlin, Hamburg and Frankfurt. There's about a twenty percent discount on these rates for those under 26.

From May to October **Busabout** operates a hop-on, hop-off service, which calls at Berlin, as well as numerous other cities in Europe. Two types of pass are available online or from STA and other affiliated tour agents (listed on the Busabout website). The Consecutive pass is available for periods of two weeks (£189/209, under/over 26) up to three months (£529/589). The Flexi Pass allows anything from seven days' travel within a month (£189/209) to twenty-four days in five months (£489/549).

Bus contacts

Anglia Lines UK ☎0870/608 8806, ⓦwww .anglia-lines.co.uk. Part of the EuroBusExpress network. Regular buses to many European cities, including Berlin.

Busabout UK ☎020/7950 1661, @www
.busabout.com.
Eurolines UK ☎08705/808 808, @www
.eurolines.co.uk, Republic of Ireland ☎01/836
6111, @www.eurolines.ie.
Gullivers International toll-free ☎00800/4855
4837, @www.gullivers.de. Part of the
EuroBusExpress network, this German operator runs
buses from London (via Eurotunnel) to Paris, Brussels,
Amsterdam, Berlin, Hamburg and Hanover, plus
connections from those cities around the continent.

By car

From the southeast of England the most
convenient way of getting across the Channel is often to take the Channel Tunnel train
shuttle – **Eurotunnel** (journey time 35–
45min). The tunnel entrance is off the M20
at Junction 11A, just outside Folkestone
(emerging outside Calais). Services operate
around the clock, 365 days a year, with four
services per hour at peak periods. Because
of the frequency of the service, you don't
have to buy a ticket in advance; just arrive
and wait to board one of the trains – promised loading time is ten minutes. Advance
tickets are available through Eurotunnel
(UK ☎0870/535 3535, @www.eurotunnel
.com) or any travel agent. Fares depend on
the time of year, time of day and length of
stay; if you travel between 10pm and 6am
outside of the summer months, you could
get a round-trip fare for just under £200 per
vehicle; the highest fares apply at weekends
and in July and August and can be as much
as £415. Bikes are carried on a specially
adapted carriage that makes the crossing
twice a day – it costs £61 for bike & person
if you are staying more than five days, £32 if
it's just a short break.

Ferries

The cheapest and most frequent (twice
daily, daytime only) Channel crossing for
Berlin is the Stena Line **ferry** from **Harwich
to the Hook of Holland** (3hr 40min).
From the Hook, the best route is Utrecht–
Amersfoort–Hengelo–Osnabrück–Hanover–
Helmstedt–Marienborn–Berlin: allow about
twelve hours to reach Berlin. Both the AA
and RAC publish route maps of the areas
you'll be passing through, which are free to
members.

The route run by **DFDS Seaways**
plies **directly** from the UK to Germany.
Once there, it's a 285-kilometre drive to
Berlin, making this the best (though more
expensive) route if you want to minimize
time actually spent driving. The service
runs from **Harwich to Hamburg** all year
round – between three and four times a
week – taking nineteen hours. From Ireland,
Irish Ferries runs services from Rosslare
to Roscoff (16hr) and Cherbourg (18hr) on
alternate days all year round. Brittany Ferries
also operates year round, once a week,
crossing from Cork to Roscoff (14hr).

Ferry prices vary according to the season
and, for motorists, the size of car. Both
crossings from Harwich cost from £120 one-
way for a car and two adults, midweek in low
season. One-way fares from Ireland begin at
around €200.

Ferry contacts

Brittany Ferries UK ☎08703/665 333,
@www.brittanyferries.co.uk; Republic of Ireland
☎021/4277 801.
DFDS Seaways UK ☎08705/333 000, @www
.dfdsseaways.co.uk.
Irish Ferries UK ☎08705/171 717, Northern
Ireland ☎00 353 818/ 300 400, Republic of Ireland
☎0818/300 400, @www.irishferries.com.
Stena Line UK ☎08704/00 67 98, Northern
Ireland ☎028/9074 7747, Republic of Ireland
☎01/204 7777, @www.stenaline.co.uk.

From North America

Despite there being numerous, generally
inexpensive, **flights** to Germany from many
major North American cities, the absence
of direct flights to Berlin means you'll need
to change planes in a major European hub.
This generally means flying via Frankfurt
using Lufthansa, London using British
Airways, Amsterdam using KLM, Paris via
Air France, or Copenhagen with SAS. For
Canadians there are no major savings to be
made by flying to the US first.

Between them the **European airlines**
above have at least daily flights from Washington, New York, Boston, Chicago, Miami,
Los Angeles and Seattle, while **US airlines**
– particularly American, Delta and United
– also have direct flights across the Atlantic
from these and many other major US cities.
Partnerships between the latter and former

mean that you may well not start and finish your trip with the same airline, although the ticket may come from either one.

The lowest discounted **scheduled fares** you're likely to get in low/high season flying midweek to Berlin is US$385/1004 from New York, Boston or Washington; US$430/1240 from Chicago; US$670/1430 from Los Angeles or Seattle; US$770/1430 from San Francisco. Canadians have fewer direct-flight options than Americans. The widest selections are out of Toronto and Montreal, with low/high season fares to Berlin from around CDN$850/$1270; from Vancouver expect to pay from CDN$1100/1410.

Airline contacts

Air Canada ☎1-888/247-2262, Ⓦwww
.aircanada.com.
Air France US ☎1-800/237-2747, Canada
☎1-800/667-2747, Ⓦwww.airfrance.com.
American Airlines ☎1-800/433-7300,
Ⓦwww.aa.com.
British Airways ☎1-800/AIRWAYS,
Ⓦwww.ba.com.
Continental Airlines ☎1-800/231-0856,
Ⓦwww.continental.com.
Delta ☎1-800/241-4141, Ⓦwww.delta.com.
KLM (Royal Dutch Airlines) See Northwest/KLM.
Lufthansa US ☎1-800/645-3880, Canada
☎1-800/563-5954, Ⓦwww.lufthansa.com.
Northwest/KLM ☎1-800/447-4747,
Ⓦwww.nwa.com, Ⓦwww.klm.com.
SAS (Scandinavian Airlines) ☎1-800/221-
2350, Ⓦwww.scandinavian.net.
United Airlines ☎1-800/538-2929,
Ⓦwww.united.com.
US Airways ☎1-800/622-1015,
Ⓦwww.usair.com.
Swiss ☎1-877/FLY-SWISS, Ⓦwww.swiss.com.

Courier flights from the US or Canada

Air Courier Association ☎1-800/282-1202,
Ⓦwww.aircourier.org. Courier flight broker.
Membership (US$35 for a year) also entitles you
to twenty percent discount on travel insurance and
name-your-own-price non-courier flights.
**International Association of Air Travel
Couriers** ☎308/632-3273, Ⓦwww.courier.org.
Courier flight broker. One year's membership costs
US$45 in the US or Canada (US$50 elsewhere).

Travel agents

Air Brokers International ☎1-800/883-3273,
Ⓦwww.airbrokers.com. Consolidator and specialist
in Round-the-World and Circle Pacific tickets.
Airtech ☎212/219-7000, Ⓦwww.airtech.com.
Standby seat broker; also deals in consolidator fares.
Airtreks ☎1-877/AIRTREKS, Ⓦwww.airtreks
.com. Round the World and Circle Pacific tickets. The
website features an interactive database that lets you
build and price your own itinerary.
Educational Travel Center ☎1-800/747-5551
or 608/256-5551, Ⓦwww.edtrav.com. Low-cost
fares worldwide, student/youth discount offers, and
Eurail passes, car rental and tours.
Flightcentre US ☎1-866/WORLD-51, Ⓦwww
.flightcentre.us, Canada ☎1-888/WORLD-55,
Ⓦwww.flightcentre.ca. Rock-bottom fares
worldwide.
New Frontiers US ☎1-800/677-0720, Ⓦwww
.newfrontiers.com. Discount firm, specializing in
travel from the US to Europe, with hotels, package
deals and especially good offers to France.
STA Travel US ☎1-800/329-9537, Canada
☎1-888/427-5639, Ⓦwww.statravel.com.
Worldwide specialists in independent travel; also
student IDs, travel insurance, car rental, rail passes,
and more.
Student Flights ☎1-800/255-8000 or 480/951-
1177, Ⓦwww.isecard.com. Student/youth fares,
plus student IDs and European rail and bus passes.
TFI Tours ☎1-800/745-8000 or 212/736-1140,
Ⓦwww.lowestairprice.com. Well-established
consolidator with a wide variety of global fares.
Travel Avenue ☎1-800/333-3335, Ⓦwww
.travelavenue.com. Full-service travel agent that
offers discounts in the form of rebates.
Travel Cuts US ☎1-800/592-CUTS, Canada
☎1-888/246-9762, Ⓦwww.travelcuts.com.
Popular, long-established student-travel organization,
with worldwide offers.
Travelers Advantage ☎1-877/259-2691,
Ⓦwww.travelersadvantage.com. Discount travel
club, with cash-back deals and discounted car rental.
Membership required ($1 for 3 months' trial).
Worldtek Travel ☎1-800/243-1723, Ⓦwww
.worldtek.com. Discount travel agency for worldwide
travel.

Tour operators in North America

Most **package holidays** combine Berlin with other German and European cities, and if you want something based in Berlin alone, you need to hunt around. A good starting point for further information on packages is the **German National Tourist Office** (DER, and, of course, your local travel agent.

Brendan Tours ☎818/786-9696 or 1-800/421-8446; ⊚www.brendanvacations.com. Eleven days in Berlin, Warsaw and Prague for around US$1,500.

Contiki ☎1-888/CONTIKI, ⊚www.contiki.com. 18- to 35-year-olds-only tour operator.

Cosmos ☎1-800/276-1241, ⊚www .cosmosvacations.com. Planned vacation packages with an independent focus.

Cross-Culture ☎1-800/491-1148 or 413/256-6303, ⊚www.crosscultureinc.com. Small-group cultural tours.

Delta Vacations ☎1-800/654-6559 ⊚www .deltavacations.com. Organizes package deals to Berlin.

DER Tours ☎1-888/337-7350 ⊚www.dertravel .com. American branch of the German national travel agency, offering tours, accommodation and rail passes.

Trafalgar Tours ☎1-800/854-0103; ⊚www .trafalgartours.com. Several bus tours take in Berlin: from 13 days for US$830.

Travel Bound ☎1-800/456-8656, ⊚www .booktravelbound.com. One of few agents to offer Berlin-only packages from around US$650 for six nights, including airfare from New York.

Vantage Travel ☎1-800/322-6677; ⊚www .vantagetravel.com. Group travel for seniors. River cruises and packages that include Berlin as part of a multi-city itinerary.

From Australia and New Zealand

There are **no direct flights** to Berlin from Australia or New Zealand; most airlines use Frankfurt or London as their European gateway. All involve either a transfer or overnight stop en route in the airline's hub city: flying times are around 24 hours via Asia and thirty hours via the US. If you're not pushed for time, stopovers are also a good way to see places along the way.

Regular return airfares are seasonally adjusted – low season is from mid-January to the end of February and October to November; high season is mid-May to August and December to January; the remainder of the year is shoulder season. Flights to Europe are generally cheaper via Asia than the US, and typical economy fares from Australia in low season start at around A$2100, in high season at A$2600.

Low season scheduled fares from Auckland start at around NZ$2300, rising to NZ$2900 upwards in the high season.

Airline contacts

Air France Australia ☎1300/361 400, New Zealand ☎09/308 3352, ⊚www.airfrance.com.

Air New Zealand Australia ☎13 24 76, ⊚www .airnz.com.au, New Zealand ☎0800/737 000, ⊚www.airnz.co.nz.

British Airways Australia ☎1300/767 177, New Zealand ☎0800/274 847 or 09/356 8690, ⊚www .britishairways.com.

Cathay Pacific Australia ☎13 17 47, New Zealand ☎0508/800 454 or 09/379 0861, ⊚www .cathaypacific.com.

Garuda Indonesia Australia ☎1300/365 330 or 02/9334 9944, New Zealand ☎09/366 1862, ⊚www.garuda-indonesia.com.

JAL (Japan Airlines) Australia ☎02/9272 1111, New Zealand ☎09/379 9906, ⊚www.jal.com.

KLM Australia ☎1300/303 747, New Zealand ☎09/309 1782, ⊚www.klm.com.

LOT Polish Airlines Australia ☎02/9244 2466, New Zealand ☎09/308 3369, ⊚www.lot.com.

Lufthansa Australia ☎1300/655 727, New Zealand ☎0800/945 220, ⊚www.lufthansa.com.

Malaysia Airlines Australia ☎13 26 27, New Zealand ☎0800/777 747, ⊚www.malaysia -airlines.com.

Malev Hungarian Airlines Australia ☎02/9244 2111, New Zealand ☎09/379 4455, ⊚www .malev.hu.

Qantas Australia ☎13 13 13, New Zealand ☎0800/808 767 or 09/357 8900, ⊚www .qantas.com.

Singapore Airlines Australia ☎13 10 11, New Zealand ☎0800/808 909, ⊚www .singaporeair.com.

SriLankan Airlines Australia ☎02/9244 2234, New Zealand ☎09/308 3353, ⊚www.srilankan.aero.

Thai Airways Australia ☎1300/651 960, New Zealand ☎09/377 3886, ⊚www.thaiair.com.

United Airlines Australia ☎13 17 77, ⊚www.united.com.

Travel agents

Flight Centre Australia ☎13 31 33, ⊚www .flightcentre.com.au, New Zealand ☎0800 243 544, ⊚www.flightcentre.co.nz. Rock-bottom fares worldwide.

Holiday Shoppe New Zealand ☎0800/808 480, ⊚www.holidayshoppe.co.nz. Great deals on flights, hotels and holidays.

OTC Australia ☎ 1300/855 118, ⓦ www.otctravel .com.au. Offers a range on holidays or flights and hotels only, with some good deals.
Silke's Travel Australia ☎ 1800 807 860, or 02/8347 2000, ⓦ www.silkes.com.au. Gay and lesbian specialist travel agent.
STA Travel Australia ☎ 1300/733 035, New Zealand ☎ 0508/782 872, ⓦ www.statravel.com. Worldwide specialists in low-cost flights, overland and holiday deals. Good discounts for students and under-26s.

Student Uni Travel Australia ☎ 02/9232 8444, ⓦ www.sut.com.au, New Zealand ☎ 09/379 4224, ⓦ www.sut.co.nz. Great deals for students.
Trailfinders Australia ☎ 02/9247 7666, ⓦ www .trailfinders.com.au. One of the best-informed and most efficient agents for independent travellers.
travel.com.au and **travel.co.nz** Australia ☎ 1300/130 482 or 02/9249 5444, ⓦ www.travel .com.au, New Zealand ☎ 0800/468 332, ⓦ www .travel.co.nz. Comprehensive online travel company, with discounted fares.

Red tape and visas

British and other EU nationals can enter Germany on a valid passport or national identity card for an indefinite period.

US, Canadian, Australian and New Zealand passport holders do not need a visa to enter Germany, and are allowed a stay of ninety days within any one year. However, you're strongly advised, if you know your stay will be longer than this, to apply for an extension visa from your local German embassy before you go. In order to extend a stay once in the country all visitors should contact the Ausländeramt (Alien Authorities) in the nearest large town: addresses are in the phone books. For more information on this complex process and finding a job see "Staying On", p.47. Visa requirements vary for nationals of other countries; contact your local German embassy or consulate for information. For details of where to find your own embassy or consulate when in Berlin, see "Directory" on p.287.

German embassies abroad

Australia 119 Empire Circuit, Yarralumla, Canberra 2600 ☎ 02/6270 1911; ⓦ www .german-embassy.org.au.
Britain 23 Belgrave Square, London SW1X 8PZ ☎ 020/7824 1300; ⓦ www.german-embassy.org.uk.

Canada 1 Waverley St, Ottawa, Ontario K2P 0T8 ☎ 613/232-1101; ⓦ www .germanembassyottawa.org.
Ireland 31 Trimelston Ave, Booterstown, Blackrock, Co Dublin ☎ 01/269 3011; ⓦ www.germany.ie.
New Zealand 90–92 Hobson St, Wellington ☎ 04/736 063. ⓦ www .deutschebotschaftwellington.co.nz.
US 4645 Reservoir Rd NW, Washington, DC 20007-1998 ☎ 202/298-4393; ⓦ www .germany-info.org.

Customs

Within the EU, **EU nationals** travelling across international borders don't have to make a declaration to Customs at their place of entry, and can effectively carry as much in the way of **duty-paid** goods as they want (as long as they're for personal use). Standard EU duty-free restrictions apply for those arriving from outside the EU. These include: 200 cigarettes (250g of tobacco, or fifty cigars), one litre of spirits and two litres of wine.

Health

As a member of the European Union, Germany has free reciprocal health agreements with other member states. To take advantage, British and Northern Ireland citizens will need form E111 (stamped), available over the counter from most post offices, which entitles you to free treatment within Germany's public healthcare system; other EU nationalities need comparable documentation. Without this form you'll have to pay in full for all medical treatment, which is expensive – currently €20 for a visit to the doctor. Non-EU residents will need to insure themselves against all eventualities, including medical costs, and are strongly advised to take out some form of travel insurance (see below). No vaccinations are needed for Berlin or Germany.

For minor ailments you'll find a local **doctor** under *Ärtze* in the Yellow Pages – surgeries don't have standard hours, but generally operate a walk-in clinic for three or four days of the week. Doctors are likely to be able to speak English, but if you want to be certain, your embassy (see "Directory", p.287) will provide a list of English-speaking ones. For an emergency doctor, call ☎030/31 00 31; for an emergency dentist, ☎030/89 00 43 33. In the event of an **emergency**, phone ☎110 for the police, who will call an ambulance (*Krankenwagen*) for you, or go straight to the casualty unit of one of the major hospitals (there's a list in the "Directory", p.287).

To get a prescription filled, go to a **pharmacy** (*Apotheke*), signalled by an illuminated green cross. Pharmacists are well trained and often speak English. Outside normal hours (usually 8.30am–6.30pm), a notice on the door of any *Apotheke* indicates the nearest one open, meaning there's a round-the-clock service. Alternatively, call ☎030/31 00 31 for the same information. You'll be served through a small hatch in the door, so don't be put off by the shop's closed appearance.

Insurance

Even though EU healthcare privileges apply in Germany, you'd do well to take out an insurance policy before travelling to cover against theft, loss and illness or injury. Before paying for a new policy, however, it's worth checking whether you are already covered: some all-risks home insurance policies may cover your possessions when overseas, and many private medical schemes include cover when abroad. In Canada, provincial health plans usually provide partial cover for medical mishaps overseas, while holders of official student/teacher/youth cards in Canada and the US are entitled to meagre accident coverage and hospital in-patient benefits. Students will often find that their student health coverage extends during the vacations and for one term beyond the date of last enrolment.

After checking out the possibilities above, you might want to contact a specialist travel insurance company, or consider the travel insurance deal we offer (see box on p.28). A typicaltravel insurance policy usually provides cover for the loss of baggage,

Rough Guides travel insurance

Rough Guides has teamed up with Columbus Direct to offer you travel insurance that can be tailored to suit your needs.

Readers can choose from many different travel insurance products, including a low-cost backpacker option for long stays; a short break option for city getaways; a typical holiday package option; and many others. There are also annual multi-trip policies for those who travel regularly, with variable levels of cover available. Different sports and activities (trekking, skiing, etc) can be covered if required on most policies.

Rough Guides travel insurance is available to the residents of 36 different countries with different language options to choose from via our website – ⓦwww .roughguides.com/insurance – where you can also purchase the insurance.

Alternatively, UK residents should call ☎0800 083 9507; US citizens should call ☎1-800 749-4922; Australians should call ☎1 300 669 999. All other nationalities should call ☎+44 870 890 2843.

tickets and – up to a certain limit – cash or cheques, as well as cancellation or curtailment of your journey. Many policies can be chopped and changed to exclude coverage you don't need – for example, sickness and accident benefits can often be excluded or included at will. If you do take medical coverage, ascertain whether benefits will be paid as treatment proceeds or only after you return home, and if there is a 24-hour medical emergency number. When securing baggage cover, make sure that the per-article limit – typically under £500/$750 and sometimes as little as £250/$400 – will cover your most valuable possession. If you need to make a claim, you should keep receipts for medicines and medical treatment, and in the event you have anything stolen, you must obtain an official statement from the police (an *Anzeige*).

Information, maps and websites

Before you set off for Berlin, it's worth contacting the German National Tourist Office, which has a lot of useful information on accommodation, what's on in town and a selection of glossy brochures. There's a wealth of resources on the Internet too, providing details, often in English, on everything from Berlin's history to its hippest nightspots – we've given a selection on p.30.

German National Tourist Offices

Australia c/o German-Australian Chamber of Industry and Commerce, PO Box 1461, Sydney NSW 2001 ☎02/8296 0488, ⓦwww.germany.org.au.
Canada 480 University Ave, Suite 1410, Toronto, Ontario M5G 102 ☎416/968 1685.
UK PO Box 2695 London W1A 3TN ☎020/7317 0908 ⓦwww.germany-tourism.de.

US 122 E 42nd St, New York, NY 10168 New York, NY 10017 ☎212/661-7200 ⓦwww .cometogermany.com.

Information

Once in the city, the **tourist office**, Berlin Tourismus Marketing (ⓦwww.berlin-tourist -information.de), can supply a wider selection of bumph than the national offices, including comprehensive listings of the higher-brow cultural events, and help with accommodation (see "Accommodation", p.221). They have several offices, but the largest, and the only one with an accommodation-booking facility, is the **Europa Center** office. BTM publishes a bilingual events magazine, *Berlin: Das Magazin*, three times a year, which details most of the mainstream cultural happenings in the city. In addition, they produce a very handy free map and a couple of brochures detailing hotels and some of the more expensive shopping and eating alternatives. All of the tourist offices feature racks of leaflets and flyers from various places and productions around town, a good way to get a quick feel for what's worthwhile.

For travel information and bookings, as well as general tips and advice, there's also the helpful **EurAide** office in Zoo Station (inside behind the Reisezentrum; Mon–Sat 8.30–noon & 1–4.30pm; ⊛www.euraide .de), set up specifically for English-speaking travellers. The office has a wealth of information and knowledgeable staff and serves as something of an oasis. Additionally, Berlin has a couple of **cultural centres**: the British Council, at Hackescher Markt 1, Mitte (Mon– Fri 11am–6.30pm, Sat 10am–4pm; ☎030/31 10 99 10; ⊛www.britishcouncil.de), has a swank information centre with magazines, books, videos, and free Internet access.

Berlin has two essential **listings magazines** – *Tip* (⊛www.tip-berlin.de) and *Zitty* (⊛www.zitty.de) – which come out on alternate weeks. *Zitty* is marginally the better of the two, with day-by-day details of gigs, concerts, events, TV and radio, theatre and film, alongside intelligent articles on politics, style and the Berlin in-crowd, and useful classified ads. Reading copies of these can be found in any bar. A third magazine, also with a good deal of listings information and possibly more useful if you don't speak any German, is the monthly English-language *ExBerliner* (⊛www.exberliner.de), which largely caters to Berlin's expat community.

Tourist offices in Berlin

The BTM runs three tourist information centres and staffs a call centre (Mon–Fri 8am–7pm, Sat & Sun 9am–6pm ☎030/25 00 25) which can provide general information as well as accommodation bookings.
Brandenburg Gate Pariser Platz (south wing; daily 10am–6pm; S-Bahn Unter den Linden).
Europa Center Budapester Str 45 (Mon–Sat 10am–7pm, Sun 10am–6pm; U- & S-Bahn Zoologischer Garten).
Fehrnsehturm Alexanderplatz (TV tower; daily 10am–6pm; U- & S-Bahn Alexanderplatz).

Maps

Having a **map** is essential for getting around Berlin; the city is full of little side streets, its long-running boulevards tend to change names every couple of blocks, and Berliners are notorious for giving the wrong directions. Your best bet is the companion edition to this book: the *Rough Guide Map: Berlin*, produced on waterproof paper, with visitor needs in mind and with the majority of the listings in this book conveniently marked. A more comprehensive map is the convenient and ingeniously folded *Falk Plan*, which contains an excellent gazetteer and enlarged plans of the city centre. It also includes a map of the U- & S-Bahn system and an index of every street in Berlin and Potsdam. It's available at most bookstores and newsagents. Those looking for complete treatment of the public transport system should pick the *BVG & S-Bahn Berlin Atlas*, which has complete listings and timetables for the U- and S-Bahn system, and bus, tram and ferry routes. It's available at the larger U-Bahn and S-Bahn stations.

Map outlets

In the UK and Ireland

Blackwell's Map Centre 50 Broad St, Oxford OX1 3BQ ☎01865/793 550, ⊛maps.blackwell .co.uk. Branches in Bristol, Cambridge, Cardiff, Leeds, Liverpool, Newcastle, Reading and Sheffield.
The Map Shop 30a Belvoir St, Leicester LE1 6QH ☎0116/247 1400, ⊛www.mapshopleicester .co.uk.
National Map Centre 22–24 Caxton St, London SW1H 0QU ☎020/7222 2466, ⊛www.mapsnmc .co.uk.
National Map Centre Ireland 34 Aungier St, Dublin ☎01/476 0471, ⊛www.mapcentre.ie.

Stanfords 12–14 Long Acre, London WC2E 9LP ⓣ020/7836 1321, ⓦwww.stanfords.co.uk. Also at 39 Spring Gardens, Manchester ⓣ0161/831 0250, and 29 Corn St, Bristol ⓣ0117/929 9966. One of the best travel bookshops in the world, with a global catalogue, expert knowledge and worldwide mail order.

The Travel Bookshop 13–15 Blenheim Crescent, London W11 2EE ⓣ020/7229 5260, ⓦwww .thetravelbookshop.co.uk.

Traveller 55 Grey St, Newcastle-upon-Tyne NE1 6EF ⓣ0191/261 5622, ⓦwww.newtraveller.com.

In the US and Canada

110 North Latitude US ⓣ336/369-4171, ⓦwww.110nlatitude.com.

Book Passage 51 Tamal Vista Blvd, Corte Madera, CA 94925 and in the historic San Francisco Ferry Building ⓣ1-800/999-7909 or ⓣ415/927-0960, ⓦwww.bookpassage.com.

Distant Lands 56 S Raymond Ave, Pasadena, CA 91105 ⓣ1-800/310-3220, ⓦwww.distantlands .com.

Globe Corner Bookstore 28 Church St, Cambridge, MA 02138 ⓣ1-800/358-6013, ⓦwww.globecorner.com.

Longitude Books 115 W 30th St #1206, New York, NY 10001 ⓣ1-800/342-2164, ⓦwww .longitudebooks.com.

Map Town 400 5 Ave SW #100, Calgary, AB, T2P 0L6 ⓣ1-877/921-6277 or ⓣ403/266-2241, ⓦwww.maptown.com.

Travel Bug Bookstore 3065 W Broadway, Vancouver, BC, V6K 2G9 ⓣ604/737-1122, ⓦwww.travelbugbooks.ca.

World of Maps 1235 Wellington St, Ottawa, ON, K1Y 3A3 ⓣ1-800/214-8524 or ⓣ613/724-6776, ⓦwww.worldofmaps.com.

In Australia and New Zealand

Map Centre ⓦwww.mapcentre.co.nz.

Map Shop (Australia) 6–10 Peel St, Adelaide ⓣ08/8231 2033, ⓦwww.mapshop.net.au.

Map World (Australia) 371 Pitt St, Sydney ⓣ02/9261 3601, ⓦwww.mapworld.net.au. Also at 900 Hay St, Perth ⓣ08/9322 5733, Jolimont Centre, Canberra ⓣ02/6230 4097 and 1981 Logan Road, Brisbane ⓣ07/3349 6633.

Map World (New Zealand) 173 Gloucester St, Christchurch ⓣ0800/627 967, ⓦwww.mapworld .co.nz.

Mapland (Australia) 372 Little Bourke St, Melbourne ⓣ03/9670 4383, ⓦwww.mapland .com.au.

Useful websites

ⓦ **www.Berlin.de** The city's official site, with loads of general information, plus the latest events.

ⓦ **www.Berlin-online.de** An excellent, all-purpose source for news, business, politics, entertainment, restaurants, listings and the like.

ⓦ **www.gotoberlin.de** General travel guide geared towards young people.

ⓦ **www.dailysoft.com/berlinwall** Illustrated history of, and facts about, the Berlin Wall.

ⓦ **www.welt.de/English** English-language articles from *Die Welt* newspaper, packed with Berlin news and culture.

ⓦ **www.berlin.world-guides.com** Online travel guide with lots of relevant advertising links.

Arrival

The major points of arrival in Berlin all lie within easy reach of the city centre by public transport. The most distant of the city's three **airports** is only about 35 minutes away by S-Bahn, and the main stations for those arriving by **train** – Bahnhof Zoologischer Garten, or Zoo Station – lie at the heart of Berlin's West End and at the western hub of the city's U- and S-Bahn network. Using this, you can reach just about anywhere in the city.

By air

Without a single large airport, Berlin's air traffic is shared between three small international air-

ports (ⓦwww.berlin-airport.de). **Tegel airport**, 7km northwest of the city centre, remains the city's largest, though **Schönefeld airport**, on the southeast side of the city, is fast catching up and is to be transformed into one large Berlin-Brandenburg airport which should serve the region's needs. In contrast, **Tempelhof airport** is fast contracting, with only a skeletal number of air services still arriving there and its closure date imminent, though, at the time of writing, uncertain. If you intend to travel into town using public transport, and expect to use public transport regularly throughout your stay see p.33 for details of the Welcome or City Tour Cards which will get you in, out and around town cheaply.

Tegel

Most scheduled and charter flights still arrive at the refreshingly small and manageable **Tegel Airport**, where you'll find currency exchange facilities, left luggage, and several car rental companies.

From Tegel, several buses head into different parts of the city. The TXL **JetExpressBus** (daily: 5am–11pm; every 15–20 minutes heads to Unter den Linden (25 minutes) and Alexanderplatz (35 minutes). **Bus X9** (daily: 5am–11.30pm every 5–10 minutes from 4.50am to 11.30pm) goes to Zoo Bahnhof (20 minutes). **Bus #109** heads to S-Bahn station Charlottenburg and #**128** to U-Bahn station Osloer Strasse. Single €2 tickets can be bought from machines outside or from the driver, and are valid for two hours. All tickets are valid for transfers onto other buses and U- and S-Bahn trains. **Taxis** cover the distance in half the time (depending on the traffic) and cost €15–20.

Schönefeld

Berlin's second airport, **Schönefeld**, lies just beyond the southeastern edge of the city and mostly serves budget flights and holiday charters. A shuttle brings you to the nearby S-Bahn and railway station. An Airport Express **train** from here reaches the city centre in 30 minutes, and the **S-Bahn** takes about 40 minutes. A **taxi** into the town centre from Schönefeld costs around €30.

Tempelhof

Tempelhof, the closest airport to the city centre, is to close in 2005, though some continue

to lobby to keep it open. From the forecourt, **bus** #119 links the airport with the Europa Center. A few minutes' walk west is Platz der Luftbrücke U-Bahn station, from where trains on line #6 take under ten minutes to reach Bahnhof Friedrichstrasse in the city centre (or change at Stadtmitte for Zoo Station). A taxi to Friedrichstrasse or Zoo Station would cost about €10, and probably take longer.

By train

Trains from European destinations generally stop at both **Zoo Station** and **Ostbahnhof** (many trains from the west also stop at Wannsee and Spandau stations). Where you alight depends on where you're staying – if your accommodation is pre-booked, check before arrival. If you have not yet arranged anything, it's probably best to get off at Zoo Station, which is handily located for the city's main tourist office, and has excellent **U- and S-Bahn links** to all parts of the city. Both principal stations have exchange offices and ATMs, lockers and left luggage facilities (see "Directory", p.288), plus the extremely helpful **EurAide office** (see p.29). A new major terminus, Lehrterbahnhof, close to the Reichstag and Scheuenviertel, is currently under construction, which, upon completion in 2006, will be Berlin's new rail hub for all train traffic, superseding Zoo Station, and will include direct airport connections. Note that some tickets into Berlin include use of zones A and B of the city's public transport system to finish your journey: check with the conductor or ticket office.

By bus

Most international **buses** and those from other German cities stop at the **Zentraler Omnibus Bahnhof** or **ZOB** (central bus station), Masurenallee, Charlottenburg, west of the centre, near the Funkturm; regular #149 buses or U-Bahn line #2 from Kaiserdamm station link it to the Ku'damm area, a journey of about fifteen minutes. Alternatively, a few minutes' walk to the Westkreuz S-Bahn station will get you there even faster. The bus station is a poor introduction to the city, shopworn and uninviting, but you'll find at least an information booth, a taxi stand, and a couple of snack places.

By car

Getting into Berlin **by car** is relatively easy: Germany's famed autobahns (*Autobahnen*) take you quite close to the heart of the city. It may, however, be a long trip – the autobahns are very congested and delays are the norm. From the south you're most likely to approach on autobahn #9, which will turn into #10 (the ring road around Berlin), from which you turn off onto #115, a highway that eases you directly into Kaiserdamm and the west side of the city, just fifteen minutes from Zoo Station. From the west you'll approach on autobahn #2, but the route once you hit the ring road is the same. Drivers coming from the Hamburg area will approach from the north on #24, which also turns into #10, but this time you turn off on the #111 road. Street **parking** can be tough in the city, but there are lots of spaces in the neighbourhood around Kurfürstendamm. Parking facilities are much scarcer on the eastern side of the city. However, almost all the larger hotels have garages.

City transport

Though Berlin ran two separate systems for forty years during its division, today's **public transport network** is well integrated, efficient and inexpensive. The cornerstone of the system is the web of fast suburban and underground trains, which are supplemented on the streets by buses and trams. All are run by the BVG, whose network looks complicated at first glance but quickly becomes easy to navigate if you bear in mind the number of the service you need and the end station of the line you want. Once onboard any service illuminated signs and announcements ensure it's easy to find the right stop. Ticket prices are fair and available from machines at stations, on the trams, or from the bus driver – but be sure to validate them by punching the ticket at the yellow machines when you travel; failure to do so will result with fines at spot checks.

Public transport

The mainstay of the transport system is the **U-Bahn** (Ⓦ www.bvg.de), which is clean, punctual and rarely overcrowded. Running both under and over ground, it covers much of the centre and stretches into the suburbs: trains run from 4am to around 12.30am, and all night on Friday and Saturday. From Friday to Sunday, U-Bahn lines # 2, 5, 6, 7, 8, 9 and 15 run every 15 minutes the night through, as does the **S-Bahn** system (Ⓦ www.s-bahn-berlin.de). This is a separate network of suburban trains, which runs largely overground and is better for covering long distances fast – say for heading out to the Wannsee lakes or Potsdam.

You never seem to have to wait long for a **bus** in the city: timetables at the stops are uncannily accurate, and the city network covers most of the gaps in the U-Bahn system, with buses converging on Zoo Station and Alexanderplatz. Buses #100 and #200, which run between the two, are good for sightseeing purposes. **Night buses** mostly run every half hour and routes often differ from daytime ones; maps of the night bus routes can be picked up in most U-Bahn ticket booths. Berlin's quiet and comfortable **trams** are found for the most part in the eastern section of the city, where the network has survived from prewar days. Some buses and trams are termed **Metro-Bus** or **MetroTram** and their numbers are preceded by the letter M: these are services that tie in closely with the U- and S-Bahn systems, running frequently whenever they do and effectively closing any gaps in their coverage.

For **more information** about Berlin's public transport system, call or check their thorough website (☎194 49, ⓦwww.bvg.de) which has complete listings and timetables for the U- and S-Bahn systems, plus bus, tram and ferry routes. Most U-Bahn stations also provide simple free maps – a larger-scale U- and S-Bahn map than the one in this guide – ask at the kiosk on the platform. A complete guide to the services is offered by the *BVG & S-Bahn Berlin Atlas*, which can be bought from the transport information offices at Zoo Station, Friedrichstrasse or Alexanderplatz.

Tickets

All BVG services are served by the same **tickets** and all are valid for transfers between different modes of transport and all other public transport services within the VBB system: which includes buses and trams in Potsdam, Oranienburg and even Regional Express trains (marked RE operating within the city limits). **Tickets** for the U- and S-Bahn system and the bus network can be bought from the machines on the platforms of their stations. These take €5 and €10 notes and all but the smallest coins, give change and have a basic explanation of the ticketing system in English. Though it's tempting to ride without a ticket, be warned that plain-clothes inspectors frequently cruise the lines, meting out on-the-spot **fines** of €40 for those without a valid ticket or pass. On buses, show your valid ticket to the driver who can sell you a ticket (including day tickets).

The transport network is divided into three zones – A, B and C – and tickets vary in price depending on which zones they are valid in. Basic **single tickets (Einzeltickets)** cost €2 and allow you to travel in Zone A and B. If you're heading for the outskirts of town or Potsdam, you'll need a ticket that covers zone C too (€2.60). Tickets are valid for two hours, enabling you to transfer across the three networks to continue your journey, but not for a return journey. A *Kurzstrecke*, or short-trip ticket, costs €1.20 and allows you to travel up to three train or six bus stops (no return journeys).

It's possible to save a little money by buying a **day ticket** (*Tageskarte*; valid until 3am the next morning) for €5.60 or an excellent-value **seven-day ticket** (*Sieben-Tage-Karte*) which costs €24.30 for zones AB and €30 for all three zones. The small **group ticket** (*Kleingruppenkarten*) is available for a whole day's travel for up to five people; it costs €14 for zones A and B and €29 for three zones. Another possibility of interest to short-term visitors is the **Welcome Card** (€21), which allows one adult and three children 72 hours' unlimited travel, and the **City Tour Card** (ⓦwww.citytourcard.com) which is also good for unlimited travel in the AB zone for 48 hours (€14.50) or 72 hours (€18.90). Both cards also give concessionary rates at a host of attractions and discounts at participating tour companies, restaurants and theatres. The main difference between the two is who their partners are, so you should have a look to see what's more appealing. Other than that, it's also worth bearing in mind that the Welcome Card has the advantage of also being valid for zone C and includes the price of taking a bicycle on board trains. If you're in Berlin for longer than a couple of weeks, you should consider buying a monthly ticket (*Monatskarte*); various types are available and explained in full in English via the information buttons on dispensing machines.

Taxis

Berlin's cream-coloured **taxis** are plentiful and are always metered, but pricey: for the first 6km it's €2.50 plus €1.50 per kilometre, after which it's €1 per kilometre. Fares rise slightly between 11pm and 6am and all day Sunday. If you're travelling in small groups, however, it can work out to be not much more expensive than public transport. Taxis cruise the city day and night and congregate at useful locations, such as outside the KaDeWe store, on Savignyplatz and by Zoo Station in the West End; and in the east at the northern entrance to Friedrichstrasse station, the entrance to Alexanderplatz S-Bahn station and in front of the nearby *Forum Hotel*. Short trips, known as *Kurzstrecke*, can be paid on a flat rate of €3 for up to two kilometres, though this only works when you hail a moving cab, and you must mention it on getting into the taxi.

Drivers are generally polite and know their way around, but you will find one or two who are student part-timers or moonlighting second-jobbers, so don't expect them necessarily to have an infallible knowledge of the city. Taxi firms include: **City Funk** (℡030/21 02 02), **Funk Taxi Berlin** (℡030/26 10 26) and **Spree Funk** (℡030/44 33 22).

Driving

Though there's practically no need for a car within the city, you may want to tour around outside Berlin, and one way of doing so is by **car**. The most important rules to bear in mind when driving in Berlin are simple. You drive on the right; main roads have a yellow diamond indicating who has priority; but if you are driving in built-up areas, traffic coming from the right normally has right of way. This is particularly important to remember in the former East Berlin, where **trams** always have the right of way. Unfamiliarity with the traffic system means that unwary visiting drivers are prone to cutting in front of turning trams at junctions – a frightening and potentially lethal error. Also, when trams halt at their designated stops, it's forbidden to overtake until the tram starts moving, to allow passengers time to cross the road and board.

Seatbelts are compulsory in front and rear seats; and children under twelve years must sit in the back. A surviving GDR traffic regulation is the "Grüner Pfeil", or green arrow attached to traffic lights at the right-hand turning lane at junctions: it means if the light is red, but no traffic is approaching from the left, you may proceed.

Thanks to a post-unification boom in car ownership and extensive road construction projects, Berlin suffers **traffic snarl-ups** that can compete with the worst any other European city has to offer. The authorities seemingly have little clue as to how to control the rush-hour jams that start at around 5pm and are particularly bad on Friday afternoons: don't be surprised if a journey you'd allowed twenty minutes for takes three or four times as long during these periods.

The recent installation of **parking meters** seems to have aided your chances of finding a place to park. The meters, identifiable

by their tall grey rectangular solar power umbrellas, generally cost €0.50 per 30min, €2 in places like Alexanderplatz. You're supposed to move after the hour, and stiff fines are handed out to those without tickets; even if you drive a car with foreign plates you can expect it to be towed away.

Car rental

All the major **car rental** agencies are represented in Berlin, although the best deals are often found through local operators – for a selection of both see "Directory", p.287. You can find local car rental firms in the Yellow Pages under *Autovermietung* (*PKW an Selbstfahrer*); phoning around should trawl in something for under €30 a day, though watch out for hidden extras such as limited mileage. Most rental places do good-value Friday afternoon–Monday morning deals, and most expect to see a credit card and passport.

Cycling

An extensive network of bike paths makes **cycling** a quick and convenient way of getting around the city. You can also take your bike on the U- or S-Bahn, should you wish to explore the countryside and lakes of the Grunewald and Wannsee areas. To take your bike on a train you'll need to buy a children's ticket for the underground system (either a single journey or a day ticket), though some monthly tickets and the Welcome Card include bike transport. One good investment if you're going to explore the city under your own steam is the cycle route map published by the **German bicycle club** ADFC, available from their shop at Brunnenstrasse 28 (Mon–Fri noon–8pm, Sat 10am–4pm ℡030/4 48 47 24) as well as most booksellers in the city. The ADFC can also provide free listings of bike rental and bike shops, with current rates and contact details. For a list of companies offering **bike tours** in and around the city, see box on p.35.

One good company for **bike rental**, with several conveniently located branches and good machines, is **Fahrradstation** at Hackesche Höfe, Hof 7 (Mon–Fri 8am–8pm Sat & Sun 10am–4pm; ℡030/28 38 48 48); Auguststr. 29 A (Mitte), (Mon–Fri 8am–8pm

Sat & Sun 10am–4pm; ☎030/28 59 96 61); Leipziger Str. 56 (Mon–Fri 8am–8pm Sat & Sun 10am–4pm; ☎030/66649 180), Bergmannstr. 9, Kreuzberg (Mon–Fri 8am–8pm Sat & Sun 10am–4pm; ☎030/215 15 66). Rates are €15 per day or €50 per week.

A recent and highly convenient innovation introduced and run by German rail (DB) is **CallBikes**, rental bikes scattered around zone A of the city, found on street corners and reliably at major points like the Brandenburg Gate and Potsdamer Platz. These silver-and-red, full-suspension bicycles can be rented at any time of day for €0.06 per minute (up to €15 per 24-hour period), with no deposit or minimum charge. To use one, or two, you first need to register a credit card (☎0700/05 22 55 22 ⓦwww.callabike .de). Registering your mobile will mean it will automatically debit your account when you call. Once you've registered, it's just a matter of calling the individual number on the side of a bike and receiving an electronic code to open the lock. To drop it off you can leave it on any street corner then ring up for a code to lock the bike and leave its location as a recorded message.

If you're planning to stay for any length of time, it works out cheaper to **buy** a secondhand machine and sell it when you leave. Of Berlin's many bike shops Froschrad, Wiener Str. 15, Kreuzberg (Mon–Fri 10am–7pm, Sat 10am–3pm; ☎030/6 11 43 68, ⓦwww.froschrad.de; U-Bahn Görlitzer Bahnhof), is one of the biggest and has the full range of secondhand bikes. Alternatively, you could try finding something under *Fahrräder* in the classified ads section of *Zweite Hand* (published Tues, Thurs & Sat), *Die Berliner Morgenpost* or *Der Tagesspiegel* (both Sun).

Boats

More an option for messing about on Berlin's numerous city-centre canals and suburban lakes than a practical mode of transport, **boats** run regularly throughout the summer. From the centre of town, Reederei Heinz Riedel, Planufer 78, Kreuzberg (April–Feb; ☎030/6 93 46 46 ⓦwww.reederei-riedel .de), runs several daily trips on the River Spree, taking in the Reichstag and the Landwehrkanal. Their Inner City Tours (€6) last around an hour and leave from the Spree just east of the Alte Nationalgalerie (see p.84); while departures for the three-hour City Tour (€14) take place at several points, including the Märkische Brücke northeast of the Märkisches Museum (see p.97) the Corneliusbrücke (see p.124) and the Potsdamer Brücke, just southwest of the Kulturforum. The same company also runs day-trips (€14) out to the Pfaueninsel and the Wannsee in the west of the city, to the Müggelsee in the east, and on other lakes surrounding Berlin.

The Stern und Kreis Schiffahrt (March–Sept ☎030/5 36 36 00; ⓦwww.sternundkreis.de) offers a variety of city-centre trips (tickets from €6) with departures from Jannowitzbrücke, Nikolaiviertel, Corneliusbrücke, and

---

Guided tours

Fierce competition between several English-language **walking tour** companies has meant that the quality of all of them is very high. All offer general four-hour city tours for around €12 plus more specialized ones of Third Reich sites and a nightlife tour. Arguably the best is Original Berlin Walks (☎030/3 01 91 94, ⓦwww.berlinwalks .com) who also offer a tour of Jewish life, Potsdam and Sachsenhausen. Insider Tour (☎030/6 92 31 49; ⓦwww.insidertour.com) also offers Cold War and bike tours. New Berlin Tours (☎0179/9 73 03 97 ⓦwww.newberlintours.com) has a Cold War Tour and excursions to Sachsenhausen; its tours of the city centre are free (tips expected), to act as tasters.

Bus tours abound: most of them depart from points on Kurfürstendamm between Breitscheidplatz and Knesebeckstrasse, making the rounds several times every day, though schedules are curtailed in the winter. Companies include Severin + Kühn (☎030/8 80 41 90, ⓦwww.severin-kuehn-berlin.de) and **Tempelhofer Reisen** (☎030/7 52 40 57, ⓦwww.tempelhofer.de). A basic two-hour tour from any company will cost about €18.

the Pergamonmuseum. They also run a number of tours around the lake systems in the Grunewald, including trips to Potsdam and tours of the waterways around Köpenick starting from Treptower Park. Other city-centre alternatives are the sailings of the cheap and cheerful Berlin Wassertaxi (April–Oct 10 daily 1hr tours from the Zeughaus; €7; ☎030/65 88 02 03 ⓦwww.berliner -wassertaxi.de) and Reederei Winker (year-round; 2 daily 3hr tours from the Schlossbrücke; ☎030/34 99 59 33 ⓦwww .reederei-winkler.de). A collection of smaller

companies also cruises Berlin's waterways, ranging as far afield as Spandau, Potsdam and Werder – details available from the Reed-erverband der Berliner Personenschiffahrt, Kronprinzessinnenweg 5, Grunewald (☎030/3 42 24 31; ⓦwww.reederverband-berlin.de). Full details and timetables for all Berlin cruise companies are available online and from city tourist offices. The largest company to trawl the western lakes is the Weisse Flotte (☎0331/2 75 92 10; ⓦwww.weisse-flotte -potsdam.de), with around a dozen daily sail-ings around the Havel lakes from Potsdam.

Costs and money

By the standards of most European capitals, prices in Berlin are reasonable and well short of the excesses of Paris and London and with quality to match. Never-theless, for those heading out to sample Berlin's famous nightspots, visiting the city has the potential to become expensive. The use of credit cards is steadily increasing in stores and accommodation, but cash is still the currency of choice, particularly in bars and restaurants.

Assuming you intend to eat and drink in moderately priced places, utilize the public transport system sparingly and not stay in the *Hilton*, the **minimum** you could get by on after you've paid for your room is €25 (around £17/US$25) a day. For this you would get a sandwich (€3), an evening meal (€10), three beers (€7) and one underground ticket (€2), with around €3 left for museums, entertainment, etc. A more realistic figure, if you want to see as much of the city as possible (and party at night), would be at least twice that amount.

Accommodation and **nightlife** are the most likely to run your budget up. The cheapest hostel dormitory is around €10, the cheapest room about €25. **Drink** is a little more expensive than most are used to, particularly in the city's more enjoyable nightspots; but the quality – especially of the beer – is significantly higher.

Eating is comparatively cheap, cheer-ful and varied (food is good value in shops

and in restaurants) for British visitors. North Americans will, however, find prices margin-ally higher than they are used to.

Youth and student discounts

As a visitor, entrance to museums and monuments is likely to swallow up a sizeable portion of your budget, but the good news, at least for those in full-time education or paying for minors, is that concessionary rates are in most cases very generous. Expect to pay around half to two-thirds of the full rate.

This means that, once obtained, various official and quasi-official **youth/student ID cards** soon pay for themselves in savings. A university photo ID might open some doors, but is not as easily recognizable as an International Student ID Card (ISIC, ⓦwww.isiccard.com), available to all full-time students, which entitles the bearer to special air, rail and bus fares and discounts at museums, theatres and other attractions.

For Americans there's also a health benefit, providing up to $3000 in emergency medical coverage and $100 a day for 60 days in hospital, plus a 24-hour hotline to call in the event of a medical, legal or financial emergency. The card costs $22 in the US; CDN$16 in Canada; A$18 in Australia; NZ$20 in New Zealand; £7 in the UK; and €13 in the Republic of Ireland.

You have to be 26 or younger to qualify for the **International Youth Travel Card**, which costs US$22/£7 and carries the same benefits. Teachers qualify for the **International Teacher Card**, offering similar discounts and costing US$22, UK£7, CDN$16, €13, A$18 and NZ$20. All these cards are available in the US from Council Travel, STA, TravelCUTS and, in Canada, Hostelling International (see p.24 for addresses); in Australia and New Zealand from STA or Campus Travel; in Ireland from USIT or STA, and in the UK from STA.

Money

On January 1, 2002, Germany was one of twelve European Union countries to change over to a single currency, the **euro**. The euro is split into 100 cents. There are seven euro **notes** – in denominations of 500, 200, 100, 50, 20, 10, and 5 euros, each a different colour and size – and eight different **coin** denominations, including 2 and 1 euros, then 50, 20, 10, 5, 2, and 1 cents. Euro coins feature a common EU design on one face, but different country-specific designs on the other. No matter what the design, all euro coins and notes can be used in twelve of the fifteen member states (Austria, Belgium, Finland, France, Germany, Greece, Ireland, Italy, Luxembourg, Portugal, Spain and the Netherlands, but not the UK, Denmark or Sweden).

Travellers' cheques

Travellers' cheques are one of the safest ways of carrying your money, as they're insured. The usual fee for their purchase is one or two percent of face value, though this fee may be waived if you buy the cheques through a bank where you have an account, and they can be cashed in any bank or exchange office. Make sure you keep the purchase agreement and a record of cheque serial numbers safe and separate from the cheques themselves. In the event that cheques are lost or stolen, the issuing company will expect you to report the loss forthwith; consequently, when you buy your travellers' cheques, ensure you have details of the company's emergency contact numbers or the addresses of their local offices. Most companies claim to replace lost or stolen cheques within 24 hours. When you cash your cheques, you'll find that almost all banks make a percentage charge per transaction on top of a basic minimum charge.

You might consider getting euro travellers' cheques rather than your own currency: they're increasingly accepted as cash in larger establishments and you will often get the face value of the cheques when you change them, so only paying commission on purchase. The most widely recognized brands are Visa, American Express and Thomas Cook.

Credit and debit cards

Debit and credit cards, once a foreign concept in Berlin, are finally becoming a part of everyday life. Debit cards are commonly accepted, whilst credit cards (at least the major ones such as American Express, Mastercard and Visa) are good in department stores, mid- to up-market restaurants, and an increasing number of shops and petrol stations. Should you want to get **cash** on your plastic, the best way is from any of the various **ATMs** around town. You can withdraw as little as €25, but they do charge a minimum fee, often around €2.50, and charge two to four percent of the withdrawal as commission. In addition to credit cards, most bank debit cards, part of either the Cirrus or Plus systems, can be used for withdrawing cash, and carry lower fees than credit cards. Various banks will also give an advance against your credit card, subject to a minimum of the equivalent of £60/$100 – stickers in the bank windows indicate which cards they're associated with. Make sure you have a personal identification number (PIN) that's designed to work overseas.

Emergency numbers for lost credit cards

Euro cheque ☎01805/02 10 21
American Express ☎069/97 97 10 00

Visa ☎0800/8 14 91 00
Mastercard / Eurocard ☎069/79 33 19 10
Citicorp (Diners Club) ☎069/26 03 58

Banks and exchange

Banking hours are usually Monday to Friday from 9am to 3pm and two days a week to 6pm (usually with a lunch break; look at the schedule posted on the door). Branches of the Berliner Bank have the longest hours: the airport branch at Tegel is open daily from 8am to 10pm, and the branch at Kurfürstendamm 24, Charlottenburg, is open Monday to Friday from 9.30am to 6.30pm, and on Saturday from 9.30am to 1.30pm. Deutsche Bank's late opening days are Tuesday and Thursday, and their branch at Potsdamer Platz is open till 4pm on Saturdays. It may be worth shopping around several banks (including the savings banks or Sparkasse), as the rates of exchange offered can vary, as can the amount of commission deducted. The latter tends to be a flat rate, meaning that small-scale transactions should be avoided whenever possible. In any case, the several **Wechselstuben** (bureaux de change) around Zoo Station, and particularly the Reisebank in the Alexanderplatz, Friedrichstrasse and Ostbahnhof stations, offer better rates, as well as being open outside normal banking hours and weekends; usually daily from 8am–8pm.

Wiring money

Having money wired from home using one of the companies listed below is never convenient or cheap, and should be considered a last resort. It's also possible to have money wired directly from a bank in your home country to a bank in Berlin, although this is somewhat less reliable because it involves two separate institutions. If you go this route, your home bank will need the address of the branch bank where you want to pick up the money and the address and telex number of the head office of the German bank, which will act as the clearing house; money wired this way normally takes two working days to arrive, and costs around £25/US$40/CDN$54/A$52/NZ$59 per transaction.

Money-wiring companies

Travelers Express/MoneyGram
US ☎1-800/444-3010, Canada ☎1-800/933-3278, UK, Ireland and New Zealand ☎00800/6663 9472, Australia ☎0011800/6663 9472, ⌨www.moneygram.com.
Western Union US and Canada ☎1-800/CALL-CASH, Australia ☎1800/501 500, New Zealand ☎0800/005 253, UK ☎0800/833 833, Republic of Ireland ☎66/947 5603, ⌨www.westernunion.com (customers in the US and Canada can send money online).

Communications

Germany's famed efficiency is apparent in its postal and telephone services: the former is speedy and the latter hassle-free. Both, however, are relatively expensive.

Mail

Central Berlin's most conveniently situated **post office** (*Postämt*) with the longest hours is at Bahnhof Friedrichstrasse (under the arches at Georgenstrasse 12; Mon–Fri 6am–10pm, Sat & Sun 8am–10pm; ⌨www.deutschepost.de). This is the easiest (and quickest) place to send letters home: mail to the UK usually takes 3 days; to North America one week; and to Australasia two weeks.

Other offices (generally Mon–Fri 8am–6pm, Sat 8am–1pm), and separate parcel offices (marked *Pakete*), usually a block or so away, are dotted around town; you can also buy stamps from the small yellow machines next to some postboxes. **Postboxes** themselves are everywhere and unmissable, painted bright yellow. When posting a letter, make sure you distinguish between the slots marked for various postal codes. Boxes marked with a red circle indicate collections late in the day and on Sunday.

The two main post offices are also the places to send and collect letters **poste restante**: letters for the Bahnhof Friedrichstrasse branch should be sent to: (Recipient's Name), Postlagernd, Postfiliale Berlin 120, 10612 Berlin; for the Budapesterstrasse branch it's Postlagernd, Postamt Rathausstrasse 5, 10178 Berlin, and collected from the counter marked "Postlagernde Sendungen" (take your passport). The major post offices also offer **fax services**, and at a cheaper rate than in copy shops and the like.

Telephones

Believe it or not, there are more **telephones** in Berlin than people. You can make **international calls** from most phone boxes in the city, which are usually equipped with basic instructions in English. Virtually every pay phone you'll find takes **cards**. These cost €5, €10 and €20 and are available from all post offices and some shops. Another option is to use the **direct phone service** facility of the main post offices: a phone booth will be allocated to you from the counter marked *Fremdgespräche*, which is also where you pay once you've finished. A large number of **phone shops** offering cheap international calling have also sprouted up and are dotted throughout the city; one central one is in the Europa Center (see p.132).

Some of the public boxes are marked *International*, with a ringing bell symbol to indicate that you can be called back on that phone. There are international and local phones in Bahnhof Friedrichstrasse and Zoo Station. The cheapest time to call abroad is between 9pm and 8am.

Mobile phones

If you want to use your mobile phone, you'll need to check with your phone provider whether it will work in Germany, and what the call charges are. In the UK, you may need to inform your phone provider before going abroad to get international access switched on. You may get charged extra for this depending on your existing

---

International dialling codes and useful numbers

Germany is one hour ahead of GMT, 9 hours ahead of US Pacific Standard Time and 6 hours ahead of Eastern Standard Time. Clocks are turned an hour forward at the end of March and an hour back at the end of September.

Phoning abroad from Berlin

Dial ☎00 + IDD country code + area code minus first 0 + subscriber number
IDD codes
Britain ☎44

Ireland ☎353
US ☎1
Canada ☎1
New Zealand ☎64
Australia ☎61

From abroad to Berlin
From the UK: dial ☎00 49 followed by the number (leaving out the first 0).
From the US: dial ☎011 49 followed by the number (leaving out the first 0).
From Australia: dial ☎0011 49 followed by the number (leaving out the first 0).
From New Zealand dial ☎00 49 followed by the number (leaving out the first 0).

Useful numbers within Berlin
Directory enquiries ☎1 18 33
English-language directory enquiries ☎1 18 37
International directory enquiries ☎1 18 34

package and where you are travelling to. You are also likely to be charged extra for incoming calls when abroad, as the people calling you will be paying the usual rate. If you want to retrieve messages while you're away, you may have to ask your provider for a new access code, as your home one is unlikely to work abroad. Most UK mobiles use GSM, which gives access to most places worldwide, except the US. For further information about using your phone abroad, check out www.telecomsadvice.org.uk/features/using_your_mobile_abroad.htm.

Unless you have a tri-band phone, it is unlikely that a mobile bought for use inside the US will work outside North America. Most mobiles in Australia and New Zealand use GSM, which works well in Europe.

If you are in Germany for a while, consider getting a local SIM card for your phone. These are available through Berlin's many phone shops (see p.39) and tend to cost around €20, often including some credit. To use a different SIM card in your phone, it will need to be unlocked, if it isn't already, to accept the cards of different providers. The phone shops will be able to advise where this is possible locally. Expect to pay around €10 for this quick service.

Email

Berlin is a very Internet-conscious city and **online access** is excellent: there are a number of local providers, and Compuserve and AOL (as well as the German T-Online service) have local nodes here. Larger hotels, and many of the growing number of Internet cafés in the city, also offer ISDN access, and WLAN hotspots – including a free one in the Sony Centre (see p.77). **Internet cafés** range from humble affairs in youth clubs to very slick techno palaces; the software is always current, but, of course, in German; costs are about €1–4 per half-hour.

One of the best (and cheapest) ways to keep in touch while travelling is to sign up for a free Internet email address – if you haven't already done so – that can be accessed from anywhere, for example Yahoo! (www.yahoo.com) or Hotmail (www.hotmail.com). Once you've set up your account, you'll be able to pick up and send mail from any Internet café, web kiosk or hostel or hotel with Internet access. For those travelling with a laptop, www.kropla.com is a useful website giving details of how to get it connected when abroad, phone country codes around the world, and information about electrical systems in different countries.

The media

English being the prevalent second language in Berlin, you'll find a good range of newspapers and magazines and – with a little searching – some English-language programmes on the TV and Radio.

Newspapers

It's relatively easy to find **British and US newspapers** in Berlin: most of the London-printed editions can be found at lunchtime on the same day and the *International Herald Tribune* is also readily available. *Internationale Presse* (inside Zoo Station; daily 9am–midnight) has a good selection of international newspapers and magazines,

as do the Alexanderplatz and Ostbahnhof stations.

Berlin has four **local newspapers**. Two of these are from the presses of the right-wing Springer Verlag: the *Berliner Morgenpost* is a staid, conservative publication, and *BZ* is a trashy tabloid. *Berliner Kurier* is another tabloid, less trashy, but more boring. The other main local paper is the *Berliner Zeitung*, originally an East Berlin publication, which covers national and international news as well as local stories.

Of the **national** dailies, the two best-sellers are also from the Springer press: *Die Welt* (Ⓦwww.welt.de), once a right-wing heavyweight, has become somewhat more centrist and now sports a back page in English, while the tabloid *Bild* is a reactionary, sleazy and sensationalist rag. Recommendable are the Berlin-based *Tagesspiegel*, a good liberal read, and the left-centre *Tageszeitung*, known as *taz* – not so hot on solid news, but with good in-depth articles on politics and ecology, and an extensive Berlin listings section on Friday. It has the added advantage of being a relatively easy read for non-native German speakers. The *Frankfurter Allgemeine*, widely available in the city, is again conservative, appealing to the business community in particular. An English-language version is included as a supplement in every issue of the *International Herald Tribune*. Hamburg-based *Die Zeit* appears every Thursday and, while left-wing in stance, includes a number of independently written reports on a variety of subjects. A few other papers from the old GDR hang on, like *Neues Deutschland*, once the Party paper. For details of Berlin's **listings magazines**, see p.29.

Television

Berlin has **five main TV channels**: ARD and ZDF somewhat approximate British channels or a down-market PBS; VOX and B1 are primarily entertainment channels; ORB is basically a local channel for Berlin and Brandenburg, risen from the ashes of the ex-GDR's two TV stations. All channels seem to exist on a forced diet of US reruns clumsily dubbed into German. With cable TV, available in larger hotels, you'll be able to pick up the locally available **cable channels** (over twenty to choose from, including MTV and BBC World). Of the cable channels, FAB (*Fernsehen aus Berlin* – "TV from Berlin") is a local channel with news footage, celebrity interviews and the infamous "Partnerwahl" dating service.

The number of **foreign films** shown in the original on the above channels has dwindled over the years but it does happen occasionally. If it's listed in the newspaper as *OF* it will be in the original language (usually English or French); *OmU* means that it has German subtitles.

Radio

The only English-speaking **radio** stations are the BBC World Service (90.2FM; Ⓦwww.bbc.co.uk/worldservice) and Star Radio (87.9FM), which daily combines American rock music with the *Voice of America* radio programme. Berlin's radio output is fairly dreadful, with a multitude of stations churning out light music and soft rock, and little else. The best local music station, depending on your taste, is Fritz Radio (102.6FM), with some decent dance music and rap shows (mainly late at night). For the latest bland pop, try L.R.S. 2 (94.3FM), and for hits from the last couple of decades try RTL (104.6FM). Also listenable is SFB4 MultiKulti (106.8FM), which has popular music from around the globe, as well as a few different foreign-language news programmes and chat shows. Best of the classical music stations is Klassik Radio (101.3FM). Jazz Radio Berlin (101.9FM) offers jazz and blues.

Opening hours, public holidays and festivals

Large shops in central Berlin are open Monday to Friday from 9 or 10am to 8pm, on Saturday from 9 or 10am to 4pm, while smaller shops or those outside the centre usually close two hours earlier.

British and American visitors will be surprised by the rigidity of Berlin's closing rules: you won't find late-night corner shops or Sunday-morning newsagent-grocers here. A few supermarkets and fruit stands, located in main stations such as Bahnhof Zoo, Bahnhof Friedrichstrasse or Alexanderplatz, are **open late** and on Sunday (see *Shopping*) though you pay for the privilege of after-hours shopping. Additionally, lots of bakers open on Sunday from 2 to 4pm.

Many **museums** follow a general pattern of opening 10am–6pm daily except Monday (although there are a few open on Monday too). This, however, cannot be taken as a rule, and to avoid disappointment it's a good idea to double-check opening times before setting off to visit a particular museum. They're open on all the **public holidays** listed (even Christmas), but usually close the following day. Remember that almost nothing else opens on public holidays other than cafés, bars and restaurants, so stock up on groceries the day before. They fall on January 1, Good Friday, Easter Monday, May 1, Ascension Day, Whitsun, October 3, November 3 and December 24–26.

Festivals and events

Berlin's festivals are, in the main, cultural affairs, with music, art and the theatre particularly well catered for. The best place to find out what's on and where (and, occasionally, to book tickets) is the tourist office in the Europa Center (see p.132): all mainstream events are well publicized in its leaflets and in brochures like Berlin Programm.

Other events, apart from the giant techno street party that is the **Love Parade** (in July), tend to be rather staid: one thing to

look out for is the Volksfeste, small, local street festivals you often come across by chance from July to September. Most city districts, in the east especially, have their own Volksfeste, which are usually an excuse for open-air music, beer-swilling and Wurst-guzzling. The Feste an der Panke in **Pankow** in September can be fun; the Köpenicker Sommer, held in **Köpenick** in the second half of June, features a re-enactment of the robbery of the Rathaus safe in 1906 by Friedrich Wilhelm Voigt, a cobbler and ex-convict who, disguised as an army officer, conned a detachment of soldiers into accompanying him.

January

Grüne Woche Berlin's annual agricultural show, held in the Messegelände, with food goodies to sample from all over the world (ⓦwww.gruenewoche.de).

Six-day Non-stop Cycle Race Late January, In the Velodrome, Paul-Heyse-Strasse. A Berlin tradition that's been going since the 1920s. (ⓦwww.sechstagerennen-berlin.de).

February

Berlin International Film Festival ("Berlinale"). The third largest film festival in the world, with around twelve days of old and new movies, arthouse cinema and more mainstream entertainment. Films are usually shown in the original versions with German (and sometimes English) subtitles. The festival is now concentrated around the multiplexes on Potsdamer Platz, though the programme repeats at various cinemas around town; check *Tip*, *Zitty* or the festival's own free daily magazine for listings. Tickets are available from booths in the Potsdamer Platz Arcade or Europa Center, or at participating theatres on the day of the screening. A limited number of season tickets go on sale a week before opening at the Galerie of the Berliner Volksbank, Linkstrasse 10, Potsdamer Platz (ⓦwww.berlinale.de).

March

Internationale Tourismus Börse (ITB).
Funkturm Exhibition Halls. Information and goodies from over a hundred countries to encourage tourism and travel (💻 www.messe-berlin.de).

May

Theatertreffen Berlin Various theatres. Large, mainly German-speaking theatre event that has tended towards the experimental in recent years. (💻 www.theathertreffen-berlin.de).
German Open Tennis Championship Ladies' Tennis Championship; see "Sport" p.274.

June

Fete de la Musique June 21. Bands from all over Europe and beyond come to play in bars, clubs, and other venues around the city (💻 www .lafetedelamusique.com).
Christopher Street Day Last Sat in June. Parade with lots of floats, music, and costumed dancers celebrating gay pride at the centre of Gay Action Week (💻 www.csd-berlin.de).

July

Love Parade Early July. Huge techno event that takes over much of the city centre and draws determined party people from all over Germany and the rest of Europe (💻 www.loveparade.de; see box p.8).
Classic Open Air Early July. The Gendarmenmarkt makes the perfect setting for this week-long series of very popular outdooor classical concerts (💻 www.classic-openair.ch).
The Bach Days Second week of July. Celebration of the great Baroque composer and musician in concerts throughout the city.
German-American Festival Truman Plaza (behind Oskar-Helene-Heim U-Bahn). One of the most popular events of the year. Eat junk food and gamble away your euros on lotteries and other carnival games.
German-French Festival Late July to mid-August. Kurt-Schumacher-Damm (near Tegel Airport). Mini-fair with food and music and a reconstruction of a different French town each year.

August

Gaukerfest Early August. Juggling and street performers' festival on Under den Linden.

Tanzfest Berlin Mid- to late August. Hebbel Theater. A series of dance performances featuring companies and artists from all over the world (💻 www.tanzfest.de).
Lange Nacht der Museen Late August. Over 100 of Berlin's museums stay open until at least midnight and put on various special events (💻 www.mdberling.de).

September

Art Forum Berlin A week-long art exposition with an international selection of galleries and dealers representing a broad spectrum of contemporary works. Takes place in Messegelände Berlin at Hammarskjöldplatz-Masurenallee (💻 www.art -forum-berlin.de).
Berlin Marathon The race begins on Strasse des 17 Juni and ends nearly 50km later, after passing through Dahlem and along the Ku'damm, back at the Kaiser-Wilhelm Memorial Church; closing date for entries is one month before the marathon (💻www .berlin-marathon.com).

October

Berlin Festival Late October to early November. Broad arts programme featuring theatre, dance, literary readings and live music – including a JazzFest; check programme available from the tourist office (💻www .berlinerfestspiele.de).

November

International Indoor Show-Jumping An annual event that attracts big names from the show-jumping world to the Deutschlandhalle.
Jewish Culture Days Second two weeks in November. Various venues. Concerts, lectures, readings and films that focus each year on Jewish culture in a particular country or place (💻 www .juedische-kulturtage.org).

December

Christmas Street Markets Twee Christmas markets dot the city with the most significant on Breitscheidplatz (see p.132), Alexanderplatz and in Spandau's old centre.
New Year's Eve Run December 31. Annual run organized by the Berlin Marathon authorities.

Crime and personal safety

The Berlin police (Polizei) maintain a low profile; they're not renowned for their friendliness, but they usually treat foreigners with courtesy. They're unlikely to make their presence much felt unless ordered to from on high (which usually happens during demonstrations), in which case the Prussian military mentality goes into automatic pilot, resulting in robotic-type gratuitous violence. But generally, in this country of rule and order it's more likely to be the ordinary citizen who'll spot you jaywalking and tick you off before the police even have a chance to get there.

Petty crime

Although crime in the city has risen rapidly since the fall of the Wall, it still remains quite modest in comparison with other European cities of the same size. The type you're most likely to encounter is **petty crime** such as pickpocketing or bag-snatching in one of the main shopping precincts. Sensible **precautions** against petty crime include: carrying bags slung across your neck and not over your shoulder; not carrying anything in pockets that are easy to dip into; having photocopies of your passport, airline ticket and driving licence, and leaving the originals in your hotel safe; and noting down travellers' cheque and credit card numbers. When you're looking for a hotel room, never leave your bags unattended.

If you do have something **stolen** (or simply lost), you'll need to register the details at the local police station (see box below): this is usually straightforward, but inevitably there'll be a great deal of bureaucratic bumph to wade through. Remember to make a note of the crime report number – or, better still, ask for a copy of the statement itself – for your insurance company.

Personal safety

As far as **personal safety** is concerned, most parts of the city are safe enough, though it's wise to be wary away from the centre, as muggings and casual violence are becoming depressingly frequent. On the whole, though, providing you use common sense, you'll be safe walking virtually anywhere alone by day in the city centre.

In the suburbs by night, particularly in the **eastern suburbs** of **Lichtenberg** or **Marzahn**, it's wise to exercise caution. As relative neo-Nazi and skinhead strongholds it's here that racial attacks are a real risk. These thugs are likely to pick on anyone who stands out – and not only because of their skin colour. Simply being "foreign" or looking unusual is reason enough to be at the rough end of their attentions. Evasive strategies include working out beforehand exactly where you're going so that you don't look lost and vulnerable, avoiding unlit areas, travelling with a friend if possible and not wearing or carrying anything obviously valuable.

Women's safety

Compared to many other European cities, Berlin is basically safe for women to visit. **Sexual harassment**, if committed at all, is generally of the verbal kind. With caution,

The police in central Berlin

The **emergency phone number** for the police is ☏110.
Headquarters:
Platz der Luftbrücke 6, Tempelhof
☏69 95
District stations:
Jägerstr. 48, Mitte ☏2 40 55
Bismarckstr. 111, Charlottenburg
☏3 30 10
Friesenstr. 16, Kreuzberg ☏69 95
Hauptstr. 44, Schöneberg ☏7 67 20
Schönhauser Allee 22, Prenzlauer
Berg ☏5 77 40

it's safe to use the U- and S-Bahn and walk around at night: streets are well lit, and dawdling for hours in late-night cafés is standard practice. Obviously you should use common sense, but even the rougher neighbourhoods (say, east Kreuzberg or Friedrichshain) feel more dangerous than they actually are: the run-down U-Bahn stations at Kottbusser Tor and Görlitzer Bahnhof (both in largely immigrant districts), or S-Bahn stations Warschauer Strasse and Ostkreuz, look alarming when compared to the rest of the system, but wouldn't stand out in most other European cities.

Women's contacts

Rape Crisis Line ☎030/2 51 28 28 (Tues & Thurs 6–9pm, Sun noon–2pm).
Women's Crisis Hotline (*Frauenkrisentelefon*) ☎030/6 15 42 43 (Mon & Thurs 10am–noon, Tues, Wed & Fri 10am–noon & 7–9pm Sat & Sun 5–7pm). Phone-in service offering sympathy and practical advice in a crisis.

Travellers with disabilities

Access and facilities for the disabled (*Behinderte*) are good in Berlin: most of the major museums, public buildings and the majority of the public transport system are wheelchair friendly, and an active disabled community is on hand for helpful advice.

Particularly good meeting places with lots of useful information are the Hotel MIT-Mensch Ehrlichstrasse 48 (☎030/5 09 69 30 ⓦwww .mit-mensch.com; S-Bahn Karlshorst; ⓢ), which provides friendly lodging run by and for the wheelchair-bound, and *Blisse* 14 Blissestr. 14 (Wilmersdorf; ☎030/8 21 20 79), a café-bar designed especially, but not exclusively, for disabled people and offering a wide range of food and non-alcoholic drinks.

A good source of more formal and advance disabled information is **Mobidat** (☎030/ 74 77 71 16; ⓦwww.mobidat.net), an activist group devoted to the issue of access for people with restricted mobility. They have a great wealth of information on wheelchair-accessible hotels and restaurants, city tours for disabled travellers and local transport services. Their online databank lists over 40,000 buildings in Berlin, including hotels, restaurants and theatres, indicating their degree of accessibility. An alternative is the **Fürst-Donnersmarck-Stiftung**, Dalandweg 19, Steglitz (☎030/7 69 70 00; ⓦwww.fdst.de), a foundation providing treatment and services for the disabled with plenty of information about accessibilty. Less useful are **Berlin Tourismus Marketing** (tourist office; see p.28), though they have listings of suitable accommodation. Lastly, if you speak German, you might like to browse the online version of the quarterly magazine *Handicap* (ⓦwww.i-motio.de), for its hundreds of articles and active forums.

Getting around

If you are registered disabled then you're allowed to use Berlin's excellent free **Telebus** service, Esplanade 17, Pankow (Mon–Fri 9am–3pm; ☎030/41 02 00), though this service is currently threatened by financial cuts, so check for the latest details on this. After being issued with a pass and number, you call the service and one of their fifty taxis or seventy buses will pick you up and take you to your destination. For people in wheelchairs, the buses need to be booked at least a day in advance, the taxis a few hours. It's also possible to use public transport with most, though not all, buses and trams equipped to allow wheelchair users on board:

look for the blue wheelchair symbol. Again, most but not all U- and S-Bahn stations are equipped with lifts; the offical U- and S-Bahn map indicates which stations are accessible by wheelchair. For advance information, check with the BVG (ⓦwww.bvg.de; see p.33) first.

Contacts for travellers with disabilities

In the UK and Ireland

Access Travel 6 The Hillock, Astley, Lancashire M29 7GW ☏01942/888 844, ⓦwww.access -travel.co.uk. Tour operator that can arrange flights, transfers and accommodation. This is a small business, personally checking out places before recommendation.

Holiday Care 2nd floor, Imperial Building, Victoria Rd, Horley, Surrey RH6 7PZ ☏0845/124 9971 or ☏0208/760 0072, ⓦwww.holidaycare.org.uk. Provides free lists of accessible accommodation abroad – European, American and long-haul destinations. Information on financial help for holidays available.

Irish Wheelchair Association Blackheath Drive, Clontarf, Dublin 3 ☏01/818 6400, ⓦwww.iwa.ie. Useful information provided about travelling abroad with a wheelchair.

Tripscope Alexandra House, Albany Rd, Brentford, Middlesex TW8 0NE ☏08457/585 641, ⓦwww .tripscope.org.uk. This registered charity provides a national telephone information service offering free advice on UK and international transport for those with a mobility problem.

In the US and Canada

Access-Able ⓦwww.access-able.com. Online resource for travellers with disabilities.

Directions Unlimited 123 Green Lane, Bedford Hills, NY 10507 ☏1-800/533-5343 or 914/241-1700. Travel agency specializing in bookings for people with disabilities.

Mobility International USA 451 Broadway, Eugene, OR 97401 ☏541/343-1284, ⓦwww .miusa.org. Information and referral services, access guides, tours and exchange programmes.

Society for the Advancement of Travelers with Handicaps 347 5th Ave, New York, NY 10016 ☏212/447-7284, ⓦwww.sath.org. Non-profit educational organization that has actively represented travellers with disabilities since 1976.

Wheels Up! ☏1-888/389-4335, ⓦwww .wheelsup.com. Provides discounted airfare, tour and cruise prices for disabled travellers, also publishes a free monthly newsletter and has a comprehensive website.

In Australia and New Zealand

ACROD (Australian Council for Rehabilitation of the Disabled) PO Box 60, Curtin ACT 2605; ☏02/6282 4333 (also TTY), ⓦwww.acrod.org.au. Provides lists of travel agencies and tour operators for people with disabilities.

Disabled Persons Assembly 4/173–175 Victoria St, Wellington, New Zealand ☏04/801 9100 (also TTY), ⓦwww.dpa.org.nz. Resource centre with lists of travel agencies and tour operators for people with disabilities.

Staying on

Berlin acts as a magnet for young people from Germany and all over Europe. Its reputation as a politicized, happening city, with a high profile in the arts and a more relaxed and tolerant attitude than its parent state, means that many people come here to live and work. That the English-speaking community – Americans, Brits and Irish – is a large one will work to your advantage when it comes to finding out the latest situation for jobs and housing, and to your disadvantage in terms of competition.

If you don't mind what you do (or what hours you do it), and are prepared to work *schwarz* ("black" – without a contract, taxes or insurance), finding **work** in Berlin shouldn't pose too much of a problem. **Work permits** (*Arbeitserlaubnis*) aren't required for EU nationals, though everyone else will need one – and, theoretically, should not even look for a job without one.

However, the paperwork and bureaucracy are complicated and tedious. The following notes cover only the initial stages of the process you'll need to follow: it's essential to seek advice from an experienced friend, especially when completing official forms – writing the wrong thing could land you in a lot of unnecessary trouble. The best official place for advice is the **Auswärtiges Amt** (German Federal Foreign Office; ☎030/01 88 81 70 ⊛www.auswaertiges-amt.de), whose website has the latest information – in English – on entry into Germany and local contact details.

All those who want to stay in Germany for longer than three months must first **register** their **residence** (*Anmeldung*) at an Einwohnermeldeamt. The documentation from this process will allow you to get an **Aufenthaltserlaubnis** ("permission to stay") from the Landeseinwohneramt, Friedrich-Krause-Ufer 24, Tiergarten (☎030/39 73 30; Mon, Tues & Thurs 7.30am–1pm, Fri 7.30am–noon). Officially you can't get one until you have a job – but you can't get a job without one. The loophole to this catch-22 situation is that most employers aren't too concerned about the *Aufenthaltserlaubnis* if you're an EU citizen. For **non-EU nationals** – North Americans, Australasians and every-

body else – finding legal work is extremely difficult, unless you've secured the job legally before arriving in Germany. The best advice is to approach the German embassy or consulate in your own country. Citizens of Australia, New Zealand and Canada between 18 and 30 can apply for a working holiday visa, enabling legal work in Germany for 90 days in a twelve-month period: contact German embassies for details.

Finding a job

High unemployment and a faltering economy can make it hard to find a decent job in Berlin, but the good news is that since long-term accommodation can work out quite cheap in Berlin, it's possible to live reasonably well on comparatively little. It's possible to get by comfortably on a take-home pay of €800–1000 a month.

Numerous **job agencies** offer both temporary and permanent work – usually secretarial – but you'll obviously be expected to have a good command of German and fast typing speeds. Check the Yellow Pages under *Arbeitsvermittlung*. Other than that, there are also several cleaning agencies (look in the Yellow Pages under *Reinigungsbetriebe*) where only a minimal knowledge of the language is needed. The Internet is now also a powerful tool for recruiters and job seekers in Germany, and key sites are: ⊛www.arbeit-online.de; ⊛www.mamas.de; ⊛jobs.de; ⊛www.jobnet.de; ⊛www.monster.de; and ⊛www.job-office.com. However, the best sources of both temporary and permanent work are certain **newspapers and magazines**: *Zweite Hand* (published on Tues, Thurs & Sat), *Tip* or *Zitty* (bi-monthly on alternate weeks, first

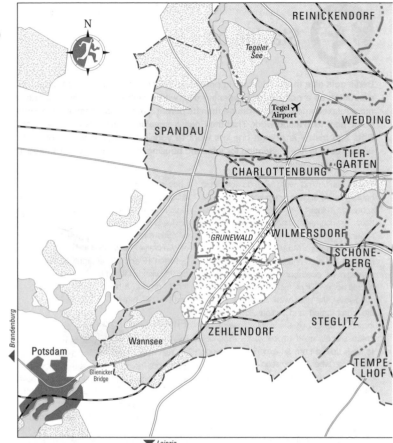

copies on sale Wed). The Sunday *Berliner Morgenpost* is also a good place to look, but be sure to pick it up late on Saturday evening around Zoo Station and scan the job (*Stelle*) section, since the best jobs always go quickly.

Other than personal contacts, these are also the best places to find English-language **teaching work** – either privately or in a school. For private work, the normal rate is €15 per hour – don't be beaten down to anything less than that. Previous experience is not always necessary (particularly for private lessons). You can place an advert for your services free in *Zweite Hand* or for a small fee in *Tip* or *Zitty*. Or you can approach the city's many language schools

directly; look in the above-mentioned magazines for names and addresses.

Working as an **au pair** is a viable option for young people between the ages of 17 and 30. Generally it's women who take up these positions which are not considered work by the state, but a cultural experience, though men are more common here than in the US or UK. Positions are relatively easy to find and can be done legally, even by non-EU citizens. A good starting point is the *Au Pair and Nanny's Guide to Working Abroad* by Susan Griffith and Sharon Legg, or surf three good general sites online: ⓦwww.au-pairs .de; ⓦwww.uapa.com; ⓦwww.iapa.org.

Otherwise, Berlin's innumerable **cafés and restaurants** often look for workers. You'll

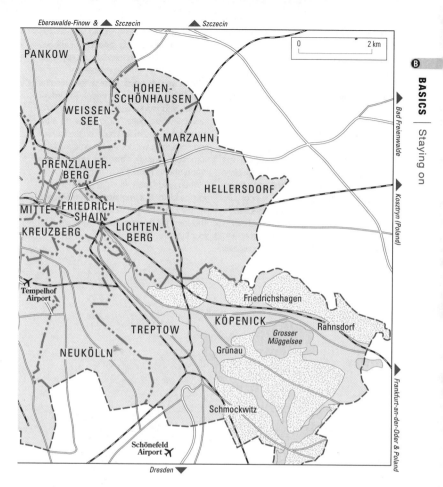

PANKOW

HOHEN-
SCHÖNHAUSEN

WEISSEN-
SEE

MARZAHN

PRENZLAUER-
BERG

HELLERSDORF

MITTE FRIEDRICH-
SHAIN

KREUZBERG LICHTEN-
BERG

Tempelhof
Airport

Friedrichshagen

KÖPENICK Rahnsdorf

TREPTOW Grosser
Müggelsee

NEUKÖLLN Grünau

Schmockwitz

Schönefeld
Airport

Dresden ▼

0   2 km

Bad Freienwalde ▶

Kostrzyn (Poland) ▶

Frankfurt-an-der-Oder & Poland ▶

need to tramp around town a bit first, and they'll expect a decent working knowledge of German, but you can often work black. If you do sign a contract with them, it's likely that you'll need a *Gesundheitspass* (health certificate), information about which can be found at any local **Bezirksamt**. These local official information offices (they're listed in the front of the Yellow Pages, and are usually located in the local town hall) can also advise on claiming social security and unemployment benefit.

Accommodation

Berlin's housing market regularly swings between glut and dearth, but currently, and despite the influx of government workers from Bonn, **apartments** are relatively easy to find, and, by the standards of European capital cities, affordable.

Although *Tip, Zitty, Zweite Hand* and the Sunday *Berliner Morgenpost* advertise apartments and rooms, it's much quicker and less traumatic to sign on at one of the several **Mitwohnzentralen**, accommodation agencies that specialize in long-term sublets in apartments throughout the city. Wherever you look, expect to pay from €400 for a self-contained one-roomed apartment, or between €150 and €300 for a room in a shared apartment. In listings or adverts, the word *Warm* means that the rent is inclusive of heating and other charges; *Kalt*, non-inclusive. Incidentally, Berlin is the only city in Germany with a large number of apartments that have coal-fuelled burners for heating (*Ofenheizung* in German). These are messy and inconvenient, as they require constant stoking up – if you're out of the house for more than a few hours, be prepared to come back to Arctic temperatures during the bitterly cold Berlin winter.

Originating in the events of 1968, the term **Wohngemeinschaft** (literally "communities") is now a firmly established part of the accommodation scene. They once described hippy communes of typically four to eight people (often with a few children thrown in), who shared rent, food and, supposedly, a few ideals, but today the term is used to describe just about any form of cohabitation that doesn't involve family or a partner and where facilities, costs of basic necessities

and cleaning duties are shared. Apartments and rooms are usually offered unfurnished and require a *Kaution* (deposit), usually in the form of three months' refundable rent.

Once you've been here a few months and made contact with people, **word of mouth** also works well if you're searching for somewhere better (or cheaper) to stay: tell everyone you meet you're on the lookout and something will usually become available surprisingly quickly – there's a high turnover in apartments here.

When you finally find a place to live, you need to first **register** your **residence** (*Anmeldung*) at an Einwohnermeldeamt. The form for this requires a signature from your landlord.

The City

The City

1

Unter den Linden and around

The natural place to start an exploration of Berlin is at its centre, in the area surrounding Unter den Linden. The broad avenues of Neoclassical buildings here formed the showpiece quarter of eighteenth-century Berlin, capital of Brandenburg-Prussia and later in its heyday as the centre of the German Empire. Now, since reunification, regeneration and the city's reinvention as Germany's capital, the street once again constitutes its nucleus. This revival has not only resurrected Unter den Linden as an important historical district, but also provided the city with the coherent centre that it lacked for so long, with a set of cultural and political attractions befitting a capital – not least its parliament, the **Reichstag**.

Berlin had been a relative backwater until the seventeenth century, but with the rise of Prussia architects were commissioned to create the trappings of a capital city – churches, theatres, libraries, palaces and an opera house – which were all set down on and around Unter den Linden. Safe **Baroque** and **Neoclassical** styles predominate, and there are no great flights of architectural fancy. These buildings were meant to project an image of solidity, permanence and power, perhaps to allay the latent insecurity of Brandenburg-Prussia as a relatively late arrival on the European stage. However, almost every one of these symbols of Hohenzollern might was left gutted by the bombing and shelling of World War II. Paradoxically, it was the postwar communist regime that resurrected them from the wartime rubble to adorn the capital of the German Democratic Republic. The result was a pleasing re-creation of the old city, though one of the motives behind this restoration was to import a sense of historical continuity to the East German state by tacitly linking it with Prussia. Whether anyone outside the Politbüro really bought into this particular conceit is doubtful, but this part of central East Berlin always compared favourably with the haphazard, soulless jumble of central West Berlin.

So successful has the **restoration** been that, looking at these magnificent eighteenth- and nineteenth-century buildings, it's difficult to believe that as recently as the 1960s large patches of the centre lay in ruins. Like archeologists trying to picture a whole vase from a single fragment, the builders took a facade, or just a small fraction of one, and set about re-creating the whole. And even though much of what can be seen today is an imitation, it's often easy to suspend disbelief and imagine an unbroken continuity.

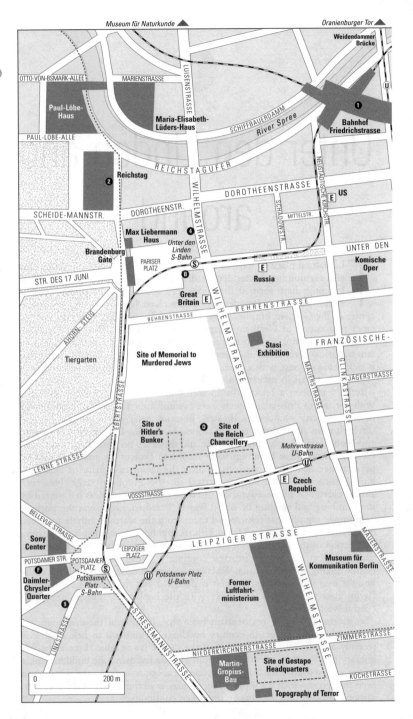

Museum für Naturkunde ▲

Oranienburger Tor ▲

Weidendammer
Brücke

OTTO-VON-BSMARK-ALLEE

MARIENSTRASSE

LUISENSTRASSE

Paul-Löbe-
Haus

Maria-Elisabeth-
Lüders-Haus

SCHIFFBAUERDAMM

River Spree

**Bahnhof
Friedrichstrasse** ❶

U

PAUL-LOBE-ALLE

REICHSTAGUFER

DOROTHEENSTRASSE

NEUSTÄDTISCHE KIRCHSTR.

SCHADOWSTR.

MITTELSTR.

E US

Reichstag ❷

SCHEIDE-MANNSTR.

DOROTHEENSTR.

WILHELMSTRASSE

UNTER DEN

Max Liebermann
Haus ❹

Komische
Oper

Brandenburg
Gate

Unter den
Linden
S-Bahn

E

STR. DES 17 JUNI

PARISER
PLATZ

Ⓢ

Russia

❸

Ⓑ

AHORN-STEIG

Great
Britain **E**

WILHELMSTRASSE

BEHRENSTRASSE

BEHRENSTRASSE

Tiergarten

Site of Memorial to
Murdered Jews

Stasi
Exhibition

FRANZÖSISCHE-

MAUERSTRASSE

GLINKASTRASSE

JÄGERSTRASSE

EBERTSTRASSE

Site of
Hitler's
Bunker

❹ Site of
the Reich
Chancellery

Mohrenstrasse
U-Bahn

Ⓤ

LENNE STRASSE

WILHELMSTRASSE

E Czech
Republic

VOSSSTRASSE

BELLEVUE STRASSE

LEIPZIGER STRASSE

MAUERSTRASSE

Sony
Center

LEIPZIGER
PLATZ

POTSDAMER STR.

POTSDAMER
PLATZ

Ⓢ

Ⓤ Potsdamer Platz
U-Bahn

Museum für
Kommunikation Berlin

Ⓕ
Daimler-
Chrysler
Quarter

Potsdamer
Platz
S-Bahn

Former
Luftfahrt-
ministerium

WILHELMSTRASSE

❾

LINKSTRASSE

STRESEMANNSTRASSE

ZIMMERSTRASSE

NIEDERKIRCHNERSTRASSE

KOCHSTRASSE

Martin-
Gropius-
Bau

Site of Gestapo
Headquarters

Topography of Terror

0   200 m

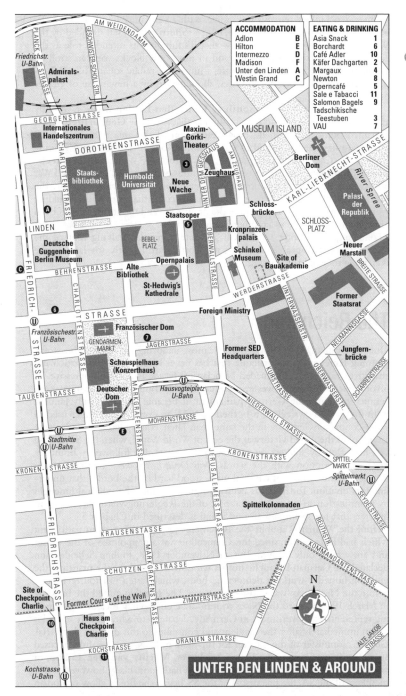

ACCOMMODATION
Adlon	B
Hilton	E
Intermezzo	D
Madison	F
Unter den Linden	A
Westin Grand	C

EATING & DRINKING
Asia Snack	1
Borchardt	6
Café Adler	10
Käfer Dachgarten	2
Margaux	4
Newton	8
Operncafé	5
Sale e Tabacci	11
Salomon Bagels	9
Tadschikische Teestuben	3
VAU	7

UNTER DEN LINDEN & AROUND

Unter den Linden remains impressive, with a surprising number of worthy buildings. The **Brandenburg Gate**, long a forlorn symbol left stranded by the Wall, has regained some stature now that it's fulfilling its intended role as the entrance to something significant, and in just a few blocks you can stroll by museums, a cathedral, an opera house, a university, public squares like **Bebel-platz**, and several other notable sites, all enlivened by a new sense of vitality on the street.

The rejuvenation continues **south of Unter den Linden** where as recently as the 1980s the twin Neoclassical churches that grace the **Gendarmenmarkt** remained bombed-out shells. Now restoration of the area is complete and the square has been returned to its position as one of Berlin's most striking corners. Less aesthetically impressive, but historically significant, is **Check-point Charlie**, further south on Friedrichstrasse; little is left of the Cold War border crossing, but the area nevertheless retains an echo of tension. Finally, the district's most dynamic and recent addition has come thanks to frantic building work on **Potsdamer Platz**, where the prewar life and soul of Berlin has been reinvented as a temple to commercialism.

Following the chapter layout will generate a circular walking tour of the district that's manageable in a day; it's worth starting early (or late) at the Reichstag to avoid the queues.

The Reichstag

One of Germany's, let alone Berlin's, most enduring landmarks, the stolid, looming **Reichstag** is a structure that has never been considered particularly attractive, though its colonnaded Neoclassical facade is suitably impressive. Its pivotal role in history, however, is unquestionable. Built in the late nineteenth century to house the German parliament, it became internationally familiar from flickering newsreels as it burned in 1933, an event which Hitler used to wrest control of Germany in the same year. Then, equally famously, it became a symbol of the Allied victory at the end of World War II, when the Soviet flag was held aloft by soldiers on its roof. In the years that followed – ironically, given its inscription with the words *Dem Deutschen Volke* ("To the German People") – this symbol of national unity stood hard by the border that under-lined its division. Today, it has been brought back into the political limelight by reunification, as it forms a vital part of the Regierungsviertel (government quarter) that has sprung up around it and is described in Chapter 5.

Until the Weimar Republic the Reichstag was home to a sham parliament which had little power, since the Chancellor was an appointee of the Kaiser and answerable only to him. But in November 1918, Philipp Scheidemann declared the German Republic from a window here, and for the first time the building hosted a working democratic body, which lasted just fourteen years before the Nazi Party was boosted to power. The **fire** that gutted the building in March 1933 allowed the Nazis to introduce emergency measures eliminat-ing representative government in Germany; debate as to who actually started it began immediately after the incident and continues to this day In a show trial, Göring, as minister of the interior for the State of Prussia, successfully accused an itinerant ex-Communist Dutch bricklayer, **Marius van der Lubbe**, of arson; he was executed the following year. What's most likely, however, is that members of the SA, the precursors of the SS, began the fire to allow draconian

The Reichstag in ribbons

In 1995, after some twenty years of lobbying, wrangling and debate, the conceptual artist **Christo** and his wife Jeanne-Claude realized their long-held dream of wrapping up the Reichstag. For two weeks in June and July, the historic building was packaged in 100,000 square metres of shiny-grey polypropylene and tied with deep-blue rope. Several hundred people were involved in the massive project, many of them mountain climbers employed to scramble along the sides of the building laying rope and tying knots. Some one million visitors saw the artwork, and even most detractors had to admit that it was indeed impressive. The price tag was said to be around $9 million.

measures to be brought in: by an emergency decree on the day after the fire, the basic civil rights guaranteed by the Weimar constitution were suspended and the death penalty was introduced for a range of political offences.

The Reichstag resumed its role as the permanent seat of the German parliament for the first time since the Third Reich on April 19, 1999. Outfitting the building to make way for the resumption of its governmental chores took several years – not only was the interior completely gutted and refashioned with a new plenary chamber and offices for the legislators, but a glass **dome**, supported by a soaring mirrored column, was set atop as well. Designed by British architect Sir Norman Foster, the cupola aroused much controversy when initially proposed, but has since proved a popular success, with hordes of visitors winding their way along the circular ramp that spirals up the inside; the **viewing deck** (daily 8am–10pm; free) at the top offers a stunning 360-degree view of the city. In clear weather you should be able to spot the Funkturm in the west (see p.138) and the high-rises of Marzahn in the east (see p.179), though it's the massive Tiergarten park (see p.123), the Sony Center (see p.77) and the Fernsehturm (see p.90), that are most attention-grabbing. Expect to queue for at least an hour, though if you arrive early or late in the day it can be a bit quicker – or, to be sure of immediate entry, make a reservation at the restaurant *Käfer im Reichstag* (see p.241).

Directly behind the Reichstag it's only just possible to make out the course of the **Berlin Wall** (see p.74), marked in the street here (and elsewhere) by a line of cobbles, which for 28 years divided the city; across the street, a poignant series of plaques marks the names (where known) of those killed trying to swim to the West across the nearby River Spree.

Unter den Linden

Unter den Linden itself is Berlin's grandest boulevard, rolling due east from the Brandenburg Gate towards Alexanderplatz. Once the main east–west axis of Imperial Berlin and site of many of the city's foreign embassies, it has been revitalized since 1989, reassuming its old role as one of Berlin's most important streets. The street – "beneath the lime trees" – was named after the trees that border its central island. The first saplings were planted by Friedrich Wilhelm, the Great Elector, during the seventeenth century to line the route that ran from his palace to the hunting grounds in the Tiergarten. The original trees were replaced by crude Nazi totem poles during the 1930s; the present generation dates from a period of postwar planting.

Until 1989 the western extremity of Unter den Linden marked the end of the road for East Berliners: a low barrier a hundred metres or so short of the Brandenburg Gate cut it off from Charlottenburger Chaussee (today known as Strasse des 17 Juni), its prewar continuation through the Tiergarten to the city's West End. From this vantage point it was possible to view the Brandenburg Gate, beyond which the discreet presence of armed border guards and the sterile white concrete of the Wall signalled the frontier with West Berlin. During this period Unter den Linden was reduced to little more than a grandiose blind alley, lined by infrequently visited embassies that gave it a strangely decorative but empty feel.

Now, however, the situation couldn't be more different. The **Brandenburg Gate** and the Reichstag, once separated, form adjacent symbols of the city's unity; the embassies have been joined by the offices of international companies and touristy shops; and traffic is heavy, as visitors heading for architectural highlights such as the **Alte Bibliothek**, and museums including the **Deutsche Guggenheim** and the **Deutsches Historisches Museum**, compete for pavement space with civil servants and business people.

The Brandenburg Gate and around

At the head of Unter den Linden is the **Brandenburg Gate** (Brandenburger Tor; S-Bahn Unter den Linden), a building dense with meaning and historical associations. Originally built as a city gate-cum-triumphal arch in 1791, it was designed by Carl Gotthard Langhans and modelled after the Propylaea, the entrance to the Acropolis in Athens. The Gate became, like the Reichstag later, a symbol of German solidarity, looking out to the monolithic Siegessäule, a column celebrating Prussian military victories and guarding the city's grandest thoroughfare. In 1806 Napoleon marched under the arch and took home with him the **Quadriga**, the horse-drawn chariot that tops the Gate. It was returned a few years later, and the revolutionaries of 1848 and 1918 met under its form; later the Gate was a favoured rallying point for the Nazis' torch-lit marches.

After the building of the Wall placed the Gate in the Eastern sector, nearby observation posts became the place for visiting politicians to look over from the West in what was a handy photo opportunity – the view was apparently emotive enough to reduce Margaret Thatcher to tears. With the opening of a border crossing here just before Christmas 1989, the east–west axis of the city was symbolically re-created and the post-Wall mood of eagerness for unification was strengthened. When the GDR authorities rebuilt the Quadriga following wartime damage, they removed the Prussian Iron Cross from the Goddess of Victory's laurel wreath, which topped her staff, on the grounds that it was "symbolic of Prussian-German militarism". When the border was reopened, the Iron Cross was replaced, which some, mindful of historical precedent, still viewed with a frisson of unease – but now it certainly seems harmless enough, presiding over a cheerful pedestrian zone, and as a popular backdrop for photos of posing tourists.

The Holocaust Memorial

The **Holocaust Memorial** (@www.holocaustmahnmal.de), officially known as the National Memorial to the Murdered Jews of Europe, has been a project fraught with delays and controversy, but is to be completed by the summer of 2005. Devoted to remembering the Nazi atrocities against Jews, the project is the brainchild of American architect Peter Eisenmann, whose design was inspired by Prague's Jewish graveyard, with its densely clustered gravestones. Consequently, it incorporates 2700 square, dark grey pillars of varying heights evenly distributed over the entire site. With no single entrance, visitors are to make their own way through the maze to the centre where the blocks are well above head height, which is thought to convey a sense of isolation and solitude. An entrance at the heart of the monument will lead to an underground centre where historical information and the personal accounts and life stories of some of the victims are presented.

Unique and strange, once built the monument will undoubtedly provoke debate, but even before its completion – a feat delayed innumerable times in the decade since its inception – it has been controversial. Its location, on prime real estate, has little historical significance, and in a city where finances are tight the price tag of around €30 million makes it unpopular. Some argue that the memorials at former camps, such as Sachsenhausen (see p.173), are adequate, and a far more poignant way of remembering the victims is by using individual golden cobbles placed outside their former homes – as has sometimes been done in the Scheunenviertel (see p.98). One final twist in the tale concerns Degussa, the company given the contract for the anti-graffiti paint on the blocks. As a daughter company of IG-Farben – who produced Cyclon-B, the gas used in the Nazi gas chambers – there were calls to remove them from the project. But after much debate, their tender was confirmed. It was argued that the whole nation was building the monument and that no organization or company should be hindered from contributing. But if the point was to avoid an exclusionary process it has begged the question why other victims of the Holocaust such as Gypsies, homosexuals, Jehovah's Witnesses and Soviet prisoners of war cannot also be remembered here.

Pariser Platz

The Brandenburg Gate looms over **Pariser Platz**, a pedestrian square where ornamental gardens have been restored and several modern office buildings erected, all with a view to reproducing a prewar feel, if not the exact look. Directly adjacent to the Brandenburg Gate on the north is the **Max Liebermann Haus** (opening times and entrance fees vary; ℡030/22 63 30 30, ⓦwww.stiftung.brandenburgertor.de). Patterned after the home of the Impressionist painter that once stood here, it now features temporary art exhibitions. On the southeast corner of the Platz, the legendary **Adlon Hotel**, once one of Europe's grandest hotels, has been rebuilt. The original was host to luminaries from Charlie Chaplin to Lawrence of Arabia and Kaiser Wilhelm II, and was regarded throughout the continent as the acme of luxury and style. The building was destroyed in the closing days of the war, and this new version, modelled closely on its predecessor – the lobby fountain, for example, was salvaged from the original – attempts the same heights of opulence. Even if you can't afford a drink here, let alone a room, have a look at the lobby and imagine the late eighteenth century when Berlin was the cultural capital of Europe. Culture of a very different sort graced the building in 2002, when Michael Jackson, who was staying in the bullet-proof presidential suite, dangled his youngest child over the balcony in front of the world's press.

Wilhelmstrasse to Friedrichstrasse

From Pariser Platz it's a short walk south along Wilhelmstrasse and past the British Embassy – along a pathway just below Behrenstrasse – to **Stasi: The Exhibition** at Mauerstrasse 38 (Mon–Sat 10am–6pm; ⓦwww.bstu.de; free) for a sobering exhibition on the feared East German Secret police. The material is presented by the government commission responsible for sifting through and reconstructing Stasi files, and whose work has included the painstaking reassembly of documents hastily shredded as the GDR's regime came to an end. The exhibition is briefer than the similar one at the former Stasi headquarters on Normannenstrasse (see p.177), but it does nevertheless contain several intriguing intelligence devices, including hidden cameras, tiny tape recorders, a big toolbox for producing counterfeit documents and even the proverbial toothpaste tube with a secret compartment. Apart from these sometimes comical tools, however, the exhibit relates (in German only) just what a powerful and frightening organization the Stasi was, and the amazing degree of observation, infiltration and control they practised in the GDR.

Back on Unter den Linden, one of the first buildings you'll see as you head east from Pariser Platz is the massive **Russian Embassy** which rears up on the right. Built in 1950 on the site of the prewar (originally Tsarist) embassy, it was the first postwar building to be erected on Unter den Linden and an example of the much maligned *Zuckerbäckerstil* or "wedding-cake style": a kind of blunted, monumental Classicism characteristic of Stalin-era Soviet architecture. Berlin has a number of such buildings, the most spectacular being those along Karl-Marx-Allee (see p.161).

The next block along from the embassy is a row of shops, which also includes the box office for the **Komische Oper**, one of Berlin's leading opera companies. The actual entrance to the theatre itself is on the street behind at Behrenstrasse 55–57, and though the building doesn't look like much from the outside, the interior is a wonderful 1890s frenzy of red plush, gilt and statuary (see Chapter 15).

Friedrichstrasse

Halfway along its length, Unter den Linden comes to its most important intersection as it crosses the busy shopping street of Friedrichstrasse. Before the war this was one of the busiest crossroads in the city, and Friedrichstrasse was a well-known prostitutes' haunt lined by cafés, bars and restaurants. Nazi puritanism dealt the first blow to this thriving *Vergnügungsviertel* ("Pleasure Quarter"), and the work was finished by Allied bombers, which effectively razed the street. The destruction caused by bombing widened Friedrichstrasse considerably, turning what had once been a narrow, slightly claustrophobic street into a broad, desolate road. Since reunification, however, Friedrichstrasse has been extensively revamped, and slipped back into its north–south axis role, becoming in the process a major shopping street with a series of high-end boutiques rubbing shoulders with more everyday shops and an antiques market around the train station.

Bahnhof Friedrichstrasse

Before the *Wende*, **Bahnhof Friedrichstrasse**, the main border crossing point for Western visitors to East Berlin, was probably the most heavily guarded train station in Europe. There was always a regular flow of main-line and S-Bahn traffic between Friedrichstrasse and Zoo Station in West Berlin (except during the Berlin Blockade of 1948–49, see p.151), but until late 1989 the East German government did all it could to keep its own citizens from joining it. Customs and passport controls and, more discreetly, armed guards separated westbound platforms from the rest of the station. Today, the station's tangle of checkpoints and guard posts have been replaced with a shopping arcade.

The Tränenpalast

Between Bahnhof Friedrichstrasse itself and the River Spree is a glass and concrete construction that was, until 1990, the **border crossing entrance** for westbound travellers, with an estimated eight million people passing through its doors each year. Known as the Tränenpalast or "Palace of Tears", this is now a concert venue, but during the days when the Berlin Wall was a very real barrier, visitors and tourists – and occasionally East German citizens who had been granted exit visas – queued inside to get through passport and customs controls before travelling by U- or S-Bahn to West Berlin.

Visitors to the East had to return to the West by midnight, and the functional entrance to the Tränenpalast was the scene of many a poignant farewell as people took leave of relatives, friends and lovers here. Within, a few reminders of its old role survive, including a cubicle with blackened glass windows overlooking the main hall, from which border guards watched those leaving the country.

Under the tracks to the east of the station, beside the Handelszentrum, is a delightful antiques market with a fascinating assemblage of old art, jewellery, books and curios.

The Admiralspalast

Just northeast of the rail bridge on Friedrichstrasse, at no. 101, is the Jugendstil **Admiralspalast**, a rare prewar survivor originally built as a variety theatre in 1910. Amid the predominantly concrete architecture of the immediate area, its partly gilded facade, divided by fluted columns and inset with bas-reliefs, comes as a real surprise. As one of the few buildings in the area to have survived the bombing, it became an important political meeting hall in the immediate postwar years and, on April 22 and 23, 1946, was the venue for the forced union of the social democratic SPD with the prewar Communist Party, the KPD. This resulted in the birth of the SED (Sozialistische Einheitspartei Deutschlands), the GDR Communist Party that controlled the country until March 1990. The building houses Die Distel theatre, a satirical cabaret whose occasionally daring performances highlighted the paradoxes and frustrations of the pre-*Wende* GDR and provided Western journalists with good intro paragraphs for state-of-the-nation pieces in the autumn of 1989.

Friedrichstrasse to Museum Island

Moving west from the Friedrichstrasse intersection along Unter den Linden, the lime trees begin to take a back seat in defining the feel of the boulevard. Instead, views open out on a string of imposing buildings, several the work of Knobelsdorf and Schinkel, which put an unyielding stamp on a strip that leads to the even grander constructions on Museum Island (covered in Chapter 2). Most are survivors of a nineteenth-century Berlin that Christopher Isherwood described as "so pompous, so very correct", and have been restored over the last 45 years or so from the postwar dereliction.

The Deutsche Guggenheim Berlin Museum

Housed in a former bank building and a far cry from the museum's architectural landmarks in New York and Bilbao, the German branch of New York's **Guggenheim Museum** (daily 11am–8pm, Thurs until 10pm; €3, Mon free; ⓦwww.deutsche-guggenheim-berlin.de; U-Bahn Französische Strasse) sits at the southern side of Unter den Linden, at the intersection with Charlottenstrasse. The disappointingly small gallery shows around four temporary exhibitions per year, focusing on top-drawer modern and contemporary art. Recent exhibitions have included looks at the work of Robert Mapplethorpe, Nam June Paik, Miwa Yanagi and Bruce Naumann. The galleries are modest in size, but are comfortably laid out and well lit. There's a small museum shop and a sleek, quiet café on site.

The Staatsbibliothek and the monument to Frederick the Great

Opposite the Deutsche Guggenheim, on Unter den Linden's northern side, the **Staatsbibliothek zu Berlin** (State Library; Mon–Fri 9am–9pm, Sat 9am–5pm; free; tours every first Sat of the month at 10.30am, also free; @www .staatsbibliothek-berlin.de; U-Bahn Französische Strasse) was first the Prussian and then GDR state library but is now twinned with the Staatsbibliothek in the Kulturforum (see p.114). A typically grandiose edifice dating from the turn of the twentieth century, its facade was extensively patched up after wartime shrapnel damage, and is now mainly the haunt of Humboldt University students. Visitors who don't feel like delving into the volumes within can sit in the ivy-clad courtyard by the fountain and have a drink or snack at the small café. As you do so, admire a GDR-era sculpture showing a member of the proletariat apparently reading a didactic Brecht poem on a relief at the other side of the fountain. The subject of the poem is the way in which the workers and soldiers who carry out the orders of kings and emperors are forgotten while the rulers themselves live on as historical figures.

Back on Unter den Linden is a statue commemorating just such a historical figure. Christian Rauch's equestrian **monument to Frederick the Great** (for more on the life of Frederick the Great see p.206) dates from the nineteenth century and shows Frederick astride a charger. Around the plinth, about a quarter of the size of the monarch, are representations of his generals, mostly on foot and conferring animatedly.

After the war, the statue of *Der alte Fritz*, as Frederick the Great is popularly known, was removed from Unter den Linden and only restored to its city-centre site in 1981 after a long exile in Potsdam. Its reinstatement reflected an odd revaluation by Erich Honecker's GDR of the pre-socialist past. No longer were figures like Frederick the Great, Blücher, Scharnhorst *et al* to be reviled as imperialistic militarists, but were to be accorded the status of historic figures worthy of commemoration. Even Bismarck, the Iron Chancellor of Wilhelmine Germany, was recognized as having "in his *Junker* way played a progressive historical role".

The Humboldt Universität

Back on the north side of the street, beside the Staatsbibliothek, stands the **Humboldt Universität**, a restrained Neoclassical building from 1748, originally built as a palace for Frederick the Great's brother. In 1809 the philologist, writer and diplomat Wilhelm Humboldt founded a school here that was to become the University of Berlin, and later renamed in his honour. Flanking the entrance gate are statues of Wilhelm and his brother Alexander, famous for his exploration of Central and South America. Wilhelm is contemplating the passing traffic, book in hand, and Alexander is sitting on a globe above a dedication to the "second discoverer of Cuba" from the University of Havana. Humboldt Universität Alumni include Karl Marx, Friedrich Engels and Karl

Liebknecht, the socialist leader and proclaimer of the first German republic who was murdered in 1919 (see p.297). The philologists Jacob and Wilhelm Grimm (better known as the Brothers Grimm) and Albert Einstein are some of the best-known former members of staff.

Bebelplatz

Directly opposite the university is **Bebelplatz**, formerly Opernplatz, the scene on May 10, 1933, of the infamous **Büchverbrennung**, the burning of books which conflicted with Nazi ideology. On the orders of Joseph Goebbels, Hitler's propaganda minister, thousands of books went up in smoke, including the works of "un-German" authors like Erich Maria Remarque, Thomas and Heinrich Mann, Stefan Zweig and Erich Kästner, along with volumes by countless foreign writers, H.G. Wells and Ernest Hemingway among them. The most fitting comment on this episode was made with accidental foresight by the Jewish poet Heinrich Heine during the previous century: "Where they start by burning books, they'll end by burning people." A recent and intriguing memorial to the book burning, *The Empty Library* by Micha Ullmann, can be seen in the middle of Bebelplatz under a glass pane set in the ground.

Bebelplatz was originally conceived by Frederick the Great as a tribute to the grandeur of ancient Rome and a monument to the greater glory of himself. He and the architect **Georg Wenzeslaus von Knobelsdorff** drew up plans for what was to be known as the Forum Fridericianum, a space that would recall the great open squares of the Classical city. It never fulfilled such lofty ambitions, and instead exhibits a rather humble and unimpressive mien. This may be changing, though, since Bebelplatz is now at the centre of a grand building project as the OpernCarrée – an adjacent block devoted to offices, shopping and luxury hotels – is being built. The area will be a building site until at least spring 2006.

The Alte Bibliothek and Staatsoper

The **Alte Bibliothek**, a former royal library, crowds the western side of Bebelplatz with a curved Baroque facade that has given it the nickname *Die Kommode* ("the chest of drawers"). Built between 1775 and 1780, its design was based on that of the Michaelertrakt in Vienna's Hofburg. Lenin spent some time here poring over dusty tomes while waiting for the Russian Revolution, and, despite the fact that only the building's facade survived the war, it has all been immaculately restored. Knobelsdorff's Neoclassical **Staatsoper**, on the eastern side of the square, looks a little plain in comparison, though it represented the pinnacle of the architect's career and was Berlin's first theatre. The building is best viewed from Unter den Linden, where an imposing portico marks the main entrance. Just under two centuries after its construction it became the first major building to fall victim to World War II bombing, on the night of April 9–10, 1941. The Nazis restored it for its bicentenary in 1943, but on February 3, 1945, it was gutted once again. Now totally reconstructed, like virtually everything else in the area, it is one of Berlin's leading opera houses (see p.257).

Sankt-Hedwigs-Kathedrale

Just behind is another Knobelsdorff creation, the stylistically incongruous **Sankt-Hedwigs-Kathedrale** (Mon–Sat 10am–5pm, Sun 1–5pm; free), which was built as a place of worship for the city's Catholic minority in 1747 and is still in use. According to popular legend it owes its circular shape and domed profile to Frederick the Great's demand that it be built in the form of an upturned teacup. This probably stems from the fact that the monarch "advised" Knobelsdorff; in truth, the building's shape was inspired by the Pantheon in Rome. Reduced to a shell on March 2, 1943, the cathedral was not reconstructed until 1963, a restoration that left it with a slightly altered dome and a modernized interior.

The **interior**, past the hazy biblical reliefs of the entrance portico, is perhaps the most unusual aspect of the whole building. The greatest feature of the vast main hall is the split-level double altar – the upper one is used on Sundays and special occasions, while the sunken altar in the crypt, reached by a flight of broad stairs, is used for weekday Masses. All this is complemented by the stainless-steel pipes of the ethereal-sounding organ above the entrance and 1970s-style globe-lamps hanging from the ceiling. If you've survived the combined effects of all this, the crypt with its eight grotto-like side chapels and near-abstract charcoal drawings is a further attraction.

The Opernpalais

Back on Unter den Linden, just east of the Staatsoper, is a lawn dotted with several dignified **statues of Prussian generals**. Scharnhorst stands at the front, while Yorck, Blücher and Gneisenau bring up the rear. Blücher, whose timely intervention turned the day at Waterloo, looks most warlike, with his foot resting on a cannon barrel and a sabre in his hand.

Next door to this martial grouping is the eighteenth-century **Opernpalais**, a Baroque palace known as the Prinzessinpalais (Princess's Palace) before the war, in memory of its role as a swanky town residence for the three daughters of Friedrich Wilhelm III. It's now home to a couple of pricey restaurants and the genteel *Operncafé* (see p.233).

The Kronprinzenpalais

Connected to its neighbour the Opernpalais via an arched bridge, the **Kronprinzenpalais** is the older of the two buildings, and dates from 1663. After a 1732 Baroque face-lift, it became a residence for Prussian princes, but with the demise of the monarchy in 1918 was converted into a national art gallery and became a leading venue for modern art exhibitions. In 1933 the Nazis closed it, declaring hundreds of Expressionist and contemporary works housed here to be examples of *entartete Kunst* or "degenerate art". Most of these were either sold off abroad or destroyed, and a number were bought at knock-down prices by leading Nazis, Göring among them. The Kronprinzenpalais has since played host to temporary exhibitions from the collections of the Deutsches Historisches Museum, as renovation took place there, and continues to house a variety of organizations and an exhibition and event space.

The Neue Wache

Schinkel's most celebrated surviving creation, the **Neue Wache**, is on Unter den Linden opposite the Opernpalais. Built between 1816 and 1818 as a guardhouse for the royal watch, it resembles a stylized Roman temple and served as a sort of Neoclassical police station until 1918. In 1930–31 it was converted into a memorial to the military dead of World War I, and in 1957 the GDR government extended this concept to include those killed by the Nazis, dedicating the building as a "Memorial to the Victims of Fascism and Militarism". Until 1990 one of East Berlin's most ironic rituals was played out in front of the Neue Wache with the regular changing of the Nationale

Volksarmee (National People's Army – the GDR army) honour guard, a much-photographed goose-stepping ritual that ended with the demise of the East German state.

These days it serves as the "National Memorial to the Victims of War and Tyranny", and inside it a granite slab covers the tombs of an unknown soldier and an unknown concentration camp victim. At the head of this memorial stone is a statue, depicting a mother clutching her dying son, an enlargement of a small sculptural piece by Käthe Kollwitz.

Maxim-Gorki-Theater

Just behind the Neue Wache, the **Maxim-Gorki-Theater** (see p.258) is a one-time singing academy converted into a theatre after World War II. The grand-looking building just to the east, the **Palais am Festungsgrab**, has had a chequered career. Originally built during the eighteenth century as a palace for a royal gentleman of the bedchamber, it later served as a residence for Prussian finance ministers, and during GDR days it was the Zentrale Haus der Deutsch-Sowjetischen Freundschaft or "Central House of German-Soviet Friendship". Today it houses the **Museum Mitte von Berlin** (Wed & Fri 1–5pm, Sat 11am–8pm, Sun 11am–5pm; free; U-Bahn Friedrichstrasse), a modest local history museum, and the *Tadschikische Teestuben*, a tearoom serving Russian specialities (see "Eating and Drinking", p.242).

The Zeughaus and the Deutsches Historisches Museum

Across Hinter den Giesshaus, opposite the Neue Wache, is one of eastern Berlin's finest Baroque buildings, the old Prussian Arsenal or **Zeughaus**, which now houses the **Deutsches Historisches Museum** (daily 10am–6pm; €2; ☎030/20 30 40, ⊛www.dhm.de; S-Bahn Hackescher Markt). The main museum is closed until mid-2005 for a major renovation, but when it reopens it will use its immense collection to chart German history from the Dark Ages to the present. One particularly impressive part of the renovation work was to add a swirling glass annexe, the **I.M. Pei Bau**, at the back of the Zeughaus to host temporary exhibitions. The annexe was designed by I.M. Pei – architect of the famous glass pyramid at the entrance to the Louvre in Paris – and the hallmark geometric glass is here too; the play of light is perhaps the most important factor in making the building work. Exhibitions here usually delve into German social history in the last couple of centuries, and vary widely, though all seem to share first-class display techniques and an even-handedness in the treatment of what is often difficult subject matter.

The original plans for the Zeughaus were drawn up by François Blondel, but the building was completed by Andreas Schlüter, who was responsible for many of the decorative elements, notably the walls of the Schlüterhof, the museum's inner courtyard, which are lined by reliefs depicting the contorted faces of dying warriors. These are vivid, realistic depictions of agony and anguish, with nothing heroic about them: death is shown cutting everyone down to size with none spared its indignities.

There was much excitement at the Zeughaus on June 14, 1848, when, during the revolutionary upheavals, the people of Berlin stormed the building looking for arms. A number of citizens were killed, and no weapons were found, but the incident gave the authorities an excuse to bring troops into the city and ban various democratic newspapers and organizations. Just over thirty years later the Zeughaus was turned into a museum devoted to the exploits of the Prussian army, and from 1953, though heavily damaged, the building was given over to the nascent Museum für Deutsche Geschichte, offering the GDR's version of German history. The highly political and subjective nature of its content was to cause problems for the directors and staff of the museum after reunification and, despite attempts to redress the balance with a special exhibition about German victims of Stalinist persecution during the period, it was closed down just after reunification. The Deutsches Historisches Museum was then established in 1991, with an exhibition entitled "Pictures and Objects from German History" that presented a West German slant on those same historical events, but it too was found wanting. After renovations, a new exhibition will be installed, but the manner in which the museum will present the tangled history of Germany is still being debated.

South of Unter den Linden

A block south of Unter den Linden begins a network of streets that is easy to explore on foot and which contains some key landmarks – particularly from Berlin's Cold War and post-reunification history. Although the war took its toll here too, much has survived or been rebuilt, including the immaculately restored **Gendarmenmarkt**, one of the architectural highlights of Berlin, with two attractive churches: the **Französischer Dom** and **Deutscher Dom**. Beside it the grid-like street pattern of Friedrichstadt on the east side of Friedrichstrasse survives as tangible evidence of the past – one of a number of seventeenth-century city extensions that took Berlin beyond its original walled core.

At the far southern end of Friedrichstrasse is the site of **Checkpoint Charlie**, the principal gateway between East and West through the **Berlin Wall**. Following the former course of the Wall west leads you to Wilhelmstrasse, Berlin's prewar Regierungsviertel or "government quarter". The area between Wilhelmstrasse and Potsdamer Platz was the site of **Hitler's Chancellery and Bunker**, where the final chapter of the Third Reich unfolded, and though little now remains, trying to figure out what was where can be a compelling activity. Just west of here is **Potsdamer Platz**, which was the city's busiest corner until pulverized by the war and then effectively erased from the Berlin landscape by the building of the Wall. A huge commercial project has recently gone up here in an attempt to re-create the area's former liveliness.

The Bauakademie and around

The block just south of Unter den Linden, on the banks of the Spree, was the site of the former bland modernist GDR Foreign Ministry building, since torn down and, for now, largely replaced by a grassy field. But before World War II it was the site of the **Bauakademie**, Karl Friedrich Schinkel's architectural school. This was reckoned to be one of his finest creations and Schinkel even moved in here, occupying a top-floor apartment until his death in 1841. Inevitably, wartime bombing took its toll and in 1962 the remains were demolished in a departure from the GDR's usual policy of restoring the city's monuments wherever possible. It's been proposed that Schinkel's Bauakademie be rebuilt, and already, as a kind of advertisement and incentive, a corner section of the

Karl Friedrich Schinkel (1781–1841)

Karl Friedrich Schinkel was an incredibly prolific architect who quite literally transformed nineteenth-century Berlin, creating some of the city's most famous Neoclassical buildings. His first ever design, the **Pomonatempel** in Potsdam (see p.215), was completed while he was still a nineteen-year-old student in Berlin. Despite this auspicious beginning, his architectural career did not take off immediately and for a while he worked as a landscape artist and set decorator for the theatre, later turning his hand to set design (an activity he pursued even after he had established himself as an architect). Towards the end of the first decade of the nineteenth century he began submitting architectural designs for the great public works of the time, and, in 1810, he secured a job with the administration of Prussian buildings.

In 1815 he was given a position in the new Public Works Department, an appointment which marked the beginning of the most productive phase of his career. During the years between 1815 and 1830, when he was made head of the department, he designed some of his most renowned buildings. Constructions like the Grecianstyle **Neue Wache** (see p.64), the elegant **Schauspielhaus** (see p.69), and the **Altes Museum** (p.85) with its striking Doric columns were just what were needed to enhance the ever-expanding capital of Brandenburg-Prussia. Other creations from this period include the **War Memorial Cross** in Kreuzberg and the **Friedrichwerdersche Kirche** (see p.67), both inspired by neo-Gothic styles that were all the rage in England at the time. Later in his career Schinkel experimented with other architectural forms, a phase marked by the Romanesque **Charlottenhof** and **Römischer Bäder** in Potsdam (see p.212).

By virtue of his own designs and the role he played in shaping Brandenburg-Prussia's building policy, Schinkel remains, without doubt, one of the most influential German architects of the nineteenth century. Nearly every town in Brandenburg has a building that Schinkel had, at the very least, some involvement in, and a lasting testimony to his importance is the fact that even today the very heart of Berlin is essentially defined by his works.

building has been reconstructed on its original site. The rest of the building has been recreated using scaffolding, wrapped in a cloth facade – the hope is to stimulate enthusiasm and raise money for its reconstruction. A statue of Schinkel himself can be seen, looking a little lost, in the middle of the field.

The Schinkel Museum

Karl Friedrich Schinkel also designed the **Friedrichwerdersche Kirche** just close by his Bauakademie in which the **Schinkel Museum** (daily: 10am–6pm; free; ⓦwww.smb.spk-berlin.de; S-Bahn Hausvogteiplatz) fittingly celebrates the work of the man, who, more than anyone, gave nineteenth-century Berlin its distinctive Neoclassical stamp (see box above). The church itself is a rather plain neo-Gothic affair, a stylistic departure for Schinkel, who was infatuated with the Classical styles he had encountered on trips to Italy. The inspiration for the Friedrichwerdersche Kirche came from churches Schinkel had seen on a visit to England in 1826.

The Schinkel Museum was opened in 1987 when postwar restoration of the building was completed to coincide with Berlin's 750th anniversary. A display in the church's upper gallery gives a full rundown of Schinkel's achievements, setting his work in the context of the times, and also details the history of the church. On the ground floor is a jumble of German Neoclassical statuary from the nineteenth century.

The Foreign Ministry and the Jungfernbrücke

Opposite the Friedrichwerdersche Kirche and beside the River Spree lies the heavily guarded **Foreign Ministry**, one of the city's many new Federal government buildings. The structure, though massive, projects an unassuming aspect by means of its plain glass facade, through which you can see a serene covered courtyard, complete with trees and fountain. It illustrates one answer to a common problem facing architects for the new German capital: how to create large and significant civic buildings whilst avoiding any hints of Nazi monumentalism. A good example of the latter, in fact, lies directly behind – an immense and imposing structure built between 1934 and 1938 for the Central Bank. Having survived the war, it was later used as SED (Socialist Unity Party of Germany) Headquarters, one-time nerve centre of the East German communist party, and is now also occupied by the Foreign Office. Heading down Unterwasserstrasse, and beside the ex-SED Headquarters, is the **Jungfernbrücke**, Berlin's oldest surviving bridge, built in 1798. It's actually a drawbridge and the creaky-looking winding gear still raises it to allow passing boats by.

The Gendarmenmarkt

A couple of minutes' walk west of the Foreign Ministry along Französische Strasse is the **Gendarmenmarkt**, a square whose present appearance belies the fact that its historic buildings were almost obliterated during the war. It's now one of the most successfully restored parts of the city, but rebuilding lasted until well into the 1980s, and it's only really in the last few years that the area has re-emerged as one of Berlin's most attractive corners. Gendarmenmarkt's origins are prosaic. It was originally home to Berlin's main market until the Gendarme regiment, who gave the square its name (recently readopted after a long GDR-era hiatus as Platz der Akademie), set up their stables on the site. With the departure of the military, Gendarmenmarkt was transformed at the behest of Frederick the Great, who ordered an architectural revamp of the two churches that stood here, in an attempt to mimic the Piazza del Popolo in Rome.

The Französischer Dom

The results of Frederick's revamp are impressive, and are at their most eye-catching in the **Französischer Dom** at the northern end of the square. Originally built as a simple place of worship for Berlin's influential Huguenot community at the beginning of the eighteenth century, the building was transformed by the addition of a Baroque tower, turning it into one of Berlin's most appealing churches.

The tower (see below) is purely decorative and not actually consecrated, but it's so striking that a lot of visitors don't actually notice the church proper, the **Französischen Friedrichstadt Kirche** (French Church in Friedrichstadt; Tues–Sun noon–5pm), which is so modest in appearance that it looks more like an ancillary building for the tower. The main entrance to the church is at the western end of the Dom, facing Charlottenstrasse. The church, reconsecrated in 1983 after years of restoration work, has a simple hall-like interior with few decorative features and only a plain table as an altar.

The Hugenottenmuseum and Dom tower

At the base of the tower next door is the entrance to the **Hugenottenmuseum** (Tues–Sat noon–5pm, Sun 11am–5pm; €2), detailing the history of the Huguenots in France and Brandenburg. There are sections dealing with the theological background of the Reformation in France, the Revocation of the Edict of Nantes leading to the flight of the Huguenots from their native country, their settling in Berlin and the influence of the new arrivals on trade, science and literature. The museum also has a short section on the destruction and rebuilding of the Dom.

A longish spiral of steps leads up to the Dom **tower** (daily 9am–7pm; €3), which was built some eighty years after the church – and only finally put to rights, after wartime damage, in 1987. Here you'll find a balcony running around the outside that offers good views of the surrounding construction sites. Another attraction is the tower bells, which ring out automatically every day at noon, 4pm and 7pm – a near deafening experience if you happen to be on the balcony at the time. At other times during the week concerts are performed by bell-ringers – ask at the desk for details.

The Deutscher Dom

At the southern end of the square, the **Deutscher Dom**, built in 1708 for the city's Lutheran community, is the stylistic twin of the Französischer Dom. The Dom now hosts the "Wege-Irrwege-Umwege" exhibition (Wed–Sun 10am–7pm, Thurs open until 10pm; free) which looks, in rather too much detail, at Germany's democratic history and is consequently fairly dull. The exhibition is in German, but a free English-language audio guide is available at the front desk (ID required). A wander up through the Dom with its labyrinth of galleries is the highlight, and the reward for reaching the top is the chance to see a few scale-models of some early Norman Foster designs for the reconstruction of the Reichstag (see p.56).

The Schauspielhaus

Between the two churches on Gendarmenmarkt stands Schinkel's Neoclassical **Schauspielhaus** (now renamed Konzerthaus Berlin). Dating from 1817, it was built around the ruins of Langhans's burned-out National Theatre, retaining the latter's exterior walls and portico columns. A broad sweep of steps leads up to the main entrance and into an interior of incredible opulence, where chandeliers, marble, gilded plasterwork and pastel-hued wall paintings all compete for attention. Gutted during a raid in 1943, the building suffered further damage during heavy fighting as the Russians attempted to root out SS troops who had dug in here. Reopened in October 1984, it's now the home of the Berlin Symphony Orchestra (see p.257). During Christmas 1989 Leonard Bernstein conducted a performance of Beethoven's Ninth Symphony here to celebrate the *Wende*, with the word *Freiheit* ("Freedom") substituted for *Freude* ("Joy") in Schiller's choral finale.

A **statue of Schiller** stands outside the Schauspielhaus. It was repositioned here in 1988, having been removed by the Nazis over fifty years earlier, returned to what was then East Berlin from the West in exchange for reliefs originally from the Pfaueninsel (see p.195) and a statue from a Tiergarten villa. Outside Germany, Friedrich Schiller (1759–1805) is best known for the *Ode to Joy* that provides the words to the final movements of Beethoven's Ninth Symphony, but in his homeland he is venerated as one of the greatest German poets and dramatists of the Enlightenment. His works, from early *Sturm und Drang* dramas like *Die Räuber* ("The Thieves") to later historical plays like *Maria Stuart*, were primarily concerned with freedom – political, moral and personal – which was probably the reason why the Nazis were so quick to bundle him off Gendarmenmarkt.

Leipziger Strasse and around

From Gendarmenmarkt, **Leipziger Strasse**, once a main Berlin shopping street running from Alexanderplatz to Potsdamer Platz, is only two short blocks south. But the most interesting route goes south via Friedrichstrasse – a block west of Gendarmenmarkt – which became an upmarket shopping district in the 1990s, and offers the usual chichi stores amid eclectic architecture.

For many years Leipziger Strasse was a lifeless housing and commercial development dating from the early 1970s "big is beautiful" phase of East Berlin town planning. The buildings on the south side of the street are higher than those on the north side – at this height they conveniently block off the huge offices of the late **Axel Springer**, extreme right-wing newspaper and publishing magnate (the newspaper *Bild* was his most notorious creation), just over the erstwhile border, which the wily old media mogul had built here to cause maximum irritation to the GDR authorities.

Until the late nineteenth century Leipziger Strasse was a quiet residential area, but by the turn of the twentieth century it had become one of Berlin's foremost shopping streets, with the establishment of Tietz and Wertheim's department stores, and a host of smaller operations and restaurants, including the celebrated *Kempinski's*. World War II put paid to all that (all three above-mentioned concerns were Jewish owned and run and were confiscated by the Nazis), relegating the street's commercial glory to the history books. Leipziger Strasse is now once again a main route leading from the heart of Berlin towards the city's West End, as thundering traffic attests.

The Spittelkolonnaden and around

Virtually nothing remains of prewar Leipziger Strasse. The only apparent survivor, the Spittelkolonnaden, a semicircular colonnade on the right towards its eastern end, on the site of what used to be Donhoffplatz, turns out to be a copy of part of an eighteenth-century structure formerly on the opposite side of the street. In front of this replica is another copy – this time of a **milepost** that once stood in the vicinity. A little further along is the **Spittelmarkt**, which marks the site of a medieval hospital. To the left of the street spouts the **Spindlerbrunnen**, a chocolate-coloured nineteenth-century fountain that was erected here in 1891. It survived the war by virtue of the fact that it was removed to the grounds of a suburban hospital in 1927 and only returned to its old site in 1980.

Museum für Kommunikation Berlin

Towards the western end of Leipziger Strasse, at the junction with Mauerstrasse, is the former Imperial postal ministry, now home to the **Museum für Kommunikation Berlin** (Tues–Fri 9am–5pm, Sat & Sun 11am–7pm; €3; ⓦwww.museumsstiftung.de; U-Bahn Mohrenstrasse). The museum traces its roots back to the world's first postal museum, which opened in Berlin in 1872 and moved into this Baroque palace to share space with the postal ministry in 1898. When the building was damaged in the war the collection dispersed, and only after reunification and several years of renovation could it reopen in its historic home in March 2000. There's a lot more here than just stamps, and if you have a keen interest in the gadgets and devices that led us to the world of the Internet, you should have a look. The interior itself, ornate Wilhelmine detailing around a wonderful, light-filled central court, is worth checking out too.

△ Potsdamer Platz

Checkpoint Charlie to Potsdamer Platz

A couple of hundred metres south of the Leipziger Strasse-Friedrichstrasse intersection is the site of **Checkpoint Charlie**, one of the most famous names associated with the Wall and Cold War-era Berlin. This Allied military post on Friedrichstrasse marked the border between East and West Berlin until July 1990, when it was removed. It can now be seen in the Allied Museum (see p.192), although a replica has been installed at the original site. While it stood it was one of Berlin's more celebrated landmarks and the building lent its name informally to the adjacent GDR border crossing (official title Grenzübergang Friedrichstrasse), which, with its dramatic "YOU ARE NOW LEAVING THE AMERICAN SECTOR" signs and unsmiling border guards, used to be the archetypal movie-style Iron Curtain crossing. In the Cold War years it was the scene of repeated border incidents, including a standoff between American and Soviet forces in October 1961, which culminated in tanks from both sides growling at each other for a few days.

The site of the border crossing itself is hardly recognizable now. The extensive **border installations** were torn down in 1991, having stood derelict since the spring of the previous year, and in their place an impromptu coach park set up. A high-profile complex of office buildings and retail shops called the American Business Center – part of it designed by American architect Philip Johnson – has gone up on the western side of Friedrichstrasse. All that remains of the border crossing is a former guard tower, now designated a historic monument.

The Museum Haus am Checkpoint Charlie

For tangible evidence of the trauma of the Wall, head for the **Museum Haus am Checkpoint Charlie** at Friedrichstrasse 44 (daily 9am–10pm; €9.50; ⓦmuseum-haus-am.checkpointcharlie.org; U-Bahn Kochstrasse). Here the history of the Wall is told in photos of escape tunnels and with the home-made aircraft and converted cars by which people attempted, succeeded, and sometimes tragically failed, to break through the border. Films document the stories of some of the 230-odd people murdered by the East German border guards, and there's a section on human rights behind the Iron Curtain, but it's a jumbled, huge and rambling collection, and not quite the harrowing experience that some visitors seem to expect. For more details, pick up a copy of *It Happened at the Wall* or *The Wall Speaks*, both on sale here.

The Luftfahrtministerium

A short walk west from Checkpoint Charlie along Zimmerstrasse, following the former course of the Wall, brings you to Hermann Göring's fortress-like **Luftfahrtministerium** (Air Ministry), one relic of the Nazi past that has survived very much intact. Göring promised Berliners that not a single

---

A chip off the old Eastern Bloc

If you're looking for a piece of the Wall as a **souvenir**, be warned that it is illegal to chip off shards from remaining portions of the wall and the pieces sold on the street by Checkpoint Charlie are almost never the real thing. Despite official-looking "certificates of authentication" often given with a purchase, a better check is to look for the tell-tale pale aggregate of flint, pebbles and other hard stones.

The uprising of June 1953

On June 16 and 17, 1953, Leipziger Strasse was the focal point of a **nationwide uprising** against the GDR's communist government. General dissatisfaction with economic and political conditions in the eastern half of the city came to a head when building workers (the traditional proletarian heroes of GDR mythology) constructing the prestigious Stalinallee project went on strike, protesting at having to work longer hours for the same pay. On June 16 they marched on the Haus der Ministerien, which was at that time the seat of the GDR government. Here they demanded to speak to GDR President Otto Grotewohl and SED General Secretary Walter Ulbricht. These two declined to make an appearance, so speakers from the crowd got up to demand the dissolution of the government and free elections. Thanks to Western radio broadcasts, the news rapidly spread across the country, and in the morning of the following day, a wave of strikes and demonstrations took place throughout the GDR. Tools were abandoned, and traffic in East Berlin came to a standstill as 100,000 demonstrators marched on the Haus der Ministerien once again; clashes with the police followed as demonstrators attacked SED party offices and state food stores. The GDR authorities proved unequal to the situation, and at 1pm the Soviet military commandant of the city declared a state of emergency. It's estimated that several hundred people died as Soviet tanks rolled in to restore order. Afterwards, Bertolt Brecht sardonically suggested that the GDR government should "dissolve the people, and elect another".

bomb would fall on the city during the war; if this were to happen, the Reichsmarschal said, he would change his name to Meyer – a common Jewish surname. Ironically, the Air Ministry was one of the few buildings to emerge more or less unscathed from the bombing and Red Army shelling. After the establishment of the GDR it became the SED regime's Haus der Ministerien (House of Ministries), and was the target of a mass demonstration on June 16, 1953 (see box above), which was to be a prelude for a general but short-lived uprising against the communist government the next day. There's a historical irony of sorts in the fact that the building became, for a number of years after reunification, the headquarters of the Treuhandanstalt, the agency responsible for the privatization of the former GDR's economy. It has again been tidied up and now houses the Federal Finance Ministry.

Wilhelmstrasse

North beyond the Luftfahrtministerium along Wilhelmstrasse the only structure that stands out – apart from the marooned apartment building that once housed high-ranking East Germans – is an apparent airport control tower that turns out to be the **Czech Embassy**. But it's really what you can't see that makes the street interesting; from 1871 onwards it was Imperial Berlin's Whitehall and Downing Street rolled into one, lined by ministries and government buildings, including the Chancellery and, after the Republic was established in 1918, the Presidential Palace. Historical markers have been placed along the street, with photos and descriptions of the former buildings.

The Nazis remodelled Wilhelmstrasse, replacing the original Chancellery with a vast **new building** designed by Albert Speer in 1938. This gigantic complex, including Hitler's underground bunker (see box, p.76), stood between Wilhelmstrasse and Ebertstrasse just north of Vosstrasse. Today nothing remains, for, even though the Chancellery building survived the war, it was torn down in a fit of revenge by the conquering Soviet army,

The Berlin Wall

After the war, Berlin was split among its conquerors, as Stalin, Roosevelt and Churchill had agreed at Yalta. Each sector was administered by the relevant country, and was supposed to exist peacefully with its neighbours under a unified city council. But, almost from the outset, antagonism between the Soviet and other sectors was high. Only three years after the war ended, the Soviet forces closed down the land access corridors to the city from the Western zones in what became known as the **Berlin Blockade**: it was successfully overcome by a massive Western **airlift** of food and supplies that lasted nearly a year. This, followed by the 1953 uprising, large-scale cross-border emigration (between 1949 and 1961, the year the Wall was built, over three million East Germans – almost a fifth of the population – fled to the Federal Republic) and innumerable "incidents", led to the building of what was known in the GDR as the "anti-Fascist protection wall".

Erected overnight on August 13, 1961 to cordon off the Soviet sector, the Wall followed its boundaries implacably, cutting through houses, across squares and rivers with its own cool illogicality. Suddenly the British, American and French sectors of the city were corralled some 200km inside the GDR.

An oddity of the Wall was that it was built a few metres inside GDR territory; the West Berlin authorities therefore had little control over the **graffiti** that covered it. The Wall was an ever-changing mixture of colours and slogans, with occasional bursts of bitterness: "My friends are dying behind you"; humour: "Why not jump over and join the Party?"; and stupidity: "We shoulda nuked 'em in 45".

Over the years, over two hundred people were **killed** endeavouring to cross the Wall. Initial escape attempts were straightforward, and often successful – hollowing out furniture, ramming checkpoint barriers and simple disguise brought many people over. However, the authorities quickly rose to the challenge, and would-be escapees were forced to become more resourceful, digging tunnels, and constructing gliders, one-man submarines and hot-air balloons. By the time the Wall came down, every escape method conceivable seemed to have been used – even down to passing through

who used marble from the site to fashion the memorial on Strasse des 17 Juni (see p.125) and the huge war memorial at the Soviet military cemetery in Treptower Park (see p.155).

The Topography of Terror

Back beside Luftfahrtministerium, and adjacent to one of the few remaining stretches of the Wall on Niederkirchenstrasse, is the former site of the Reich Security offices, which included the headquarters of the Gestapo and SS. Little has been done with the plot since the destruction of the offices at the end of the war, though the outdoor exhibition, **The Topography of Terror** (Tues–Sun 10am–6pm; free but bring ID for deposit to hire audio-guide, @www.topographie.de), is worth investigating. A numbered series of noticeboards with photographs and German texts (the audioguides are in English) indicate the sites of the most important buildings and reveal just how massive a machine the Nazi organization became: it was here that Himmler planned the Final Solution – the deportation and genocide of European Jews – and organized the Gestapo, the feared secret police. The ground underneath the exhibition once held the cellars of the Gestapo headquarters, which stood at Prinz-Albrecht-Str. 8 (now Niederkirchnerstrasse), where important prisoners were interrogated and tortured. The staff of the SS were based in the former *Hotel Prinz Albrecht* next door, and just around the corner in the Prinz-Albrecht-Palais (opposite the entrance

Checkpoint Charlie in the stomach of a pantomime cow – and those desperate to get out of the GDR preferred the long wait and complications of applying to leave officially to the risk of being gunned down by a border guard. The guards, known as Grepos, were under instructions to shoot anyone attempting to scale the Wall, and to shoot accurately: any guard suspected of deliberately missing was court-martialled, and his family could expect severe harassment from the authorities.

Late in 1989 the East German government, spurred by Gorbachev's *glasnost* and confronted by a tense domestic climate, realized it could keep the impossible stable no longer. To an initially disbelieving and then jubilant Europe, travel restrictions for GDR citizens were lifted on November 9, 1989 – effectively, the Wall had ceased to matter, and pictures of Berliners, East and West, hacking away at the detested symbol filled newspapers and TV bulletins around the world. Within days, enterprising characters were renting out hammers and chisels so that souvenir hunters could take home their own chip of the Wall.

Today, especially in the city centre, it's barely possible to tell exactly where the Wall ran: odd juxtapositions of dereliction against modernity, an unexpected swathe of erstwhile "Death Strip", are in most cases all that's left of one of the most hated borders the world ever knew. The simple row of cobbles that has been placed along much of the former course of the wall acts as a necessary reminder. Few significant stretches remain, the sections devoted to the East Side Gallery (see p.154) and the Berlin Wall Memorial (see p.104) being the most notable exceptions.

One sad postscript to the story of the Wall hit the headlines in spring 1992. Two former **border guards** were tried for the murder of Chris Gueffroy, shot dead while illegally trying to cross the border at Neukölln in February 1989. Under the GDR government the guards had been treated to a meal by their superiors and given extra holiday for their patriotic actions; under the new regime, they received sentences for murder – while those ultimately responsible, the former leaders of the GDR, have largely evaded punishment.

to Kochstrasse) was the SS security service headquarters, where extensive records of all "enemies of the state", a category that included Jews and homosexuals, were kept.

The Martin-Gropius-Bau

The magnificently restored building on the southern side of Niederkirchnerstrasse is the **Martin-Gropius-Bau** (times and prices vary; ☎030/25 48 60, @www.gropiusbau.de; S&U-Bahn Potsdamer Platz). Designed in 1877 by Martin Gropius, a pupil of Schinkel and the uncle of Bauhaus guru Walter (see p.124), the Gropius-Bau was, until its destruction in the war, home of the museum of applied art. In recent years it has been rebuilt and refurbished, and now houses changing exhibitions of art, photography and architecture. The *Gropius Restaurant* serves snacks and meals and is a useful stopping-off point and necessary pick-me-up after tackling the adjacent Topography of Terror exhibition.

Potsdamer Platz

Said to have been the busiest square in prewar Europe, **Potsdamer Platz** was once surrounded by stores, bars and clubs and pulsed with life day and night. The war left Potsdamer Platz severely battered, though it soon regained some of its vitality in the first chaotic postwar years as a black market centre

Hitler's bunker

Just above An der Kolonnade (slightly to the north of the Chancellery site) is the site of **Hitler's Bunker**, where the Führer spent his last days, issuing meaningless orders as the Battle of Berlin raged above. Here Hitler married Eva Braun and wrote his final testament: he personally was responsible for nothing; he had been betrayed by the German people, who had proved unequal to his leadership and deserved the future he could now envisage ahead of them. On April 30, 1945, he shot himself, and his body was hurriedly burned by loyal officers. In a 1992 postscript to the story, the KGB released film showing a gaunt corpse with a toothbrush moustache, allegedly Hitler, claiming that the dictator's body had in fact survived destruction in the war's final days and fallen into Soviet hands. Subsequently, so the tale went, the body was transported to Russia where it exerted a near-obsessional fascination for Stalin and many others who saw it. The supposed corpse was ferried around various secret locations until the 1970s, when it was finally destroyed on the orders of Leonid Brezhnev.

For several years after reunification there was debate about what to do with the remains of the bunker. Some said they should be preserved as a memorial; others claimed that they would become a shrine for rightists and neo-Nazi groups and should be destroyed. Finally it was decided to leave the bunker buried and unmarked.

at the junction of the Soviet, American and British occupation sectors. Later, West Berliners watched from their side of the dividing line as the Soviets put down the East Berlin uprising of 1953. During the rest of the decade the Cold War was played out here in words, with the Western authorities relaying their version of the news to East Berliners by means of an electronic newsboard – countered by an Eastern billboard exhorting West Berliners to shop in cheap East Berlin stores. This ended with the coming of the Wall, which finally put a physical seal on the ideological division of Potsdamer Platz. On the Eastern side all the buildings (which were mostly war vintage wrecks) were razed to give the GDR's border guards a clear field of fire, while in the West only a couple of battered survivors, including the hulk of the *Hotel Esplanade*, once one of the city's finest, were left as a reminder of the way things used to be. For many years tourists were able to gaze out at the East from a viewing platform here, and ponder the sight of prewar tramlines disappearing at the base of the Wall.

The dismantling of the Wall produced one of Europe's most valuable lots, a huge empty site smack in the middle of the city. It was no surprise, therefore, that the land was bought up by huge corporations, Sony and DaimlerChrysler principally, with equally huge plans for sprawling **commercial complexes**. Building this now-completed mini-city from scratch represents a feat of engineering: an entire infrastructure for power, water and sewage was created; subway tunnels were drilled and new S- and U-Bahn stations built; the surviving Weinhaus Huth, a landmarked building, was picked up and trundled to another spot; and the remaining interior portions of the *Hotel Esplanade* were incorporated into a new restaurant. For several years the area, sporting a thicket of huge cranes and dominated by the incessant sounds of building, was touted as "Europe's largest construction site". Despite all the fuss, however – and the huge amounts of money – the new Potsdamer Platz offers little more than most large malls, though some of the modern architecture is certainly worth a second look.

The DaimlerChrysler Quarter

DaimlerChrysler hired, among others, Renzo Piano and Richard Rogers to create an ensemble of disparate buildings that includes several restaurants, a stage theatre, a movie multiplex, a 3D big-screen movie theatre, and the obligatory shopping mall. The decision to use a variety of forms and facades was a good one, but inevitably the results on street level aren't all that stimulating.

Rise above the street, though, to the **Panorama Punkt** (Tues–Sun 11am–7.30pm; €3) at the top of its largest skyscraper and via Europe's fastest elevator, and the views are among the best in the city. This is mainly due to the immense height and ideal central location, but the exposed nature of the outdoor viewing deck gives an immediacy of experience that you won't find in the Fernsehturm (see p.90), the other main contender.

The Sony Center

The **Sony Center** (⊛www.sonycenter.de), designed by Helmut Jahn, is more uniform than the DaimlerChrysler Quarter, with several similar glass-sheathed buildings grouped around a capacious, circular courtyard. Its rotunda, topped by a conical glass roof, is perhaps the most impressive showpiece in the platz, open to the elements but at the same time providing a remove from the surrounding urban racket. It has the same touristy pulls as the Daimler-Chrysler complex, but does include a couple of worthwhile attractions. The **Filmmuseum Berlin** (Tues–Sun 10am–6pm; Thurs until 8pm; €6; ⊛www .filmmuseum-berlin.de) contains an excellent presentation on the history of the movies, concentrating on the German film industry, from *The Cabinet of Dr. Caligari* to *Run, Lola, Run*. No fewer than three rooms are devoted to artefacts – costumes, letters, photos, and the like – of Germany's biggest international star, Marlene Dietrich.

2

Schlossplatz and the Museum Island

At the eastern end of Unter den Linden the Schlossbrücke leads onto **Schlossplatz** and the island in the middle of the River Spree that formed the core of the medieval twin town of Berlin-Cölln. By virtue of its defensive position, this island later became the site of the Hohenzollern *Residenz* – location of the fortress-cum-palace and church of the family who controlled Berlin and Brandenburg from the fifteenth century onwards. Centred roughly on present-day Schlossplatz, this was originally a martial, fortified affair, as much for protection from the perennially rebellious Berliners as from outside enemies, but over the years domestic stability resulted in the reshaping of the *Residenz* on a slightly more decorative basis.

With the consolidation of their authority during the nineteenth century and the rise of Brandenburg-Prussia to great power, the Hohenzollerns decided it was time to add a museum quarter to their increasingly bombastic capital. This was duly carried out, over eighty years or so, on the northern tongue of the mid-Spree island, an area which became known as the Museumsinsel or **Museum Island**. A few of the world's greatest museums reside here: the **Pergamonmuseum**, with a jaw-dropping collection of antiquities, the **Altes Museum**, with its selection of superlative Greek vases, and the **Altes Nationalgalerie**, boasting a world-class assortment of nineteenth-century European paintings. Perhaps it was to bask in the reflected glory of such cultural monuments that the GDR government felt impelled to build its most important civic buildings, **the Palast der Republik** and the **Staatsrat**, nearby.

The easiest way to reach Museum Island by public transport is to take the frequent bus #100, which stops at Schlossplatz, from Bahnhof Zoo or Alexanderplatz. Alternatively, **U- and S-Bahn station** Friedrichstrasse and S-Bahn Hackescher Markt are both within easy walking distance.

Schlossbrücke and the Schlossplatz

Schlossplatz (known as Marx-Engels-Platz until 1994) is reached from Unter den Linden via Schinkel's **Schlossbrücke**. When it was opened on November 28, 1823, the bridge was not fully completed, lacking among other things a fixed balustrade, and 22 people drowned when temporary wooden barriers collapsed. Eventually cast-iron balustrades were installed, featuring graceful dolphin-, merman- and sea-horse motifs designed by Schinkel. The very pristine-looking Classical statues of warriors and winged figures lining each side of the bridge represent scenes from ancient Greek mythology and earned the bridge the popular epithet Puppenbrücke or "Puppet Bridge". Once wartime bombing started they were removed for safe-keeping; after the division of the city they ended up in West Berlin, and were only returned to the East in 1981.

SCHLOSSPLATZ AND THE MUSEUM ISLAND

Schlossplatz

Beyond the bridge is **Schlossplatz** itself, former site of the Berliner Schloss, the old Imperial Palace, the remains of which were demolished by the Communists after the war, and which, along with the Berliner Dom (see p.68), formed the Imperial *Residenz*. Work began on the palace in 1443 and the Hohenzollern family were to live there for nearly half a millennium. Over the centuries the Schloss was constantly extended and reshaped, the first major overhaul coming in the sixteenth century when it was transformed from a fortress into a Renaissance palace. Later it received a Baroque restyling, and subsequently virtually every German architect of note, including Schlüter, Schinkel and Schadow, was given the opportunity to add to it. For centuries the Schloss dominated the heart of Berlin, and until the 1930s no city centre building was allowed to stand any higher.

On November 9, 1918, the end of the Hohenzollern era came when Karl Liebknecht proclaimed a "Free Socialist Republic" from one of the palace balconies (now preserved in the facade of the Staatsrat building, see p.80), following the abdication of the Kaiser. Almost simultaneously, the Social Democrat Phillip Scheidemann was proclaiming a democratic German republic from the Reichstag, and it was in fact the latter that prevailed, ushering in the pathologically unstable Weimar Republic of the 1920s.

After the war the Schloss, as a symbol of the still recent Imperial past, was an embarrassment to the SED authorities and they ordered the dynamiting of its ruins in 1950, despite the fact that it was no more badly damaged than a number of other structures subsequently rebuilt. Today the Berliner Schloss can only be appreciated in photographs and there is, predictably, great nostalgia for it, with some even calling for it to be re-created – despite the fact that its piecemeal construction and bombastic architectural style made it a rather unattractive building. Notwithstanding, during the summers of 1993 and 1994 the pro-Schloss lobby erected a spectacular scaffolding and canvas replica of the building here, to mobilize public support for their aims. Tepid response and a lack of money have put the project on the back burner. Currently, a series of placards on the square surrounds a few basic archeological excavations and charts the history of the Schloss and square from 1443 to the present.

The Palast der Republik

It was no coincidence that the GDR authorities chose the space formerly occupied by the Schloss for their **Palast der Republik**, which was built on the southeastern side of Schlossplatz during the early 1970s to house the Volkskammer, the GDR's parliament. Irreverently dubbed "Ballast der Republik", this huge angular building with its bronzed, reflecting windows was completed in less than a thousand days, and was a source of great pride to the Honecker regime. As well as the former Volkskammer, it also housed an entertainment complex, including restaurants, cafés, a theatre and a bowling alley. The interior is a masterpiece of tastelessness and the hundreds of lamps hanging from the ceiling of the main foyer gave rise to its other nickname, Erichs Lampenladen – "Erich's lamp shop". Shortly before unification an asbestos hazard was discovered in the building, and on October 3, 1990, it was closed indefinitely. Today it stands as an unmissable reminder of the old GDR, and though its future and even its existence are uncertain, for now it sometimes plays host to diverse temporary exhibitions and shows that require a vast floor space.

The Staatsrat and Neue Marstall

A slightly less jarring reminder of the GDR survives on the southern side of Schlossplatz in the form of the one-time **Staatsrat**, or State Council, an early 1960s building with some stylistic affinities to the *Zuckerbäcker* architecture of the Stalin era. It's enhanced by the inclusion in its facade of a big chunk of the Berliner Schloss, notably the balcony from which Karl Liebknecht proclaimed the German revolution in 1918. Immediately to the east of the Staatsrat lies the **Neue Marstall**, an unimaginative turn-of-the-twentieth-century construction, built to house the hundreds of royal coaches and horses used to ferry the royal household around the city.

From this building revolutionary sailors and Spartacists beat off government forces during the November Revolution of 1918, when the building was headquarters of the revolutionary committee. A couple of plaques commemorate this deed of rebellious derring-do and Liebknecht's proclamation of the socialist republic. One shows Liebknecht apparently suspended above a cheering crowd of sailors and civilians, while the other, to the left of the entrance, has the head of Marx hovering over some excited but purposeful-looking members of the proletariat. At present the building is under development, being adapted as a campus for the European School of Management and Technology (@www.esmt.org) from late 2005 onwards.

Breite Strasse sweeps south beside the Neue Marstall, but before it arrives at the intersection with Mühlendamm – just over the Spree from the Nikolaiviertel (see p.94) – it passes the delicately gabled **Ribbeckhaus**. This late-Renaissance

△ Alte Nationalgalerie

palace from the seventeenth century is one of the city's oldest surviving buildings and now houses a branch of Berlin's public library.

The Lustgarten

A large flat green expanse leading up to the Altes Museum on the northern side of the Schlossplatz, the **Lustgarten** was originally a garden built by the Great Elector. Later King Friedrich Wilhelm I, Prussia's "Soldier-King", turned it into a parade ground as part of his general attempt to transform the city into a vast barracks. In 1942 resistance fighters under the Jewish communist Herbert Baum set fire to an anti-communist exhibition that was being held here, an action that cost them their lives. It is commemorated by a stone cube at the centre of the greenery which, despite the inscription "forever bound in friendship with the Soviet Union", still attracts wreath-layers. At the northern end of the Lustgarten, at the foot of the steps leading up to the Altes Museum (see p.85), is what looks like a large granite saucer. This was carved from a huge glacier-deposited boulder found near Fürstenwalde, just outside Berlin, and brought here in 1828 to form part of the Altes Museum's rotunda. A mistake in Schinkel's plans meant that its seven-metre diameter made it too large, so, for want of a better plan, it was left here to become an unusual decorative feature.

The Berliner Dom

Opposite the Palast der Republik and adjacent to the Lustgarten, The **Berliner Dom** (April–Sept Mon–Sat 9am–8pm, Sun noon–8pm; Oct–March Mon–Sat 9am–7pm, Sun noon–7pm; €5) is a hulking symbol of Imperial Germany that managed to survive the GDR era. It was built at the turn of the twentieth century on the site of a more modest cathedral, as a grand royal church for the Hohenzollern family. Fussily ornate with a huge dome flanked by four smaller ones, it was meant to resemble that of St Peter's in Rome, but somehow it comes across as little more than a dowdy neo-Baroque imitation.

The Berliner Dom served the House of Hohenzollern as a family church until 1918, and its vault houses ninety sarcophagi containing the remains of various members of the line. The building was badly damaged during the war, but has undergone a long period of reconstruction, leaving it looking like a simpler version of its prewar self, with various ornamental cupolas missing from the newly rounded-off domes.

The main entrance leads into the extravagantly overstated **Predigtkirche**, the octagonal main body of the church. From the marbled pillars of the hall to the delicate plasterwork and gilt of the cupola, there's a sense that it's all meant to reflect Hohenzollern power rather than serve as a place of worship. As if to confirm this impression, six opulent Hohenzollern sarcophagi, including those of Great Elector Wilhelm I, and his second wife, Dorothea, are housed in galleries at the northern and southern ends of the Predigtkirche. The spiritual underpinnings of the society they ruled are less ostentatiously represented by statues of Luther, Melanchthon, Calvin and Zwingli, along with four German princes favourable to the Reformation, in the cornices above the pillars in the main hall.

For an overhead view, head for the **Kaiserliches Treppenhaus** (Imperial Staircase), a grandiose marble staircase at the southwest corner of the building, which leads past pleasantly washed-out paintings of biblical scenes to a balcony looking out onto the Predigtkirche. Here you'll also find a small exhibition on the history of the building. Back downstairs and to the south of the Predigtkirche is the restored **Tauf- and Traukirche**. At first sight this appears to be a marbled souvenir shop, but it is in fact a side chapel used for baptism and confirmation ceremonies.

The Museum Island

Northwest of Schlossplatz, extending peninsula-like from the square, is an area known as the **Museum Island** (Museumsinsel), location of eastern Berlin's most important museums: the **Pergamonmuseum**, the **Altes Museum**, the **Alte Nationalgalerie** and the **Bodemuseum**. Their origins go back to 1810, when King Friedrich Wilhelm III decided Berlin needed a museum to house the then rather scant collection of royal treasures. He ordered the reclamation of a patch of Spree-side marsh and commissioned Schinkel to come up with a suitable building, which resulted in the Altes Museum at the head of the Lustgarten.

Things really started to take off when German explorers and archeologists began plundering the archeological sites of Egypt and Asia Minor. The booty brought back by the Egyptologist Carl Richard Lepsius during the 1840s formed the core of what was to become a huge collection, and the **Neues Museum** was built to house it at the behest of King Friedrich Wilhelm IV. Later in the century the Imperial haul was augmented by treasures brought from Turkey by Heinrich Schliemann, for which the vast Pergamonmuseum was constructed.

During World War II the contents of the museums were stashed away in bunkers and mine shafts for protection from bombing, and in the confusion of 1945 and the immediate postwar years it proved difficult to recover the scattered works. Some had been destroyed, others ended up in museums in the Western sector and others disappeared to the East with the Red Army. Gradually, though, the various pieces were tracked down and most of what had survived was returned to the Museum Island, which has become a major Berlin attraction.

One important collection that has not been returned, though, is the lost gold of Priam, Schliemann's most famous find and alleged to have come from the ruins of the fabled city of Troy. This collection of nine thousand gold chains, elaborate silver pictures, gold coins and other amazing artefacts hit the front pages in 1993 when it finally resurfaced in Moscow, where it remains today.

Yet reunification has brought the opportunity of bringing together the remaining, impressive, and long-divided, collections. The ambitious plan is currently in progress to **restructure and renovate** Museum Island, which, by 2010, will

---

Visiting the state museums

The state-run museums of Museum Island exhibit only part of Berlin's collections, which also has groups of museums in the Kulturforum (p.114), Charlottenburg (p.136) and Dahlem (p.187). In all these groupings, the basic ticket to enter a museum (€4–8) is termed a Standortkarte (literally "location ticket") which is also good for all the other museums in that grouping on the same day. Alternatively, you can buy a **day ticket** (€10), valid for all the state museums or a **three-day ticket** (€12), which may be better value since visiting more than one large museum in a day can be wearing. Entry to all state museums is **free** during the last four opening hours on Thursdays; but be aware that on some summer Thursdays some museums have late-opening nights, making the times of free entry later than usual. Best to call or check the website first. In all cases entrance to **special exhibitions** costs extra. Also note that all the museums are closed on Mondays.

Most exhibits are in German only, but some collections do provide explanations and information sheets in English and many have excellent, multilingual **audio tours** included in the entrance price.

result in one of the world's greatest museum complexes. Thus, for several years, art works are reshuffled and galleries renovated, some museums will be closed and various collections inaccessible – see each museum for details.

The Pergamonmuseum

The **Pergamonmuseum** (Tues–Sun 10am–6pm, until 10pm on Thurs; €8; ⊛www.smb.spk-berlin.de; S-Bahn Friedrichstrasse) is accessible from Am Kupfergraben on the south bank of the River Spree. It's a massive structure, built in the early part of the twentieth century in the style of a Babylonian temple to house the treasure trove of the German archeologists who were busy plundering the ancient world, packaging it up and sending it back to Berlin. The Pergamonmuseum will close sometime in 2005, with piecemeal opening of some sections until 2010, when it formally reopens with its collections reunited and reordered, and its courtyard roofed over to exhibit large architectural pieces.

The museum is divided into three sections, the most important of which, the **Department of Antiquities** on the main floor, contains the **Pergamon Altar**. A huge structure dedicated to Zeus and Athena, dating from 180 to 160 BC, it was unearthed at Bergama in western Turkey by the archeologist Carl Humann and brought to Berlin in 1903. The **frieze** shows a battle between the gods and giants and is a tremendously forceful piece of work, with powerfully depicted figures writhing in a mass of sinew and muscle. To the rear of the Altar is the **Telephos Frieze**, another amazing Pergamon find, which originally adorned the interior of the Pergamon Altar; its depiction of the life story of Telephos, the legendary founder of Pergamon, is a bit more sedate. The section also contains other pieces of Hellenistic and classical architecture, including the two-storey **market gate** from the Turkish town of Miletus. Built by the Romans in 120 AD, the gate was destroyed by an earthquake just under a thousand years later and brought to Berlin in fragmentary form for reconstruction during the nineteenth century.

The **Middle Eastern Section**, also on the main floor, has items going back four thousand years to Babylonian times. The collection includes the enormous **Ishtar Gate**, the **Processional Way** and the facade of the **Throne Room** from Babylon, all of which date from the reign of Nebuchadnezzar II in the sixth century BC. It's impossible not to be awed by the size and the remarkable state of preservation of the deep-blue enamelled bricks of the Babylon finds, but at the same time it's worth bearing in mind that much of it is a mock-up, built around the original finds. Look out for the weird mythical creatures that adorn the Ishtar Gate, and check the small model of the whole structure to get some idea of its enormous scale.

Pride of place in the museum's **Islamic Section** goes to the relief-decorated facade of a Jordanian **Prince's Palace** at Mshatta, from 743 AD, presented to Kaiser Wilhelm II by the sultan of Turkey. On a slightly more modest scale is a thirteenth-century **prayer niche** decorated with turquoise, black and gold tiles, from a mosque in Asia Minor. Also worth seeking out is the **Aleppo Room**, a reception chamber with carved wooden wall decorations, reassembled in Berlin after being removed from a merchant's house in present-day Syria. The section is also home to a host of smaller but no less impressive exhibits from Arabia and Persia, including carpets, ceramics, leatherwork, and wooden and ivory carvings.

The Alte Nationalgalerie

Roughly behind the Pergamonmuseum and Neues Museum is the **Alte Nationalgalerie** (Tues–Sun 10am–6pm, until 10pm on Thurs; €8;

⚛www.smb.spk-berlin.de; S-Bahn Friedrichstrasse), a slightly exaggerated example of post-Schinkel Neoclassicism that contains the **nineteenth-century** section of Berlin's state art collection. The main body of the museum is a grandiose interpretation of a Corinthian temple, built in 1876 and placed atop a huge pediment fronted by a statue of its royal patron, Friedrich Wilhelm IV – who is commemorated by an equestrian statue at the entrance above a double flight of stairs.

Particularly noteworthy among the Alte Nationalgalerie's collection are several works of the **"German Romans"**, mid-nineteenth-century artists like Anselm Feuerbach and Arnold Böcklin, who spent much of their working lives in Italy – Böcklin's eerie, dreamlike *Isle of the Dead* retains its power even today. A highlight of this school is the Casa Bartholdy **frescoes**, softly illuminated paintings by Peter Cornelius, Wilhelm Veit and others that illustrate the story of Joseph. The broad canvases of Adolph von Menzel strike a rather different note: though chiefly known during his lifetime for his detailed depictions of court life under Frederick the Great, it's his interpretations of Berlin on the verge of the industrial age, such as *The Iron Foundry*, that make more interesting viewing today.

Though arguably less interesting, other rooms contain important **Impressionist** works by van Gogh, Degas, Monet and native son Max Liebermann, plus statues by Rodin. But it's on the top floor, in the **Galerie der Romantik**, with its collection of nineteenth-century paintings from the German Romantic, Classical and Biedermeier movements, that the collection is at its most powerful. The two central rooms on this floor contain work by **Karl Friedrich Schinkel** and **Caspar David Friedrich**. Schinkel was the architect responsible for the Neoclassical design of the Altes Museum (see below) and his paintings are meticulously drawn Gothic fantasies, often with sea settings. *Gothic Church on a Rock by the Sea* is the most moodily dramatic and didactic in purpose: the medieval knights in the foreground ride next to a prayer tablet – Schinkel believed that a rekindling of medieval piety would bring about the moral regeneration of the German nation. But more dramatic are the works of **Caspar David Friedrich**, all of which express a powerful elemental and religious approach to landscape. Particularly evident of the brooding and drama of his Romantic sensibility is the *Abbey Among Oak Trees* of 1809, perhaps the best known of his works. *Moonrise at Sea* reveals something of Friedrich's philosophy; initially a straightforward seascape, on closer study the painting unfolds its deeper meaning, the moon that illuminates the scene and guides the ships represents Christ, while the rock on which the figures sit is a symbol of the constancy of Christian faith. In the next room is *Der Watzmann*, where it seems as if some massive, primeval force is about to leap forth from the earth.

The Altes Museum

At the head of the Lustgarten the **Altes Museum** (Tues–Sun 10am–6pm; €8; ⚛www.smb.spk-berlin.de; U-Bahn Friedrichstrasse) is perhaps Schinkel's most impressive surviving work, with an 87-metre-high facade fronted by an eighteen-column Ionic colonnade. Along with the Schauspielhaus (see p.69), this is one of Berlin's most striking Neoclassical buildings. Originally opened as a home for the royal collection of paintings in 1830, the Altes Museum is now host to the **Collection of Classical Antiquities**: small sculpture and pottery from the city's famed Greek and Roman collections. These small works perhaps lack the power and drama of the huge pieces on view at the Pergamon, but there are some captivating items well presented here: *The Praying Boy*, a lithe and delicate bronze sculpture from

Rhodes dating back to 300 BC, is the collection's pride and joy. Look, too, for the vase of Euphronios, decorated with an intimate painting of athletes in preparation – the series of Greek vases here is considered to be among the finest in the world.

Until 2005, the first floor of the Altes Museum will be used for special exhibitions, after which (and until 2009) it will house the Egyptian rooms of the Neues Museum (see below).

The Bodemuseum

At the northeastern tip of the Museumsinsel stands an intimidating, turn-of-the-twentieth-century neo-Baroque building that houses the **Bodemuseum**. It's presently closed (see p.83), but, when restored, the impressive building will house the **Sculpture Collection**, an excellent, chiefly German collection of sculpture particularly authoritative in its sections detailing the Middle Ages – including work by the masters Tilman Riemenschneider, Nicolaus Gerhaert, Michael Erhart and Hans Multscher. Also finding a home here will be the **Museum for Byzantine Art**, with an extensive range of objects, mainly religious in nature, from the pre-medieval eastern Mediterranean. At present only the collection's manifold coin collection is open to visitors – appealing mainly to those with a specialist interest – but the entire museum should be accessible by late 2006.

The Neues Museum

Between the Altes Museum and the Pergamonmuseum is the **Neues Museum**, originally built to house the Egyptian Collection. Bombed out in the war, the building is slowly being rebuilt and is scheduled to open in 2009 as the new home of the Egyptian Museum and the Museum for Pre- and Early History. Until then, its Egyptian collection can be seen at the Altes Museum (see p.85), while the Museum for Pre- and Early History currently resides in Charlottenburg (see p.136).

Alexanderplatz and around

With the adjacent gigantic TV tower looming over all Berlin, the vast sweeps of dreary concrete that constitute **Alexanderplatz**, the unmistakeable product of the old East Germany, are easy to find. During East Berlin's forty-year existence, while Unter den Linden was allowed to represent the glories of past Berlin, Alexanderplatz and its environs were meant to represent the glories of a modern socialist capital city. It's hard to imagine, though, that the concrete gigantism of the GDR era will wear as well as the efforts of Schinkel and his contemporaries. This is one part of town where there's little point in trying to spot what remains of prewar Berlin. Elsewhere at least a few buildings have made it through to the postwar period, but around Alexanderplatz there's almost no trace of what stood here before 1945. Whole streets have vanished – the open area around the base of the **TV tower** for example, used to be a dense network of inner-city streets – and today only a few survivors like the **Marienkirche** and **Rotes Rathaus** remain standing amid the modernity.

This is not to say that Alexanderplatz should be passed by. If you can let your sensibilities take a back seat, it's worth exploring not only the area's handful of historic buildings but also the ugly East German creations that have their own place in Berlin's architectural chronology.

If it all gets too much, relief from the concrete is on hand in the nearby **Nikolaiviertel**, an attempt to re-create the destroyed medieval heart of Berlin; and also in the area to the immediate east, which has a clutch of secluded old buildings and a stretch of Berlin's first wall – built to keep people out rather than in. Also close by are a few interesting museums, detailing the history of the city itself.

Alexanderplatz

A huge, windswept, pedestrianized plaza surrounded by high-rises, **Alexanderplatz** has long been an important business and traffic centre. During the eighteenth century routes to all parts of Germany radiated out from here, and a cattle and wool market stood on the site. It acquired its present name after the

The Berlin that never was

As you survey what has replaced the destroyed city centre around Alexanderplatz, ponder on a couple of paths that history nearly took: one school of thought considered that Berlin in 1945 was simply not worth rebuilding, and proposed to build a **new Berlin** from scratch, 60km away, as had been done at Stalingrad. More disturbing, though, was the wartime plan by the Allies to drop **anthrax bombs** on the city, which would have killed all the inhabitants but left the buildings standing. Had this happened, it would now be possible (presumably having donned protective gear) to wander the streets of a ghost city, completely unchanged since the day the bomb dropped.

Russian tsar Alexander I visited Berlin in 1805, and was made famous beyond the city by Alfred Döblin's unreadable novel (see p.336) of life in the Weimar era, *Berlin Alexanderplatz*, subsequently filmed by Fassbinder. Today, in addition to the S-Bahn line running overhead, three underground lines cross beneath the Platz, various bus routes converge on the area, and several tram lines course through it, making it one of central Berlin's busiest corners.

From the main doors of the railway station, the route onto "Alex" leads through a gap between a couple of prewar survivors: the **Alexanderhaus** and the **Berolinahaus**, two buildings designed at the beginning of the 1930s by the architect and designer Peter Behrens, whose ideas influenced the founders of the Bauhaus. These two buildings are the only Alexanderplatz buildings not to have been destroyed in the war. Today Behrens' buildings, once the tallest in the area, have been put in the shade by the ugly *Park Inn* and various other local high-rises. At the centre of things is the sorry-looking, communist-era **Brunnen der Völkerfreundschaft** ("Friendship of the Peoples Fountain"), which used to be a hangout for prostitutes and is now covered in graffiti. A more renowned monument is the **Weltzeituhr** (World Clock) in front of the Alexanderhaus. Central Berlin's best-known rendezvous point, it tells the time in different cities throughout the world, and is a product of the same architectural school responsible for the Fernsehturm.

Despite its drab contemporary appearance, Alexanderplatz has figured prominently in city upheavals ever since revolutionaries (including the writer Theodor Fontane) set up barricades here in 1848. In 1872 it was the site of a demonstration by an army of homeless women and children, and half a century later, during the revolution of 1918, sailors occupied the Alexanderplatz police headquarters (a feared local landmark that lay just to the southeast of the Platz – a plaque marks the spot) and freed the prisoners. More recently, it was the focal point of the million-strong city-wide **demonstration** of November 4, 1989, which formed a prelude to the events of November 9 (see p.323) when hundreds of thousands of people crammed into the square to hear opposition leaders speak. Veteran writer Stefan Heym summed up the mood in his speech to the crowd: "Power belongs not to one, not to a few, not to the Party and not to the State. The whole people must have a share."

Before the war, Alexanderplatz was one of the city's main shopping centres with two expensive department stores in the vicinity: Hermann Tietz, a neo-Baroque palace between the Berolinahaus and what is now the *Park Inn*, and Wertheim, the biggest department store in Germany, which stood on the opposite side of the S-Bahn tracks to the Alexanderhaus. Both were Jewish-owned until "Aryanized" by the Nazis. The Kaufhof department store facing the fountain was, as Centrum, one of the best-stocked shops in East Germany,

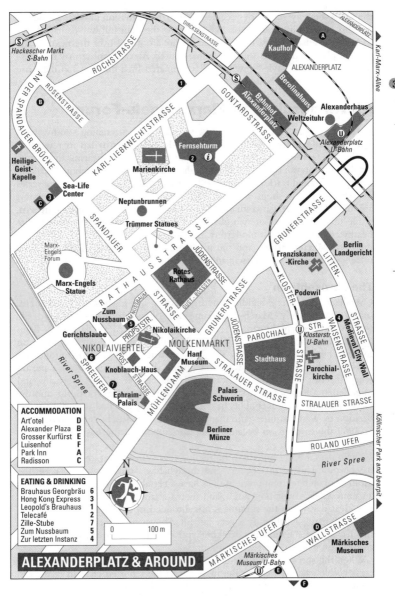

ALEXANDERPLATZ & AROUND

though these days it's just another run-of-the-mill big store. Today commercial life on Alexanderplatz seems to happen more at street level, with stalls and snack bars jostling for space in the plaza.

Throughout its existence the face of Alexanderplatz has undergone many transformations. A major reshaping at the end of the 1920s cleaned up what had turned into a rather sleazy corner of the city, and during the early 1960s the GDR-era city authorities decided to realize their vision of what a modern, socialist metropolis should look like by giving the then still war-damaged area the form it retains today. Further changes are afoot and over the next decade or so, if plans under discussion are implemented, Alexanderplatz may be transformed into a US-style "downtown", dominated by a dozen or so high-rise office and apartment buildings.

Alexanderplatz to Marx-Engels-Forum

Despite its apparent concrete aridity, the vast plaza stretching southwest of the **Alexanderplatz** S-Bahnhof to **Marx-Engels-Forum** has its rewarding corners. The station is one of the few buildings around here bearing any resemblance to its prewar appearance – though it's actually a 1960s rebuild. Walking below its elevated tracks along the pedestrianized Rathausstrasse – past a series of largely missable shops and cafés – brings you to several sights. Foremost among them is the gargantuan GDR vintage TV tower or **Fernsehturm**, while surprisingly, one or two older landmarks have managed to cling to life nearby amid the brutalist modernity. These include the city's oldest church, the medieval **Marienkirche**, and the nineteenth-century **Rotes Rathaus**, now once again seat of Berlin's civic administration.

The Fernsehturm

Overshadowing every building in the vicinity, the gigantic **Fernsehturm**, or TV tower (daily: March–Oct 9am–1am; Nov–Feb 10am–midnight; €7; ⓦwww.berlinerfernsehturm.de), just southwest of the Alexanderplatz S-Bahn station, dominates the eastern Berlin skyline like a displaced satellite sitting on top of a huge factory chimney. The highest structure in Western Europe, this 365-metre-high transmitter was built during the isolationist 1960s, a period when the east part of the city was largely inaccessible to West Germans, and intended as a highly visible symbol of the permanence of East Berlin and the German Democratic Republic. Its construction was watched with dismay and derision by West Berliners (and many people in the East), but after completion in 1969 the tower soon became a popular stopoff on the East Berlin tourist circuit.

These days, having outlasted the regime that conceived it, the Fernsehturm has become part of the scenery, and though few would champion it on the grounds of architectural merit, it does have a certain retro appeal. It also makes an unmissable orientation point, and there's a tremendous **view** (40km on a rare clear day, when the summit is not shrouded in cloud) from the observation platform – reached by a very fast lift. Above the observation platform is the *Tele-café* (see "Eating and drinking", p.233), whose main attraction is that it revolves on its own axis twice an hour.

When the sun shines on the globe of the tower, the reflected light forms a cross visible even in western Berlin, much to the reported chagrin of the old GDR authorities and amusement of Berliners, who call it the "pope's revenge". If you want to go up, bear in mind that there are sometimes long queues (the evening is your best bet).

The Marienkirche

Once hemmed in by buildings, and now oddly alone in the shadow of the huge Fernsehturm, stands the **Marienkirche** (daily 10am–6pm; free; U & S-Bahn Alexanderplatz), Berlin's oldest parish church. The Gothic nave in stone and brick dates back to about 1270, but the tower is more recent, having been added in 1466, with the verdigris-coated upper section tacked on towards the end of the eighteenth century by the designer of the Brandenburg Gate, Carl Gotthard Langhans. This uncontrived combination of architectural styles somehow makes the Marienkirche one of Berlin's most appealing churches, its simplicity a reminder of the city's village origins.

The **interior** is an excellent place to escape the increasingly frenetic street life of the area and listen to a free organ recital (Sat 4.30pm). Near the main entrance at the western end of the church is a small cross erected by the citizens of Berlin and Cölln as penance to the pope, after a mob immolated a papal representative on a nearby marketplace. There are five holes in the cross and, according to tradition, during the Middle Ages convicted criminals wishing to prove their innocence could do so by inserting the fingers of one hand into the holes simultaneously – not too many escaped punishment, though, as the feat is virtually an anatomical impossibility. Just inside the entrance, look out for the fifteenth-century *Totentanz*, a twenty-two-metre frieze showing the dance of death. It's very faded, but accompanied by a representation of how it once looked, with Death shown as a shroud-clad mummy popping up between people from all levels of society.

The vaulted nave is plain and white but enlivened by some opulent decorative touches. Foremost among these is Andreas Schlüter's magnificent **pulpit**, its canopy dripping with cherubs and backed by a cloud from which gilded sunrays radiate. Complementing this are the white marble altar with a huge triptych altarpiece and the eighteenth-century organ, a riot of gilded filigree and yet more cherubs, topped by a sunburst.

The Neptunbrunnen

Walking a short way south across the large open plaza from the **Marienkirche** brings you to the **Neptunbrunnen**, an extravagantly imaginative fountain incorporating a statue of a trident-wielding Neptune sitting on a shell. A serpent, seal and alligator spray the god of the sea with water, and he is supported by strange fish and eel-draped aquatic centaurs with webbed feet instead of hooves. Around the rim of the fountain sit four female courtiers, symbolizing what were at the time the four most important German rivers: the Rhine, the Vistula, the Oder and the Elbe. The statue was built in 1891 and originally positioned on Schlossplatz (see p.79).

The Rotes Rathaus

Across Rathausstrasse from the Neptunbrunnen is a rare survivor of Hohenzollern-era Berlin in the shape of the **Rotes Rathaus**, Berlin's "Red Town Hall". So called because of the colour of its bricks rather than its politics, the Rotes Rathaus has a solid angularity that contrasts sharply with the finicky grandeur of contemporaries like the Dom (see p.82). This is perhaps because it's a symbol of the civic rather than the Imperial Berlin of the time: a city in the throes of rapid commercial expansion and industrial growth. The building has lost some of its impact now that it's been hemmed in by new structures, but it remains a grandiose, almost Venetian-looking, structure; look out for the intricate bas-relief in terracotta, illustrating episodes from the history of Berlin, that runs around the building at first-floor level. The Rathaus was badly knocked around in 1945, but made a good comeback following restoration during the 1950s. During GDR days it was headquarters of the East Berlin city administration (West Berlin was administered from Schöneberg town hall,

△ Berliner Rathaus

see p.145), but since October 1991 it's been the seat of the united Berlin city administration.

The reconstruction of the Rathaus and thousands of other Berlin buildings is largely due to the *Trümmerfrauen* or "rubble women", who set to work in 1945 clearing up the 100 million tons of rubble created by wartime bombing and shelling. Their deeds are commemorated by the **statue** of a robust-looking woman facing the eastern entrance to the Rathaus on Rathausstrasse. Women of all ages carried out the bulk of the early rebuilding work, since most of Berlin's adult male population was dead, disabled or being held in PoW camps by the Allies. Despite this, the male contribution to the work is also marked by a statue of a man looking wistfully towards his *Trümmerfrau* counterpart from the western end of the Rathaus.

The Sea-life Center and Heilige-Geist-Kapelle

Spandauer Strasse, once one of the city's more important streets, cuts through the plaza beside the Rathaus. Though almost all its historic buildings were destroyed during the war, it is still worth a quick exploration. At its north-western corner stands a large modern colossus that incorporates the *Radisson Hotel* (see p.93), a touristy mall and Berlin's **Sea-life Center**, Spandauer Strasse 3 (daily: April–Aug 10am–7pm, Sept–March 10am–6pm; €13.50, concessions €12.60; ☎030/99 28 00, ⊛www.sealifeeurope.com; S-Bahn Hackescher Markt), a fiercely commercial aquarium that displays the fairly dreary aquatic life of the region's rivers and the North Atlantic. But at least the species here, highlights of which include sea horses, jellyfish, small sharks and manta rays, are elegantly displayed, particularly in the **Aquadom**. This gigantic tubular tank, located in the lobby of the *Radisson* next door, has an elevator through which Sea-life visitors can slowly rise. Others might sneak a peek at it from the hotel lobby, with its swish bar and comfy chairs.

Beyond the Sea-life Center, on the way to Hackescher Markt (see p.111), is one of Berlin's oldest surviving buildings. Now quaintly incongruous, the red-brick Gothic **Heilige-Geist-Kapelle** (Holy Ghost Chapel) is a remnant of the fourteenth century. Unfortunately, the chapel is dwarfed by a larger, newer building (originally a trade school, now part of Humboldt University) that was grafted onto it at the turn of the twentieth century, and the original interior has not survived. But it's a miracle that the chapel is still standing at all: during the course of the last six hundred years, it has endured a huge city fire in 1380, the enormously destructive explosion of a nearby gunpowder magazine in 1720, and, above all, wartime bombing.

The Marx-Engels-Forum

Back south down Spandauer Strasse and on the southern side of Karl-Liebknecht-Strasse, is the **Marx-Engels-Forum**, a severely well-ordered patch of city-centre greenery. At its heart sits a lumpen bronze representation of the founders of the "scientific world view of the working class", as pre-*Wende* guidebooks used to refer to Karl Marx and Friedrich Engels. Facing the monument are eight steel pillars bearing photogravure images of uplifting scenes from Soviet and East German life and events from various revolutionary struggles. These have been partly vandalized, and someone has made a determined effort to scratch out the face of Erich Honecker on one of them. Nearby are blurred bronze reliefs of men and women doing nothing in particular, and between the Marx-Engels statue and the Palast der Republik are similarly unclear stone reliefs showing muscular men standing around.

Nikolaiviertel and around

Slightly to the southwest of the Rotes Rathaus lies the **Nikolaiviertel**, a recent development that attempts to re-create the old prewar heart of Berlin on the site of the city's **medieval** core, which was razed overnight on June 16, 1944. To the east of here is the **Molkenmarkt** where a few historic buildings and one of the city's oldest *Gaststätten* survive. It's also worth heading south across the River Spree where the **Märkisches Museum** has some excellent material on the history of the city.

The Nikolaiviertel

The compact network of streets that forms the **Nikolaiviertel** was a radical architectural departure for the old-style GDR. No longer, it seems, did the city planners feel compelled to build enormous monuments to the concrete-pourer's art; most of the Nikolaiviertel buildings are no more than four or five storeys high, and a concerted effort was made to inject a bit of vernacular individuality into the designs. One or two original buildings aside, the Nikolaiviertel consists partly of exact replicas of historic Berlin buildings that didn't make it through to the postwar era and partly of stylized buildings not based on anything in particular, but with a vaguely "old Berlin" feel. Sometimes it doesn't quite come off, and in places the use of typical East German *Plattenbau* construction techniques, with prefabricated pillars and gables, isn't too convincing, but all in all the Nikolaiviertel represents a commendable effort to get away from the monumentalism of earlier postwar construction projects. It also represents an attempt to attract big-spending tourists, with a series of expensive restaurants, cafés and *Gaststätten* (see p.233, p.239 & p.242).

Around the Nikolaikirche

At the centre of it all, on Nikolaikirchplatz, just off Propststrasse, is the Gothic **Nikolaikirche** (Tues–Sun 10am–6pm; €1.50, Wed free, combined ticket with Knoblauch-Haus and Ephraim-Palais €5; @www.stadtmuseum .de), a thirteenth-century church, restored to its twin-towered prewar glory. The Nikolaikirche is one of the city's oldest churches and it was from here on November 2, 1539, that news of the Reformation was proclaimed to the citizens of Berlin. The distinctive needle-like spires date from a nineteenth-century restoration of the church, or rather their design does – the building was thoroughly wrecked during the war, and what you see today is largely a rebuild, as extensive patches of lighter, obviously modern, masonry show.

The church is now a **museum** that traces the building's history, although it is often given over to temporary exhibitions. An unusual feature of its interior is the bright colouring of the vault ribbings: the orange, purple, green, and other vivid lines look like a Sixties Pop Art addition, but actually follow a medieval pattern discovered by a restorer in the 1980s. There are also a number of intricately carved tombs inside, most notably those of Daniel Männlich and Johann Andreas von Kraut, the former designed by Andreas Schüter.

Some of the most attractive **Nikolaiviertel houses** are around the Nikolaikirche, along Propststrasse and on the southern side of Nikolaikirchplatz, behind the church itself. The last are particularly convincing – it's hard to believe that these pastel-facaded town houses are fakes dating back only as far as the beginning of the 1980s.

For a little light relief head for **Zum Nussbaum** (see p.233) on the corner of Propststrasse and Am Nussbaum, a handily located copy of a celebrated sixteenth-century *Gaststätte* that stood on the nearby Fischerinsel until destroyed during the bombing. The original is said to have been the local haunt of Berlin artists Heinrich Zille and Otto Nagel, and the replica is a faithful copy, right down to the walnut tree in the tiny garden. It's a little touristy but still a good place for a beer, particularly in summer if you can get a table outside.

Propststrasse runs all the way down to the River Spree and ends in a rather clichéd statue of St George and the Dragon. Before here a right turn into Poststrasse will take you past the **Gerichtslaube**, another Nikolaiviertel replica, this time of Berlin's medieval courthouse. The original was dismantled in 1870 in order to create the space needed for the building of the Rotes Rathaus, and was removed to the grounds of Schloss Babelsberg in Potsdam where it can still be seen (see p.217). The copy houses a couple of pricey tourist restaurants.

The Knoblauch-Haus

Poststrasse is more rewarding, leading to the **Knoblauch-Haus** at no. 23 (Tues–Sun 10am–6pm; €1.50, Wed free, combined ticket with Nikolaikirche and Ephraim-Palais €5; www.stadtmuseum.de), a Neoclassical town house built in 1759 and a rare survivor of the war. It was home to the patrician Knoblauch family, who played an important role in the commercial and cultural life of eighteenth- and nineteenth-century Berlin, and now contains an exhibition about their activities. While the careers of Eduard Knoblauch, Berlin's first freelance architect, and Armand Knoblauch, founder of a major city brewery, are mildly interesting, the real appeal here is the **interior** of the house, furnished in the grand-bourgeois style of the times, which gives a good impression of upper middle-class life in Hohenzollern-era Berlin. The ground floor and vaulted basement of the Knoblauch-Haus are home to the *Historische Weinstuben*, a reconstruction of a nineteenth-century wine-restaurant once favoured by the playwrights Gerhart Hauptmann, August Strindberg and Henrik Ibsen.

The Ephraim-Palais

There's another relic of Berlin bourgeois high life at the southern end of Poststrasse, where the elegant Rococo facade of the **Ephraim-Palais**, Poststrasse 16 (Tues–Sun 10am–6pm; €3, Wed free, combined ticket with Nikolaikirche and Knoblauch-Haus €5; www.stadtmuseum.de), curves round onto Mühlendamm. A rebuild of an eighteenth-century merchant's mansion, this now houses a museum of Berlin-related art from the seventeenth to the beginning of the nineteenth centuries, with numerous pictures, prints and maps giving a good impression of how the city looked in its glory days.

The Ephraim-Palais was built by Veitel Heine Ephraim, court jeweller and mint master to Frederick the Great, and all-round wheeler-dealer. He owed his lavish lifestyle primarily to the fact that – on Frederick's orders – he steadily reduced the silver content of the Prussian *thaler*. This earned a great deal of money for Frederick and Ephraim himself but ruined the purchasing power of the currency. Ephraim's palace housed a museum of sport from 1925 to 1934, before being dismantled in 1935 as part of a road-broadening scheme; much of the facade, however, was preserved and later turned up in West Berlin, whence it was returned to be incorporated into the 1980s rebuild.

The Hanf Museum

Nearby, in another reconstructed Berlin house, is the **Hanf Museum** (Hemp Museum), Mühlendamm 5 (Tues–Fri 10am–8pm, Sat & Sun noon–8pm; €3; ⓦwww.hanfmuseum.de), a somewhat amateurish museum dedicated to cannabis. It's filled with an odd assortment of glass cases and ill-framed exhibits, but there is a surprisingly large amount of information about the history, uses and cultural significance of the plant. Devotees may find it interesting, but all captions are in German. There's a small shop and a café in the basement.

The Molkenmarkt

The area where Mühlendamm meets Stralauer Strasse is known as the **Molkenmarkt**, one of the oldest public spaces in Berlin. The two pompous and dull buildings on the southern side of Mühlendamm are the **Berliner Münze** (Berlin Mint) and the former **Palais Schwerin** (built for Otto Schwerin, a minister of Friedrich I of Prussia). The latter is completely missable and the only redeeming feature of the former is a replica of a frieze depicting coining techniques by Gottfried Schadow, designer of the Brandenburg Gate Quadriga.

The Stadthaus and around

A couple of minutes' walk northeast of Palais Schwerin brings you to Jüdenstrasse – "Jews' Street" – running north from Stralauer Strasse in the shadow of the domed **Stadthaus**. Reminiscent of the Französischer Dom but dating from as recently as 1911, this building is a relic of the area's days as an administrative district of Wilhelmine Berlin and now houses federal government offices. The area around Jüdenstrasse was Berlin's original ghetto, a role that ended when the Jews were driven out of Brandenburg in 1573. On being allowed back into Berlin in 1671 the Jews settled mainly around what is now Oranienburger Strasse (see p.106).

A right turn midway along Jüdenstrasse leads into Parochialstrasse, where the first stone of Communist control over postwar eastern Berlin was laid at **Parochialstrasse 1**. The building hosted the opening meeting of Berlin's post-Nazi town council, headed by future SED chief Walter Ulbricht, even as fighting still raged a little to the west. Ulbricht and his comrades had been specially flown in from Soviet exile to sow the seeds for a future communist civil administration and moved in here, having been unable to set up shop in the still-burning Rotes Rathaus. Further along the street and right into Klosterstrasse brings you to the **Parochialkirche**, a Baroque church that dates back to the sixteenth century. The bare brick interior (legacy of the usual wartime gutting) is a venue for changing, but often low-key and dull, art exhibitions (free).

Around Klosterstrasse

On the northeastern side of the Parochialstrasse–Klosterstrasse (named after a long-vanished local monastery) junction is **Podewil**, an eighteenth-century residence that's now home to an arts centre, music venue (see p.254) and pleasant café. Not far away at the top of Klosterstrasse is the gutted thirteenth-century **Franziskaner-Kirche**, destroyed by a land mine in 1945 and left a ruin as a warning against war and fascism. Behind here, at Littenstrasse 14–15, is the **Berlin Landgericht**, a courthouse whose neo-Baroque facade conceals a wonderful Jugendstil interior of strange interlocking stairwells that seem to owe their structure to organic processes rather than the work of an architect. A rather more functional piece of Berlin architectural history can be seen towards the southern end of Littenstrasse in the shape of a fragment of Berlin's medieval **Stadtmauer** or city wall.

South of the Spree

From Klosterstrasse it's a short U-Bahn hop to Märkisches Museum station on the **southern side of the Spree** (you can also walk via Mühlendamm and along Fischerinsel, a shoddy GDR-era showpiece housing development), where you'll find the Märkisches Museum, an institution dating from before reunification. There is little else in the neighbourhood to attract attention. East of the museum, old factories and large industrial yards line the banks of the Spree. Southwards lies a swathe of residential buildings.

The Märkisches Museum

Looking like a red-brick neo-Gothic cathedral, the **Märkisches Museum**, Am Köllnischen Park 5 (Tues–Sun 10am–6pm; €4; ⓦwww.stadtmuseum .de; U-Bahn Märkisches Museum), covers the history of Berlin and the Mark Brandenburg, though its treatment is episodic: eighteenth- and nineteenth-century culture is definitely its forte, while coverage of the Third Reich and postwar years is inadequate.

The museum has an old-fashioned flavour to it, with lots of small rooms crammed with paintings, gadgets and glass vitrines. The **ground floor** covers early history, starting with pottery pieces from the first prehistoric settlers and ending with copies of royal proclamations from Friedrich Wilhelm, the Great Elector, who died in 1688 – but is the least rewarding section. The two **upper floors** are more engaging, with rooms devoted to themes such as "Industrialization", "Intellectual Life", "Woman", and "the Military". Particularly noteworthy is the **Gottische Kapelle**, a room resembling a small chapel and filled with wonderful pieces of medieval sacred art from (usually) unknown local artisans, including the expressive sculpture, *Spandauer Madonna*. Slightly more secular in theme is the room devoted to the "Panorama", a huge arcade-like machine, built over a hundred years ago: as you peer through the eyepiece, a huge drum rotates to show you in turn dozens of fascinating 3D photographs of old Berlin.

In the late nineteenth century, Berlin was a centre of **barrel organ** production, an industry established by Italian immigrants, and many examples of these music-makers are on display in the museum, as well as their increasingly large and more intricate progeny. Organ-grinding performances are given every Sunday at 3pm in the exhibition room devoted to the devices.

Another bit of Berliniana is on view outside the museum: a **statue** of **Heinrich Zille**, the Berlin artist who produced earthy satirical drawings of Berlin life around the turn of the twentieth century. Behind him is a leafy park, the Kollnischer, with a **bearpit**, home to a couple of sleepy brown bears. Nearby, at Märkisches Ufer 10, is the Baroque **Ermeler Haus**, an eighteenth-century mansion transplanted here from nearby Breite Strasse.

The Scheunenviertel and around

The **Scheunenviertel** is the name commonly given to the northern periphery of central Berlin, a crescent-shaped area running roughly from just north over the Spree from Bahnhof Friedrichstrasse (see p.60) to Rosa-Luxemburg-Platz – just north of Alexanderplatz (see p.87). After the *Wende* this quarter emerged as one of the most intriguing parts of the unified city, its appeal based on both its history as Berlin's prewar **Jewish quarter** and a contemporary nightlife boom that makes it one of the city's premium after-hours destinations.

The district has its origins in the Spandauer Vorstadt, one of a number of suburbs built beyond Berlin's walled centre during the seventeenth century. Meaning "barn quarter", *Scheunenviertel* originally described a district built following a decree that flammable hay and straw could no longer be stored in the city centre. Jews settled here after they were permitted to return to Berlin in 1671, following expulsion orders a century before. From that point on the area became a refuge for Jews fleeing persecution and pogroms in eastern Europe and Russia, and by the nineteenth century the Scheunenviertel was the cultural and spiritual centre of Berlin's by then well-established and influential Jewish community.

The melting-pot atmosphere made the area an ideal refuge for those at odds with the Prussian and later the Imperial German establishment, and it became a notorious centre of revolutionary and criminal activity, so much so that the authorities were constantly trying to find ways to justify pulling it down. At one point they refused to put cobblestones down in the heart of the Scheunenviertel for fear that the inhabitants would rip them up and use them to build barricades.

The Scheunenviertel's vibrant nature also attracted **artists** and **writers** who created their own bohemian enclave here, and during the 1920s local bars and dives attracted personalities like Bertolt Brecht, Marlene Dietrich and the actor Gustav Gründgens as patrons. During these years the Scheunenviertel became a regular battleground for the street gangs of the left and right, who had their own *Kneipen* and meeting halls in the area.

Deportation of the Jews under the Nazis did much to take the soul out of the Scheunenviertel; this was followed in the GDR era by a general shutting down of what little business life remained. From the 1950s until the *Wende* the quarter was not much more than a network of decrepit prewar streets punctuated by the occasional slab of GDR-era housing. Few visitors strayed here from Unter den Linden, and apart from a couple of pockets of restoration the area was allowed to decay quietly – forgotten almost as much by the authorities as by visitors to East Berlin. Today the Scheunenviertel has undergone a dramatic revival, with restoration projects putting the infrastructure to rights and new bars and restaurants appearing almost every week. Though the brightly painted squatted houses in the backstreets have almost all given way to the ever-encroaching forces of renovation, it's still one of the more rewarding corners of the city to explore.

For the visitor the main points of interest are centred around the neat segment formed by Oranienburger Strasse, Auguststrasse and Rosenthalerstrasse. **Oranienburger Strasse** itself is home to countless bars and restaurants, as well as the **Neue Synagoge**, with its exhibitions on Jewish culture, while just to the east is the newly renovated **Hackesche Höfe**, a sort of "art mall" and a major hub of activity for both tourists and locals. The whole area acts as a centre for a busy café, gallery and trendy shopping scene. The main hubs for entering the district are U- & S-Bahn Friedrichstrasse, or S-Bahn Hackescher Markt; once there it's easiest to get around on foot.

Around Oranienburger Tor

These days the streets around Oranienburger Tor, across the Spree just north of Bahnhof Friedrichstrasse, are home largely to shops and apartments, belying the fact that this is where the industrial revolution first hit Berlin. As the loose centre of a **theatre district**, the area's main attractions have artistic associations – particularly with **Bertolt Brecht** whose home, workplace and grave are all here. A short walk up the road are a couple of worthwhile museums: the **Museum für Naturkunde** with its impressive natural history collection, and **Hamburger Bahnhof**, the city's premier contemporary art venue. Also at the very northern boundary of the district is one of the few remaining sections of the Wall – now the **Berlin Wall Memorial**.

Around Upper Friedrichstrasse

By day there's not much to see in Berlin's theatre district, but keen fans might like to pop past the **Berliner Ensemble**, where Bertolt Brecht worked upon his postwar return to Berlin, and have a quick look at the revamped and influential nearby **Deutsches Theater**. Otherwise you can't fail to notice the giant **Friedrichstadt Palast** (see "The Arts") as you head up to Oranienburger Tor along Friedrichstrasse. This clumsy GDR-era Jugendstil pastiche rears up opposite; it's perfect if you're into big, splashy, scantily clad revues, but otherwise eminently missable.

The Berliner Ensemble

A walk across Weidendammer Brücke from Bahnhof Friedrichstrasse brings you into central Berlin's vague theatre land. Veer immediately west and you'll find the **Berliner Ensemble** theatre (see p.258), tucked away on Bertolt-Brecht-Platz. Built in the early 1890s, its rather austere exterior hides a much more rewarding and opulent neo-Baroque interior. Generally thought of as Berlin's "Brecht theatre" – complete with a statue of the man himself in front – this is where, on August 31, 1928, the world premiere of his *Dreigroschenoper* ("The Threepenny Opera") was staged. This

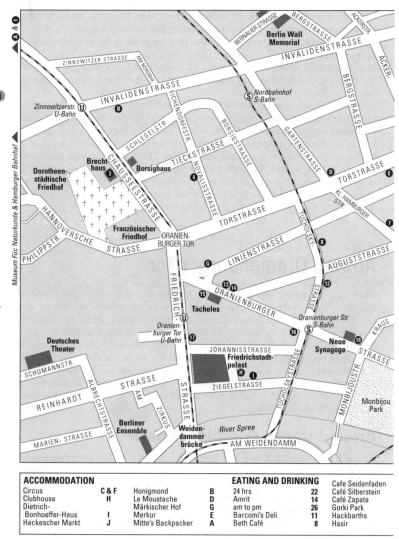

ACCOMMODATION		EATING AND DRINKING		
Circus	C & F	Honigmond	B	24 hrs	22	Cafe Seidenfaden
Clubhouse	H	Le Moustache	D	Amrit	14	Café Silberstein
Dietrich-Bonhoeffer-Haus	I	Märkischer Hof	G	am to pm	26	Café Zapata
Hackescher Markt	J	Merkur	E	Barcomi's Deli	11	Gorki Park
		Mitte's Backpacker	A	Beth Café		Hackbarths
					8	Hasir

was the first of 250 consecutive performances in a ritualistic tribute to one of the few world-renowned German writers East Germany could claim as its own. After spending much of the Nazi era in American exile, Brecht returned in 1949 with his wife, Helene Weigel, to take over direction of the theatre, marking his return by painting a still-visible red cross through the coat of arms on the royal box. During box office times (Mon–Fri 8am–6pm, Sat & Sun 11am–6pm) you can view the foyer of the theatre, but the rest is only open to the public during performances. These still include regular performances of Brecht, though the bulk of the programme is now given over to a range of reliable pieces by Henrik Ibsen, Friedrich Schiller and the like.

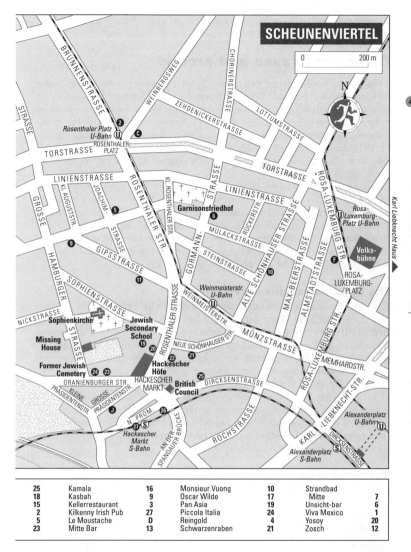

25	Kamala	16	Monsieur Vuong	10	Strandbad	
18	Kasbah	9	Oscar Wilde	17	Mitte	7
15	Kellerrestaurant	3	Pan Asia	19	Unsicht-bar	6
2	Kilkenny Irish Pub	27	Piccola Italia	24	Viva Mexico	1
5	Le Moustache	D	Reingold	4	Yosoy	20
23	Mitte Bar	13	Schwarzenraben	21	Zosch	12

The Deutsches Theater

A few streets to the northwest, at Schumannstrasse 13, is the elegant **Deutsches Theater** founded in 1883. In 1905 Max Reinhardt, who was to dominate the theatre scene for nearly three decades, took over as director (moving on from the Theater am Schiffbauerdamm); and in 1922 a young and unknown Marlene Dietrich made her stage debut here. A couple of years later Bertolt Brecht arrived from Munich and began his energetic conquest of Berlin's theatre world. In time for its 1983 centenary, millions were spent on restoring the interior to its original splendour; and in contrast to the Berliner Ensemble, the Deutsches Theater is going from strength to strength, and is now widely regarded as one of the city's best (see p.258).

Chausseestrasse and around

Things start to get more interesting a little further to the north along Friedrichstrasse, beyond **Oranienburger Tor**. During the nineteenth century this area was the location of one of Berlin's densest concentrations of heavy industry. Development had begun during the 1820s with the establishment of a steam-engine factory and iron foundry in Chausseestrasse. In 1837 August Borsig built his first factory, and by the 1870s his successors were churning out hundreds of steam engines and railway locomotives each year.

Other industrial concerns were also drawn to the area, earning it the nickname Feuerland – "Fireland". However, by the end of the century most had outgrown their roots and relocated en masse to the edges of the rapidly expanding city. A reminder of the past, and of Borsig's local influence, is the **Borsighaus** at Chausseestrasse 9. Once the central administration block of the Borsig factories, this sandstone building, its facade richly decorated with bronze figures, looks like a displaced country residence.

The Dorotheenstädtische Friedhof

Roughly opposite here sits the **Dorotheenstädtische Friedhof** (daily: May– Aug 8am–8pm, Sept–April 8am–4pm; U-Bahn Oranienburger Tor), eastern Berlin's VIP cemetery. Here you'll find the graves of Bertolt Brecht and Helene Weigel; the architect Karl Friedrich Schinkel, his last resting place topped by an appropriately florid monument; John Heartfield, the Dada luminary and interwar photomontage exponent, under a headstone decorated with a runic H; the philosopher Georg Hegel, whose ideas influenced Marx; the author Heinrich Mann; and many other Berlin worthies. A plan detailing who lies where is located beside the cemetery administration offices (on the right at the end of the entrance alley). The Dorotheenstädtische Friedhof also encloses the **Französischer Friedhof** (entrance on Chausseestrasse), originally built to serve Berlin's Huguenot community.

The Brecht-Haus

Just past the Dorotheenstädtische Friedhof entrance is the **Brecht–Haus**, Chausseestrasse 125 (guided tours every 30min: Tues–Fri 10am–noon, Thurs also 5–7pm, Sat 9.30am–2pm, Sun 11am–6.30pm, last entrance 30min before closing; €3, book afternoon tours in advance on ☏030/2 83 05 70 44; U-Bahn Oranienburger Tor), final home and workplace of Brecht and Helene Weigel, his wife and collaborator. The guided tours take in the seven simply furnished rooms – an absolute must for Brecht fans, but not so fascinating if you're only casually acquainted with his works. The Brecht-Haus also has a Bertolt Brecht **archive** (Tues–Fri 9am–3pm) and the basement is home to the *Kellerrestaurant im Brechthaus* (see p.243), which dishes up Viennese specialities, supposedly according to Weigel's recipes.

A little way past the Brecht-Haus stands a brutalist **pillar commemorating the Spartakusbund**, the breakaway antiwar faction of the SPD formed by Karl Liebknecht in 1916, which later evolved into the KPD, Germany's Communist Party. The inscription, a quote from Liebknecht, says, "Spartakus means the fire and spirit, the heart and soul, the will and deed of the revolution of the proletariat." The modern-day proletariat, however, seems little interested in this relic of its revolutionary past.

Invalidenstrasse

Heading north, the Chausseestrasse leads to **Wedding**, an industrial and working-class residential suburb whose charms are few, despite its prewar fame as a socialist heartland known as "Red Wedding". You're better off turning onto Invalidenstrasse: west to get to two impressive and very different museums – the educational **Museum für Naturkunde** and the thought-provoking **Hamburger Bahnhof** and a noteworthy small graveyard, the **Invalidenfriedhof** – or east to see the only remaining complete section of the Berlin Wall, enshrined as the **Berlin Wall Memorial**.

Museum für Naturkunde

Walking northwest on Chausseestrasse, a left turn into Invalidenstrasse quickly leads to the **Museum für Naturkunde** at no. 43 (Tues–Fri 9.30am–5pm; €3.50; U-Bahn Zinnowitzer Strasse), one of the world's largest natural history museums. The museum's origins go back to 1716, though the present building, and the nucleus of the collection it houses, date from the 1880s.

High point of the sixteen-room display (exhibits are not labelled in English) is the reconstructed brachiosaurus skeleton in the main hall. The museum is also home to the fossil remains of an archaeopteryx, the oldest known bird. Elsewhere, amid the endless glass cases containing stuffed animals, fossils, and insects pinned on card, the rooms devoted to the evolution of vertebrates and the ape family stand out, as does the interesting if slightly ghoulish section on how the numerous stuffed animals were "prepared for exhibition", as the commentary delicately puts it. The museum also boasts a vast mineralogy collection, including a number of meteorites.

The Invalidenfriedhof

A short walk west along Invalidenstrasse there's the opportunity for a pleasant little offbeat walk along a canal towpath to the **Invalidenfriedhof**, a one-time important Prussian military cemetery that spent the latter half of the twentieth century within the death strip of the Berlin Wall. The path begins alongside the Humboldthafen, which runs beside the Hamburger Bahnhof (see below), and soon leads to the cemetery whose earliest graves date from the mid-eighteenth century, but whose most impressive ones belong to prominent Prussian figures, like Count Tauentzien and Generals Winterfeldt and Scharnhorst. These all remained largely undisturbed until the building of the Berlin Wall, when parish boundaries dictated that the death strip would surround the graves. Some of the graveyard was levelled and given over to access tracks which still remain, but a good number of memorials – all those here today – were preserved and provided a surreal and macabre touch to the death strip. This section of the Berlin Wall was also famed for another depressing reason, since it was here that Günter Litfin, the first victim of the Wall, was shot and killed on 24 August 1961 as he attempted to swim across the canal. A modest information board commemorates the events.

Hamburger Bahnhof

Running along the opposite bank of the Humboldthafen canal from the Invalidenfriedhof lies Berlin's premier contemporary art venue, the

Bertolt Brecht is widely regarded as one of the leading German dramatists of the twentieth century. Born in Augsburg, the son of a paper-mill manager, he studied medicine, mainly to avoid full military service in World War I. Working as an army medical orderly in 1918, his experiences helped shape his passionate anti-militarism. Soon he drifted away from medicine onto the fringes of the theatrical world, eventually winding up as a dramaturg at the Munich Kammerspiele in 1921. Increasingly he was drawn to Berlin, and a few years later took up a similar position at the Deutsches Theater under Erwin Piscator, where he began his speedy ascent to the heights of German theatre. Brecht's earliest plays were anarchic semi-Expressionistic pieces: his first work, *Baal*, depicted life as an intensely sensual yet ultimately futile and doomed experience. Although his work attracted the attention of the critics and his first performed play, *Trommeln in der Nacht* ("Drums in the Night"), won the prestigious Kleist prize in 1922, it wasn't until the premiere of the *Dreigroschenoper* ("The Threepenny Opera"), co-written with the composer Kurt Weill, six years later, that Brecht's real breakthrough came.

The *Dreigroschenoper* marked the beginning of a new phase in Brecht's work. A couple of years earlier he had embraced Marxism, an ideological step that had a profound effect on his literary output, leading him to espouse a didactic "epic" form of theatre. The aim was to provoke the audience, perhaps even move them to revolutionary activity. To this end he developed the technique of **Verfremdung** ("alienation") to create a sense of distance between spectators and the action unfolding before them. By using effects such as obviously fake scenery, monotone lighting, and jarring music to expose the sham sentimentality of love songs, he hoped constantly to remind the audience that what they were doing was watching a play – in order to make them judge, rather than be drawn into, the action on stage. The result was a series of works that were pretty heavy-going, though the opera *Aufstieg und Fall der Stadt Mahagonny* ("Rise and Fall of the City of Mahagonny") and *Die Heilige Johanna der Schlachthöfe* ("St Joan of the Stockyards") from this period are reasonably accessible.

Hamburger Bahnhof at Invalidenstrasse 50–51 (Tues–Fri 10am–6pm, Sat & Sun 11am–6pm; €6, free Thurs 2–6pm and first Sun of each month; ⓦwww.smb.spk-berlin.de; U-Bahn Zinnowitzer Strasse or S-Bahn Lehrter Stadtbahnhof). Like the Anhalter Bahnhof (see p.146), the Hamburger station was damaged in the war, though it had ceased functioning as a station as early as 1906. Fortunately, it didn't suffer its twin's fate in postwar redevelopment, and is today the home of the new **Museum for Contemporary Art**. The collection here represents a thorough survey of postwar art: Rauschenberg, Twombly, Warhol, Beuys, Lichtenstein, right on up to Keith Haring and Donald Judd. And the old railway station makes a spacious, effective setting, particularly the main hall, where large sculptures by Judd, Anselm Kiefer and Richard Long, among others, are displayed. It's well worth a visit, though there are disappointingly few surprises – Beuys is rather over-represented, while the Warhol collection is excellent. When you need a break, there's a good bookstore and café on the premises.

The Berlin Wall Memorial

Heading east along Invalidenstrasse from Chausseestrasse soon brings you to S-Bahn Nordbahnhof, from where it's a couple of minutes' walk (up

In 1933, unsurprisingly, Brecht went into self-imposed exile, eventually ending up in the States. His years away from Germany were among his most productive. During this time he wrote some of his greatest parable-plays, works that benefited from a tempering of the writer's more overt didactic intent: *Leben des Galilei* ("The Life of Galileo"), *Der gute Mensch von Sezuan* ("The Good Woman of Szechuan"), *Mutter Courage und ihre Kinder* ("Mother Courage and her Children"), *Der Kaukasische Kreidekreis* ("The Caucasian Chalk Circle"). The political message was still very much present in his work, but somehow the dynamic and lyrical force of his writing meant that it was often largely lost on his audience – at the Zürich premiere of *Mutter Courage* in 1941, Brecht was dismayed to learn that the audience in fact identified with his heroine, whom he had intended to serve as an unsympathetic symbol of the senselessness of wartime sacrifice.

In America Brecht had tried to make a living as a Hollywood scriptwriter, though not with much success – only one film made it to the screen, *Hangmen Also Die*, directed by another German-in-exile, Fritz Lang. In 1947 Brecht came before the Committee for Un-American Activities, but was able to defend himself without implicating any of his friends. Returning to Europe, he finally settled in East Berlin in 1949, after a brief period in Switzerland. His decision to try his luck in the Soviet-dominated Eastern sector of Germany was influenced by the offer of the chance to take over at the Theater am Schiffbauerdamm, the theatre where the *Dreigroschenoper* had been premiered more than twenty years earlier. However, before heading east, Brecht first took the precaution of gaining Austrian citizenship and lodging the copyright of his works with a West German publisher.

The remainder of Brecht's life was largely devoted to the running of what is now known as the Berliner Ensemble and facing up to his own role in the fledgling GDR. The workers' uprising of 1953 prompted a private ironic outpouring (see p.73), but did not prevent him from accepting the Stalin Peace Prize the following year. Two years later Brecht died, and though he never did break with the workers' and peasants' state, it's interesting to reflect on what might have happened had he lived a few years longer.

Gartenstrasse and Bernauerstrasse) to the **Berlin Wall Memorial**. Bernauerstrasse was a street literally bisected by the Wall. Before the Wall was erected you could enter or exit the Soviet Zone just by going through the door of one of the buildings, which is why, on August 13, 1961, some citizens, who woke up to find themselves on the wrong side of the newly established "national border", leapt out of windows to get to the West. Over the years, the facades of these buildings were cemented up and incorporated into the partition itself, until they were knocked down and replaced by the Wall proper in 1979. A short section of it, now the **Berlin Wall Memorial** (Berliner Mauer Gedenkstätte), remains at the corner of Bernauerstrasse and Ackerstrasse. Across the street at Bernauerstrasse 111, the **Wall Documentation Centre** (Wed–Sun 10am–5pm; free; ⓦwww.berliner -mauer-dokumentationszentrum.de) keeps alive the story of the Wall using photos, sound recordings and info-terminals. Diagonally across the street is the site of the **Versöhnungskirche** (Church of Reconciliation), blown up by the GDR border patrol in 1985 and now in the process of being rebuilt, using various salvaged relics from the old building. Originally built in 1894, its new incarnation is intended to symbolize a reconciliation of East and West.

Oranienburger Strasse and around

The area around **Oranienburger Strasse**, which runs southeast from its beginning close to Oranienburger Tor, forms the start of the Scheunenviertel proper and heart of Berlin's prewar **Jewish district**. Although Berlin's Jewish population numbers only around twelve thousand today, it has an enduring symbol in the shape of the **Neue Synagoge**, which over the last couple of years has been restored and is now a museum not a working synagogue. With the opening of a number of Jewish cafés and a cultural centre, Oranienburger Strasse has regained a little of its pre-Nazi identity.

A few streets away on **Grosse Hamburger Strasse** are further reminders of Jewish Berlin, although here the past is recalled more by the absence of certain landmarks than by their presence. Just behind Grosse Hamburger Strasse, **Sophienstrasse** ranks as one of Berlin's best-restored nineteenth-century streets, taking its name from the nearby **Sophienkirche**, the city's finest Baroque church. The big draw here, however, is the **Hackesche Höfe**, a restored series of early twentieth-century courtyards.

Oranienburger Strasse

Until 1989 **Oranienburger Strasse** was one of central Berlin's more desolate streets, but since the *Wende* it has been through a phase as an atmospheric bar-crawling strip, and is now principally known for its upscale **restaurants**. With a host of stylish watering holes both here and on the surrounding streets, it is as much a trendy tourist haunt as part of the new eastern Berlin *Szene* (see p.231). Prostitutes still openly solicit along the entire road, and as the area succumbs to the lights of suave restaurants and cafés it has produced a surreal combination of uses, with hints of Amsterdam's red-light district.

Tacheles and around

The revitalization of Oranienburger Strasse began with **Tacheles** (ⓦwww.tacheles.de), a group of young international artists who took over a spectacularly ruined building on the southern side of the street, just beyond the Oranienburger Tor junction, in early 1990. The exterior is usually festooned with works-in-progress, and the building has become home and workplace to an ever-changing band of painters, sculptors, kindred spirits and hangers-on. Inside is a café/bar (see p.234) and regular gigs and events take place here (see p.253).

The Tacheles building itself has an interesting past, reflecting the history of the city in which it stands. Built in 1907, it was one of the first reinforced concrete structures in Europe, originally housing the Friedrichstrassepassagen shopping centre, then between the wars it became the AEG's exhibition hall for all its electrical products. From 1934 onwards the building was used by the SS and the Deutsche Arbeitsfront, a Nazi labour organization. After the war it housed a cinema and work space for art students, before suffering partial demolition and standing vacant for many years until the Tacheles collective moved in. Rumours of its demise have been rampant in the last few years, as speculators eager to swallow up a big chunk of prime real estate (which it helped bring to life) have zoned in on the building, but, after much political wrangling, it seems that Tacheles has ensured its future as a permanent fixture in the cultural landscape. Indeed, it's come a long way since its anarchic beginnings, much to the disappointment of those involved in the early days, who inevitably claim the new-look Tacheles with its plate-glass windows is not the place it once was.

A little way along from Tacheles, on the opposite side of the street, is an important-looking building that turns out to be a nineteenth-century **post office administration building**. It's built in the mock-Moorish style so favoured by Berlin civic architects during the nineteenth century. They decked out everything from stations to breweries in alternating bands of orange and yellow brick, with generously arched doorways and windows and fanciful turrets with decorative cupolas. These days it's home to a yearly festival of new experimental art, held in May.

Auguststrasse

Auguststrasse, which branches off from Oranienburger Strasse opposite Tacheles, is another street that's undergone a breathtaking transformation since 1989, and is now the centre of a thriving arts scene. The galleries on and around Auguststrasse attract artists from all around the world and feature some of the most interesting and controversial work you're likely to see in Berlin. The city authorities have provided an enviable level of financial support. In June 1992 they stumped up for the "37 Rooms Exhibition", in which the whole of Auguststrasse was turned into a giant gallery, an event widely viewed as having given artistic life on the street an air of legitimacy.

The Neue Synagoge and around

Before the war Oranienburger Strasse and its immediate environs were at the heart of Berlin's main **Jewish quarter**. During the initial waves of Jewish immigration from the seventeenth century onwards the area was a densely populated and desperately poor ghetto, but by the nineteenth century Berlin's Jews had achieved a high degree of prosperity and assimilation. This was reflected in the building of the grand **Neue Synagoge**, to a design by Eduard Knoblauch, halfway down Oranienburger Strasse just off the corner of Krausnickstrasse. The synagogue was inaugurated in the presence of Bismarck in 1866, a gesture of official recognition which, coming at a time when Jews in Russia were still enduring officially sanctioned pogroms, must have made many feel that their position in German society was finally secure. The acceptance that they had enjoyed in Wilhelmine Germany contributed to the sense of disbelief many Jews felt at the rise of Nazism during the 1920s and 1930s.

Like the post office building near the Tacheles, the Neue Synagoge was built in mock-Moorish style, with the conspicuous addition of a bulbous gilt and turquoise dome. It was Berlin's central synagogue for over sixty years, serving also as a venue for concerts, including one in 1930 by Albert Einstein in his lesser-known role as a violinist. A Jewish museum was opened next door on January 24, 1933, just six days before the Nazi takeover. Neither museum nor synagogue survived the Third Reich. Both were damaged on *Kristallnacht* (see p.108), though the synagogue wasn't actually destroyed thanks to the intervention of the local police chief who chased off SA arsonists and called the fire brigade to extinguish the flames. It remained in use as a place of worship until 1940 when it was handed over to the Wehrmacht, who used it as a warehouse until it was gutted by bombs on the night of November 22, 1943.

After the war the synagogue remained a ruin and in 1958 the main hall, which was thought to be on the verge of collapse, was demolished, leaving only the building's facade and entrance rooms intact. For many years these stood here largely overlooked, a plaque on the shattered frontage exhorting the few passers-by to: *Vergesst es nie* – "Never forget". The Jewish community pressed for what was left to be turned into a museum, but the authorities did

Kristallnacht and Berlin's Jews

Kristallnacht ("Crystal Night"), so called after the sound of breaking glass as Jewish businesses and institutions were wrecked, marked an intensification of Nazi attacks on the Jews. The murder of Ernst vom Rath, a German official in Paris, by Herschel Grynszpan, a young German-Jewish refugee protesting at his parents' forced deportation to Poland with ten thousand other Jews, gave the Nazis the excuse they had been waiting for to unleash a general pogrom on German Jews. (Ironically, vom Rath was an anti-Nazi whom Grynszpan had mistaken for his intended target, the German ambassador.) At a party meeting on November 9, 1938, Nazi propaganda minister Joseph Goebbels, having broken the news of the assassination, ordered Reinhard Heydrich, chief of the Reich's Security Head Office, to organize "spontaneous" anti-Jewish demonstrations. Heydrich directed the police to ensure that attacks on the German-Jewish community, mainly instigated by SA men in civilian clothes, were not hindered. *Kristallnacht* resulted in the deaths of at least 36 Berlin Jews and the destruction of 23 of the city's 29 synagogues, with hundreds of shops and businesses wrecked. After the attacks the Nazi government fined the German-Jewish community one billion marks, ostensibly to pay for the damage, and enacted new laws confiscating Jewish property.

Kristallnacht was the violent public culmination of a process of state-backed persecution of German Jews that had started when the Nazis assumed power in 1933. The first step was the SA-enforced boycott of Jewish shops, businesses, and medical and legal practices that began on April 1 of that year. A series of laws passed in the years that followed banned Jews from most of the professions, and in September 1935 the Nürnberg laws effectively deprived Jews of their German citizenship, introducing apartheid-like classifications of "racial purity". There was a brief respite in 1936 when Berlin hosted the Olympic Games and the Nazis, wishing to show an acceptable face to the outside world, eased up on overt anti-Semitism, but by the following year large-scale expropriation of Jewish businesses had begun. After *Kristallnacht* all remaining Jewish businesses were forcibly "Aryanized", effectively excluding Jews from German economic life. With the outbreak of war in September 1939, Jews were forced to observe a night-time curfew and were forbidden to own radios. Forced transport of Jews to the East (mainly occupied Poland) began as early as February 1940, and September 1941 saw the introduction of a law requiring Jews to wear the yellow Star of David, heralding the beginning of mass deportations.

In January 1942, the **Wannsee Conference** held in a western suburb of Berlin (see p.194) discussed the *Endlösung* or "Final Solution" to the "Jewish Question", drawing up plans for the removal of all Jews to the East and, implicitly, their extermination. As the Final Solution began to be put into effect, daily life for Berlin's Jews grew ever more unbearable: in April they were banned from public transport, and in September their food rations were reduced. By the beginning of 1943 the only Jews remaining legally in Berlin were highly skilled workers in the city's armaments factories, and in February deportation orders began to be enforced for this group, too. Most Berlin Jews were sent to Theresienstadt and Auschwitz concentration camps, and only a handful survived the war. By the end of the war Berlin's 160,564-strong Jewish population (1933 figure) had been reduced, by the combined effects of emigration and genocide, to about 6500; 1400 survived as "U-boats", hidden by Gentile families at great personal risk, and the rest had somehow managed to evade the final round-ups, usually as a result of having irreplaceable skills vital to the war effort.

not respond until 1988, when it was decided to resurrect the shell as a "centre for the promotion and preservation of Jewish culture".

A new plaque was affixed to the building amid much official pomp and ceremony on November 9, 1988, the fiftieth anniversary of *Kristallnacht*, and work began on restoration of the facade and the reconstruction of the gilded dome. In 1995, the extensive renovation work was completed and the building was reopened as a museum and cultural centre, officially called **Centrum Judaicum – Neue Synagoge** (Tues–Thurs 10am–6pm, Fri 10am–5pm, Sun & Mon 10am–8pm; €3 plus extra for special exhibitions). Inside there are two permanent exhibitions: one on the history and restoration of the synagogue itself, and another on the Jewish life and culture that could once be found in the surrounding area. Already the synagogue's dome, visible from far and wide, has become a Berlin landmark once again.

In order to get in you'll have to pass through airport-type magnetic detectors – a sad reflection of the continuing threat to Jewish institutions from terrorist attack and the home-grown far right. Once in you can also visit the headquarters of Berlin's Jewish community (Mon–Thurs 9am–4.30pm, Fri 9am–1.30pm), who have literature about the synagogue and a map showing important Jewish sites in the city past and present – English-language versions of both available.

Towards the southern end of Oranienburger Strasse is **Monbijoupark**, once the grounds of a Rococo royal palace, reduced to rubble by the war and, like so many Hohenzollern relics, never rebuilt. Today this park makes an unexpected and shady refuge from the unrelentingly urban landscape of the area. A footbridge at its southwestern corner links it to the Museumsinsel. Just after it meets the park, Oranienburger Strasse veers off to the left to become a strip of small and trendy clothes shops.

Grosse Hamburger Strasse and Sophienstrasse

Toward the eastern end of Oranienburger Strasse is the junction of **Grosse Hamburger Strasse**. The site of some poignant reminders of the area's Jewish past, it also offers access to **Sophienkirche**, one of Berlin's prettiest churches and the attractively restored adjacent **Sophienstrasse**.

The Jewish Cemetery and around

On the immediate right, just into Grosse Hamburger Strasse, is the location of Berlin's oldest **Jewish cemetery**, established in 1672, and the first **Jewish old people's home** to be founded in the city. The Nazis used the building as a detention centre for Jews, and 55,000 people were held here before being deported to the camps. A memorial tablet, on which pebbles have been placed as a mark of respect (following the Jewish practice for grave-site visits), and a sculpted group of haggard-looking figures, representing deportees, mark the spot where the home stood.

The grassed-over open space behind is the site of the cemetery itself. In 1943 the Gestapo smashed most of the headstones and dug up the remains of those buried here, using gravestones to shore up a trench they had excavated through the site. A few cracked headstones with Hebrew inscriptions line the graveyard walls. The only freestanding monument was erected after the war to commemorate Moses Mendelssohn, the philosopher and German Enlightenment figure. Also adorned with pebbles, it's on the spot where he is thought to have been buried, with an inscription in German on one side and in Hebrew on the other. Just to the north of the cemetery at **Grosse Hamburger Strasse 27** is a former Jewish boys' school, recently reopened as a Jewish secondary school for both sexes. Above its entrance a still-visible sign from prewar days reads, in German, "Jewish Community Boys' School". On the facade a plaque pays homage to Mendelssohn, who was a founder of Berlin's first Jewish school here in 1778, and who, until 1938, was commemorated by a bust in the school garden.

On the other side of the street is the **Missing House**, a unique and effective monument to the wartime destruction of Berlin. A gap in the tenements marks where house number 15–16 stood until destroyed by a direct hit during an air raid. In the autumn of 1990 the French artist Christian Boltanski put plaques on the side walls of the surviving buildings on either side as part of an installation, recalling the names, dates and professions of the former inhabitants of the vanished house.

The Sophienkirche

Continuing north along the street, past turn-of-the-twentieth-century neo-Baroque apartment buildings, brings you to the entrance gateway of the **Sophienkirche** on the right-hand side.

Dating back to 1712, this is one of the city's finest Baroque churches, and was the only central Berlin church to survive the war more or less undamaged. Its clear, simple lines come as a welcome change after the monumental Neo-classicism and fussy Gothic revivalism of so much of Berlin's architecture. The church's seventy-metre-high tiered tower is one of the area's most prominent landmarks and was added during the 1730s.

The ground on which the church was built was a gift from the Jewish community to the Protestant community, who at the time were slightly financially embarrassed. The church itself was paid for by Princess Sophie Louise, in

△ Jewish memorial tablets

Wartime scars

Like the old houses around Grosse Hamburger Strasse, nearly all the buildings that remain from the war, and which have not had their facades redone since the *Wende*, show the damage inflicted during the Battle of Berlin: take a look at Kraus-nickstrasse, Auguststrasse, or on the side streets of Prenzlauer Berg (see Chapter 8), and you'll see scores of bullet and shell marks.

order to provide a parish church for the neighbourhood, then an outlying area known as the Spandauer Vorstadt. The **interior**, in washed-out shades of green and grey, is a simple but pleasing affair, and you can't help but feel that this is one church where restoration could only have a detrimental effect. The one note of aesthetic exuberance is a pulpit with a crown-like canopy, set on a spiral pillar, which makes it look exactly like a chalice.

Sophienstrasse

Just beyond the Sophienkirche, a sharp turn to the right takes you into **Sophienstrasse**, first settled at the end of the seventeenth century and once the Spandauer Vorstadt's main street.

During the 1980s the street was extensively restored and its buildings now house a mix of retailers and arts and crafts workshops. In places, however, the restoration is only skin-deep and the pastel frontages of the old apartment houses conceal squalid, crumbling courtyards. House no. 11 dates back to 1780, and the vaguely Gothic-looking **Handwerkervereinshaus** at no. 18 used to be the headquarters of the old Craftsmens' Guild. Until the founding of the German Social Democrat Party (SPD), this had been the main focus of the Berlin workers' movement, and thereafter its headquarters continued to play an important role as a frequent venue for political meetings, including, on November 14, 1918, the first public gathering of the Spartakusbund (Spartacus League), the breakaway anti-war faction of the SPD that later evolved into the KPD (Communist Party of Germany).

At Sophienstrasse 21, a doorway leads to the **Sophie-Gips Höfe**, a recently renovated retail and office complex that houses the Sammlung Hoffman, a private art collection – some of the larger pieces of which are on display outside – and *Barcomi's Delicatessen*, a fashionable coffee and cake establishment representative of the current climate of the neighbourhood. A walk through the colourful, neon-lit passageway brings you to neighbouring Gipsstrasse, a rather quiet side street but a night-time favourite, with a couple of trendy bars.

Hackescher Markt

At the eastern end of Oranienburger Strasse is the small jumbled and slightly chaotic crossroads of **Hackescher Markt**, which over the last decade or so has steadily become a major tourist centre in Berlin. Other than the **Hackesche Höfe**, a series of beautifully restored early-twentieth-century courtyards, it's the many restaurants and cafés – with plentiful outdoor seating in a pedestrian plaza – adjacent to the **Hackescher Markt S–Bahnhof** that bring people here.

The Hackesche Höfe

Among the most significant forces of revitalization in the area are the Hack-esche Höfe, a series of nine courtyards built between 1905 and 1907 to house businesses, flats and places of entertainment. Restored to their former Art Deco glory, the Höfe (courtyards) bustle with crowds visiting the several cafés, stores, galleries, theatres and cinemas within. The Höfe were originally intended as a centre for the city's emerging artists but the result is all a bit too premeditated to be of any use to up-and-coming talent, most of whom gravitate to the network of galleries on and around Auguststrasse. That said, it's one of the main draws of the neighbourhood, and definitely worth a look-in, if nothing else for the architecture and people-watching opportunities. The first courtyard, decorated with blue mosaic tiles, is home to the Chamaleon Varieté, a venue at the forefront of the revival of the city's interwar cabaret tradition (see p.259). The second courtyard contains the Hackesche Höfe Theater, which regularly plays host to klezmer concerts and Jewish-themed theatre pieces.

A parallel courtyard, accessed via an entrance at no. 39 Rosenthaler Strasse, is the **Museum Blindenwerkstatt Otto Weidt** (Mon–Fri noon–8pm, Sat & Sun 11am–8pm; €1.50; ☎030/28 59 94, 07 ⊛www.blindes-vertrauen.de; U- & S-Bahn Hackescher Markt), entry to which is included in tickets to the Jewish Museum (see p.147). As tiny as it is poignant, this museum occupies the former rooms of a broom and brush factory run by one Otto Weidt, whose employees were mostly deaf, blind and Jewish. Luckily the factory was considered important to the war effort, so for a long time Weidt was able to protect his workers from deportation to concentration camps. But in the 1940s, as pressure grew, he resorted to producing false papers, bribing the Gestapo, and providing food and even hiding places to keep them alive, all at considerable personal risk. One small room, whose doorway was hidden by a cupboard, was the refuge for a family of four, until their secret was discovered and they were deported and murdered at Auschwitz. The exhibition has relics of the war-time era factory: brushes, photos and letters from the workers, but all is in German so be sure to ask for the free English translation on entry.

Directly opposite Sophienstrasse is Neue Schönhauserstrasse, another street with a concentration of shops displaying a young and fashionable assortment of clothing and footwear, in addition to a couple of sleek and rather expensive restaurants – all a very long way from the old GDR.

Hackescher Markt S-Bahnhof

Just to the south of **Hackescher Markt** is its **S-Bahnhof**, a nineteenth-century construction retaining an original red-tile facade, with mosaic decorative elements and rounded windows typical of the period. Now a protected building, its architectural features are best appreciated by walking through the station itself and taking a look at the northern facade. On both sides you'll see that the arches under the S-Bahn tracks have now been renovated to house trendy restaurants, bars and clothes shops. The station has undergone several name changes during the last century. Until the *Wende* it was called S-Bahnhof Marx-Engels-Platz; before the war it was known as Bahnhof Börse, thanks to its proximity to Berlin's long-since-vanished Stock Exchange. This stood behind the Humboldt Universität building on Spandauer Strasse (the site is now occupied by the *Radisson*), was gutted during the war and suffered an unlikely fate: it was demolished and its granite blocks were used to build the panorama wall of East Berlin's zoo, behind the polar bear enclosure.

North and east of Hackescher Markt

If you've developed a taste for wandering the backstreets of central Berlin, you might like to seek out a few lesser-known attractions **north and east of**

Hackescher Markt. These include the **Garnisonsfriedhof**, a small military cemetery, and the district around Rosa-Luxemburg-Platz, which was the traditional heart of the old Scheunenviertel quarter, and one-time centre of the city's scrap-iron and rag-and-bone trades. Little of this remains now, and the **Volksbühne** theatre is its most obvious attraction.

Up Rosenthaler Strasse

The leafy **Garnisonsfriedhof** on Kleine Rosenthaler Strasse is a military cemetery dating from the eighteenth century, full of rusting cast-iron crosses with near-obliterated inscriptions commemorating the officers and men of the Prussian army. Also here is the rather grander tomb of Adolph von Lützow, a general who found fame during the Napoleonic Wars, contrasting sharply with the overgrown wooden crosses commemorating victims of the Battle of Berlin, hidden away in a far corner. Information about the history of the cemetery is available from the administration offices near the entrance, which also house a small **exhibition** (Mon–Thurs 10am–5.50pm, Fri 10am–3.30pm; free).

The Volksbühne and around

On Rosa-Luxemburg-Platz the most prominent landmark is the **Volksbühne** theatre, built in 1913 with money raised by public subscription. Under the directorship of the ubiquitous Max Reinhardt, it became Berlin's people's theatre and, daringly for that time, put on plays by Hauptmann, Strindberg and Ibsen. Erwin Piscator continued the revolutionary tradition from 1924 to 1927, and immediately after the war in September 1945 a production of Lessing's plea for tolerance, *Nathan the Wise*, was put on here. The theatre was officially reopened in 1954 and became one of the ex-GDR capital's best theatres. These days it's still one of the most exciting and innovative theatres in the city, under director Frank Castorf (see "The Arts", p.259).

Nearby, at Weydingerstrasse 14 and Kleine Alexanderstrasse 28, is the **Karl-Liebknecht-Haus**, the former KPD central committee headquarters, which also housed the editorial offices of the Communist newspaper *Rote Fahne* ("Red Flag"). From the late 1920s onwards this was an important centre of resistance to the increasingly powerful Nazis: 100,000 pro-Communist workers demonstrated here on January 25, 1933, just a few days before Hitler came to power. After the Reichstag fire in February 1933 the KPD was broken up and its headquarters ransacked.

A couple of nearby streets, Almstadtstrasse and Mulackstrasse, though fairly unremarkable today, were important parts of the Scheunenviertel scene during its heyday. **Almstadtstrasse**, formerly known as Grenadierstrasse, became a magnet for Jewish migrants from eastern Europe and Russia at the end of the nineteenth century and it was here that a bustling street market grew up, echoing the *Schtetl* districts where Jewish traders did business in eastern European and Russian towns. During the inflationary period of 1923–24 the street gained notoriety as a black-market centre, with dealers trading illegally in everything from currency to precious stones.

Mulackstrasse was home to a famous Scheunenviertel *Gaststätte*, the *Mulack-Ritz*, whose clientele encompassed pimps, prostitutes and small-time gangsters, as well as artists and actors. The establishment survived until the general closing down enforced by the GDR authorities in the 1960s, though the interior has been preserved in the Gründerzeitmuseum in Mahlsdorf (see p.181).

The Tiergarten and around

A huge swathe of peaceful green smack in the middle of Berlin, the **Tiergarten** stretches west from the Brandenburg Gate and Reichstag, its beautifully landscaped meadows, gardens and woodlands a great antidote to the bustle and noise of the city. Yet at the same time the park and its immediate surroundings are very much part of the city's central *Mitte* district, forming a sub-district also known as Tiergarten. This spreads west from Potsdamer Platz (see p.75) and contains a number of attractions, the most high-profile of which is the **Kulturforum** complex just southeast of the park. Highlights of this superb agglomeration of museums and venues are the **Gemäldegalerie** with its internationally renowned collection of European art, the twentieth-century art of the **Neue Nationalgalerie** and the **Kunstgewerbemuseum**'s fine applied arts exhibition.

The **diplomatic district** begins just west of the Kulturforum. Here the **Bendlerblock**, site of several July Bomb Plot executions (see p.122), houses the interesting **Gedenkstätte Deutscher Widerstand**, a museum to **German resistance** against the Nazis. Further east, one architecturally impressive **embassy** lies beside another as far as the **Bauhaus Archive** where the elements of this influential art and design movement are covered. A couple of quick stops on the bus north of here and you are at the Tiergarten's proud centrepiece: the **Siegessäule**, a huge column that celebrates Prussian military victories and delivers fine views over the park and Berlin.

While Potsdamer Platz, with its U- and S-Bahn station, is the main **transport** hub for the Tiergarten district, Bahnhof Zoo and Alexander Platz are equally useful as the extremely frequent #100 and #200 buses link the two and stop at or near the main sites: #200 stops at the Kulturforum, while #100 stops at all the major points in the Tiergarten. But the best way to explore this area, particularly the park itself, is by bike (see p.34 for rental information).

The Kulturforum

The **Kulturforum** (U- or S-Bahn Potsdamer Platz) is a mixture of museums and cultural spaces that could easily fill a day of your time. Many of the buildings

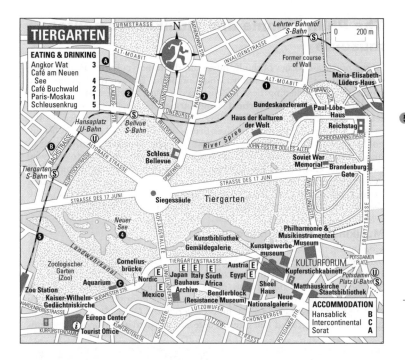

here were designed in the 1960s by Hans Scharoun – with the exception of the impressive Mies van der Rohe Neue Nationalgalerie – but mostly the area lay dormant on the fringe of West Berlin, until after the *Wende* when building work here was completed.

The Staatsbibliothek

Walking west from Potsdamer Platz, the first building on your left is the **Staats-bibliothek** (Mon–Fri 9am–9pm, Sat 9am–7pm; free 90min tours on third Sat of month 10.30am; €0.50; ⓦwww.sbb.spk-berlin.de), which has over three and a half million books, occasional exhibitions, a small concert hall, a reasonable café and a wide selection of British newspapers. As the final building to be designed by Hans Scharoun, and the most popular of his works among his fans, the *Staabi*'s most recent claim to fame came when it was used as an important backdrop in Wim Wenders' poetic film elegy to the city, *Wings of Desire*.

Entrance to the Kulturforum

A *Standortkarte* (€6) can be bought at any of the museums in the Kulturforum: the Gemäldegalerie, Kunstbibliothek, Kunstgewerbemuseum, Kupferstichkabinett, Neue Nationalgalerie and Musikinstrumenten Museum. It gives you entry to all others and the Hamburger Bahnhof (see p.103) on the same day. You will be sold this ticket automatically at all museums except the Musikinstrumenten Museum. For information on day tickets, valid in all of Berlin's municipal museums, see p.83.

The Philharmonie and Musikinstrumenten museum

At the northeast corner of the Kulturforum the honey-coloured **Philharmonie** is home of the Berlin Philharmonic orchestra, frequently considered the world's best. Conducting here is considered a huge privilege, and to be the resident conductor – as **Herbert von Karajan** (see opposite) was until he retired and subsequently died in 1989 – the ultimate accolade, since it's the members of the orchestra themselves that vote for this. Looking at the gaudy gold-clad building, designed in the 1960s by Hans Scharoun, and bearing in mind von Karajan's famously short temper with artists, it's easy to see why Berliners nicknamed it "Karajan's circus". However, Scharoun's complicated floor plan around the orchestra offers top-notch acoustics and views, regardless of your seat. Other than visiting a performance (see p.258), you can also view the interior of the building on free tours (in German), held daily at 1pm.

Musikinstrumenten museum

Continuing the musical theme, the **Musikinstrumenten museum** (Tues–Fri 9am–5pm, Sat & Sun 10am–5pm; €3, free Thurs 1–4pm), in the same building as the Philharmonie, comes as something of a disappointment. Yet there are a few high points in its comprehensive collection of (mostly European) keyboards, wind and string instruments from the fifteenth century to the present day, including the flute Frederick the Great played to entertain his guests. Pre-recorded tapes give a taste of the weird and wonderful sounds

△ Haus der Kulturen der Welt

Herbert von Karajan (1908–89)

The success of Austrian conductor **Herbert von Karajan** in the postwar years obscured a murky past that included a close association with the Nazi Party, though it seems that their ideals were not his and that his musical influences came from more eclectic sources. Born in 1908 into an aristocratic Austrian family, von Karajan soon became a child prodigy and quickly rose to success, becoming Germany's youngest ever Director of Music in 1935. Von Karajan's career rose with the Nazis, whose party he joined, though beyond that his relationship with them is unclear. He certainly organized a number of concerts for the Führer – including an occasion when he had the audience seating arranged in the form of a swastika – and, consequently, few of the world's great Jewish soloists ever performed or recorded with him. It seems probable, though, that his Nazi associations were the result of ambitions rather than beliefs, and his second marriage, to Anita Gutermann, a Jew, had him expelled from the Party in 1942.

The end of the war pushed his career into the doldrums, as he found himself banned by the Allies, including at the Salzburg festival, where he nevertheless found a way of participating anonymously. These postwar career difficulties made this period one of von Karajan's most intriguing and one in which he became inspired by Zen Buddhism, which he claimed brought teachings of mindfulness and concentration into his conducting. In an interview he summed the influence up: "The language of Buddhism says not 'I shoot' or 'I operate'. It says 'it shoots – it operates'. The 'it' indicates that something behind you is governing every thing. You are only giving it the first control, then you must let it go. When I forget I make music, I know that it is right."

By the 1950s the ban on Karajan was fully lifted, allowing him to rocket to prominence once again, and in 1955 he became musical director for the Berlin Philharmonic. From the 1960s to the 1980s von Karajan ruled the Berlin Philharmonic with a rigid discipline that alienated many who worked under him, but proved fabulously successful in the field of popularizing classical music. Under the Deutsche Gramophon label, they recorded just about everything that had a chance of selling, all in the highly polished von Karajan style – and one which rarely saw him refer to music sheets.

of the instruments, the most memorable of which are the seventeenth-century cembalo, a nineteenth-century glass harmonica, consisting of liquid-filled glasses, and a three-storey-high 1929 Wurlitzer organ.

The Kunstgewerbemuseum

Over the road from the Philharmonie is the **Kunstgewerbemuseum** (Museum of Applied Arts; Tues–Fri 10am–6pm, Sat & Sun 11am–6pm; €6, free from 2pm on Thurs ⊛www.smb.spk-berlin.de/kgm/) with its encyclopedic, but seldom dull, collection of European arts and crafts. The top floor contains Renaissance, Baroque and Rococo pieces (wonderful silver and ceramics), along with Jugendstil and Art Deco objects, particularly furniture. Among the many impressive pieces is a massive silver buffet that once resided in the Berlin City Palace, one of the very few surviving artefacts from that residence, and, of course, the museum has a superb collection of Meissenware and KPM porcelain. The ground floor holds the Middle Ages to Early Renaissance collections, with some sumptuous gold pieces. The highlights are Lüneburg's municipal silver and the treasures from the Stiftskirche in Enger and, in the basement, a small but great assembly of Bauhaus furniture, glittering contemporary jewellery, and a display on the evolution of product design.

The Gemäldegalerie

Beside the Kunstgewerbemuseum is the **Gemäldegalerie** (Picture Gallery; Tues–Sun 10am–6pm, Thurs until 10pm; €6, including audio tour, free Thurs 6–10pm ☏030/2 66 29 51 ⊛www.smb.de) whose stupendous collection of early European paintings makes it the real jewel of the Kulturforum. Almost nine hundred paintings are on display, arranged in chronological order, and subdivided by region.

The German section

A dignified introduction to the gallery's treasures, the collection of **German work** from the Middle Ages and Renaissance begin just to the right of the entrance on the north side of the building. Highlights include the large *Wurzach Altar* of 1437, made in the workshop of the great Ulm sculptor Hans Multscher; its exaggerated gestures and facial distortions mark it out as an ancient precursor of Expressionist painting. An interesting contrast is offered by the far more subtle *Solomon before the Queen of Sheba*, painted in the same year by Konrad Witz, while the exquisite *Nativity* by Martin Schongauer is the most important surviving panel by the father figure of the German Renaissance.

These apart, the best works here are by Albrecht Altdorfer, one of the first fully realized German landscape painters, and Albrecht Dürer – among others, *The Madonna with the Siskin* and *Hieronymous Holzschuher* – with an impressive group of works by Dürer's eccentric pupil Hans Baldung, notably an exotic *Adoration of the Magi* triptych. Holbein the Younger is represented by several superbly observed portraits, the most celebrated being *The Danzig Merchant Georg Gisze*, with a still-life background that's a real *tour de force* of artistic virtuosity. Notable among the many examples of Cranach are his tongue-in-cheek *The Fountain of Youth*, and his free reinterpretation of Bosch's famous triptych *The Garden of Earthly Delights*.

The Netherlandish section

A lighter, less crude, treatment of religious subjects is apparent in the **Netherlandish section**. Particularly illustrative is Jan van Eyck's beautifully lit *Madonna in the Church*, crammed with architectural detail and with the Virgin lifted in the perspective for gentle emphasis. Petrus Christus is thought to have been a pupil of van Eyck, and certainly knew his work, as *The Virgin and Child with St Barbara and a Carthusian Monk* reveals; in the background are tiny Flemish houses and street scenes, the artist carefully locating the event in his native Bruges. Dieric Bouts' figures tend to be stiff and rather formalized, but his *Christ in the House of Simon the Pharisee* is filled with gesture, expression and carefully drawn detail.

Also on show are some pieces by Rogier van der Weyden, which show the development of the Eyckian technique to a warmer, much more emotional treatment of religious subjects. The figures in his *Middelburg Altar* reveal a delicacy of poise and an approachable humanity that was to greatly influence German painting in the fifteenth century. Albert van Ouwater was also influential, although his *Raising of Lazarus* is the only complete work to have survived; it's a daring picture, the richly dressed merchants on the right contrasting strongly with the simplicity of the Holy Family on the left. Geertgen tot Sint Jans was Ouwater's pupil, though his *St John the Baptist* is quite different from his master's painting – the saint sits almost comically impassive against a rich backdrop of intricately constructed landscape. Two other major paintings nearby are both by Hugo van der Goes: the *Adoration of the Shepherds* (painted when the artist was in the first throes of madness) has the scene unveiled by two characters representing the prophets, while the shepherds stumble into the frame; the *Adoration of the Magi* – also known as the *Monforte Altarpiece* – has a superbly drawn realism that marks a new development in Netherlandish art, carrying precision over into a large-scale work with a deftly executed, complex perspective. The small altarpiece *Triptych with the Adoration of the Magi* by Joos van Cleve reveals how these techniques were absorbed by Goes' successors. The collection then moves into the sixteenth century and the works of Jan Gossaert, Quentin Massys and Bruegel the Elder, whose *Netherlandish Proverbs* is an amusing, if hard-to-grasp, illustration of over a hundred sixteenth-century proverbs and maxims – a key and English translation help you pick out a man armed to the teeth, banging his head against a brick wall and casting pearls before swine.

The Dutch and Flemish collections

The next section reveals the gallery's second strength in the **Dutch and Flemish collections**. This contains the large portraits of Van Dyck and the fleshy canvases of Rubens, as well as a fine group of Dutch interiors. The paintings of Vermeer are the most easily identifiable, though his *Woman with a Pearl Necklace* is not one of his greater works. Better is *Man and Woman Drinking Wine*, which displays his usual technique of placing furniture obliquely in the centre of the canvas, the scene illuminated by window light. His contemporary, Pieter de Hooch, is represented by *The Mother*, a masterly example of Dutch interior painting. Other rooms trace the development of Dutch art through the works of Nicholas Maes, Gerrit Dou, Jan Steen and Frans Hals.

The high points of this section, hung in a large octagonal room, are the paintings of **Rembrandt**. The most famous picture here, *The Man in the Golden Helmet*, was recently proved to be the work of his studio rather than the artist himself, though this does little to detract from the elegance and power of the portrait, its reflective sorrow relieved by the bright helmet. Other (verified) works include a 1634 *Self-Portrait*, painted at the height of the artist's wealth and fame; *The Mennonite Preacher Anslo and His Wife*, from 1641; a beautifully warm and loving *Portrait of Hendrickje Stoffels*, the artist's later, common-law wife; and several other religious paintings.

Interrupting the chronology somewhat are three rooms – numbers 20, 21 and 22 – in the southwest corner displaying, respectively, eighteenth-century French, English (including several Gainsborough portraits) and German paintings.

Italian paintings

The galleries on the museum's southern side contain, for the most part, **Italian paintings** from the Renaissance to the eighteenth century. This collection is particularly strong on works from the Florentine Renaissance: Fra Filippo Lippi's *The Adoration in the Forest* is a mystical image of unusual grace and beauty, rightly one of the most admired paintings of the period, while Correggio's playfully suggestive *Leda with the Swan* is a good example of the Classical preoccupations of the period. Classical themes again crop up in Piero de Cosimo's *Venus, Mars, and Cupid*, completed about two decades before Correggio's painting; though not one of the eccentric artist's better-known works, it is an intimate rendering of a popular scenario. There's work here, too, by Giotto, Verrocchio, Masaccio, Mantegna, Raphael and Titian, and, most importantly, two by Botticelli: *Madonna with Saints* and *Mary with the Child and Singing Angels*.

Other noteworthy painters represented in the museum include Caravaggio (*Cupid Victorious*, heavy with symbolism and homoeroticism), Poussin (the important *Self-Portrait*), Claude and Canaletto.

The Kupferstichkabinett

Sharing its main entrance with the Gemäldegalerie, the **Kupferstichkabinett** (Engraving Cabinet; Tues–Fri 10am–6pm, Sat & Sun 11am–6pm; €6, free Thurs 2–6pm; ☎030/2 66 20 02, ☒www.kupferstichkabinett.de) at Matthäikirchplatz 4 holds an extensive collection of European medieval and Renaissance prints, drawings and engravings, many kept under protective lighting. Founded by William Humboldt in 1831, the collection includes Botticelli's exquisite drawings for Dante's *Divine Comedy*. The museum organizes exhibitions on all aspects of print-making, drawing and related design.

Kunstbibliothek

Also beside the Gemäldegalerie is the **Kunstbibliothek** (Art Library; Tues–Fri 10am–6pm, Sat & Sun 11am–6pm ☎030/20 90 55 55; free; ☒www.smb.spk -berlin.de) a gigantic resource for those with interest in art, photography and graphic design, thanks to its 350,000 volumes and over 1,300 international periodicals. The library also has its own galleries for temporary exhibitions, which are almost always worth at least a quick look.

Matthäuskirche

The clear odd-man-out in the Kulturforum is the brick neo-Romanesque **Matthäuskirche** (Matthias Church; Tues–Sun noon–6pm; €1), built between 1844 and 1846 and the only survivor of the war here. It houses temporary exhibitions and you can climb the tower for some aerial views of the other, far more modern and angular, Kulturforum buildings.

The Neue Nationalgalerie

By far the finest building here – architecturally speaking – is the **Neue Nationalgalerie**, Potsdamer Strasse 50 (Tues–Fri 10am–6pm, Sat & Sun 11am–6pm; ☒www.smpk.de; €6, free Thurs 2–6pm), behind the Matthäuskirche. A black-rimmed glass box, its ceiling seems almost suspended above the ground, its clarity of line and detail having all the intelligent simplicity of the Parthenon. Designed by Mies van der Rohe in 1965, the upper section is used for temporary exhibits, often of contemporary art, while the underground galleries contain paintings from the beginning of the twentieth century onwards. Included among the permanent collection are the paintings of the "Brücke" group, such as Ernst Kirchner and Karl Schmidt-Rottluff. **Kirchner** spent time in Berlin before World War I, and his *Potsdamer Platz* dates from 1914, though, given the drastic changes to it since then, it might as well be in another country instead of just down the road. The galleries move on to the portraits and Berlin cityscapes of **Grosz** and **Dix**, notably Grosz's *Gray Day* and Dix's *Maler Family*. Cubism is represented by work from **Braque**, **Gris** and **Picasso** (though the latter is seen in greater number and to better effect in the Berggruen Collection in Charlottenburg; see p.137). There are also pieces by, among others, Klee, Max Beckmann and Lyonel Feininger.

The diplomatic district

Leaving the Kulturforum behind, a short walk west down Sigismund Strasse leads to Stauffenbergstrasse, which takes its name from Count Claus Schenk von Stauffenberg, one of the instigators of the July Bomb Plot (see p.122). Stauffenbergstrasse is the eastern edge of the **diplomatic district**, a term coined by Hitler's architect, Albert Speer, to describe an area of villas where several embassies had begun to congregate in the 1920s and 1930s. The concept was strengthened in the 1940s when close Nazi allies Japan and Italy were invited to build embassies here. The war saw most of the district comprehensively destroyed, and while the German government was in Bonn, there was little rebuilding here. But with the move in government back to Berlin many countries have re-established their presence here, leading to a stimulating showcase of modern architecture – best admired by walking along Tiergartenstrasse – which conveniently lines the way to the **Bauhaus Archive**.

The Bendlerblock and the Gedenkstätte Deutscher Widerstand

At Stauffenbergstrasse 13–14 stands the **Bendlerblock**, once the home to the Wehrmacht headquarters – where Stauffenberg was chief of staff – and now the German Defence Ministry. The floors where Stauffenberg worked are occupied by the absorbing exhibition **Gedenkstätte Deutscher Widerstand** (Memorial to German Resistance; Mon–Wed & Fri 9am–6pm, Thurs 9am–8pm; Sat & Sun 10am–6pm; free), a huge collection of photos and documents covering the many and wide-ranging groups who actively opposed the Third Reich – an eclectic mix which included communists, Jews, Quakers and aristocrats – (see "Resistance against the Nazis", p.306). Most of the exhibition is in German, though the English audio tour (for which you need to leave ID) gives a good taste by covering the highlights in around forty minutes.

The Shell-Haus

Further south down Stauffenbergstrasse, on the corner of Reichspietschufer, is the **Shell-Haus** – now known as the Bewag building – one of Berlin's great edifices that substantially survived World War II. A procession of tiered levels, this office building was designed by Emil Fahrenkamp in 1931 and was a leading piece of modernist architecture.

The embassies

The **diplomatic district** kicks off properly at the northern end of Stauffenbergstrasse, site of the dignified **Egyptian** and flamboyant **Austrian** embassies, both built around the beginning of the millennium, with the latter the work of Viennese architect Hans Hollein. Turning the corner to head west along Tiergartenstrasse, and beyond the South African Embassy, brings you to the reconstructed 1940s **Italian** and **Japanese** embassies, two rather gloomy and foreboding Nazi-era edifices. Thankfully, relief is at hand around the next corner on Kinglehoferstrasse, location of the architecturally brilliant **Nordic Embassy**, which provides offices for Denmark, Sweden, Finland, Iceland and Norway, with each housed in a separate building designed to represent their different cultural identities. Further down the street, the avant-garde **Mexican Embassy** features slanting supports that create a vertical blind effect and a

The July Bomb Plot

The **July Bomb Plot** that took place in the summer of 1944 at Hitler's Polish HQ, the "Wolf's Lair" in Rastenburg, was the assassination attempt that came closest to success. The plot, led by **Count Claus Schenk von Stauffenberg**, an aristocratic officer and member of the General Staff, had gained the support of several high-ranking members of the German army. Sickened by atrocities on the eastern front, and rapidly realizing that the Wehrmacht was fighting a war that could not possibly be won, von Stauffenberg and his fellow conspirators decided to kill the Führer, seize control of army headquarters on Bendlerstrasse and sue for peace with the Allies. Germany was on the precipice of total destruction by the Allies; only such a desperate act, reasoned the plotters, could save the Fatherland.

On July 20, Stauffenberg was summoned to the Wolf's Lair to brief Hitler on troop movements on the eastern front. In his briefcase was a small bomb, packed with high explosive: once triggered, it would explode in under ten minutes. As Stauffenberg approached the specially built conference hut, he triggered the device. Taking his place a few feet from Hitler, Stauffenberg positioned the briefcase under the table, leaning it against one of the table's stout legs less than two metres away from the Führer. Five minutes before the bomb exploded, the Count quietly slipped from the room unnoticed by the generals and advisers, who were absorbed in listening to a report on the central Russian front. One of the officers moved closer to the table to get a better look at the campaign maps and, finding the briefcase in the way of his feet under the table, picked it up and moved it to the other side of the table leg. This put the very solid support of the table leg between the briefcase and Hitler.

At 12.42pm the bomb went off. Stauffenberg, watching the hut from a few hundred metres away, was shocked by the force of the explosion. It was, he said, as if the hut had been hit by a 155mm shell; there was no doubt that the Führer, along with everyone else in the room, was dead.

Stauffenberg hurried off to a waiting plane and made his way to Berlin to join the other conspirators. Meanwhile, back in the wreckage of the conference hut, Hitler and the survivors staggered out into the daylight: four people had been killed or were dying from their wounds, including Colonel Brandt, who had moved Stauffenberg's briefcase and thus unwittingly saved the Führer's life. Hitler himself, despite being badly shaken, suffered no more than a perforated eardrum and minor injuries. After being attended to, he prepared himself for a meeting with Mussolini later that afternoon.

It quickly became apparent what had happened, and the hunt for Stauffenberg was on. Hitler issued orders to the SS in Berlin to summarily execute anyone who was slightly suspect, and dispatched Himmler to the city to quell the rebellion.

massive concrete and marble entranceway, making it another architectural breath of fresh air. A public exhibition area within its atrium is a homage to a Mayan observatory, the first cylinder construction in the Americas.

The Bauhaus Archive

Further south down the road, at Klingelhöferstrasse 14, and on the bus route of the #100 bus between the Tiergarten and Bahnhof Zoo, is the **Bauhaus Archive** (Mon & Wed–Sun 10am–5pm; €4; ℗www.bauhaus.de). The Bauhaus school of design, crafts and architecture was founded in 1919 in Weimar by Walter Gropius. It moved to Dessau in 1925 and then to Berlin, to be closed by the Nazis in 1933. The influence of Bauhaus has been tremendous, but you only get a very small impression of this from the modest collection here. Marcel Breuer's seminal chair is still (with minor variations) in production today, and

Back in the military Supreme Command headquarters in Bendlerstrasse, the conspiracy was in chaos. Word reached Stauffenberg and the two main army conspirators, Generals Beck and Witzleben, that the Führer was still alive. They had already lost hours of essential time by failing to issue the carefully planned order to mobilize their sympathizers in the city and elsewhere, and had even failed to carry out the obvious precaution of severing all communications out of the city. After a few hours of tragicomic scenes as the conspirators tried to persuade high-ranking officials to join them, the Bendlerstrasse HQ was surrounded by SS troops, and it was announced that the Führer would broadcast to the nation later that evening. The attempted coup was over.

The conspirators were gathered together, given paper to write farewell messages to their wives, taken to the courtyard of the HQ (a memorial stands on the spot) and, under the orders of one General Fromm, shot by firing squad. Stauffenberg's last words were "Long live our sacred Germany!" Fromm had known about the plot almost from the beginning, but had refused to join it. By executing the leaders he hoped to save his own skin – and, it must be added, save them from the torturers of the SS.

Hitler's revenge on the conspirators was severe even by the ruthless standards of the Third Reich. All the colleagues, friends and immediate relatives of Stauffenberg and the other conspirators were rounded up, tortured and taken before the "People's Court" (the building where the court convened, the Kammergericht building, still stands – see p.145), where they were humiliated and given more or less automatic death sentences, most of which were brutally carried out at **Plötzensee prison** to the northwest of the city centre (see p.140). Many of those executed knew nothing of the plot and were found guilty merely by association. As the blood lust grew, the Nazi Party used the plot as a pretext for settling old scores, and eradicated anyone who had the slightest hint of anything less than total dedication to the Führer. General Fromm, who had ordered the execution of the Bendlerstrasse conspirators, was among those tried, found guilty of cowardice and shot by firing squad. Those whose names were blurted out under torture were quickly arrested, the most notable being Field Marshal Rommel, who, because of his popularity, was given the choice of a trial in the People's Court – or suicide and a state funeral.

The July Bomb Plot caused the deaths of at least five thousand people, including some of Germany's most brilliant military thinkers and almost all of those who would have been best qualified to run the postwar German government. Within six months the country lay in ruins as the Allies advanced; had events at Rastenburg been only a little different, the entire course of the war – and European history – would have been altered incalculably.

former Bauhaus director Mies van der Rohe's designs and models for buildings show how the modernist Bauhaus style has changed the face of today's cities. There's work, too, by Kandinsky, Moholy-Nagy, Schlemmer and Klee, all of whom worked at the Bauhaus. Gropius designed the building himself.

The Tiergarten

Flanking both the Kulturforum and Diplomatic District is the **Tiergarten**, a restful expanse of woodland and lakes, but which was originally designed by Peter Lenné, as a hunting ground under Elector Friedrich III. The 1945 Battle of Berlin destroyed most of it, and after the war it was used as farmland, largely

Bauhaus, a German word whose literal meaning is "building-house", has become a generic term for the aesthetically functional design style that grew out of the art and design philosophy developed at the Dessau school. The origins of the Bauhaus movement lie in the Novembergruppe, a grouping of artists founded in 1918 by the Expressionist painter Max Pechstein with the aim of utilizing art for revolutionary purposes. Members included Bertolt Brecht and Kurt Weill, Emil Nolde, Eric Mendelsohn and the architect **Walter Gropius**. In 1919 Gropius was invited by the new republican government of Germany to oversee the amalgamation of the School of Arts and Crafts and the Academy of Fine Arts in Weimar into the **Staatliche Bauhaus Weimar**. It was hoped that this new institution would break down the barriers between art and craft, creating a new form of applied art. It attracted over two hundred students who studied typography, furniture design, ceramics, wood-, glass- and metalworking under exponents like Paul Klee, Wassily Kandinsky and Laszlo Moholy-Nagy.

Financial problems and opposition from the conservative administration in Weimar eventually forced Gropius to relocate to Dessau, 120km southwest of Berlin, chosen after the town authorities offered financial and material support and because it was home to a number of modern industrial concerns, notably an aeroplane factory and a chemical works. Dessau's **Bauhausgebäude**, designed by Gropius and inaugurated on December 4, 1926, is one of the classic buildings of modern times – a forerunner of architectural styles that would not come into their own until the 1950s and 1960s.

Towards the end of the 1920s, the staff and students of the Bauhaus school became increasingly embroiled in the political battles of the time. As a result, Gropius was pressurized into resigning by the authorities and replaced by the Swiss architect Hannes Meyer. He, in turn, was dismissed in 1930 because of the increasingly left-wing orientation of the school. His successor **Ludwig Mies van der Rohe** tried to establish an apolitical atmosphere, but throughout the early 1930s Nazi members of Dessau town council called for an end to subsidies for the Bauhaus. Their efforts finally succeeded in the summer of 1932, forcing the school to close down. The Bauhaus relocated to the more liberal atmosphere of Berlin, setting up in a disused telephone factory in Birkbuschstrasse in the Steglitz district. However, after the Nazis came to power, police harassment reached such a pitch that on July 20, 1933, Mies van der Rohe took the decision to shut up shop for good. He and many of his staff and students subsequently went into exile in the United States.

growing potatoes for starving citizens, but since then replanting has been so successful that these days it's hard to tell it's not original.

It's most easily accessed using bus #100 which cuts through the park on its way from Bahnhof Zoo to Alexanderplatz via all the main sights, but the best way to appreciate it is on foot or by bike. At the very least, try wandering along the Landwehrkanal, an inland waterway off the River Spree that separates the park from the zoo. It's an easy hour's walk between **Corneliusbrücke** – just up Cornelius-Strasse from the Bauhaus Archive (see p.122) – and Bahnhof Zoo, via a popular beer garden *Schleusenkrug* (see p.235). At Corneliusbrücke a small, odd sculpture commemorates the radical leader **Rosa Luxemburg**. In 1918, along with fellow revolutionary Karl Liebknecht (see p.79), she reacted against the newly formed Weimar Republic and especially the terms of the Treaty of Versailles, declaring a new Socialist Republic in Berlin along the lines of Soviet Russia (she had played an important part in the abortive 1905 revolution). The pair were kidnapped by members of the elite First Cavalry Guards: Liebknecht was gunned down while "attempting to escape", Luxemburg was knocked unconscious and shot, her body dumped in the Landwehrkanal at this point.

Just to the north of the Landwehrkanal, and deeper inside the park, is a pretty little group of ponds that makes up the grand-sounding **Neuer See**. In summer there's another popular beer garden here, the *Café am Neuen See* (see p.234), and it's possible to rent **boats** by the hour.

The Siegessäule

In the midst of the park and approached by four great boulevards is the **Siegessäule** (April–Oct Mon–Fri 9.30am–6.30pm, Sat & Sun 9.30am–7pm; Nov–March Mon–Fri 10am–5pm, Sat & Sun 10am–5.30pm; €2.20; bus #100), a victory column celebrating Prussia's military victories (chiefly that over France in 1871). It was shifted to this spot on Hitler's orders in 1938 from what is today known as Platz der Republik in front of the Reichstag. The move was part of a grand design for Berlin as capital of the Third Reich, and with the same forethought Hitler had the monument raised another level to commemorate the victories to come in what became World War II. Though the boulevard approaches exaggerate its size, it's still an eye-catching monument: 67m high and topped with a gilded winged victory that symbolically faces France. The summit offers a good view of the surrounding area, but climbing the 585 steps to the top is no mean feat. Have a look, too, at the mosaics at the column's base, which show the unification of the German peoples and incidents from the Franco-Prussian War: they were removed after 1945 and taken to Paris, only to be returned when the lust for war spoils had subsided. Dotted around the Siegessäule are **statues** of other German notables, the most imposing being that of Bismarck, the "Iron Chancellor", under whom the country was united in the late nineteenth century. He's surrounded by figures symbolizing his achievements; walk around the back for the most powerful.

Strasse des 17 Juni

East and west of the Siegessäule, the **Strasse des 17 Juni** is the broad, straight avenue that cuts through the Tiergarten to form the continuation of Unter den Linden beyond the Brandenburg Gate (see p.58). Originally named Charlottenburger Chaussee, it was also once known as the East–West Axis and a favourite strip for Nazi processions. Indeed, Hitler had the stretch from the Brandenburg Gate to Theodor-Heuss-Platz (formerly Adolf-Hitler-Platz) widened in order to accommodate these mass displays of military might and Nazi power; on his birthday in 1938, 40,000 men and 600 tanks took four hours to parade past the Führer. Later, in the final days of the war, Charlottenburger Chaussee became a makeshift runway for aeroplanes ferrying Nazi notables to and from the besieged capital. Now called Strasse des 17 Juni, its name commemorates the day in 1953 when workers in the East rose in revolt against the occupying Soviet powers, demanding free elections, the removal of all borders separating the two Germanys, and freedom for political prisoners. Soviet forces were quickly mobilized, and between two and four hundred people died; the authorities also ordered the execution of twenty-one East Berliners and eighteen Soviet soldiers – for "moral capitulation to the demonstrators". But today it's moral capitulation of a different sort for which the Strasse des 17 Juni is best known: by night it's lined by prostitutes and every summer it forms the prime venue for the hedonistic Love Parade (see p.8).

Schloss Bellevue and the Kongresshalle

From the Siegessäule it's a long hike down to the Brandenburg Gate and Reichstag, so it's worth hopping on the #100 bus. If you do travel this way, look out for **Schloss Bellevue**, an eighteenth-century building that was once a guesthouse for the Third Reich and is today the Berlin home of the Federal President. Further east, on John-Foster-Dulles-Allee, sits the oyster-shaped **Kongresshalle**, an exhibition centre whose concept couldn't be matched by available technology: its roof collapsed in 1980, and it has since been rebuilt and reopened as the **Haus der Kulturen der Welt**, a venue for theatre, music, performance art and exhibitions – chiefly from Africa, South America and the Far East. South from here, on the north side of Strasse des 17 Juni, is the **Soviet War Memorial** to the Red Army troops who died in the Battle of Berlin. Built from the marble of Hitler's destroyed Berlin HQ, the Reich's Chancellery, it's flanked by two tanks that were supposedly the first to reach the city.

Regierunsviertel

Beyond the Kongresshalle and all the way past the Reichstag (see p.56) lies the **Regierungsviertel** (government quarter), site of several new and strikingly modern buildings. At its western end is the **Bundeskanzleramt** (Federal Chancellery), a huge, modern, strangely inspired building that was a pet project of Helmut Kohl. Designed by Axel Schultes and Charlotte Frank, it is based around a nine-storey white cube, shaped in such a way as to earn the building the nickname "the washing machine". It's best appreciated from its northern side on the banks of the Spree and the Moltebrücke. To get here you'll need to pass in front of the **Paul–Löbe–Haus** which stretches away to the east and is joined, via a footbridge, to the **Maria–Elisabeth–Lüders–Haus** on the opposite bank of the Spree. Following the designs of Stefan Brunfels, who sought to pick up themes from the Bundeskanzleramt, both buildings were officially completed in 2001 and are used as government offices and conference rooms. Note how large windows make the latter entirely visible from outside in a conscious effort to underline the importance of transparency in government.

Charlottenburg and Wilmersdorf

Since reunification the former centre of West Berlin, just west of Tiergarten and in the districts of **Charlottenburg** and **Wilmersdorf**, has gradually reverted to its prewar role. This was based, as now, on the shops of the **Kurfürstendamm** (universally called the Ku'damm). Even in the grim first few years after the war, a few retailers managed to struggle on here, but it was with the coming of the Berlin Wall that the area got a real boost. With Berlin's true centre snatched away by the communists, this area quickly became an awkward surrogate. Large amounts of modern showcase building ached to transform the area into the heart of a great late twentieth-century metropolis, but the work was largely in vain. Once the Wall came down the city hastily reverted to its old centre. Now, with the balance of the city restored, this quarter has had to slowly reinvent itself and seems to have settled on a mix of slick and fairly bland high-street shops.

Shopping aside, the Ku'damm area also has several other deserving attractions – particularly the iconic semi-derelict church tower of the **Kaiser-Wilhelm-Gedächtniskirche** and a stimulating multi-media museum of the city's history, the **Berlin Story**.

From the Ku'damm, **Charlottenburg** and **Wilmersdorf** stretch north and west of the town centre and encompass the northern forests of the Grunewald. Their most significant attraction is the **Schloss Charlottenburg** – Berlin's pocket Versailles with opulent chambers inside, wanderable gardens out, and beside several of Berlin's excellent municipal **museums**. Further out, Charlottenburg has strong reminders of the 1930s and wartime Berlin, with the **Funkturm**, **Olympic Stadium** and **Plötzensee Prison Memorial** the main draws. Wilmersdorf's chief attraction is the Grunewald on its western edge – covered in Chapter 10 – though you might find yourself staying on one of its pleasant leafy streets close to the centre of town, particularly if you book a private room.

The Ku'damm is easily explored on foot, while points west are best visited using **bus services** from Bahnhof Zoo: Bus #145 stops in front of Schloss Charlottenburg; #149 heads to the Funkturm where you can pick up #218 to the Olympia Station. From here you have a choice of U- and S-Bahn stations to whizz you back into the centre.

Bahnhof Zoo, the Ku'damm and around

As the district's main gateway, **Bahnhof Zoo** – squeezed between a couple of scruffy shopping precincts and surrounded by third-rate modern architecture – makes for a convenient, albeit unprepossessing, start to a day's sightseeing. Thankfully, distractions are close at hand in the form of the engaging photographic exhibits of the **Museum für Fotographie**, home to the **Helmut Newton Stiftung**; **Berlin Zoo**, one of Europe's best; and a sensationalist but quirkily comprehensive **Erotik Museum**.

Walk two blocks south and things get considerably swisher, as you're on the **Ku'damm**, a 3.5-kilometre strip of ritzy shops, cinemas, bars and cafés. In among the consumer jungle are two good museums, the **Käthe Kollwitz Museum** with displays of Kollwitz's anti-war art inspired by her tortured life, and **The Story of Berlin**, the best place in the city to get up to speed on its history.

At its eastern end the Ku'damm homes in on Breitscheidplatz, location of the landmark **Kaiser-Wilhelm-Gedächtniskirche** and the forgettable adjacent **Europa Center** shopping mall, location of the city's main **tourist information** office. This is a ten-minute walk away from **KaDeWe**, Berlin's most prestigious department store – whose excellent top-storey food court provides the necessary resuscitation after a hard shop.

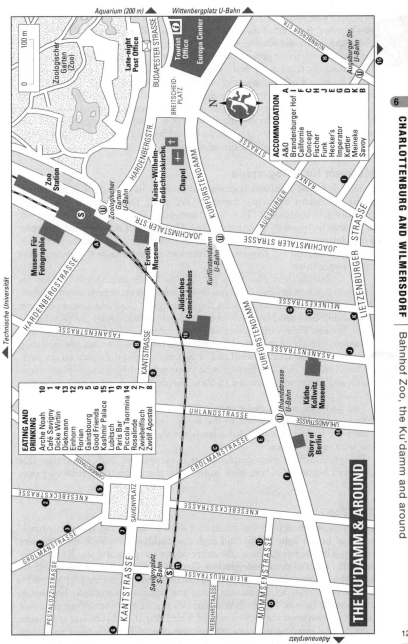

Aquarium (200 m) ▲   Wittenbergplatz U-Bahn ▲

ACCOMMODATION

A&O	A
Brandenburger Hof	I
California	F
Concept	C
Fischer	H
Funk	J
Hecker's	E
Imperator	G
Kettler	D
Meineke	K
Savoy	B

Zoologischer Garten (Zoo)

Late-night Post Office

Tourist Office

Europa Center

Technische Universität ▲

Museum Für Fotographie

Zoo Station

Zoologischer Garten U-Bahn

Kaiser-Wilhelm-Gedächtniskirche

Chapel

Erotik Museum

Jüdisches Gemeindehaus

Kurfürstendamm U-Bahn

Uhlandstrasse U-Bahn

Käthe Kollwitz Museum

Story of Berlin

Savignyplatz

Savignyplatz S-Bahn

EATING AND DRINKING

Arche Noah	10
Café Savigny	1
Dicke Wirtin	4
Diekmann	13
Einhorn	12
Florian	3
Gainsbourg	5
Good Friends	6
Kashmir Palace	15
Lubitsch	11
Paris Bar	9
Piccola Taormina	14
Rosalinde	2
Zwiebelfisch	7
Zwölf Apostel	8

THE KU'DAMM & AROUND

Adenauerplatz ▲

Bahnhof Zoo

Whether you come by train, or on the bus from Tegel airport, chances are you'll arrive at Bahnhof Zoologischer Garten – **Zoo Station**. Perched high above the street, and with views across to the zoo itself, the train station conjures up memories of prewar steam trains as you pull in under its glassy roof. Unfortunately, that's as far as the nostalgia goes: Zoo Station is comparatively small, without a large lobby or grand entrance portal, so overall it rather lacks presence. More importantly, though, at street level it has been smartened up quite a bit, and despite the retinue of urban casualties permanently posted by the entrance, it's a far cry from the days, a decade or so ago, when it was a marketplace for heroin dealing and child prostitution. A few glossy, late-opening stores contribute to the new look.

Museum für Fotographie

Behind Bahnhof Zoo, and best reached through its back door, is another of Berlin's excellent municipal museums (see p.83), the **Museum für Fotographie**, Jebenesstrasse 2 (Tues–Sun 10am–6pm, Thurs open until 10pm; €6, free Thurs 6–10pm; ☏030/20 90 55 66). The home of the **Helmut Newton Foundation**, it exhibits the work of this world-famous fashion and nude photographer, and has temporary exhibitions of lesser-known photographers on its upper floors.

The collection was Newton's gift to his home city shortly before his untimely death in January 2004 and divides into two main permanent exhibits. The first, **Us and Them**, explores the fascinatingly close and almost obsessive relationship between Newton and his wife, who works under the pseudonym Alice Springs. Their cameras seem rarely to have been far from their eyes and attentions to each other's naked forms unswerving. Self-portraits give revealing insights into their state of mind and images from Newton's deathbed are stark. "Them" are the rich and famous who commissioned Newton to photograph them, and one room is devoted to these heavily stylized, yet nonetheless quite brilliant, portraits.

The odd **Sex and Landscapes** gallery forms the other permanent exhibition and is largely devoted to the more risqué of Newton's provocatively perceptive trademark nudes. Some landscape shots break up the sexual tension, but with mixed success.

The ground-floor photography **shop** is exceptional, with a coverage that goes well beyond Newton, with many of its glut of books at reduced prices (see p.279).

The Zoo

Step out east through the main entrance of Zoo Station and you're in a maelstrom of bright lights, traffic and high-rise buildings, but walk over the area occupied by the bus station to the other side of the plaza and you'll find yourself at the gates of the **Zoologischer Garten** (daily: April–Sept 9am–6.30pm; Oct–March 9am–5pm; zoo €10, aquarium €10, combined ticket €15; ⓦwww.zoo-berlin.de), containing a zoo and aquarium. Originally laid out in 1844 on the basis of Friedrich Wilhelm IV's private zoo from Pfaueninsel (see p.195), this survived the destruction of World War II, and subsequent pressure from a local starving populace, to become one of Europe's most important zoos, with over 1,500 species represented. It's a pleasantly landscaped place with reasonably large compounds for the animals, some peaceful nooks for quietly observing animal behaviour, and lots of benches that make it ideal for picnicking. Unusual highlights are the *Nachttierhaus*, an underground nocturnal environment, whose principle attraction is the bat cave, and a large glass-sided hippo-pool. In addition, amid all the usual cast of characters there's the chance to see a couple of rare giant pandas – both gifts from China. The zoo's **aquarium** also lives up to its international reputation, with more species than any other in the world. The large, humid crocodile hall is the most memorable part, though almost all of the tanks are well cared for and appealingly laid out, making it an excellent rainy-day option. Despite the attractive combination price, avoid trying to get around both the zoo and aquarium in a day, as this can be quite a rush.

The Erotik-Museum

Wildlife of a different sort is on show on the short block immediately south of Bahnhof Zoo, home, beyond a sleazy strip of sex shops, to the **Erotik-Museum** (daily 9am–midnight; €5, over-18s only). It's run by Beate Uhse, a household name in Germany: once a Luftwaffe test pilot, she began selling sex education pamphlets after the war and now heads a multimillion-euro corporation dedicated to all things sexual. Located on three floors above her sex shop, the museum is really an assemblage rather than an organized exhibition, but it does present a surprisingly extensive collection of prints, paintings and objects – including Japanese silk paintings, Balinese fertility shrines, Indian reliefs in wood and Chinese bordello tokens, to name but a few. The assortment of 1920s and 1930s artwork from Europe, including charcoal sketches of cabaret artist Anita Berber, and pieces by George Grosz and local favourite Heinrich Zille, is particularly good, suggesting – albeit faintly – something of the atmosphere of Weimar Berlin.

Ku'damm

A short walk two blocks south of Bahnhof Zoo lies the **Ku'damm**'s litany of shops and cafés, which blaze the trail at night in a dazzle of neon. Built under Bismarck in the nineteenth century, the avenue was described by Thomas Wolfe as "the largest coffee-house in Europe" in the 1920s. These days there's little left from either man's time and the street is lined with a combination of international chain stores and smaller, more exclusive shops that make it, together with the adjacent **Tauentzienstrasse**, the main downtown shopping locale for Berliners.

The Käthe Kollwitz Museum

West along the Ku'damm, just prior to Uhlandstrasse U-Bahn station, lies Fasanenstrasse where the one cultural attraction, the **Käthe Kollwitz Museum**, is at no. 24 (Mon & Wed–Sun 11am–6pm; €5; ⓦwww .kaethe-kollwitz.de; U-Bahn Uhlandstrasse). The drawings and prints of Käthe Kollwitz are among the most moving works from the first half of the twentieth century. Born in 1867, she lived for almost all her life in Prenzlauer Berg in the eastern part of the city (see Chapter 8), where her work evolved a radical left-wing perspective. Following the death of her son in World War I, her woodcuts, lithographs and prints became explicitly pacifist, often dwelling on the theme of mother and child – her most famous print, *No More War*, a stark, furious work depicting a protesting mother, is a perfect example. Her sculptures, too, often deal with this subject: two of her bronzes, *Tower of Women* and the pietà *Mother with Dead Son*, can be seen here. When her grandson was killed in World War II her work became even sadder and more poignant. A staunch pacifist and committed socialist, the Nazis kept a careful watch over her and forced her resignation from a prestigious post at the Faculty of Arts, while at the same time using some of her work for their own propaganda purposes. She died in 1945, shortly before the end of the war. The museum's comprehensive collection of her work makes it possible to trace its development, culminating in the tragic sculptures on the top floor.

The Story of Berlin

Back on the Ku'damm and just west of the Uhlandstrasse U-Bahn, **The Story of Berlin**, at no. 207–208 (daily 10am–8pm, last admission 6pm; €9.30; ⓦwww.story-of-berlin.de), is an excellent multimedia exhibition and an ideal first step in unravelling Berlin's history. Tucked away in the back of a mall, the museum uses its odd layout to its advantage, with each subsection extensively labelled in English and designed with an inventiveness generally reserved for stage sets. On the way around you'll be confronted with life-size dioramas, film clips, noises, flashing lights, smoke and smells, which illustrate the trawl through the highs and lows of the city's turbulent past. The end result will entertain all ages and will take at least two hours to complete, not including the additional bonus: a taste of the Cold War given on the frequent guided tours of the 1970s Allied-built nuclear bunker below the mall. It's still functional and designed for around 3,500 people to shelter in the first few weeks after a nuclear attack. If you've run out of time or energy having visited the museum, it's possible to use your ticket to come back another day to view the bunker.

The Kaiser-Wilhelm-Gedächtniskirche

Retracing your steps east, the Ku'damm homes in on the **Kaiser-Wilhelm-Gedächtniskirche** (Kaiser Wilhelm Memorial Church), one of Berlin's great landmarks and a postcard favourite. Built at the end of the nineteenth century, it was destroyed by British bombing in November 1943. Left as a reminder, it's a strangely effective memorial, the crumbling tower providing a hint of the old city. It's possible to go inside what remains of the nave (Mon–Sat 10am–4pm): there's a small exhibit showing wartime destruction and a "before and after" model of the city centre. Adjacent, a modern **chapel** contains a tender, sad charcoal sketch by Kurt Reubers, *Stalingrad Madonna*, dedicated to those that died – on both sides – during the battle of Stalingrad. The blue-glass campanile on the opposite side of the ruined church to the side of the chapel has gained the nickname the "Lipstick" or the "Soul-Silo" because of its tubular shape; its base contains a shop selling Third World gifts.

Breitscheidplatz and the Europa Center

The area around the church acts as a magnet for vendors, caricaturists and street musicians, while **Breitscheidplatz**, the square behind, often hosts fairs or festivals in the summer that feature much the same cast of characters – otherwise it serves as an outdoor annexe to the **Europa Center** shopping mall. There's nothing much of interest in this rather generic mall, which was built in the 1960s as a capitalist showcase for West Berlin, topped by a huge, rotating Mercedes-Benz symbol. An intriguing sculpture entitled *Flow of Time*, an alternative clock consisting of an elaborate series of liquid-filled glass pipes,

△ Taunzienstrasse

does, however, attract some attention down in the lobby. On the northern side of the mall – but accessible only from the street – is the Berlin **tourist office** (see p.28).

Tauentzienstrasse

East of the Kaiser-Wilhelm-Gedächtniskirche, the Ku'damm becomes the rather bland chain-store shopping street **Tauentzienstrasse**, which is also arranged around a wide boulevard. At its eastern end, and claiming to be the largest department store on the continent, is **KaDeWe**. An abbreviation of Kaufhaus Des Westens – "the Department Store of the West" – it's an impressive statement of the city's standard of living, and the sixth-floor food hall is a mouth-watering inducement to sample the many exotic snacks sold there. A little further down, **Wittenbergplatz U-Bahn station** has been likeably restored to its prewar condition both inside (1920s kitsch) and out (Neoclassical pavilion). Near the entrance, a tall sign reminds passers-by of the wartime concentration camps: it states that the German people must never be allowed to forget the atrocities that were carried out there, and lists the names of some of the camps. It's an odd memorial, neither terribly poignant nor at a significant site, and one that goes largely unnoticed by shoppers.

Schloss Charlottenburg and around

Allow at least a day to cover **Schloss Charlottenburg** and the clutch of good museums opposite the palace – which include the outstanding **Ägyptisches Museum**. And even if Baroque palace interiors aren't to your taste and you're museumed-out, the extensive **Schloss Gardens** are a worthy target and a fine way to idle away a sunny Berlin morning or take a break from sightseeing. The Schloss is best reached using bus #145 from Bahnhof Zoo, since U-Bahn Richard-Wagner-Platz and S-Bahn Westend, the nearest train stations, are each a ten-minute walk away.

Schloss Charlottenburg

Schloss Charlottenburg (@www.spsg.de) comes as a surprise after the unrelieved modernity of the city streets. Commissioned as a country house by the future Queen Sophie Charlotte in 1695 (she also gave her name to the district), the Schloss was expanded and added to throughout the eighteenth and early nineteenth centuries to provide a summer residence for the Prussian kings; master builder Karl Friedrich Schinkel (see p.67) provided the final touches. Approaching the sandy elaborateness of the Schloss through the main courtyard, you're confronted with Andreas Schlüter's **statue** of Friedrich Wilhelm, the Great Elector, cast as a single piece in 1700. It's in superb condition, despite (or perhaps because of) spending the war years sunk at the bottom of the Tegeler See for safekeeping.

The various parts of the Schloss can be visited and paid for separately, but **combined tickets** are the best value and available as day tickets (€7) or two-day tickets (€12); concessionary rates are €5 and €9 respectively. These tickets give access to all Schloss buildings, but do not cover the tour of the royal apartments in the Altes Schloss, nor entry to the Museum für Vor- und Frühgeschichte one of Berlin's municipal museums (see p.83).

The Altes Schloss

Immediately behind the statue of Friedrich Wilhelm is the entrance to the **Altes Schloss** (Tues–Fri 9am–5pm Sat & Sun 10am–5pm, last tour 4pm; tour of lower-floor royal apartments and upper floors €8; upper floors only €2). The upper floors are open to independent viewing and include the apartment of Friedrich Wilhelm IV and a collection of silver and tableware. But to view the lower floor, which includes the Baroque rooms of Friedrich I and Sophie Charlotte and an ancestral portrait gallery, you're obliged to go on the conducted **tour** that's in German only – though free English pamphlets are available. The tour is a traipse through increasingly sumptuous chambers and bedrooms, filled with gilt and carvings. Look out for the **porcelain room**, packed to the ceiling with china, and the **chapel**, which includes a portrait of Sophie Charlotte as the Virgin ascending to heaven.

The Neuer Flügel

It's just as well to remember that much of the Schloss is in fact a fake, a reconstruction of the buildings following wartime damage. This is most apparent in the Knobelsdorff-designed **Neuer Flügel** (New Wing; Tues–Fri 9am–6pm Sat & Sun 11am–6pm; €5 including audio guide) to the right of the Schloss entrance as you face it; the upper rooms, such as the elegantly designed Golden Gallery, are too breathlessly perfect, the result of intensive restoration. Better is the adjacent White Hall, whose eighteenth-century ceiling, made grungy by regular clouds of candle soot during festivities, was replaced at the end of the nineteenth century by a marble and gold confection with full electric illumination. Next door, the Concert Room contains a superb collection of works by **Watteau**, including one of his greatest paintings, *The Embarcation for Cythera*, a delicate

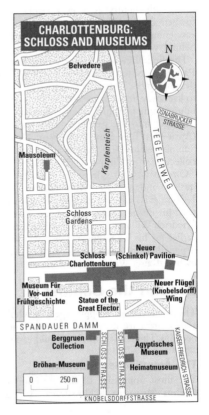

CHARLOTTENBURG: SCHLOSS AND MUSEUMS

N

Belvedere

OSNABRÜCKER STRASSE

Karpfenteich

TEGELERWEG

Mausoleum

Schloss Gardens

Neuer (Schinkel) Pavilion

Schloss Charlottenburg

Neuer Flügel (Knobelsdorff) Wing

Museum Für Vor-und Frühgeschichte

Statue of the Great Elector

SPANDAUER DAMM

Berggruen Collection

Ägyptisches Museum

Bröhan-Museum

Heimatmuseum

SCHLOSS STRASSE

KAISER-FRIEDRICH-STRASSE

0   250 m

KNOBELSDORFFSTRASSE

Rococo frippery tinged with sympathy and sadness. Also here is his *The Shop Sign*, painted for an art dealer in 1720.

The Museum für Vor- und Frühgeschichte

The western wing of the Schloss once contained an orangerie (much depleted after the war) and the **gallery** there now houses major exhibitions. Also in the west wing is the **Museum für Vor- und Frühgeschichte** (Museum of Pre- and Early History; Tues–Fri 9am–5pm, Sat & Sun 10am–5pm; €6, free Thurs 1–5pm; ®www.smpk.de), an unexciting collection of archeological discoveries from the Berlin area, along with general European prehistoric finds. There are, though, some interesting pieces from the Schliemann excavations of Troy, though the best pieces (some represented here in reproductions) remain in Russia, carted away as spoils of war. Delicate negotiations for the return of the Schliemann treasures continue, with the German authorities hoping that they will have them back in Berlin by the time this collection moves to the Neues Museum on Museum Island (see p.86).

The Schloss Gardens

Laid out in the French style in 1697, the **Schloss Gardens** (usually open daily 9am–5pm, till 9pm in the summer months – check at the Schloss complex) were transformed into an English-style landscaped park in the early nineteenth century; after severe damage in the war, they were mostly restored to their Baroque form. Though it's possible to buy a map in the Schloss, it's easy enough to wander through the garden to the lake and on to the grounds behind, which do indeed have the feel of an English park.

The first place to head for, before hitting the gardens proper, is the **Neuer Pavillon**, just to the east of the Schloss (Tues–Sun 10am–5pm; €2), which was designed by Schinkel for Friedrich Wilhelm III, and where the king preferred to live, away from the excesses of the main building. Square and simple, it today houses some of Schinkel's drawings and plans.

Deeper into the gardens, on the north side of the lake, is the **Belvedere** (April–Oct Tues–Sun 10am–5pm; Nov–March Tues–Fri noon–4pm Sat & Sun noon–5pm; €2), built as a teahouse in 1788 and today housing a missable collection of Berlin porcelain.

On the western side of the gardens a long, tree-lined avenue leads to the hushed and shadowy **Mausoleum** (April–Oct Tues–Sun 10am–noon & 1–5pm; €1), where Friedrich Wilhelm III is buried: his sarcophagus, carved with his image, makes him seem a good deal younger than his seventy years. Friedrich Wilhelm had commissioned the mausoleum to be built thirty years earlier for his wife, Queen Luise, whose own delicate sarcophagus apparently depicts her not dead but sleeping, though it's hard to tell. Later burials here include Kaiser Wilhelm I, looking every inch a Prussian king.

Around the Schloss

Though you could happily spend a whole day wandering around the Schloss and its gardens, just across the way another group of excellent **museums** beckons. These in themselves could easily take an afternoon of your time.

The Ägyptisches Museum

The most impressive of the museums opposite the Schloss is the **Ägyptisches Museum**, Schlossstrasse 70 (Egyptian Museum; daily 10am–6pm;

€6, €4 on Mon, free Thurs 2–6pm; ⊛www.smpk.de), the result of innumerable German excavations in Egypt from the early part of the twentieth century. The museum's pride and joy is the *Bust of Nefertiti* on the first floor, a treasure that has become a symbol for the city as a cultural capital. There's no questioning its beauty – the queen has a perfect bone structure and gracefully sculpted lips – and the history of the piece is equally interesting. Created around 1350 BC, the bust probably never left the studio in Akhetatenin which it was created, acting as a model for other portraits of the queen (its use as a model explains why the left eye was never drawn in). When the studio was deserted, the bust was left there, to be discovered some 3000 years later in 1912. In the last few days of the war, the bust was "removed" from the Soviet sector of Berlin, and until recently wrangles continued over its return. Elsewhere in the museum, atmospheric lighting complements the uniformly high standard of the exhibits. The light is used to particularly good effect on the Expressionistic, almost Futuristic, *Berlin Green Head* of the Ptolemaic period, and the Kalabsha Monumental Gate, given to the museum by the Egyptian government in 1973.

The Heimatmuseum Charlottenburg and Museum Berggruen

Immediately south of the Ägyptisches Museum at Schlossstrasse 69, the **Heimatmuseum Charlottenburg** (Tues–Fri 10am–5pm, Sun 11am–5pm; free) isn't anything special, but worth ducking into for a quick look at a few evocative photos of Charlottenburg from the Weimar and wartime eras. Across Schlossstrasse, however, is the wonderful **Museum Berggruen** (Tues–Sun 10am–6pm; €6, free Thurs 2–6pm; ⊛www.smpk.de). Heinz Berggruen, a young Jew forced to flee Berlin in 1936, wound up as an art dealer in Paris, where he got to know Picasso and his circle and assembled a collection of personal favourites. In 1996 the city gave him this building to show off, in a comfortable, uncrowded setting, his revered collection, which includes a dozen or so Picassos. Most of these have rarely been seen before and steal the show – highlights include the richly textured Cubist work *The Yellow Sweater* and large-scale *Reclining Nude* – but the collection also boasts a handful of Cézannes and Giacomettis and a pair of van Goghs. The top floor is very strong on Paul Klee, with works spanning the entire interwar period and so offering a meaningful insight into the artist's development. Be sure to pick up the audio tour, which is in English and included in the price of entry.

The Bröhan-Museum

Just south of the Berggruen Collection, the **Bröhan-Museum** at Schlossstrasse 1a (Tues–Sun 10am–6pm; €4; ⊛www.broehan-museum.de) houses a fine collection of Art Deco and Jugendstil ceramics and furniture, the assembly of which was the passion of Karl Bröhan (1921–2000), who selflessly donated all the pieces he had amassed to the city to commemorate his sixtieth birthday. Each of the museum's period rooms is dedicated to a particular designer and hung with contemporary paintings – worthiest of which are the pastels of Willy Jaeckel and the resolutely modern works of Jean Lambert-Rucki. Small, compact and easily taken in, the Bröhan forms a likeable alternative to the more extensive Ägyptisches Museum or the Schloss collections.

The Funkturm, Olympic Stadium and around

Western Charlottenburg is best known for its **Olympic Stadium**, the focus of world attention in the 1936 Games and which has recently been revamped for its next big appearance on the international stage in the 2006 Football World Cup. Also in the vicinity is the skeletal transmission mast, the **Funkturm**, Berlin's Eiffel Tower, and the **Teufelsberg**, Berlin's highest hill, built entirely out of rubble remains at the end of World War II.

The Funkturm

The **Funkturm** (Tues–Sat 10am–11pm; €3.60; U-Bahn Kaiserdamm) was built in 1928 as a radio and, eventually, a TV transmitter. One of Dr Goebbels's lesser-known achievements was to create the world's first regular TV service in 1941. Transmitted from the Funkturm, the weekly programme could only be received in Berlin; the service continued until just a few months before the end of the war. Today the Funkturm only serves police and taxi frequencies, but the mast remains popular with Berliners for the toe-curling views from its 126-metre-high **observation platform**. With the aluminium-clad monolith of the **International Congress Centre** (ICC) immediately below, it's possible to look out across deserted, overgrown S-Bahn tracks to the gleaming city in the distance – a sight equally mesmerizing at night.

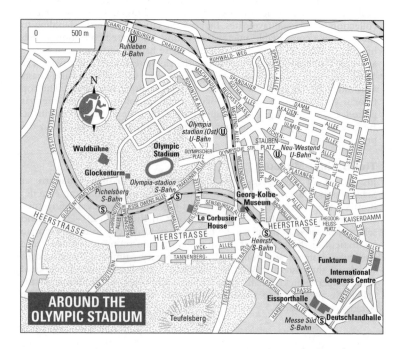

AROUND THE OLYMPIC STADIUM

The Olympic Stadium

To reach the **Olympic Stadium** (Wed & Sun 10am–6pm; exhibition €2.50; ☎030/3 01 11 00; U- and S-Bahn Olympiastadion) from the Funkturm, catch bus #218. A short way beyond the Funkturm it crosses **Theodor-Heuss-Platz**, a huge square formerly known as Adolf-Hitler-Platz; in its centre flickers an eternal flame that used to be dedicated to the reunification of East and West Germany – and which is still, rather oddly, alight. As Berlin's best football team, Hertha BSC's home ground (see p.274), the stadium is sometimes closed for sporting events or team practice, so it's best to call before trudging out. Calling ahead may also get you onto a tour (€5) of the stadium that requires a ten person minimum.

Built for the 1936 Olympic Games, the Olympic Stadium is one of the few fascist-era buildings left intact in the city, and remains very much in use. Whatever your feelings about it, the building is impressive, the huge Neoclassical space a deliberate rejection of the modernist architecture that began to be in vogue in the 1930s.

Inside the stadium the sheer size of it comes as a surprise, since the seating falls away below ground level to reveal a much deeper auditorium than you would imagine. On the western side, where the Olympic flame was kept and where medal winners are listed on the walls, it's easy to see how this monumental architecture, and the massive sculptures dotting the grounds outside, some of which are still extant, could inspire the crowds. During the Olympics, Berliners were kept up to date with commentary on the games, interspersed with stirring music, from hundreds of loudspeakers that ran all the way from the Museum Island via Unter den Linden and the Brandenburg Gate, through the Tiergarten and out to the stadium. Standing here, looking back out to the city, you realize what an achievement this was.

The 1936 Olympic Games

Hitler used the international attention the 1936 **Olympics** attracted to show the "New Order" in Germany in the best possible light. Anti-Semitic propaganda and posters were suppressed in the city, German half-Jewish competitors were allowed to compete, and when (for the first time in the history of the games) the Olympic flame was relayed from Athens, the newsreels and the world saw the road lined with thousands wearing swastikas and waving Nazi flags. To the outside world, it seemed that the new Germany was rich, content, and firmly behind the Führer.

Though the games themselves were stage-managed with considerable brilliance – a fact recorded in Leni Riefenstahl's poetic and frighteningly beautiful film of the events, *Olympia* – not everything went according to official National Socialist doctrine. Black American athletes did supremely well in the games, **Jesse Owens** alone winning four gold medals, disproving the Nazi theory that blacks were "subhuman" and the Aryan race all-powerful. But eventually Germany won the most gold, silver and bronze medals (there's a memorial at the western end of the stadium), and the games were deemed a great success.

At the medal ceremony Hitler did not shake Owens's hand, not, as is usually stated, because of any racist reasons (though they were undoubtedly there), but because, as patron of the games, he had been told that he must either congratulate all the medal winners (which would have been impractical) or none. Owens must have been more upset when he got back to the States, since President Roosevelt also refused to shake his hand.

Around the Olympic Stadium

If you cut south and west around the stadium, down the road named after Jesse Owens, and take a right into Passenheimer Strasse, you reach the **Glockenturm** or bell tower (April–Oct daily 9am–6pm; €2.50), the spot where Hitler would enter the stadium each morning, state business permitting. Rebuilt after wartime damage, it's chiefly interesting for the stupendous view it gives, not only over the stadium but also north to the natural amphitheatre that forms the Waldbühne, an open-air concert site (see p.255), and across the beginnings of the Grunewald to the south. Also easy to spot is the **Teufelsberg** (Devil's Mountain), a massive mound that's topped with a faintly terrifying fairytale castle that used to be a US signals and radar base, built to listen in to Eastern bloc radio signals; no longer needed, it's scheduled to be dismantled – though no one seems in a hurry. The mountain itself is artificial: at the end of the war, the mass of debris that was once Berlin was carted to several sites around the city, most of the work being carried out by women known as *Trümmerfrauen* – "rubble women" (see p.93). Beneath the poplars, maples and ski runs lies the old Berlin, about 25 million cubic metres of it, presumably awaiting the attention of some future archeologist. In the meantime, it's popular as a place for weekend kite flying, and skiing and tobogganing in winter.

Le Corbusier house and Georg-Kolbe-Museum

If you're a fan of the French architect Le Corbusier, you may want to make a pilgrimage to the **Le Corbusier house**, between Flatowallee, the street leading directly south of the stadium, and Heilsberger Allee. Built as part of the International Building exhibition in 1957, it contains more than five hundred apartments. Once heralded as a modernist vision of the ideal living environment, it now seems similar to all the other depressing concrete boxes thrown up in the 1960s. More rewarding is the **Georg-Kolbe-Museum** at Sensburger Allee 25 (Tues–Sun 10am–5pm; €4; ⊛www.george-kolbe-museum.de). Kolbe, a sculptor who died in 1947, never achieved the eminence of his contemporary Ernst Barlach – a judgement that perhaps seems reasonable when you view some of the 180 bronze figures and numerous drawings in what was the artist's home.

The Plötzensee Prison Memorial

Berlin sometimes has the feel of a city that has tried, unsuccessfully, to sweep its past under the carpet of the present. When concrete reminders of the Third Reich can be seen, their presence in today's postwar city becomes all the more powerful. Nowhere is this more true than in these buildings where the Nazi powers brought dissidents and political opponents for imprisonment and execution – preserved today as the **Plötzensee Prison Memorial** (Gedenkstätte Plötzensee; daily: March–Oct 9am–5pm; Nov–Feb 9am–4pm; free; ⊛www.gedenkstaette-ploetzensee.de).

Plötzensee stands in the northwest of the city, on the border between the boroughs of Charlottenburg and Wedding. To **get there**, take a thirty-minute ride on bus #123 from Tiergarten S-Bahn station to stop "Gedenkstätte Plötzensee", and walk away from the canal along the wall-sided path of Hüttigpfad.

The former prison buildings have been refurbished as a juvenile detention centre, and the memorial consists of the buildings where the executions took place. Over 2500 people were hanged or guillotined here between 1933 and 1945, usually those sentenced in the Supreme Court of Justice in the city. Following the July Bomb Plot (see p.122), 89 of the 200 people condemned were executed here in the space of a few days. The hangings were carried out with piano wire, so that the victims would slowly strangle rather than die from broken necks, and it is claimed (though there is no evidence to support this) that Hitler spent his evenings watching movie footage of the executions. Today the execution chamber has been restored to its wartime condition: on occasion, victims were hanged eight at a time, and the hanging beam, complete with hooks, still stands. Though decked with wreaths and flowers, the atmosphere in the chamber is chilling, and in a further reminder of Nazi atrocities an urn in the courtyard contains soil from each of the concentration camps. Perhaps more than at any other wartime site in Berlin, it is at Plötzensee that the horror of senseless, brutal murder is most palpably felt.

The Maria Regina Martyrum church

From the memorial hop back on the #123 bus for four more stops and you'll arrive a short walk from the **Maria Regina Martyrum** at Heckerdamm 230, a purposefully sombre memorial church dedicated to those who died under the Nazis. Completed in 1963, the church's brutally plain exterior is surrounded by a wide courtyard whose walls are flanked by abstract *Stations of the Cross* modelled in bronze. The interior is a plain concrete shoebox, adorned only with an abstract altarpiece that fills the entire eastern wall. It's a strikingly unusual design, and one that successfully avoids looking dated.

7

Schöneberg, Kreuzberg and around

D irectly south of Berlin's central district *Mitte* lie the boroughs of **Schöneberg** and **Kreuzberg**. Both are, in the main, residential: Schöneberg and West Kreuzberg are more middle class and less ethnically mixed, while East Kreuzberg, sometimes called **SO 36** after its old postal code, is more unkempt and famed for its large immigrant community and self-styled "alternative" inhabitants (a mix of punks, old hippies and students), nightlife and happenings. Throughout the 1970s and 1980s, this was where the youth of the Federal Republic came to get involved in alternative politics and avoid national service, making it West Berlin's "hip" quarter, and the place to hang out and hit the raucous nightspots.

If you've taken pension accommodation or found a private room via the tourist office, you might well end up in **Schöneberg** or **Kreuzberg**, and while there's little in the way of things to see, both do have their attractions and are close to the adjacent districts of Tempelhof and Treptow which contain two huge and impressive monuments to crumbled regimes: the Nazi **Tempelhof Airport** and **Soviet Memorial** respectively.

But most importantly, if you're staying in this part of the city, the **nightlife** is excellent. The bars and clubs around Schöneberg's Nollendorfplatz are where smart people (and particularly smart gay people) hang out; while Kreuzberg's reputation as home to some of the city's more avant-garde nightspots still rings true, even if Prenzlauer Berg and Friedrichshain have begun to overshadow it.

The best way to **get around** Schöneberg is on foot from Nollendorfplatz, with most sights of interest an easy walk away. The exception here is Rathaus Schöneberg, but this is easily reached using bus #204, which travels just south of Winterbergfeldt Platz and then along the main artery Potsdamer Strasse before terminating at the Rathaus. West Kreuzberg's main sights are strung along the route of bus #M41, which can be picked up a short walk south of Potsdamer Platz and which terminates at Tempelhof airport. In East Kreuzberg the U-Bahn Kottbusser Tor or Schlessisches Tor are the best way in, after which it's mostly a matter of walking around – though the Soviet Memorial in Treptower Park is a bus ride from the latter.

Schöneberg

Once a separate suburb, **SCHÖNEBERG** was swallowed up by Greater Berlin as the city expanded in the late eighteenth and nineteenth centuries. Blown to pieces during the war, it's now a mostly middle-class residential area. Things to see are few, but what is here is both fascinating and moving.

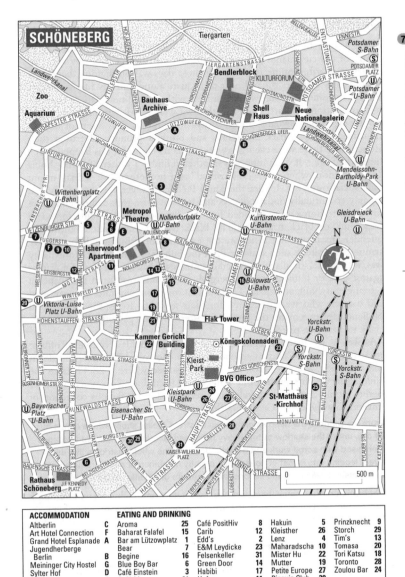

ACCOMMODATION		EATING AND DRINKING							
Altberlin	C	Aroma	25	Café PositHiv	8	Hakuin	5	Prinzknecht	9
Art Hotel Connection	F	Baharat Falafel	15	Carib	12	Kleisther	26	Storch	29
Grand Hotel Esplanade	A	Bar am Lützowplatz	1	Edd's	2	Lenz	4	Tim's	13
Jugendherberge		Bear	7	E&M Leydicke	23	Maharadscha	10	Tomasa	20
Berlin	B	Begine	16	Felsenkeller	31	Mister Hu	22	Tori Katsu	18
Meininger City Hostel	G	Blue Boy Bar	6	Green Door	14	Mutter	19	Toronto	28
Sylter Hof	D	Café Einstein	3	Habibi	17	Petite Europe	27	Zoulou Bar	24
Tom's House	E	Café M	21	Hafen	11	Pinguin Club	30		

The obvious gateway to the district is **Nollendorfplatz**, a long-standing centre in the city's gay and lesbian community. Schöneberg's main drag, Potsdamer Strasse, runs a block or so east of here and was once lined by the **Sportpalast** and **Kammergericht**, the scenes of several important chapters in the city's history. A bus ride on #204 down the road brings you to **Rathaus Schöneberg** where John F. Kennedys made his "Berliner" speech.

Nollendorfplatz

In the Weimar Berlin of the 1920s and early 1930s, **Nollendorfplatz** was the centre of the city's large **gay and lesbian community**. Even by contemporary standards, Berlin's gay scene in those days was prodigious: there were around forty gay bars on and near this square alone, and gay life in the city was open, fashionable and well organized, with its own newspapers, community associations and art. The city's theatres were filled with plays exploring gay themes, homosexuality in the Prussian army was little short of institutionalized, and gay bars, nightclubs and brothels proudly advertised their attractions – there were even gay working men's clubs. All this happened at a time when the rest of Europe was smothered under a welter of homophobia and repression, when to be "discovered" as a homosexual or lesbian meant total social ostracism. Under the Third Reich, however, homosexuality was quickly and brutally outlawed: gays and lesbians were rounded up and taken to concentration camps, branded for their "perversion" by being forced to wear pink or black triangles. (The black triangle represented "antisocial" offenders: in an attempt to ignore the existence of lesbianism, lesbians were arrested on pretexts such as swearing at the Führer's name.) As homosexuality was, at the time, still illegal in Allied countries, no Nazis were tried for crimes against gays or lesbians at Nürnberg. A red granite plaque in the shape of a triangle at Nollendorfplatz U-Bahn station commemorates the gay men and women who were murdered for their sexuality. Today, the area around Nollendorfplatz remains the focus of western Berlin's gay nightlife and especially its bars (see p.269).

As well as its first-rate nightlife, Nollendorfplatz holds a couple of offbeat attractions by day. Walk past the proto-Deco **Metropol Theater**, and down Maassenstrasse, which leads on to Nollendorfstrasse, where at no. 17 stands the building in which **Christopher Isherwood** lived during his years in prewar Berlin, a time that was to be elegantly recounted in his famous collection of stories about the city – *Goodbye to Berlin*:

From my window, the deep solemn massive street. Cellar shops where lamps burn all day, under the shadow of top-heavy balconied facades, dirty plaster frontages embossed with scroll work and heraldic devices. The whole district is like this: street leading into street of houses like shabby monumental safes crammed with the tarnished valuables and secondhand furniture of a bankrupt middle class.

Schöneberg has since been reborn as a fancy, even chic, neighbourhood; the would-be Isherwoods of the moment hang out in East Kreuzberg, or Prenzlauer Berg.

The Sportpalast

Heading south from Nollendorfplatz, it's worth turning off Potsdamer Strasse at Pallasstrasse and heading west for a block. This was the site of the famed

Sportpalast, a sports centre that was the main venue for Nazi rallies in the 1930s. Hitler delivered some of his most famous speeches in the Sportpalast: most of the old newsreels showing the Führer working himself up into an oratorical fever were filmed here, and it was also the place where Goebbels asked the German people if they wanted "total war" – the affirmative reply failing to comprehend the force of destruction that would be unleashed on the city.

The Sportpalast was demolished in 1974 to make way for the huge and undistinguished apartment building that straddles the road. Beneath it, on the south side of the road, is one of the city's remaining **flak towers**. Several of these were built to defend the city from Allied raids: the largest, the Tiergarten tower, was severely damaged by bombing (the raid also destroyed the best of the city's collection of Egyptian ceramics, which had been stored in the tower for safekeeping). After the war, the Pallasstrasse tower proved impervious to demolition attempts, and the lower levels, which had been air-raid shelters, were used by NATO troops to store food and provisions in case of a Soviet invasion. Ironically, from the Cold War years until recently, supplies that were reaching the end of their shelf life were sold off – usually on the cheap to the Soviet Union.

Kleistpark and around

South of Pallasstrasse is the **Kleistpark**, which, fronted by the **Königskolonnaden**, a colonnade from 1780 that originally stood on Alexanderplatz, gives this stretch of Potsdamer Strasse a touch of dignity: on a misty morning you might be fooled into thinking you were in Paris. The **Kammergericht building** behind the park was once the Supreme Court of Justice. Here the Nazi courts under the infamous Judge Freisler held the "People's Court" following the July Bomb Plot, as well as show trials of their political opponents, a prelude to the inevitable executions, which often took place in Plötzensee prison (see p.140). Freisler met his unlamented end here in the final few weeks of the war: on his way from the courtroom a bomb from an American aircraft fell on the building, dislodging a beam that crushed his skull. Today much restored, only thirty of the building's 486 rooms are in use, formerly as a meeting place of the Allied Air Control, which oversaw safety in the air corridors leading to the city. Until the meetings came to an end with unification, a place was always set for Soviet representatives – even though they ceased to attend meetings in 1948. The building is now used by NATO.

Over Potsdamer Strasse from the Kleistpark, at the end of Grossgörschenstrasse, lies the **Sankt-Matthäus-Kirchhof**, a graveyard that contains the bodies of the Brothers Grimm, united in death as they were in copyright. The bodies of Stauffenberg and his co-conspirators were also buried here following the July Bomb Plot, only to be exhumed a few days later and burned by Nazi thugs.

Rathaus Schöneberg

Schöneberg's most famous attraction actually offers the least to see: the **Rathaus Schöneberg** on Martin-Luther-Strasse, the penultimate stop on U-Bahn line #4. Built just before World War I, the Rathaus became the seat of the West Berlin parliament and senate after the last war, and it was outside here in 1963 that **John F. Kennedy** made his celebrated speech on the Cold War political situation, just a few months after the Cuban missile crisis:

There are many people in the world who really don't understand, or say they don't, what is the great issue between the free world and the Communist world. Let them come to Berlin. There are some who say that Communism is the wave of the future. Let them come to Berlin. And there are some who say in Europe and elsewhere we can work with the Communists. Let them come to Berlin. And there are even a few who say it is true that Communism is an evil system, but it permits us to make economic progress. Lässt sie nach Berlin kommen. Let them come to Berlin ... All free men, wherever they may live, are citizens of Berlin, and, therefore, as a free man, I take pride in the words "Ich bin ein Berliner".

Rousing stuff. But what the president hadn't realized as he read from his phonetically written text was that what he had said could be misinterpreted as "I am a doughnut", since *Berliner* is a name for jam doughnuts – though not in Berlin, where it is usually known as a *Pfannkuchen*. What emerged years later was an urban myth that peals of laughter greeted this embarrassing error. People did laugh at the time, after applauding, but because the President thanked his interpreter, who had simply repeated his quote, for translating his German. The common understanding that he had erroneously called himself a jam doughnut was largely the work of pedants long after the event. The day after Kennedy was assassinated, the square in front of the Rathaus was given his name – a move apparently instigated by the city's students, among whom the president was highly popular.

If you've time and interest you can climb the Rathaus tower (daily 10am–5pm) and see the replica **Liberty bell** donated to the city by the US in 1950, though it's more pleasant, and certainly less strenuous, to take a stroll in the small **Volkspark**, a thin ribbon of greenery that runs southwest from here.

West Kreuzberg

West Kreuzberg, the area bounded by Schöneberger Strasse in the west, Viktoriapark in the south and Südstern in the east, is a richer, fancier, more sedate area than grungier East Kreuzberg – though in the past the latter has tended, mistakenly, to shape the image of the entire district. But West Kreuzberg certainly has its bohemian touches, which are best displayed not in the rather bland residential areas around its two top-draw museums – the **Technikmuseum** and the **Jüdisches Museum** – but in the area around **Viktoriapark** whose offbeat shops make it good for a wander. On the southern fringe of this area is **Tempelhof airport**, an impressive Nazi edifice whose future is uncertain.

The Anhalter Bahnhof

From Potsdamer Platz (see p.75) it's only a short walk south, cutting down Stresemannstrasse, to the remains of the **Anhalter Bahnhof**, a sad reminder of misguided civic action that some would term civic vandalism. The Anhalter Bahnhof was once one of the city's (and Europe's) great rail termini, forming Berlin's gateway to the south. Completed in 1870, it received only mild damage during World War II and was left roofless but substantial in 1945. Despite attempts to preserve it as a future museum building, it was blown up in 1952 – essentially because someone had put in a good offer for the bricks. Now only a fragment of the facade stands, giving a hint at past glories. The patch of land that the station once covered is today devoted to a park – the rear portion of which sports the **Tempodrom** (see p.255).

The Gruselkabinett and S-Bahn

If you look to one side of the Anhalter Bahnhof, you'll see a blunt and featureless building, a fortified bunker-storehouse built during the war and one of a handful of Nazi buildings that remain in the city. It's now given over to the **Gruselkabinett**, at Schöneberger Strasse 23a (Mon, Tues, Thurs & Sun 10am–7pm, Fri 10am–8pm, Sat noon–8pm; €7; ⓦwww.gruselkabinett -berlin.de; S-Bahn Anhalter Bahnhof), an amateurish "chamber of horrors" type of exhibit, of which the only vaguely interesting part is that given over to the bunker itself, with a few odd artefacts found here and in Hitler's bunker further north.

The Nazis also excavated the stretch of the **S-Bahn** that runs underground south of the Anhalter Bahnhof and heads north below Potsdamer Platz to Bahnhof Friedrichstrasse. It was built in 1935 and was supposed to be ready in time for the 1936 Olympics; however, the furious pace at which it was excavated meant that safety measures were skimped: when part of the tunnel between Potsdamer Platz and the Brandenburg Gate collapsed, nineteen workers were killed, and the line was only finally completed in 1939. The tunnel passes under the River Spree, the Landwehrkanal and the U-Bahn line #2, which, during the war, sheltered Berliners from bombing raids. When on May 2, 1945, it was thought that the Soviets were preparing to use the S- and U-Bahn systems to send shock troops directly into the city centre, the Nazis blew up the bulkheads where the tunnel passes under the Landwehrkanal, flooding the tunnel and the local U-Bahn system. As a result, many civilians sheltering in the U-Bahn died horrific deaths, drowning in the choking muddy waters that surged through the tunnels.

The Deutsche Technikmuseum Berlin

A fifteen-minute walk south from the Anhalter Bahnhof, down Möckenstrasse, leads to the **Deutsche Technikmuseum Berlin** at Trebbiner Strasse 9 (German Technology Museum of Berlin; Tues–Fri 9am–5.30pm, Sat & Sun 10am–6pm; €3; ⓦwww.dtmb.de; U-Bahn Möckernbrücke). This is one of the city's most interactive museums: a children's and button-pushers' delight. The technology section has plenty of experiments, antiquated machinery and computers to play with, alongside some elegant old cars and planes. The museum's collection of ancient steam trains and carriages is even more impressive; the polished behemoths have been brought to rest in what was once a workshop of the old Anhalter Bahnhof.

The Jüdisches Museum Berlin

A brisk twenty-minute walk east of the Technikmuseum, through streets once levelled by wartime bombing, takes you to the **Jüdisches Museum Berlin**, Lindenstrasse 14 (Jewish Museum Berlin; Mon 10am–10pm, Tues–Sun 10am–8pm, tour times vary; ☎030/25 99 33 00; €5, tours €3; ⓦwww.jmberlin.de;

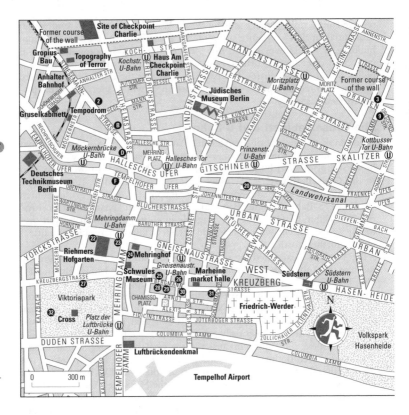

U-Bahn Halleschees Tor), a phenomenal silver fortress in the midst of residential northern Kreuzberg that's one of the city's most exciting pieces of architecture. The building's uncomfortable angles and severe lines create a disturbed and uneasy space to mirror the difficult story portrayed inside: that of the history and culture of German Jewry. To **get here by public transport** take bus #248 or #M41 from the Technikmuseum or Anhalter Bahnhof respectively: both services stop at the southern end of Lindenstrasse, a couple of minutes' walk from the museum. Alternatively, bus #143 goes to the museum's entrance from Alexanderplatz.

The extraordinary museum **building** is by Daniel Libeskind: the ground plan is in the form of a compressed lightning bolt (intended as a deconstructed Star of David), while the structure itself is sheathed in polished metallic facing, with windows – or, rather, thin angular slits – that trace geometric patterns on the exterior. There's no front door and entry is through an underground tunnel connected to the **Kollegienhaus** – the Baroque building next door that serves as an annexe to the museum and is used for temporary exhibitions.

The museum **interior** is just as unusual, manifesting Libeskind's ideas about symbolic architecture, whilst retaining a sculptural symmetry: a "void" – an empty and inaccessible diagonal shaft – cuts through the structure, while three long intersecting corridors, each representing an element of Jewish experience,

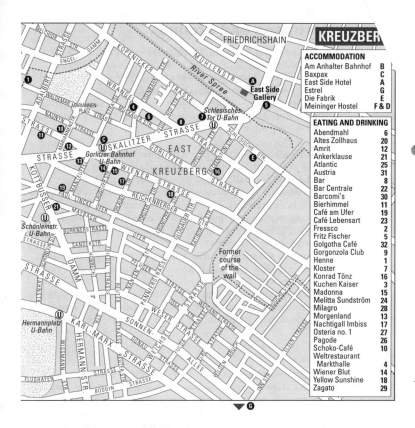

FRIEDRICHSHAIN **KREUZBER**

River Spree

East Side Gallery

Schlesisches Tor U-Bahn

SKALITZER STRASSE
Görlitzer Bahnhof U-Bahn
EAST
WIENER KREUZBERG
STRASSE
REICHENBERGER
Schönleinstr. U-Bahn
Hermannplatz U-Bahn
KARL-MARX STRASSE
Former course of the wall

ACCOMMODATION	
Am Anhalter Bahnhof	B
Baxpax	C
East Side Hotel	A
Estrel	G
Die Fabrik	E
Meininger Hostel	F & D

EATING AND DRINKING	
Abendmahl	6
Altes Zollhaus	20
Amrit	12
Ankerklause	21
Atlantic	25
Austria	31
Bar	8
Bar Centrale	22
Barcomi's	30
Bierhimmel	11
Café am Ufer	19
Café Lebensart	23
Fressco	2
Fritz Fischer	5
Golgotha Café	32
Gorgonzola Club	9
Henne	1
Kloster	7
Konrad Tönz	16
Kuchen Kaiser	3
Madonna	15
Melitta Sundström	24
Milagro	28
Morgenland	13
Nachtigall Imbiss	17
Osteria no. 1	27
Pagode	26
Schoko-Café	10
Weltrestaurant Markthalle	4
Wiener Blut	14
Yellow Sunshine	18
Zagato	29

7

SCHÖNEBERG, KREUZBERG AND AROUND | West Kreuzberg

divide the space at **basement** level. Next, at the foot of the basement stairs the "axis of exile" leads outside to a garden of pillars; the "axis of the Holocaust" crosses it, connecting with the Holocaust Tower, dimly lit and, again, completely empty; the "axis of continuity" follows, which leads to a trudge up several flights of stairs leading to the permanent exhibition space. Part way up the stairs, the first floor contains the so-called **Memory Void**, an eerie space filled with the sounds of clanking as visitors walk across a space scattered with piles of thousands of grimacing iron masks; a powerful, and certainly not silent, reminder of the Holocaust.

The **permanent exhibition** begins on the top floor of the museum and focuses, in a broadly chronological way, on pre-1900 German-Jewish history before moving to the second floor to deal with the painful twentieth century, and ending with the present day.

Though expertly crafted, the exhibition suffers from being a bit convoluted – an irony of the deliberately disorientating building is that it has spawned countless signs and stickers directing you around its halls – and that, despite its engaging layout and many interactive devices, it's too big to comfortably absorb in one go. If you still have the energy afterwards you can go on to the Museum Blindenwerkstatt Otto Weidt (see p.112), entry to which is included in your ticket – but thankfully this offer is valid for two days after purchase.

Bergmannstrasse and around

Bergmannstrasse, the vague centre of West Kreuzberg's "downtown" area, is a twenty-minute walk south of the Jewish Museum along Lindenstrasse and Zossener Strasse, a route plyed by the #M41 bus. The buildings around here are among the few that housed working-class families at the end of the nineteenth century to have survived in what was West Berlin: restoring them to their original design has been painstaking, and though the area is now thoroughly gentrified, there's no denying that it's a pleasant place to live.

The area has a laid-back bohemian feel and Bergmannstrasse itself is lined with cafés, bistros and *Trödelläden* (junk shops and occasionally antiques), as well as **Marheineke market hall**, a good indoor grocery market.

Along the eastern stretches of Bergmannstrasse lie several large eighteenth- and nineteenth-century **cemeteries**. They're full of forgotten Berlin worthies, the only name of any real note being Gustav Stresemann, chancellor and foreign minister in the Weimar years – he's in Luisenstädtischen Kirchhof, the most southeasterly of the four cemeteries here.

Also worth a look is **Chamissoplatz**, just south of Bergmannstrasse, for its well-preserved, tidily balconied nineteenth-century houses and, a block south, water tower. The square also boasts one of Berlin's few remaining Wilhelmine *pissoirs* – ornate public toilets, characteristically dark green in colour, erected in an early attempt at sanitation. This one has been recently renovated, and gents can pop in for a Bismarckian moment of relief.

The Viktoriapark

Just to the west of Bergmannstrasse is Mehringdamm, location of the **Schwules Museum** (Gay Museum) at no. 61 (see p.267), which runs a programme of thoroughly researched temporary exhibits on a huge variety of gay issues and history. On the opposite side of Mehringdamm a short walk along Kreuzebergstrasse leads to **Viktoriapark** (the "Kreuzberg", as it's popularly known). Draped across the slopes of a hill, the park is one of the city's most likeable, a relaxed ramble of trees and green space with a pretty brook running down the middle. To one side is the *Golgotha Café* and disco (see p.251), packed on summer evenings; on another side is what claims to be Germany's northernmost vineyard; and atop the hill is the **Cross** (though it's more of a Neoclassical spire) from which Kreuzberg gets its name, designed by Schinkel to commemorate the Napoleonic Wars. The view is a good one, too.

The well-restored streets around the hill, along with Yorckstrasse to the north, have a scattering of cafés, their tone and clientele reflecting the residents of the neighbourhood, who are on the whole slightly older than those of East Kreuzberg. Between Hagelbergerstrasse and Yorckstrasse, the **Riehmer's Hofgarten** is an impressive turn-of-the-twentieth-century bourgeois residential building, though the steel-and-glass Yorck Cinema doesn't fit well in the ensemble.

Tempelhof Airport

Just south of West Kreuzberg, in the adjacent district of Tempelhof, housing fades away to the flatlands containing **Tempelhof Airport** (U-Bahn Platz der Luftbrücke). The airport was opened in the 1920s and

The Berlin Blockade (1948–49)

The **Berlin Blockade** was the result of an escalation in tensions between East and West in the late 1940s. These came to a head when the Western zone introduced the Deutschmark as currency in June 1948; the Soviets demanded that their own Ostmark be accepted as Berlin's currency, a move that was rejected by the city's parliament. Moscow's answer to this was an attempt to bring West Berlin to its knees by severing all road and rail links to the Western zones and cutting off the power provided by plants on the Eastern side. West Berlin had to "import" almost all of its food and fuel: when the Soviets pulled the plugs the city had only a month's supply of food and ten days' supply of coal.

Rather than use military force, it was decided to try and supply the city by air: the Soviets, it was gambled, would not dare risk an international incident – possibly even war – by shooting down Western aircraft. The airlift thus began on June 26, 1948, and at its height nine months later, planes were landing or taking off every thirty seconds and bringing 8000 tons of supplies to the city each day.

The Soviets called off the Blockade in May 1949, but they had been defeated in more ways than one. For the occupying British and American forces the propaganda value was enormous: aircrews who a few years previously had been dropping bombs on the city now provided its lifeline. Photographs of the "candy bomber" – a USAF captain who dropped chocolate bars and sweets from his plane on small parachutes for the city's children – went around the world. No longer were the occupiers seen as enemies, but rather as allies against the Soviet threat.

was once Germany's largest; the present complex was built in 1936–41 and is one of the best surviving examples of Nazi architecture. A huge bronze eagle that surmounted the building was removed in the 1960s, ostensibly to make way for a radar installation (the eagle's head can still be seen at the entrance to the airport), but you can't help thinking that its removal probably had more to do with its being an ugly reminder of the Nazi past. Until recently, the airport was used for visiting dignitaries and the military, but today it handles only a light load of small carrier flights. Sadly, the airport is scheduled to close; what will become of the building and the land is a matter for heated debate.

It was to Tempelhof that the Allies flew in supplies to beat the **Berlin Blockade** of 1948–49 (see box above) – an act that was to strengthen anti-Soviet feeling among West Berliners and increase the popularity of the occupying forces. At the height of the airlift a plane landed here every minute and the **Luftbrückendenkmal**, a memorial at the entrance to the airport, commemorates the seventy airmen and eight ground crew who died in crashes while attempting to land. The memorial represents the three air corridors used, and forms half of a bridge: the other half, "joined by air", is in Frankfurt. Inside the airport a small exhibition shows photographs of its building and the Blockade – mostly publicity shots of gleaming USAF pilots and scruffy kids, with little on the role of Tempelhof in the war years.

Having seen the airport you might want to have a quick look at the **Polizei-historische Sammlung** (Police History Collection; Mon–Wed 9am–3pm; free) next door at Platz der Luftbrücke 6; worth dipping into for its nine-teenth-century uniforms and illustrations intended to help police determine "typical criminal types".

With cheap rents and squatting opportunities in abundance, Kreuzberg readily became West Berlin's hive for squatters, radicals and non-conformists. Until the wall came down, to say you lived in Kreuzberg was something of a political statement: left-wing generally and anti-establishment specifically. At that time, if you wanted to gauge the political temperature of West Berlin, you had only to see what was happening on the streets here. Even as late as 1988, Kreuzberg constituted enough of a threat for the authorities to seal the area off during the annual conference of the IMF – though, despite the provocation, things remained calm.

One reason for the presence of so many young alternative types in the city was because of a national service loophole. Its "occupied" status meant Berlin was the only place in Germany where the eighteen months' **national service**, compulsory for all males between the ages of 18 and 32, could be evaded (an anomaly abolished after reunification). Consequently in the 1960s, 1970s and 1980s, especially when anti-war feelings were running high, the city became a haven for those avoiding service.

Service dodgers were attracted to Kreuzberg partly because of its cosmopolitan feel – given the numbers of *Gastarbeiter* here – but mainly due to the cheap rents and **squatting opportunities**. The latter came from a ruling that pre-1950s-built apartments were subject to rent restrictions, which meant that speculators often allowed them to fall into disrepair so that they could erect new buildings and charge whatever rent they pleased; squatters who maintained and developed these old apartments thus saved some of the city's old architecture.

By the 1980s Kreuzberg was the focus and point of reference for squatters throughout the Federal Republic, and the Social Democratic city government adopted a liberal approach to them, offering subsidies to well-organized squats and giving them some security of tenure. Projects like the Mehringhof (Gneisenaustrasse 2; U-Bahn Mehringdamm), a home for alternative industries and arts, flourished.

All went well until the Christian Democrats took over the city in 1981. Using arguments over the role of city property – many of the buildings here are owned by the government – and the growing problems of crime and drug dealing, the right-wing minister of the interior ordered the riot police to enter Kreuzberg and forcibly close down the squats. There were riots in the streets, demonstrations all over the city, and intense political protest, which reached its peak with the death of a fifteen-year-old boy, hit by a bus during a demonstration. Activists called a strike and the city government had to back down.

Today, the city government occasionally clears out a building, but generally the squatters themselves have moved on – Prenzlauer Berg being a major target immediately after the *Wende* – of their own volition, and less than a handful of squats remains.

The political climate has also changed and only the occasional uprising still occurs, usually on May Day, when an annual demonstration ritually turns into a riot between police and demonstrators, but the atmosphere is more subdued and less political than it was pre-*Wende*. It remains to be seen to what extent activists here will again turn their attention away from local matters towards national issues.

East Kreuzberg

In the 1830s, Berlin's industries started recruiting peasants from the outlying countryside to work in their factories and machine shops. It was to the small village of **Kreuzberg** that many came, to work in the east of the city and live in buildings that were thrown up by speculators as low-rent accommodation. Kreuzberg was thus established as a solidly working-class area and, in time, a suburb of Greater Berlin. Siemens, the electrical engineering giant, began life in one of Kreuzberg's rear courtyards. In the 1930s local trade unionists and workers fought street battles with the Nazis, and during the war it was one of the very few areas to avoid total destruction, and among the quickest to revive in the 1950s. When the Wall was built in 1961, things changed: Kreuzberg became an eastern outpost of West Berlin, severed from its natural hinterland in the East. Families moved out, houses were boarded up, and Kreuzberg began to die. At the same time, the city, deprived of cheap East Berlin labour to work in its factories, began to look further afield for the migratory workers generally known as *Gastarbeiter*. At first these came from countries like Yugoslavia, Greece, Spain and Italy, but later, and most in evidence today, are Turks, who began to move to the city in large numbers, in time bringing their families and Islamic customs. Throughout the 1960s and 1970s Kreuzberg – having Berlin's cheapest rentable property – developed as West Berlin's Turkish enclave, though few landlords welcomed the new workers. Into Kreuzberg, too, came the radicals, students and dropouts of the 1968 -generation – attracted to the city because of the national service loophole, and to Kreuzberg because it offered vast potential for squatting (see box opposite).

Over the last half-decade, the squatter movement has died a natural death and the left-wing radicalism of the area has begun to wane, in line with the political climate generally. Some Turks and other immigrant communities still thrive, but strong signs of gentrification have begun to appear, stimulated in part by its vibrant café and **nightlife** scene which is still among the city's wildest (see p.236 & p.251).

Eastern Kreuzberg's main drag is the **Oranienstrasse**, close to U-Bahn **Kottbusser Tor**, but the whole area is enjoyable to wander through by day: stopping off at one of the innumerable Turkish snack bars for a kebab, breakfasting on a 9am vodka-and-beer special at a café (see p.236), or just taking in the feel of the place – think Istanbul market in an Eastern-bloc housing development. To the east and hard on the former border to East Berlin is **Schlesisches Tor**, now a practical gateway for visiting the **East Side Gallery** over the River Spree – murals on the longest remnant of the Wall – and the **Soviet Memorial** in **Treptower Park** a short bus ride away.

Kottbusser Tor and around

Catching U-Bahn line #1 (unkindly named the "Istanbul Express" in this stretch) to **Kottbusser Tor** is a good introduction to eastern Kreuzberg. The area around the station is typical: a scruffy, earthy shambles of Turkish street vendors and cafés, the air filled with the aromas of southeast European cooking. Cutting through Dresdener Strasse, past the Babylon Cinema (see p.261), takes you to Kreuzberg's main strip, **Oranienstrasse**, which from Moritzplatz east is lined with café-bars, art galleries and clothes shops, and in a way forms an "alternative" Kurfürstendamm.

South of Kottbusser Tor U-Bahn, it's less than ten minutes' walk down Kottbusser Strasse to the Landwehrkanal and Kottbusser Brücke. Turn left beyond the bridge down Maybachufer and you'll find a food **market** that's alive in a myriad colours and a babble of noise and excitement on Tuesday and Friday afternoons.

Schlesisches Tor and around

Around the **Schlesisches Tor** (the "Silesian Gate", which gave the station its name, was the former entrance to the city for immigrants from Silesia) things are more residential, although for years the nearness of the Wall heightened tension in the area. The River Spree here was in GDR territory, a strange situation for those residents of West Berlin whose apartments backed directly onto it. Times have changed, though, and now the Spree is a popular summer hangout, with a basic beach beside the **East Side Gallery**, a series of murals painted onto the longest remaining stretch of Berlin Wall. More intentional is the memorial a short way south, just within the district of Treptow in the form of the **Trep-tower Park**, home to the huge and impressive **Soviet Memorial**.

The East Side Gallery

Crossing the River Spree by way of the Oberbaumbrücke, just north of U-Bahn Schlesisches Tor, brings you to the southern edge of the district of Friedrichshain (see p.160) and the **East Side Gallery**. This 1.3-kilometre surviving stretch of Wall runs along Mühlenstrasse as far as the Ostbahnhof and has been daubed with various political/satirical images, some imaginative, some trite and some impenetrable. One of the most telling shows Brezhnev and Honecker locked in a passionate kiss, with the inscription, "God, help me survive this deadly love."

Treptower Park

Schlesisches Tor is only ten minutes' walk or a quick bus ride away (#265) from **Treptower Park** (S-Bahn Treptower Park) and the huge and sobering **Soviet Memorial** to troops killed in the Battle of Berlin. As Berlin expanded rapidly during the nineteenth century, the park was one of the places where the city's tenement-dwellers could let off steam, and by 1908 there were thirty-odd dance halls and restaurants here. Later, during the interwar years, the park became a well-known assembly point for revolutionary workers about to embark on demonstrations or go off to do battle with the Brownshirts.

Until the *Wende* most of the visitors to the park were either East Berliners out for a day at **Spreepark**, the GDR-era amusement park still in use today, or Soviet citizens who came here by the busload to pay their respects at the memorial. But since the beginning of the 1990s increasing numbers of former West Berliners have discovered the place, and the park has become a popular Sunday promenade destination for the space-starved inhabitants of Neukölln and Kreuzberg.

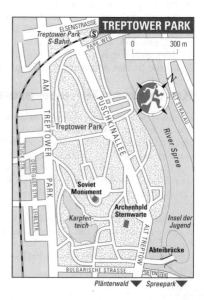

The Soviet Memorial

At the heart of the park, the **Soviet Memorial** (Sowjetisches Ehrenmal) commemorates the Soviet Union's 305,000 estimated casualties during the Battle of Berlin in April and May 1945 and is the burial place of 5000 of them. It's best approached from the arched entrance on the south side of Puschkinallee. A little way to the south of here is a sculpture of a grieving woman representing the Motherland, to the left of which a broad concourse slopes up towards a viewing point flanked by two vast triangles of red granite, fashioned from stone bought from Sweden by the Nazis to furnish Berlin with projected victory monuments. From the viewing point, a long sunken park of mass graves of the Red Army troops is lined by sculpted frescoes of stylized scenes from the Great Patriotic War and quotes from Stalin with German translations. These lead the way to the centrepiece: a vast symbolic statue and typical piece of Soviet gigantism, built using marble from Hitler's Chancellery. Over 11m high, and set on top of a hill modelled on a *kurgan* or traditional warriors' grave of the Don region, it shows an idealized Russian soldier clutching a saved child and resting his sword on a shattered swastika.

Inside the plinth is a memorial crypt with a mosaic in true Socialist Realist style, showing Soviet citizens (soldiers, mother, worker, peasant, and what looks like an old-age pensioner) honouring the dead. One significant aspect of the crypt and memorial generally is the lack of religious iconography – eschewed by the Soviet state – showing that grandiose memorials needn't depend on pious objects for their spiritual power.

In January 1990 the monument hit the headlines briefly when it was defaced, allegedly by neo-Nazis, despite the fact that the place was guarded around the clock. Many East Berliners suspected a put-up job, engineered by the still-communist government or its supporters, ostensibly to combat rising neo-Nazism. Either way, the monument remains an important part of the Berlin cityscape, its sheer scale imparting a sense of the Soviet Union's colossal losses during World War II, losses that shaped Soviet defence and foreign policy, and explain as much as anything why history unfolded as it did in postwar Berlin.

Around the rest of the park

The rest of the park conceals a couple of low-key attractions, including the **Karpfenteich**, a large carp pool just south of the memorial, and, a little to the east of here, the **Archenhold Sternwarte**, Alt-Treptow 1 (Wed–Sun 2–4.30pm; tours Thurs 8pm, Sat & Sun 3pm; €3.10 ☎030/5 34 80 80, ⓦwww.astw.de), an observatory with the longest refracting telescope in the world.

The park continues north of Puschkinallee, where you'll also find the *Eierschale-Zenner* (see p.240), a riverside *Gaststätte* whose origins go back to the eighteenth century. Just to the east is the **Insel der Jugend**, a small island in the Spree reached via the **Abteibrücke**, an ornamental footbridge built by French prisoners of war in 1916 to link the island to the mainland. The end of Treptow's summer festival is marked by a firework display from this bridge, an event known as *Treptow in Flammen* or "Treptow in Flames". The island was originally the location of an abbey, but now the main attraction is *Die Insel*, a tower-like clubhouse that houses a café, cinema and gallery and is a regular venue for club nights and gigs, with occasional outdoor raves in summer (see p.253). Returning across the bridge, walk northwest back to the S-Bahn station via a grass-lined boardwalk good for picnicking or just relaxing by the water – there's boat rental nearby, providing rowing boats and paddle boats (from €5 per hour). At the beginning of the boardwalk, you'll find a very tasty *Imbiss* stand serving fresh smoked fish.

For something a bit more frenetic, head southeast from the bridge to the **Spreepark**, a popular amusement park in the GDR days and recently refurbished, featuring the usual rides, *Bockwurst* stands and a big wheel. It's all part of the **Plänterwald** woods, which cover a couple of square kilometres and offer good, untaxing strolling. Just to the southwest of Neue Krug is the *Plänterwald*, a largish *Gaststätte* that makes a good place to interrupt your wanderings. If you're in the mood for something more elaborate, you can take a cruise around the surrounding waterways (see "Boats", p.35).

Friedrichshain, Prenzlauer Berg and around

F anning out immediately east of the city centre, the two former East Berlin boroughs **Friedrichshain** and **Prenzlauer Berg** could barely look more different. Though both were overwhelmingly residential, Friedrichshain was comprensively destroyed during the war, losing over two thirds of its buildings – as much as any Berlin district – and so today virtually all its buildings are of GDR vintage. The old working-class district Prenzlauer Berg in comparison, fared much better in the war. The densely populated tenement district was fought over street-by-street so that many of its hallmark turn-of-the-twentieth-century tenement blocks, though battle-scarred, survived fairly well, leaving a tight network of leafy cobbled streets that are unusual in Berlin. But what unites the two districts is that both have been thrust into the city's limelight since the *Wende*, when their central location and low rents quickly turned them into lively "in" districts, giving them some of the best cafés, bars and nightlife in the city.

Prenzlauer Berg in particular has long been a centre of **bohemian culture**; even in GDR days it was a uniquely vibrant and exciting corner of East Berlin, home to large numbers of artists and young people seeking an alternative lifestyle, who chose to live here on the edge of established East German society (literally as well as figuratively – the district's western boundary was marked by the Berlin Wall). Given the all-embracing nature of the state, this was not as easy as in "alternative" West Berlin: in the GDR even minor acts of non-conformism, or actions that wouldn't have been regarded as out of the ordinary at all in the West, such as organizing an unofficial art exhibition or concert, could result in a run-in with the police or attract the unwelcome attentions of the Stasi.

Since 1989 countless new bars, restaurants and clothes shops have opened, thriving partly because the area's original inhabitants have been joined by an influx of people once drawn from the West by cheap accommodation and squatting opportunities; though now even the days of finding a cheap apartment are over. Gentrifying forces have changed all this, although the area's

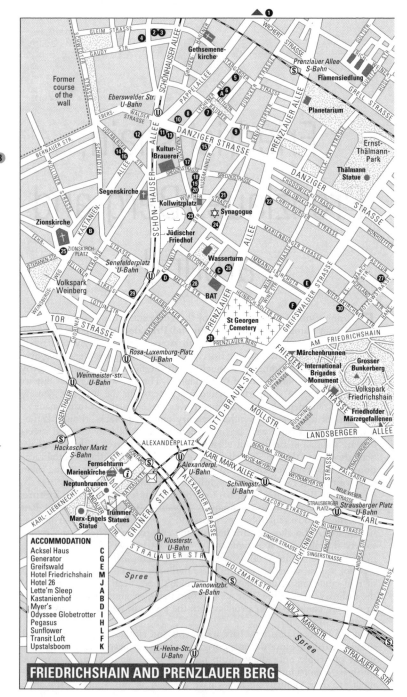

ACCOMMODATION

Acksel Haus	C
Generator	G
Greifswald	E
Hotel Friedrichshain	M
Hotel 26	J
Lette'm Sleep	A
Kastanienhof	B
Myer's	D
Odyssee Globetrotter	I
Pegasus	H
Sunflower	L
Transit Loft	F
Upstalsboom	K

FRIEDRICHSHAIN AND PRENZLAUER BERG

▲ *Der Weissesee*

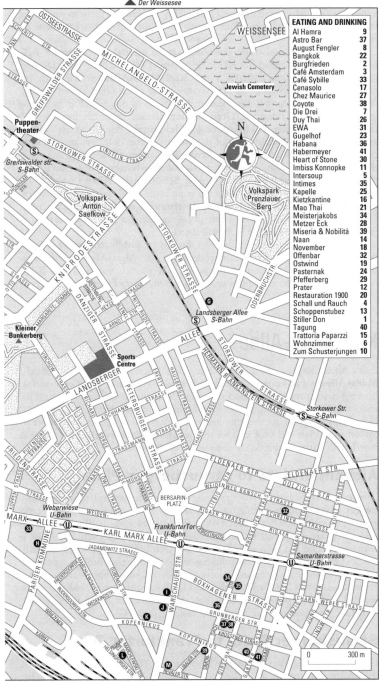

EATING AND DRINKING	
Al Hamra	9
Astro Bar	37
August Fengler	8
Bangkok	22
Burgfrieden	2
Café Amsterdam	3
Café Sybille	33
Cenasolo	17
Chez Maurice	27
Coyote	38
Die Drei	7
Duy Thai	26
EWA	31
Gugelhof	23
Habana	36
Habermeyer	41
Heart of Stone	30
Imbiss Konnopke	11
Intersoup	5
Intimes	35
Kapelle	25
Kietzkantine	16
Mao Thai	21
Meisterjakobs	34
Metzer Eck	28
Miseria & Nobilità	39
Naan	14
November	18
Offenbar	32
Ostwind	19
Pasternak	24
Pfefferberg	29
Prater	12
Restauration 1900	20
Schall und Rauch	4
Schoppenstubez	13
Stiller Don	1
Tagung	40
Trattoria Paparzzi	15
Wohnzimmer	6
Zum Schusterjungen	10

venues can still have some freshness and energy that enables them to supersede their more established equivalent haunts of Kreuzberg and Schöneberg in West Berlin.

The two districts are strung out along several arterial roads that are well served by public transport from Alexanderplatz or Hackescher Markt. Doubtless the grandest thoroughfare is the **Karl-Marx-Allee**, which with its fascinating examples of Stalinist architecture is one of the GDR's most notable contributions to today's Berlin. Also an extension to one of the great boulevards around Alexanderplatz, **Greifswalder Strasse** heads northeast out of the centre passing close to **Volkspark Friedrichshain**, one of the city's oldest and best parks, and resting place of the victims of the 1848 revolution. From here you pass the bland, GDR-era **Ernst-Thälmann-Park** before touching the fringe of the tidy middle-class district of **Weissensee**, where you'll find the city's largest Jewish cemetery. Finally, **Schönhauser Allee** runs close to the former East–West border and is the main route to all the trendiest parts of Prenzlauer Berg. These include the **Kulturbraueri** and **Kollwitzplatz**, near which some Jewish elements of the city – including a large **cemetery** and still-functioning **synagogue** – are still intact.

The quickest way to explore the two districts by **public transport** is from Alexanderplatz. You can U-Bahn-hop along the Karl-Marx-Allee to Friedrichshain; take tram M#4 up Greifswalder Strasse to Weissensee; and take the U-Bahn to Senefelder Platz, an ideal place to start a walking tour of Prenzlauer Berg.

Karl-Marx-Allee

From Alexanderplatz the main gateway into Friedrichshain is along **Karl-Marx-Allee**, a vast boulevard lined with model 1950s and 1960s communist housing developments. No buses or trams run along the road, and it's hard to make the distance on foot, so consider renting a bike or taking a taxi a few U-Bahn stops to appreciate the immensity of it. At the very least, try to get off at Strausberger Platz and walk east for ten minutes to **Café Sybille**, which has a worthwhile little exhibition on the history of the street.

Alexanderplatz to Strausberger Platz

The section of Karl-Marx-Allee running between Alexanderplatz and **Strausberger Platz** went up during the early to mid-1960s and is predictably stark and angular; this is where the GDR Politbüro and Eastern Bloc dignitaries took the salute during the military parades held every year to mark the GDR's anniversary. The last such occasion was on October 7, 1989, when Mikhail Gorbachev warned that "Life punishes those who arrive late" – a pointed reference to the East German leadership's rejection of his liberalization plans. It was already too late for Honecker and his Politbüro though, and the event sparked a series of demonstrations across the country that led to the downfall of the SED regime and the subsequent collapse of the GDR.

Strausberger Platz to Frankfurter Tor

From Strausberger Platz onwards, where the district of Friedrichshain begins, the architecture recalls an earlier era and things get more interesting. The

△ Karl-Marx-Allee

prefabricated blocks of the 1960s give way to the *Zuckerbäckerstil* (wedding-cake style) of the previous decade.

In September 1951, work began on a scheme to turn Karl-Marx-Allee, then known as Stalinallee, into "Germany's first socialist street", providing modern flats that would be "palaces for the people". The first foundation stone of what was to become an ornate high-rise apartment building, the **Hochhaus an der Weberwiese**, was laid at Marchlewskistrasse 25, just south of Weberwiese U-Bahn station. Over the next few years similar buildings were constructed from Strausberger Platz to the Frankfurter Tor U-Bahn station, which marked the eastern limit of the old Stalinallee. Flanking these two ends of the strip – 1500m apart – are two twin-tiered towers. At Frankfurter Tor the ecclesiastical-looking domes stand on the site of an earlier customs gate.

These buildings epitomize the *Zuckerbäckerstil*, a mutated Classicism that was repeated across the Soviet bloc throughout the 1950s, most famously in Warsaw's Palace of Culture and Moscow's so-called seven sisters, which include its university and foreign ministry. Though the style was and is much derided in the West, the buildings of Stalinallee were a well-thought-out and relatively soundly constructed attempt at housing that would live up to the great architectural tradition of Berlin. The Stalinallee apartments with their central heating and parquet floors also provided an enviable level of comfort at a time when most Berliners were crowded into bomb-shattered tenement blocks or makeshift temporary housing.

Ironically, it was striking workers from the Stalinallee construction project, angered by increased work norms, who sparked off the uprising of June 1953 (see p.73). Later, when the project was completed, the apartments were given over mainly to SED functionaries and high-ranking members of the security services. Most tenants are now old and the whole street has been bought by a Wiesbaden-based property company that's begun a much-needed renovation of the blocks. The inhabitants have been assured that no one will be thrown out but it seems likely that sooner or later the former Stalinallee housing will be transformed into up-market apartments, conveniently located for city-centre offices, institutions and ministries.

Café Sybille

After looking around the avenue itself the **Café Sybille**, Karl-Marx-Allee 72 (daily 10am–8pm; free; ☏030/29 35 22 03; U-Bahn Weberwiese), is the best way of getting a handle on the history of the area's development. This stylish, minimalist café is a pleasant stop in its own right, but it's the exhibits in the back that are the big draw. These begin by charting the beginnings of the Stalinallee: rubble clearance and early plans for redevelopment, which suggested small-scale, self-contained, community-focused housing. But political agendas decided its fate, and it was decided to create something grand to honour Stalin's seventieth birthday. The buildings were to be "palaces for workers, not American eggboxes", and architectural plans were quickly shipped direct from the USSR. From then on it was all about model workers putting in overtime and even donating a portion of their wages to see the project through. A few of the lucky even got to live in the apartments, but mostly these were for the well connected.

Beyond Frankfurter Tor

Beyond Frankfurter Tor, Karl-Marx-Allee becomes Frankfurter Allee, a bleak arterial road lined by high-rises, rolling out into the suburbs in the direction of Frankfurt an der Oder and Poland. The only real attraction anywhere along its length is the former Stasi Headquarters in the neighbouring Bezirk of

Lichtenberg (see p.176). On either side of Frankfurter Allee, however – just after the Frankfurter Tor – the kind of eclectic **bar scene** that sprang up in Prenzlauer Berg and Mitte in the early 1990s still blooms: on Simon-Dach-Strasse and around Boxhagener Platz to the south, and around Rigaer Strasse to the north (see p.237).

Greifswalder Strasse and around

Running roughly parallel to Schönhauser Allee and Prenzlauer Allee, **Greifswalder Strasse** is the other major artery through Prenzlauer Berg. It still looks very neat with its freshly painted facades, and in pre-*Wende* days traffic came to a standstill along the side streets a couple of times a day as a convoy of black Citroëns and Volvos sped by, whisking high-ranking government members (notably Erich Honecker himself) from the Palast der Republik (see p.80) to their homes in the now infamous lakeside town of Wandlitz to the north of Berlin. But behind the immaculate facades, the *Hinterhöfe* of Greifswalder Strasse were just as run-down as those in the backstreets.

From Greifswalder Strasse you can reach the **St Georgen** cemetery (see p.168) and a series of fine civic spaces in the form of the **Volkspark Friedrichshain** and the very GDR **Ernst-Thälmann-Park**, behind which lurks the **Zeiss Planetarium** and the **Flamensiedlung**, a modest late-1920s model housing development. Beyond here you reach the limits of Prenzlauer Berg and enter the residential district of **Weissensee**, whose highlight is Berlin's largest **Jewish cemetery**.

Volkspark Friedrichshain

By the start of Greifswalder, where Friedenstrasse and Am Friedrichshain Strasse meet, is **Volkspark Friedrichshain**. Just within the limits of the Friedrichshain district, it's one of the city's oldest and largest parks (and a well-known gay cruising area). At the western entrance to the park is the **Märchenbrunnen** (Fairytale Fountain), a neo-Baroque arcade and fountain with statues of characters from Brothers Grimm stories. Intended as a gift to tenement-dwelling workers, it was put up in 1913 at the instigation of Social Democratic members of the city council, in direct contravention of the Kaiser's wishes.

The Spanish Civil War Monument and the March 1848 graveyard

A few hundred metres to the southeast of the Märchenbrunnen stands the **Gedenkstätte für die Deutschen Interbrigadisten**, a monument to the German members of the International Brigades who fought against the Fascists in Spain in the Spanish Civil War. Of the five thousand Germans (including many leading Communists) who went to Spain, only two thousand returned. There's another monument to the east of here (just off Landsberger Allee), this time to victims of an upheaval closer to home. The **Friedhof der Märzgefallenen** is where many of the 183 Berliners killed by the soldiers of King Friedrich Wilhelm IV during the revolution of March 1848 were buried, their interment attended by 80,000 of their fellow citizens. Only a few of the original gravestones survive, but the dead of 1848 have been joined by 33 of those killed in the November Revolution of 1918, commemorated by a statue of a *Rote Matrose* or "Red Sailor" at the cemetery entrance, reflecting the role played in the revolution by Imperial Navy sailors.

The Bunkerbergs

The final resting place of the revolutionaries is overshadowed by the **Grosser Bunkerberg** and **Kleiner Bunkerberg**, two artificial hills created when a million cubic metres of rubble from bombed-out Berlin were dumped over a couple of wartime bunkers. In between the two is a small, tree-shaded lake, and nearby you'll find the kind of worthy sporting amenities (**Sport und Erholungszentrum**, see p.273) and giant outdoor chess sets that keep many Germans amused during their free hours. Set on a grassy slope a little to the east is a **monument** commemorating the joint fight of the Polish army and German resistance against the Nazis. Given the feelings most Germans and Poles had for each other, the sentiments expressed seem rather unconvincing.

Ernst-Thälmann-Park and around

At the northeastern end of Greifswalder Strasse is another example of former-GDR civic window-dressing in the shape of the **Ernst-Thälmann-Park** (a one-kilometre walk from the Heinrich-Roller-Strasse and Greifswalder Strasse intersection, or take tram #M4). This is a model housing development, set in a small park and fronted by a gigantic marble sculpture of the head and clenched fist of Ernst Thälmann, the pre-1933 Communist leader who was imprisoned and later murdered by the Nazis. Floodlit and guarded round the clock by police in pre-*Wende* days, his likeness is now daubed with graffiti, and the concrete terrace on which it stands is favoured by local skateboarders. About 4000 people, mostly from the ex-GDR elite, live here in high-rise buildings with restaurants, shops, nurseries and a swimming pool all immediately at hand.

Zeiss Planetarium and the Flamensiedlung

On foot it's possible to cut through the Ernst-Thälmann-Park past several miserable high-rises to the silver-domed **Zeiss Planetarium** (show times vary; €5; ☎030/42 18 45 12 ⓦwww.astw.de; S-Bahn Prenzlauer Allee) on Prenzlauer Allee, with its imaginative assortment of narrated (German-only) music and children's shows on the universe. Nearby is Prenzlauer Allee's distinctive, yellow-brick 1890s S-Bahn station, one of the best-looking in the city, and just northeast of here, between Sültstrasse and Sodtkestrasse, is the so-called **Flamensiedlung** (Flemish Colony), a model housing development built in 1929–30 according to plans by the architect Bruno Taut. With his associate Franz Hillinger, Taut wanted to create mass housing that broke away from the tenement-house concept. Basing their design on work already done in Holland, they diffused the angularity of their apartment blocks with corner windows and balconies, and left open areas between them to create cheerful bright back yards.

Weissensee

Moving further northeast, Greifswalder Strasse becomes Berliner Allee as it leaves Prenzlauer Berg and enters the neighbouring borough of **Weissensee**. A predominantly middle-class area, Weissensee has a slightly sleepy atmosphere, which hints at the open countryside only a few kilometres away. The main attraction here is Germany's largest **Jewish cemetery**, another indicator of Berlin's high-profile but now all-but-vanished Jewish community.

The Jewish Cemetery

The **Jüdischer Friedhof Weissensee** (May–Oct Sun–Thurs 8am–5pm Fri 8am–3pm, Nov–April Sun–Thurs 8am–4pm Fri 8am–3pm) lies at the end of Herbert-Baum-Strasse (named after the Jewish resistance hero executed for his part in an attack on a Nazi propaganda exhibition in the Lustgarten in 1942, see p.82), ten minutes south of Berliner Strasse. Opened in 1880, when the Schönhauser Allee cemetery had finally been filled to capacity, this is one of Europe's largest Jewish cemeteries, and certainly the biggest in Germany. At the entrance to the cemetery a sign requests male visitors to cover their heads before entering; you can borrow a skullcap from the cemetery office to the right.

Immediately beyond the entrance is a memorial "to our murdered brothers and sisters 1933–45" from Berlin's Jewish community. It takes the form of a circle of tablets bearing the names of all the large concentration camps. Like many memorials to the war years in the city, it's a poignant monument to the horrors that occurred, and succeeds in being less inflated and militaristic than many others. Nearby is a memorial to Herbert Baum.

Beyond here are the cemetery administration buildings (where information about the cemetery is available), constructed in a similar mock-Moorish style to the synagogue on Oranienburger Strasse. The cemetery itself stretches back from the entrance for about 1km: row upon row of headstones, with the occasional extravagant family monument in between, many for those systematically wiped out by the Third Reich.

A handful of well-tended postwar graves near the administration buildings are, paradoxically, symbols of survival, witness to the fact that a few thousand Berlin Jews did escape the Holocaust and that the city still has a small, though active, Jewish community of around ten thousand people.

The Weisser See and around

Back on Berliner Allee, it's only a few minutes' walk to the shady park containing the **Weisser See**, the lake that gives the district its name. Near the park entrance is a **monument** commemorating the struggle against fascism. The communist authorities tried to foster a tradition whereby newly engaged couples would lay flowers at the memorial, but this is an activity that has declined drastically in popularity since 1989. In the park itself it's possible to rent boats on the lake (which features a fairly unspectacular fountain), and there's an open-air stage and a *Gaststätte* nearby. Adjacent to the lake is an outdoor swimming pool, which is fed by an underground spring. To the north of the park, off Radrennbahnstrasse, is the **Radrennbahn Weissensee**, a cycle track where rock concerts were occasionally held. In the old days the SED administration brought in big-name Western acts like James Brown and ZZ Top at great expense, as a sop to the nation's disaffected youth. The initial impetus for this came after young people clashed with police who had attempted to move them on from streets near the Wall in the city centre, where they had been listening to a Eurythmics concert going on just over the border in West Berlin.

Along Pistoriusstrasse

After Berliner Allee, Weissensee's main street is the mostly residential **Pistoriusstrasse**, which branches off northwest from the former just before the Weisser See itself. Roughly halfway along it is Pistoriusplatz, site of a weekend market and prelude to another Berlin architectural experiment, the

Gemeindeforum Kreuzpfuhl, which lies just to the right of the street, set around a small lake called the **Kreuzpfuhl**. It looks like no other development in the city, benefiting heavily from its position on the tree-lined lakeshore, and is perhaps the most aesthetically successful of the many attempts to break away from the dreadful housing conditions of the *Mietskaserne*. These four-storey apartment blocks with their decorative red-brick facades and distinctive gabled roofs were built in 1908 and have been officially designated a "valuable monument of social history".

Schönhauser Allee and around

The quickest way to explore the two districts by **public transport** is to take the U-Bahn from Alexanderplatz to either Eberswalder Strasse or Schönhauser Allee. For a more atmospheric approach, take tram #M2 from Hackescher Markt, which, going up Prenzlauer Allee, is the most direct route to the Kollwitzplatz area, or try tram #M1, which will take you through some of eastern Berlin's lesser-known backstreets before dropping you at Eberswalder Strasse, the district's central hub. Walking to Prenzlauer Berg from Rosa-Luxemburg-Platz involves a walk uphill but takes in a couple of interesting sights.

It's a fairly easy walk to Prenzlauer Berg from central Berlin. The district starts just north of Rosa-Luxemburg-Platz at the beginning of **Schönhauser Allee**, and if you follow this street for about 600m you'll find yourself on **Senefelderplatz**, previously known as Pfefferberg (Pepper Hill), but later renamed after the inventor of the lithographic process (printing from engraved stone), Alois Senefelder. A statue of Senefelder stands on the square, with his name appearing on the base in mirror script, as on a lithographic block. The name Pfefferberg, incidentally, is still in use, and applies to a former factory complex just below Senefelderplatz that features a nightclub and *Biergarten* – a favourite spot in summer for late-night drinking, snacking or just hanging out (see "Eating and Drinking", p.240).

The Jewish Cemetery

A little further along Schönhauser Allee, just past the police station, is the **Jüdischer Friedhof**, Schönhauser Allee 23–25 (Mon–Thurs 10am–4pm, Fri 10am–1pm; male visitors are requested to keep their heads covered), Prenzlauer Berg's Jewish cemetery, which opened when space ran out at the Grosse Hamburger Strasse cemetery. Over 20,000 people are buried here, but for most, this last resting place is an anonymous one: in 1943 many of the gravestones were smashed and a couple of years later the trees under which they had stood were used by the SS to hang deserters found hiding in the cemetery during the final days of the war. Today many of the stones have been restored and repositioned, and a memorial stone near the cemetery entrance entreats visitors: "You stand here in silence, but when you turn away do not remain silent."

The Segenskirche and around

Further along Schönhauser Allee, on the left near the junction with Wörtherstrasse, is the confused **Segenskirche**, a bizarre mix of Gothic and neo-Renaissance styles. But it's in the maze of streets on either side of Schönhauser Allee that Prenzlauer Berg's real attractions lie: here, you'll find some of the best **cafés**, **bars** and **restaurants** in the eastern part of Berlin (see p.237 & p.246).

Starting at the intersection just north of the Segenskirche, a turn left into Oderbergerstrasse leads you to **Kastanienalle**, a lively area of bars and shops, or you could continue along Oderbergerstrasse and find a strip buzzing with eating and drinking joints.

Alternatively, you can turn right into Sredzkistrasse from Schönhauser Allee and find the **Kulturbrauerei**, a former Schultheiss brewery, built in the 1890s in the pseudo-Byzantine style much favoured by Berlin's architects during that era. The grounds of the former brewery have been transformed into the Kulturbrauerei, which, despite a recent facelift involving the addition of a movie multiplex, supermarket and family restaurants, remains a cultural centre with an alternative slant. Passing through the entrance around the corner at Knaackstrasse 97, you'll discover an inner courtyard with a live-music venue, a theatre and various exhibition spaces where there's almost always something – cultural, political or just entertaining – going on.

Kollwitzplatz and around

Just opposite the Segenskirche, Wörther Strasse leads to **Kollwitzplatz**, focal point for Prenzlauer Berg's main sights. It is named after the artist **Käthe Kollwitz**, who lived in nearby Weissenburgerstrasse (now called Kollwitzstrasse) from 1891 to 1943. Her work embraced political and pacifist themes and can be best appreciated in the Käthe Kollwitz Museum (see p.131). There's also an unflattering statue of Kollwitz in the little park on the square.

The Wasserturm

A left turn at the southern corner of Kollwitzplatz will land you on Knaackstrasse, where, after 50m or so, the huge red-brick **Wasserturm** (water tower) looms over the surrounding streets. Built in 1875 on the site of a pre-industrial windmill, the tower has been designated a historic monument and converted into apartments with room plans that follow the circular shape of the building. After the Nazis came to power the SA turned the basement into a torture chamber, and later the bodies of 28 of their victims were found in the underground pipe network. A memorial stone on Knaackstrasse commemorates them: "On this spot in 1933 decent German resistance fighters became the victims of fascist murderers. Honour the dead by striving for a peaceful world." Before the construction of the Wasserturm, Prenzlauer Berg's water requirements had been provided by the slim tower at the southern end of the square. Before that, people had to lug their water up from wells, and open sewers had taken their waste back downhill to the Spree, with the unsurprising result that disease was rife.

Synagogue Rykestrasse

From Knaackstrasse, a left turn into Rykestrasse brings you to a still-functioning **synagogue**, an ornate edifice in the courtyard of house no. 53. Originally built in 1904–5, this survived both *Kristallnacht* and use as a stables by the SA. It was designated a "Temple of Peace" in 1953 but today, poignantly, its capacity exceeds the Jewish population of the eastern part of the city.

BAT and the St. Georgen cemetery

On the southwestern side of the water tower is Belforter Strasse, where at no. 15 you'll find the **BAT** or **Studiotheater der Hochschule für Schauspielkunst Ernst Busch**, which is part of the School of Dramatic Art (see p.259). At the end of Belforter Strasse, cross Prenzlauer Allee into Heinrich-Roller-Strasse, which leads down to Greifswalder Strasse. On the right is the **St. Georgen** cemetery, a venerable and overgrown affair dating back to the early nineteenth century (access from Greifswalder Strasse), with some elaborate tombstones and vaults. Many of the memorials bear shrapnel and bullet scars, an indication of just how intense the fighting during the Battle for Berlin must have been; even the city's graveyards were fought for inch by inch.

Along Husemannstrasse

Running north of Kollwitzplatz is **Husemannstrasse**, a nineteenth-century tenement street that was restored to its former glory in late-GDR days and turned into a kind of living museum in an attempt to recall the grandeur of old Berlin. Since the *Wende*, restoration projects have transformed neighbouring streets too, covering raddled facades with fresh stucco and installing new wrought-iron balconies.

Husemannstrasse is now home to a lively restaurant and bar scene, anchored by the well-known and well-regarded *Restauration 1900*, which was established long before the Wall came down (see p.246).

Beyond Eberswalder Strasse

From the northern end of Husemannstrasse it's about 300m west along Danziger Strasse to the busy junction below **Eberswalder Strasse** U-Bahn station on Schönhauser Allee. North of the junction, Schönhauser Allee assumes its true identity as Prenzlauer Berg's main drag, an old-fashioned shopping street which, thanks to its cobbled streets and narrow shop facades, still retains a vaguely prewar feel. This effect is enhanced by the U-Bahn, which runs overground and becomes an elevated railway. Supported by ornate steel pillars, it leaves much of Schönhauser Allee in the shadows and was nicknamed the *Magistratschirm* or "municipal umbrella" at the time of its construction.

Gethsemanekirche

From Eberswalder Strasse, Schönhauser Allee extends northwards for a couple of kilometres towards Pankow, lined by shops and street stalls. Just to the southeast of Schönhauser Allee U-Bahn station, at the intersection of Stargarder Strasse and Greifenhagener Strasse, is the **Gethsemanekirche**, which was a focal point for reformist activities during the summer 1989 exodus from the GDR, and in the months leading up to the *Wende*. Given the peaceful nature of Schönhauser Allee today, it's hard to imagine that on October 7, 1989, the police were beating non-violent demonstrators here, during the anti-government street protests that followed the celebrations of the GDR's fortieth anniversary. Just over a month later, however, the nightmare was over, and it was in Prenzlauer Berg that ordinary East Germans first experienced the reality of the passing of the old order. At 9.15pm on November 9, 1989, a couple walked through the nearby Bornholmer Strasse border crossing into West Berlin, becoming the first East Berliners to take advantage of the opening of the Wall.

The eastern suburbs and beyond

f you've enough time, head out to Berlin's **eastern suburbs** whose face has significantly changed in the fifteen years since the *Wende*. Projects designed to iron out the differences between the two sides of the city have resulted in a strange mixture of past and present here: old GDR-style socialist architecture sits alongside the clean-cut lines and flashy design of new buildings. These elements have settled into a state of coexistence, even if they don't quite gel – often, of course, it's the incongruity that appeals. Beyond this, visiting these primarily residential areas partially moulded by almost fifty years of communist rule, unpleasant as this sometimes is, is an important part of getting a complete picture of Berlin – and on their southern fringes some genuine rural breathers offer a break from the city.

Moving north from the inner city, the tidy bourgeois district of **Pankow**, once home to the GDR capital's elite, has some pleasant parks but few really worthwhile sights. But it does makes a good stopoff on the way to or from the former concentration camp of **Sachsenhausen** – itself part of the town of Oranienburg and beyond Berlin's city limits, though still reachable via the S-Bahn. After World War II the camp became a Soviet Special Camp, as did the **Stasi Prison Hohenschönhausen** back in town in the district of **Lichtenberg**, before it was taken over by the *Stasi*, the East German secret police. The **Stasi Headquarters** were also in Lichtenberg, but the district also has some more pleasant and decidedly offbeat attractions as well as eastern Berlin's sprawling zoo **Tierpark Friedrichsfelde**. Northeast of Lichtenberg is **Marzahn**, a mid-1970s satellite town and perhaps Berlin's least obvious sightseeing destination. Silo-like apartment blocks and soulless shopping precincts stretch for miles out towards the edge of the city in what has to be one of the most desolate of the city's boroughs. However, this *is* Berlin for tens of thousands of Berliners, and worth a look for this reason alone. But probably the most pleasant day out in the eastern suburbs is to explore the surprisingly unspoiled lakes and woods in the far southeast – around **Köpenick** with its attractive small-town feel.

All of the places described in this chapter are easily reached on **public transport**: by S- or U-Bahn, though you may like to take a slower tram or bus on your journey out just to see a bit more of the city; links are suggested throughout the chapter.

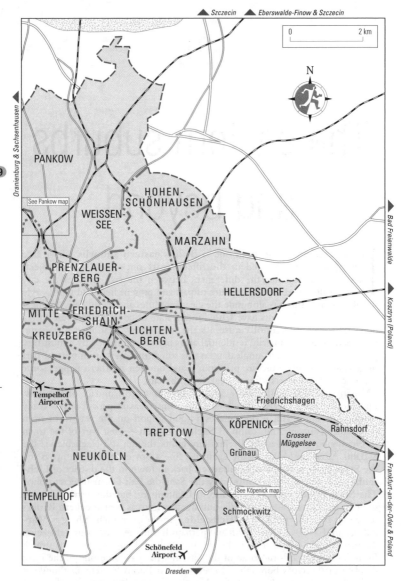

Pankow and Sachsenhausen

Pankow, Berlin's northernmost eastern borough before the city gives way to open countryside, has a slightly different atmosphere to other Berlin suburbs with an almost village-like feel, contrasting sharply with the grimier inner city. Though there's not much in the way of sights, its broad streets and parks make for an hour or two's pleasant strolling, and a brief sortée here can easily be fitted into a day that takes in the former concentration camp at **Sachsen-hausen**, since the two both lie off the same S-Bahn route (S1). If you do decide to visit Pankow on your way back from Sachsenhausen, consider getting off at S-Bahn Wilhelmsruh, close to the Soviet Memorial, and working your way southeast into the centre of the borough via the Schlosspark – the reverse of the order below.

Pankow

PANKOW, directly to the north of Prenzlauer Berg, was always more than just another East Berlin suburb. For years its villas and well-maintained flats were home mainly to members of the upper reaches of East Berlin society: state-approved artists and writers, scientists, East Berlin resident diplomats and the *Parteibonzen* (party bigwigs) of the old regime. Up until the 1960s the area was perceived in the West as being the real centre of power in the old GDR: Schloss Niederschönhausen, an eighteenth-century palace on the edge of the *Bezirk*, was the official residence of the GDR's first president, Wilhelm Pieck, and later of SED General Secretary Walter Ulbricht, the man who took the decision to build the Wall. The name of the suburb was also appropriated by one of the ex-GDR's best-known rock bands, in a satirical dig at the social hierarchy of the workers' and peasants' state. Today, it's a pleasant, very middle-class borough, focused on the large shopping street **Breite Strasse**, and is most attractive for the belt of parks – the **Schlosspark**, **Bürgerpark** and **Volkspark Schönholzer Heide** – that lies a block or so to the north of this main road.

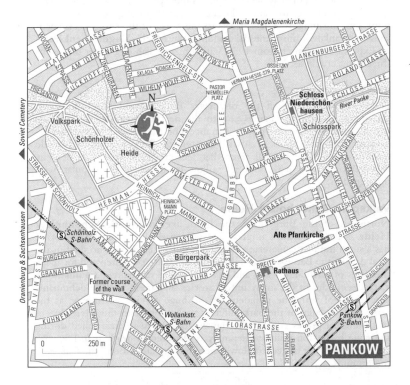

Breite Strasse is best reached by taking the **U-** or **S-Bahn** to Pankow station. From Pankow station it's a short walk north along Berliner Strasse to Breite Strasse. Alternatively, tram #M1 from Hackescher Markt will take you directly there, and give you good views of the streets of Prenzlauer Berg.

Breite Strasse and around

At the junction of Berliner Strasse and Breite Strasse, on a mid-road island that used to be the village green, is the **Alte Pfarrkirche**, Pankow's parish church and oldest building. It dates back to the fifteenth century but was extensively restored in 1832, a project in which Schinkel had a hand, resulting in an unusual-looking neo-Gothic jumble. At the western end of Breite Strasse, at the end of the main strip of chain stores and boutiques, is the turn-of-the-twentieth-century neo-Baroque **Rathaus**, a red-brick affair of fanciful gables, towers and cupolas, with a good *Ratskeller* in its basement.

The Schlosspark

A short walk north of Breite Strasse is the **Schlosspark**, in whose leafy grounds lurks **Schloss Niederschönhausen**, former home of Elisabeth Christine, the estranged wife of Frederick the Great. The Schloss was built at the beginning of the eighteenth century and given an extensive but run-of-the-mill face-lift in 1764. During GDR days it could only be admired from a distance, as it served first as official residence of the GDR president, from 1949 to 1960, and then as the old regime's most prestigious state guesthouse; these days you're free to wander the slightly dreary grounds (daily 9am–7pm, until 9pm in summer). A few streets to the north of the park on Platanen-strasse is Pankow's most unusual building, the **Maria-Magdalenenkirche**, an Expressionist church from 1930, with a bizarre slab of a tower topped by three giant crucifixes.

The Bürgerpark

Following the course of the tiny river Pank beyond the Schlosspark, walking via Parkstrasse brings you to the neat **Bürgerpark**, a one-time private park with an impressive entrance portal symbolic of nineteenth-century Pankow's status as a villa quarter for Berlin's more well-to-do citizens. The Pank, a small river that lent its name to the settlement, flows through the park, and its willow-lined banks are popular with promenaders.

Volkspark Schönholzer Heide

Northwest of the Bürgerpark, the heath-like **Volkspark Schönholzer Heide** is Pankow's most impressively wild park. In its southwest corner lies a small humble cemetery; a burial ground for civilians who died in the final days of the Battle of Berlin. Most are women or children and for many the dates of birth and death, and in some cases even names, are unknown, a stark reminder of the many untold stories that are lost in the dehumanizing chaos of war. The grandeur of the huge **Soviet cemetery**, at the northwestern edge of the park, offers a stark contrast to this. Here dozens of communal graves contain the remains of 13,200 soldiers killed during the same battle and military hierarchy is observed in death as in life, with officers occupying the central lower tiers and privates around the fringes of the grounds.

Gedenkstätte Sachsenhausen

A beastly vehicle for two of the twentieth century's most powerful and oppressive regimes, the **Gedenkstätte Sachsenhausen** (Sachsenhausen Memorial; mid-March to mid-Oct 8.30am–6pm; mid-Oct to mid-March 8.30am–4.30pm; free; ⊛www.gedenkstaette-sachsenhausen.de), based at the impressively gloomy and unremittingly miserable eponymous former concentration camp, forms a key historical site in Berlin's hinterland. The camp was one of the Nazis' main internment camps, a prototype upon which all others were based. It was, however, never designed specifically for extermination, and only at the end of the war was the camp used to systematically kill thousands of Soviet POWs and Jewish prisoners on death marches. After the war the Soviets continued to use the infrastructure for similar purposes.

The information centre and the New Museum

To enter the camp visitors pass through an **information centre** packed with books and a handful of displays on the camp. Here you could pick up the audio tour (€3), which uses unnecessarily long-winded descriptions to delve into the minutiae of camp life and the rather dull mechanics of preserving the camp as a monument. Better to make do with the free leaflet, which has a plan of the camp on it.

From the information centre you approach the camp along **Lagerstrasse**, as most prisoners would have done. Close to the entrance of the outer perimeter of the camp the track passes a large green wooden building, formerly the **SS command centre** and dubbed the green monster by prisoners.

The largest structure in the outer perimeter of the camp, the **New Museum**, houses exhibits on the origins of the camp and the process of constructing the memorial. Once inside the building, be sure to take a left – past the GDR-era stained glass to those who fought and suffered for "the freedom and independence of the fatherland" – to tackle the exhibits in sequence. Both exhibitions are impossibly detailed and furnished with enough resources to keep you occupied for days, but are also worth skimming and have plenty of pointers in English. Particularly fascinating is the big-screen projection of celebrations in Potsdam as Hitler came to power, with the *Führer* at the head of the military parade and the crowd going berserk. But this has only an indirect bearing on the camp, which was converted from a deserted brewery into a prison by the SA when they incarcerated political prisoners from the local area here; a process which in many cases involved the imprisonment of classmates, colleagues and neighbours.

Inside the camp

The camp proper begins under the main **watchtower** and beyond a **gate** adorned with the ominous sign *Arbeit macht frei* ("work makes you free"). In the early days of the camp its triangular layout meant the watchtower could effectively guard the entire camp, but soon its expansion required guard towers to be dotted around the entire perimeter. Either side of the guard tower is the **death strip**, a piece of land surrounding the entire camp: a no-go zone for prisoners, who would be shot without warning if they ventured here. Beyond it the perimeter fence was a high-voltage electric one, typical of all the Nazi camps, and the site of frequent suicides by despairing prisoners.

Overlooked by the main watchtower is the **parade ground** and, to the right, the few remaining **prison blocks** – largely reconstructions of the originals.

One houses a thoughtful museum (with exhibits in English) which follows the fortunes of a selection of the camp's prisoners – recounting their personal journeys to and from the camp. Beside is the **camp prison**, from which internees seldom returned and about which there is little information in English. The cells were mostly used for solitary confinement in rudimentary conditions, with prisoners fed just enough to keep them alive. One cell, marked with a British flag, housed two captured British officers who were held manacled to a concrete block at the centre of their cell in near darkness for six months before being taken around the back of the prison and summarily shot. The prison yard is also the site of several tall wooden poles to which prisoners would be tied by their hands until their arms separated from their shoulder joints – a routine punishment for minor misdemeanours.

Moving anticlockwise around the main **parade ground** brings you to another two blocks at the heart of the complex. In front of them and at the head of the parade ground lies a public execution site. Prisoners would be hung here in front of the assembled inmates as an example to all. At Christmas the SS put a decorated tree here. Only one of the blocks behind the parade ground is open to the public and currently houses a sensationalist, and somewhat misleading, **GDR-era exhibition** on the camp. From it you would assume the camp was directly involved in mass executions of Jews, which it never was; however, near the end of the war and immediately afterwards many died here as a result of forced marches and disease, and an untold number of Soviet POWs were executed here.

This exhibition is due to disappear soon as the memorial is redeveloped and its history told in a more accurate and objective way. Another result of this drive is that much of the rest of the former camp is still under reconstruction. Memorials are being placed on the mass graves of the Soviet dead and a museum is under development on the Soviet Special Camp (1945 and 1950), where the Russians imprisoned 60,000 people with suspected links to the Nazi regime, of which at least 12,000 died.

Practicalities

Tucked away in a northeastern suburb of the small town of Oranienburg, the former camp can be **reached** via the S-Bahn (S1 from Berlin; around an hour's journey). From the S-Bahn station hourly buses (#M804 or #M821; BVG day tickets valid) ply the route to the *Gedenkstätte*, but you may find it faster to make the twenty-minute walk to the site. The walk heads north from the square beside the S-Bahn station a couple of hundred metres along Stralsunder Strasse to reach Bernauer Strasse. A ten-minute walk east along this brings you to a major crossroads, where you turn north up Strasse der Einheit and then east onto Strasse der Nationen, past a small plaque devoted to the 6000 who died on the *Todesmarch* – the march away from the front line to which the Nazis subjected prisoners as the Russians approached.

After visiting the camp, there is little else to keep you in Oranienburg so you're best off hopping on the S-Bahn and wandering around Pankow (see p.171), but if you've worked up an appetite, you might try the mediocre fast **food** and traditional German dishes of the adjacent *Café Talk* (Tues–Fri 9am–6pm, Sat & Sun 10am–6pm), though a much better bet is to head back to the *Vietnam Bistro*, Straslunder Strasse 1 (Mon–Fri 10am–10pm; Sat & Sun 11am–10pm), just north of the railway station, which serves up tasty Thai and pan-Asian dishes at extraordinarily low prices (mostly around €4–5 a dish) and has an English menu.

△ Soviet memorial

Lichtenberg

Beyond the eastern reaches of Friedrichshain lies the district of **Lichtenberg**, a sprawling working-class district, part prefabricated postwar mass dwellings and part traditional tenement blocks, with heavy concentrations of industry in the north and south. Until the mid-nineteenth century Lichtenberg was little more than a country town and popular Sunday-outing destination for Berliners. With industrialization, however, the familiar Berlin tenements sprang up and the area's rustic past was soon forgotten. In these post-unification days Lichtenberg has been hard hit by the collapse of the old order, with unemployment running high. A nasty side effect of all this is a reputation for mindless, often racially motivated, violence, making it a place to avoid at night. By day, however, head here for the Stasi prison at **Hohenschönhausen** and headquarters at **Normannenstrasse**; both served the GDR's all-pervasive secret police and have been turned into important, though slightly ghoulish, tourist attractions. The borough also has a good zoo, **Tierpark Friedrichsfelde**, in the eastern sector. Of more esoteric appeal are the memorials to various figures from the socialist past in Lichtenberg proper, and the **museum in Karlshorst**, in the building where the Wehrmacht surrendered to the Soviet armed forces in 1945.

With the exception of the Gedenkstätte Hohenschönhausen, which is best reached by **tram** from Hackescher Markt, most of Lichtenberg is linked to Alexanderplatz via the U5 **U-Bahn** line.

Gedenkstätte Hohenschönhausen

A potent antidote for the so-called *Ostalgie* – nostalgia for the GDR – is a visit to the grim former Stasi prison at **Gedenkstätte Hohenschönhausen**, Genslerstrasse 66 (Memorial Hohenschönhausen daily 9am–4pm, tours in German Mon–Fri 11am & 1pm; €3; Sat & Sun hourly until 4pm – tours in English by arrangement ☎030/98 60 82 30, ⊛www.stiftung-hsh.de), which offers an insight into the fear and oppression upon which the regime was founded. Exhibitions in the prison are still being developed, with signs explaining parts of the compound gradually appearing, but even after this process is complete, the clear highlight of a visit will likely remain the **guided tours** by former prisoners. To get here take tram #M5 or from Hackescher Markt or, if you're already in Lichtenberg, bus #256 from U-Bahn Lichtenberg. Get off either tram or bus at Freienwalder Strasse at the end of which is the entrance to the former jail.

Hohenschönhausen began life in 1945 as a **Soviet Special Camp**: an assembly and transit camp, with 4200 inmates penned in together in horrendous living conditions. It is estimated that by 1946 around 3000 detainees had died here. Officially most of these were interned because of suspected association with the Nazis, but in fact the bulk were thought to have little or no active involvement in the collapsed regime. In consequence torture chambers were an important means of acquiring "confessions" from prisoners and these can be seen in the underground prison nicknamed the "*U-Boot*" (submarine). The lights were constantly on in the damp, windowless cells here and interrogations lengthy and intimidating. If that brought no results, water torture was used to force confession, while as a last resort prisoners were put into a tiny air-tight cell where, once the oxygen ran out, they would have around three minutes before suffocation to agree to confess. The consequences of confession were usually decades of forced labour – though almost all the condemned were declared innocent by the Russian authorities in the 1990s.

The Stasi

East Germany's infamous **Staatssicherheitsdienst** (State Security Service), or Stasi, kept tabs on everything that happened in the GDR. Its job was to ensure the security of the country's borders, carry out surveillance operations on foreign diplomats, business people and journalists, and monitor domestic and foreign media. It was, however, in surveillance of East Germany's own population that the organization truly excelled. Very little happened in the GDR without the Stasi knowing about it: files were kept on millions of innocent citizens and insidious operations were orchestrated against dissidents, real and imagined. By the time of the *Wende* the Stasi had a budget of £1 billion and 91,000 full-time employees and 180,000 informers within the East German population; figures brought into context by the comparatively puny, though even more ruthless, 7000-strong Nazi Gestapo.

At the beginning of 1991 former citizens of the GDR were given the right to apply to see their Stasi files. Tens of thousands availed themselves of the opportunity to find out what the organization had recorded about them, and, more importantly, who had provided the information; many a friendship and not a few marriages came to an end as a result.

In 1951, the Russians ceased to use the compound, handing it over to the Ministry of State Security (*Ministerium für Staatssicherheit*, commonly known as the Stasi; see box above) for whom it became a **remand prison**. The complex formed the centre of a district taken over by the secret services where no ordinary citizens were allowed and which was omitted from city maps. The smallest sign of resistance or opposition to the state, including comments written in letters – which were all routinely steamed open – could have you put in prison here. Typically, you'd be caught unawares on your way to work, bundled into an unmarked van and then brought here, with no idea why.

The tours look at many facets of the prison – padded cells, tiny exercise facilities, endless corridors of interrogation rooms – but the methods employed remain the most fascinating. The former prisoners deliver an absorbing insight into the psychological rather than physical abuse involved: how they were held without charge, demeaned, cut off from the world and other prisoners and subjected to lengthy daily interrogations – routinely twelve hours at a time – for months on end to get incriminating statements.

Stasi headquarters and Gedenkstätte Normannenstrasse

The former **Stasi headquarters** comprises a huge complex bounded by Frankfurter Allee, Ruschestrasse, Normannenstrasse and Magdalenenstrasse – an area approximately the size of London's Whitehall – with another slightly smaller complex a few streets to the north.

Part of the building from which all this was controlled now houses a museum with an unwieldy title, the **Forschungs- und Gedenkstätte Normannenstrasse** (Normannenstrasse Research and Memorial Centre; Ruschestrasse 103, Haus 1; Mon–Fri 11am–6pm, Sat & Sun 2–6pm; €3.50; ⊛www .stasimuseum.de; U-Bahn Magdalenenstrasse), which covers the GDR political system and the way in which the massive surveillance apparatus of the Stasi helped maintain it. Walking along the bare, red-carpeted corridors and looking at the busts of Lenin and Felix Dzerzhinsky – founder of the Soviet Cheka, forerunner of the KGB and model for the Stasi – it all seems to belong to a much more distant past, rather than an era which came to an end only at the beginning of 1990. But then the obsessively neat office and apartment of **Erich Mielke**, the minister of state security who oversaw Stasi operations from 1957 to October 1989, somehow makes it all the more immediate. Everything is just as he left it: white and black telephones stand on the varnished wooden desk as though awaiting incoming calls, and Mielke's white dress uniform hangs in a wardrobe.

On the floor above Mielke's offices various rooms are devoted to different aspects of the history of the Stasi and the GDR. The commentary is in German only (an accompanying booklet in English costs €3), but the displays of Stasi surveillance apparatus, most of it surprisingly primitive, speak for themselves. The extensive array of bugging devices and cameras reveals the absurd lengths the GDR went to in order to keep tabs on what its citizens were doing – included in the display are watering cans and plant pots concealing toy-like cameras. You'll also find a couple of rooms stuffed with medals, badges, flags and other items of GDR kitsch. The sections on political terror during the Stalin years and forced resettlement from border zones throw light on otherwise little-known aspects of GDR history.

Dorfkirche and Gedenkstätte der Sozialisten

At its western end, two blocks from the Stasi headquarters, Normannenstrasse comes to a junction with Möllendorffstrasse, close to where the rather sinister-looking Rathaus Lichtenberg looms. Just north of here, marooned amid the traffic, is an improbably rustic **Dorfkirche**, a church dating back to Lichtenberg's village origins. The stone walls date from the original thirteenth-century structure, but the rest is more modern, the spire having been tacked on as recently as 1965. The only other attraction in Lichtenberg itself is the **Gedenkstätte der Sozialisten** or "Memorial to the Socialists", a kilometre or so northeast of Lichtenberg U- and S-Bahn station, at the end of Gudrunstrasse, and perhaps only for die-hard fans of GDR relics. Its centrepiece is a four-metre chunk of red porphyry bearing the inscription *Die Toten mahnen uns* – "The dead remind us" – commemorating the GDR's socialist hall of fame from Karl Liebknecht and Rosa Luxemburg onwards. A tablet bears a list of names that reads like the street directory of virtually any town in pre-*Wende* East Germany, recording the esoteric cult figures of the workers' and peasants' state in alphabetical order, and until 1989 the East Berlin public were cajoled and coerced into attending hundred-thousand-strong mass demonstrations here. The whole thing actually replaced a much more interesting Mies van der Rohe-designed memorial that stood here from 1926 until the Nazis destroyed it in 1935. Altogether more uncompromising, featuring a huge star and hammer and sickle, the original memorial caused problems for Mies van der Rohe when he came before Joseph McCarthy's Un-American Activities Committee in 1951. The Gedenkstätte is also the burial place of Walter Ulbricht, the man who took the decision to build the Wall, and Wilhelm Pieck, the first president of the GDR.

Tierpark and Schloss Friedrichsfelde

To reach Lichtenberg's sprawling zoo, **Tierpark Friedrichsfelde** (daily 9am–sunset or 7pm; €10; ⊛www.tierpark-berlin.de; U-Bahn Tierpark), the entrances are on the eastern side of Am Tierpark. The Tierpark ranks as one of the largest zoos in Europe and a thorough exploration of its wooded grounds could easily absorb the better part of a day. It's an ideal destination for families, though some visitors may balk at the traditional nature of the place and the fact that some of the animals are kept in very small cages. However, others have much more space to roam around and virtually every species imaginable, from alpaca to wisent, can be found here, including rare Przewalski horses, which have been bred in the zoo in great numbers over the years, bringing the breed back from the edge of extinction.

Hidden away in the grounds of the zoo, just beyond an enclosure of lumbering pelicans, is **Schloss Friedrichsfelde** (Tues–Sun 10am–6pm; €0.50 on top of zoo entrance; ⑩www.stadtmuseum.de), a Baroque palace housing an exhibition of eighteenth- and nineteenth-century interior decor. Theodor Fontane described it as the Schloss Charlottenburg of the East, but he was exaggerating – the best thing about it is its pretty, ornamental grounds.

Karlshorst and the Museum Berlin-Karlshorst

From the Tierpark, a stroll south down Am Tierpark, bearing left along Treskowerallee for about a kilometre, will bring you to the sub-district of **Karlshorst**. For many years you were more likely to hear Russian than German spoken on the streets around here, as the area was effectively a Russian quarter, thanks to the presence of large numbers of Soviet soldiers and their dependants. The Russians accepted the unconditional surrender of the German armed forces in a Wehrmacht engineer's school here on May 8, 1945, and went on to establish their Berlin headquarters nearby. For many years after, Karlshorst was a closed area, fenced off and under armed guard, out of bounds to ordinary East Germans. Later, they were allowed back into parts of the area, but Karlshorst retained an exclusive cachet, its villas given over to the elite of GDR society – scientists and writers – or used as foreign embassy residences.

The Russians finally left in the summer of 1994, but a reminder of their presence endures in the shape of the **Museum Berlin-Karlshorst** in Zwieseler Strasse 4 (Tues–Sun 10am–6pm; free; ⑩www.museum-karlshorst .de; S-Bahn Karlshorst), the building where the German surrender was signed. When the GDR still existed, this museum was officially known as the "Museum of the Unconditional Surrender of Fascist Germany in the Great Patriotic War 1941–45". Since then it has been renamed and rearranged to suit post-Cold War sensibilities. It features an exhibition on the long and tumultuous German-Russian relationship, obviously focusing on the treaty that ended the war.

Marzahn and around

To see the most enduring legacy of East Berlin – **MARZAHN** – it's probably best to go by day and preferably not looking too much like a tourist, as the area has a reputation for violence. It's in places like Marzahn, all across the former GDR, that people are bearing the economic brunt of reunification's downside – unemployment, *Kurzarbeit* or "short-time working", and low wages – and where you'll see the worst effects caused by the collapse of a state that, for all its faults, ensured a certain level of social security for its citizens. Ironically, Marzahn was one of the GDR's model new towns of the 1970s – part of Honecker's efforts to solve his country's endemic housing shortage by providing modern apartments in purpose-built blocks with shopping facilities and social amenities to hand. The result here was a six-kilometre by two-kilometre area of high-rise developments, stretching from Springpfuhl in the south to Ahrensfelde, which house 150,000 people. But, like similar developments in Western countries, it never quite worked out according to plan, with the usual crime and drugs surfacing.

Most people will see enough of Marzahn by travelling on the S-Bahn to Springfuhl and then taking tram #M8 to Alt-Marzahn, the original, slightly quaint and now hugely incongruous centre of this district. It still has some of the feel of a traditional village – complete with green, pub, cobbled streets, war memorial and parish church. From here you can wander between the high-rises, taking in the immensity of it all, or take bus #195 to the **Erholungspark Marzahn**, a large park with a collection of exotic ornamental gardens. This bus goes on into the administratively linked borough of **Hellersdorf**, location of the **Gründerzeitmuseum Mahlsdorf**, a museum that brings together a fine collection of late nineteenth-century furnishings from the time of the beginning of the German Empire.

Alt-Marzahn

More or less in the middle of Marzahn, with endless high-rises stretching out north and south, is **Alt-Marzahn** (tram #M8 from S-Bahn Springfuhl), where something of the area's village past survives. Admittedly it's not a very pleasant past: from 1866 the fields of the area were used as *Rieselfelder*, specially designated for the disposal of Berlin's sewage. Despite this malodorous development, Marzahn acquired a Dorfkirche in neo-Gothic style a few years later, built by Schinkel's pupil Friedrich August Stüler. Nearby, at Alt-Marzahn 31, is the somewhat curious **Handwerksmuseum und Friseurmuseum** (Handicrafts Museum and Barber Museum; Tues, Wed, Sat & Sun 10am–6pm; €2; ⓦwww .stadtmuseum.de). The former is devoted mainly to an exhibit of woodworking tools and a huge collection of locks and keys, while the latter consists of the many and varied haircutting, shaving and surgical tools employed by barbers throughout history.

Erholungspark Marzahn

Opened in 1987 as part of the city's 750th birthday celebrations, the **Erholungspark Marzahn**, Eisenacher Strasse 98 (daily: March & Oct 9am–5pm; April 9am–7pm; May–Sept 9am–8pm; Nov–Feb 9am–4pm; €2; ☏030/54 69 80 ⓦwww.erholunspark-marzahn.de), a large tidy park, forms an attractive oasis amid the high-rises of one of Berlin's most notoriously unattractive neighbourhoods. The park is dotted with decorative features, pleasant nooks and playgrounds, but its star turns are the trio of exotic gardens, of which two are largely the result of Berlin's twinning with Beijing and Tokyo. The sprawling and ornate **Chinese Garden** is perhaps the best known in the park, being the biggest in Europe, and has a restaurant, snack bar and a teahouse where you can take part in a traditional tea ceremony (reservation necessary, call ☏0179/3 94 55 64).

A much tighter affair is the **Japanese Garden** (mid-April to Oct Mon–Fri 1pm–garden closing; Sat and Sun opens 9am), where water and rock features compete for space with the shrubs and bonsai trees, and tidy attention to detail is evident throughout. The newest of the park's exotic gardens is the **Balinese Garden** in a warm damp greenhouse where you'll find a simple rural family home amid the ferns and orchids.

The Gründerzeitmuseum Mahlsdorf

The suburb of **Mahlsdorf** (in the neighbouring *Bezirk* of Hellersdorf), about 5km southeast of Marzahn, is no cultural centre, but it does boast one of the city's most notable museums, the excellent **Gründerzeitmuseum Mahlsdorf**, Hultschiner Damm 333 (Wed & Sun 10am–6pm; €4.10; ☏030/8 67 83 29, ⊛www.gruenderzeitmuseum.de; S-Bahn Mahlsdorf where bus #195 from Alt-Marzahn and the Erholungspark stops), a collection of furniture and household gear from 1880–1900, the period known as the *Gründerzeit* or "foundation time" when the newly united Germany was at its Imperial peak. The founder of the museum, Lothar Berfelde (better known in Germany as a writer under his pseudonym, Charlotte von Mahlsdorf), got the collection together during GDR days when such an undertaking was by no means an easy task, creating a representative *Gründerzeit* apartment by taking the complete contents of rooms and relocating them in this eighteenth-century manor house. Depending on your tastes the result is either exquisite or over the top, but either way the museum is fascinating and certainly worth the long haul out to the suburbs. In the basement are furnishings from the *Mulack-Ritz*, a famous turn-of-the-twentieth-century Berlin *Kneipe* that originally stood on Mulackstrasse in the Scheunenviertel (see p.113). Lothar Berfelde was awarded the Bundesverdienstkreuz, Germany's equivalent of the OBE, in the summer of 1992 for his services to the preservation of the city's cultural and social heritage; he is, incidentally, one of Berlin's better-known transvestites.

Köpenick and around

Köpenick is one of eastern Berlin's more pleasant *Bezirke*, located on the banks of the River Spree towards the southeast edge of the city, and easily reached by S-Bahn line #3 from Alexanderplatz, Friedrichstrasse Station and Zoo Station. The town of Köpenick is a slow-moving little place, but ideal to visit as an escape from the city centre. It also makes a convenient base for exploring Berlin's southeastern lakes, in particular the **Müggelsee**, with its appealing shoreline towns of Friedrichshagen and Rahnsdorf. Also easily accessible are the **Müggelberge**, Berlin's 150-metre-high "mountains", and the towns of **Grünau** and **Schmöckwitz** on the banks of the Lange See, which gives access to the Zeuthener See and Krossinsee.

Köpenick

KÖPENICK itself was a town in its own right during medieval times, and though it has since been swallowed up by Greater Berlin, it still retains a distinct identity. The presence of a number of major factories in the area meant that Köpenick always had a reputation as a "red" town. In March 1920, during the Kapp putsch attempt, workers from Köpenick took on and temporarily drove back army units who were marching on Berlin in support of the coup. The army later returned, but its success was short-lived as the putsch foundered – thanks mainly to a highly effective general strike. This militancy was to continue into the Nazi era: on January 30, 1933, the day Hitler came to power, the red flag could be seen flying from the chimney of the brewery in the suburb of Friedrichshagen. This defiance was punished during the *Köpenicker*

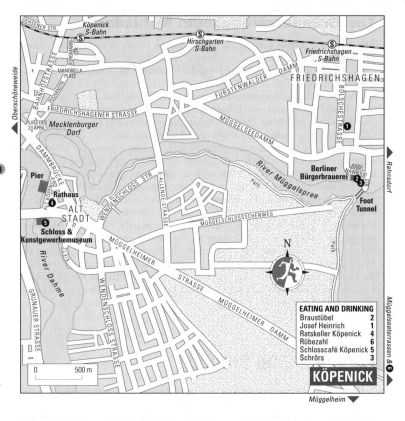

Oberschöneweide ◀

Rahnsdorf ▶

Müggelseeterrassen & ⑥ ▶

EATING AND DRINKING
Braustübel	2
Josef Heinrich	1
Ratskeller Köpenick	4
Rübezahl	6
Schlosscafé Köpenick	5
Schrörs	3

KÖPENICK

Müggelheim ▼

Blutwoche ("Köpenick Week of Blood") in June, during which the SA swooped on Social Democrats and Communists. Five hundred people were imprisoned and 91 murdered.

The Altstadt

At the heart of Köpenick is the Altstadt or old town. To walk there from the S-Bahn station, follow Borgamannstrasse to Mandrellaplatz, location of Köpenick's **Amtsgericht** (District Court), in whose execution chamber the victims of the *Köpenicker Blutwoche* were killed. From Mandrellaplatz, Puchanstrasse leads to Am Generalshof and the **Platz des 23 April**, which commemorates the arrival in Köpenick of the Soviet army – liberators or conquerors, depending on your point of view. On the Platz a sculpted clenched fist on top of a stone tablet honours those killed by the Nazis in 1933.

From the Platz, the Dammbrücke (you can rent boats by the foot of the bridge from €3 per hour) leads across the Spree into Köpenick's **Altstadt** (linked to the S-Bahn station by tram #60 and #62 or bus #M69). Situated on an island between the Spree and Dahme rivers, the Altstadt's streets run more or less true to the medieval town plan.

The most prominent building is the early twentieth-century neo-Gothic **Rathaus** on Alt Köpenick, a typically over-the-top gabled affair with an imposing clock tower. Eight years before World War I, an incident took place here that would capture the imagination of the world's press and provide the inspiration for a play that would make Köpenick famous far beyond the city limits of Berlin. On October 16, 1906, an unemployed shoemaker named **Wilhelm Voigt**, who had spent some time in prison, disguised himself as an army officer and commandeered a troop of soldiers. He marched them to the Köpenick Rathaus and, with their assistance, requisitioned the contents of the municipal safe. Having ordered his detachment to take Köpenick's mayor and book-keeper to the Neue Wache guardhouse in the city centre, he disappeared. Although Voigt was soon caught, the story was seized on abroad as an example of the Prussian propensity to blindly follow anyone wearing uniform. Later, the playwright Carl Zuckmeyer turned Voigt's exploits into a play, *Der Hauptmann von Köpenick* ("The Captain of Köpenick"). The robbery is re-enacted every summer in the second half of June during the Köpenick summer festival, and a statue of Voigt now stands by the entrance of the Rathaus.

In **Grünstrasse** and **Böttcherstrasse** are a number of typical nineteenth-century *Bürgerhäuser* with restored facades, and given the sometimes down-at-heel nature of the Altstadt it's not hard to picture this area as it must have been a century or so ago.

Schloss Köpenick

At the southern end of the Altstadt island a footbridge leads to the Schlossinsel, site of the Baroque **Schloss Köpenick**, a fortified manor house dating back to the seventeenth century. The Schloss houses the **Kunstgewerbemuseum** (Museum of Applied Art; Tues–Fri 10am–6pm, Sat & Sun 11am–6pm; €4, free Thurs 2–6pm; ☎030/2 26 29 02, ⊛www.smpk.de), another of Berlin's fine state museums (see p.83), with an attractive and beautifully exhibited collection of interior decorations from the sixteenth to eighteenth centuries. In general its collection is perhaps slightly less impressive than that of the Kulturforum's Kunstgewerbemuseum (see p.183; tickets bought at either are valid in both on the same day), though the museum takes advantage of its setting by integrating many pieces into the original interiors of the Baroque manor. Appreciation of these is greatly enhanced by a first-class audio tour, included in the price of admission.

The **exhibition** has been laid out to tell the story of Renaissance, Baroque and Rococo styles, and makes most sense when followed in sequence. A plan with the route marked on is available at the ticket office. From a small number of items on the ground floor the tour ascends the south wing up to the attic before dropping down the north wing back to the start. The basement contains information about the history of the manor and its restoration and is only of passing interest to most.

Beginning on the **ground floor**, the self-guided tour starts with the Italian Renaissance, an example Europe soon followed, particularly as it was quickly bolstered by the French version as shown by the grand pieces of furniture in the next room. But these exhibits really serve only as a preamble to the museum's strong point: the German Renaissance.

On the first floor of the **south wing** themes of love, marriage and fertility are explored in sturdy Teutonic furniture, and an eye-catching series of ornate sixteenth-century backgammon boards. After a brief foray into Dutch Baroque, the suggested route leads to the floor above, where the Germanic nature of the collection is underlined by a group of gigantic beer mugs. Next, a few Polish influences on the Renaissance offer distraction before you arrive at the museum's most famous pieces: a silver buffet originally found in the ruling Hohenzollern family's Berliner Schloss – one of the few treasures from there to survive intact.

Having visited this wing, you can pop up to the **attic** of the manor to view an eye-glazing collection of Baroque glassware and porcelain, but it's the impressive old beams which hold up the roof that make the climb worthwhile.

Back on the second floor the suggested route ducks into the **north wing** and then into a room of Chinese artefacts. Seventeenth-century Dutch and British trade with the Orient brought items like these vases and commodes back to Europe and helped inspire elements of Rococo, as some of the following rooms illustrate. The next room, the impressive *Wappensaal* (coat of arms hall), is a complete festival hall, with the original ceiling and wall stucco decorations restored, and silverware and porcelain laid out on a huge banquet table. Moving on from here, the Rococo movement is looked at in more depth, with glimpses particularly at the German and French branches, and ending in the porcelain gallery. Much of the items here were the private possessions of Frederick II and sport particularly heavy oriental influences. Clearly he was a big fan of the style, since the *pièce de résistance* here – a gaudy and excessively flamboyant porcelain lampshade – was one of a series that Frederick liked to bestow as gifts (probably not one that would win him too many friends today).

Frauentog and the Kietz

Just beside the Schloss Köpenick and its attendant Schlossplatz are views out over the **Frauentog**, a small bay where Köpenick's fishermen used to cast their nets, which becomes the Langer See further south (see p.185). This sheltered bay is now home to the Solarbootpavilon (Mon–Fri noon–8pm, Sat & Sun 10am–8pm; ☎060/6 30 99 97, ☞www.solarworld.de), a boat-hire company that offers the novelty of hiring out solar-powered craft from €10/1hr.

On the east side of this small bay and just to the southeast of the Altstadt is the **Kietz**, a cobbled street of fishing cottages whose origins go back to the early thirteenth century. Recent renovation has brightened up the shutters and whitewashed facades of most of these cottages, making it a pleasant street for a stroll.

The Grosser Müggelsee and around

From Luisenhain, opposite the Rathaus in Köpenick Altstadt, it's possible to take a Stern und Kreisschiffahrt boat trip (see p.35) around the nearby **Grosser Müggelsee**, one of Berlin's main lakes, just a few kilometres east of Köpenick itself. Although the lake lies within the city limits of Berlin, the atmosphere of suburbs like Friedrichshagen and Rahnsdorf is distinctly small-town, and wandering the shores of the lake and the surrounding woods is a welcome relief from pounding Berlin's relentless urban streets. Beware, though, the Müggelsee area gets very crowded at all times of the year – in summer, people swarm here for sun and sailing, and in winter to ice-skate.

Friedrichshagen and the Müggelsee shore

Another way of reaching the Grosser Müggelsee is to take tram #60 from Köpenick's Schlossplatz or the S-Bahn to **FRIEDRICHSHAGEN**, a small town founded in 1753 as a settlement for Bohemian cotton spinners who, as a condition of their being allowed to live here, were required by law to plant mulberry trees for the rearing of silkworms. Both tram and train stop beside Friedrichshagen's main drag, **Bölschestrasse**, where a number of single-storey houses survive from the original eighteenth-century settlement, dwarfed by later nineteenth-century blocks, and a few vestigial mulberry trees still cling to life at the roadside. About halfway down this otherwise attractive street the **Christophoruskirche**, a gloomy neo-Gothic church in red brick, puts a Lutheran damper on things.

To get away from it, make for the lake, which is reached via Josef-Nawrocki-Strasse, passing the extensive buildings of the **Berliner Bürgerbrauerei**, from whose chimney the red flag flew provocatively the day Hitler was sworn in as chancellor. Following the road around leads to a small park at the point where the Spree flows into the Grosser Müggelsee. Here there's a cruise-ship pier and a foot tunnel that takes you under the river. At the other side a path through the woods follows the lakeshore that's perfect for strolling and leads to the **Müggelberge** 2km away (see below).

Back to the north of the Spree and halfway between Friedrichshagen and Rahnsdorf is the **Museum im Wasserwerk**, Müggelseedamm 307 (March–Oct Tues–Fri 10am–4pm, Sun 10am–5pm; Nov–Feb Tues–Fri 10am–3pm, Sun 10am–4pm; ⊛www.museum-im-wasserwerk.de; €2 S-Bahn Friedrichshagen then tram #60 to terminus), an old waterworks building that's been turned into a museum detailing the history of Berlin's water supply.

Rahnsdorf

At the east end of the Grosser Müggelsee, the little town of **RAHNSDORF** can be reached by S-Bahn or by tram #61 from Friedrichshagen. Rahnsdorf itself is one of eastern Berlin's more delightful hidden corners, a sprawl of tree-shaded lakeside houses with an old fishing village at its core. Head for **Dorfstrasse**, a cobbled street at the southern end of the village (bus #161 from the S-Bahn station for seven stops, then follow the signs for Altes Fischerdorf or ask directions), lined by fishermen's cottages and centred around a small parish church. The best way to explore Rahnsdorf is to simply wander the lakeside and soak up the atmosphere. Just off Fürstenwalder Damm, on the western edge of town, there's an FKK (*Freikörperkultur*) **nudist beach** for hardy souls.

The Müggelberge

Accessed via a two-kilometre lakeshore path from Friedrichshagen (see opposite) or bus #M69 from Köpenick S-Bahn, the **Müggelberge** are a series of rolling forested hills overlooking the Grosser Müggelsee. From bus stop Rübezahl, a path leads south through the woods up to the summit of the **Müggelberge** hills. Around about the halfway mark is the **Teufelsee** (Devil's Lake), a small pool with a glass-smooth surface, which acts as a focus for various nature trails. More information on these, and on the flora and fauna of the area, can be obtained at the nearby **Lehrkabinett** information centre (May–Sept Wed–Fri 10am–4pm, Sat & Sun 10am–5pm; Oct–April Wed, Thurs, Sat & Sun 10am–4pm). Pushing on and up through the woods leads to the **Müggelturm** (closed for renovations), a functional-looking observation tower offering great views of the lake and woods, plus a café, bar and restaurant (also closed for renovations). Incidentally, both the Teufelsee and Müggelturm are accessible by car and bike (if you've got the stamina) along reasonably well-surfaced tracks from the main road.

Grünau and the Langer See

Another possible local destination is **GRÜNAU** on the River Dahme, just to the south of Köpenick. There isn't a great deal in terms of sights, but you could do worse than go for a walk along the quiet banks of the **Langer See**, as the

Dahme is called beyond Grünau. Tram #68 runs directly from Köpenick and on past Grünau S-Bahn station to Schöckwitz.

The Langer See itself is a watersports centre, and the **Strandbad Grünau**, a beach of sorts, lies just outside town, with numerous *Gaststätten* nearby. To reach it, head along Regattastrasse past the **Regattatribüne**, starting point for boat races along this stretch and venue for part of the 1936 Olympics.

Gartenstadt Falkenberg

A couple of hundred metres' walk southwest of S-Bahn Grünau is the **Gartenstadt Falkenberg**, a settlement of model housing designed by Bruno Taut in response to slum conditions in the city-centre tenements. To get there, take the S-Bahn to Grünau station, from where it's a short walk southwest along Bruno-Taut-Strasse to the houses on the western end of that street and Akazienhof. The best examples are along Akazienhof: pastel-painted, cottage-like dwellings that must have seemed paradise to their first inhabitants, newly escaped from the filth and industry of the inner *Bezirke*. A plaque at Akazienhof used to state, without irony: "Many of the founder members [of the settlement] were active opponents of war and fascism. Their ideals have become reality in the German Democratic Republic."

Schmöckwitz

Tram #68 also passes through the tranquil villa settlement of Karolinenhof to **Schmöckwitz**, which has been inhabited since prehistoric times. Again, there aren't any real sights, but you can spend a pleasant hour or two wandering through the **Schmöckwitzer Werder**, a woodland area occupying a finger of land several kilometres square between the Zeuthener See and Krossinsee, southeast of Schmöckwitz. On the shores of the Krossinsee (and accessible by occasional buses from Schmöckwitz) are a couple of decent **campsites** (see "Accommodation", p.228).

The western suburbs

While there's more than enough to detain you in Berlin's centre, it's worth heading to the laid-back **western suburbs** for a disparate group of attractions of considerable cultural and historical interest, as well as the lakes and woodlands beyond them that feel a world away – not just a half-dozen S-Bahn stops – from the centre of town.

Culturally speaking, the important target in the west is the **Dahlem museum complex**, in the suburb of the same name, which contains a world-class ethnological museum as well as museums of Indian and East Asian Art. A short bus ride west of here are some other interesting museums including the **Allied Museum**, where the original Checkpoint Charlie booth is kept. Beyond here the lakes and verdant woodlands of the **Grunewald**, the city's very own eco-friendly playpen, begin in earnest and come as a surprise after the claustrophobic city – a reminder of Berlin's position in *Mitteleuropa* – and of the fact that one-third of the city is greenery and parkland. The Grunewald is flanked by the huge Havel lake, where one bay, the **Wannsee**, is famed for its summer-time bathing and as the location of the **Wannsee Villa**, where a Nazi conference sealed the fate of millions of Jews. At the northern end of the Havel, where it joins the Spree, lies **Spandau**, which has a small-town feel far removed from Berlin, a sense that is only enhanced by the presence of its **Zitadelle**, one of the world's best preserved Renaissance fortifications.

Thanks to the efficient **U- and S-Bahn** systems, it's possible to reach Berlin's western edges in under three-quarters of an hour, but once there the best, and often only, form of public transport is **bus**. This is particularly so in the Grune-wald where the double-deckers are great for sightseeing. Also included on the BVG public transport system and in the price of a day ticket is the hourly **ferry** across the Havel. This, linked with bus #134 from Alt-Kladow on the opposite side of the lake, is a picturesque way of getting to Spandau. Given these trans-port links it's possible to have a good day out by picking a museum to visit in Dahlem, going for a short hike in the Grunewald, then rounding the day off with a visit to Spandau's Zitadelle. Alternatively, you can try a programme offered by the private boat trips on the Havel, summarized on p.35.

Dahlem and around

The suburb of **Dahlem** lies to the southwest of central Berlin in the district of Zehlendorf, a neat village-like enclave that feels a world away from the technoflash city centre. Mostly residential, it's home to the Free University, the better-off bourgeoisie and an excellent **Dahlem museum complex**, Lansstrasse 8 (Museen Dahlem; Tues–Fri 10am–6pm, Sat & Sun 11am–6pm; €4, free 2–6pm on Thurs; ☏030/8 30 14 38, ☜www.smb.spk-berlin.de),

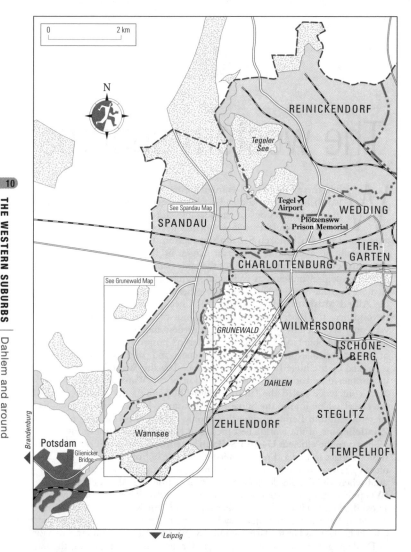

which is clearly signposted from the entrance to U-Bahn Dahlem-Dorf. Here, you'll find the **Museum of Ethnology**, the **Museum of Indian Art**, and the **Museum of East Asian Art**. A block in the opposite direction from the underground station at Im Winkel 6/8 is the **Museum of European Cultures**. For information on day and multi-day tickets that cover all of Berlin's state museums see p.83.

While you're in the vicinity you might like to visit the **Domäne Dahlem**, a working pre-industrial farm-cum-museum, the local parish church **Dorfkirche St Annen** and the city's impressive **Botanical Gardens**. When you've begun to feel heavy on your feet, you should investigate the good beer gardens of the area (see p.240) – popular thanks to the local presence of the Free University's student population.

The Museum of Ethnology

On display at the **Museum of Ethnology** (Ethnologisches Museum) is a small portion – imaginatively and strikingly laid out – of one of the world's most extensive collections of ethnological artefacts. Covering three continents – Asia, Africa and the Americas, plus the Pacific and South Sea Islands – the museum details the varying cultures of dozens of civilizations and ethnic groups, each with their own traditions, religious beliefs and artistic forms. In particular, look out for the dramatically lit group of sailing boats from the South Sea Islands; the huge and macabre engraved stone stele from Guatemala; and the thoughtful exhibition on North American Indians, which not only contains artefacts such as clothing and weapons, but also examples of the non-Indian literature and ephemera – dime novels, advertising signs, rodeo posters and the like – that created many of our perceptions of indigenous American life. Equally imposing is a wall of painted ceremonial masks from South Asia and an exhibit of huts from Polynesia, Micronesia, New Guinea and New Zealand. But many of the smaller pieces, such as bronzes from Benin and carved figures from Central America, are also captivating.

The Museums of Indian Art and East Asian Art

Exceptional, too, is the **Museum of Indian Art** (Museum für Indische Kunst), with its assortment of intricate bronze, wood or jade religious sculptures. Many of these crafted pieces are from the Buddhist temples and monasteries that lined the northern Silk Route, and indeed religious art naturally comprises the great bulk of the collection. There is, however, an intriguing series of miniature paintings on display, in which the artists were clearly free to explore more secular themes; with subjects such as court scenes and nature studies, the works are characterized by a certain informality and playfulness.

The **Museum of East Asian Art** (Museum für Ostasiatische Kunst) concentrates on art from China, Japan and Korea, devoting separate sections to each of these countries. The collections of calligraphy from China and Japanese woodcuts are particularly impressive, but other exhibits worth seeking out are a stunning seventeenth-century gold and lacquer throne inlaid with mother-of-pearl, and a Japanese tearoom, built by Japanese carpenters as part of the museum's recent renovations.

The Museum of European Cultures

A short signposted walk down Archivstrasse directly opposite U-Bahn Dahlem brings you to the modest **Museum of European Cultures**, Im Winkel 6, (Museum Europäischer Kulturen; ☎030/83 90 12 87), which uses its collection of handicrafts, paintings, prints and the like to put together changing exhibitions on subjects such as religious practices, handicrafts, modernization and commerce, of the regional and national cultures of the continent. Generally the collection is strongest in representing German culture, though typically exhibitions also include plenty of French and Russian artefacts.

The Domäne Dahlem and Dorfkirche St Annen

Just west of and over the road from Dahlem U-Bahn station, the working farm and handicrafts centre **Domäne Dahlem**, Königin-Luise-Strasse 49 (Mon & Wed–Sun 10am–6pm; €1.50; ☎030/8 32 50 00, ⓦwww.snafu.de/~domaene-dahlem), attempts to show the skills and crafts of the pre-industrial age. The old estate house has a few odds and ends, most interesting of which are the thirteenth-century swastikas, but the collection of agricultural instruments in an outbuilding is better, with some good early twentieth-century inducements to farmers from grain manufacturers. Elsewhere are demonstrations of woodcarving, wool and cotton spinning and various other farm crafts, but it's best to come at the weekend, when some of the old agricultural machinery is fired up and the animals are paraded round – call first to see what's on.

A little further down Königin-Luise-Strasse, at no. 55, is the **Dorfkirche St Annen**, a pretty little brick-built church that dates back to 1220. If it's open (officially Mon, Wed & Sat 2–5pm, but seemingly random), pop in for a glimpse of the Baroque pulpit and gallery, and carved wooden altar. If not, content yourself with the old gravestones.

The Botanical Gardens

Another way to escape the cultural overload in Dahlem is to catch the #183 bus heading east to the **Botanical Gardens**, Königin-Luise-Strasse 6–8 (daily: 9am–dusk or 9pm; greenhouse closes 30min before garden; €5; ⊛www.bgbm .org; S-Bahn Botanischer Garten), where you'll find palatial, sticky hothouses sprouting every plant you've ever wondered about (some 18,000 species, including several gruesome fly-eating plants, lots of vicious-looking cacti, and a huge variety of tulips), enticingly laid-out gardens and an uninspiring **Botanical Museum** (daily 10am–6pm; €2).

The Grunewald and the Havel

Few people associate Berlin with hikes through dense woodland or swimming from crowded beaches, though that's just what the **Grunewald** forests and the adjacent **Havel** lakes have to offer. In all, the Grunewald makes up around 32 square kilometres of mixed woodland between the suburbs of Dahlem and Wilmersdorf. More than two thirds were cut down in the postwar years for badly needed fuel, but subsequent replanting has replaced pine and birch with oak and made it more attractive and popular with Berliners for its bracing air and walks.

The eastern edge of the Grunewald, where the wealthy suburbs of Zehlendorf begin, is dotted with a series of modest but unusual **museums** that can be combined with time spent hiking in the forest to make a pleasant well-rounded day out. The museums include the **Brücke Museum**, which showcases German Expressionism, the **Jagdschloss Grunewald** with its small collection of old masters, the **Allied Museum**, which has important relics of Cold War Berlin, and the **Museumsdorf Düppel**, which re-creates medieval village life.

All these museums are connected with the city centre by bus #115 which can be picked up at the U-Bahn stations Günzelstrasse and Fehrberliner Platz and S-Bahn station Hohenzollern. But for those who fancy a pleasant lakeside walk through the forest, a better way is via **Grunewald S-Bahn station**. The flat forty-five-minute walk to the Jagdschloss Grunewald follows Fontanestrasse to its intersection with Königsalle then turns southwest (right) down this road before heading into the forest on a broad track opposite the police station at the bottom of the hill.

The other main cluster of attractions in the Grunewald is at its southern edge – around the **Wannsee** lake, known for its large sand beach and forming an idyllic backdrop for the agreeable landscaped island **Pfaueninsel** and the **Wannsee Villa**, where one of Berlin's most sinister events took place at

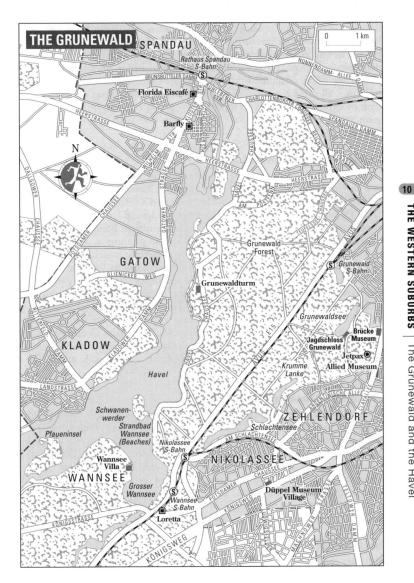

the Wannsee conference when the Nazis decided the fate of Europe's Jews, remembered today in an excellent exhibition. All these Wannsee-area attractions are reachable by bus from S-Bahn Wannsee.

The Brücke Museum

Bus 115 stops at Pücklerstrasse, just outside the **Brücke Museum**, Bussardsteig 9 (Mon, Wed–Sun 11am–5pm; €4 ⓦwww.bruecke-museum .de), which displays German Expressionist works by the group known as Die

Brücke ("The Bridge"), who worked in Dresden and Berlin from 1905 to 1913, and whose work was banned by the Nazis. The big names are Kirchner, Heckel and Schmidt-Rottluff, who painted Expressionist cityscapes – using rich colours and playful perspectives – and who had a large influence on later artists. Many of their works were destroyed during the war, making this collection all the more interesting. The museum's exhibitions change every sixth months, but always try to include early and later works from the movement, which is considered to have come into its own with its own distinctive style after 1909.

Jagdschloss Grunewald

From the Brücke Museum it's a ten-minute walk west along Pücklerstrasse into the depths of the Grunewald and the royal hunting lodge **Jagdschloss Grunewald**, Hüttenweg 10 (mid-May to mid-Oct Tues–Sun 10am–5pm; mid-Oct to mid-May Sun tours at 11am, 1pm & 3pm; €2; ☎030/9 69 42 02), built in the sixteenth century and enlarged by Friedrichs I and II. Today it's a museum housing old furniture; Dutch and German paintings, including works by Cranach the Elder and Rubens; and a small hunting museum in the outbuildings. Additionally, the Jagdschloss grounds are regularly used for concerts on summer evenings. But in truth it's more refreshing to walk by the adjacent lake **Grunewaldsee** than see the collections, though at weekends it can be too busy with dog-walkers to be relaxing. The Jagdschloss is a good starting point for longer hikes into the Grunewald: a forty-five-minute ramble along the eastern side of the Grunewaldsee brings you to S-Bahn Grunewald (see p.190); or you can walk south to U-Bahn Krumme Lanke in about an hour, crossing Hutten Weg and then Onkel-Tom-Strasse to then walk around the shores of Krumme Lanke lake.

The Allied Museum

If you would rather see another museum than explore the Grunewald, and you have an interest in Cold War Berlin, you should walk fifteen minutes southeast of the Jadgschloss Grunewald along Im Jagen to the **Allied Museum**, Clayallee 135 (Alliierten Museum; Mon, Tues & Thurs–Sun 10am–6pm; free; ⊕www.alliiertenmuseum.de). The highlights here are a segment of the Wall, a guardtower, and, most impressively, the original Checkpoint Charlie guardpost. The rest of the museum delivers a well-presented, but nevertheless somewhat turgid exhibition on Cold War Berlin, enlivened only occasionally by a spy story.

Museumsdorf Düppel

You can see a Berlin of a very different sort at the reconstructed medieval country village **Museumsdorf Düppel**, Clauertstrasse 11 (April–Oct Thurs 3–7pm, Sun & holidays Sun 10am–5pm; €2; ☎030/8 02 66 71; ⊕www .dueppel.de; bus #115 to Ludwigsfelderstrasse), in the far southwest edge of the city. The open-air museum attempts to give an impression of what things might have looked like hereabouts 800 years ago with its dozen thatched buildings built on the actual site of a twelfth–century settlement. Here traditional local breeds of sheep are reared and old strains of rye grown, and demonstrations of handicrafts and farming techniques from the Middle Ages take place. If you've still time and energy afterwards, explore the surrounding, attractive and little-visited Düppel Forest.

Wannsee

Of the many lakes which dot, surround and generally enhance the Grunewald, the best known is the **Wannsee**. The main attraction here is the **Strandbad Wannsee**, a kilometre-long strip of pale sand that's the largest inland beach in Europe, and one that's packed as soon as the sun comes out. From here it's easy to wander into the forests and to smaller, less populated beaches along the lakeside road **Havelchaussee**. The main tourist destination around the Wannsee is, however, the **Wannsee villa**, the venue for the Wannsee Conference in which the Nazis elected to send millions of Jews to gas chambers as a "final solution". The villa is now a memorial, with its exhibition remembering the conference and giving an overview of the atrocities. A useful nearby pick-me-up comes in the form of the infinitely more pleasant **Pfaueninsel**, an island that was once the playground of royals and is now a bucolic park in which peacocks roam.

Most destinations around the Wannsee are best reached by **public transport** from S-Bahn Wannsee, whence various buses radiate. The only exception to this is the Strandbad Wannsee which is a ten-minute walk from S-Bahn Nikolassee Station, one stop earlier on the line from the city centre. Cross the main road outside S-Bahn Wannsee and you're a couple of minutes' walk through a park away from regular ferries over to Alt-Kladow (and included in the price of a BVG day-ticket).

Strandbad Wannsee and the Havelchaussee

In essence Berlin's seaside, the **Strandbad Wannsee**, has changed little in character since the drawings of Heinrich Zille sketched the working classes at play here in the late-nineteenth century, with the beach still packed out with all shapes and sizes on every sunny summer day. It's the right place to find a busy commercial beach scene, but if you are looking for a quieter sandy spot by the water, you should head north along the shore, following the **Havelchaussee**. Usefully, bus #218 from S-Bahn Wannsee and Nikolassee goes this way and runs along 6km of sandy coves where there are few facilities. This area is also a good one for a spot of hiking – both along the lakeshore and inland into the forest.

One possible start or terminus of a hike is the **Grunewaldturm** (daily 10am–dusk; €1), an observation tower around 4km north of the Strandbad and right next to the Havel. Built at the end of the nineteenth century as a memorial to Kaiser Wilhelm I, this 55-metre-high tower has a restaurant and fine views out across the lakes.

The Wannsee villa

While it can't be described as the most enjoyable of sights, the one place that should on no account be missed on a trip here is the house overlooking the lake, where, on January 20, 1942, the fate of European Jewry was determined: the **Wannsee villa** at Am Grossen Wannsee 56–58 (Haus der Wannsee Konferenze; Mon–Fri 10am–6pm, Sat & Sun 2–6pm; free; ⊛www.ghwk.de). To get here, catch a #114 bus (about a 5min journey) from S-Bahn Wannsee and get off at "Haus der Wannsee-Konferenz".

The villa, which is entered through strong security gates, contains an exhibition showing the entire process of the Holocaust, from segregation and persecution to the deportation and eventual murder of the Jews from Germany, its allies and all the lands the Third Reich conquered. Each room examines a different part of the process, and there's an English-language translation of the

The Wannsee Conference

The conference at the **Wannsee villa** on January 20, 1942, was held at the instigation of Reinhard Heydrich, Chief of Reich Security Head Office and second only to Himmler. Göring had ordered Heydrich to submit plans for the rounding up, deportation and destruction of the Jews in Reich territory. Heydrich summoned SS and government officials, including Adolf Eichmann and Roland Freisler, later to gain infamy as the judge at the Volksgerichtshof (see Kammergericht, p.145). Eichmann kept a complete set of minutes of the meeting, and these documents, discovered after the war – despite the fact that all recipients had been requested to destroy their copies – played an important part in the later Nürnberg trials of war criminals.

The problem Heydrich delineated was that Europe contained eleven million Jews: the "Final Solution" to the "Jewish Question" was that these people should be taken to camps and worked to death, if they were able-bodied, murdered on arrival if not. Those who survived would eventually be executed, since, under Nazi principles of natural selection, they would be the toughest, and in Heydrich's words could be "regarded as the germ cell of a new Jewish development". In these early stages the systematic killing machines like Auschwitz and Treblinka were not yet fully operational. More discussion was spent on how the Jews should be rounded up: great deception was to be used to prevent panic and revolt, and the pretence that Jews were being moved for "resettlement" was extremely important. Heydrich charged Eichmann with this task, a job that would eventually cost him his life when he was sentenced to death for war crimes in Israel in 1960.

At no time during the conference were the words "murder" or "killing" written down, only careful euphemisms to shield the enormity of what was being planned. Reading through the minutes (copies are kept in the villa's library), it's difficult not to be shocked by the matter-of-fact manner in which the day's business was discussed, the way in which politeness and efficiency absorb and absolve all concerned. When sterilization was suggested as one "solution", it was rejected as "unethical" by a doctor present; and there was much self-congratulation as various officials described their areas as "Judenfrei" (free of Jews).

Heydrich himself died following an assassination attempt in Prague a few months later; some of the others present did not survive the war either, but, in contrast to the millions who were destroyed by their organizational ability, many of the Wannsee delegation lived on to gain a pension from the postwar German state.

exhibits available from the ticket desk. Inevitably, it's deeply moving: many of the photographs and accounts are horrific, and the events they describe seem part of a world far removed from the quiet suburban backwater of Wannsee – which, in many ways, underlines the tragedy. Particularly disturbing is the photograph of four generations of women – babe-in-arms, young mother, grandmother and ancient great-grandmother – moments before their execution on a sand dune in Latvia.

The room where the conference took place is kept as it was, with documents from the meeting on the table and photographs of participants ranged around the walls, their biographies showing that most lived on to comfortable old age. Even fifty years after the event, to stand in the room where the decision was finally formalized to coldly and systematically annihilate a race of people brings a shiver of fear and rage. The vast scale of the Holocaust sometimes makes it hard to grasp the full enormity of the crime: looking into the faces of the guilty, and then of those they destroyed, makes the crimes more immediate.

The villa also has a library containing reference material such as autobiographies, first-hand accounts, slides, newspapers and much else concerning the Holocaust and the rise of neo-fascist groups across Europe.

The Pfaueninsel

Originally designed as a royal fantasy getaway on one of the largest of the Havel islands, the **Pfaueninsel** (Peacock Island; daily: May–Aug 8am–8pm; April & Sept 9am–6pm; Oct 9am–5pm; Nov–March 10am–4pm; ferry €1 ⓦwww.spsg.de) is now a conservation zone with a flock of peacocks scattered around its landscaped park. No cars are allowed on the island (nor, incidentally, are dogs, ghetto-blasters or smoking), which is accessed by a regular passenger ferry from the terminus of bus #316 which shuttles to and fro from S-Bahn Wannsee. The island's attractions include a mini-Schloss, built by Friedrich Wilhelm II for his mistress and today containing a small **museum** (April–Oct Tues–Sun 10am–5pm; €2). Most enjoyable, though, are the gardens, landscaped by Peter Lenné, the original designer of the Tiergarten. The Pfaueninsel was a favourite party venue for the Nazis: in the 1930s, Joseph Goebbels, minister of propaganda, hosted a massive "Italian evening" here for over a thousand guests, including many famous German film stars and celebrities of the day and hundreds of foreign visitors including British MPs.

Spandau

SPANDAU, situated on the confluence of the Spree and Havel rivers, about 10km as the crow flies northwest of the city centre, is Berlin's oldest suburb. Granted a town charter in 1232, it managed to escape the worst of the wartime bombing, preserving a couple of old village-like streets – at their best during the Christmas market – and an ancient moated fort, the **Zitadelle**. But the word Spandau immediately brings to mind the name of its jail's most famous – indeed in later years only – prisoner, **Rudolf Hess**. However, there's little connection between Hess and Spandau itself. The jail, 4km away from the centre on Wilhelmstrasse, was demolished after his death to make way for a supermarket for the British armed forces.

The Altstadt

Spandau's **Altstadt** or old town is of minor interest but worth the ten-minute walk through that it takes to get to the Citadel, particularly if you've arrived at S-Bahn Spandau or the bus stop Rathaus Spandau where the #134 from Alt Kladow stops. The Altstadt begins just to the northeast of the Rathaus and is at its best around the **Nikolaikirche**, which dates from the Middle Ages; the Reformationsplatz (where there's a good *Konditorei*), where playful sculptures adorn the modern marketplace; and in the restored street called **Kolk** (turn

---

Rudolf Hess (1894–1987)

Rudolf Hess marched in the Munich Beer Hall *Putsch* of 1923 and was subsequently imprisoned with Hitler in Landsberg jail, where he took the dictation of *Mein Kampf*. For a time he was the **deputy leader** of the Nazi party, second only to the Führer himself. An experienced World War I airman, he flew himself to Scotland in 1941, ostensibly in an attempt to sue for peace with King George VI and ally Great Britain with Germany against the Soviet Union. It remains unclear whether he did this with Hitler's blessing, but there is evidence to suggest that the Führer knew of Hess's plans. Either way, he was immediately arrested and Churchill refused to meet him; he was held until he was sentenced to life imprisonment at the Nürnberg trials. He finally committed suicide in 1987 in his Spandau jail – the only inmate in a jail designed for six hundred – hanging himself on a short piece of lamp flex, aged 93.

△ Peacock, Peacock Island

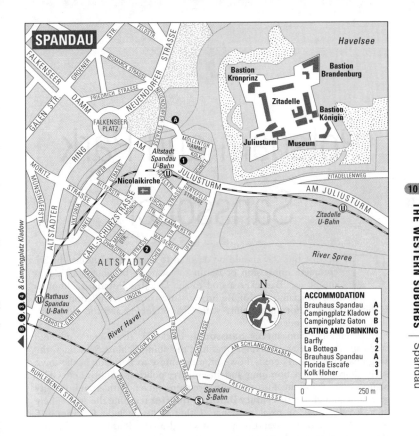

ACCOMMODATION
Brauhaus Spandau	A
Campingplatz Kladow	C
Campingplatz Gaton	B

EATING AND DRINKING
Barfly	4
La Bottega	2
Brauhaus Spandau	A
Florida Eiscafe	3
Kolk Hoher	1

right off Am Juliusturm, opposite Breite Strasse). Also here is the **Brauhaus**, Neuendorfer Strasse 1, a nineteenth-century brewery that produces beer to a medieval recipe, and has tours explaining the brewing process.

The Zitadelle

The postcard-pretty **Zitadelle** (Citadel; Tues–Fri 9am–5pm, Sat & Sun 10am–5pm; €2.50; U-Bahn Zitadelle), just northeast over the Havel from the Altstadt, was established in the twelfth century to defend the town. Its moat and russet walls were built during the Renaissance by an Italian architect and it's an explorable, if not totally engrossing, place with a small local history museum, a pricey restaurant and the thirteenth-century **Juliusturm**, from which there's a good view over the ramshackle Zitadelle interior and the surrounding countryside.

Potsdam and Park Sanssouci

"The first fine day should be devoted to Potsdam, without which a complete impression of Berlin can scarcely be obtained," claims the prewar Baedeker, a nod to the fact that **Potsdam**, although not officially part of Berlin, was the natural completion of the Hohenzollern city, forming a unity with Charlottenburg and the old centre along Unter den Linden.

Above all, Potsdam means **Sanssouci**, Frederick the Great's splendid landscaped park of architectural treasures, including Schloss Sanssouci, the king's palace retreat. There is, however, much more to Potsdam: in the town itself, despite Allied bombing and insensitive, politically motivated GDR planners, much of the historic centre remains intact, with grandiose city gates and an eighteenth-century **Baroque quarter** recalling the atmosphere of a *Residenzstadt* or royal residence. Other sights include **Cecilienhof**, where the fate of postwar Europe was sealed at the Potsdam conference; **Russische Kolonie Alexandrowka**, a nineteenth-century Russian collection of timber houses overlooked by an Orthodox chapel; the **Pfingstberg**, with its forlorn Jewish cemetery and ruined Belvedere; another Schloss across the River Havel in **Babelsberg**, which also boasts a film studio prominent in the history of German cinema; and myriad smaller attractions in between.

Though Potsdam makes for a good day out from Berlin, you'll probably find that you need two or three days to take everything in, so practical details and listings are in this chapter.

Potsdam

Like most towns in the Berlin area, **POTSDAM**'s origins are Slavonic and its first documented mention was as Poztupimi during the tenth century, making it older than Berlin by a couple of hundred years. In 1160 a castle was built here, marking the first step in the town's gradual transformation from fishing backwater, though for the next couple of centuries it remained a relatively sleepy place.

Under the Hohenzollerns, Potsdam became a **royal residence** and **garrison town**, roles which it enjoyed right up until the abdication of Kaiser Wilhelm II in 1918. World War II left Potsdam badly damaged: on April 14, 1945, a bombing raid killed four thousand people and reduced the town centre to ruins, destroying many fine Baroque buildings (the raid was so heavy that it could be heard and seen from Bernau, over 40km to the northeast). Immediately after the war, Potsdam was chosen by the victorious Allies as the venue for a conference where, on August 2, 1945, the division of Germany and Europe was confirmed. Subsequently, under the SED regime, it was decided to demolish the ruins of much of the old town and undertake extensive modern building programmes in pursuit of a "new, socialist Potsdam". These account for the unattractive and confused appearance of the eastern half of the town centre, and although attempts were made to preserve the architectural integrity of the town during the 1980s, the Communists always felt ill at ease with its historical role and Imperial associations.

With the opening of the border in 1989, Potsdam's links with the rest of Berlin were once again revived, and it has since traded well on its tourist appeal. The influx of cash has allowed the town to be polished up considerably, not least through the destruction of the surrounding red-brick *Uhlan* barracks that used to house Russian soldiers. Nevertheless, it's surprising how many dilapidated buildings remain; capitalist élan will no doubt soon refurbish – or remove – even these structures, but for now they stand as reminders of the long historical road trodden by the city.

Arrival, getting around and information

Excellent transport links from Berlin mean visiting Potsdam couldn't be easier. The frequent **S-Bahn** S1 takes around 40 minutes to get here from Berlin's Bahnhof Friedrichstrasse, or you can take the S7 to Wannsee from Bahnhof Zoo and change to the S1 there. A more atmospheric approach is provided by the cruise boats from Wannsee (see pp.35–36).

S-Bahn trains, like regional trains, arrive in Potsdam's Hauptbahnhof which incorporates a sizeable mall. The southern entrance delivers you to the city's main bus station, where you should pick up **bus** #695 run by the Verkehrsbetrieb Potsdam (ViP; ⊛www.vip-potsdam.de) if you wish to hightail it straight to Park Sanssouci. If you're bound for the town centre, you could take **tram** #92 from the Hauptbahnhof's west entrance, though it might be quicker and more interesting to simply head north for ten minutes' **walk** across the Lange Brücke into the centre of town. Use of Potsdam's local bus and tram services is covered by a zone C BVG day ticket, making this the most economical way to get here and around. But the most interesting, rewarding and practical way to explore Potsdam is to rent a **bike**. Sturdy urban models can be hired from Rebhah Rent-a-Bike (⊕0331/27 06 210; daily Mon–Fri 9am–7pm, Sat & Sun 9am–8pm; €11/day), a friendly company operating out of a container in a park outside the Hauptbahnhof's northern entrance. They will happily mark a good seventeen-kilometre route on a free map that takes in all the main sites in a day.

Just north of the Lange Brücke is Potsdam's well-equipped **tourist office**, at Friedrich-Ebert-Strasse 5 (April–Oct Mon–Fri 9.30am–6pm, Sat & Sun 9.30am–4pm; Nov–March Mon–Fri 10am–6pm, Sat & Sun 9.30am–2pm; ⊕0331/27 55 80; ⊛www.potsdamtourismus.de). It can furnish you with maps, multilingual information and can book accommodation.

Accommodation

Ideally, you should spend at least a couple of days in Potsdam, though local accommodation can be hard to come by in summer. If you're on a budget the best bet is to book a **private room** (around €30–55) through the tourist office (see p.199). Alternatively, you could try a large **hostel** – **Jugendgästehaus Siebenschläfer**, Lotte-Puewka-Str. 43 (☏0331/74 11 25, ⊛www.jgh-potsdam .de), located on the Babelsberg side of the Havel, is a fifteen-minute walk from the Hauptbahnhof: take the north exit and head east down Babelsberger Strasse to Lotte-Puewka-Str. Dorms start at €12 per night in high season, doubles for €30. The closest **campsite** is *Campingpark Sanssouci Gaisberg*, An der Pirschheide 1 (☏0331/9 51 09 88, ⊛www.campingpark-sanssouci-potsdam .com), just south of Potsdam and connected to the city centre by tram #94.

Hotels and Pensions

Apartment-Hotel Bornimer Hof Rückerstr. 31 ☏0331/54 96 60, ⊛www .apartmenthotel-bornimerhof.de. A hotel complex offering two-room suites and bungalows, some quite spacious, in a very quiet wooded setting north of town. Wide range of prices depending on size of apartment and its facilities. ❷
Froschkasten Kiezstr. 4 ☏0331/29 13 15. No-nonsense pine-furnished en-suite doubles above an inn, with a decent restaurant (see p.205), on the edge of the town centre. ❸
Mercure Potsdam Lange Brücke ☏0331/27 22, ⊛www.mercure.com. A typical GDR-era high-rise with central location, good views over town and standard hotel rooms. ❹

Schloss Cecilienhof Im neuen Garten ☏0331/29 24 98, ⊛www.relexa-hotels .de. Housed in a wing of Schloss Cecilienhof (see p.215), this is the place to head for if you want a little luxury. Rooms have touches of old-fashioned class and pleasant views over the surrounding park and garden. Rates start at €242 and include an excellent buffet breakfast. ❾
Schlossgarten Hotel Geschwister-Scholl-Str. 41a ☏0331/97 17 00, ⊛www.schloss -gartenhotel-garni.de. Plain but pleasant new hotel in a leafy suburb beside Sanssouci Park. Prices include a good buffet breakfast. ❺

The Altstadt

Walking from the railway station across the Lange Brücke to the **Altstadt**, you'll pass high above the **Freundschafts Insel**, a leafy mid-Havel island which makes a good place to take a break from street-pounding, with its ornamental garden and boat rental facilities. But it's the buildings ahead, around the triangular plaza **Alter Markt**, which will draw your attention, with the stately domed **Nikolaikirche** and the startlingly unattractive, GDR-era *Hotel Mercure* both arresting, albeit in starkly different ways. Between the two, in a modern building that's another representative of the high-rise chicken-coop school of GDR architecture, is Potsdam's **tourist office** (see p.199). Far more attractive are the dignified old royal stables, the **Marstall**, across the road from the tourist office, which house Potsdam's worthwhile **Filmmuseum**. From the Marstall you can head west along **Breite Strasse** to a few minor attractions in what was once the heart of Potsdam's old town – including Potsdam's reasonable **natural history museum** and an ornate **pump house** – or head deeper into the modern centre of town, via a handful of Altstadt relics in and around **Am Neuen Markt** and the soulless **Platz der Einheit**.

The Nikolaikirche and around

Though the most elegant form in Postdam's riverside skyline, the Neoclassical lines of the **Nikolaikirche** (Mon 2–5pm, Tues–Sat 10am–5pm, Sun 11.30am–5pm) are at dramatic odds with its surroundings. It was originally built according to plans drawn up by Schinkel, and the impact of its exterior is echoed within – the walls are decorated with paintings of New Testament scenes and the effect of the dome is, if anything, more impressive than from the outside. Much of what can be seen, however, is a restoration, as the church was very badly damaged during the war.

The **obelisk** in front of the church was designed by Knobelsdorff and in its original form bore four reliefs depicting the Great Elector and his successors. When it was re-erected during the 1970s these were replaced with reliefs of architects whose work did much to shape Potsdam: Schinkel, Knobelsdorff, Gontard and Persius. Beside it and the Nikolaikirche is Potsdam's former **Rathaus** (daily Tues–Sun 10am–6pm; free), which was built in Palladian Classical style during the mid-eighteenth century, when it must have represented something of a departure for Brandenburg's municipal architecture. Until 1875 the circular Rathaus tower, on top of which a gilded Atlas supports the globe, served as the town jail. The Rathaus lost its town-hall function in 1885, and was taken over by a bank, which remained there until the bombs came. Under the old authorities the building became a *Kulturhaus* or arts centre, a role it retains to this day.

The Marstall and the Filmmuseum

Across the main road, Friedrich-Ebert-Strasse, from the Nikolaikirche, lies the squat but elegant **Marstall**, the oldest town-centre survivor. Originally built as an orangerie towards the end of the eighteenth century and converted into a stables by that scourge of frivolity, Friedrich Wilhelm I, the building owes its subsequent appearance to Knobelsdorff, who extended and prettified it during the eighteenth century.

Today the Marstall houses Potsdam's **Filmmuseum**, Breite Strasse 1a (daily 10am–6pm; €3, special exhibits €5; ☎0331/2 71 81 12, ⊛www.filmmuseum -potsdam.de), visits to which can make for an interesting hour or so. Drawing on material from the UFA studios in nearby Babelsberg (later DEFA, the GDR state film company), the museum presents both a technical and artistic history of German film from 1895 to 1980, with some particularly fascinating material concerning the genres of the immediate postwar period. There's a vaguely hands-on feel, with a few visitor-operated bioscopes and numerous screens playing clips. The museum **cinema** is the best in Potsdam and there's also a good **café**.

The Stadtschloss

If you think the area around the Alter Markt looks a bit incomplete with the Nikolaikirche on one side and the Marstall on the other, then you'd be right, since the *Hotel Mercure* stands on the site of the **Stadtschloss** that completed the picture here until World War II. This Baroque residence was built at the behest of the Great Elector between 1662 and 1669 but was reduced to a bare, roofless shell in 1945. Demolition of its last skeletal remains in 1960 then removed the last vestiges of what, judging by prewar photographs, was a not unappealing building, although a number of its statues have since been discovered languishing in a local wood. Like the royal palace in eastern Berlin, the Stadtschloss, with its Hohenzollern connections, was an embarrassment to the communist authorities – so they quite simply erased it.

Along Breite Strasse

Traffic from the Alter Markt surges west along the broad bleak **Breite Strasse**, which is today lined with such dreary modern buildings that at first glance it's hard to believe the road linked some of Potsdam's quaintest corners. But before the war Breite Strasse was the town's main promenade and one of its premier landmarks was the **Garnisonkirche**, which lay on a site a little to the west of the Marstall now occupied by a prefabricated office building. This Baroque garrison church was the last resting place of many prominent members of the Hohenzollern family and the place where on March 23, 1933, the Reichstag was reconvened following the fire and the subsequent elections that had given the Nazis a small majority (see p.303). The building was later wrecked during the bombing, and its burnt-out shell finally demolished in 1968, despite protest from both home and abroad – like the Stadtschloss, a victim of the old regime's discomfort with relics of the Prussian and Imperial German past.

Also vanished from the town plan is the **Stadtkanal** or city canal, a tree-lined remnant of a fortification system that once ran around the core of old Potsdam, following modern Dortustrasse, turning east into Yorckstrasse, and then running the length of Am Kanal. An address here was highly desirable, despite the stench from the stagnant waters, but in 1972 public hygiene won the day and the canal was filled in. Just west of the point where Breite Strasse intersects with Dortustrasse is the **Militärwaisenhaus**, a late eighteenth-century military orphanage that looks positively palatial, despite the fact that it's obviously lost its dome. The present building replaced an earlier half-timbered one and its main purpose was to provide a home for the illegitimate offspring of grenadiers and local girls.

A little further along is the **Naturkundemuseum**, Breite Strasse 13 (Tues–Sun & first Mon of each month 9am–5pm; €2, free first Mon of each month; ☎0331/2 89 67 07), Potsdam's reasonably good natural history museum, whose strong point is its aquariums of local aquatic life. The museum building was constructed in 1769 with the architecture of Whitehall in London as its model, at the instigation of Friedrich II.

From here it's worth making a quick detour down **Kiezstrasse**, where a number of eighteenth-century Rococo houses have been beautifully restored, including no. 4 which houses *Der Froschkasten*, a traditional, and recommended *Kneipe*. The nearby high-rises on the Neustädter Havelbucht don't compare very favourably, but do hide in their midst the **Dampf-maschinenhaus** (guided tours mid-May to mid-Oct Sat & Sun 10am–5pm; €2), which ranks as the most imaginative pump house in Germany. At first sight it looks like a mosque, which is what the architect, Ludwig Persius, intended when he built it at the beginning of the 1840s. The chimney takes the form of a minaret, and the striped stonework and tiling look wildly incongruous. The pump originally supplied water to a reservoir on the Ruinenberg hill near Sanssouci.

Am Neuen Markt and Platz der Einheit

Along with the Breite Strasse, the other main road out of Alter Markt is Friedrich-Ebert-Strasse, which heads north into the centre of present-day Potsdam. En route and just off the main drag, you can find a few tangible vestiges of old Potsdam. **Am Neuen Markt**, in particular, has a couple of good-looking survivors. These include, on its west side behind the *Waage* restaurant, some improbably grand (but decrepit) eighteenth-century coaching stables with an entrance in the form of a triumphal arch, which are now home to a haulage firm. At Am Neuen Markt 1 is the **Kabinetthaus**, a small mansion that was the birthplace of Friedrich Wilhelm II, the only member of the Hohenzollern family actually born in Potsdam. Take a look too at Werner-Seelenbinder-Strasse, at the southern end of Am Neuen Markt, where the Baroque buildings on the north side of the street are stunning, especially so in contrast to the dreary modern structures on the south side – old and new Potsdam in microcosm. **Yorckstrasse**, just to the north of Am Neuen Markt, also boasts a number of fine **Baroque houses**, as does **Wilhelm-Staab-Strasse**.

Just to the east **Platz der Einheit** is modern Potsdam's largest square, but few non-concrete buildings survive in its immediate vicinity. The fancy-looking building at the southeast corner of the square is a neo-Baroque **post office**, to the immediate north of which stood the Wilhelm III Synagogue until it was wrecked on *Kristallnacht*, and later completely demolished – a plaque marks the spot. From the square's southeast corner Am Kanal runs east, but only a few ailing eighteenth-century townhouses survive here despite this area technically being the oldest part of Potsdam: at the southern end of Fischerstrasse is the site of what was once the Slavonic island settlement of Poztupimi, the forerunner of the modern town.

The Baroque quarter and the Holländisches Viertel

North of the Platz der Einheit, the area bounded by Schopenhauerstrasse, Hegelallee, Hebbelstrasse and Charlottenstrasse is Potsdam's **Baroque quarter**, built between 1732 and 1742 on the orders of Friedrich Wilhelm I. **Bassinplatz**, though disfigured by a huge modern bus station, offers the best introduction to this episode of Potsdam's architectural history. At the southeastern corner of the square is the **Französische Kirche**, completed according to plans by Knobelsdorff in 1753, in imitation of the Pantheon in Rome, a recurring theme in German architecture of the period. At its western end, Bassinplatz is graced by the nineteenth-century **Peter-Pauls-Kirche**, a replica of the campanile of San Zeno Maggiore in Verona, and the first large Catholic church to be built in the town.

The main concentration of ornate Baroque houses, built with slight variations in detail to avoid monotony, lies to the west of here, on and around **Brandenburger Strasse**, Potsdam's pedestrianized main shopping street. The whole quarter was intended as a settlement for trades people in the then rapidly expanding town. Some 584 houses were built in all, and this area, unlike the Altstadt, survived the war substantially intact. Turning into Lindenstrasse from Brandenburger Strasse, the Dutch-style former **Kommandantenhaus**, at nos. 54–55, is a building with uncomfortably recent historical associations: until the *Wende* it served as a Stasi detention centre known as the "Lindenhotel". Handed over to the embryonic political opposition groups in November 1989, it now houses **Gedenkstätte Lindenstrasse** (Tues–Thurs & first and third Sat of the month 9am–5pm; €0.50), part of the Potsdam Museum, with an exhibition on the history of the building: it was used as a Nazi "hereditary-health court", which made decisions about compulsory sterilization, and a prison for the Nazi "Peoples' Court", before its more recent function – viewing the cells in the back building is a chilling experience.

To the north and west of the Baroque quarter are the most impressive of Potsdam's three surviving town gates – the **Jägertor** or "Hunter's Gate" (at the end of Lindenstrasse), surmounted by a sculpture of a stag succumbing to a pack of baying hounds, and the **Brandenburger Tor** (at the western end of Brandenburger Strasse), a triumphal arch built by Gontard in 1733, with a playfulness lacking in its Berlin namesake.

The Holländisches Viertel

Just to the north of Bassinplatz is the **Holländisches Viertel** or "Dutch quarter", the best-known and most appealing part of Friedrich Wilhelm I's town extension. In the area bounded by Gutenbergstrasse, Kurfürstenstrasse, Friedrich-Ebert-Strasse and Hebbelstrasse are 134 gabled, red-brick houses put up by Dutch builders for immigrants from Holland who were invited to work in Potsdam by the king. In fact, not many Dutch took up the invitation and many of those who did returned home when the promised employment dried up following Friedrich Wilhelm's death, allowing Germans to move into their houses.

Under the old regime it was decided to renovate the quarter, which even at the time of its building was recognized as one of the most attractive in the town. Restoration work has so far been only a partial success: modern builders lacked the skills to restore the carved gables, and bad planning meant that in some cases inhabitants were moved out but work was never started. As a result, a few of the houses look derelict, but some excellent restored examples can be found along **Mittelstrasse**, particularly at the junction with Benkertstrasse. Mittelstrasse has been gentrified to a large extent, with a number of trendy shops and cafés attracting both locals and tourists. Finally, at the top of Friedrich-Ebert-Strasse, at the northwestern corner of the Holländisches Viertel, is the **Nauener Tor**, a stylistically messy-looking town gate inspired by English architectural trends of the mid-eighteenth century.

Eating, drinking and nightlife

Eating and drinking pose few problems in Potsdam. There's a good array of **restaurants**, and most places are pleasant enough, though few would gain any stars in a gourmet's guide to the Berlin area. In town the major and most convenient concentration of possibilities is along Brandenburger Strasse, although it pays to go a little further afield.

Restaurants

Arco Friedrich-Ebert-Str. ☎0331/2 70 16 90. Small, fancy Italian restaurant occupying the east wing of the Nauener Tor, with some outdoor seating in summer. Serves excellent Pan-Continental food (mains around €9) and a sumptuous Sunday brunch buffet (€8). Daily 10am–3pm, buffet €8.

Café im Filmmuseum Breite Str. 1a ☎0331/2 01 99 96. Atmospheric Lebanese restaurant with a small menu of tasty specialities (starters €6; mains €10) best sampled by ordering a range of smaller dishes to try. A good place to take a break after visiting the museum, for a Lebanese tea or coffee or a suck on the water pipe. Tues–Sun noon–midnight.

Logenhaus Kurfürstenstr. 52 ☎0331/2 37 03 45. In a restored former Freemasons' building, this moderately priced pub-restaurant features German and Mediterranean food – piled high for the excellent Sunday brunch (10am–3pm). The *Happy Hour* bar (see opposite) is in the same

building, enabling a seamless continuation into a night out. Mon–Fri 4pm–midnight, Sat noon–midnight, Sun 10am–midnight.
Seconda Luise Luisenplatz 6 ☏0331/90 36 63. Mid-priced Italian food served in casual surroundings overlooking a plaza and the Brandenburg Gate. If you don't fancy the pasta, pizza and *pesce* served

here, you can pick from other good options alongside – all perfect places to eat before tackling Sanssouci, just up the road. Daily noon–late.
Zur Linde Lindenstr. 50 ☏0331/2 80 50 31. No scene-maker, but a personable and relaxing restaurant with typical German food. Four local beers on tap. Daily noon–late.

Cafés and bars

Babette Brandenburger Str. 71 ☏0331/29 16 48. Pleasant café with outdoor seating in the shade of the Brandenburg gate that's a good place to rest weary feet and have an indulgent *Torte* after trekking around Sanssouci Park. The large menu is also available in English and has a range of simple snacks (€7) and main meals (€9). Mon–Sat 9am–late, Sun 10am–late.
Drachenhaus Maulbeerallee ☏0331/5 05 38 08. Genteel little café in the grounds of Schloss Sanssouci itself, housed in a pagoda-style building once used by royal vintners. You can also eat well here. March–Oct Tues–Sun 11am–7pm, Nov–Feb Tues–Sun 11am–6pm.
Froschkasten Kiezstr. 4 ☏0331/29 13 15. One of the oldest and most authentic bars in Potsdam, this *Kneipe* also serves good traditional German food. They've a good line in fish dishes, too, particularly the grilled salmon fillet (€19). Mon–Sat noon–midnight, Sun noon–10pm.
Happy Hour II Kurfürstenstr. 52. Sports bar in the Logenhaus (see opposite) where you can play pool and darts until the small hours. Daily 5pm–4am.

La Leander Benkertstr. 1 ☏0331/2 70 65 76. Predominantly gay and lesbian bar in the Holländisches Viertel, location for most of Potsdam's hip bars. There's a short menu, with some good sandwiches, but mainly this is a place to come drinking and the cocktails are correspondingly good. 12.30pm–2.30am.
La Madeleine Lindenstr. 9 ☏0331/2 70 54 00. A small creperie featuring over thirty variations – some decidedly odd (chick curry) – of the French speciality. Prices run from €2.50–7.50. Daily noon–10pm.
Lapis Lazuli Benkertstr. 21 ☏0331/2 80 23 71. Hippyish café with old wooden tables and candles. Light snacks only; including the very good tomato and mozzarella baguette (€6). Noon–late.
Matschkes Galerie Café Alleestr. 10 ☏0331/2 80 03 59. A quiet, leafy courtyard provides a wonderfully restful spot to enjoy authentic Russian cuisine. Daily noon–10pm.
Pancha Mama Sellostr. 15a ☏0331/9 67 81 32. High-ceilinged and stylish Spanish café, with excellent tapas €3–5 – choose the fresh mussels when they're offered – and excellent cocktails. Mon–Fri 4pm–late, Sat & Sun noon–late.

Nightlife

For **nightlife** the best bet is the *Lindenpark*, Stahnsdorfer Str. 76–78 (☏0331/74 79 70 ⊛www.lindenpark.de), over in Babelsberg, with regular "alternative" discos and live bands. Also recommended is the *Waschhaus*, Schiffbauergasse 1 (☏0331/2 71 56 26, ⊛www.waschhaus.de), just off Berliner Strasse on the way into town from the Glienicker Brücke, a large complex with live music, galleries and an open-air cinema, often hosting various parties and events. At the same address is *Fabrik* (☏0331/2 80 03 14, ⊛www.fabrikpotsdam.de), a theatre for contemporary dance and music. For German-speakers the Hans-Otto-Theater, Zimmerstrasse 10 (☏0331/9 81 18, ⊛www.hot.potsdam.de), is Potsdam's main **theatre**, with a programme worth investigating. The town also boasts a **cabaret**, the *Kabarett Obelisk*, Schopenhauerstrasse 27 (☏0331/29 10 69, ⊛www.kabarett-potsdam.de).

Park Sanssouci

Park Sanssouci (ⓦwww.spsg.de), Frederick the Great's fabled retreat, stretches out for 2km west of Potsdam town centre, and its gardens and palaces are what draw most visitors to the town. In 1744 Frederick ordered the construction of a residence where he would be able to live "without cares" – "sans souci" in the French spoken in court. The task was entrusted to the architect Georg von Knobelsdorff, who had already proved himself on other projects in Potsdam and Berlin. **Schloss Sanssouci**, on a hill overlooking the town, took three years to complete, while the extensive parklands to the west – the **Rehgarten** – were laid out over the following five years. As a finishing touch Frederick ordered the construction of the **Neues Palais** at the western end of the park, to mark the end of the Seven Years' War. Over the following 150 years or so, numerous additions were made, including the **Orangerie** and the laying of Jubiläumstrasse (now known as Maulbeerallee) just south of the Orangerie in 1913. The park is at its most beautiful in spring, when the trees are in leaf and the flowers in bloom, but these days it's usually overrun by visitors. To avoid the crowds, visit on a weekday, preferably outside summer, when you'll be better able to appreciate the place. The main **visitors' centre**

Frederick the Great

Frederick the Great (1740–1786) had the great misfortune to be born the son of Friedrich Wilhelm I, Brandenburg-Prussia's "Soldier King", a stern militarist whose attitude to his children seems to have been much the same as his attitude to the conscripts in his army. Frederick was subjected to a strict and unforgiving regime from the earliest age. His education included the Lutheran catechism and military drill but precious little else, certainly no hint of the arts or humanities.

Frederick's interest in the latter emerged despite his father's best efforts, leading to conflict between the king and the young crown prince. Friedrich Wilhelm I's odious treatment of his son – he frequently thrashed him and forced him to kiss his boots in public – eventually prompted Frederick to try to flee the country in 1730, enlisting the aid of two friends, Hans Hermann von Katte and Karl Christoph von Keith. At the last moment von Keith hesitated, betraying the conspiracy before escaping himself. Frederick and Katte (with whom the prince had a very close, possibly homosexual, relationship) were arrested and stripped of rank and privileges. Both were court-martialled; Katte was sentenced to two years' imprisonment, but the court declared itself unable to sit in judgement over a crown prince.

At this point the old king intervened to drastic effect. Katte was sentenced to death and Frederick was forced to watch his beheading from his cell, having been led to understand that he too was under sentence of death. When news of his shattered state was conveyed to the king by a priest, the monarch, having achieved his intended effect, granted Frederick a conditional pardon.

As penance and a test of his remorse, Frederick had to serve in his father's civil administration pending restitution of rank and freedom. There was a marked improvement in his circumstances when in 1733 he was sent to the north Brandenburg town of Rheinsberg where, away from his father's hypercritical eyes, he was able to renew his interest in the arts. Only an arranged marriage to Elizabeth Christine, daughter of the Duke of Brunswick-Bevern, blighted what had become a relatively idyllic existence.

In 1740 the king died and Frederick acceded to the throne, much to the delight of the populace, who had been worn down by Friedrich Wilhelm I's austere style (daily: March–Oct 8.30am–5pm; Nov–Feb 9am–4pm) is by the historic windmill (see p.210).

Schloss Sanssouci

To approach **Schloss Sanssouci** as Frederick the Great might have done, make for the eighteenth-century **obelisk** on Schopenhauerstrasse, which marks the main entrance to the park. Beyond, Hauptallee runs through the ornate Knobelsdorff-designed **Obelisk-Portal** – two clusters of pillars flanked by the goddesses Flora and Pomona – to the **Grosse Fontäne**, the biggest of the park's many fountains, around which stands a host of Classical statues, notably those of Venus and Mercury. The approach to the Schloss itself leads up through the Weinbergterrassen, whose terraced ranks of vines are among the northernmost in Germany.

Frederick had very definite ideas about what he wanted and worked closely with Knobelsdorff on the design of his palace, which was to be a place where the king, who had no great love for his capital, Berlin, or his wife Elizabeth Christine, could escape both. It's a surprisingly modest one-storey Baroque affair, topped by an oxidized green dome and ornamental statues, looking out over the vine terraces towards the high-rises of the Neustädter Havelbucht. Freder-

of rule. Initially Frederick lived up to early expectations, abolishing torture and censorship, establishing ostensible freedom of worship, and recalling exiled scholars. With the aid of Voltaire he published his **Antimachiavel**, a treatise expounding a princely ethic based on virtue, justice and responsibility. However, Frederick inclined towards enlightened despotism, and as his rule progressed he introduced increasingly unpopular measures such as the establishment of state monopolies for certain commodities. His first notably un-progressive act, however – the invasion of and subsequent annexation of Silesia – came in 1740 at the very beginning of his reign.

In 1756 Austria, Saxony, France and Russia, alarmed at the growing strength of Prussia, began squaring up for the **Seven Years' War**. Frederick struck first, attacking Saxony, and, though initially successful, was later beaten at the Battle of Kolin. Encouraged, the French invaded Prussia, and, though able to beat them back, Frederick could not prevent military defeat at the Battle of Kunersdorf, after which the Russian army occupied Berlin. With British aid Frederick was able to push out the invaders, gaining important victories in 1760 and 1761, but eventually the war fizzled out with all sides exhausted, and a general peace was concluded in 1763.

Frederick's 1740–1745 acquisitions were confirmed, the Habsburg hold on the now-crumbling Holy Roman Empire had been lessened and Prussia was the leading German state. The remaining 23 years of Frederick's reign were a period of reconstruction, marked by increasing eccentricity on the part of the monarch, who during this period came to be known as **Der alte Fritz** ("Old Fritz"). He retreated to Schloss Sanssouci and, in the company of Voltaire, honed his Francophile tendencies while overseeing the upkeep of his army (and extraction of punitive taxes from his people to finance it).

In 1772 he successfully secured a chunk of Poland for Prussia during the First Partition of that country and in 1777 launched his final military action, an unsuccessful campaign against Bavaria. When he died in 1786, he was, like his father, not mourned.

ick loved the Schloss so much that he intended to be buried here, and had a **tomb** excavated for himself in front of the eastern wing, near the graves of his Italian greyhounds, animals whose company he preferred to that of human beings during the last, increasingly eccentric, years of his life. When he died, however, his nephew Friedrich Wilhelm II had him interred in the Garnisonkirche in Potsdam itself, next to the father Frederick hated. Towards the end of World War II, the remains of Frederick and his father were exhumed and eventually taken to Schloss Hohenzollern in Swabia for safekeeping from the approaching Soviet army. Only in August 1991, after reunification, were the remains returned and buried with much pomp at the site Frederick had chosen. He lies there now, his last resting place marked by a simple stone bearing the terse inscription *Friedrich der Grosse*.

The interior

The interior of Schloss Sanssouci (April–Oct Tues–Sun 9am–5pm; Nov–March Tues–Sun 9am–4pm; €8) can only be visited as part of a **guided tour**. These take place every twenty minutes and tickets for the whole day go on sale at 9am – get there as early as possible, as demand is high.

Once inside the Schloss, you'll find a frenzy of Rococo, spread through the twelve rooms where Frederick lived and entertained his guests – a process that usually entailed quarrelling with them. The most eye-catching rooms are the opulent **Marmorsaal** (Marble Hall) and the **Konzertzimmer** (Concert Room), where the flute-playing king forced eminent musicians to play his own works on concert evenings. Frederick's favourite haunt was his library where, surrounded by his two thousand volumes – mainly French translations of the classics and a sprinkling of contemporary French writings – he could oversee the work on his tomb. One of Frederick's most celebrated house guests was Voltaire, who lived here from 1750 to 1753, acting as a kind of private tutor to the king, finally leaving when he'd had enough of Frederick's bizarre behaviour, damning the king's intellect with faint praise and accusing him of treating "the whole world as slaves". In revenge Frederick ordered that Voltaire's former room be decorated with carvings of apes and parrots.

The **Damenflügel**, the west wing of the Schloss (mid-May to mid-Oct Sat & Sun 10am–5pm; €1), was added in 1840, and its thirteen rooms housed ladies and gentlemen of the court. Nearby on the terrace is a wrought-iron summerhouse protecting a weather-beaten copy of a Classical statue, while just to the south an eighteenth-century sculpture of Cleopatra looks over the graves of Frederick's horses.

Around the Schloss

East of Schloss Sanssouci, overlooking the ornamental Holländischer Garten or Dutch Garden, is the **Bildergalerie** (mid-May to mid-Oct Tues–Sun

---

Combination tickets for Park Sanssouci buildings

If you plan to visit several buildings in the Sanssouci Park, consider getting a **combination ticket**. A **Premium-Tageskarte** (€15; concession €10) allows entry to all buildings in the Park and is available only at Schloss Sanssouci. The regular **Tageskarte** (€12; €9 concessions) is also sold here, as well as at the visitors' centre, and will get you into all buildings in Park Sanssouci except Schloss Sanssouci itself. Despite calling themselves *Tageskarten* (day tickets), both are valid for two consecutive days.

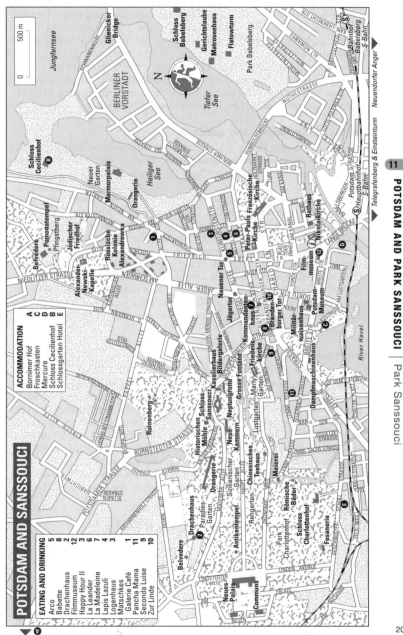

10am–5pm; €2), a restrained Baroque creation, which, it's claimed, was the first building in Europe to be erected specifically as a museum. Unfortunately, wartime destruction and looting scattered the contents, but a new collection was put together after the war, comprising paintings from around the GDR that had survived, including Caravaggio's wonderful *Incredulity of St Thomas* and several works by Rubens and Van Dyck.

Just to the right of the Holländischer Garten is the **Neptungrotte**, a Knobelsdorff-designed architectural oddity: a grotto with a Rococo entrance and a ring of empty statue pediments in front. The statues, representing Moorish figures, are currently in Schloss Sanssouci awaiting renovation.

The Neue Kammern and gardens

On the opposite side of the Schloss, from a point near the Cleopatra statue, steps lead down to the **Neue Kammern** (April to mid-May Sat & Sun 10am–5pm; mid-May to mid-Oct Tues–Sun 10am–5pm; €3), the architectural twin of the Bildergalerie, originally used as an orangerie and later as a guesthouse. Immediately to the west of the Neue Kammern is the prim **Sizilianischer Garten** or Sicilian Garden, crammed with coniferous trees and subtropical plants, complementing the **Nordischer Garten**, another ornamental garden just to the north, whose most interesting feature is the strange-looking **Felsentor** or Rock Gate, a gateway fashioned out of uncut stones and topped by a lumpen-looking eagle with outstretched wings.

Frederick was prepared to go to some lengths to achieve the desired carefree rural ambience for Sanssouci and retained an old wooden windmill as an ornament just north of the Neue Kammern. Four years after his death, this was replaced by a rustic-looking stone construction, the **Historische Mühle**, which is now a restaurant.

The Ruinenberg

The **Ruinenberg**, rising to the north of Schloss Sanssouci, looks like a cluster of Classical ruins, but in fact these fragments are artificial, designed to render a little more interesting a small reservoir built during the eighteenth century to feed the fountains in the park. However, it was a long time before this reservoir fulfilled its purpose, as attempts to fill it with water from the Havel proved fruitless. It worked briefly in 1754 when Frederick the Great (in a characteristic fit of manic inventiveness) allowed it to be filled with snow. When the snow melted the locks were opened and water coursed through the system, giving the fountains in the park a few minutes' life. It wasn't until the building of the mosque-shaped pump house in the town centre that the problem was solved.

The Orangerie to the Neues Palais

From the western corner of the Sizilianischer Garten, **Maulbeerallee** (Mulberry Alley), a road open to traffic, cuts through the park to the ascent of the **Orangerie** (mid-May to mid-Oct Tues–Sun 10am–5pm; €3).

This Italianate Renaissance-style structure with its belvedere towers is perhaps the most visually impressive building in the park, and is certainly more outwardly imposing than the Schloss. A series of terraces, with curved retaining walls sporting waterspouts in the shape of lions' heads, lead up to the sandy-coloured building, whose slightly down-at-heel appearance lends it added character.

It was built at the behest of Friedrich IV and, like the Friedenskirche (see p.212), inspired by the architecture seen on his travels in Italy. The facade is lined with allegorical statues – some of which have been removed for renovation – set in niches, depicting figures like "Industry" holding a cog wheel. The western wing of the building is still used for its original purpose, as a refuge for tropical plants in winter, and during the summer it's possible to ascend the western tower, from where there are great views of the Neues Palais and depressing vistas of Potsdam's high-rises to the east. The Orangerie also houses a gallery, the Raphaelsaal, with copies of paintings looted by Napoleon. Part of the Orangerie is given over to private flats, occupied by members of the park staff – which must be just about the best address in Potsdam.

Below the Orangerie, south of Maulbeerallee, is the Jubiläumsterrasse, with a large goldfish-inhabited pool, beyond which are statues of Mercury and an equestrian Frederick the Great, a replica of the bronze one on Unter den Linden (which incidentally stood for many years in Potsdam).

The Belvedere, Drachenhaus and Antikentempel

From the western wing of the Orangerie, the arrow-straight Krimlindenallee, lined with lime trees, leads up towards a Rococo **Belvedere**, the last building to be built under Frederick the Great. It was the only building in the whole park to suffer serious war damage, but has recently been restored to its former glory. A couple of hundred metres short of the Belvedere, a path branches off to the left, leading to the **Drachenhaus**, a one-time vintner's house built in the style of a Chinese pagoda for the small vineyard nearby. Today there's a genteel café inside, an ideal point to interrupt your wanderings. Southwest of the Drachenhaus, a pathway leads across the park to the **Antikentempel**, originally built in 1768 to house part of the art collection of Frederick the Great. This domed rotunda is now the last resting place of a number of members of the Hohenzollern family, including the Empress Auguste Victoria, and Hermine, the woman Wilhelm II married in exile, who came to be known as the "last Empress".

The Neues Palais

To the west through the trees rises the **Neues Palais** (April–Oct Mon–Thurs, Sat & Sun 9am–5pm; Nov–March Mon–Thurs, Sat & Sun 9am–4pm; €5), another massive Rococo extravaganza from Frederick the Great's time, built between 1763 and 1769 to reaffirm the might of Prussia and its king after the Seven Years' War. At the centre of the palace is a huge green-weathered dome, topped by a crown, while the edges of the roof around the entire building are adorned by lines of Classical figures, specially mass-produced by a team of sculptors to adorn Frederick's new creation.

The main entrance to the palace is in the western facade, approached via gates flanked by stone sentry boxes. Once inside, you'll find the interior predictably opulent, particularly as you enter; almost immediately, the vast and startling **Grottensaal** on the ground floor is decorated entirely with shells and semi-precious stones to form images of lizards and dragons. The other highlight is the equally huge **Marmorsaal**, with its beautiful floor of patterned marble slabs. The southern wing contains Frederick's apartments and the theatre where the king enjoyed Italian opera and French plays. A Francophile to the point of near mania, Frederick believed that the Germans were philistines incapable of producing great art. It was said that he'd "rather a horse sang him an aria, than allow a German in his opera". The last Imperial resident of the Neues Palais was Kaiser Wilhelm II, who packed sixty train carriages with the contents of the palace when he and his family fled in November 1918, following the revolution and abdication. Facing the Neues Palais entrance are the **Communs**, a couple of pointless Rococo fantasies joined by a curved colonnade. They look grandiose, but their purpose was mundane: they were built for the serving and maintenance staff of the palace.

The Rehgarten and Charlottenhof

From the Neues Palais, Ökonomieweg leads east through the **Rehgarten** or Deer Garden, the former court hunting ground (and still home to a few deer), where you'll find the slightly kitsch-looking **Chinesisches Teehaus** (mid-May to mid-Oct Tues–Sun 10am–5pm; €1), a kind of Rococo pagoda housing a small museum of Chinese and Meissen porcelain and surrounded by eerily lifelike statues of Oriental figures.

The broad expanse of rough parkland to the south of Ökonomieweg is **Charlottenhof**, a park created by Friedrich Wilhelm III as a Christmas present for his son, and today one of Sanssouci's quieter corners. A path leads over a bridge past a small farm building to the **Römische Bäder** (mid-May to mid-Oct Tues–Sun 10am–5pm; €2), built by Schinkel and Persius in convincing imitation of a Roman villa.

Across the lawns to the south is **Schloss Charlottenhof** (mid-May to mid-Oct Tues–Sun 10am–5pm; €4), another Roman-style building, once again designed by Schinkel and Persius for Friedrich IV. Though designated a palace, it is, in reality, little more than a glorified villa, but its interior, unlike most Sanssouci buildings, is original. The effect is impressive: the hallway is bathed in blue light filtered through coloured glass decorated with stars, a prelude to the **Kupferstichzimmer**, or print room, whose walls are now covered in copies of Italian Renaissance paintings. Immediately east of Schloss Charlottenhof is the **Dichterhain** (Poets' Grove), an open space dotted with busts of Goethe, Schiller and Herder, among others. West of here through the woods and across a racetrack-shaped clearing called the **Hippodrom** is the **Fasanerie**, another Italian-style edifice built between 1842 and 1844.

The Grünes Gitter and around

At the southeastern corner of Sanssouci is the **Grünes Gitter** or Green Gateway entrance to the grounds, where there's an **information kiosk** with a few leaflets about the park and its environs. Immediately to the north of here is the Italianate **Friedenskirche** (mid-May to Oct daily 10am–6pm; free), designed by Persius for Friedrich Wilhelm IV and completed in 1850. With its 39-metre-high campanile and lakeside setting, it conjures up the southern European atmosphere that Friedrich Wilhelm was striving to create when he ordered the construction of the church using the St Clemente Basilica in Rome as a model, with the design centred on the magnificent Byzantine apse mosaic that was brought here from Murano. Adjoining the church is a domed Hohenzollern mausoleum containing the tombs of Friedrich Wilhelm IV and his wife Elizabeth, and Friedrich III and his wife Victoria. Directly to the west of the Friedenskirche is the **Marly-Garten**, once the kitchen garden of Friedrich I, who named it, with intentional irony, after Louis XIV's luxurious Marly park.

North of the centre

Heading north along Friedrich-Ebert-Strasse will bring you to some of Potsdam's most fascinating, yet least-known, corners, set in and around the woodland areas of **Pfingstberg** and, just to the east, the **Neuer Garten**. Architectural curiosities hereabouts include the **Alexander Newski Kapelle**, but the real crowd puller is the **Schloss Cecilienhof**, scene of the postwar Potsdam conference.

Russische Kolonie Alexandrowka

The beginnings are inauspicious as you head north from Nauener Tor – on the left is a mid-nineteenth-century Italianate villa, once the residence of a royal gardener, behind which the former district headquarters of the Stasi rise up, while the neo-Baroque affair a little to the north is a turn-of-the-twentieth-century local government office. However, after about fifteen minutes' walking you'll reach **Russische Kolonie Alexandrowka**, a settlement of Russian-style wooden houses, built for a group of Russian military musicians who found themselves marooned here after the Napoleonic Wars. Its incongruity makes it one of the most intriguing sights in town, a collection of two-storey dwellings with steeply pitched roofs laid out in the form of a St Andrew's cross. The buildings are in fact half-timbered, but plank cladding gives them the look of birch-log cabins.

△ Neues Palais

Their inhabitants were originally prisoners of war, among five hundred captured when the Prussians were fighting with the French in Kurland (part of modern Poland). Sixty-two of these men were selected to form a Russian choir for the entertainment of the troops, and after the Prussians joined forces with the Russians to combat Napoleon's armies, their services were retained. At the end of the Napoleonic Wars they were stationed in Potsdam, consumed by homesickness but forbidden to return to Russia.

Eventually, in 1826, Friedrich Wilhelm III gave the order that houses should be built for these men and their families. Eight houses were constructed on the arms of the cross, four more at the semicircular linking roads at each end, with an overseer's residence in the middle. The names of the original occupants and subsequent inhabitants (a few of them descendants of the Russians, even today) are carved into the housefronts. Some of the oldest inscriptions are in Cyrillic script.

For many years this whole area was the focus of the Russian presence in Potsdam. The Red Army occupied huge barrack buildings along Voltaireweg and Pappelallee, formerly the property of the Wehrmacht and before that the Imperial German army, while Soviet officers and their families lived in the nearby flats.

The Alexander Newski Kapelle

Directly to the north of the settlement is the **Kapelle des heiligen Alexander Newski**, a church built for the Russians in 1829, set on top of the closely wooded Kapellenberg hill. Access is either by scrambling up the hillside, or via a track branching to the right off Nedlitzer Strasse, which leads to a rudimentary car park. The chapel is a fragment of Russia transplanted to Brandenburg: a compact building in pink stucco edged with white, topped by a central onion-domed tower, with smaller domes at each corner.

The chapel is usually accessible at weekends, but if there's anyone about during the week it's often possible to take a look around. The interior is festooned with icons, many of them gifts from the Tsarina Alexandra, who started life as Princess Charlotte of Prussia. The priest's wife oversees a little stall selling replica icons and holy medals, and often plays Russian Orthodox choir tapes, which enhance the already ethereal effect.

The first service held here, in 1829, was attended by Tsar Nicholas I, and the chapel remained in use for well over a century, boosted by the arrival in Berlin of thousands of Russian émigrés after the Russian Revolution of 1917. During the 1960s the chapel lost its priest, but in 1986 the patriarchate of Moscow sent a new one, and regular church services are held for Potsdam's handful of Orthodox families.

The Pfingstberg

Immediately to the north of the Kapellenberg is the wooded **Pfingstberg**, another little-known Potsdam curiosity which, like the Russian settlement and the Kapellenberg, has been rediscovered over the past few years. At the foot of the Pfingstberg is the walled **Jüdischer Friedhof** or Jewish cemetery. Only organized visits are possible – enquire at the tourist office in town for details. The cemetery was given by the town to Potsdam's growing Jewish population in 1763 – until then they had had to bury their dead in Berlin. As recently as 1933 the Jewish community of Potsdam numbered several hundred, of whom just two returned after the war.

From the cemetery the path leads on up the hill to the ruined nineteenth-century **Belvedere**, a vast and improbable-looking edifice, built to plans drawn up from Friedrich Wilhelm IV's sketches of the folly-like castles constructed in Italy during the Renaissance. As the name suggests, this unusual building was erected as a kind of viewing terrace for the royal inhabitants of nineteenth-century Potsdam and their guests. Its walkways and towers give great views of Potsdam itself, and of the landscape north as far as Spandau and Charlottenburg, and west as far as the town of Brandenburg.

Although virtually undamaged by the war, the Belvedere was allowed to collapse into ruin by the pre-*Wende* city authorities, because (according to some Potsdamers) it afforded such good views of the border and West Berlin – renovation of the structure is only now going ahead. Just to the southeast of the Belvedere is the **Pomonatempel** (April–Oct Sat & Sun 3–6pm; free), a small Neoclassical building that's fronted by a four-columned portico. This neat temple was Schinkel's (see p.67) first-ever finished building, constructed in 1800 when he was a nineteen-year-old student of architecture.

The Neuer Garten

To the east of the Pfingstberg is the **Neuer Garten** (⊛www.spsg.de), another large park complex – the main entrance is at the eastern end of Alleestrasse (which branches off Friedrich Ebert-Strasse at the southern end of the Alexandrowka settlement), beyond which a road snakes through the park. A couple of hundred metres east of the road, overlooking the Heiliger See, stands the **Marmorpalais** or Marble Palace (April–Oct Tues–Sun 10am–5pm; Nov–March Sat & Sun 10am–4pm; €2), built for Friedrich Wilhelm II, who died a premature death here in 1797, allegedly as a consequence of his dissolute lifestyle. In more recent years it was home to the GDR's main military museum, and until 1990 visitors were greeted by the incongruous sight of a MiG-17 parked in the palace grounds. It has now been restored to an approximation of its original royal condition and the sumptuous rooms can be seen once again.

Schloss Cecilienhof

Towards the end of the road through the wooded grounds of the Neuer Garten is **Schloss Cecilienhof** (April–Oct Tues–Sun 9am–5pm; Nov–March Tues–Sun 9am–4pm; with guided tour €5; without guided tour €4; ⊛www.spsg.de; tram #92 from Platz der Einheit north to Alleestrasse, then change to bus #692), which looks like a mock-Elizabethan mansion transplanted from the English Home Counties. Building work on this, the last palace to be commissioned by the Hohenzollerns, began in 1913 and was completed in 1917, the war having evidently done nothing to change the architectural style. Cecilienhof would only rate a mention in passing, were it not for the fact that the **Potsdam Conference**, confirming the decisions made earlier that year at Yalta about the postwar European order, was held here from July 17 to August 2, 1945. The conference was as much symbolic as anything else, providing a chance for Truman, Stalin and Churchill (replaced mid-conference by Clement Attlee) to show the world that they had truly won the war by meeting in the heart of the ruined Reich.

Centre of attraction within is the **Konferenzsaal** or conference chamber, where the Allied delegates worked out the details of the division of Europe, and which resembles the assembly hall of a British minor public school. Everything has been left pretty much as it was in 1945, with the huge round table specially made in Moscow for the conference still in place, despite the fact that in July 1990 there was an arson attack on the hall. The fire brigade arrived within a few minutes and extinguished the fire, but not before considerable damage had been done. A remarkably quick restoration job has left few traces of what happened. It's still not known who was responsible for the attack, but local *Faschos* – neofascists – are thought to be the most likely culprits.

It's also possible to visit the delegates' workrooms, furnished in varying degrees of chintziness. The study of the Soviet delegation is about the most tasteless, but the British room (with a bronze stag at bay in the fireplace and furniture that looks like it was bought as a job lot from a defunct presbytery) comes a close second. Cecilienhof has been used as a hotel since 1960, and there's an expensive restaurant which is also only for the deep of pocket (see p.200).

The Berliner Vorstadt and Glienicker Brücke

On the opposite shore of the Heiliger See to the Neuer Garten is the **Berliner Vorstadt**, formerly an elegant Potsdam suburb, whose crumbling villas were given over to various party and social institutions under the SED regime. Here, too, were numerous Imperial army barracks, housing elite units like the Garde du Corps and Hussars, which until the summer of 1994 were in Russian hands. At the end of Berliner Strasse, leading back to Berlin, is the **Glienicker Brücke**, the famous spy-swap bridge which inspired many a Cold War film scene. Here, in 1962, U-2 pilot Gary Powers was traded for a Soviet agent, while more recently, in 1986, Jewish dissident Anatoly Scharansky was freed into the West by the Soviet authorities in an early manifestation of Gorbachev's *glasnost*. The bridge was reopened to normal traffic at the beginning of 1990, and today there are few reminders of the era when people living in the immediate vicinity needed special permits simply to come and go from their own homes. From the Potsdam side of the bridge, tram #93 leads back to Platz der Einheit, while bus #116 crosses over and ends in Wannsee.

Babelsberg

On the eastern bank of the Havel is the town of **BABELSBERG**, now officially part of the Potsdam administrative district. Crossing the Lange Brücke from Potsdam, it's hard not to notice a square tower rising up out of the trees atop the **Brauhausberg** hill on the Babelsberg side. This is the former local SED headquarters or "**Kreml**" (Kremlin), to give it its local nickname. Originally built as a military college at the turn of the twentieth century, it later served as a state archive building – a dark oval patch on the side of the tower marks where the SED symbol used to be.

The Telegrafenberg and the Einsteinturm

Like Potsdam, Babelsberg has a few secrets ripe for rediscovery. Above the Lange Brücke, Albert-Einstein-Strasse leads up onto the **Telegrafenberg**. This was the site chosen in 1832 for a telegraph station, one of a whole network positioned between Berlin and Koblenz to relay messages by means of mechanical signal arms. Just over forty years later, when the mechanical system had been rendered obsolete, it was decided to build an astronomical observatory here. The complex still stands, finished in the orange- and yellow-striped brickwork typical of the late nineteenth century.

Beyond the observatory, a path leads to the nearby **Einsteinturm**, a twenty-metre-high observatory tower designed by Erich Mendelsohn in 1920. An unrepentently phallic piece of Expressionist architecture, it looks like an element from a Dalí dreamscape and is the most remarkable modern building in the Potsdam area. Experiments testing the Theory of Relativity were carried out here in the presence of Einstein, and scientific work continues here today with research into the sun's magnetic field.

On the eastern side of the Telegrafenberg are a couple of musts for cemetery fans: the **Neuer Friedhof**, laid out in 1866 according to plans drawn up by the architect Lenné, and, below it on the other side of Heinrich-Mann-Allee, the eighteenth-century **Alte Friedhof** with its Classical mausoleum and numerous overgrown monuments, including one to Eleonore Prochaska, who joined the Prussian army in 1813 disguised as a man, successfully fooling her comrades, and later fell in the war against Napoleon.

Nowawes and Park Babelsberg

From the junction of Heinrich-Mann-Allee and Friedrich-Engels-Strasse, bus #698 follows the latter to the centre of Babelsberg. Alighting just north of Lutherplatz, it's a short walk south across this square to **Neuendorfer Anger**, once the heart of the old town, with now only the shell of the **Neuendorfer Dorfkirche** as a reminder. Follow Karl-Liebknecht-Strasse northwards; on either side of the road is an area known as **Nowawes**, where single-storey cottages survive from a settlement of Protestant Czech weavers founded by Friedrich Wilhelm II. The name Nowawes came from *Nowa Ves*, a derivation of the Czech for Neuendorf – "new village" – and the streets either side of Karl-Liebknecht-Strasse today have names like Spindelallee and Jutestrasse, bearing witness to the trades once plied here. A right turn onto Weberplatz brings you to the pretty eighteenth-century **Friedrichskirche**, one of the most appealing buildings in Nowawes.

Between Alt Nowawes and the Tiefer See is the **Park Babelsberg**, Potsdam's third great park complex, designed by Lenné, and neglected by most visitors in favour of Sanssouci. The main entrance is at the end of **Allee nach Glienicke**, the northern extension of Alt Nowawes, although until 1989 this was closed because of the proximity of the border fortifications. A roadway leads through the hilly, roughly wooded park to **Schloss Babelsberg** (closed for renovation; ⓦwww.spsg.de), a neo-Gothic architectural extravaganza built by Schinkel at the behest of Prince Wilhelm, brother of Friedrich Wilhelm IV, and inspired by England's Windsor Castle. A couple of nineteenth-century architectural oddities lurk in the park: the **Flatowturm** (April to mid-Oct Tues–Sun 10am–5pm; €2; ⓦwww.spsg.de), an improbable-looking neo-Gothic guest house and lookout tower, and the **Matrosenhaus**, a bizarrely styled gabled house built for the men who crewed the royal boats and barges of the Hohenzollerns. The park is also home to the thirteenth-century **Gerichtslaube**, Berlin's Gothic courthouse building, brought here in 1872 after the Rotes Rathaus had displaced it.

The Filmpark Babelsberg and Jagdschloss Stern

Babelsberg has a couple of other curiosities. At the eastern end of town, served by buses #690 from Babelsberg's S-Bahn station and #601 and #602 from Potsdam's Hauptbahnhof, is the **Filmpark Babelsberg**, Grossbeeren Strasse (mid-March to Oct daily 10am–6pm; ☎0331/7 21 27 55; €17; concessions €15.50; ⓦwww.filmpark.de), a huge complex, which is mainly of interest to those who have a good knowledge of the German film industry. Originally founded in 1917, this was the premises of the UFA film studios and during the 1920s the heart of the German film industry, rivalling Hollywood as a centre of cinematic innovation. Films produced during the heyday of UFA included Robert Wiene's Expressionist masterpiece *Das Kabinett des Dr Caligari* ("The Cabinet of Dr Caligari"), Fritz Lang's *Metropolis* and *Der Blaue Engel* ("The Blue Angel") starring the young Marlene Dietrich. Under the Nazis the anti-Semitic *Jud Süss* was filmed here in 1940, followed a few years later by the special effects-laden colour epic *Münchhausen*. Later, as the DEFA studios, it was the heavily subsidized centre of the East German film industry, which didn't last much longer than the GDR itself after the *Wende*. These days, Babelsberg has reinvented itself as the "Film Experience Park", and visitors can wander through the costume and props departments and watch technicians going through the motions of shooting film scenes for their benefit. It's also possible to visit the hangar-like studio where Fritz Lang may have filmed *Metropolis* (no one is quite sure of the exact location) and admire a reproduction of his futuristic set. Aside from the film-related attractions, there are fairground rides, several featuring German cartoon characters, and animal shows.

If you have the time or the inclination for yet another royal leftover, take the bus as far as the stop just before Steinstrasse on the eastern edge of town, then follow Jagdhaus Strasse on foot to the **Jagdschloss Stern** (by appointment only – call ☎0331/9 69 42 40, ⊕www.jagdschloss-stern.de), a former royal hunting lodge in gabled Dutch style, built in 1732 by Friedrich Wilhelm I. The Schloss is quite plain, a reflection of the soldier king's preferences, and comes as a surprise after the splendour of Potsdam's other royal palaces. East of the Schloss, well-signposted trails lead through the wooded **Parforceheide**, a one-time hunting ground of the king.

Listings

Listings

Accommodation

Berlin has a range of **hotels**, **hostels** and **campsites**, and it's also possible to stay in a **private room** or **an apartment**, which are both among the most cost-effective options. Even though the city's accommodation is continually increasing in both quality and quantity, you should try to book at least a couple of weeks in advance to be assured of getting exactly what you want, and at least a month or two in advance to stay during important trade fairs, festivals – such as the Love Parade (early July), the Berlin Marathon (first Sun in Oct) and the Berlin Film Festival (Feb) – and at Easter, Christmas and New Year.

If you are stuck for accommodation at short notice, try the **reservation service** of Berlin Tourismus Marketing (see p.28). At no extra charge, staff can take same-day personal bookings for hotels and pensions listed in their authoritative *Hotels und Pensionen* booklet, available from them for free. Staff can also arrange private rooms free of charge, but have a fairly limited selection on their books. Much better are the accommodation agencies listed on p.229.

Hotels and pensions

Broadly speaking, a **pension** is smaller than a **hotel**, and usually cheaper, although the categories are not strictly applied. There are also "Hotel-Pensions", which may be either or both, so don't take too much notice of the labels. Moderate and budget establishments continue to be found in much greater numbers in the west of the city, although a clutch of new places have opened on the eastern side in the past couple of years. Look out for good deals at many of the more upmarket hotels, which slash their tariffs at the weekend. If you're after a **single room**, note that these are usually, at best, only a third cheaper than doubles.

Accommodation price codes

Hotels, pensions and hostels reviewed in this book have been graded according to the following price codes, indicating the cost of the **cheapest double room** in **high season** (May–Sept). For dorm beds in hostels, actual prices are given in the reviews.

❶ Under €50	❹ €70–80	❼ €100–150
❷ €50–60	❺ €80–90	❽ €150–200
❸ €60–70	❻ €90–100	❾ Above €200

Women looking for single-sex hotel accommodation should try the *Intermezzo* (see below) and the *Frauenhotel Artemisia* (p.224). For hotels and pensions run predominantly by and for the **gay** community, see p.268.

Unter den Linden and around

Accommodation in this section is marked on the map on pp.54–55.

Adlon Unter den Linden 77 ☎030/2 26 10, 🕸www.hotel-adlon.de. The jewel of Berlin's prewar luxury hotels has been re-created in all its excessive splendour. Prices are fit for a Kaiser, with rooms starting at €240; you'll part with at least €8500 per night for the presidential suite. U- & S-Bahn Unter den Linden. ➒

Hilton Mohrenstr. 30 ☎030/2 02 30, 🕸www.hilton.com. Luxurious, expensive and not much different to any other *Hilton* hotel in the world. Facilities include a sauna, swimming pool and squash court. U-Bahn Stadtmitte. ➑

Hotel Unter den Linden Unter den Linden 14 ☎030/23 81 10, 🕸www.hotel-unter-den-linden.de. A survivor of the GDR, this is a simply furnished but comfortable place at the junction of Friedrichstrasse and Unter den Linden. The rooms are on the small side but are well kept enough. U- & S-Bahn Friedrichstrasse. ➏

Intermezzo Gertrude-Kolmar-Str. 5 ☎030/22 48 90 96, 🕸www.hotelintermezzo.de. Spartan pension for women only, within walking distance of Potsdamer Platz and Unter den Linden. Breakfast is included. U-Bahn Mohrenstrasse. ➌

Madison Potsdamer Str. 3 ☎030/20 29 20, 🕸www.madison-berlin.de. Swish Potsdamer Platz hotel with a range of modern suites and great views over Tiergarten park – particularly good from the deck of its Finnish sauna. U- & S-Bahn Potsdamer Platz. ➐

Westin Grand Hotel Friedrichstr. 158–164 ☎030/2 02 70, 🕸www.westin.com/berlin. Fully living up to its name, this GDR-era hotel originally served party bigwigs but has since been overhauled to provide oodles of traditional upmarket luxury. Consequently it's a little more atmospheric than some of its rivals. U-Bahn Französische Strasse. ➐

Alexanderplatz and around

Accommodation in this section is marked on the map on p.89.

Alexander Plaza Rosenstr. 1 ☎030/24 00 10, 🕸www.alexander-plaza.com. Once housing a fur atelier, this building survived the war and the GDR, and has been beautifully renovated to become a sleek, bright, dynamic hotel. Some rooms have kitchenettes; all are decorated with modern art. U- & S-Bahn Hackescher Markt. ➐

art'otel Berlin Mitte Wallstr. 70–73 ☎030/24 06 20, 🕸www.artotel.de. Smart, lively hotel with quirky decor – lots of contemporary and modern art – in a quiet corner of Berlin, close to the U-Bahn. When reserving, you can pick the colour of your room: green, blue, red or aubergine. U-Bahn Märkisches Museum. ➐

Grosser Kurfürst Neue Ross-Str. 11 ☎030/24 60 08 43, 🕸www.deraghotels.de. Luxury hotel in a renovated building from the turn of the last century. Facilities include coin-op laundry, wireless Internet access, and a sauna and steambath. Discounts for longer stays available. U-Bahn Märkisches Museum. ➐

Luisenhof Köpenicker Str. 92 ☎030/2 41 59 06, 🕸www.luisenhof.de. This restored 1822 coaching company building is one of the best options in its price range. It's a little off the beaten track, though within walking distance of the U-Bahn and Nikolaiviertel. The rooms have all mod cons and are immaculate. U-Bahn Märkisches Museum. ➐

Park Inn Alexanderplatz ☎030/2 38 90, 🖷23 89 43 05. Big, ugly block bang in the middle of things, with unbeatable views over the city and hard to beat for convenience. The nine hundred en-suite rooms are nothing special though. U- & S-Bahn Alexanderplatz. ➏

Radisson SAS Karl-Liebknecht-Str. 3 ☎030/23 82 80, 🖷2 38 28 10. One of Berlin's newest and most impressive hotels. When booking, it's a tough choice between a room with views over the Spree and the Dom, or one facing inwards, looking out onto 2,500 tropical fish in the vast aquarium that's housed in the lobby-cum-atrium. The hypnotic fish (part of the Sea-life Center; see p.93), spa and the range of good restaurants here might not encourage venturing out, but Museum Island and the Hackescher Markt are both only short walks away. U- & S-Bahn Hackescher Markt. ➑

The Scheunenviertel

Accommodation in this section is marked on the map on pp.100–101.

Dietrich-Bonhoeffer-Haus Ziegelstr. 30 ⊤ 030/28 46 71 86, Ⓦ www.hotel-dbh.de. This small, church-affiliated hotel and conference centre is where the first round of talks between the GDR regime and the opposition – which led to free elections and reunification – were held in December 1989. The airy en-suite rooms are simple, quiet and equipped with desk and TV. A good buffet breakfast is included in the rate. U- & S-Bahn Friedrichstrasse. ❼

Hackescher Markt Grosse Präsidentenstr. 8 ⊤ 030/28 00 30, Ⓦ www.hotel-hackescher-markt.de. Quirky little hotel with an eclectic mix of furnishings on a quiet side street, in the midst of the Hackescher Markt bar scene. Pleasant touches include under-floor heating in the en-suite bathrooms and some non-smoking rooms. The rooms overlooking the courtyard are quieter. U- & S-Bahn Hackescher Markt. ❻

Honigmond Garden Hotel Invalidenstr. 122 ⊤ 030/28 44 55 77, Ⓕ 28 44 55 88. Downtown bargain in a charming 1845 building. The rooms are sparsely furnished, but their original wooden floors help generate an authentic elegance. Guests have access to the relaxing back garden. U-Bahn Zinnowitzer Strasse. ❹

Märkischer Hof Linienstr. 133 ⊤ 030/2 82 71 55, Ⓦ www.maerkischer-hof-berlin.de. Within strolling distance of Unter den Linden, this offers comfortable but unexciting rooms with TV and mini-bar. U-Bahn Oranienburger Tor. ❺

Merkur Torstr. 156 ⊤ 030/2 82 95 23, Ⓦ www.hotel-merkur-berlin.de. Budget place with fairly comfortable rooms, most of which have showers. There are a small number of good-value singles. U-Bahn Rosenthaler Platz. ❸

Tiergarten and around

Accommodation in this section is marked on the map on p.115.

Hansablick Flotowstr. 6 ⊤ 030/3 90 48 00, Ⓦ www.hotel-hansablick.de. A short hop from the Tiergarten, this is one of the few "alternative" hotels in town, run by a collective. Rooms sport cheerful multicoloured furnishings and preside over all the usual mod cons. The rate includes a good buffet breakfast. S-Bahn Tiergarten. ❼

Intercontinental Budapester Str. 2 ⊤ 030/2 60 20, Ⓦ www.interconti.com. Plush modern stopover for high-powered business people and visiting rock stars. It's in a relatively dull corner of town, but has legion amenities, among them a fully equipped fitness centre, sauna and pool. Absolute luxury. Doubles start at €250. U- & S-Bahn Zoologischer Garten. ❾

Sorat Hotel Spreebogen Alt-Moabit 99 ⊤ 030/39 92 00, Ⓦ www.sorat-hotels.de/spree-bogen. A spirited hotel housed in a former dairy and filled with postmodern chic. Its position across the Spree River, though attractive, means it's isolated from most of the action. U-Bahn Turmstrasse. ❽

Charlottenburg and Wilmersdorf

Accommodation in this section is marked either on the map on p.128 or, in the case of hotels on or just off the Ku'damm (including those around Savignyplatz), on the map on p.129.

Alsterhof Augsburgerstr. 5 ⊤ 030/21 24 20, Ⓦ www.alsterhof.com. Central enough, though removed from the bustle of the Ku'damm, this is a pleasant modern hotel with a top-notch gym, pool and sauna. U-Bahn Augsburger Strasse. ❼

art'otel Berlin City Centre West Lietzenburger Str. 85 ⊤ 030/887 77 70, Ⓦ www.artotels.de. This sleek hotel is one for Andy Warhol fans, with over two hundred originals of his scattered about the place. His style extends to the staff uniforms and the furniture – white leather beds and purple chairs. U-Bahn Uhlandstrasse. ❽

Bogota Schlüterstr. 45 ⊤ 030/8 81 50 01, Ⓦ www.bogota.de. Pleasant down-to-earth place offering a touch of affordable luxury in an historic nineteenth-century building – that once served as the Nazi Chamber of Culture. Many of the rooms share facilities. The photos on the third floor are by the photographer known only as YVA, who tutored Helmut Newton (see p.130) in the 1930s. S-Bahn Savignyplatz. ❹

Dittberner Wielandstr. 26 ⊤ 030/8 84 69 50, Ⓕ 8 85 40 46. Friendly old-fashioned pension, boasting spacious rooms, stuccoed ceilings, antiques and plush upholstery. S-Bahn Savignyplatz. ❻

Frauenhotel Artemisia Brandenburgische Str. 18 ⓣ030/8 73 89 05, ⓦ www.frauenhotel-berlin .de. Popular women-only hotel, with modern rooms, most of which are en suite, a sociable roof garden and artworks as part of the decor. Fills up quickly, so book well in advance. Breakfast is included in the rate. U-Bahn Konstanzer Strasse. ❹

Herberge Grosse Kantstr. 71 ⓣ030/3 24 81 38, ⓦ www.herbergegrosse.de. Friendly pension with just three rooms perched high above a busy street. Guests are overwhelmed by excellent facilities and service: Internet access, cable TV and use of the communal kitchen and laundry are all included in the price, and bike rental is available. Free pickup can be arranged from the train stations and the airport. S-Bahn Wilmersdorfer Strasse. ❸

Hotel Gates Knesebeck Strasse 8–9 ⓣ030/31 10 60, ⓦ www.hotel-gates.com. Slick modern business hotel with functional rooms. The main selling piont is free high-speed Internet access in every room, on PCs equipped with flat screens. U-Bahn Ernst-Reuter-Platz. ❼

Ibis Brandenburgische Str. 11 ⓣ030/86 20 20, ⓦ www.ibishotel.com. One of ten branches of this international chain in Berlin. As ever, the rooms are small but aggressively priced. U-Bahn Fehrbelliner Platz. ❸

München Güntzelstr. 62 ⓣ030/8 57 91 20, ⓦ www.hotel-pension-muenchen-in-berlin.de. Straightforward, unpretentious pension with simple, bright modern decor and friendly management. U-Bahn Günzelstrasse. ❹

Propeller Island City Lodge Albrecht-Achilles -Str. 58 ⓣ030/8 91 90 16, ⓦ www.propeller -island.de. Entertainingly wacky hotel where the furnishings in every room have been handcrafted by the owner according to individual themes: check the website to choose from among the likes of the Space Cube, the Mirror Room, Two Lions, Forest, Temple, Electric Wallpaper, Nudes, or Upside Down. U-Bahn Adenauerplatz. ❻

The Ku'damm and around

Brandenburger Hof Eislebener Str. 14 ⓣ030/21 40 50, ⓦ www.brandenburger-hof.com. This hotel is an architectural and design *tour de force*, a bright nineteenth-century mansion reworked with Bauhaus influences. The staff ooze suave attentiveness, and there's a Michelin-starred restaurant and a beautiful Japanese-influenced garden to enjoy.

Doubles cost around €260. U-Bahn Augsburger Strasse. ❾

California Kurfürstendamm 35 ⓣ030/88 01 20, ⓦ www.hotel-california.de. With its huge chandeliers and elegant cornicing, there's not much that's particularly Californian in this well-appointed hotel in the thick of the Ku'damm. The large en-suite rooms have becoming nineteenth-century touches, though the cheaper rooms just seem dated and a little plain. The rate includes an excellent buffet breakfast. U-Bahn Uhlandstrasse. ❼

Concept Grolmanstr. 41–43 ⓣ030/88 42 60, ⓦ www.concept-hotel.com. Large business hotel just south of the Savignyplatz restaurant district. The rooms are in two buildings, the newer one more stylish and with better facilities – including ports for your laptop. To relieve stress, take advantage of the sauna, solarium, massage facilities or rooftop terrace. U-Bahn Uhlandstrasse. ❼

Fischer Nürnberger Str. 24a ⓣ030/2 18 68 08, ⓕ2 13 42 25. Small and very basic pension. Breakfast is not included. U-Bahn Augsburger Strasse. ❶

Funk Fasanenstr. 69 ⓣ030/8 82 71 93, ⓦ www .hotel-pensionfunk.de. Interesting re-creation of a prewar flat, with furniture and objects from the 1920s and 1930s, when this was the home of Danish silent-movie star Asta Nielsen. Given this and its location, it's a great bargain. The cheapest rooms share bathrooms. U-Bahn Uhlandstrasse. ❸

Hecker's Grolmannstr. 35 ⓣ030/8 89 00, ⓦ www.heckers-hotel.de. Swanky boutique hotel close to the restaurants of Savigny-platz, with a range of classy suites and rooms. Pride of the hotel are its three luxuriously furnished, themed suites (Bauhaus, Tuscany and Colonial), costing upwards of €350 per night. U-Bahn Uhlandstrasse. ❽

Imperator Meinekestr. 5 ⓣ030/8 81 41 81, ⓕ8 85 19 19. Great-value, intimate hotel, situated on one of the most exclusive yet friendly streets in the city. The rooms are spacious and stylishly decorated; the cheapest rooms share facilities. U-Bahn Kurfürstendamm. ❸

Kettler Bleibtreustr. 19 ⓣ030/8 83 49 49, ⓕ8 82 42 28. A tiny, charming 1920s-style pension on a lively, café-lined street. A multitude of knick-knacks, Berlinana and patterned wallpaper give the place character. S-Bahn Savignyplatz. ❹

Savoy Hotel Fasanenstr. 9–10 ☎030/31 10 30, ⓦ www.hotel-savoy.com. Luxury hotel whose traditional, old-world atmosphere has been happily married with some Cuban decorative flair; there's even a cigar shop in the lobby. U- & S-Bahn Zoologischer Garten. ❾

Schöneberg

Accommodation in this section is marked on the map on p.143.

Altberlin am Potsdamer Platz Potsdamer Str. 67 ☎030/2 61 29 99, ⓦ www.altberlin.de. Large pension, recently refurbished with trappings from the turn of the nineteenth century. It's just a few minutes' walk from the Tiergarten museums. U-Bahn Kurfürstenstrasse. ❺

Grand Hotel Esplanade Lützowufer 15 ☎030/25 47 80, ⓦ www.esplanade.de. Sleek and streamlined top-class hotel close to the Tiergarten park with all the facilities most people could want and a flashy New York-style cocktail bar, Harry's. Doubles start at €230. U-Bahn Nollendorfplatz. ❾

Sylter Hof Berlin Kurfürstenstr. 116 ☎030/2 12 00, ⓦ www.sylterhof-berlin.de. Well-appointed eighteen-storey hotel just behind Wittenbergplatz and the Ku'damm. All accommodation has network access. The suites are spacious and well priced, and come with kitchen. U-Bahn Wittenbergplatz. ❻

Kreuzberg and Southern Friedrichshain

The hotels in this section are marked on the map on pp.148–149.

East Side Hotel Mühlenstr. 6 ☎030/29 38 33, ⓦ www.eastsidehotel.de. Small, laid-back modern hotel just over the Spree from Kreuzberg in Southern Friedrichshain and overlooking the East Side Gallery. The service is exceptional and the absence of rules refreshing: you can check in or out, order room service, or have breakfast in the café 24 hours a day. Original artwork in the hotel includes quirky murals by Birgit Kinder, who famously painted the Trabant. Under-15s stay free in their parents' rooms. Video games are available to rent. U- and S-Bahn Warschauer Strasse. ❺

Hotel Am Anhalter Bahnhof Stresemannstr. 36 ☎030/2 51 03 42, ⓦ www.hotel-anhalter -bahnhof.de. Not a pretty hotel, but a pleasant one, with friendly staff. The cheaper rooms share bathrooms, but all the rooms are a good deal considering the location, just south of Potsdamer Platz and the Kulturforum. S-Bahn Anhalter Bahnhof. ❹

Friedrichshain

The hotels in this section are marked on the map on pp.158–159.

Hotel 26 Grünberger Strasse 26 ☎030/2 97 77 80 ⓦ www.hotel26.de. Simple, bright and modern hotel close to Friedrichshain's many bars. All rooms are en suite. U- and S-Bahn Warschauer Strasse. ❹

Hotel Fredrichshain Warschauer Strasse 57 ☎030/97 00 20 30, ⓦ www.boardinghouse -berlin.com. Straightforward modern hotel with uncluttered rooms and a kitchen on every floor. A good deal for longer stays: prices drop after your third night and almost halve after your fifteenth. U- and S-Bahn Warschauer Strasse. ❹

Upstalsboom Hotel Gubener Strasse 42 ☎030/29 37 50, ⓦ www.upstalsboom-berlin .de. Upmarket hotel whose particular strong point is its spa. The rooms are bland, if spacious, and are available in four categories, the largest of which has a kitchenette. U- and S-Bahn Warschauer Strasse. ❼

Prenzlauer Berg

Accommodation in this section is marked on the map on pp.158–159.

Acksel Haus Belforter Str. 21 ☎030/44 33 76 33, ⓦ www.ackselhaus.de. Small offbeat hotel on an attractive residential street in the midst of the lively Prenzlauer Berg scene. Besides rooms, it offers fully equipped and individually themed apartments with network access and spacious kitchens. ❸

Greifswald Greifswalder Str. 211 ☎030/4 42 78 88, ⓦ www.hotel-greifswald.de. An informal pension, tucked away in a quiet rear courtyard. The en-suite rooms are tidy, if fairly basic. Breakfast is served right up until 1pm, though it isn't included in the rate. ❹

Kastanienhof Kastanienallee 65–66 ☎030/44 30 50, ⓕ44 30 51 11. Small hotel in a nineteenth-century tenement house, with spacious, well-appointed rooms, and convenient for the area's nightlife. Prices include a continental breakfast. ❼

Myer's Hotel Metzer Str. 26 ☎030/44 01 40, ⓦwww.myershotel.de. Small upmarket hotel in the quiet courtyard of a renovated building from the turn of the nineteenth century. The rooms are elegant and tastefully furnished, though a little on the small side. ❼

Am Weissen See Parkstr. 78 ☎030/9 78 90 10, ⓕ97 89 01 99. Tiny and rather too chintzy pension out in a leafy residential area, with good public transport links to the centre. The rooms are en suite and come with TV, phone and minibar. ❸

Hostels

In recent years Berlin has seen a wave of new, independently run **hostels**, which have swept aside many of the old-fashioned, unfriendly pensions and overtaken the established IYH hostels in standards of service. At these newer hostels, the reception desk is almost always a bountiful source of information and frequently doubles as a 24-hour bar for the communal area, where you'll often find several Internet terminals. Common rooms are usually available for relaxing and meeting other travellers, and the universal absence of curfews makes the newer hostels much more user-friendly. Though traditional facilities such as a laundry and kitchens are unusual in these places, in Berlin the nearest laundry or snack bar is never far away.

All the hostels welcome travellers of any age, though most cater mainly to 20-something visitors (the larger establishments are also periodically overwhelmed by school groups). The actual accommodation comprises various mixed-sex, multiple-occupancy dorm rooms, plus singles, doubles and triples. Prices reflect the number of people sharing: a twenty-bed dorm may be priced at around €10 per person, while five sharing a room might pay double that per person, and singles and doubles typically go for around €40–60. Bedding is provided in most instances, though sometimes there's a small one-off fee of around €3 for this, or you can use a sleeping bag. Most hostels offer a simple buffet breakfast for around €5.

The hostels in this section are marked on the map on pp.100–101.

Circus Hostel Weinbergsweg 1a and Rosa-Luxemburg-Str. 39–41 ☎030/28 39 14 33, ⓦwww.circus-berlin.de. A pair of popular, top-notch hostels in fantastic locations, with particularly helpful staff and good facilities. Rooms are plain though bright, with large windows and high ceilings. The Weinbergsweg hostel has its own, decent bar, *Goldman's*, downstairs. U-Bahn Rosenthaler Platz and Rosa-Luxemburg-Str. Besides dorms, a few singles, doubles and triples are available. Dorms €15–18; ❶

Clubhouse Kalkscheunenstr. 4–5 ☎030/28 09 79 79, ⓦwww.clubhouse-berlin.de. Small, slightly grungy hostel with too few bathrooms, but whose faults are more than made up for by its fantastic location, close

to the bars of Oranienburger Strasse and a 10min walk from Unter den Linden. U- and S-Bahn Friedrichstr. Dorms are spacious and cost around €15, and there are also workaday singles, doubles and triples. Dorms €15; ❶

Mitte's Backpacker Chausseestr. 102 ☎030/28 39 09 65, ⓦwww.baxpax.de. Imaginatively decorated converted factory within walking distance of the Scheunenviertel bar scene. Facilities include bike rental and a communal kitchen. U-Bahn Zinnowitzer Str. Some dorms are single-sex. Dorms from €13; ❶

A&O Joachimstaler Str. 1–3 ☎030/2 97 78 10, ⓦwww.aohostels.com. Vast multistorey hostel beside Zoo station (reached by the stairs beside *Hanne's* bar; see the map on p.129) and consequently very handy for the public transport network. It's sociable, with its own large outdoor bar, but is often a bit overrun by school groups. The cheapest dorm beds might seem like bargains, but you'll be sharing with twenty people and there are no lockers available. The singles and doubles are pricey, but they do have en-suite facilities. U-Bahn Zoologischer Garten. Dorms €10–17; ❷

Berolina Backpacker Stuttgarter Platz 17 ☎030/32 70 80 72, ⓦwww.berolinabackpacker .de. Converted former pension with none of the sociable atmosphere you'd expect from a hostel, and virtually no communal facilities – but some of the dorm beds are among the city's cheapest, and it's close to the S-Bahn and airport bus route. A good place to try when most other hostels are full. See the map on p.128 for the location; S-Bahn Charlottenburg. Dorms €8–15; ❶

Schöneberg

The hostels in this section are marked on the map on p.143.

Jugendherberge Berlin Kluckstr. 3 ☎030/2 61 10 97, ⓦwww.jugendherberge.de. The best of Berlin's IYH youth hostels, thanks mainly to its location, a stone's throw from the Kulturforum museum complex and Potsdamer Platz. The HI card that you need to stay here can be purchased via a small premium paid for the first six nights, after which you become a member. There's no curfew, and breakfast is included in the price. U-Bahn Kurfürstenstr. Dorms from around €20.

Meininger City Hostel Meininger Str. 10 ☎030/66 63 61 00, ⓦwww.meininger-hostels .de. A large, reasonable but unremarkable hostel. But the low prices, particularly for the sparkling singles and doubles (whose rates include a good buffet breakfast), make it a recommended choice. Films are screened nightly for free, but the common room lacks the requisite cosiness. U-Bahn Schöneberg. Dorms from €12,50; ❶

Kreuzberg

The hostels in this section are marked on the map on pp.148–149.

BaxPax Skalitzer Str. 104, ☎030/69 51 83 22, ⓦwww.baxpax.de. Cheerful and convivial

beatnik hostel in a happening area of Kreuzberg, whose claim to fame is its bed in a pink VW Beetle parked in one of the rooms. Otherwise it's unremarkable and the communal facilities are a bit overstretched. Besides dorms, there are some double rooms and one single. U-Bahn Görlitzer Bahnhof. Dorms from €15; ❶

Die Fabrik Schlesische Str. 18 ☎030/6 11 71 16, ⓦwww.diefabrik.com. Hip but quiet hostel in a converted factory. Unusually, the dorm beds aren't bunk beds. Bedding is included in the price, though the breakfasts aren't. U-Bahn Schlesisches Tor. Dorms from €18; ❷

Meininger City Hostels Hallesches Ufer 30 and Tempelhofer Ufer 10 ☎030/66 63 61 00, ⓦwww.meininger-hostels.de. A pair of well-run hostels on either side of the Landwehrkanal, in one of Kreuzberg's duller corners. The dorms and private rooms come with a shower and toilet, while single and twin rooms (though not the triples) also have a TV and phone. Rates include a great buffet breakfast. U-Bahn Hallesches Tor. Dorms from €14; ❷

Friedrichshain

The hostels in this section are marked on the map on pp.158–159.

Odyssee Globetrotter Hostel Grünberger Str. 23 ☎030/29 00 00 81, ⓦwww.globetrotterhostel .de. Imaginatively decorated and sociable hostel hard by the Friedrichshain scene and with a happening bar of its own – making the hostel's late checkout times especially convenient. Some doubles and triples and one single room are available. U-Bahn Frankfurter Tor. Dorms €15; ❷

Pegasus Strasse der Pariser Kommune 35 ☎030/29 35 18 10, ⓦwww.pegasushostel .de. Well-run establishment set around a garden-cum-courtyard that comes into its own in the summer as a place to enjoy your free welcome drink. It's a bit out of the way, though the U-Bahn is just a 5min walk away. Singles, doubles and triples available. U-Bahn Weberwiese. Dorms €15; ❶

Sunflower Hostel Helsingforserstr. 17 ☎030/44 04 42 50, ⓦwww.sunflower-hostel.de. Sociable hostel tucked away in a residential part of Friedrichshain. The reception doubles as a bar, while the hostel itself is fairly handy for transport and the local bar scene. The dorms are good value, but the singles and doubles are dingy and uninviting. U- and S-Bahn Warschauer Str. Dorms €13; ❶

Prenzlauer Berg

The hostels in this section are marked on the map on pp.158–159.

Lette'm Sleep Lettestr. 7 ☎030/44 73 36 23, ⓦwww.backpackers.de. Quirky hostel with comfy if basic rooms, just steps away from the action in Prenzlauer Berg. A big plus point is the cosy living room with free coffee, tea and Internet access, and the communal kitchen. There are discounts for longer stays. U-Bahn Eberswalder Str. Dorms from €15; ❶

The Generator Storkower Str. 160 ☎030/4 17 24 00, ⓦwww.generatorhostels.com. This gargantuan place is the largest hostel in Germany, part of an international chain. It's modern, clean, friendly and efficient, but rather out of the way. Singles and doubles have their own toilet and shower. S-Bahn Landsberger Allee. Dorms from €12; ❶

Transit Loft Greifswalder Str. 219 ☎030/48 49 37 73, ⓦwww.transit-loft.de. Part budget hotel, part hostel, this uncluttered establishment occupies the top floor of a converted factory building, the floors below housing a cinema, café, fitness club and billiards hall. Both dorms and private rooms are large and cheerful, and the nightlife of Kollwitzplatz is a stroll away. A buffet breakfast is included in the price. U-Bahn Rosa-Luxemburg Platz. Dorms €20; ❷

The Grunewald

Jetpak Pücklerstr. 54 ☎030/030/83 25 011, ⓕ83 22 79 05, ⓦwww.jetpak.de. One-of-a-kind hostel with a laid-back international vibe, out in the woods on the south-western edge of Berlin (see the map on p.191). The large communal spaces offer lots, including free nightly big-screen movies, free Internet access and lots of indoor and outdoor games. Bring supplies as there are no stores in the vicinity. U-Bahn Günzelstrasse or Fehrberliner Platz then bus 115 to Pückerstrasse; night buses from the centre stop a 10min walk from the hostel (though note that it's a dark walk through the woods). Dorms €12; ❶

Campsites

None of Berlin's **campsites** is close to the centre; if you're looking to cut costs, bear in mind that hostels will probably work out cheaper once you've added the cost of travel to a campsite. That said, all the campsites are well run and inexpensive – expect to pay €4 per tent and then €10 per person per night. Further afield, the Brandenburg region that surrounds Berlin has innumerable sites; the various tourist offices can give you a complete list.

During the summer season, from April until the end of September, the campsites are open between 6am and 1pm and from 3pm to 10pm; during the winter season they open one hour later and close one hour earlier, unless otherwise stated in the reviews.

Backpackers Paradise Ziekowstrasse 161, Reinickendorf ☎030/4 33 86 40, ⓦwww .backpackersparadise.de. Budget youth camp with sociable vibe around the nightly camp-fire and a lake for swimming that's only a bike ride (rentals available) away. U-Bahn Tegel or S-Bahn Alt-Tegel, then bus #222 to Titusweg (get off on Berliner Strasse). Open mid-June to Aug only. It charges €7 per night for floor space in the communal tent, or to pitch your own, plus an extra €1.50 extra to rent a bed in a tent.

Campingplatz Am Krossinsee Wernsdorfer Str. 38 ☎030/6 75 86 87. Pleasantly located in the woods just outside the southeastern suburb of Schmöckwitz, *Am Krossinsee* offers easy access to local lakes. It's also possible to rent a bungalow here. From S-Bahn Grünar take tram #68 to Schmöckwitz, and from there catch bus #463 to the grounds.

Campingplatz Gatow Kladower Damm 207–213, Spandau ☎030/36 80 84 92. New facilities not far from the Kladow campsite, with showers, laundry and a restaurant. U-Bahn Rathaus Spandau, then bus #134 or #X34 directly to Flugplatz Gatow stop.

Campingplatz Kladow Krampnitzer Weg 111–117, Spandau ☎030/3 65 27 97. Friendly campsite on the western side of the Havel Lake, with the best facilities of all the sites, including a free crèche, bar, restaurant, shop and showers. U-Bahn Rathaus Spandau, then bus #134 to Kladow; at the southern end of Kladower Damm (Alt-Kladow stop), change to the #234, get off when the bus swings off Krampnitzer Weg and walk west to the end of the road.

Campingplatz Kohlhasenbrück Neue Kreis Str. **36, Zehlendorf** ☎ **030/8 05 17 37**. Has all the basic facilities (showers, laundry etc), a children's playground and a restaurant. A 10min walk from S-Bahnhof Griebnitzsee. June–Sept only.

Private rooms and apartments

Private rooms are usually of a good standard: clean and simple, often self-contained, and there's quite a lot of privacy – you may barely see your host. Breakfast is sometimes included in the price, in which event it's most likely a case of helping yourself to bread and what's in the fridge.

The typical charge for a private room is €20–30 per person per night, while monthly rents for an apartment start at €350 if it's self-contained, or about half to two-thirds that if you're prepared to share kitchen and bathroom facilities.

The accommodation agencies listed below are divided according to whether they specialize in **short-term** lets – usually considered to be up to a month in length – or **long-term** lets, exceeding a month. The agency fee is usually 20–25 percent of the monthly rent quoted.

Mostly short term

Bed & Breakfast Privatzimmervermittlung ☎ 030/78 91 39 71, ⓦ www.bed-and-breakfast .de. Part of a national chain, offering rooms ranging from the simple to the luxurious.

Bed & Breakfast in Berlin ☎ 030/44 05 05 82, ⓦ www.bed-and-breakfast-berlin.de. Single and double rooms starting at around €28 a night.

Citybed ☎ 030/23 62 36 30, ⓦ www.citybed.de. Primarily an online booking tool for accommodation, with prices starting at around €20 per person.

Stadtbett ☎ 030/69 56 50 00, ⓦ www.stadtbett .de. Another good way of finding rooms and apartments online, via a request service.

Zimmervermittlung Dentler ☎ 030/55 51 11, ⓦ www.zimmer-berlin.de. Wide range of rooms and apartments all over the city with vast online search engine; prices start from around €30 per person.

Mostly long term

Agentur Wohnwitz ☎ 030/8 61 82 22, ⓦ www .wohnwitz.com. Agency offering rooms in shared flats and apartments.

Fine & Mine ☎ 030/2 35 51, ⓦ www .fineandmine.de. Search engine in German only; some short-term lets available.

Home Company ☎ 030/1 94 45, ⓦ www .homecompany.de. A long-established agency, best for long-term lets, though the booking tool handles lets of less than a month too.

Room with a Loo ☎ 030/47 37 29 64, ⓦ www .roomwithaloo.com. Accommodation agency run by *Exberliner*, Berlin's English-language monthly listings magazine.

Wohnagentur am Mehringdamm ☎ 030/7 86 20 03, ⓦ www.wohnung-berlin.de. A good selection of rooms and apartments, many in Kreuzberg and Schöneberg. The website is in German only.

Zeitraum Wohnkonzepte ☎ 030/4 41 66 22, ⓦ www.zeit-raum.de. Helpful agency with rooms and apartments all over the eastern part of the city.

Eating and drinking

Berlin has all the possibilities you'd expect from a major European capital city, with virtually every imaginable type of food represented: indeed, the national cuisine generally takes a back seat to Greek, Turkish, Balkan, Indian and Italian fare. Berliners tend to eat out regularly, so prices are reasonable – a main dish typically costing around e6 to e10 – though you can easily triple this figure by dining at top-end places serving Neue Deutsche Küche (see below); or halve it, by eating a perfectly reasonable meal at an Imbiss (budget eatery).

In line with Berlin's rolling nightlife timetable, you can pretty much **eat and drink around the clock**. The majority of restaurants will happily serve until around 11pm, and even later than this it's not hard to find somewhere in most neighbourhoods. Another common feature in Berlin is how many places morph from one **type of venue** into another throughout the day. A good place to slurp a morning coffee and read a paper may well turn into a

---

German cuisine

To enjoy traditional **German cuisine**, it does help if you share the national penchant for solid, fatty food accompanied by compensatingly healthy fresh vegetables and salad.

The **pig** is the staple of the German menu – it's prepared in umpteen different ways, and just about every part of it is eaten. Sausages are the country's most popular snack, while *Kassler Rippen* (smoked and pickled pork chops) and *Eisbein* (pig's trotters) are Berlin favourites – although the fatty *Eisbein* tends to be more of a winter speciality. *Königsberger Klopse* (meat dumplings in a caper- and lemon-flavoured sauce) can also be found on many menus.

Unusual things are done with **potatoes**, too: try *Kartoffelpuffer* (flour and potatoes mixed into a pancake) or *Pellkartoffeln mit Quark und Leinöl*, a stomach-churning combination of baked potatoes, low-fat cheese and linseed oil that's best digested with lashings of beer or schnapps.

Surprisingly for a country known for its cakes, **desserts** in Berlin's German restaurants are something of an anticlimax. *Rote Grütze* (mixed soft berries eaten hot or cold with vanilla sauce) is one of the few distinctive dishes. Otherwise, it's the usual selection of fresh and stewed fruits, cheeses and ice creams; if you have a sweet tooth, you're best off heading for a café that serves one of the delicious cakes or gateaux of which Germans are so fond.

Modern German cuisine, known as **Neue Deutsche Küche**, the German equivalent of *nouvelle cuisine*, is a reaction against heavy traditional cooking. While not as minimalistic as the French or Californian versions, like any food trend it tends to be expensive – particularly so for the quantity you get.

restaurant later on before rolling out the decks for a DJ until the small hours, when it closes to repeat the process all over again two or three hours later. This opportunistic approach, and the integration of the activities of eating and drinking in German culture, means that the distinction between restaurants, cafés, bars and even clubs can be difficult to make: outside busy periods, many restaurants are perfectly happy to serve you just a coffee, and some of the tastiest food you'll eat on your trip may be from a café.

We have divided the **listings** below into **cafés and bars** – for a drink, a light bite, and generally hanging out; **restaurants** – recommended for a full meal; **snack bars** – for something quick and cheap; and **Hausbrauereien** (microbreweries) and **beer gardens** – venues for the kind of concerted beer drinking Germany is famous for. These are in turn split by neighbourhood; generally speaking, the more established restaurants are in the west, though in the last decade the eastern districts of the city have experienced a restaurant boom, which caters to a younger crowd and emphasizes modern and foreign cuisine. Both drinking and eating are generally best done away from the obvious tourist strips like Unter den Linden and the Ku'damm, where standards tend to be lower and prices higher.

Cafés and bars

Nowhere in Berlin is more than a stone's throw away from a **bar**. The basic, no-frills drinking hole (known as a *Kneipe*) is found on street corners throughout the city and is identifiable by its general gloom and all-male clientele. *Kneipen* are the cheapest places to drink – a small beer costs around €2 – and can be fun if the regulars decide to befriend you. Unaccompanied women should bear in mind that such befriending may have unwanted overtones; as a rule, local women do not frequent these places, choosing instead to head for more mixed and upmarket bars and cafés – often referred to as *Szene* ("Scene") hangouts – that make up the bulk of our listings. Here, stylish decor appeals to the in-crowd and pose (or self-conscious lack of it) is all. While the trendier-looking bars are more expensive, few are outrageously so; and, given their tendency to cluster, it's easy to barhop until you find a favourite. Almost all the better places serve food, too, and this can be a bargain – though beware the most chic places, where that interesting-looking item on the menu turns out to be a plate of asparagus tips for €15.

Most bars stay open later than elsewhere in Germany and there are no last-orders in Berlin. Typically, however, bars will close between 1am and 5am, often to reopen around 9am to become part of Berlin's well-established **café scene**, with hundreds of coffee houses acting as additional social hangouts.

Afternoon is traditionally time for **Kaffee und Kuchen** (coffee and cakes) in one of the self-consciously elegant (and, therefore, ultra-expensive) cafés in the city centre. Although indelibly associated with Austria, these places are just as popular an institution in Germany, serving various types of coffee, cream cakes, pastries and handmade chocolates – ideal for when your blood sugar level needs pepping up.

Bars and cafés are dotted across Berlin, but many areas have clusters of particularly good ones. Cafés on **Unter den Linden** and in the Nikolaiviertel, near **Alexanderplatz**, are mostly traditional, there to provide sightseers with large slabs of rich cake and coffee. The stretch along Oranienburger Strasse in the **Scheunenviertel**, just north of the city centre, fairly heaves with places also catering primarily, though not exclusively, to visitors. But the scene here

Wine

Many people's knowledge of German **wine** starts and ends with *Liebfraumilch*, the medium-sweet easy-drinking wine. Sadly, its success has obscured the quality of other German wines, especially those made from the *Riesling* grape, and it's worth noting that the *Liebfraumilch* drunk in Germany tastes nothing like the bilge swilled abroad.

The vast majority of German wine is white, since the northern climate doesn't ripen red grapes regularly. If you're pining for a glass of red, try a *Spätburgunder* (Germany's answer to the *pinot noir* of Burgundy).

First step in any exploration of German wine should be to understand what's on the label: the predilection for Gothic script and gloomy martial crests makes this an uninviting prospect, but the division of categories is intelligent and helpful – if at first a little complex.

Wine categories

Like most EU wine, German wine is divided into two broad categories: *Tafelwein* ("table wine", for which read "cheap plonk") and *Qualitätswein* ("quality wine"), equivalent to the French *Apellation Controllée*.

TAFELWEIN

Tafelwein can be a blend of wines from any EU country; *Deutscher Tafelwein* must be 100-percent German. *Landwein* is a superior *Tafelwein*, equivalent to the French *Vin de Pays*, and medium dry. Like all German wines, *Tafelwein* can be *trocken* (dry), *halb-trocken* (medium dry) or *lieblich* (sweet).

QUALITÄTSWEIN

There are two basic subdivisions of *Qualitätswein*: **QbA** (*Qualitätswein eines bestimmten Anbaugebietes*) and **QmP** (*Qualitätswein mit Prädikat*). "QbA" wines come from eleven delimited regions and must pass an official tasting and analysis. "QmP" wines are further divided into six grades:

Kabinett The first and lightest style.

Spätlese Must come from late-picked grapes, which results in riper flavours.

Auslese Made from a selected bunch of grapes, making a concentrated medium-sweet wine. If labelled as a *trocken*, the wine will have lots of body and weight.

Beerenauslese Wine made from late-harvested, individually picked grapes. A rare wine, made only in the very best years, and extremely sweet.

Trockenbeerenauslese *Trocken* here means dry in the sense that the grapes have been left on the vine until some of the water content has evaporated. As with *Beerenauslese*, each grape will have been individually picked. This is a very rare wine that is intensely sweet and concentrated.

Eiswein Literally "ice wine", this is made from *Beerenauslese* grapes – a hard frost freezes the water content of the grape, concentrating the juice. *Eiswein* is remarkably fresh, due to its high acidity.

---

is very different: this is the primary visitor nightlife district – most cafés double as bars and are open late. In the western part of the city, the majority of bars and cafés congregate around the **Ku'damm** (traditional coffee houses), and Savignyplatz, in **Charlottenburg** (showier modern places). South of the centre, the scene in **Schöneberg** and **Kreuzberg** revolves around three distinct and fairly bohemian areas, which attract an older, less image-conscious crowd: Winterfeldplatz is a popular gay centre, Bergmannstrasse a conventionally alternative neighbourhood, and the Oranienstrasse a bit of a grittier counter-cultural stronghold – you could spend weeks bar-crawling these last two districts before you began to exhaust the possibilities. Presently, the new frontier for Berlin's clubbers and bar-hoppers is **Friedrichshain**, where the Simon-Dach-Strasse has become

Breakfast and Sunday brunch

Breakfast (*Frühstück*) will often be provided with your accommodation but can also be bought at many cafés, which frequently continue to serve breakfast throughout the afternoon and into the evening. Prices start at around €3 for a basic bread, eggs and jam affair, rising to €13 for more exotic, champagne-swigging delights.

Typically, you'll be offered a small platter of **cold meats** (usually sausage-based) and **cheeses**, along with a selection of marmalades, jams and honey, and, occasionally, muesli or another cereal. You're generally given a variety of **breads**, one of the most distinctive features of German cuisine. Both brown and white rolls are popular, often baked with caraway, coriander, poppy or sesame seeds. The rich-tasting black rye bread, known as *Pumpernickel*, is a particular favourite.

Coffee (usually freshly brewed) is the normal accompaniment, though **tea** – whether plain or herbal – and **hot chocolate** are common alternatives. A glass of **fruit juice** – almost invariably orange – is sometimes included as well.

A developing Berlin tradition is the trip to a café, bar or restaurant for **Sunday brunch**. These are invariably busy and sociable affairs, offering first-class people-watching and often excellent food – and are particularly good value when offered as part of a **buffet**. Expect to pay €5–9 for unlimited food; drinks are paid for separately.

---

the city's student nightlife quarter. As Berlin's alternative yuppie district, **Prenzlauer Berg** is good for late-night nightlife, but is particularly recommended for its well-balanced mix of cafés by day.

Unter den Linden and around

Café Adler Friedrichstr, 206 ☎030/251 89 65. Small café whose popularity comes from its position by the site of Checkpoint Charlie, but which somehow avoids being too touristy. Serves breakfast and other meals: the soups are excellent, packed with fresh ingredients, and look out for the well-priced daily specials (€4–9). U-Bahn Kochstrasse. Mon–Sat 10am–midnight, Sun 10am–7pm.
Newton Bar Charlottenstr. 57, MI ☎030/20 29 54 21. Helmut Newton's life-size shots of nude Amazons stare out at the black leather and dark green marble interiors of this highly chic bar: perfect for watching Berlin's sharp dressers smoking cigars and sipping expertly-made cocktails. U-Bahn Stadtmitte. Fri 10am–4am, Sat 10am–4am, Sun–Thurs 10am–3am.
Operncafé Opernpalais, Unter den Linden 5 ☎030/20 26 83. In a former royal palace, this elegant café evokes the atmosphere of Imperial Berlin, and its coffee and amazing cakes make it a recommended stopping-off point after seeing the local sights. U-Bahn Französische Str. Daily 8am–midnight.
Sale e Tabacci Kochstr. 18 ☎030/25 29 50 03. Authentic and beautiful Italian café

near Checkpoint Charlie where journalists and architects linger over espresso and cigarettes. Food is contemporary and uses top-notch ingredients, but is a little over-priced, with mains around €15–22. U-Bahn Kochstrasse. Mon–Fri 9am–2am, Sat & Sun 10am–2am.

Alexanderplatz and around

Tele-café Alexanderplatz Panorama Str. ☎030/242 33 33. This café, 207m above Berlin in the upper reaches of the TV tower, rotates so you can enjoy a wonderful panoramic view of the city while tucking into a pricey ice cream or an international menu (mains €9–14). But the daily specials, particularly the soups, are the best options. An essential Berlin tourist experience: make reservations or wait for a table. U- & S-Bahn Alexanderplatz. Daily 10am–11.30pm.
Zum Nussbaum Am Nussbaum 3 ☎030/242 30 95. In the heart of the Nikolaiviertel, this is a convincing copy of a prewar bar – destroyed in an air raid – that stood on the Fischerinsel and was favoured by the artists Heinrich Zille and Otto Nagel. This replica verges on the expensive, but it's a

good place to soak up a bit of ersatz old-Berlin ambience. Daily noon–11pm.

The Scheunenviertel

am to pm Am Zwirngraben 2 ☏ 030/24 08 53 01. Open nonstop, this café-cum-bar-cum-club under the Hackescher Markt S-Bahn station helps support Berlin's reputation for nonstop nightlife. It's a good people-watching spot during the day, and a convenient way to start, or finish, a night out. U- & S-Bahn Hackescher Markt. Open 24hrs.

Barcomi's Deli Sophienstr. 21 ☏ 030/28 59 83 63. Situated in a pleasant courtyard, Barcomi's is a nice place to rest while gallery-hopping, serving interesting soups and American-style baked goodies. It also offers great breakfasts. U-Bahn Weinmeisterstrasse. Daily 9am–10pm.

Café Silberstein Oranienburger Str. 27 ☏ 030/2 81 20 95. Great place, usually packed with party people and celebrated for its weird welded chairs (for sale), which mutates into a club from 11pm at weekends. U-Bahn Oranienburger Tor. Daily 10am until late.

Gorki Park Weinbergsweg 25 ☏ 030/4 48 72 86. Artsy street café with tasty and affordable Russian dishes such as blini and pelmeni. Large Milchcafé comes with a delicious molasses cookie, and the weekend brunch buffet is a treat. U-Bahn Rosenthaler Platz. Daily 9.30am until late.

Hackbarths Auguststr. 49a ☏ 030/2 82 77 06. Dominated by a huge triangular bar, Hackbarths attracts a very mixed crowd. The good choice of food includes tasty breakfasts and excellent quiche. U-Bahn Rosenthaler Platz. Daily 9am until late.

Kilkenny Irish Pub Am Zwirngraben 17–20 ☏ 030/2 83 20 84. Large, very "oirish" pub, sprawling across several rooms and with a menu that includes Irish stew and that well-known Irish dish tzatziki. Popular with expat construction workers. U- & S-Bahn Hackescher Markt. Daily 10am until late.

Mitte Bar Oranienburger Str. 46 ☏ 030/283 38 37. Relaxed by day, for a late breakfast or coffee, but best for a cocktail in the evenings when it's a favourite with bartenders after hours. Also has a small dance floor with music ranging from 1980s to experimental electronica. U-Bahn Oranienburger Tor. Daily 10am–1am.

Oscar Wilde Irish Pub Friedrichstr. 112a ☏ 030/282 81 66. Generic Irish bar and something of a social club for Berlin's English-speaking community, with quiz nights, karaoke, SkySports on the big screen and live music on Friday and Saturday nights. The all-day breakfasts and Irish stews aren't bad, particularly if you're homesick. U-Bahn Oranienburger Tor. Mon–Fri noon–1am, Sat 1pm–3am, Sun 1pm–2am.

Reingold Novalisstr. 11 ☏ 030/21 75 16 45. Sophisticated Art Deco cocktail lounge with a twenty- and thirty-something clientele lounging on the leather and velvet seating. U-Bahn Oranienburger Tor. Sun–Mon 6pm–2am Fri & Sat 7pm–4am.

Strandbad Mitte Kleine Hamburger Str. 16 ☏ 030/24 62 89 63. At the end of a small street off the beaten tourist track, this inviting café and bar, with some outdoor seating, makes a good retreat when it all gets too much. Excellent breakfasts served 9am–4pm. U-Bahn Rosenthaler Platz. Daily 9am–2am.

Zapata Oranienburger Str. 54–56 ☏ 030/281 61 09. Part of the Tacheles complex, the addition of plate-glass windows and permanent fixtures and fittings has toned this once-wild place down a little, but it's still fairly shambolic. Tip the bar staff and the dragon spits fire. If this doesn't suit, try the beer garden in the back yard and the various bars on almost every level of the building. U-Bahn Oranienburger Tor. Daily 10am–late.

Zosch Tucholskystr. 30 ☏ 030/2 80 76 64. Alternative place that started as a squat when the wall came down, and one of the few places to have changed little since: a good place for gigs and club nights in the cellar. U-Bahn Oranienburger Tor. Daily 4pm–5am.

Tiergarten and around

Café am Neuen See Lichtensteinallee 2 ☏ 030/2 54 49 30. A little piece of Bavaria smack in the middle of the Tiergarten park; this beer garden is next to a picturesque lake where you can hire a rowing boat. The usual snacks served alongside frothing jugs. Daily 10am–11pm.

Café Buchwald Bartningallee 29 ☏ 030/3 91 59 31. This old-fashioned konditorei has been serving its famed Baumkuchen since 1852, and is good for a respite from a hard session of strolling around the Tiergarten.

S-Bahn Tiergarten. Daily: March–Oct 11am–11pm, Nov–Feb 11am–6.30pm.
Schleusenkrug Müller-Breslau-Str. ☎030/313 99 09. Wedged between a canal lock, the zoo, and Tiergarten, this is a great spot to spend a last hour before hopping on a train at Zoo Bahnhof. Chairs are easy to manoeuvre for optimal sunning, and anything off the small daily menu is a safe bet. Inside, the Krug is modern diner chic. U-Bahn Zoologischer Garten. Daily: March–Oct 10am–late, Nov–Feb 10am–6pm.

The Ku'damm and around

Café Savigny Grolmanstr. 53 ☎030/31 51 96 12. Bright café serving superb coffee to an arty/media, mixed gay and straight crowd. Excellent for breakfast 10am–4pm. U-Bahn Ernst-Reuter Platz. Daily 9am–1am.
Dicke Wirtin Carmerstr. 9 ☎030/312 49 52. Traditional Berlin *Kneipe*, here since the 1920s and spruced up to make it more attractive to visitors who can pick from nine draught beers and basic snacks like Schmalzbrot (lard on bread). S-Bahn Savignyplatz. Daily noon–2am.
Gainsbourg Savignyplatz 5 ☎030/3 13 74 64. The name may pay homage to the master of risqué chansons, but the cocktails (€7–9) and food are more like *An American in Paris*. Nevertheless, they're some of the best drinks in the neighbourhood. S-Bahn Savignyplatz. Daily 5pm until late.
Galerie Bremer Fasanenstr. 37 ☎030/881 49 08. Pricey cocktail bar in a 1950s gallery – with interior features by Hans Scharoun, architect of the Berlin Philharmonic, see p.116 – that's a meeting point for actors and artists. U-Bahn Spickernstrasse. Mon–Sat 8pm until late.
Lubitsch Bleibtreustr. 47 ☎030/8 82 37 56. Slick bistro-style café that's a bit on the expensive side and very popular with business people. U-Bahn Uhlandstrasse. Mon–Sat 9.30am–1am, Sun 8pm–1am.
Rosalinde Knesebeckstr. 16 ☎030/313 59 96. Upmarket café with an unusual variety of breakfasts, served until noon: the Fitness Frühstück (muesli, fresh fruit and nuts) does the trick after a heavy night out, and there's hot food until 2am. The prices here take some beating, too: breakfasts from €3, mains from €4. S-Bahn Savignyplatz. Daily 7.30am–2am.

Zwiebelfisch Savignyplatz 7 ☎030/312 73 63. Corner bar that's a bit of a 1970s throwback for would-be arty and intellectual types. Jazz, earnest debate and good cheap grub, like goulash and Swabian Maultaschen (ravioli), served until 3am. S-Bahn Savignyplatz. Daily noon–6am.

Schöneberg

Bar am Lützowplatz Lützowplatz 7 ☎030/2 62 68 07. Distinguished by having the longest bar in the city, this place also has Berlin's best selection of whiskies (63 kinds), 150 kinds of champagne and a superb range of moderately priced cocktails (€6–14). A dangerously great bar. U-Bahn Nollendorfplatz. Daily 2pm–4am.
Café Einstein Kurfürstenstr. 58 ☎030/2 61 50 96. Housed in a seemingly ancient German villa, this is about as close as you'll get to the ambience of the prewar Berlin Kaffeehaus, with international newspapers and breakfast served until 2pm. Occasional live music, and a good garden. Expensive, though, and a little snooty. U-Bahn Nollendorfplatz. Daily 9am–midnight.
Café M Goltzstr. 34 ☎030/2 16 70 92. Though littered with tatty plastic chairs and precious little else, M is Berlin's most favoured rendezvous for self-styled creative types and the conventionally unconventional – the cool thing to drink is Flensburger Pils. Usually packed, particularly for its famous breakfasts. U-Bahn Nollendorfplatz. Mon–Fri 8am until late; Sat & Sun 9am until late.
E&M Leydicke Mansteinstr. 4 ☎030/2 16 29 73. Claiming to be the oldest *Kneipe* in western Berlin – though some of the decor looks suspiciously modern – this place is famed for its fruitwines and theme-nights: rockabilly to belly-dancing. U- and S-Bahn Yorkstrasse. Daily 7pm until late.
Felsenkeller Akazienstr. 2 ☎030/7 81 34 47. An unpretentious old bar, recently discovered by a young hip crowd. Unchanged by the experience, it continues to pour beer and dish up cheap food. U-Bahn Eisenacher Strasse. Mon–Fri 4pm–2am, Sat noon–2am, Sun 6pm–2am.
Green Door Winterfeldtstr. 50 ☎030/2 15 25 15. Somewhat snobby, dimly-lit cocktail bar, attracting a well-dressed crowd of young professionals and party-goers. Press the buzzer to get in; once you're past the pretension the place can be fun, and they

mix a really good cocktail. U-Bahn Nollendorfplatz. Mon–Fri 6pm–3am Sat & Sun 6pm–4am.

Kleisther Hauptstr. 5 ☏ 0303/7 84 67 38. Neighbourhood institution perennially crowded with style-conscious alternative types. Does a good Sunday buffet brunch (10am–4pm; €7.50). U-Kleistpark. Daily 8am–5am.

Mister Hu Goltzstr. 39 ☏ 030/2 17 21 11. Warm red cocktail bar with a great range of drinks (€5–9.50) mixed by some of the city's best bartenders. U-Bahn Eisenacher Strasse. Daily 5pm–4am.

Mutter Hohenstaufenstr. 4 ☏ 030/2 6 49 90. Large but usually crowded café-bar with loud music. Breakfast is served until 6pm, when Asian food including sushi takes over. U-Bahn Nollendorfplatz. Daily 10am–4am.

Pinguin Club Wartburgstr. 54 ☏ 030/7 81 30 05. Tiny and friendly bar with 1950s and 1960s Americana decor. Doesn't really get going until after midnight. U-Bahn Eisenacher Strasse. Daily 9pm–4am.

Tomasa Motzstr. 60 ☏ 030/2 13 23 45. Rather tacky 1970s-style interior design, but excellent Mediterranean food and popular for breakfast (until 4pm) and brunch. Reservations essential. U- & S-Bahn Viktoria-Luise-Platz. Daily 8am–2am.

Toronto Crellestr. 17 ☏ 030/7 81 92 30. Classy wood-panelled café spilling onto a large leafy plaza. Perfect on a fine summer day and excellent for homemade cake and the Sunday brunch buffet (10am–3pm; €8.70). U-Bahn Kleistpark. Mon–Sat 9am–12.30am, Sun 10am–midnight.

Zoulou Bar Hauptstr. 5. No phone. Wonderfully low-key bar packed after 11pm with sociable Schönebergers, quaffing draught *Kölsch*, Cologne's famous beer, and a few good cocktails. U-Bahn Kleistpark. Daily 8pm–6am.

Kreuzberg

Ankerklause Maybachufer 1 ☏ 030/6 93 56 49. This nautically themed pub overlooking a bucolic canal has been transformed into a hip place playing a mixture of techno and easy listening. Great breakfast choice (served until 4pm) with first-class French toast and a Mexican breakfast that will tide you over until dinner. Usually packed by 11pm. U-Bahn Kottbusser Tor. Tues–Sun 10am–4am, Mon 4pm–4am.

Atlantic Bergmannstr. 100 ☏ 030/6 91 92 92. Kreuzberg's attempt at an upmarket and chic New York bar: good for people-watching along Bergmannstrasse from the outside tables, and busy at any time of day – good snacks. U-Bahn Mehringdamm. Daily 9am until late.

Bar Skalitzerstr. 64 ☏ 030/6 12 43 88. Normally packed – chiefly because the bar staff are apt to forget to measure the drinks – and serving a good line in non-alcoholic cocktails (€4.50). U-Bahn Schlesisches Tor. Mon–Sat 10am until late, Sun 11am until late.

Barcomi's Bergmannstr. 21 ☏ 030/28 59 83 63. American-style coffee house with exotic blends accompanied by bagels, brownies and other oversized American baked goods – great cheese and carrot cake. Scattered copies of the *New Yorker* as well. U-Bahn Gneisenaustrasse. Mon–Sat 9am–10pm Sun 10am–11pm.

Bierhimmel Oranienstr. 183 ☏ 030/6 15 31 22. Candlelit bar with a cosy 1950s cocktail lounge out back. Great atmosphere, and a second home to many locals, it's good for coffee and cakes in the afternoon and cocktails later on. U-Bahn Kottbusser Tor. Daily 1pm–3am.

Café am Ufer Paul-Lincke-Ufer 43 ☏ 030/61 62 92 00. Good views of the Landwehrkanal if you sit outside and of the frequent fights if you stay inside. Nevertheless a fun place, with reasonable bar food and €6 breakfast buffets at weekends. U-Bahn Kottbusser Tor. Daily 10am until late.

Café Lebensart Mehringdamm 40 ☏ 030/7 86 84 80. A very traditional kind of café, with a long glass counter of exceptional cakes and cookies in front, and several smoky rooms for breakfast and lunch out back. U-Bahn Mehringdamm. Mon–Fri 7am–7.30pm, Sat 8am–7.30pm, Sun 9am–7.30pm.

Kloster Skalitzerstr. 76 ☏ 030/6 18 64 62. Loud and raucous night bar with a religious icon theme, located close to the former border by the Oberbaumbrücke. Also does reasonable breakfasts. U-Bahn Schlesisches Tor. Daily 10am–4am.

Konrad Tönz Falckensteinstr. 30 ☏ 030/6 12 32 52. Cheesy bar with 1970s trappings; sip cocktails (€3–7) while grooving to beat and easy listening. U-Bahn Schlesisches Tor. Tues–Sun 8.15pm until late.

Madonna Wiener Str. 22 ☏ 030/6 11 69 43. Grimy paint job, a sparse interior, and waning popularity, but this still remains one of Berlin's "in" places. Check out the ceiling fresco of the seven deadly sins, pick from the extensive whisky selection and vibrate to the loud music. U-Bahn Görlitzer Bahnhof. Daily 3pm until late.

Milagro Bergmannstr. 12 ☎030/6 92 23 03. Superb café-cum-restaurant that's become fiercely popular for its imaginative food and huge breakfasts (9am–4pm). Kloster beer on tap. U-Bahn Gneisemaustrasse. Daily 9am–1am.

Wiener Blut Wienerstr. 14 ☎030/6 18 90 23. Former studenty bar that has aged along with its clientele, though there's still table football and a buoyant, spirited atmosphere. U-Bahn Görlitzer Bahnhof. Mon–Fri 6pm until late, Sat 3pm until late, Sun 6pm until late.

Yellow Sunshine Wienerstr. 19 ☎0178/4 87 74 48. Vegetarian self-service burger bar, with set meals including fries and a drink from €6. The toasties are good for breakfast. U-Bahn Görlitzer Bahnhof. Mon–Thurs 9am–1am, Fri 9am–2am, Sat 11am–2am, Sun 11am–1am.

Friedrichshain and Prenzlauer Berg

Al Hamra Raumerstr. 16 ☎030/42 85 00 95. Comfortable Arab café with shabby decor but decent Mediterranean food, beer, water pipes, backgammon and chess, plus Internet access (€2 per hour). U-Bahn Eberswalder Strasse. Daily 10am–3am.

Astro Bar Simon-Dach-Str. 40. No phone. Enduring Friedrichshain favourite, with its 1970s sci-fi trappings and DJs most nights; gets busy when its neighbours begin to shut. U- and S-Bahn Warschauer Strasse. Daily 6pm until late.

August Fengler Lychner Str. 11 ☎030/44 35 66 40. Classic neighbourhood bar – with table football and even a Kegelbahn (German nine-pin bowling: call ahead to book, €13 per hour) – that's been taken over by a trendy disco bar set who dance in the small back room to soul, disco and funk. U-Bahn Eberswalder Strasse. Daily 7pm–6am.

Café Sybille Karl-Marx-Allee 72 ☎030/29 35 22 03. Airy café with a fin-de-siècle feel – it's been here over a century – and a diverting exhibition on the Karl-Marx-Allee in the back. Worth a visit for the cakes and ice creams alone. U-Bahn Strausberger Platz. Daily 10am–8pm.

Coyote Grünbergerstrasse 64 ☎030/29 77 14 99. Tex-Mex café with the usual finger foods and burgers, plus good cocktails at low prices. It really comes alive after about 3am, with bar staff from elsewhere heading here after closing. Good cocktails at low prices. U- and S-Bahn Warschauer Strasse. Daily 3pm–7am.

Dachkammer Simon-Dach-Str. 39 ☎030/2 96 16 73. The largest and arguably most sociable place on the strip, the combination of a rustic bar downstairs and retro bar upstairs has made this a local classic. U- and S-Bahn Warschauer Strasse. Mon–Fri noon–1am, Sat & Sun 10pm–1am.

Habana Grünberger Str. 57 ☎030/26 94 86 61. Latin-themed bar with some decent Tex-Mex food – especially the large plado variado mixed starter – and lengthy happy hours (3pm–9pm & 1–2am) when the cocktails (from €7) are half-price. U- and S-Bahn Warschauer Strasse. Daily 9am–2am.

Habermeyer Gärtnerstr. 6 ☎030/29 77 18 87. Another of Berlin's 1970s spots but with free snacks and an unusual mix of music from the DJ – from rockabilly to electronica – that give it the edge over similar places nearby. U- and S-Bahn Warschauer Strasse. Daily 7pm until late.

Intersoup Schliemannstr. 31 ☎030/23 27 30 45. Mellow den with an encyclopedic collection of excellent soups (€3.50–5) and a relaxing vibe. S-Bahn Prenzlauer Allee. Daily noon–4am.

Intimes Boxhagener Str. 107 ☎030/29 66 64 57. Laid-back studenty bar, a good place to read the paper while chomping through the grilled meats on the menu. It does a fine Sunday brunch buffet, too (10am–4pm; €8). U- and S-Bahn Warschauer Strasse. Daily 10am until late.

Kapelle Zionskirchplatz 22–24 ☎030/44 34 13 00. High ceilings and apricot walls in the shadow of the hulking Zionskirche. A little off the beaten track but worth the detour particularly if you're heading to the flea market on the Arkonaplatz. Breakfasts, snacks, cakes and great frozen fruit juices available. U-Bahn Rosenthaler Platz. Daily 9am–3am.

Metzer Eck Metzer Str. 33 ☎030/4 42 76 56. Founded in 1913, this *Kneipe* was a well-known Szene haunt during GDR times, as the signed celebrity photos that adorn the walls attest. Its old-fashioned feel makes a change from the slicker, newer places in the neighbourhood, and it serves inexpensive traditionals like sausages, Boulette and fried potatoes. (€5–9). U-Bahn Senefelderplatz. Mon–Fri 4pm–1am, Sat & Sun 6pm–1am.

November Husemannstr. 15 ☎030/4 42 84 **25.** Uncluttered exposed wood place, just north of Kollwitzplatz, with imaginative daily German specials (€7–13), a reasonable Sunday brunch (9am–4pm; €8) and outdoor seating in a pleasantly quiet residential street. U-Bahn Senefelderplatz. Mon–Fri 9am–2am, Sat & Sun 9am–3am.

Pasternak Knaackstr. 24 ☎030/4 41 33 99. Authentic upmarket Russian place that recalls the cafés and restaurants founded by Berlin's large Russian émigré community during the 1920s. A nice spot for caviar and champagne, a Milchcafé or a more substantial meal from the good selection of Russian dishes, including borscht, pelmeni and blini. The range of vodkas is suitably extensive. U-Bahn Senefelderplatz. Daily 10am until late.

Tagung Wühlischstr. 29. Friendly bar with GDR kitsch and memorabilia and a kitchen that's limited to sausage and excellent Russian stew *Soljanka* (€3). U- and S-Bahn Warschauer Strasse. Daily 7pm until late.

Wohnzimmer Lettestr. 6 ☎030/4 45 54 58. The rumpled and ramshackle living room atmosphere helps make this a relaxed and sociable hangout at any time of day – and the comfy sofas make leaving hard. Breakfast served until 4pm. U-Bahn Eberswalder Strasse. Daily 10am–4am.

Köpenick

Braustübel Müggelseedamm 164 ☎030/6 45 57 16. Waterside pub of the Berliner Bürgerbräu brewery, serving German and well-priced international dishes (mains around €8) and the fine local beer Rot Händel. S-Bahn Friedrichshagen and tram 60 or 61. Tues–Sat noon–midnight, Sun 11am–midnight.

Josef Heinrich Bölschestrasse 11. No phone. Simple modern café-bar, at the southern end of Friedrichshagen's main drag, with basic modern pub fare, soups, nachos and a cheese platter (all at around €5), and a good Sunday buffet brunch (€7.50). S-Bahn Friedrichshagen and tram 60 or 61. Mon–Fri 5pm until late; Sat 2pm until late; Sun 10pm until late

Schlosscafe Köpenick Schlossinsel ☎030/65 01 85 85. Elegant café beside Schloss Köpenick, with lake-views and excellent fresh daily dishes (mains €8–17), good cake and a wonderful Sunday brunch (10am–2pm; €13). S-Bahn Köpenick and bus M69, tram 67 or 68.

Spandau

Florida Eiscafe Klosterstr. 15 ☎030/3 31 56 **66.** Ice-cream parlour with a Berlin-wide reputation; you'll need to wait in line to see what the fuss is all about but that gives you time to choose from the forty-one flavours. U- & S-Bahn Rathaus Spandau. Daily noon–11pm.

Barfly Brüderstr. 47 ☎030/3 31 55 55. Laid-back, living-room-style café with a good, ever-changing selection of food. All meats are organic and the weekend brunch buffet (10am–2pm; €9.50) is a winner. U- & S-Bahn Rathaus Spandau. Mon–Fri 8am–3am, Sat & Sun 9am–3am.

Hausbrauereien and beer gardens

Prussian beers aren't anywhere near as famous as their Bavarian counterparts, and even play second fiddle to the beers of northwestern Germany, yet Berlin, like the rest of Germany, has seen a mini renaissance of its **Hausbrauereien** (microbreweries). The house beers in these places are generally top quality, and the decor is suitably shiny vat brewery-chic. **Beer gardens** play a significant role in Berlin, once they emerge from hibernation around the end of March, becoming convivial gathering points for outdoor beery overindulgence – always accompanied by sausages and pretzels and various other solid foods.

Many of the best places to head for are out in the suburbs, particularly **Köpenick** (eastern) and **Zehlendorf** (western), and the summer beer gardens that line the shores of the city's lakes.

Beer

For serious beer drinkers, Germany is the ultimate paradise. Wherever you go, you can be sure of getting a product made locally, often brewed in a distinctive style. The country boasts around forty percent of the world's breweries, with some 800 (about half the total) in Bavaria alone. It was in this state in 1516 that the **Reinheitsgebot** ("Purity Law") was formulated, laying down stringent standards of production, including a ban on chemical substitutes. This has been rigorously adhered to ever since. It was not so scrupulously followed by the communists, but has since been reintroduced in those East German breweries that survived closure.

Unfortunately, the law fell foul of EU bureaucrats, who deemed it a restriction on trade, since very few foreign beers met the criteria laid down (and so could not be imported), and is now unenforceable. Thankfully though, it hasn't obliged the Germans into lowering their own standards, the entire brewing industry having reaffirmed its commitment to the *Reinheitsgebot*.

There's also an encouraging continuation of old-fashioned **top-fermented** brewing styles. Until the twentieth century, all beers were made this way, but the interaction of the yeasts with a hot atmosphere meant that brewing had to be suspended during the summer. It was the Germans who discovered that the yeast sank to the foot of the container when stored under icy conditions, and thereafter, brewing took on a more scientific nature, and yeast strains were bred so that beer could be bottom-fermented, thus allowing its production all year round. While the *Reinheitsgebot* has ensured that bottom-fermented German brews are of a high standard, the technique has been a major factor in the insipidity of so much beer in other countries, including Britain. The top-fermentation process, on the other hand, allows for a far greater individuality in the taste (often characterized by a distinct fruitiness), and can, of course, now be used throughout the year, thanks to modern temperature controls. All wheat beers use this process.

Berlin beer specialities include *Berliner Weisse*, a top-fermented "young beer" that's only just fermented and still quite watery and sour, and must be drunk with a shot of fruity syrup or *Schuss*. Ask for it *mit grün* and you get a dash of woodruff, creating a greeny brew that tastes faintly like cough syrup; *mit rot* is a raspberry-flavoured drink that works wonders at breakfast time.

Alexanderplatz and around

Brauhaus Georgbräu Spreeufer 4 ℡030/242 42 44. A merry touristy locale, also popular among locals for its excellent beer and traditional German food. U-Bahn Klosterstrasse. Daily 10am–midnight.

Leopold's Brauhaus Karl-Liebknecht-Str. 13, Mitte ℡030/24 78 38 31 11. All the trappings of a Bavarian beer hall including the excellent beers – try the delicious Weissen, a cloudy Bavarian speciality– re-created in the heart of Berlin. Good for basic pub-food with well-priced lunch specials for €6. U- & S-Bahn Alexanderplatz. Mon–Sat 10am–midnight, Sun 10am–11pm.

Charlottenburg and Wilmersdorf

Luisenbräu Luisenplatz 1 ℡030/341 93 88. Large microbrewery, within sight of Schloss Charlottenburg, that's popular with locals and almost a German cliché for its muscular bar staff carrying large numbers of frothing mugs. The menu of traditional staples – sausage salad, pepper steak, pork chops – fits in perfectly, is reasonably priced and available until 11pm. Note the beer will keep coming unless you put your beer mat on the glass. U-Bahn Richard Wagner Platz. Mon–Thurs & Sun 9am–1am, Fri & Sat 9am–2am.

Kreuzberg

Golgotha Dudenstr. 48–64 ℡030/7 85 24 53. Enormous and hugely popular summer-only beer garden and disco (from 10pm) perched in the Viktoriapark near the top of Kreuzberg's hill. Breakfast served until 3pm. U- & S-Bahn Yorkstrasse. April–Sept daily 10am–late.

Prenzlauer Berg

Pfefferberg Schönehauser Alle 176 ☎ 030/2 82 92 89. This popular outdoor beer garden, in the courtyard of a former brewery, offers Czech and Bohemian tipples among its range of draught beers. Food is limited to meaty items from a couple of stalls. U-Bahn Senefelderplatz. Daily 11am until late.

Prater Kastanienallee 7–9 ☎ 030/4 448 56 88. In summer you can swig beer, feast on bratwurst and other native food, and listen to Seventies German rock in the traditional beer garden; in winter the beer hall offers a similarly authentic experience. U-Bahn Eberswalder Strasse. Beer hall Mon–Sat 6pm until late, Sun 10am until late; beer garden April–Sept daily noon till late.

Treptow

Haus Zenner in der Eierschale Alt-Treptow 14–17, Treptow ☎ 030/5 33 73 70. A large and popular beer garden by the shore of the Spree river. S-Bahn Treptower Park. Daily 10am–late.

Köpenick

Müggelseeterrassen Rübezahl Am grossen Müggelsee, Köpenick ☎ 030/65 88 24 70. Unreliable food and hideous Alexanderplatz-style architecture, but a good place for a beer looking out over the Müggelsee. S-Bahn Köpenick and bus M69. Daily 11.30am–late.

Schrörs am Müggelsee Josef-Nawrocki-Strasse 16, Friedrichshagen ☎ 030/64 09 58 80. Water-front beer garden, at the northern end of the Spreetunnel, ideally placed for a beer before or after a wander along the lake shore. After 7pm you can buy cheap local specialities like herring and fried potatoes (€5.50). S-Bahn Friedrichshagen and tram 60 or 61. Daily 11am–late.

Zehlendorf

Alter Krug Königin-Luise-Str. 52 ☎ 030/84 31 95 40. Rustic pub opposite Domäne Dahlem and close to the U-Bahn station, the big beer garden here makes it an ideal counterbalance to the nearby museums – or prepare yourself for your culture fix with breakfast or the Sunday brunch buffet (10am–2pm; €8). Later on there's lots of traditional meat and potatoes fare to choose from: mains around €12. U-Bahn Dahlem-Dorf. Daily 9am–11pm.

Loretta am Wannsee Kronprinzessinweg 260 ☎ 030/8 03 51 56. Inviting tree-lined beer garden with Wannsee views enjoyed by a mixed crowd digging into snacks and beer – let down by a confusing ordering system that requires items to be ordered at different tills. S-Bahn Wannsee. Daily 11pm–late.

Spandau

Brau Haus in Spandau Neuendorfer Str. 1, Spandau ☎ 030/353 9070. Brewery with beer garden and various beer halls. U-Bahn Altstadt Spandau. Mon 4pm–1am, Tues–Thurs 11am–1am, Fri 11am–2am, Sat 10am–2am, Sun 10am–midnight.

Restaurants

Restaurant eating in Berlin need not be expensive: a sit-down meal starts at around €6 for a single main course, and drinks aren't hiked up much more than they are in bars. When it comes to **tipping**, add a euro or so to the bill, since a fifteen percent service charge is already added. A tip should be given directly to your server when paying, rather than left on the table.

It's worth noting that Italian, Yugoslav and – especially – Greek eateries often provide the best bargains, while if you're on a *very* tight budget, try the city's *Imbiss* restaurants, which offer rock-bottom prices (see p.247).

German restaurants, on the other hand, are generally expensive. The *Gaststätte*, or traditional German eating places, with their dark wood-panelled walls, waitresses in *dirndls* and huge beer mugs, almost always have a kitsch atmosphere, and the food served is heavy and old-fashioned – dumplings,

Berlin ohne Speck – a guide for vegetarians

In the 1930s, Berlin had over thirty vegetarian restaurants, and while the city can't field anything like that amount today, it's still the best place for a vegetarian to be in a country that seems overwhelmingly to sustain itself on dead pig. There's a list of exclusively vegetarian places below: otherwise, you should generally steer clear of pubs and German restaurants, whether traditional or Neue Deutsche Küche – lard and beef stock are used ubiquitously, and there's an unwritten convention that no meal is really complete until sprinkled with small pieces of *Speck* (bacon). Refuse your plain omelette because it's been so garnished and you'll be treated with incredulity. Thankfully, the city's cosmopolitan spread of cuisines means that choosing an Italian, Indian or Thai option will usually yield something without meat on the menu, and most upmarket cafés have a flesh-free option.

Useful phrases

Ich bin Vegetarier. I am a vegetarian.
Ich esse keinen Fleisch oder Fisch. I don't eat meat or fish.
Ich möchte keinen Speck oder Fleischbrühe essen. I don't want to eat bacon or meat stock.
Gibt's Fleisch drin? Has it got any meat in it?
Gibt's was ohne Fleisch? Do you have anything without meat in it?

Vegetarian restaurants

Abendmahl (see p.245)
Beth Café (see p.242)
Einhorn (see p.248)
Hakuin (see p.245)
Yellow Sunshine (see p.237)

13

roast pork, sauerkraut, and the like. However, they are good places to meet the natives, and at the best restaurants the food can be good.

Most of the restaurants listed below are walk-in establishments; though on weekend nights or at the most expensive places, booking is recommended.

The **Nikolaiviertel**, Berlin's old quarter, is replete with restaurants, particularly of the traditional German variety, though some can be a bit touristy. There are a good variety of places in the **Scheunenviertel**, making it the best district for browsing if you're unsure what you're after. In the last decade, **Prenzlauer Berg** has gone decidedly upmarket, with pricey restaurants catering to the district's incumbent yuppies.

Unter den Linden and around

Borchardt Französische Str. 47 ☎030/20 38 71 10. A re-creation of an elegant prewar French restaurant of the same name, with original high ceilings and tile floors, and widely considered one of the top restaurants in the city. Delectable beef dishes (mains €20–30) make regular appearances, though the menu changes every day. U-Bahn Stadtmitte. Daily noon–2am.

Käfer Dachgarten Platz der Republik 1 ☎030/22 62 99 33. Famous for its location on the roof of the Reichstag and its 180-degree view of eastern Berlin, this restaurant specializes in gourmet renditions of regional German dishes (mains €7–26). A reservation here also means you get to nip in a side entrance and avoid the consistently long line at the front entrance. S-Bahn Unter den Linden. Daily 9.30am–midnight, with last orders taken at 9.30pm.

Margaux Unter den Linden 78 (entrance on Wilhelmstr.) ☎030/22 65 26 11. Onyx walls, marble floors and burgundy upholstery set the stage for this upscale restaurant, whose daily menu is dictated by the quality of available supplies. The gracious and friendly maitre d' will happily recommend wines from their selection of seven hundred; prices are harder to swallow, with mains from €18–48, but a budget alternative is offered in the form of set meals, with three-course lunches (€35) and six-course dinners (€95). S-Bahn Unter den Linden. Mon–Wed 7–10.30pm, Thurs–Sat noon–2pm, 7.30–10.30pm.

Tadschikische Teestuben Palais am Festungs-graben ☎030/2 04 11 12. More famous for its tea specialities, but also serving up tasty Russian and Tajik dishes (the latter mainly involving lamb), with most mains around the €10 mark. The intricately decorated interior is a protected monument and is festooned with oriental carpets: 1974 gifts from the USSR to the GDR. U- & S-Bahn Friedrich-strasse. Mon–Fri 5pm–midnight, Sat & Sun 3pm–midnight.

VAU Jägerstr. 54–55 ☎030/2 02 97 30. Sleek and fiercely popular high-end restaurant that specializes in utilizing ingredients from the Berlin area. The menu changes often, but expect to see intriguing combinations such as scallops, red beets, dove and polenta, or halibut, spiced taboule, carrot and apple – with prices hovering around the €35 mark. For a budget sample, try the selection of €12 lunchtime specials. U-Bahn Hausvogteiplatz. Mon–Sat noon–2.30pm & 7–10.30pm.

Alexanderplatz and around

Zille-Stube Spreeufer 3 ☎030/242 52 47. Traditional German restaurant and homage to Berlin life – and artist Heinrich Zille, in particular. Zille used to drink nearby at Zum Nussbaum (see p.233), and his illustrations line the wood-clad walls. Recommended on the menu of old Berlin favourites are the Kohlroulade (beef-stuffed cabbage leaves) and Sauerbraten (marinated pot roast); both around €10. U-Bahn Klosterstrasse. Daily noon–10pm.

Zur letzten Instanz Waisenstr. 14–16 ☎030/2 42 55 28. Berlin's oldest *Kneipe*, with a wonderfully old-fashioned interior, including a classic tiled oven, and a great beer garden. Reasonably priced traditional dishes, all with legal-themed names like Zeugen-Aussage ("Eyewitness account"), a reminder of the days when people used to drop in on the way to the nearby court-house. Considered so authentically German that foreign heads of state are often brought here: Mikhail Gorbachev

dined at Zur letzten in 1989, as has, more recently, Jacques Chirac. If all the meaty dishes (€8–13) look too heavy, try the simple Boulette, Berlin's homemade mince and herb burger, done here to perfection. U-Bahn Klosterstrasse. Mon–Sat noon–11pm, Sun noon–9pm.

The Scheunenviertel

Amrit Oranienburger Str. 45 ☎030/28 88 48 40. A cut above most of Berlin's very average Indian restaurants, delivering good-quality ingredients and fresh spices at reasonable prices (mains €7–12) and in clean-cut contemporary surroundings. Lots of veggie choices. U-Bahn Oranienburger Tor. Sun–Thurs 11am–1am, Fri & Sat 11am–late.

Beth Café Tucholskystr. 40 ☎2 81 31 35. Small and spartan, yet slightly snooty, vegetarian kosher café run by a small Orthodox Jewish congregation, with pretty courtyard seating outside and no-smoking inside. The snacks and light meals are mostly Israeli and traditional eastern European specialities, and run around €2–9. S-Bahn Oranienburger Str. Sun–Thurs midday–8pm.

Hasir Oranienburger Str. 4 ☎030/28 04 16 16. Opulent Turkish restaurant with liveried waiters, tucked away in a courtyard near the Hackescher Höfe. Look for the Grand Bazaar-style hawker to find the entrance, but don't be put off: inside is one of Europe's finest Turkish restaurants. Predictably, you can't go wrong with any of the many lamb dishes – prepared either over a wooden coal grill or in a stone oven – and there are plenty of veggie options too. Main courses mostly run around the €12–15 mark; very reasonable, given the quality. S-Bahn Hackescher Markt. Daily 11.30am–1am.

Kamala Oranienburger Str. 69 ☎030/2 83 27 97. Deservedly popular Thai restaurant in a cramped basement, where fresh and crisp ingredients produce rich curries (mains €7–15) that are enhanced rather than consumed by chillies. S-Bahn Oranienburger Str. Mon–Thurs noon–11.30pm, Fri & Sat noon–midnight, Sun 11am–11.30pm.

Kasbah Gipsstr. 2 ☎030/27 59 43 61. Fabulous little Moroccan eatery with atmospheric dimness, and a certain Arabic charm – not least when the waiter washes your hands in rosewater. Pick from an unusual mix of starters that include zaalouk, a fruity aubergine dip, and pastilla, a flaky pastry filled with chicken and onion and coated with cinnamon and icing sugar. The choice of mains (€8–13) revolves around couscous variations, kofte (spicy meatballs) and a number of first-class tajines (clay-pot stews). Clubby music and cocktails encourage lingering after dinner. U-Bahn Weinmeisterstr. Tues–Sun 4pm–midnight.

Kellerrestaurant im Brechthaus Chausseestr. 125 ☎030/282 38 43. Atmospheric restaurant in the basement of Brecht's old house, decorated with Brecht memorabilia, including models of his stage sets. Viennese specialities (mains €9–15) from recipes said to have been dreamt by Brecht's wife Helene Weigel. U-Bahn Oranienburger Tor. Daily 6pm–1am.

Monsieur Vuong Alte Schönhauser Str. 46 ☎030/30 87 26 43. Snazzy Vietnamese place with delicious soups and noodle dishes (€7–10) from a tiny menu – look out also for the daily specials on the blackboard, which are available without meat. Bench dining means you'll sometimes have to squeeze together with other diners – expect queues at peak times. Don't miss the delicious jasmine or artichoke teas, and zesty fruit smoothies. U-Bahn Weinmeisterstr. Mon–Sat noon–midnight, Sun 2pm–midnight.

Pan Asia Rosenthaler Str. 38 ☎030/27 90 88 11. Large, hip Asian restaurant, with long communal tables and simple modern decor, hidden in a courtyard beside the Hackescher Höfe. The Pan–Asian menu (mains €5–14) is huge, but avoid the pricey sushi, dull soups and bland Thai options and stick to the outstanding Chinese choices, such as Pad Puk (noodles with duck and vegetables). S-Bahn Hackescher Markt. Mon–Thurs 11am–midnight, Fri & Sat 11am–1am.

Schwarzenraben Neue Schönhauser Str. 13 ☎030/28 39 16 98. The in-crowd flock to this elegant café-restaurant in the graceful former hall of a nineteenth-century soup kitchen. Pick between the frequently changing Italian specialities, (the homemade pasta is particularly good), and wash it down with one of the vast number of wines available by the glass. On a sunny day, the back garden's a delight to sit in. U-Bahn Weinmeisterstrasse. Daily noon–3.30pm & 6.30pm–midnight.

Unsicht-bar Gormannstr. 14 ☎030/24 34 25 00. Hugely successful novelty restaurant (run by an organization of the blind and visually impaired), where you eat in total darkness. First, pick from one of several three- or four-course fixed menus (€40–60), including a vegetarian option, then follow your blind or partially sighted waiter into the pitch black for your meal. The idea is that without your eyesight, your other senses will be heightened, but you're likely to make other discoveries, too, including how hard it is to judge the amount of food that's on your plate or fork, or even down your front. U-Bahn Weinmeisterstr. Daily 6pm–midnight.

Viva Mexico Chausseestr. 36 ☎030/2 80 78 65. Authentic, family-owned Mexican restaurant with a vivacious vibe, fresh ingredients, moderate prices, and salsa to die for. U-Bahn Zinnowitzer Str. Mon–Thurs noon–11pm, Fri noon–midnight, Sat & Sun 5pm–midnight.

Yosoy Rosenthaler Str. 37 ☎030/28 39 12 13. Inexpensive tapas bar, with beautiful tile work and a Spanish staff, perfectly placed for before-drinking or after-clubbing dinners (€9–15). S-Bahn Hackescher Markt. Daily 11am–2am.

Tiergarten and around

Angkor Wat Paulstr. 22 ☎030/3 93 39 22. Excellent place, serving subtle variations on traditional Cambodian food at moderate prices (mains €10–15). The two-person set meals (from €30) are a great way to sample a cross-section of delicious dishes. S-Bahn Bellevue. Daily 8–11pm.

Paris-Moskau Alt-Moabit 141 ☎030/3 94 20 81. Housed in a former train station on the Paris to Moscow line, this French gourmet restaurant is popular with politicians and civil servants from the nearby government district and manages to be elegant without being too snooty. But it's expensive: dishes such as the rack of lamb with roasted artichokes and gnocchi, or the pigeon-breast pie with fired goose liver on chicory with new potatoes, cost around €20–25. S-Bahn Lehrter Bahnhof. Daily 6–11.30pm.

Charlottenburg and Wilmersdorf

Casa Portuguesa Helmholtzstr. 15 ☎030/3 93 55 06. Rustic, family-run Portuguese place, with well-above-average food, musicians some evenings, and the freshest of fish. Menu prices range widely, with the cheapest mains around €6, the priciest €17. U-Bahn Turmstrasse. Mon–Sat 5pm–midnight, Sun 4pm–midnight.

Hitit Knobelsdorffstr. 35 ⊕030/3 22 45 57. Proof that Turkish cuisine offers much more than doner kebabs, with an equal mix of meat and vegetarian choices. Prices are barely higher, though, with mains running at €4–12. Reservations recommended. U-Bahn Sophie-Charlotte-Platz. Daily 8am–midnight.

The Ku'damm and around

Arche Noah Fasanenstr. 79–80 ⊕030/8 82 61 38. Wonderful kosher delights served up in a great atmosphere. Mains are a bit pricey at €10–16; but the €18 buffet (Tues only) is highly recommended for its thirty different dishes. U- & S-Bahn Zoologischer Garten. Daily 11.30am–3.30pm & 6.30–11pm.

Diekmann Meinekestr. 7 ⊕030/8 83 33 21. Longstanding Berlin bistro, with French colonial touches in the decor and on the menu; the €10 three-course business lunches are a bargain, otherwise you'll pay €15–21 for oft-changing mains that are always fresh and reliable – the oysters are particularly good. U-Bahn Kurfürstendamm. Mon–Sat noon–11.30pm, Sun 6–11.30pm.

Florian Grolmanstr. 52 ⊕030/313 91 84. Leading light of the Neue Deutsche Küche movement in Berlin (see box on p.230), this is as much a place for Berlin's beautiful people to be seen in as it is a place to eat in. The food, similar to French nouvelle cuisine, is light and flavourful and only moderately expensive at €12–20 for main courses. S-Bahn Savignyplatz. Daily 6pm–3am.

Good Friends Kantstr 30. ⊕030/3 13 26 59. One of the city's few really authentic Cantonese restaurants, with many unusual items (mains €7–19) as well as Peking Duck (24hrs' notice required), a rarity in Berlin's Chinese restaurants. Always busy; evening bookings recommended. S-Bahn Savignyplatz. Daily noon–2am.

Kashmir Palace Marburger Str. 14 ⊕030/2 14 28 40. Upmarket Indian offering as authentic a cuisine as you'll find in Berlin – thanks, in part, to the Tandoori oven – but a general toning down for the German

palate may require you asking for things to be spiced up a little. Prices are a bit steep, with basic main dishes starting at €10. U-Bahn Augsburger Str. Mon 5pm–midnight, Tues–Fri noon–3pm & 6pm–midnight, Sat & Sun noon–midnight.

Paris Bar Kantstr. 152 ⊕3 13 80 52. Once the city's most famous meeting place for artists, writers and intellectuals, high prices mean that it's now wholly the preserve of the moneyed middle classes – and visiting celebrities including Madonna, Robert de Niro and Mikhail Gorbachev. The food is French and Viennese in style and the service immaculate, but it's probably not worth the €16–24 charged for the mains; weekday lunches, however, are a bargain at €10.50 each. U-Bahn Uhlandstrasse. Daily noon–2am.

Zwölf Apostel Bleibtreustr. 49 ⊕030/3 12 14 33. This deluxe pizzeria has been packing them in for years, with out-of-the-ordinary toppings like smoked salmon and cream cheese and five types of calzone (mains: €8–24). The €5 weekday lunch (noon–4pm) is excellent. Booking recommended. S-Bahn Savignyplatz. Open 24hrs.

Schöneberg

Aroma Hochkirchstr. 8 ⊕7 82 58 21. Quality Italian restaurant with photo gallery that shows Italian films on Tuesday nights. One of the best options in this part of town, it's advisable to book ahead. Mains cost between €7 and €15; the top-notch Sunday brunch buffet (until 4pm) costs €9.50. U- & S-Bahn Yorckstrasse. Mon–Fri 5.30pm–1am, Sat noon–1am, Sun 11am–1am.

Carib Motzstr. 31 ⊕030/2 13 53 81. Classic Caribbean cuisine fused with European dishes (mains €11.50–15.50) and served by the friendly Jamaican owner. Reservations recommended. U-Bahn Nollendorfplatz. Daily 5pm–midnight.

Edd's Thailändisches Lutzowstr. 81 ⊕2 15 52 94. Huge portions of superbly cooked fresh Thai food make this a sumptuous place, popular all week. Bearing in mind the quality and authenticity – many family recipes stem from Edd's gran, who cooked in Bangkok's Royal Palace – the prices are very reasonable, with mains from €8 to €15. Booking is essential and credit cards not accepted. U-Bahn

Kurfürstenstrasse. Tues–Fri 11.30am–4pm & 6pm–midnight, Sat 5pm until late, Sun 2pm–midnight.

Hakuin Martin-Luther-Str. 1 ☎2 18 20 27. Exceptional Japanese vegetarian-macrobiotic, run by a Buddhist order, featuring tofu and tempura dishes (€15–19), often complemented by a seaweed salad. Quiet and no smoking, so booking recommended. U-Bahn Wittenbergplatz. Tues–Sat 5–11.30pm, Sun midday–11.30pm.

Maharadscha Fuggerstr. 21 ☎030/2 13 88 26. Though the ambience is that of a German farmhouse, the food is pure Indian, with dishes (€6–10) from every part of the subcontinent. Gets packed out for the Sunday buffet (noon–5pm; €6.90). U-Bahn Nollendorfplatz. Sun–Thurs 11.30am–midnight, Fri & Sat 11.30am–1am.

Petite Europe Langenscheidtstr. 1 ☎7 81 29 64. Unpretentious Italian place that dishes up filling homemade pastas and stone-oven pizzas (€4–12) in an informal, lively atmosphere. Usually full, so booking is advised. U-Bahn Kleistpark. Daily 5pm–1am.

Storch Wartburgstr. 54 ☎7 84 20 59. Rustic eatery serving cuisine from the Alsace region in what was once – they claim – a brothel. The excellent food, a mix of French and German and often including wild boar (mains €14–18), is served at long communal tables. Bookings advisable, though none is taken after 8pm. U-Bahn Eisenacher Strasse. Daily 6pm–1am (kitchen closes at 11.30pm).

Tim's Canadian Deli Maassenstr. 14 ☎030/21 75 69 60. One of the best North American restaurants in Berlin, featuring hearty meals, including burgers, ribs, club sandwiches and buffalo meat. There's also a good line in baked goods, particularly brownies, pastries and bagels. Known for its generous breakfasts, including, of course, maple-syrup-soaked pancakes. U-Nollendorfplatz. Mon–Thurs 8am–1am, Fri & Sat 8am–3am, Sun 9am–1am.

Kreuzberg

Abendmahl Muskauerstr. 9 ☎030/6 12 51 70. Predominantly vegetarian restaurant (it also serves fish), magnificent in every respect: excellent food (especially the soups – try the Kürbis or pumpkin) and a busy but congenial atmosphere. Main courses (€10.50–17.50) have funky names and the

Flaming Inferno, a spicy fish curry, is well worth trying, as is the fine selection of so-called Deadly Ice Creams. U-Bahn Görlitzer Bahnhof. Daily 6pm–1am.

Altes Zollhaus Carl-Herz-Ufer 30 ☎6 92 33 00. Very classy place located in an old half-timbered building overlooking a canal, serving modern German food such as duck from Brandenburg with Kartoffelpuffer, and zander from the Havel. The three-course set menus cost €35. U-Bahn Prinzenstrasse. Tues–Sat 6pm–1am.

Amrit Oranienstr. 202 ☎030/28 88 48 40. The seating is always a bit of a squeeze at this busy Indian restaurant, where the huge portions are inexpensive (mains €7–14) and delicious. Not the sort of place to linger after a meal, and reservations are recommended in the week and essential at weekends. U-Bahn Görlitzer Bahnhof. Sun–Thurs noon–midnight, Fri & Sat noon–1am.

Austria Bergmannstr. 30 ☎030/694 44 40. Generous portions of excellent Austrian food – particularly Wiener Schnitzel – are served up on solid wood tables in dark, rustic surrounds. Mains range between €8 and €17. U-Bahn Gneisenaustrasse. Daily 7pm–midnight.

Bar Centrale Yorckstr. 82 ☎030/7 86 29 89. Chic Italian locale, popular with the affluent young, and exiled Italians. Lots of fresh antipasti, pasta, fish and meat dishes (mains €13–18) and an international wine list. U-Bahn Mehringdamm. Mon–Thurs noon–2am, Fri & Sat noon–3am.

Gorgonzola Club Dresdener Str. 121 ☎030/6 15 64 73. Classy pizzas and freshly made pasta (€8–14) – choose any sauce with any pasta – in a rustic, fun atmosphere that's also, unfortunately, often very smoky. U-Bahn Kottbusser Tor. Daily 6pm until late.

Henne Leuschnerdamm 25 ☎030/6 14 77 30. Pub-style restaurant serving the best fried chicken (€6) in Berlin. The interior is original – it hasn't been changed, the owners claim, since 1905. Reservations essential. Daily 7pm–midnight.

Kuchen Kaiser Oranienpl. 11–13 ☎030/61 40 26 97. Well-rounded café, overlooking a green platz, serving a mixed bag of items in a laid-back atmosphere. Great for cakes at any time, but otherwise at its best during the Sunday brunch buffet (€8; 10am–4pm) with special kids' rates, and its "Chicken, wings and ribs" buffet (Thurs 8pm; €7.50). U-Bahn Moritzplatz. Daily 9am until late.

Morgenland Skalitzer Str 35 ☎ 030/6 11 31 83. Relaxed café with a mix of European snacks and welcoming vibe. The amazing Sunday brunch buffet (until 3pm; €7.50) seems to attract most of the neighbourhood. U-Bahn Görlitzer Bahnhof. Daily 9.30am–2am.

Osteria No. 1 Kreuzbergstr. 71 ☎ 030/7 86 91 62. Classy and popular Italian, run by a collective, dishing up quality pizzas and oft-changing pastas (€7–17) in a lush courtyard. Particularly child-friendly (kids under eight eat for free on Sun). Booking recommended. U-Bahn Mehringdamm. Daily 10am–2pm.

Weltrestaurant Markthalle Pücklerstr. 34 ☎ 030/6 17 55 02. Spacious restaurant with long communal tables, offering German food in hearty portions. Popular with a young crowd. Look out for the €7.50 daily special and leave space for the phenomenal cakes. U-Bahn Görlitzer Bahnhof. Daily 9am until late.

Zagato Bergmannstr. 27 ☎ 030/6 91 34 68. Tiny, unassuming Italian joint, with plastic tablecloths and basic but delicious dishes. U-Bahn Gneisenaustrasse. Mon–Sat 6pm–midnight.

Friedrichshain and Prenzlauer Berg

Bangkok Prenzlauer Alle 46 ☎ 030/4 43 94 05. Authentic and very good Thai food. First choice in Prenzlauer Berg for inexpensive dining (dishes €3.30–9), and consequently often a bit too busy for its own good. U-Bahn Senefelderplatz. Daily 11am–11pm.

Cenasolo Sredzkistr. 23 ☎ 030/44 04 47 43. Stone-oven pizzas and fresh pasta (€5–15) don't get much better than at this inexpensive bistro – and the open kitchen lets you watch the mouth-watering preparation process. U-Bahn Eberswalder Strasse. Daily noon–1am.

Chez Maurice Botzowstr. 39 ☎ 030/4 25 05 06. A little out of the way but worth it for the totally authentic food and theatrics of the manic French chef Maurice. Service can be slow, so count on spending the better part of an evening here. Mains €12–16; reservations recommended. S-Bahn Griefswalder Strasse. Tues–Sat noon–4pm, daily 6.30pm–late.

Fritz Fischer Stralauer Allee 1 ☎ 030/5 20 07 22 02. Classy waterfront restaurant with views of the Oberbaumbrücke, Spree and Treptow, and delicious, if pricey (€14.50–21.50), fish dishes; lunchtime specials are a bargain (€2.50–5), though. U- and S-Bahn Warschauer Strasse. Mon–Fri noon–3pm & 6.30pm until late, Sat 6.30pm until late.

Gugelhof Knaackstr. 37 ☎ 030/4 42 92 29. Lively Alsatian restaurant put on the map by Bill Clinton's surprise visit in 2000, and successful ever since. Serves inventive and beautifully presented German, French and Alsatian food (mains €7–17) – worth trying is the unusual Flammekuchen, a thin-crust Alsatian pizza. U-Bahn Senefelderplatz. Daily 6pm–midnight, Sat & Sun 10am–midnight.

Mao Thai Wörther Str. 30 ☎ 030/4 41 92 61. Perhaps a bit overpriced, but the Thai food is excellent, garnished with delightful little sculpted vegetables, and the service, in traditional garb, unfailingly polite. Mains €8–15. U-Bahn Senefelderplatz. Daily noon–midnight.

Miseria & Nobiltà Kopernikusstr. 16 ☎ 030/29 04 92 49. Lively and highly personable low-key Sardinian restaurant, with flamboyant staff and phenomenal homemade food. Booking recommended. U- and S-Bahn Warschauer Strasse. Tues–Thurs 5pm–midnight, Fri–Sat 5pm until late.

Naan Oderbergerstr. 49 ☎ 030/44 05 84 14. South of Kastanienallee, an authentic Indian restaurant with low prices – no dish over €5 – that's always jam-packed with Prenzlauer Berg's art and student crowd. U-Bahn Eberswalder Strasse. Daily noon–midnight.

Ostwind Husemannstr. 13 ☎ 030/4 41 59 51. Serene setting for superb modern and traditional (and MSG-free) Chinese dining. Prices are a little above average (mains €6.50–13.50), but justified by the quality of the ingredients and preparation. The Sunday brunch (all day; €8) is as good as it is unusual. U-Bahn Eberswalder Strasse. Mon–Sat 6pm–1am, Sun 10am–1am.

Restauration 1900 Husemannstr. 1 ☎ 030/4 42 24 94. A Kollwitzplatz culinary highlight, serving traditional German dishes that spring a few surprises, as well as some pasta and vegetarian options (€9–15). It's also another good option for a Sunday buffet brunch (10am–4pm; €8). Check out the photographs of the neighbourhood before and after reunification. U-Bahn Eberswalder Strasse. Daily 10am–midnight.

Trattoria Paparazzi Husemannstr. 35 ☎030/4
40 73 33. Top-rated place with outstanding
Italian food and a large wine list. Prices are
reasonable, given the quality, with mains
€10–61. U-Bahn Eberswalder Strasse. Daily
8pm–1am (kitchen until 11.30pm).
Zum Schusterjungen Danziger Str. 9 ☎030/4
42 76 54 Large portions of no-nonsense
German food served in the back room of
a locals' *kneipe*. The plastic and Formica
decor has echoes of the GDR and, at
around €8 per dish, the prices are almost
as cheap as back then, too. U-Bahn
Eberswalder Str. Daily 11am–midnight.

Köpenick

Ratskeller Köpenick Alt Köpenick 21 ☎030/6 55
56 52. Authentic Ratskeller full of locals, and
serving decent, value-for-money German
food from €6 per dish. Occasional live jazz.
S-Bahn Köpenick. Daily 11am–11pm.

Spandau

Kolk Hoher Steinweg 7 ☎030/3 33 88 79.
Popular family-run restaurant in an old fire
station, serving regional dishes, including
good vegetarian versions (mains €8–16).
Its outdoor seating is beside the old city
walls. U-Bahn Altstadt Spandau. Daily
11.30am–midnight.
La Bottega Breite Str. 56–58 ☎030/36 75
01 71. Unpretentious Italian trattoria with
exceptional food and prices for every
budget; mains are in the €4.50 to €13.50
range. U-Bahn Altstadt Spandau. Mon–Sat
9am–midnight.

Snack bars

For cheap, on-the-hoof snacks, head for one of the ubiquitous **Imbiss stands**
found on street corners, where for a couple of euros you can fill up on *Currywurst* – a chubby smoked pork sausage smothered in curried ketchup – which
originated in Berlin – and French fries (*Pommes Frites*); or try a *Boulette*, a
hamburger pattie made from ground beef, eggs, butter and onions, which
was first introduced into the city by the French Huguenots in the late 1600s.
Even more common are Turkish *Imbiss* stands selling doner or chicken kebabs
– in pitta bread with salad. Greek stands are also popular, selling Greek doner
kebabs, known as *Gyros*, in a puffy pitta-style bread, generally with a tzatziki-
type sauce; these are great value at around €1.50–3.

For something more substantial but barely more expensive, **Imbiss restaurants** – a step up from the *Imbiss* street stall, and usually with some seating
– charge between €3.50 and €6 for a meal, and are handy if you want to
refuel cheaply. They come in many guises – some serving German sausages,
others Turkish, Greek or Chinese food – with major concentrations of all types
around the main train stations.

Unter den Linden and around

Asia Snack Bahnhof Friedrichstrasse. For
once, dishes closely resemble the menu
photos at this small eatery selling quick
fixes of Thai and pan-Asian food to hungry
diners. It's one of a number of such places
under the S-Bahn tracks, and good for a
quick lunch. U- & S-Bahn Friedrichstrasse.
Daily 10am–late.
Salomon Bagels Potsdamer Platz Arkaden, 1st
floor. Good selection of bagels,
sandwiches and sweets, but as with all
of the many cheap eateries in this mall
– there's a concentration of them in the
basement – the noise and bustle don't
exactly create a relaxing atmosphere.
U- & S-Bahn Potsdamer Platz. Daily
9am–late.

Alexanderplatz and around

Hong Kong Express Karl-Liebknecht-Str. 5
☎030/40 05 48 83. Good slap-up Cantonese
cooking accessed from a courtyard beside
the Radisson. Most dishes are around
the €6.50 mark, and there's a surprisingly
good line in cocktails, both alcoholic and
soft. U- & S-Bahn Hackescher Markt. Daily
11am–11pm.

The Scheunenviertel

Piccola Italia Oranienburger Str. 6 ☏ 030/2 83 58 43. The constant stream of snackers who mill around the steps of this place can't be wrong: the thin-based pizza's excellent and, at €1.50 a slice, well priced. U- & S-Bahn Hackescher Markt. Sun–Thurs 11am–1am, Fri & Sat 11am–3am.

The Ku'damm and around

Einhorn Mommsenstr. 2 ☏ 030/8 81 42 41. Vegetarian wholefood at its best, with a daily changing international menu and a fabulous lunch-bar. Low prices (€3–6 per dish) mean it's often packed to standing, yet the atmosphere remains friendly and relaxed. U-Bahn Uhlandstrasse. Mon–Fri 10am–5pm.

Piccola Taormina Uhlandstrasse 29 ☏ 030/8 81 47 10. Enduringly popular wafer-thin pizza specialist with a strange setup: order what you want and pay at the bar, find a seat in the back room, listen up for a tannoy announcement when it's ready, then head back to the bar to collect. It's all a bit chaotic and very Italian, but well worth it for the food – slices from €1. U-Bahn Uhlandstrasse. Daily 10am–2am.

Schöneberg

Baharat Falafel Winterfeldtstr. 37 ☏ 030/2 16 83 01. The best falafels this side of Baghdad. U-Bahn Nollendorfplatz. Daily 11am–2am.

Habibi Goltzstr. 24 ☏ 030/2 15 33 32. Amiable late-night falafel shop with seating. U-Bahn Nollendorfplatz. Fri 11am–5am, Sat–Thurs 11am–3am.

Tori Katsu Winterfeldtstr. 7 ☏ 030/2 16 34 66. Slightly chaotic Japanese Imbiss – here long before sushi became popular – specializing in dishes with breaded chicken. U-Bahn Nollendorfplatz. Daily 11am–10pm.

Kreuzberg

Nachtigall Imbiss Ohlauerstr. 10 ☏ 030/6 11 71 15. Arab specialities, including the delicious Schwarma kebab – lamb and hummus in pitta bread. Good salads for vegetarians as well. U-Bahn Görlitzer Bahnhof. Daily 11.30am–1.30am.

Pagode Bergmannstr. 88 ☏ 030/6 19 26 40. The Thai meals dished up here enjoy a high reputation among Berlin's Imbiss aficionados. U-Bahn Gneisnaustrasse. Daily noon–midnight.

Friedrichshain and Prenzlauer Berg

Duy Thai Prenzlauer Allee 226. No phone. Inexpensive and tasty Thai cuisine, including crispy duck with fruit, as well as many vegetarian and noodle dishes. U-Bahn Senefelderplatz. Mon–Fri noon–midnight, Sat & Sun 1pm–midnight.

Imbiss Konnopke Schönhauser Allee 44a ☏ 030/4 42 77 65. Pre-fab shack under the S-Bahn lines, serving some of Berlin's best Currywurst and unbeatable fries – a simple formula, but one that ensures queues at any time of day. U-Bahn Eberswalder Strasse. Mon–Fri 6am–8pm.

Kietzkantine Oderberger Str. 50 ☏ 030/4 48 44 84. Choose from just two or three excellent daily specials at rock-bottom prices in this hugely popular bistro. There's always something vegetarian, and students get a discount – order and pay at the till, the food will then be brought to your seat. U-Bahn Eberswalder Strasse. Mon–Fri 9am–4pm.

EATING AND DRINKING | Snack bars

Clubs and live music

S ince the time of the Weimar Republic, and even through the lean postwar years, Berlin has had a reputation for having some of the best – and steamiest – nightlife in Europe, an image fuelled by the cartoon-like drawings of George Grosz and films like *Cabaret*. Today the big draw is the clubs that have grown up out of the city's techno scene. In a remarkably short space of time these places, many housed in abandoned buildings on or around the former no-go area of the East–West border strip, have spawned a scene that ranks among the most exciting in Europe. As well as this manic dance music scene, Berlin has a wide range of more traditional clubs and discos, ranging from slick hangouts for the trendy to raucous punky dives – where you'll find live music of just about every sort. The way to find out exactly what's on and where is by checking the listings magazines *Tip* (Ⓦwww.tip-berlin.de) and *Zitty* (Ⓦwww.zitty.de), available at any newsstand, and by looking out for posters and flyers. Two free leaflets, Flyer (Ⓦwww .flyer.de) and *guide*, or *030*, list parties and clubs. They can be picked up in record shops, clubs, bars and cafés. On the web, Ⓦwww.clubcommission.de is another useful source of German-only listings information. In common with most major cities, Berlin's turnover in nightspots is rapid: expect the following listings to have changed at least slightly by the time you arrive – this applies particularly to the newer places on the east side of town.

Clubbing

Berlin's clubs and discos are smaller, cheaper and less exclusive than their counterparts in London or New York – and fewer in number. Most of the in-places are in former East Berlin, where glitz is out and raving is in. For the slightly older crowd, Schöneberg and Kreuzberg tend to be where it's happening. Don't bother turning up until midnight at the earliest, since few places get going much before then, and note that at most places closing time will depend on how busy it is and the mood of the staff – though 6am is a fairly typical time to shut. Admission is often free – though cover charges tend to run from €5 to €11 on weekends and can change dramatically depending on the event. Some places have strict door policies, but in the main, if you look the part you'll probably get in. If you're in Berlin primarily to go clubbing, consider getting the 19 Clubshuttle Berlin pass, available from the tourist office (see p.28). It gives you entry to a dozen big-name clubs and includes a transport service on a Saturday night.

Unter den Linden and around

Tresor & Globus Leipziger Str. 126a ⓣ030/229 06 11, ⓦwww.tresorberlin.de. A key player in the burgeoning of Berlin's dance music scene since 1990, though regulars claim that it's not as good as it used to be. Nevertheless, trouser-shaking techno in the steamy basement and slightly mellower house and hip-hop beats upstairs still attract clubbers from all over Europe. U- and S-Bahn Potsdamer Platz. Wed–Sat 11pm–6am.

Alexanderplatz and around

Sternradio Alexanderplatz 5 ⓣ030/2 46 25 93 20, ⓦwww.sternradio-berlin.de. Compact all-in-one club-bistro-lounge package on the inhospitable strip between the TV Tower and the Rotes Rathaus. Music runs the full spectrum of electronic dance music, house, techno, and drum 'n' bass, often with big-name guest DJs and local heroes such as Clé and Mitja in residency. U- and S-Bahn Alexanderplatz. Fri & Sat 11pm until late.

The Scheunenviertel

Delicious Doughnuts Rosenthaler Str. 9, Mitte ⓣ2 83 30 21, ⓦwww.delicious-doughnuts.de. Beautiful party people grooving to acid jazz, trip-hop and funk beats. Best as a pre- or post-club venue, though the little dance floor can be busy until 10am. U-Bahn Rosenthaler Platz. Entry €3. Daily 10pm until late.

Grüner Salon Rosa-Luxemburg-Pl. 2 ⓣ030/24 59 89 36, ⓦwww.gruener-salon.de. All-green club beside the Roter Salon (see below) that preserves something of the 1920s in its chandeliers and velvet. Renowned for its Thursday tango, Friday swing and Saturday cabaret (8–10pm) evenings. Entry €4–15. U-Bahn Rosa-Luxemburg-Platz. Mon–Sat 7pm until late.

Kaffee Burger Torstr. 60 ⓣ030/28 04 64 95, ⓦwww.kaffeeburger.de. Russian-owned smoky 1970s retro-bar legendary for its Russian disco nights, but good anytime, not least for the mad mix of genres – Balkan, surf rock, samba, rockabilly – that fills the small dance floor. Readings and poetry often start evenings off, but it really fills up later on. Entry €3–5. U-Bahn Rosa-Luxemburg-Platz. Daily 7pm until late.

Kingkongklub Brunnenstr. 173 ⓣ030/28 59 85 38. Rock club with massive dark leather sofas and DJs spinning just about any genre of rock from Elvis through Hendrix to the sounds of contemporary local bands; draws an older thirty-something crowd. Popular rock 'n' roll nights on Fridays. Entry €8. U-Bahn Rosenthaler Platz. Mon–Sat 9pm until late.

Kurvenstar (K-Star) Kleine Präsidentenstr. 3 ⓣ030/28 59 97 10, ⓦwww.kurvenstar.de. Beautifully decorated retro 1970s club with a bar and lounge up front and dance floor in the back. Caters now to a young, not very gregarious, crowd: Tuesday is Jazz Radio night, Wednesday break beats, Thursday live music, and Saturday hip-hop. S-Bahn Hackescher Markt. Daily midday till late.

Mudd Club Grosse Hamburger Str. 17 ⓣ030/443 62 99. Brick basement bar at the back of a courtyard based on the New York club of the same name. Furnishings are of the comfy 70s variety and the best nights are offered by Balkan Beats events which scout talent from Eastern Europe. S-Bahn Hackescher Markt. Wed–Sun 9.30pm until late.

Roter Salon Rosa-Luxemburg-Pl. 2 ⓣ030/24 06 58 06. Tatty club within the Volksbühne theatre, with lurid red decor and chintzy furniture giving it the feel of a 1950s brothel. Readings, concerts and club nights are held here. Wednesday is soul and funk night, other nights a mix of Electronica, ska and Brit-pop. Entry €5–6. U-Bahn Rosa-Luxemburg-Platz. Most nights 11pm–4am.

Sophienclub Sophienstr. 6 ⓣ2 82 45 52. Small, functional and rather nondescript club with a couple of cramped, well-populated dance floors and a mixed crowd. At its best on Tuesdays' Brit-pop nights, otherwise patrons survive on a mixed diet of soul, funk, house and indie. Entry €3–5. S-Bahn Hackescher Markt. Tues & Thurs–Sun 10pm until late.

Tiergarten and around

Polar TV Heidestr. 73, cnr Invalidenstr. ⓣ030/246 25 93 20, ⓦwww.polar.tv. Large cutting-edge warehouse techno club, in the middle of nowhere – in terms of other nightlife – that attracts big-name DJs. One floor's generally reserved for experimental and deep house, the rest has more hectic beats, and there's a refreshing outdoor area. Entry €10.

S-Bahn Hauptbahnhof Lehrter Bahnhof.
Wed–Sat 11pm until late.

Charlottenburg & Wilmersdorf

Abraxas Kantstr. 134, Charlottenburg ☎ 030/3
12 94 93. Hot and sweaty dance floor,
specializing in funk and hip-hop and Latin
American. Gregarious and lots of fun. Entry
€3–5. S-Bahn Savignyplatz. Tues–Sat
10pm until late.

Far Out Kurfürstendamm 90, Wilmersdorf
☎ 030/32 00 07 23, Ⓦ www.farout-berlin.de.
Formerly a Bhagwan disco, now a friendly
and very mainstream nightspot for a mix
of offbeat conservatives and tourists. Gets
crowded. Entry €3–5; Wed over-30s free.
U-Bahn Adenauer Platz. Mon 8pm until
late, Tues 7pm until late, Wed 9pm until
late, Thurs–Sun 10pm until late.

Schöneberg

90° ("Neunzig Grad") Dennewitzstr. 37,
Kreuzberg ☎ 030/2 62 89 84, Ⓦ www.90
-grad.de. Glamorous jet-set and celebrity
magnet with strict door policies: unless
you look like one of the stylish beautiful
people, you've got no chance. Entry
€5–10. U-Bahn Kurfürstenstrasse. Wed
7pm until late, Fri & Sat 11pm until late.

Havanna Hauptstr. 30 ☎ 030/784 85 65,
Ⓦ www.havanna-berlin.de. Up-beat Latin
disco, with seven bars and three dance
floors: one for salsa and merengue, and the
others to groove to funk and R&B. Dance
classes available; entry €2.50–7. U-Bahn
Kleistpark. Wed 9pm until late, Fri & Sat
10pm until late (typically 4am).

Kit-Kat Club Bessemerstr. 2–14. No phone,
Ⓦ www.kitkatclub.de. Famously debauched
club, not for voyeurs but those looking for
casual and public liaisons. The door policy
is strict: wear something revealing or fet-
ishistic – check the website for guidelines,
and for details of theme evenings. Gay
parties are usually held during the week, at
weekends it's a free-for-all – starting at 8am
on Sundays. S-Bahn Priesterweg. Fri & Sat
11pm until late, Sun 8am until late.

Kumpelnest 3000 Lützowstr. 23 ☎ 030/261 69
18. Carpeted walls and a mock-Baroque
effect attract a rough-and-ready crew of
thirty-somethings to this erstwhile brothel.
Gets going around 2am, by which time
there's standing room only. Good fun, and
the best place in the area and infamous as

a hook-up bar. U-Bahn Kurfürstenstrasse.
Sun–Thurs 5pm–5am, Fri & Sat 5pm until
late.

Kreuzberg

Avastar Nostitzstr. 12, Kreuzberg ☎ 030/69 53
36 08. Relaxing and hip little place in western Kreuzberg, with wild video collages on
the wall and an mp3 jukebox. Entry free
and via a doorbell. U-Bahn Merhingdamm.
Daily 8pm until late.

Ankerklause Kottbusser Damm 104 ☎ 030/6 93
56 49. A little café, perched by the Land-
wehr canal, turns into a funk and soul club
by night. Very trendy and very crowded.
Thursday is 60s night. Mon 4pm until late,
Tues–Sun 10am until late. U-Bahn
Kottbusser Tor.

Golgotha Dudenstr. 48–64 ☎ 030/7 85 24 53.
Kreuzberg's popular hillside café (see p.239)
hosts a daily alfresco disco from 10pm
April–Sept; good fun on warm evenings.
U- & S-Bahn Yorckstrasse. April–Sept daily
10am until late.

Privatclub Pücklerstr. 34 Kreuzberg ☎ 030/6 11
30 02, Ⓦ www.privatclub-berlin.de. Cellar club
below Weltrestaurant Markthalle, which is
notable for weekend theme parties – that
attract a wide range of ages – ranging
from 1970s disco trash and new wave to
blaxploitation funk, often guest-DJ-ed by
local celebrities such as splatter-flick director Jörg Buttgereit. Local bands often play
here. €6–7. U-Bahn Görlitzer Bhf. Fri & Sat
11pm until late.

Sage Club Köpenicker Str. 76 ☎ 030/278 98
30, Ⓦ www.sage-club.de. One of Berlin's
premier clubs, with multiple dance floors
and a good range of sounds: Thursdays
is rock night; Fridays hip-hop and R 'n' B,
Saturdays mainstream techno and Sundays
a tremendously popular hard house, trance
and progressive mix. Always a good vibe,
but perhaps a bit too popular with teenag-
ers – the bouncers regularly dress in drag
to scare them away. U-Bahn Heinrich-
Heine-Str. Thurs 10pm until late, Fri–Sun
11pm–9am.

SO36 Oranienstr. 190, Kreuzberg ☎ 030/61 40
13 06, Ⓦ www.so36.de. Kreuzberg institution,
whose heyday may have been the 1980s,
but is still going strong. Offers everything
from gay-oriented house nights, Turkish and
oriental pop to the odd punk concert – but
avoids the mainstream like the plague.

U-Bahn Kottbusser Tor. Mon 11pm, Wed & Fri 10pm, Sat 9pm, Sun 7pm until late.

Watergate Falckensteinstr. 49, Kreuzberg ⊤030/61 28 03 95, ⓦ www.watergate.de. Latest contender for top spot among Berlin's club scene, with a glorious location by the Oberbaumbrücke overlooking the waters of the Spree. The club sprawls over two levels: a large main floor and a floor with a lounge. Music is varied but mostly electronic. Entry €6–10. U- and S-Bahn Warschauer Str. Thurs–Sat 11pm until late.

Prenzlauer Berg

Dunckerclub Dunckerstr. 64 ⊤030/4 45 95 09 ⓦ www.dunkerclub.de. Indie, industrial and unashamedly Goth refuge from the mainstream and techno. €2.50–3.50. S-Bahn Prenzlauer Alle. Mon–Thurs 10pm until late, Fri & Sat 11pm until late.

Geburtstagsclub Friedrichshain 33 ⊤030/42 02 14 05, ⓦ www.geburtstagsklub.de. Hit-and-miss club that's always reinventing itself, though the Monday reggae-night is one of Berlin's best, otherwise it's mostly house and disco. S-Bahn Greifswalder Str. Mon, Fri & Sat 11pm until late.

Icon Cantianstr. 15 ⊤030/61 28 75 45, ⓦ www .iconberlin.com. Arguably the finest drum 'n' bass club in town, with local DJs being regularly joined by international bigwigs. The club is divided into several bars, lounges and dance areas, making it easy to find your niche. Admission €3–6. U-Bahn Eberswalder Str. Mon & Sun 8pm until late, Fri 10.30pm until late, Sat 11.30pm until late.

Nbi Schönhauser Alle 157 ⊤030/44 05 16 81. The residential neighbourhood keeps the volume of the music here down, which the lounge-cum-club has used to its advantage, creating a comfortable environment for the appreciation of cutting-edge electronic music. DJs come here to hear each other experiment. U-Bahn Eberswalder Str. Daily 10pm until late.

Soda Knaackstr. 97, Prenzlauer Berg ⊤030/44 05 87 07, ⓦ www.soda-berlin.de. Club in the Kulturbrauerei cultural centre located in the grounds of a former brewery. The usual diet of Soul, house and funk is interrupted on Thursdays and Sundays by well-attended salsa nights. Occasional live acts, too. U-Bahn Eberswalder Str. Mon from 8.30pm, Thurs & Sun from

8pm, Fri from 10.30pm, Sat from 11pm until late.

Friedrichshain

Casino Mühlenstrasse 26–30 ⊤030/29 00 97 99, ⓦ www.casino-bln.com. Housed in the grounds of a former baked-goods factory, Casino is the rave joint du jour, with star DJs like Paul Van Dyk packing the early-twenties in. Lately has been softening around the edges and offering house, rock and more mainstream tunes. Entry €5–10. U- and S-Bahn Warschauer Str. Fri & Sat 11pm until late.

Maria am Ostbahnhof Str. der Pariser Kommune 8–10, Friedrichshain ⊤030/29 00 61 98, ⓦ www.clubmaria.de. Cutting-edge club whose electronic music is mirrored by the industrial minimalism of its interior. There's a good live music programme here, too. S-Bahn Ostbahnhof. Fri & Sat 11pm until late.

Matrix Warschauer Pl. 18 ⊤030/29 49 10 47, ⓦ www.matrix-berlin.de. Once a temple for pill-poppers, the club has now gone mainstream with top-40, hip-hop and reggae entertaining three colourful dance floors beneath vaulted stone-and-brick arches and Warschauer Strasse railway station. Drinks promotions on Tuesdays and Thursdays fill the place with students, and on Saturdays the 80s and disco nostalgia draw an older crowd. U- and S-Bahn Warschauer Str. Tues & Thurs from 9pm, Wed, Fri & Sat from 10pm until late.

Pavillon Friedenstrasse in Volkspark ⊤0172/7 50 47 24, ⓦ www.pavillon-berlin.de. Beer garden by day and café by night in the laid-back greenery of Volkspark Friedrichshain, this venue is best in the summer months when its hundred-person dancefloor packs out to the sounds of funk, Nu Jazz and soul. U-Bahn Strausberger Platz. Fri & Sat 11pm until late (beer garden from 11am).

WMF (Café Moskau) Karl-Marx-Allee 34 ⓦ www.mfclub.de. Reliable, long-standing major player in the Berlin club scene, with a nomadic existence that makes this – a former restaurant that catered to the GDR's elite – the club's fifth location. The hip groove to electronic music, with big-name DJs regularly playing sets. Entry €7.50–10. U-Bahn Schillingstr. Thurs–Sun 10pm until late.

Live music

By recently establishing itself as the centre of the German record industry, Berlin has assured itself of a healthy **live music** scene, one that covers the breadth of tastes and is rarely expensive. As ever, it's the city's grittiness that gives the nightlife its colour. It's also worth remembering that, in addition to the places below, many bars and cafés put on live music; venues for opera and classical music are listed in Chapter 15, "The Arts".

Rock music venues

Acud Veteranenstr. 21, Mitte ☎ 030/44 35 94 97, ℗ www.acud.de. Rock and blues are the mainstay of this ramshackle venue, with hip-hop and drum 'n' bass thrown in for good measure. There's also a gallery and movie theatre tucked inside. U-Bahn Rosenthaler Platz.

Bastard Kastanienallee 7–9, Prenzlauer Berg ☎ 030/44 04 96 69. Small club and live-music venue nestled in the Prater beer garden and theatre complex. Caters to the intelligent electronica and post-rock crowd, with poetry slams and surreal offbeat performances, good pot-luck choice. U–Bahn Eberwalder Str. Fri & Sat 11pm until late, occasional week-nights.

Die Insel Alt-Treptow 6, Treptow ☎ 030/5 33 71 69, ℗ www.insel-berlin.net. Reliable venue for thrash/punk gigs and club nights, with occasional outdoor raves on the large terrace in summer. On a Spree island that's part of Treptower Park. S-Bahn Plänterwald. Daily from 3pm.

Junction Bar Gneisenaustr. 18, Kreuzberg ☎ 030/6 94 66 02, ℗ www.junction-bar.de. Nightly live music covering the full spectrum of sounds, played to a very mixed crowd in a basement club. Always busy, and DJs keep the night going after the bands finish. Bands start around 9–10pm. Entry €3–6. U-Bahn Gneisenaustr.

Knaack-Club Greifswalderstr. 224, Prenzlauer Berg ☎ 030/4 42 70 60, ℗ www.knaack-berlin .de. One-time GDR youth centre that pioneered the club-land explosion in the east. Now a bit past its prime and pretty average, but excellent to see some of the local band scene, with regular indie acts dropping in. Entry €2.50–5. S-Bahn Greifswalder Str. Fri–Sat 9pm until late.

Kulturbrauerei Knaackstr. 97, Prenzlauer Berg ☎ 030/48 49 44, ℗ www.kulturbrauerei-berlin .de. Nineteenth-century brewery that's been turned into a multi-venue arts and cultural centre attracting frequent visits by local and mid-level bands. U-Bahn Eberswalder Str.

Magnet Club Greifswalderstr. 212–213 ☎ 030/42 02 14 07. Exceptionally friendly club to which up-and-coming bands come for exposure. DJs spin after the gig and there's another dance floor, too. Music styles vary, but the crowd is always in its twenties. Entry €3–8. U-Bahn Senefelder Platz. Tues, Fri & Sat 9pm until late, Sun 8pm until late.

Schokoladen Ackerstr. 169–170 ☎ 030/2 82 65 27, ℗ www.schokoladen-mitte.de. The spartan, bare-brick interior of this former chocolate factory is a hangover from its time as a squatted building in the early post-*Wende* days. Now a venue for theatrical and art events: with live music on Saturdays and decent contemporary cabaret on Sunday evenings – the latter particularly recommended, if your German's up to it. U-Bahn Rosenthaler Platz. Daily 8pm until late.

Tacheles Oranienburger Str. 53–56, Mitte ☎ 030/2 81 61 19, ℗ www.tacheles. de. Occasional concerts feature as part of the cultural programme of this multi-venue artists' collective. The performers are likely to be pretty eclectic, ranging from guitar bands to industrial noise merchants. U-Bahn Oranienburger Tor.

Tränenpalast Reichstagsufer 17, Mitte ☎ 030/2 38 62 11. A former waiting room at the border between East and West is now a medium-sized hall featuring rock, soul and jazz. U- & S-Bahn Friedrichstr.

Wild at Heart Wiener Str. 20 ☎ 030/6 11 70 10, ℗ www.wildatheartberlin.de. Cornerstone live music venue for rock 'n' roll, indie and punk, with something always going on well into the small hours. U-Bahn Görlitzer Bahnhof. Daily 8pm until late.

Jazz and world music venues

A-Trane Bleibtreustr./Pestalozzistr., Charlottenburg ☎ 030/3 13 25 50, ℗ www.a -trane.de. Slick forum of the Berlin jazz scene and a good place to see both up-

and-coming and well-known jazz artists in a comfortable, intimate setting. Best during Saturday-night jams, when musicians arrive from other venues and join in at will throughout the evening. Entry €5–20, free on Mon and Sat. U-Bahn Savignyplatz. Daily 9pm until late.

Badenscher Hof Badensche Str. 29, Wilmersdorf, ☎030/8 61 00 80 ⓦ www.badenscher-hof.de. Lively café-restaurant and long-standing jazz venue that draws in the Schöneberg crowd for its frequent concerts. Expect any type of jazz – from mainstream to modern – or some blues. U-Bahn Blissestrasse. Mon–Fri 4pm until late, Sat 6pm until late.

b-flat Rosenthaler Str. 13, Mitte ☎030/28 38 68 35, ⓦ www.b-flat-berlin.de. Roomy and modern with live jazz and acoustic music every night; Wednesday is reserved for the local jam session and Sunday for dancing Tango. Entry €4–10. U-Bahn Weinmeister Str. Mon–Thurs 9pm–12.30am, Fri & Sat 10pm–12.30am.

Flöz Nassauische Str. 37, Wilmersdorf ☎030/8 61 10 00. Basement club that's the meeting point for Berlin's jazz musicians and a testing ground for the city's new bands. Also offers occasional salsa and cabaret. Can be wild. U-Bahn Blissestrasse. Daily 9am until late, live music from 9pm.

Haus der Kulturen der Welt John-Foster-Dulles-Allee 10, Tiergarten ☎030/39 78 71 75, ⓦ www.hkw.de. The city's number one venue for world music. Always worth checking out. S-Bahn Lehrter Bahnhof.

Pfefferberg Schönhauser Allee 176, Prenzlauer Berg ☎030/2 82 92 89, ⓦ www.pfefferberg.de. Summer beer garden (see p.240) where non-European beats will regularly whisk you away from hectic Berlin, at least mentally. U-Bahn Senefelderplatz. Daily 11am until late.

Podewil Klosterstr. 68–70, Mitte ☎030/24 74 96, ⓦ www.podewil.de. Avant jazz, world music and occasional classical concerts – check the website for details. Less lively than some other venues but dedicated to the music. U-Bahn Klosterstrasse.

Quasimodo Kantstr. 12a, Charlottenburg ☎030/3 12 80 86, ⓦ www.Quasimodo.de. Casual smoky cellar bar that's one of Berlin's best jazz spots, with nightly programmes starting at 10pm. A high-quality mix of international, usually American, stars and up-and-coming names. Small, with a good atmosphere. Often free on weekdays.

Entry €5–25. U- & S-Bahn Zoologischer Garten. Mon–Fri 5pm until late, Sat & Sun noon until late.

Soultrane Kantstr. 17, Charlottenburg ☎030/3 15 18 60, ⓦ www.soultrane.de. One of Berlin's top jazz bars and one which many of the top visiting jazz musicians will play. Free, though entry to special events €10–25. S-Bahn Savignyplatz. Mon 10am–2am, Tues 10am–2am, Fri & Sat 10am–3am, Sun 8pm–1am.

Major venues

At the **major venues** you can expect to find international supergroups playing, and you will need to book well in advance for anything even vaguely popular. In most cases you can't buy tickets from the places themselves, so you'll need to go to one of the ticket offices listed on p.256.

There are two particularly notable and unusual live music venues in the city: the *Waldbühne* is a large outdoor amphitheatre on the Hollywood Bowl model, just west of the Olympic Stadium. It presents everything from opera to movies to rock – unbeatable in summer.

Arena Eichenstr. 4, Treptow ☎030/5 33 73 33, ⓦ www.arena-berlin.de. Located almost in the middle of nowhere, this medium-sized hall usually offers rappers, teenie groups and other popular bands for a young audience. Adjacent Glashaus hosts regular Sunday-morning house breakfasts and hip-hop jams. S-Bahn Treptower Park.

Columbiahalle Columbiadamm 13–21, Tempelhof ☎030/6 98 09 80, ⓦ www.columbiahalle. Right across the street from the Tempelhof airport, this venue hosts crowd-pleasing international acts. U-Bahn Platz der Luftbrücke.

ICC Berlin Messedamm 26, Charlottenburg ☎030/30 38 30 00, ⓦ www.icc-berlin.de. Vast, soulless hall for trade fairs that often hosts gigs. S-Bahn Eichkamp.

Parkbühne Wuhlheide Wuhlheide Park, Eichgestell, Köpenick ☎030/5 30 79 530, ⓦ www.wuhlheide.de. Smaller than the Waldbühne (see below), this open-air stage tucked away in the forest has hosted REM and Iggy Pop and is a favourite for summertime festivals. S-Bahn Wuhlheide.

CLUBS AND LIVE MUSIC | Live music

Velodrom Paul-Heyse-Str. 29, Prenzlauer Berg ☎ 030/44 30 45, ⓦ www.velomax.de. Home of mega sports events such as the six-day bicycle race, this is also the place to go to see the likes of Britney Spears or Janet Jackson. S-Bahn Landsberger Allee.

Waldbühne Glockenturmstr./Passenheimer Str., Charlottenburg ☎ 030/3 04 06 76. Open-air spot in a natural amphitheatre near the Olympic Stadium that features movies, bands, classical concerts and other entertainments. Great fun on summer evenings, but arrive early as it often gets crowded. U-Bahn Olympia–Stadion, S-Bahn Pichelsberg.

Tempodrom Möckernstrasse 10, Kruezberg ☎ 030/6 95 33 85, ⓦ www.tempodrom.de. Tent-shaped venue hosting mid-level rock and world music acts. Hosts a free music festival each summer. S-Bahn Anhalter Bahnhof.

Classical music, theatre, dance and film

When Berlin was a divided city, the West German government poured in subsidies for all kinds of **art**: the annual sum given to the western half of the city by the government (DM550 million) was over half the federal budget for culture for the entire United States. Now, in the mood of glum post-unification realism, things are very different: the plugs have been pulled on almost all subsidies, and orchestras and theatres are being forced to look elsewhere for funding; many companies have folded.

Which is not to say that all is black in Berlin: there are high-quality dance groups performing everything from classical ballet to contemporary experimental works, and scores of mainstream and art-house cinemas. The art gallery scene is thriving, and the city still has one of the world's finest **symphony orchestras**. Unification has left it with a "doubling" of facilities, three magnificent opera houses and one of the liveliest arts scenes of any European city. Berlin's reputation as a leader of the avant-garde is reflected in the number of small, often experimental, theatre groups working here. The scene is active, though it's worth remembering that many **theatre companies** take a break in July and August.

Online booking and payment for most events can be done via the Tourist Information (Ⓦwww.btm.de) or by visiting one of their offices (see p.28),

Ticket offices

Box office Theatrekasse Nollendorfplatz 7, Schöneberg ☎030/2 15 54 63. U-Bahn Nollendorfplatz.

Hekticket Charlottenburg Hardenberg Str., Charlottenburg ☎030/2 30 99 30, Ⓦwww.hekticket.de. U- and S-Bahn Zoologischer Garten.

Hekticket Mitte Karl-Liebknecht-Strasse, Mitte ☎030/24 31 24 31, Ⓦwww .hekticket.de. U- and S-Bahn Alexanderplatz.

Ko Ka 36 Oranienstr. 29, Kreuzberg ☎030/6 15 88 18, Ⓦwww.koka36.de. U-Bahn Kottbusser Tor.

otherwise Ticket offices or *Theaterkassen* are usually the easiest way of buying tickets for all major music, theatre and dance events. Open during working hours (or longer), they charge a hefty commission (up to 17 percent) on the ticket price. The first place to try, especially for fringe-type theatre, less popular classical concerts and dance, is *Hekticket* (see box opposite for details), which sells half-price tickets from 4pm, and charges only €1 commission on tickets for the same day's performance.

Classical music

For years classical music in Berlin meant one man and one orchestra: Herbert von Karajan and the Berlin Philharmonic. Since his death in 1989, the **Philharmonie** has had its former supremacy questioned by the rise of the excellent **Deutsches Symphonie Orchester** under Vladimir Ashkenazy. Yet the Philharmonic still remains arguably the world's best orchestra, directed since 2002 by Simon Rattle. The Philharmonie and Deutsche Symphonie Orchester are by no means the only options. Many smaller orchestras play at sites in and around the city, and museums and historic buildings often host chamber concerts and recitals. As elsewhere in the arts, though, cutbacks in state and senate funding have brought about a more cautious and conservative atmosphere in the classical music world.

It's possible to pick up inexpensive tickets for many performances from *Hekticket* (see box opposite). As ever, see *Zitty* and *Tip* for full and up-to-date listings.

Orchestras and venues

Berlin Symphonie Orchester ⓦ www.berliner -symphoniker.de. Founded in 1952 and based in the Konzerthaus (see below), this used to be East Berlin's main symphony orchestra, and it maintains its fine reputation today, though it does not compare to the Philharmonic. Tickets €7–30.

Deutsche Oper Berlin Bismarckstr. 35, Charlottenburg; box office ⓣ 030/3 43 84 01 (Mon–Sat 11am–6pm), ⓦ www .deutscheoperberlin.de. Formerly West Berlin's premier opera house, built in 1961 after the Wall cut access to the Staatsoper. Once the city's most prestigious venue in terms of visiting performers, it now shares that honour with its eastern cousin. This is the place to hear Wagner and Strauss. Tickets €10–112. U-Bahn Deutsche Oper.

Deutsches Symphonie Orchester ⓦ www.dso -berlin.de. Shares the Konzerthaus (see below) with the Berlin Symphonie Orchester. Currently under conductor Kent Nagano and with no permanent base: often at the Konzerthaus or Tempodrom. Tickets €10–55.

Staatsoper Unter den Linden 5–7, Mitte; box office ⓣ 030/20 35 45 55 (Mon–Sat 10am–8pm, Sun 2–8pm), ⓦ www.staatsoper-berlin.de. The city's oldest and grandest music venue, built for Frederick the Great in 1742 to a design by Knobelsdorff. While little remains from that time (the building was bombed out in 1941, rebuilt, destroyed again in 1945 and rebuilt to the current specifications in 1955), the interior is all you'd expect a grand opera house to be. During the GDR years, political isolation meant that performers didn't match the glamour of the venue. The appointment of Daniel Barenboim in 1992 as musical director was an attempt to bring the Staatsoper to the forefront of the international opera scene and it certainly seems to be working. Tickets €8–120. U-Bahn Französische Strasse.

Komische Oper Behrenstr. 55–57, Mitte; ⓣ 030/47 99 74 00, ⓦ www.komische-oper -berlin.de. Less traditional than the Staatsoper, but a reliable venue for well-staged operatic productions, under the direction of Harry Kupfer. Expert cutting-edge interpretation of modern works alongside the usual fare – and tickets at half the price of the Deutsche Oper. Box office at Unter den Linden 41, Mitte. S-Bahn Unter den Linden.

Konzerthaus Berlin (Schauspielhaus) Gendarmenmarkt, Mitte; box office

☎030/20 30 90, ⓦ www.konzerthaus.de. A super venue, not only for performances by resident Deutsche Symphonie and Berlin Symphonie orchestras, but also the Rundfunk Symphonieorchester Berlin and other visiting musicians, orchestras and ensembles. Two concert spaces occupy the Schinkel-designed building: the Grosser Konzertsaal for orchestras and the Kammermusiksaal (not to be confused with that of the same name in the Philharmonie) for smaller groups and chamber orchestras. Look out for performances on the Konzerthaus's famed organ. Tickets €5–40. U-Bahn Stadtmitte.

Philharmonie Matthäikirchstr. 1, Tiergarten; box office ☎030/25 48 89 99, ⓦ www .Berliner-philharmoniker.de. Home to the world-famous Berlin Philharmonic, Hans Scharoun's indescribably ugly building is acoustically near-perfect, and while you'll have to be near-loaded to enjoy it, it's definitely worth it. Conductor Simon Rattle is slowly creating his own distinctive sound with the orchestra, moving them away from their traditional Germanic comfort zone of Brahms and Beethoven and into more contemporary music like that of the Finnish composer Magnus Lindberg. At first this caused the orchestra concern, but tremendous success of the eventual execution of these pieces has strengthened the relationship between the director and orchestra. The Philharmonie also contains the smaller Kammermusiksaal for more intimate performances, and your best chance of getting a ticket is when guest orchestras are playing. Tickets €8–61. U- and S-Bahn Potsdamer Platz.

Rundfunk Symphonieorchester Berlin ⓦ www .rsb-online.de. After the Philharmonic, the second-oldest orchestra in Berlin and a little more daring than its older sister. The orchestra appears at both the Philharmonie and the Konzerthaus, and director Marek Janowski often lends his baton to guest conductor Michael Jurowski.

Theatre

Sad to say, the mainstream **civic and private theatres** in Berlin are, on the whole, dull, unadventurous and expensive – though it's often possible to cut costs by buying student standby tickets – and in recent years, many professional people have left the birthplace of experimental theatre and returned to Munich and the lure of the film business.

However, Berlin's reputation as Germany's **Theaterstadt** still holds firm for the thousands of eager young Germans who flock to the city every year, rent a space, and stage their work. The city is still a major venue for **experimental work**, and if your German is up to it, a number of groups are worth the ticket price; check under "Off-Theater" in *Tip* or *Zitty* for up-to-the-minute listings. Groups that have the word *Freie* in their name are not dependent on city or state subsidies, which often impose creative constraints on a group's output.

You'll find little in English at the mainstream theatres, but you may have more luck with the small roving theatre groups.

Civic and private theatres

Berliner Ensemble Bertold Brecht Platz 1, Mitte ☎030/2 82 31 60, ⓦ www.berliner-ensemble .de. Brecht's old theatre now seems a little adrift, performing pieces without a strong sense of artistic direction. Brecht still forms the staple fare here, though thankfully the productions are a little livelier than in GDR days. There are also occasional experimental productions on the Probebühne (rehearsal stage). Tickets €4–32. U- and S-Bahn Friedrichstrasse.

Deutsches Theater Schumannstr. 13a, Mitte ☎030/28 44 12 21, ⓦ www.deutsches-theater .de. Good, solid productions taking in everything from Schiller to Mamet make this one of Berlin's best theatres. Invariably sold out. Also includes a second theatre, the Kammerspiele des Deutschen Theaters and Die Baracke, an experimental stage. Tickets €4–42. U-Bahn Oranienburger Tor.

Maxim-Gorki-Theater Am Festungsgraben 2, Mitte ☎030/20 22 11 15. Consistently good productions of modern works like Tabori's *Mein Kampf* and Schaffer's *Amadeus*. More experimental works are staged on the Studiobühne (studio stage). Tickets €12–26. U- and S-Bahn Friedrichstrasse.

Prater der Volksbühne Kastanienallee 7–9, Prenzlauer Berg ☎030/2 47 67 72, ⓦwww .volksbuehne-berlin.de. Second stage of the Volksbühne (see below). Performance, experimental works and modern adaptations of classics. Tickets €10–21. U-Bahn Eberswalder Strasse.

Renaissance Theater Knesebeckstr. 100, Charlottenburg ☎030/3 12 42 02, ⓦwww .renaissance-theatre.de. Contemporary pieces of theatre from Ayckbourn to Reza, readings and musical revues. Tickets €10–30. U-Bahn Ernst-Reuter-Platz.

Schaubühne am Lehniner Platz Kurfürstendamm 153, Wilmersdorf ☎030/89 00 23, ⓦwww.schaubuehne.de. State-of-the-art theatre that hosts performances of the classics and some experimental pieces. The new directorship that began in 2000 promises to bring an infusion of young energy – expect more of an accent on dance. Its high reputation means booking ahead is advisable. Tickets €10–30. U-Bahn Adenauerplatz.

Theater des Westens Kantstr. 12, Charlottenburg ☎030/8 82 28 88, ⓦwww.theater-des -westens.de. Musicals and light opera, the occasional Broadway-style show, sometimes in English. Housed in a beautiful fin-de-siècle building. Often sold out. Tickets €27–85. U- and S-Bahn Zoologischer Garten.

Volksbühne Rosa-Luxemburg-Platz, Mitte ☎030/2 47 67 72, ⓦwww.volksbuehne-berlin .de. Under director Frank Castorf, this has become one of Berlin's most adventurous and interesting theatres. Castorf has gone all out to bring in young audiences, with the result that performances are often highly provocative – nudity and throwing things at the audiences crop up fairly regularly and there's a high chance of witnessing a partial audience walkout. Tickets €10–21. U-Bahn Rosa-Luxemburg-Platz.

Experimental and free theatre

BAT (Studiotheater der Hochschule für Schauspielkunst) Belforter Str. 15, Prenzlauer Berg ☎030/4 42 79 96, ⓦwww.bat-berlin.de. Originally a "workers' and students' theatre", founded in 1975, this one can usually be relied on to come up with challenging experimental offerings, including drama student graduation projects. A meeting point for everyone interested in theatre. Tickets €8. U-Bahn Senefelder Platz.

Freunde der Italienischen Oper Fidicinstr. 40, Kreuzberg ☎030/6 91 12 11, ⓦwww .thefriends.de. Tiny courtyard theatre specializing in fringe productions performed in English. Tickets €8–14. U-Bahn Platz der Luftbrücke.

Hebbel Am Ufer Hallesches Ufer 32, Kreuzberg ⓦwww.hebbel-am-ufer.de. Hosts short runs of a variety of theatre, performance and dance productions, sometimes in English. Puts up the large-scale shows of Freunde der Italienischen Oper (see above). Often interesting, modern and experimental. Tickets €6–15. U-Bahn Hallesches Tor.

Schaubude Greifswalder Str. 81–84, Prenzlauer Berg ☎030/4 23 43 14, ⓦwww.schaubude -berlin.de. Former GDR puppet theatre now presenting shows for adults and children – from *Hansel and Gretel* to *Faust* and performances on atomic physics. Tickets €4–10. S- and U-Bahn Greifswalder Str.

Stükke Palisadenstr. 48, Friedrichshain ☎030/71 58 11 43. International selection of contemporary theatre and performance works. Tickets €18–25. U-Bahn Weberwiese.

Theater 89 Torstr. 216, Mitte ☎030/2 82 46 56, ⓦwww.theater89.de. A small venue putting on modern works in a simple and unaffected style. Tickets €7.50–14. U-Bahn Oranienburger Tor.

Cabaret

In the 1920s and 1930s, Berlin had a rich and intense **cabaret scene**: hundreds of small clubs presented acts that were often deeply satirical and political. When the Nazis came to power these quickly disappeared, to be replaced by anodyne entertainments in line with Party views. Sadly, the cabaret scene has never recovered: most of what's on show today is either semi-clad titillation for tourists or drag shows. However, a few places are worth trying, notably the

Chamäleon Variete, which plays host to some very eclectic acts. Check out the *Mitternachtshow* ("Midnight Show") on Friday and Saturday. Be warned that most cabaret venues make their money by charging very high prices at the bar.

Cabaret venues

Bar Jeder Vernunft Scharperstr. 24, Wilmersdorf ☎030/8 83 15 82, ⒲www.bar-jeder-vernuft. de. Among the city's best, younger and hipper than most. Tickets €14–30. U-Bahn Spichernstrasse.

Chamäleon Variete Rosenthaler Str. 40–41, Mitte ☎030/2 82 71 18, ⒲www.chamaeleon -variete.de. Very lively, with jugglers, acrobats and the like. Tickets €4–27. S-Bahn Hackescher Markt.

Friedrichstadt Palast Friedrichstr. 107, Mitte ☎030/23 26 24 74, ⒲www.friedrichstadtpalast .de. Big, flashy variety shows with leggy chorus girls, but the real stuff is to be found in their small café theatre. Tickets €12–59. U-Bahn Oranienburger Tor.

Hackesches Hof Theater Rosenthaler Str. 40–41, Mitte ☎030/2 83 25 87. Musical theatre, often with Jewish themes, and klezmer music every week. Tickets €15–20. S-Bahn Hackescher Markt.

Kalkscheune Johannisstr. 2, Mitte ☎030/28 39 00 65. Creative shows – authentic but without the nostalgia. Tickets €12–18. U-Bahn Oranienburger Tor.

Kleine Nachtrevue Kurfürstenstr. 116, Schöneberg ☎030/2 18 89 50, ⒲www.kleine -nachtrevue.de. Berlin Burlesque, intimate

and dimly lit, going for that 1920s feel. Tickets €15. U-Bahn Kurfürstenstrasse.

La Vie en Rose Flughafen Tempelhof, Kreuzberg ☎030/69 51 30 00. A drag variety revue with lots of glitter and lots of skin. There's also a piano bar. Tickets €10–15. U-Bahn Platz der Luftbrücke.

Mehringhof Theater Gneisenaustr. 2a, Kreuzberg ☎030/6 91 50 99, ⒲www .mehringhoftheater.de. Mixed bag of alternative cabaret. Tickets €10–15. U-Bahn Mehringdamm.

Roter/Grüner Salon in the Volksbühne, Rosa-Luxemburg-Platz, Mitte ☎030/24 06 58 07. Lots of interesting and varied goings on, with occasional performances in English (see p.250)

Scheinbar Variete Monumentenstr. 9, Schöneberg ☎030/7 84 55 39, ⒲www .scheinbar.de. Hip, experimental and fun; open stage on Wed nights. Tickets €6–11. U- and S-Bahn Yorckstrasse.

Wintergarten Potsdamer Str. 96, Tiergarten ☎030/23 08 82 30, ⒲www.wintergarten -variete.de. A glitzy attempt to re-create the Berlin of the 1920s, with live acts from all over the world – cabaret, musicians, dance, mime, etc. Tickets €18–35. U-Bahn Kurfürstenstrasse.

Dance

Though there are few **dance groups** in the city, those that exist are of a high quality: you can expect to see plenty of original, oddball and unusual performances. Apart from those regular venues listed below, expect dance performances to pop up at *Podewil* (see p.254), as well as at various theatres such as Balhaus Nauenystrasse, UFA-Fabrik, Volksbühne and especially the Schaubühne (see p.259).

Dance companies and venues

Die Etage Ritterstrasse 12–14, Kreuzberg ☎030/6 91 20 95, ⒲www.dieetage.de. Contemporary dance and mime; also runs dance classes. Tickets €5–7. U-Bahn Moritzstrasse.

Hebbel Am Ufer Hallesches Ufer 32, Kreuzberg ⒲www.hebbel-am-ufer.de. While not primarily

a dance venue, this theatre features four major annual contemporary dance festivals; see "Experimental and free theatre". U-Bahn Hallesches Tor.

Komische Oper Behrenstr. 55–57, Mitte; ☎030/47 99 74 00, ⒲www.komische-oper -berlin.de. Modern ballet and experimental works, arguably the most interesting of the established heavyweights.

Staatsballett ⓦ www.staatsballett-berlin.de.
Berlin's premier ballet company performs at the Staatsoper and Deutsche Oper: see "Orchestras and venues".
Tanzfabrik Berlin Möckernstr. 68, Kreuzberg ⓣ 030/7 86 58 61, ⓦ www.tanzfabrik-berlin

.de. Experimental and contemporary works, usually fresh and exciting. This is also Berlin's biggest contemporary dance school. Tickets €10. U- and S-Bahn Yorckstrasse.

Film

When the all-night drinking starts to get too much, it's always possible to wind down in front of the silver screen. Art-house cinemas, unfortunately, are facing very hard times, but for those who like the mainstream, the corresponding rise of the multiplex theatres means there is more English-language fare available. The two surest bets for English-language films are Cinemaxx at Potsdamer Platz and the UFA Arthouse Kurbel, though old standbys such as Odeon and Babylon, and the newly renovated Neues Off, soldier on with somewhat more interesting choices. There are still some **smaller cinemas** showing art-house and independently made movies, and some of the more interesting places are listed below.

Tip and Zitty have listings of all the films showing each week and tell you which language the film is in. If a film is listed as **OF** or **OV** (Originalfassung) it's in its original language; **OmU** (Originalfassung mit Untertiteln) indicates German subtitles. Otherwise, the film will have been dubbed into German. You may occasionally see films listed as **OmE** – original with English subtitles. **Ticket** prices range from €5 to €10; the price we give below is a full-price ticket, but there are always reductions for children and sometimes for students, too. Ticket prices are also reduced one day a week, designated Kinotag. The day varies from venue to venue, but it's commonly a Monday, Tuesday or Wednesday, and the price is usually around €4.

In February, the **Berlinale** (ⓦ www.berlinale.de) Film Festival dominates the city's cultural life. Second only to Cannes among European festivals, it was once the showcase for East German and East European films, and still offers a staggering number of films from all around the world. A limited number of season tickets (around €130) go on sale a week before the opening. Otherwise, advance tickets can be purchased at the ticket booths centrally located in the Potsdamer Platz Arcaden shopping mall, the second floor of the Europa Center or at the International (see p.262). Tickets for the day of the show must be purchased at the cinema box office. During the festival, programming information is available in the regular listings magazines or the festival's own daily magazine, Berlinale, available at all participating theatres.

Cinemas

The following are the usual venues for English-language films, but it pays to look through the listings in Tip and Zitty, as there are always surprises.
Arsenal Potsdamer Str. 2 in the Sony Filmhaus at Potsdamer Platz ⓣ 030/26 95 51 00.
Specializes in retrospectives, series and experimental work. Sometimes in English,

and foreign films, particularly Asian, may have English subtitles. Tickets €5. U- & S-Bahn Potsdamer Platz.
Babylon Dresdener Str. 126, Kreuzberg ⓣ 030/61 60 96 93. New films in English, with and without subtitles. Tickets €7. U-Bahn Kottbusser Tor.
Babylon Mitte Rosa-Luxemburg-Str. 30, Mitte ⓣ 030/2 42 50 76. Central Berlin's best repertory cinema in a landmark theatre. Occasional films with English subtitles.

Tickets €6.50. U-Bahn Rosa-Luxemburg-Strasse.

Brotfabrik Prenzlauer Promenade 3, Weissensee ☎030/4 71 40 02. Art-house cinema that's worth checking out. Occasional films in English. Tickets €5. S-Bahn Prenzlauer Allee.

Central Rosenthalerstr. 39, Mitte ☎030/2 85 99 93. Main programme is almost all German, but bizarre midnight events are often held and are often in English. Tickets €6.50. S-Bahn Hackescher Markt.

Cinemaxx Potsdamer Platz Potsdamer Platz 5, Tiergarten ☎030/44 31 63 16. Monster nineteen-screen multiplex with at least two screens in English. Tickets €8. U- & S-Bahn Potsdamer Platz.

Cinestar Sony Center Potsdamer Str. 4, Tiergarten ☎030/ 26 06 62 60. Eight-screen cinema in the bowels of the Sony Center, with almost every screen in the original (usually English) language; most films are of the Hollywood blockbuster variety. Tickets €8. U- & S-Bahn Potsdamer Platz.

Eiszeit-Kino Zeughofstr. 20, Kreuzberg ☎030/6 11 60 16. Tiny cinema tucked away in a Hinterhof, specializing in retrospectives and alternative films. Less English than before but still the home of innovative programming. Tickets €6.50. U-Bahn Görlitzer Bahnhof.

Hackesche Höfe Rosenthalerstr. 40–41, Mitte ☎030/2 83 46 03. Five-screen multiplex on the top floor of the busy Hackesche Höfe.

Upscale independent foreign films and documentaries, sometimes in English. Often sold out at weekends, but they take phone reservations. Tickets €7. S-Bahn Hackescher Markt.

High End 54 Oranienburgerstr. 54–56, Mitte ☎030/2 83 14 98. Mostly foreign and indie films, sometimes in English. Tickets €6.50. U-Bahn Oranienburger Tor.

International Karl-Marx-Allee 33/Schillingstr., Mitte ☎030/24 75 60 11. A big, comfortable GDR landmark cinema showing new releases. The Monday-night gay programme often shows films in their original language. Tickets €7.50. U-Bahn Schillingstrasse.

Moviemento I Kottbusser Damm 22, Kreuzberg ☎030/6 92 47 85. Less innovative than before but still worth a look. Tickets €6. U-Bahn Schönleinstrasse.

Odeon Hauptstr. 116, Schöneberg ☎030/78 70 40 19. If you're after the more intelligent English-language releases, the Odeon will have them first. Tickets €7.50. U-Bahn Innsbrucker Platz.

Xenon Kolonnenstr. 5, Schöneberg ☎030/7 82 88 50. Often screens English-language independent films with an accent on Queer Cinema. Tickets €6. U-Bahn Kleistpark.

Zeughaus-Kino Unter den Linden 2, Mitte. Cinema in the Zeughaus which often unearths fascinating films from the pre- and postwar years. Tickets €5. S-Bahn Hackescher Markt.

CLASSICAL MUSIC, THEATRE, DANCE AND FILM | Film

Kids' Berlin

A ttitudes to young children in Berlin strike the outsider as oddly ambivalent. While the city has a large number of single-parent families and excellent social-service provisions for them, Berliners aren't too tolerant of kids in "adult" places, such as restaurants or bars; and though the city consists of a higher proportion of lakes, parks and woodland than any other European capital, there's little in them directly geared to entertaining children. If you're bringing kids, be prepared to do Berlin versions of the obvious things – zoos, museums and shops – rather than anything unique to the city. On a day-to-day basis, check the listings in *Tip* and *Zitty* (under "Kinder") for details of what's on.

Parks and zoos

With over a third of Berlin being forest or parkland, often with playgrounds dotted around, there's no shortage of spaces for children to go and let off steam. The most central and obvious choice is the **Tiergarten**, northeast of Zoo Station, though this is rather tame compared to the rambling expanses of the **Grunewald** (S-Bahn Grunewald). In both parks paddle and rowing boats can be rented. The Grunewald borders the **Wannsee** lake, and it's fun to take the ferry over to the **Pfaueninsel** (Peacock Island), where there's a castle and plenty of strutting peacocks; see p.195 for details. Alternatively, **Freizeitpark Tegel** (U-Bahn Alt-Tegel, walk to the lake, then turn right) has playgrounds, trampolines, table tennis and paddle boats, while the **Teufelsberg** (Devil's Mountain; bus #149 to Preussenallee stop, then walk for 20min south down Teufelsseechaussee), a large hill to the west of the city, is the place to go

---

Babysitting services

Berlin has a couple of reliable agencies that can supply English-speaking **babysitters** and a multilingual **day-care centre** where kids can stay overnight. Auggepasst (☎030/030/8 51 37 23, ⓦaufgepasst.de) is a babysitting and day-care agency whose rates are around €10 per hour, plus a €10 booking fee. Another child-care option is Kinderinsel, Eichendoffstrasse 17 (☎030/41 71 69 28, ⓦwww.kinderinsel .de; U-Bahn Zinnowitzer Str.), where parents can leave their children (0–14 years) in good hands for anything from a couple of hours to several days. The programme of outings and activities offered by the friendly and dynamic centre ensures the kids won't get bored; rates are €12 per hour, €99 for an overnight stay.

kite-flying at weekends. On the southeastern edge of the city, the woods around the **Grosser Müggelsee** (S-Bahn to Friedrichshagen) offer lakeside walking trails, and there's also a good nature trail around the **Teufelssee** (S-Bahn to Köpenick, then bus #M69 for five stops), just south of the Müggelsee. Educationally oriented **Kinderbauernhöfen**, or children's farms, can also be fun without knowing the language: they're to be found at Domäne Dahlem (see p.189); in Görlitzer Park at Wiener Str. 59, Kreuzberg (Mon, Tues, Thurs & Fri 10am–5pm, Sat & Sun 11am–5pm; U-Bahn Görlitzer Bahnhof); and in the UFA-Fabrik, Viktoriastr. 13–18, Tempelhof (Mon–Fri 10am–5pm, Sat & Sun noon–3pm; U-Bahn Ullsteinstrasse).

Zoologischer Garten Hardenbergplatz 8, Charlottenburg ☏030/25 40 10, ⊛ www.zoo -berlin.de (U- & S-Bahn Zoologischer Garten). Daily: April–Sept 9am–6.30pm; Oct–March 9am–5pm; admission zoo €10, aquarium €10, combined ticket €15; children zoo €4.50, aquarium €4.50, combined ticket €7. Near the train station of the same name, this zoo keeps exotic animals in surroundings that attempt to mimic their natural habitat. Of most interest to kids will be the monkeys, orang-utans and gorillas; the hippo house; the nocturnal rooms (a darkened area where varieties of gerbil-type creatures, and bats, do their thing; pony and horse-and-trap rides around the zoo; a playground and a children's zoo where farm animals can be petted and fed. The **aquarium**, also in the grounds, but with a separate entrance at Budapester Str. 32, is well worth the money, with a dazzling array of fish and a humid crocodile hall.

Sea-life Center Spandauer Strasse 3 ☏030/99 28 00, ⊛ www.sealifeeurope.com (S-Bahn Hackescher Markt). Daily: April–Aug 10am–7pm; Sept–March 10am–6pm; admission €13.50, children €10. An educational and entertaining aquarium; kids can test their knowledge with quiz questions dotted around the facility (in English) and get to touch manta rays and star-fish in a tank. The elevator ride through the Aquadom, a gigantic tubular tank, is also a sure-fire hit.

Tierpark Friedrichsfelde ☏030/51 51 10, ⊛ www.tierpark-berlin.de (U-Bahn Tierpark). Daily 9am–sunset or 7pm at the latest; €10; children €9. This sprawling zoo will be enough to exhaust even the most demanding child; all the usual suspects are here, but it's the several new monkey enclosures that are likely to provide most of the entertainment.

Circuses, leisure complexes and funfairs

Professional circus troupes and small funfairs visit the city regularly during the summer months, setting up in the parks that dot the city.

UFA-Fabrik Viktoriastr. 10, Tempelhof ☏030/75 50 30, ⊛ www.ufafabrik.de (U-Bahn Ullsteinstrasse). Residential circus offering an inventive alternative – jugglers, acrobats, magicians – to the usual lions-and-clowns stuff. **Cabuwazi Zirkus** Weiner Str. 59h, Kreuzberg ☏030/6 11 92, ⊛ www.cabuwazi.de (U-Bahn Görlitzer Bahnhof), and Bouchéstr. 74, Alt-Treptow ☏030/5 33 70 16 (U-Bahn Treptower Park). Another resident circus, in which youngsters perform. Also a popular venue for visiting circuses. **Blub Baderparadis** Buschkrugallee 64, Neukölln ☏030/6 06 60 60, ⊛ www.blub-berlin.de (U-Bahn Grenzallee). Daily 10am–11pm; admission €11–14, children €9–12. Of the city's sports facilities, this slick indoor and outdoor pool complex in Neukölln is probably of most interest to kids. It's a bit of a trek out, and expensive to boot, but is worth it for the waterfalls, whirlpools, twelve-metre chute and wave machine, to name but a few attractions. There's a similar complex in the eastern suburb of Friedrichshain, the SEZ-Sport und Erholungszentrum (see p.273), which is currently undergoing renovation, but when it reopens will offer several pools with slides, chutes and diving boards. **FEZ Wuhlheide** Wuhlheide, Köpenick ☏030/53 07 11 46, ⊛ www.fez-berlin.de (S-Bahn to Wühlheide). Summer Tues–Thurs 10am–9pm, Fri 10am–10pm, Sat 1–6pm, Sun 10am–6pm;

during the school year Tues–Fri 10am–6pm, Sat 1–6pm, Sun 10am–6pm. A large GDR-era recreation park, packed with play- and activity-areas for kids of all ages and including a popular narrow-gauge railway, the seven-kilometre-long Berliner Parkeisenbahn (ⓦwww.parkeisenbahn.de), which is operated by children.

Museums and sights

Almost all museums give a discount for children; the following are the most interesting in terms of special areas for kids, interactive exhibits and fun things to do. Depending on your children's level of interest, some sightseeing might also be enjoyable. A ride on the #100 or #200 bus will take in all the main sights between Alexanderplatz and Bahnhof Zoo and also connects several places with superb views of Berlin from on high. The Siegessäule (see p.125) is fun but has a lot of steps, making it hard work for little legs; the Reichstag dome (p.56) is of some interest; but the Fernsehturm (p.90) and the Panorama Punkt (see p.77) are probably going to go down better – though the exposed outdoor nature of the latter could be unnerving for some smaller children.

Deutsches Technikmuseum Berlin Trebbiner Strasse 9 ⓣ030/90 205 40, ⓦwww.dtmb.de (U-Bahn Möckernbrücke). Tues–Fri 9am–5.30pm, Sat & Sun 10am–6pm; admission €3, children €1.50. The German Technology Museum of Berlin has lots of gadgets to experiment with, plus a great collection of old steam trains and carriages. Highly diverting; the perfect thing for a wet afternoon. See also p.147.

Domäne Dahlem Königin-Luise-Str. 49, Zehlendorf ⓣ030/8 32 50 00, ⓦwww.snafu .de/~domaene-dahlem (U-Bahn Dahlem Dorf). Wed–Mon 10am–6pm; admission €1.50, children €0.80. This working farm and craft museum has plenty to entertain kids besides farmyard animals, especially at weekends when craft fairs are held here, and there are games and shows especially for children. Phone ahead to see what's on. See p.189.

Düppel Museum Village Clauertstr. 11, Zehlendorf ⓣ030/8 02 66 71, ⓦwww.dueppel .de (bus #115 to Ludwigsfelderstrasse). April to early Oct Thurs 3–7pm, Sun & holidays 10am–5pm; admission €2, children €1.50. Reconstruction of a medieval country village, with demonstrations of the handicrafts and farming methods of those times. Better for older children. See p.192.

Juniormuseum im Ethnologischen Museum Lansstrasse 8 ⓣ030/8 30 14 38, ⓦwww.smb .spk-berlin.de (U-Bahn Dahlem Dorf) Tues–Fri 10am–6pm, Sat & Sun 11am–6pm; admission €4, free 2–6pm on Thurs; children free. A section of the Ethnological Museum in Dahlem (see p.189), this museum teaches children about different cultures through playful activities and interactive temporary exhibits.

Labyrinth Kindermuseum Berlin Osloer Str. 12, Wedding ⓣ030/49 30 89 01, ⓦwww .kindermuseum-labyrinth.de (U-Bahn Pankstr.). Outside school holidays Tues–Sat 1–6pm, Sun 11am–6pm; in school holidays Mon–Fri 9am–6pm, Sat 1–6pm, Sun 11am–6pm; admission €3.50, children €3. A converted factory building that offers temporary exhibits, usually very inventive and thoughtful, geared towards hands-on learning and fun.

Museum für Kommunikation Berlin Leipziger Str. 16, Mitte ⓣ030/20 29 40, ⓦwww .museumsstiftung.de (U-Bahn Stadtmitte). Tues–Fri 9am–5pm, Sat & Sun 11am–7pm; admission €3, children free. Robots career around the main lobby in this hands-on communications museum that offers older kids lots of computers and devices to play with. See p.70.

Museum für Naturkunde Invalidenstr. 43, Mitte ⓣ030/20 93 85 91 (U-Bahn Zinnowitzer Str). Tues–Fri 9.30am–5pm; €3.50, children €2. The main attraction at this natural history museum is the gigantic Brachiosaurus skeleton, and once that's been admired the rest of the display is a bit of an anticlimax. However, it should keep animal-crazy kids happy for an hour or so. See p.103.

The Story of Berlin Kurfürstendamm 207–208 ⓣ030 88 72 01 00, ⓦwww.story-of-berlin.de. Daily 10am–8pm, last admission 6pm; €9.30, children €3.50. Easily the most captivating of the city's history museums, with lots of multimedia gimmicks to bring the experience alive, as well as the rare chance to visit a nuclear bunker – recommended for kids with anything more than a glimmer of interest in Berlin's past.

Theatres and cinemas

Most cinemas show **children's films** during the school holidays but these are likely to be German-language only. The one time you're likely to catch English-language kids' films is during the Berlin Film Festival in February (see p.261), which always offers a children's programme (*Kinderprogramm*). Berlin supports an astonishing number of **puppet theatres**, most of which put on worthwhile performances that kids don't need a knowledge of German to enjoy. For details of children's films and theatre performances, check the listings magazines or call the venues.

Charlottchen Droysenstr. 1, Charlottenburg ☎030/3 24 47 17. A child-friendly café with a theatre offering funny fairytales and original pieces in the back. S-Bahn Charlottenburg.

Fliegendes Theater Berlin Urbanstr. 100, Kreuzberg ☎030/6 92 21 00. Puppet theatre for kids of 4 and over. U-Bahn Schönleinstrasse.

Grips Theatre Altonaer Str. 22, Tiergarten ☎030/39 74 74 77. Top-class children's/young people's theatre; usually all improvised. U-Bahn Hansaplatz.

Narrenspiegel Otto-Suhr-Allee 94, Charlottenburg ☎030/7 81 45 49. Children's theatre presenting fairytales and original productions. U-Bahn Richard-Wagner-Platz.

Shops

There's a fair but not overwhelming selection of **children's shops** in Berlin, with an emphasis on wooden toys, ecological themes and multicultural education. Plastic pistols and toy soldiers are definitely out of favour and hard to find. For a full list of shops, see Chapter 19.

Anagramm Mehringdamm 50, Kreuzberg ☎030/7 85 95 10, ⍟www.anagram-buch .de. Neighbourhood bookstore with an excellent children's section and a reading corner. U-Bahn Mehringdamm. Mon–Fri 9am–6.30pm, Sat 10am–3pm.

Bella, Boss & Bulli Trafohaus auf dem Helmholtzplatz ☎030/44 67 41 34. Café, playground and secondhand children's wear all in one: very Prenzlauer Berg bohemian. U-Bahn Eberswalder Strasse. Daily 2–7pm.

Emma & Co Niebuhrstrass 2 ☎030/88 67 67 87. Designer knitwear and other children's fashions, lots of unique and interesting pieces and a good selection of shoes. S-Bahn Savignyplatz. Mon 11am–7pm, Sat 11am–4pm.

Grober Unfug Zossener Str. 32, Kreuzberg ☎030/69 10 14 90, ⍟www.groberunfug .de. Large display of international comics. U-Bahn Gneisenaustrasse. Mon–Fri 11am–7pm, Sat 11am–4pm.

Jonglerie Körtestr. 26, Kreuzberg ☎030/6 91 87 69, ⍟www.jonglerie.de. Magic tricks, balloons and toys. U-Bahn Südstern. Mon–Fri 11am–6.30pm, Sat 10am–2pm.

Speilbrett Körtestr. 27, Kreuzberg ☎030/6 92 42 50. Massive selection of games and puzzles with some picture books, too. U-Bahn Südstern. Mon–Fri 10am–6.30pm, Sat 10am–2pm.

Tabularium Krausenickstr. 23, Mitte ☎030/2 80 82 03. One half of this store is dedicated to Judaica, the other half to wooden toys, sophisticated puzzles and children's books. S-Bahn Hackescher Markt. Mon–Sat 11am–8pm.

Flying Colors Eisenacher Str. 81, Schöneberg ☎030/78 70 36 36, ⍟www.flying-colors.de. Kites – the place to come before heading off for the Teufelsberg hill. U-Bahn Eisennacher Strasse. Mon–Fri 10am–1pm & 2.30–8.30pm, Sat 10am–2pm.

Zauberkönig Hermannstr. 84, Neukölln ☎030/6 21 40 82. Illusions and tricks for magicians and their apprentices. U-Bahn Leinestrasse. Mon–Thurs 1–6pm, Fri 10am–6pm, Sat 10am–1pm.

Gay and lesbian Berlin

Despite the horrors of the past, Berlin has a good record for tolerating an open and energetic gay and lesbian scene. As far back as the 1920s, Christopher Isherwood and W.H. Auden both came here, drawn to a city where, in sharp contrast to the oppressiveness of London, there was a gay community which did not live in fear of harassment and legal persecution. Today, Berlin's gay and lesbian communities are among the most vibrant in the world.

The easy-going, easy-living attitude stretches into the straight community, too, and it's not uncommon to see transvestites at their glitziest dancing atop tables at even the most conservative of bashes. The best time to arrive and plunge yourself into the hurly-burly is during **Gay Pride Week**, centred around the **Christopher Street Day parade** (@www.csd-berlin.de) on the last Saturday in June every year. The Love Parade held annually in July (see p.8) also has a strong gay presence.

Berlin does also boast an interesting gay museum, the relatively low-profile **Schwules Museum**, Mehringdamm 61, Kreuzberg (Mon, Wed–Fri & Sun 2–6pm, Sat 2–7pm; €5; @www.schwulesmuseum.de), with changing exhibitions on local and international gay history, and library material to browse through. There's also the **Spinnboden** ("Archive and Treasury for Womanlove"), Anklamer Str. 38, Mitte (Mon & Fri 2–9pm; donation expected), providing a comprehensive archive of every aspect of lesbian experience, with a beautifully housed collection of books, videos, posters and magazines.

Contacts and resources

The German/English-language *Berlin von Hinten* (€12) is the city's most useful gay **guide**. *Siegessäule* (@www.siegessaeule.de), a monthly gay **magazine**, has listings of events and an encyclopedic directory of gay and lesbian contacts and groups; it's available free from all of the groups below and most gay bars, as well as at the Prinz Eisenherz bookshop. *Blattgold* (@www.blattgold-berlin .de), a monthly publication listing all lesbian groups and events, is available from feminist meeting places and bookshops. The German-language website @berlin.gay-web.de is good for practical advice and general information.

Contact organizations

AHA–Lesben- und Schwulenzentrum
Mehringdamm 61, Kreuzberg ☎030/6 92 36 00
@www.aha-berlin.de. Non-profit organization

that provides premises for gay and lesbian groups and organizes workshops and events. U-Bahn Mehringdamm.
Begine Potsdamer Str. 139, Schöneberg
☎030/2 15 14 14, @www.begine.de.

Women's centre with a programme of earnest lectures and films (Sept–May), and excellent performances by women musicians and dancers. U-Bahn Kurfürstenstrasse. Daily 6pm until late.

EWA Prenzlauer Allee 6, Prenzlauer Berg ☎030/4 42 55 42. The first post-Wall women's centre in east Berlin, EWA offers courses and counselling, as well as various cultural events and computer and media facilities. Good for what's-on information and flyers. U-Bahn Rosa-Luxemburg-Platz. Daily except Fri 6–11pm.

Lesbenberatung Kulmer Str. 20a, Schöneberg ☎030/2 17 27 53. Lesbian advisory service for those coming out. U- and S-Bahn Yorckstrasse. Mon–Thurs 5–8pm.

Mann-0-Meter Motzstr. 5, Schöneberg ☎030/2 16 80 08, ⓦwww.mann-o-meter.de. One of the city's main gay information centres and

meeting points. U-Bahn Nollendorfplatz. Mon–Sat 5–10pm, Sun 4–10pm.

Schokofabrik Mariannenstr. 6, Kreuzberg ☎030/6 15 29 99. One of Europe's largest women's centres, with a café/gallery, sports facilities (including Hamam, a women-only Turkish bath; see p.274) and diverse events. U-Bahn Kottbusser Tor. Mon–Fri & Sun 11am–10pm.

Vorspiel Naumanstrasse 33, Schöneberg ☎030/3 32 17 77, ⓦwww.vorspiel-berlin.de. Berlin's gay sports club, offering a variety of activities for every level of fitness and ability. S-Bahn Papestrasse. Tues 5–8pm, Thurs 10am–1pm.

Weiberwirtschaft Anklamer Str. 38, Mitte ☎030/4 40 22 30, ⓦwww.weiberwirtschaft .de. Complex housing businesses or services owned by, and for, women. U-Bahn Bernauer Strasse.

Bookshops and galleries

Ana Koluth Karl-Liebknecht-Str. 13 ☎030/24 72 69 03, ⓦwww.anakoluth.de. Exceptionally well-stocked lesbian bookstore, which also puts on regular exhibitions and readings; check the website for details. U-Bahn Alexanderplatz. Mon–Fri 10am–8pm, Sat 10am–4pm.

Das Verborgene Museum Schlüterstr. 70, Charlottenburg ☎030/3 13 36 56. A gallery founded by women artists for the research, documentation and exhibition of women's art. S-Bahn Savignyplatz. Wed & Fri 3–7pm, Sat & Sun noon–4pm.

Galerie Janssen Pariser Str. 45, Wilmersdorf ☎030/8 81 15 90. Men's art gallery, also

selling posters, postcards and some art books. The building next door contains Janssen's photographic gallery, devoted to exhibiting "classical and contemporary" gay photography. U-Bahn Hohenzollernplatz. Mon–Fri 11am–6.30pm, Sat 11am–2pm.

Prinz Eisenherz Buchladen GmbH Bleibtreustr. 52, Charlottenburg ☎030/3 13 99 36, ⓦwww .prinz-eisenherz.com. Friendly and informative gay bookstore with helpful assistants. Excellent for relaxed browsing and for free magazines, what's-on posters and leaflets about current gay happenings in the city. U-Bahn Wittenbergplatz. Mon–Sat 10am–8pm.

Accommodation

Most **accommodation** in Berlin is gay-friendly, though you may find the options below more comfortable as they are run for and by the gay community. There are no hotels or pensions in Berlin specifically for lesbians, though there are two women-only hotels, the *Artemisia* (see p.224) and *Intermezzo* (see p.222).

Art Hotel Connection Fuggerstr. 33, Schöneberg ☎030/2 17 70 28, ⓦwww.arthotel-connection .de. Located above the well-known Connection club (see map, p.143). Most rooms are large and en suite; breakfast is included in the rate. U-Bahn Wittenbergplatz. ⑤

Charlottenburger Hof Stuttgarter Platz 14, Charlottenburg ☎030/32 90 70, ⓦwww .charlottenburger-hof.de. Bright contemporary hotel (see map, p.128), replete with modern art, Bauhaus design and multicoloured furniture. Perks include free Internet access in every room and a 24hr café. S-Bahn Charlottenburg. ❸

Le Moustache Gartenstr. 4 ☎ & ⓕ **030/2 81 72 77,** ⓦ **www.lemoustache.de.** Basic hotel next door to the leather bar of the same name (see p.270; for the location, see the map on pp.100–101). The rate includes entry to the

adjacent swimming pool, Stadtbad Mitte. U-Bahn Oranienburger Tor. ❷

Tom's House Eisenacherstr. 10, Schöneberg ☎ **030/2 18 55 44,** ⓕ **2 13 44 64.** Friendly and somewhat eccentric gay hotel, popular with those into leather. See map on p.143 for the location. U-Bahn Nollendorfplatz. ❺

Cafés and bars

The longest-standing and most concentrated area of **gay bars** is in Schöneberg between Wittenbergplatz and Nollendorfplatz, though in the last decade or so the area south of Kleiststrasse, along Schönhauser Allee in Prenzlauer Berg, has become an eastern gay centre.

As in many other large cities, **lesbians** in Berlin have a much lower profile than gay men. Perhaps because of this, there's no real distinction between bars and cafés for lesbians and straight women, and many of Berlin's women-only bars have a strong lesbian following.

Schöneberg

See the map on p.143 for the locations of the venues below.

Mostly men

Bear Fuggerstr. 34, Schöneberg ☎ **030/21 96 87 53.** If you're in Berlin for the S&M leather action, look no further than this wicked leather bar: service is from behind a grille and handcuffs line the walls. U-Bahn Wittenbergplatz. Daily 7pm until late.

Blue Boy Bar Eisenacherstr. 3, Schöneberg ☎ **030/2 18 74 98.** Tiny, convivial bar, far less raucous than many that surround it. U-Bahn Nollendorfplatz. Daily noon–6am.

Lenz Eisenacher Str. 3, Schöneberg ☎ **030/2 17 78 20.** Straightforward, likeable Szene bar with comfortable couches and huge flower arrangements. Attracts a good-looking crowd; specializes in cocktails (there are 150 on its list), with happy hour running until 9pm every evening. U-Bahn Nollendorfplatz. Daily 6pm–3am.

Prinzknecht Fuggerstrasse 33, Schöneberg ☎ **030/23 62 74 44.** A refined version of an American sports bar, all bare brick and gleaming chrome, attracting a broad range of gays and some women. The men-only cellar darkroom is underused. U-Bahn Wittenbergplatz. Daily 3pm–3am.

Mixed

Café PositHiv Bülowstr. 6, Schöneberg ☎ **030/2 16 86 54.** Quiet self-help café run by and

for PWAs and men and women who are HIV-positive. U-Bahn Nollendorfplatz. Tues, Thurs, Fri & Sun 3–11pm, Wed 1–11pm, Sat 6–11pm.

Hafen Motzstr. 19, Schöneberg ☎ **030/2 11 41 18.** Adjacent to Tom's Bar (see p.271), this is a long-established, cruisey bar for 20- and 30-somethings, and always packed. U-Bahn Nollendorfplatz. Mon–Sat 8pm–4am, Sun 3pm–4am.

Prenzlauer Berg

See the map on pp.158–159 for the locations of the venues below.

Mostly men

Burgfrieden Greifenhagener Str. 31, Prenzlauer Berg ☎ **030/44 71 53 45.** An established haunt that's been going since the Sixties, with a 35-plus crowd that takes in everyone from leathermen to transvestites and all points in between. Two bars, one serving beer, the other cocktails. U- & S-Bahn Schönhauser Allee. Mon–Fri & Sun 7pm–1am, Sat 7pm–3.30am.

Schoppenstube Schönhauser Allee 44, Prenzlauer Berg ☎ **030/4 42 82 04.** The best-known gay place in eastern Berlin, this is really two very different bars: a pleasant wine bar upstairs, and a steamy cruisers' haven downstairs. Knock for entry, and if the doorman likes the look of you you're in. U-Bahn Eberswalder Strasse. Mon–Thurs 8pm until late, Fri–Sun 10pm until late.

Stiller Don Erich-Weinert-Str. 67, Prenzlauer Berg. An accessible intro to the scene in the former East, like a slightly intellectual neighbourhood bar and with a clientele running right across the age spectrum. U-Bahn Schönhauser Allee. Daily 8pm until late.

Mixed

Café Amsterdam Gleimstrasse 24, Prenzlauer Berg ☎ 030/44 00 94 54. Popular café and bar, as well as a weekend house and techno club. U-Bahn Schönhauser Allee. Mon–Thurs 9am–3am Fri, Sat 9am–5am, Sun 9am–3am.

Schall und Rauch Gleimstr. 23, Prenzlauer Berg. Tasteful designer elegance in this hip young bar. A place to see and be seen – and eat, thanks to an imaginative and ever-changing menu. U-Bahn Schönhauser Allee. Daily 10am–3am.

Women

EWA Frauencafé In the EWA Frauenzentrum, Prenzlauer Allee 6, Prenzlauer Berg ☎ 030/4 42 55 42. An airy café-gallery with a children's play area. Offers advice, discussion and events. Women only. U-Bahn Rosa-Luxemburg-Platz. Mon–Thurs 6–11pm.

The Scheunenviertel

See the map on pp.100–101 for the locations of the venues below.
Café Seidenfaden Dircksenstr. 47 ☎ 030/2 83 27 83. Gentle women-only café with inexpensive lunch specials (€3). No alcohol. U-Bahn Weinmeisterstrasse. Mon, Tues, Thurs & Fri noon–7pm, Wed noon–9pm, Sat 11am–8pm.

Le Moustache Gartenstr. 4. Men-only leather bar in the tiled surroundings of an old butcher's shop. It's quite average, but is a popular haunt in a part of town with few other gay venues, though it doesn't usually get going until around 11pm. Has a pension attached (see p.269). U-Bahn Rosenthaler Platz. Tues–Sun from 8pm.

Kreuzberg

See the map on pp.148–149 for the locations of the venues below.
Melitta Sundström Mehringdamm 61. Small and pleasant mixed café that's low-key and comfortable – often a warm-up for the basement, location of the legendary Schwuz club (see opposite). Food served until 11pm. U-Bahn Mehringdamm. Daily 10am–4am.

Schoko Café Mariannenstr. 6 ☎ 030/6 15 15 61. Alternative women-only place in a converted warehouse, housing a health-conscious café and offering information on the many activities organized by the Schokofabrik collective. The cliquey atmosphere can be a little intimidating if you're new to the place. U-Bahn Kottbusser Tor. Daily 3pm until late.

Friedrichshain

Offenbar Schreinerstr. 5 ☎ 030/4 26 09 30. Mixed hangout with a good Sunday brunch, and good for a latte any day, though it's a bit hit-and-miss at night. See the map on pp.158–159 for the location. U-Bahn Samariterstrasse. Daily 10am–4am.

Clubs

Many mainly straight clubs have gay nights – see *Tip*, *Zitty* or *Siegessäule* for details.

Connection Fuggerstr. 83, Schöneberg ☎ 030/2 18 14 32, ⓦ www.connection-berlin.dom. Very popular gay disco playing house and techno and attracting a largely leather-clad crowd. U-Bahn Wittenbergplatz. Fri & Sat from 11pm–6am.

Die Zwei Am Wasserturm, Spandauer Damm 168, Charlottenburg ☎ 030/39 83 89 69. An exuberantly tacky and determinedly (but not exclusive) lesbian bar, popular particularly among older women, with music from Marlene Dietrich to Madonna, via Iron Butterfly. U-Bahn Birkenstrasse. Fri & Sat 10pm until late.

Pick ab! Greifenhagener Str. 16, Prenzlauer Berg ☎ 030/4 45 85 23. As the name suggests, this place is anything but restrained. "Porn videos will be shown", they claim, and there's a darkroom at the back. U-Bahn Schönhauser Allee. Daily 10pm–6am.

Roses Oranienstr. 187, Kreuzberg ☎030/6 15 65 70 22. Kitsch gay club with a strong lesbian presence. One of the locales of choice for a solo night out for either sex. U-Bahn Kottbusser Tor. Daily 9.30pm–5am.

Scheune Motzstr. 25, Schöneberg ☎030/2 13 85 80. Very popular leather club with regular theme parties for devotees of rubber, uniforms or sheer nakedness. Darkroom, baths and other accoutrements. U-Bahn Nollendorfplatz. Mon–Thurs 9pm–7am, nonstop Fri 9pm–Mon 7am.

Schwuz Mehrindamm 61, Kreuzberg ☎030/69 50 78 89. Dance club well loved by all stripes of the gay community, and always crowded and convivial. One floor has the usual Eighties and disco mixes, the other more experimental tunes. Highly recommended. U-Bahn Mehringdamm. Fri & Sat from 11pm–4am.

Tom's Bar Motzstr. 19, Schöneberg ☎030/2 13 45 70. Dark, sweaty and wicked cruising establishment with a large back room. Possibly Berlin's most popular gay bar, and a great place to finish off an evening. Drinks are two for the price of one on Monday night. Men only. U-Bahn Nollendorfplatz. Daily 10pm–6am.

GAY AND LESBIAN BERLIN | Clubs

18

Sport

W hile Berliners go in for healthy eating in a big way, they're not famous for being fitness fanatics – they need all their energy for the frenetic nightlife. Nonetheless there is a surprising variety of **participatory sports** available in the city and, despite a shortage of international-quality teams, the **spectator sports** scene is vibrant, with fanatical support in evidence for virtually every team. Major and some minor sporting events are listed in the *Tip* and *Zitty* what's on magazines (see p.29), but the best index of facilities and events is on the web on the German-only ⓦwww.sport-berlin.de.

Participatory sports

Municipal facilities for many sports are excellent across the city, as this is one area the GDR was always keen to invest in. Wherever you are in the city, it shouldn't be hard to find somewhere to jog and swim – with many outdoor pools opening for the summer. Berlin is also a cycle-friendly city (see "Basics" p.34).

Ice-skating

Small open-air rinks sprout near Christmas markets in the centre of town, but the proper rinks are all a little way out. These usually have several three-hour sessions per day which usually cost around €4 and the same again to rent skates. The city's largest rink is the Horst-Dohn-Eisstadion, Fritz-Wildung-Strasse 9, Wilmersdorf (☎030/8 24 10 12; U–Bahn Heidelberger Platz), an outdoor facility, with a track surrounding the central rink.

Jogging

Its many parks make it easy to find a good place to jog in Berlin. Particularly suited are the Tiergarten, Volkspark Friedrichshain, Treptower Park and the gardens of Schloss Charlottenburg. The lakes around the city are also popular with joggers: try the Schlachtensee, Krumme Lanke or Grunewaldsee. If you're into long-distance running there's always the **Berlin Marathon** on the last weekend in September.

In-line skating and skateboarding

In-line skating is extremely popular in Berlin, as evidenced by the success of Skate Night (May–Sept; ⓦwww.skate-night-berlin.com) when thousands take to cordoned-off streets in the city centre. The event usually starts at 8.30pm on Sundays and runs until dusk, returning skaters back to the start point. It's a magnificent opportunity to see some of Berlin's streets from an unusual viewpoint. Skateparks, ramps and pipes are scattered around the city's parks, with one of the best being at the old Radrennbahn in Weissensee and Grazer Platz in Schöneberg. A full overview is given on the website ⓦwww.skate -spots.de.

Sports centres

Berlin's private gyms are generally members-only and you'll usually need to be a guest of a member to qualify for a day pass, which is likely to run around €25.

FEZ Wuhlheide An der Wuhlheide 197, Köpenick ☎030/53 07 15 04, ⓦwww.fez-berlin.de. Large leisure complex some way out of town with some unusual facilities, such as a BMX track, that make the trek out of town worthwhile. S-Bahn Wuhlheide.

Freisportanlage Am Südpark, Spandau ☎030/3 61 52 01. Massive outdoor sports complex on the edge of town, with lots of free facilities including basketball and volleyball courts, table tennis, tennis and an in-line skating area. Also crazy golf (€3 per round). May–Sept. S-Bahn Spandau and bus #131 or #134.

SEZ (Sport- und Erholungszentrum) Landsberger Allee 77, Friedrichshain ☎030/42 08 79 20. Gigantic sports complex with a multitude of facilities, most of which are undergoing renovation, due to be completed by 2007. There will be piecemeal reopening until then of facilities, which include several swimming pools, a wave machine, an ice- and roller-skating rink, a sauna, a bowling alley, a sports hall and fitness area, plus various cafés. The entrance is near the junction of Danziger Strasse and Landsberger Allee. S-Bahn Landsberger Allee.

Swimming pools

Most districts throughout the city have both indoor and outdoor **swimming pools** (not necessarily in the same place). Most municipal pools charge around €4 for a swim, €10–14 for a sauna, and have complicated opening hours – from as early as 7am to as late as 10pm on some days – and some men- and women-only times

which can all be found out by calling ☎01813/10 20 20 or checking the web at ⓦwww.berlinerbaederbetriebe.de. Many pools have special women- or families-only days or evenings. Watch out too for **Warmbädetag**, when the water is warmer than usual – and admission usually more expensive.

Bad am Spreewaldplatz Wiener Str. 59h, Kreuzberg ☎030/6 12 70 57. Popular indoor pool complete with sauna and wave machine. U-Bahn Görlitzerbahnhof.

Blub Baderparadis Buschkrugallee 64, Neukölln ☎030/6 06 60 60, ⓦwww.blub-berlin .de. Magnificent indoor and outdoor pool with wave machine, 120-metre chute, whirlpools, waterfalls, sauna and fitness centre. Entry €11–14. U-Bahn Grenzallee. Daily 10am–11pm.

Sommerbad Olympia-Stadion Olympischer Platz (Osttor), Charlottenburg ☎030/30 06 34 40. Outdoor pool, part of the Olympic Stadium complex. U-Bahn Olympia Stadion.

Stadtbad Charlottenburg (Alte Halle) Krumme Str. 10, Charlottenburg ☎030/34 38 38 60. A delightful, old-fashioned tiled pool with sauna, which is relatively unknown and as a result seldom crowded. Women only Mon & Thurs. Mon–Sat from 7am, Wed from noon, irregular closing time. U-Bahn Bismarckstrasse.

Stadtbad Mitte Gartenstr. 5, Mitte ☎030/30 88 09 10. Centrally located old-fashioned fifty-metre pool. S-Bahn Nordbahnhof.

Stadtbad Neukölln Ganghoferstr. 3, Neukölln ☎030/68 09 26 53. Swim and relax in a setting resembling a Hungarian spa. Two pools (one heated, one cool) decorated with fountains and mosaic tiles, encased in a maze of archways and colonnades. Sauna and steamroom available.

Strandbad Wannsee Wannseebadweg 25, Zehlendorf ☎030/8 03 56 12. Outdoor pool with beach nearby, lots of activities in the summer and usually packed. May–Sept daily 7am–8pm. S-Bahn Nikolassee.

Saunas and spas

Leave your Anglo-Saxon prudishness at home in Berlin's saunas and spas, which are inevitably mixed-sex and naked affairs. Women who feel uncomfortable with this arrangement should look out for women-only sessions offered regularly at most facilities, while men should be aware that somewhere advertising itself as a men's sauna is a gay venue, where some cruising is likely.

Hamam Mariannenstrasse 6, Kreuzberg
☎030/6 15 14 64. Women-only (but not lesbian) Turkish-style bathhouse, where three hours of sweating in the steam costs €12. Various beauty treatments also available. U-Bahn Kottbusser Tor. Mon 3–11pm, Tues–Sun noon–11pm.

Liquidrom Möckernstrsse 10, Kreuzberg
☎030/74 73 71 71. Cutting-edge health spa, whose claim to fame is its atmospheric saltwater pool into which ambient music is piped. The amazing underwater sound experience is complemented by mildly psychedelic projections on the ceiling and floors. There's also a couple of hot tubs – one outdoor – a sauna and steam room and civilized bar. Two hours cost €15, €4 per hour thereafter. S-Bahn Anhalter Bahnhof. Sun–Thurs 10am–10pm, Fri & Sat 10am–midnight.

Spectator sports

Though none of Berlin's sporting teams is world-class, all play in competitive leagues and have a loyal and entertaining fan base. The most successful and high-profile team is the city's major **soccer team** Hertha BSC, though within their leagues Eisbären Ice hockey team and the Berlin Thunder American Football team have excelled in recent times. The biggest sporting spectacles, however, are the city's annual events, including the **Six-day Non-stop Cycle Race** (see p.42) in late January, the late-September **Berlin Marathon** (see p.43) and the **German Open Women's Tennis Tournament** (ⓦwww .german-open-berlin.de) in May, a highly popular event that's a major date on the ladies' circuit.

Teams and venues

Alba Berlin ☎030/3 00 90 50 ⓦwww .albaberlin.de. Berlin's premier basketball team, and one of the top dozen in Europe, plays in the Max-Schmeling-Halle in Prenzlauer Berg in Oct–June; tickets €6.50–50. U-Bahn Eberswalder Strasse.

Berlin Thunder ☎030/30 06 44 00, ⓦwww .berlin-thunder.de. American football team, which has often been a strong contender in NFL Europe league, with a couple of World Bowl titles under its belt and topping the league in 2004. The quality is a far cry from its stateside cousin, but at least the Olympic stadium venue is as impressive as they come. Season April–June; tickets €8–32. U-Bahn Olympia Stadion.

Berliner Schlitschue-Club Preussen ☎030/30 81 18 29, ⓦwww.bschc-preussen.de. Western Berlin's ice-hockey team plays second fiddle to the Eisbären, and in a lower league, but there's loads of passion and atmosphere in the Deutschlandhalle and the quality of the hockey is reasonable. The stands have the best atmosphere and

views. Don't go if you find the idea of a thousand fans chanting "Prussia" unnerving. Season Sept–March; tickets €8–18. S-Bahn Eichkamp.

EHC Eisbären ☎030/97 18 40 40 ⓦwww .eisbaren.de. Fanatically supported eastern Berlin ice-hockey team, which has been competitive at the top of the premier German division for some years. The Sportforum Berlin is a good venue, with decent views from all the seats and good atmosphere in the stands. The razzmatazz surrounding the teams and players brings it close to the likes of the NHL and the game quality is not too far off. Season Sept–March; tickets €15–30. S-Bahn Hohenschönhausen.

Hertha BSC ☎01805/18 92 00 ⓦwww .hertahabsc.de. Berlin's Bundesliga also-rans, who always seem to evade real glory, despite lots of promise and the occasional successful European outing. But the Olympic Stadium is glorious whatever the team or result. Tickets are generally easy to come by, either online or via the Hertha fan-shop in the Europa Center (see p.132).

Season August–May; tickets €10–60. U-Bahn Olympia Stadion.

Trabrennbahn Karlshorst Treskowerallee 129, Lichtenberg ☎030/50 01 71 21. Enjoy a day at the races Berlin-style, watching trap-and-dog racing: usually Wed 6pm, sometimes Sat 2pm & Tues 6pm. The racetrack is to the left of Treskowerallee, just south of the S-Bahn bridge. Tickets €1. S-Bahn Karlshorst.

Union Berlin ☎030/6 56 68 80 ⓦ www.fc-union-berlin.de. Eastern Berlin's football team, with a fiercely loyal working-class following, plays in the second division. Despite some shock success in German cup matches and even in Europe, the day-to-day picture is fairly bleak. Matches are played in the Stadion an der alten Förterei, An der Wuhlheide in Köpenick. Season August–May; tickets €7.50–23. S-Bahn Köpenick.

Shopping

The majority of Berliners visit the city's many multistorey **department stores** for most of their shopping, but that's not to say that Berlin doesn't possess more interesting shops. In fact, a remarkable number of small and quirky specialist shops have survived the onslaught of the big retailers. Below is a selection of some of the more interesting, but the list is far from extensive. The yellow pages (*Gelbe Seiten*) can be useful in finding further specialist shops in a given field, but the best way is to ask around at similar shops. The level of shop-assistant training is invariably excellent – and if a shop can't supply your needs they will not hesitate to suggest alternatives. If you like browsing and foraging you'll find a second home in the city's many **flea markets** – good places to find relics of the Eastern Bloc – and **secondhand clothes shops**.

Glitz and dazzle are the prerogatives of **Wittenbergplatz** and the **Kurfürstendamm**, with its two miles of large chain stores, while the recently rebuilt **Friedrichstrasse** in the east, though more modest in size, is more opulent in wares. Many of the city's funkiest speciality shops and expensive boutiques are concentrated in **Charlottenburg**, **Mitte** and **Prenzlauer Berg**. Ethnic foods and "alternative" businesses are mostly in **Kreuzberg**, along Oranienstrasse and Bergmannstrasse.

Normal **shop opening hours** are Monday to Friday 9am to 8pm & Saturday 9am to 4pm. Smaller shops outside of the major shopping districts tend to close earlier: 6pm on weekdays and 2pm on Saturdays. Except for chains and the larger places, **credit cards** are not widely accepted.

Art and design

Like most Berlin phenomena, the city's art scene divides sharply into east and west, the latter containing the expensive, more established galleries in **Charlottenburg** and **Tiergarten** and the former reflecting the current energy and attention. The area around **Auguststrasse** in Mitte, which became the breeding ground of experimental art in the first years after the Wall came down, is now known as the "Art Mile" – after the many galleries that have sprung up along its streets. It seems to be settling down, though, as it becomes more commercialized. A useful and comprehensive source of information about **what's on** in the city's galleries is the English/German monthly magazine *artery berlin*, found in most galleries. You can pick up the free *Galerien Berlin* listings brochure put out by the Berlin Art Dealers Association in galleries as well, or visit their website at ⓦwww .berliner-galerien.de. The quarterly *Berliner Kunstblatt* has selective listings.

Zitty and *Tip* (under "Galerien" in "Ausstellungen") are also worth checking for up-to-the-minute details.

Galleries

Aktions Galerie Auguststrasse. 20, Mitte ☎030/28 59 96 54, ⓦwww.aktionsgalerie.de. Experimental and conceptual art and generally outrageous happenings. Also organizer of the always interesting Und ab die Post show at the Postfuhramt, Oranienburgerstr. 19–21, every May & June. U-Bahn Weinmeisterstrasse. Tues–Sat 2–7pm.

Arndt & Partner Auguststr. 35, Mitte ☎030/2 80 81 23, ⓦwww.arndt-partner.de. International contemporary art and young local artists. U-Bahn Stadtmitte. Tues–Sat noon–6pm.

Asian Fine Arts Berlin Sophienstr. 18 (1st Hof), Mitte ☎030/28 39 13 88, ⓦwww.asianfinearts.de. Focus on new Asian art with a strong international profile. U-Bahn Weinmeisterstrasse. Tues–Sat noon–7pm.

DAAD Galerie Kurfürstenstr. 58, Tiergarten ☎030/2 02 20 80 26, ⓦwww.Berliner-kuenstlerprogramm.de. Exhibitions and occasional readings by big-name artists working in the city on fellowships awarded by the Berlin Artist Exchange of the Deutsche Akademischer Austausch Dienst (German Academic Exchange Service). U-Bahn Nollendorfplatz. Daily 12.30–7pm.

EIGEN+ART Auguststr. 26, Mitte ☎030/2 80 66 05, ⓦwww.eigen-art.com. Run by Gerd Harry Lybke, who opened the first private gallery in the GDR back in the 1980s, this is one of the most important Auguststrasse galleries. Though originally a showcase for East German talent, the programme now covers painting, installations and photography by (predominantly young) international artists. S-Bahn Hackescher Markt. Tues–Sat 11am–6pm.

Fine Art Rafael Vostell Knesebeckstr. 30, Charlottenburg ☎030/8 85 22 80, ⓦwww.vostell.de. International artists of the 1960s with a mix of young Berlin painters. S-Bahn Savignyplatz. Mon–Fri 11am–7pm, Sat 11am–4pm.

Galerie Anselm Dreher Pfalzburgerstr. 80, Wilmersdorf ☎030/8 83 52 49, ⓦwww.galerie-anselm-dreher.com. One of the city's top galleries, showing international avant-garde artists. U-Bahn Hohenzollernplatz. Tues–Fri 2–6.30pm, Sat 11am–2pm.

Galerie Barbara Thumm Dirksenstr. 41, Mitte ☎0302/8 39 03 47, ⓦwww.bthumm.de. British and Berlin-based artists working in all media. S- & U-Bahn Alexanderplatz. Tues–Fri 1–7pm, Sat 1–6pm.

Galerie Thomas Schulte Mommsenstr. 56, Charlottenburg ☎030/3 24 00 44, ⓦwww.galeriethomasschulte.de. Well-presented photographic exhibitions and installations, frequently featuring established artists from America. S-Bahn Charlottenburg. Mon–Fri 11am–6pm, Sat 11am–3pm.

Galerie Paula Böttcher Klein Hamburgerstr. 15, Mitte ☎2 81 12 36, ⓦwww.galeriepauaboettcher.de. Young energetic presentation of young energetic artists – local and international. U-Bahn Weinmeisterstrasse. Wed–Fri 2–6pm, Sat 1–6pm.

Galerie Springer & Winckler Fasanenstr. 13, Charlottenburg ☎030/3 12 70 63, ⓦwww.springer-winckler.de. Top-class contemporary painting. One of the galleries foremost in establishing the Berlin art scene after World War II. U- and S-Bahn Zoologischer Garten. Mon–Fri 2–7pm, Sat 11am–2pm.

Galerie Wohnmaschine Tucholskystr. 36, Mitte ☎030/87 20 15, ⓦwww.wohnmaschine.de. Young gallery-owner Friedrich Loock opened his first gallery in his flat (he's one of the few people involved in the Scheunenviertel art scene who actually comes from the area) and now specializes in promoting the works of young, predominantly local, artists. U-Bahn Oranienburger Tor. Tues–Sat 11am–6pm.

Kunst-Werke Berlin Auguststr. 69, Mitte ☎030/2 43 45 90, ⓦwww.kw-berlin.de. Large gallery overrunning a former factory building, heavily subsidized by the city. Varies from has-been American artists carpetbagging their way into the city arts scene to astute reflections on contemporary Berlin. Principal organizer of the Berlin Biennale (ⓦwww.berlinbiennale.de). U-Bahn Oranienburger Tor. Tues–Sun 2–6pm.

Raab Galerie Potsdamer Str. 58, Tiergarten ☎030/2 61 92 17, ⓦwww.raab-galerie.de. Avant-garde and contemporary art; popular meeting place for the art in-crowd. U- and S-Bahn Zoologischer

Garten. Mon–Fri 10am–7pm, Sat 10am–4pm.

Zwinger Gallerie Gipsstr. 3, Mitte ☏ 030/28 59 89 07. One of the city's most important galleries, presenting a mixture of the avant-garde and conventional. U-Bahn Weinmeisterstrasse. Tues–Fri 2–7pm, Sat 11am–2pm.

Ararat Bergmannstr. 99a, Kreuzberg ☏ 030/6 93 50 80, ⓦ www.ararat.de. Huge selection of greetings cards and postcards; posters and prints are across the street at Bergmannstr. 9 ☏ 030/6 94 95 32. U-Bahn Gneisenaustrasse. Mon–Sat 10am–8pm.

Books, newspapers and magazines

Berlin boasts a great variety of new and secondhand bookstores, and it's an ideal city for leisurely, unharassed browsing. There are quite a few places to find **English-language books**, most of them situated in or around Knesebeckstrasse, the street with Berlin's highest concentration of bookstores.

Almost any decent-sized magazine shop in the central districts of Berlin will stock a few English-language newspapers, usually at least *The Guardian*, *Financial Times* and *The New York Herald-Tribune*. Several places selling international newspapers and magazines cluster around the Zoo Station area, the best stocked being **Internationale Presse**, Joachimstalerstr. 1, Charlottenburg, open daily until midnight, which has every London–printed morning newspaper by 1pm; a branch just inside the main entrance to Zoo Station also has a wide selection of newspapers and magazines. Alternatively, try the store on the first floor of the **Europa Center**, open daily until 10pm. See also "Information and maps" in "Basics".

Books in Berlin Goethestr. 69, Charlottenburg ☏ 030/3 13 12 33, ⓦ www.booksinberlin .de. Small bookstore with a good selection of English-language history and popular fiction, some secondhand. U-Bahn Ernst-Reuter-Platz. Mon–Fri noon–8pm.

Dussmann Friedrichstr. 90, Mitte ☏ 030/20 25 24 00, ⓦ www.kulturkaufhaus.de. A huge emporium of books, CDs, videos and software. U- & S-Bahn Friedrichstrasse. Mon–Sat 10am–10pm.

Hugendubel Tauentzienstr. 213, Charlottenburg ☏ 030/21 40 60, ⓦ www.hugendubel.de. Huge general bookstore with a section devoted to English-language paperback fiction. Branches at Friedrichstr. 83, Mitte ☏ 030/20 63 51 00, and in the Potsdamer Platz shopping mall, Tiergarten ☏ 030/2 53 91 70. U-Bahn Kurfürstendamm. Mon–Sat 10am–8pm.

Marga Schoeller Knesebeckstr. 33, Charlottenburg ☏ 030/8 81 11 12. Small shop, packed with English fiction and nonfiction: the best place for esoteric topics in English. S-Bahn Savignyplatz. Mon–Wed 9.30am–7pm, Thurs–Fri 9.30am–8pm, Sat 9.30am–4pm.

Berlin Story Unter den Linden 40, Mitte ☏ 030/20 45 38 42. The city's most extensive bookshop on itself, with everything from travel guides to specialist histories, and offered in a range of languages. U- & S-Bahn Friedrichstrasse. Daily 10am–7pm.

Another Country Riemannstr. 7, Kreuzberg ☏ 030/69 40 11 60. A living-room atmosphere pervades this intimate shop of English-language used books, run by a British expat. The cellar is full of science fiction. U-Bahn Gneisenaustrasse. Mon–Fri 11am–8pm, Sat 11pm–4pm.

Artificium Rosenthaler Str. 40–41, in the Hackeschen Höfen, Mitte ☏ 030/30 87 22 80, ⓦ www.artificium.com. Nineteenth- and twentieth-century art, architecture, photography and the like. S-Bahn Hackescher Markt. Mon–Thurs 10am–9pm, Fri & Sat 10am–10pm.

Bücherbogen Stadtbahnbogen 593–594, Charlottenburg ⊙ 030/31 86 95 11, ⓦ www .buecherbogen.com. Situated under the S-Bahn arches, a nevertheless airy and spacious setting for specialist books on art, architecture, film and photography. S-Bahn Savignyplatz. Mon–Fri 10am–8pm, Sat 10am–6pm.

Museum für Fotografie Jebensstr. 2 ⊙ 030/20 90 55 66. Small bookshop in the foyer of the museum – you can browse without paying admission – with a glut of books on photography, art and design – many at reduced prices. U- and S-Bahn Zoologischer Garten. Wed & Fri–Sun 10am–6pm, Thurs 10am–10pm.

Comics and science fiction

Grober Unfug Zossener Str. 32, Kreuzberg ⊙ 030/69 10 14 90, ⓦ www.groberunfug.de. Large display of international comics, plus T-shirts and cards on sale. Prides itself on being the number-one place for cartoon enquiries. Often has exhibitions of cartoonists' work in the small gallery upstairs. U-Bahn Gneisenaustrasse. Mon–Fri 11am–7pm, Sat 11am–4pm.

Modern Graphics Oranienstr. 22, Kreuzberg ⊙ 030/6 15 88 10, ⓦ www.modern-graphics .de. Small, serious shop stuffed with sci-fi comics, cards and posters. U-Bahn Kottbusser Tor. Mon–Fri 10am–8pm, Sat 10am–6pm.

Gay, feminist and radical

Prinz Eisenherz Buchladen GmbH Bleibtreustr. 52, Charlottenburg ⊙ 030/3 13 99 36, ⓦ www.prinz-eisenherz.com. The city's best-known gay bookstore, with a large selection of fiction and nonfiction, much in English. U-Bahn Wittenbergplatz. Mon–Sat 10am–8pm.

Travel

Chatwins Goltzstr. 40, Schöneberg ⊙ 030/21 75 69 04, ⓦ www.chatwins.de. Friendly bookshop run for and by travellers with a vast array of guidebooks and travel writing. U-Bahn Nollendorfplatz. Mon–Fri 10am–8pm, Sat 10am–4pm.

Schropp Potsdamer Str. 129, Schöneberg ⊙ 030/23 55 73 20, ⓦ www.schrop.de. Specialist travel-book and map store, with a large, well-chosen selection. Also stocks detailed cycling maps of Berlin and Germany. U-Bahn Bülowstrasse. Mon–Fri 9.30am–8pm, Sat 10am–4pm.

Music

Berlin doesn't have a large number of general record stores but there are plenty of smaller shops dedicated to just one style.

DaCapo Kastanienallee 96, Prenzlauer Berg ⊙ 030/4 48 17 71, ⓦ www.da-capo-vinyl.de. Vinyl-only new and used record shop with a wide selection of jazz, 1960s–80s rock and releases on East German label Amiga. U-Bahn Eberswalderstrasse. Mon–Fri 11am–7pm, Sat 11am–4pm.

DNS Records Alte Schonhauser Str. 39, Mitte ⊙ 030/2 47 98 35. Listening stations and a large selection of the newest of club dance music on CD and vinyl. U-Bahn Weinmisterstrasse. Mon–Fri 11am–8pm, Sat 11am–6pm.

Down-Beat Dresdener Str. 19, Kreuzberg ⊙ 030/61 60 93 26, ⓦ www.downbeat-store .de. Reggae specialist with a good selection of soul, R&B and jazz, including some rare items. U-Bahn Kottbusser Tor. Mon–Fri noon–8pm, Sat noon–4pm.

Dussmann Friedrichstr. 90, Mitte ⊙ 030/20 25 24 00, ⓦ www.kulturkaufhaus.de. Good selection of rock, jazz, dance, world and international vocalists. The basement is devoted entirely to classical. You can spend a whole afternoon listening to CDs without salesperson interference if you like. U- & S-Bahn Friedrichstrasse. Mon–Sat 10am–10pm.

Hard Wax Paul-Lincke-Ufer 44a, Kreuzberg ⊙ 030/61 13 01 11, ⓦ www.hardwax.com. Premier dance music specialist. Techno, trance: you name it, they should have it. And if they haven't, they'll get it for you. U-Bahn Görlitzer Bahnhof. Mon–Sat noon–8pm.

L&P Classics Knesebeckstr. 33–34, Charlottenburg ⊙ 030/88 04 30 43, ⓦ www .lpclassics.de. Store devoted entirely to classical music. U-Bahn Uhlandstrasse. Mon–Wed 10am–7pm, Thurs & Fri 10am–8pm.

Mr Dead & Mrs Free Bülowstr. 5, Schöneberg ☏030/2 15 14 49, ⊛www.deadandfree .com. Primarily pop, folk, indie and country records on independent labels, mostly on vinyl. U-Bahn Nollendorfplatz. Mon–Fri 11am–7pm, Sat 11am–4pm.

Scratch Records Zossener Str. 31, Kreuzberg ☏030/69 81 75 91. A large selection of club, world and alternative music. If you can't find what you're looking for, they will order it for you. U-Bahn Gneisenaustrasse. Mon–Wed 11am–7pm, Thurs & Fri 11am–8pm, Sat 10am–4pm.

Soul Trade Sanderstr. 29, Kreuzberg ☏030/6 94 52 57. Specialists in black music including soul, hip-hop, funk, house and jazz. U-Bahn Schönleinstrasse. Mon–Fri 11am–8pm, Sat 11am–4pm.

WOM Augsburger Str. 35–41, Charlottenburg ☏030/8 85 75 40, ⊛www.wom.de. Huge general shop behind Wertheim on the Ku'damm with all kinds of music, including good selections of folk and world music, blues and soundtracks. U-Bahn Kurfürstendamm. Mon–Fri 10am–8pm, Sat 10am–4pm.

Clothes

Although they like to think of themselves as such, Berliners aren't exactly trendsetters. The city is not short of innovative fashion designers but their work is mostly small-scale, rarely cutting edge, and tend to lack international impact. Still, it's possible to pick up superb **bargains** at the many **secondhand** clothes stores: you'll find unusual (and trendy) items here at very low prices. Easier access to the discarded wardrobes of the East has brought into the shops many odd items of official uniform and clothing since the Wall fell.

The main shopping areas at Wilmersdorferstrasse U-Bahn, Wilmersdorf, and Walter-Schreiber-Platz U-Bahn, Steglitz, have plenty of inexpensive name-brand styles. Ku'damm and Friedrichstrasse boast designer clothes shops, but unless you're very rich and very conservative, these aren't worth the time. A couple of exceptions are leather outlets, which have both cheap and good-quality jackets, and the excellent and stylish shoe shops.

Secondhand

Upmarket and designer secondhand clothing (Jill Sander, Yves Saint Laurent etc) can be found by perusing **Mommsenstrasse**, starting at the **Knesebeckstrasse** end, in Charlottenburg.

Garage Ahornstr. 2, Schöneberg ☏030/2 11 27 60. Largest secondhand clothes store in Europe; good for jackets, coats and jeans. Prices are according to weight (the clothes', not yours). U-Bahn Nollendorfplatz. Mon–Wed 11am–7pm, Thurs–Fri 11am–8pm, Sat 10am–4pm.

Humana Frankfurter Tor 3 ☏030/4 22 20 18. Gigantic branch of a local secondhand chain, offering great bargains on items that are (again) in style. One of a dozen stores in Berlin, with another under the S-Bahn tracks at Alexanderplatz. U-Bahn Frankfurter Tor. Mon–Fri 10am–7pm, Sat 10am–4pm.

Secondo Mommsenstr. 61, Charlottenburg ☏030/8 81 22 91. Exclusively designer clothes at massively knockdown prices: most items are in top condition, though of course many designs are a bit dated. S-Bahn Savignyplatz. Mon–Fri 11am–7pm, Sat 11am–3pm.

Sgt. Peppers Kastanienallee 91, Prenzlauer Berg ☏030/4 48 11 21. Mixed bag of vintage 1960s and 1970s, and the store also has its own label of retro-wear. U-Bahn Eberswalder Strasse. Mon–Fri 11am–7pm, Sat 11am–4pm.

New and designer labels

Clothes shops open, close and change hands almost as fast as bars in Berlin. To find the latest additions, wander down **Bleibtreustrasse** between the Ku'damm and Kantstrasse. This area is also great to browse in during the sales in January (*Winterschluss* *verkauf*) and July/August (*Sommer-schluss verkauf*), when designer and less well-known names are on offer at knockdown prices – the length of **Pestalozzistrasse** (as far as Wilmersdorfer Strasse), **Oranienstrasse**, **Stuttgarter Platz** and **Ludwigkirschstrasse**, off Uhlandstrasse.

Berlinomat Frankfurter Allee 89 ☎030/42 08 14 45, ⓦwww.berlinomat.com. The showcase for more than thirty Berlin designers. You'll find a large and varied assortment of clothing and accessories here – lots of unique souvenirs – and the prices, considering they're designer duds, are reasonable. U- & S-Bahn Frankfurter Allee. Mon–Fri 11am–8pm, Sat 10am–6pm.

Claudia Skoda Linien Str. 156, Mitte ☎030/2 80 72 11, ⓦwww.claudiaskoda.com. Berlin's knitmaster and most famous designer. U-Bahn Weinmeisterstrasse. Mon–Fri noon–8pm, Sat 11am–7pm.

Eisdieler Kastanienallee 12, Prenzlauer Berg ☎030/28 38 87 25. Innovative, international collection of urban streetwear. U-Bahn Eberswalder Str. Mon–Sat noon–8pm.

Lisa D. Rosenthaler Str. 40–41 (in the Hackescher Höfe), Mitte ☎030/2 82 90 61, ⓦwww.lisad.com. One of Berlin's very few local designers to have made a name for herself, Lisa D. favours fitted dresses in muted colours. S-Bahn Hackescher Markt. Mon–Sat 11am–7.30pm.

Mientus Wilmersdorfer Str. 73, Charlottenburg ☎030/3 23 90 77, ⓦwww.mientus.com. Casual and formal up-to-the-minute menswear, ranging in price from reasonable to outrageously expensive. U-Bahn Wilmersdorfer Str. Mon–Fri 10am–7pm, Sat 10am–6pm.

Molotow Gneisenaustr. 112, Kreuzberg ☎030/6 93 08 18, ⓦwww.molotowberlin.de. The best of west and east Berlin designers; mid-price range. U-Bahn Mehringdamm. Mon–Fri 2–8pm, Sat noon–4pm.

Nix Auguststr. 86, Mitte ☎030/2 81 80 44, ⓦwww.nix.de. Unusual, robust and practical designs for women from a couple of young east Berliners. S-Bahn Oranienburger Str. Mon–Sat 11am–8pm.

Respectmen Neu Schonhauser Str. 14, Mitte ☎030/2 83 50 10, ⓦwww.respectmen.de. Good tailoring and nice design mark this men's store featuring suits and casual wear. S-Bahn Hackescher Markt. Mon–Fri noon–8pm, Sat noon–6pm.

Soma Alte Schonhauser Str. 27, Mitte ☎030/2 81 93 80, ⓦwww.soma-berlin.de. Young Berlin designers and club-wear in the front of the shop, secondhand in the rear. S-Bahn Hackescher Markt. Mon–Fri noon–8pm, Sat noon–6pm.

Shoes

Barfuss oder Lackschuh Oranienburgerstr. 89, Mitte ☎030/28 39 19 91, ⓦwww.barfussoderlackschuh.de. The place to head for everything from designer shoes to workboots. S-Bahn Hackescher Markt. Mon–Sat 11am–8pm.

Budapester Schuhe Kurfürstendamm 199, Charlottenburg ☎030/8 81 17 07. World-class, expensive designer shoes such as Prada, Dolce & Gabbana etc. U-Bahn Uhlandstrasse. Mon–Fri 10am–7pm, Sat 10am–6pm.

Luccico Goltzstr. 34, Schöneberg ☎030/2 16 65 17, ⓦwww.luccico.de. Wild and wacky Italian shoes, plus plainer varieties. Also at Zossenerstr. 32, Kreuzberg; and Bergmannstr. 97, Kreuzberg. U-Bahn Eisenacer Strasse. Mon–Fri noon–8pm, Sat 11am–6pm.

Ludwig Reiter Fasanenstr. 29, Charlottenburg ☎030/88 68 17 76, ⓦwww.ludwig-reiter.com. Luxurious formal wear and well-made sports shoes. U-Bahn Uhlandstrasse. Mon–Fri 11am–7pm, Sat 11am–4pm.

Mad Flavor Krumme Str. 58, Charlottenburg ☎030/3 12 49 63, ⓦwww.madflavor.de. Trendy sneakers for the hip-hop and club crowd. U-Bahn Wilmersdorfer Strasse. Mon–Fri noon–7pm, Sat 11am–4pm.

Trippen Hackescher Höfe, Rosenthaler Str. 40, Mitte ☎030/28 39 13 37, ⓦwww.trippen.com. Hot Berlin design specializing in wooden-soled shoes with a rounded toe. S-Bahn Hackescher Markt. Mon–Fri 11am–7pm, Sat 10am–5pm.

Underwear

Körpernah Massanenstr. 8 ☎030/2 15 74 71. Fashionable underwear and lingerie for both sexes in every possible size. U-Bahn Nollendorfplatz. Mon–Thurs 10.30am–7.30pm. Fri 10.30am–8pm, Sat 10am–6pm.

Accessories

Fiona Bennett Grosse Hamburger Str. 25, Mitte ☎030/28 09 63 30, ⓦwww.fionabennett.com.

Unique and avant-garde designer hats for men and women. S-Bahn Hackescher Markt. Mon–Fri 10am–6pm, Sat noon–6pm.

Rio Bleibtreustr. 52, Charlottenburg ☎030/3 13 31 52. Decorative costume jewellers, with lots of unusual offerings from Paris and Milan, as well as its own line. Also specializes in earrings at affordable prices.

S-Bahn Savignyplatz. Mon–Wed & Fri 11am–6.30pm, Sat 10am–4pm.

Sack und Pack Kantstr. 48, Charlottenburg ☎030/3 12 15 13, ⓦwww.taschenladen.de. Specializes in natural- and black-leather bags in sporty styles, but there's a whole gamut of luggage here too. U-Bahn Wilmersdorfer Strasse. Mon–Fri 10am–7pm, Sat 10am–4pm.

Hair and beauty

There are plenty of places to get made up and perfumed in Berlin, though note that as a rule hairdressers are closed on Monday. As well as the *parfumiers* listed below there are also branches of Parfumerie Douglas (several on Kurfürstendamm – notably on the corner of Uhlandstr. and Fasanenstr.), which carry an extensive range of up-to-date and established perfume lines. KaDeWe department store has the largest cosmetic floor in the city, and Quartier 206 on Friedrichstrasse the most exclusive.

Hair

Ponyclub Kopernikusstr. 13 ☎030/29 00 32 61, ⓦwww.ponyclubberlin.de. Salon that uses Vidal Sassoon techniques to create natural-looking cuts that more or less look after themselves. U- and S-Bahn Warschauer Strasse. Mon noon–8pm, Tues–Fri 10am–8pm, Sat 10am–4pm.

Schnittstelle Kollwitzstr. 70, Prenzlauer Berg ☎030/44 04 98 70, ⓦwww.eitelkeiten.de. Good cuts and colour to the sound of techno. U-Bahn Senefelderplatz. Mon 11am–3pm, Tues–Fri 10am–8pm, Sat 11am–3pm.

Beauty

Belladonna Bergmannstr. 101, Kreuzberg ☎030/6 94 37 31, ⓦwww.bella-donna.de. Large choice of natural cosmetics. U-Bahn Mehringdamm. Mon–Fri 10am–7pm, Sat 10am–5pm.

Harry Lehman Kantstr. 106, Charlottenburg ☎030/3 24 35 82. Mix your smells then take them away, for €3–4. Over fifty different brews, including one aptly named "Berlin". U-Bahn Wilmersdorfer Strasse. Mon–Fri 9am–6.30pm, Sat 9am–2pm.

Travel equipment

Bannat Lietzenburger Str. 65, Charlottenburg ☎030/8 82 76 01, ⓦwww.bannat.de. A great selection of travel equipment, particularly for the backpacker and camper. Mon–Fri 10am–8pm, Sat 10am–6pm.

Camp 4 Karl-Marx-Allee 32, Mitte ☎030/2 42 66 34, ⓦwww.camp4.de. Everything necessary for hiking and mountain climbing, including a particularly good selection of backpacks. U-Bahn Schillingstrasse. Mon–Fri 10am–8pm, Sat 10am–4pm.

Farradbüro Berlin Hauptstr. 146 (next to Kleiststr. U-Bahn), Schöneberg ☎030/78 70 26 00, ⓦwww.fahrradbuero.de. Every

conceivable piece of equipment for bikes. U-Bahn Kleistpark. Mon–Fri 10am–7pm, Sat 10am–2pm.

Globetrotter Schlossstrasse 78–82 ☎030/850 89 20 ⓦwww.globetrotter.de. Massive outdoor shop with several gimmicks – like the pool to try out kayaks and a freezer at –25°C to try out jackets and sleeping bags – as well as lots of well-priced stock. A bit of a trek out of the centre on the subway, but directly above the station. U- & S-Bahn Rathaus Steglitz. Mon–Fri 10am–8pm, Sat 9am–8pm.

Department stores

There are no surprises inside Berlin's **department stores** and, with the exception of KaDeWe and Galeries Lafayette, they're only worth popping into to stock up on essentials. Listed below are the most central ones; check the phone book for outlying branches.

Galeries Lafayette Französische Str. 23, Mitte ☏030/20 94 80, ⓦwww.Lafayette-berlin. de. Branch of the upscale Paris-based department store. Surprisingly small, but packed with beautiful and expensive things and including a food department with imports from France. U-Bahn Französischer Strasse. Mon–Sat 10am–8pm.

KaDeWe Tauentzienstr. 21, Schöneberg ☏030/2 12 10. Content rather than flashy interior decor rules the day here. From designer labels to the extraordinarily good displays at the international delicatessen, where you can nibble on some piece of exotica or stock up on double-price El Paso taco mix, everything the consumer's heart desires can be found at this, the largest department store on the Continent. U-Bahn Wittenbergplatz. Mon–Sat 10am–8pm.

Kaufhof Alexanderplatz 9, Mitte ☏030/24 74 30. Once the location of the GDR's showcase department store, this is now a quite typical emporium. U- and S-Bahn Alexanderplatz. Mon–Sat 10am–8pm.

Wertheim Kurfürstendamm 231, Charlottenburg ☏030/88 00 30. A smaller and cheaper version of KaDeWe. Everything is beautifully laid out, with a particularly good menswear department. U-Bahn Kurfürstendamm. Mon–Sat 10am–8pm.

Food and drink

Of the city's **supermarket chains** Pennymarkt, Lidl and Aldi, all budget grocery stores, are by far the cheapest for food and drink, although they offer less choice than the rest. Ullrich, on Hardenbergstrasse, underneath the railway bridge by Zoo Station, has an excellent selection of foods, wines and spirits and is very cheap despite its central location. The city's **speciality food shops** are spread throughout the town, though the majority of Turkish shops are in Kreuzberg. Health food is very popular, particularly organically grown fruit and vegetables, and almost every neighbourhood has its own health-food shop (*Naturkostladen*), with vegetarian goodies, chemical-free beers and wines.

Bread and cakes

Freshly baked **bread** is one of the delights of Berlin, where small neighbourhood bakeries provide wholemeal loaves fresh from their ovens. For cakes, it's hard to beat the quality and selection on offer at KaDeWe – you may end up paying slightly more here than elsewhere, but you won't regret it.

Einhorn Wittenbergplatz 5, Schöneberg ☏030/21 47 51 80. Excellent wholegrain breads and cakes, baked in-house at this popular veggie eatery (see p.248). U-Bahn Uhlandstrasse. Mon–Fri 10am–5pm.

KaDeWe Tauentzienstr. 21, Schöneberg ☏030/2 12 10. The sixth-floor food hall has over 400 different breads. U-Bahn Wittenbergplatz.

Mon–Sat 10am–8pm.

Leysieffers Kurfürstendamm 218, Charlottenburg ☏030/8 85 74 80, ⓦwww.leysieffer-berlin.de. Best selection of cakes, chocolates and biscuits in town. U-Bahn Kurfürstendamm. Mon–Fri 10am–8pm, Sat 10am–7pm, Sun 11am–7pm.

Operncafé Unter den Linden 5, Mitte ☏030/20 26 83. An amazing array of baroque extravaganzas in cakes and gateaux. Select one from the display, collect a ticket and give it to the waiter. U-Bahn Französische Strasse. Daily 8am–midnight.

Weichardt Mehlitzstr. 7, Wilmersdorf ☏030/8 73 80 99, ⓦwww.weichardt.de. Probably the best Vollkorn (wholegrain) bakery in town: delicious cakes and breads. U-Bahn Blissestrasse. Tues–Fri 7am–6pm, Sat 7am–1pm.

Night shops

In general, few shops open beyond normal hours, and those that do charge considerably for the convenience. The exception to this are the many **Turkish shops** open Saturday afternoons and Sundays 1–5pm, and **petrol stations** often have shops with basics that are open seven days a week until late. The best place to head if you need basic groceries and toiletries after hours is one of the main train stations: particularly Bahnhof Zoo, the Ostbahnhof and Bahnhof Friedrichstrasse. All these have some kind of convenience store open between 8am and 10pm every day of the week.

Coffee and tea

Barcomi's Bergmannstr. 21, Kreuzberg
☎030/28 59 83 63, ⊛www.barcomis.de.
A good selection of top-notch, house-roasted coffee, including organic and caffeine-free varieties. U-Bahn Gneisenaustrasse. Mon–Sat 9am–10pm, Sun 10am–11pm.

Tchibo Kurfürstendamm 11, Charlottenburg
☎030/8 81 11 94 (many other branches around the city). The city's most popular stand-up coffee with good-quality beans and the chance to mix your own blend from a small choice at the counter. U-Bahn Kurfürstendamm. Mon–Sat 8am–8pm.

Teesalon Invalidenstr. 160 ☎030/28 04 06 60, ⊛www.tee-import.de. Offers a glut of exotic teas and all the paraphernalia they cry out for to be enjoyed in style. U-Bahn Rosenthaler Platz. Mon 2–7pm, Tues & Wed 10am–6.30pm, Thurs & Fri 10am–8pm, Sat 9.30am–1.30pm.

Delicatessens and ethnic foods

Alimentari e Vini Skalitzer Str. 23, Kreuzberg
☎030/6 11 49 81, ⊛www.alimentari.de. A slick shop in scruffy Kreuzberg offering wines, pastas and other Italian deli items. U-Bahn Kottbusser Tor. Mon–Fri 9am–8pm, Sat 9am–4pm.

Aqui Espana Kantstr. 34, Charlottenburg
☎030/3 12 33 15, ⊛www.aqui-espana.de.
Spanish and South American foods, though rather pricey. S-Bahn Savignyplatz. Mon–Fri 9am–8pm, Sat 9am–6pm.

Galeries Lafayette Französische Str. 23, Mitte
☎030/20 94 80, ⊛www.Lafayette-berlin.de.
Like the larger KaDeWe, this swank department store offers a gourmet food section with delectables from around the world. U-Bahn Französischer Strasse. Mon–Sat 10am–8pm.

KaDeWe Tauentzienstr. 21, Schöneberg
☎030/2 12 10. The sixth-floor food hall (Feinschmecker Etage) of the giant department store is a gourmets' delight: 400 types of bread, 1200 cheeses and 1400 meats, plus cafés where you can sample lots of the goodies on sale. The dough for their French bakery, Le Notre, is flown in from Paris daily. U-Bahn Wittenbergplatz. Mon–Sat 10am–8pm.

Fish and meat

Fleischerei Klaus Gerlach Greifswalder Str. 205, Prenzlauer Berg ☎030/4 42 61 83. One of the few butchers located in the eastern part of the city to offer organically raised meat. S-Bahn Greifswalder Strasse. Mon–Fri 8am–6.30pm, Sat 8am–4pm.

Rogacki Wilmersdorfer Str. 145–146, Charlottenburg ☎030/3 43 82 50, ⊛www.rogacki.de. Great selection of fresh and smoked fish, with an eat-in Imbiss. U-Bahn Bismarckstrasse. Mon–Wed 9am–6pm, Thurs 9am–7pm, Fri 8am–7pm, Sat 8am–3pm.

Health food

Himmel und Erde Naturkost Skalitzer Str. 46, Kreuzberg ☎030/611 60 41, ⊛www.naturkostlieferservice.de. The city's best organic supermarket, around for over two decades. U-Bahn Görlitzer Bahnhof. Mon–Fri 9am–7pm, Sat 9am–2pm.

Wines and spirits

Vineyard Salzufer Salzufer 13–14, Tiergarten
☎030/390 49 00, ⊛www.vineyard.de.
Specializes in rare New World wines, with a choice of over 300 sorts. U-Bahn Ernst-Reuter Platz. Mon–Fri noon–6pm.

Wein & Glas Compagnie Prinzregentenstr. 2, Schöneberg ☎030/2 35 15 20, ⊛www

.weinundglass.com. German and French wines (and some glasses). U-Bahn Eisenacher Strasse. Mon–Fri 10am–6.30pm, Sat 9.30am–4pm.
Wein & Whisky Eisenacherstr. 64 ☎**030/7 84 50 10,** ⊛**www.world-wide-whisky.de.** Though far from the source, this whisky specialist has an almost definitive collection encompassing over 2000 varieties of the water of life. U-Bahn Eisenacherstrasse. Mon 1–6pm, Tues–Fri 11am–6pm, Sat 10am–2pm.
Weinkeller Gneisenaustrasse. 15, Kreuzberg ☎**030/6 93 46 61,** ⊛**www.weinkeller-berlin**

.de. Spanish, French, Italian and German-wines, and sherries and whiskies from the cask. U-Bahn Gneiseanaustrasse. Mon–Thurs 2–8pm, Fri 11am–8pm, Sat 10am–4pm.
Die Weinliferanten Mohrenstr. 30, Mitte ☎**030/20 62 68 20,** ⊛**www.die -weinliferanten.com.** Interesting place to pick up an unusual bottle of wine. The staff are extremely knowledgeable and bring delicious rarities to your attention; particularly good on Austrian wines. U-Bahn Stadtmitte. Mon–Fri noon–8pm, Sat 10am–2pm.

Markets

There are several food markets within each quarter of the town, too numerous to mention here; listed below is a selection of the best **flea markets** and **outdoor food markets**. For **junk shops**, Suarezstrasse in Charlottenburg, Gotzstrasse in Schöneberg and Bergmannstrasse in Kreuzberg are the places to head.

Flea markets

Antiquitäten- und Flohmarkt Bahnhof Friedrichstrasse (under the railway arches 190–203), Mitte. Tending more towards the antique end of things, with numerous little shops selling everything from books to jewellery. Not particularly cheap. U- and S-Bahn Friedrichstrasse. Wed–Sun 11am–6pm.
Flohmarkt am Arkonaplatz Arkonaplatz, Prenzlauer Berg. Popular fleamarket in the city's yuppie district, thick with 1960s and 70s junk and cult objects in equal measure. U-Bahn Bernauer Strasse. Sun 10am–5pm.
Flohmarkt am Boxhagener Platz Boxhagener Platz, Friedrichshain. Small flea market catering to the needs of the student quarter and good for old East Bloc memorabilia. U- and S-Bahn Warschauer Strasse. Sun 9am–4pm.
Flohmarkt am Tierfarten Strasse des 17 Juni, north side of road near Ernst-Reuter-Platz, Charlottenburg. Pleasant enough for a Sunday-morning stroll, but the most expensive of the flea markets, and with horribly tourist-oriented wares. Good for embroidery and lace, though. S-Bahn Tiergarten. Sat & Sun 10am–5pm.
Flohmarkt an der Museumsinsel by the Bode and Pergamon Museums, Mitte. A good mix of real antiques, schlock souvenirs, used books and bootleg CDs. S-Bahn Hackescher Markt. Sat & Sun 11am–5pm.

Flohmarkt Schöneberg in front of the Schöneberg City Hall, Schöneberg. Some professionals here selling books and collectables, but also a good number of amateur vendors who have cleared out the garage or attic and are selling the motley results. U-Bahn Rathaus Schöneberg. Sat & Sun 8am–4pm.
Hallentrödelmarkt Treptow Eichenstr. 4, Treptow. Ideal rainy-day option: there's something of everything in this huge indoor flea market. The stalls are all permanent fixtures and thoroughly chaotic. From the S-Bahn head north along Hoffmannstrasse, parallel to the Spree river. S-Bahn Treptower Park. Sat & Sun 11am–4pm.
Zille-Hof Fasanenstr. 14, Charlottenburg. Not so much a flea market as an overgrown junkshop with reproduction curios, old street signs and a miscellany of interesting junk. Not especially cheap, but the pleasure is in rummaging as much as in buying. Mon–Fri 8am–5pm, Sat 8am–1pm.

Food markets

Türken-Markt Kottbusser Damm/Maybachufer, Neukölln. Definitely worth a visit, especially on Friday when there's a real Oriental flavour. Handy for all things Turkish, especially cheese, bread, olives and dried fruits, all at rock-bottom prices. U-Bahn Kottbusser Tor. Tues & Fri noon–6pm.

Flowers and plants

Flowers are frequently given as gifts, and are almost a prerequisite for birthdays and other special occasions. When looking for flowers, avoid the Ku'damm, where prices are steep and quality is poor, and take a look instead along some of the side streets. It's more fun choosing your own bouquet. Simply explain roughly what colours you'd like and the price you'd prefer to pay – around €10 should get you a respectable bunch. The city's many open-air markets also sell interesting arrangements at affordable prices.

Blumen Röwer S-Bahnhof Friedrichstrasse, Mitte ☏030/20 45 43 49. Conveniently located in the Friedrichstrasse train station. U- & S-Bahn Friedrichstrasse. Mon–Fri 10am–8pm, Sat 10am–4pm.

Miscellaneous

As Germany's largest and most cosmopolitan city, Berlin offers a cross-section of unusual and quirky stores – from the trendy to the merely odd.

Ampelmann Galerie Shop Hackescher Höfe V ☏030/44 04 88 01, ⓦ www.ooxo-berlin .de. Celebration of the traffic-light man (Ampelmann) that reigns supreme on the eastern side of the city. He was threatened by replacement with the svelte West Berlin counter part and has since become a cult object. Pick up T-shirts, mugs, lights and so on here. S-Bahn Hackescher Markt. Mon–Fri noon–6pm, Sat noon–4pm.

Atzert Kleiststr. 33, Schöneberg ☏030/2 12 98 41. Do-it-yourself radio and electronics paradise. U-Bahn Nollendorfplatz. Mon–Fri 9.30am–7pm, Sat 10am–4pm.

Dritte-Welt-Laden inside the Gedächtniskirche, Charlottenburg ☏030/8 31 54 32. Non-profit organization selling handicrafts from the developing world. U-Bahn Kurfürstendamm. Mon–Fri 10am–6pm, Sat 10am–4pm.

Küchenladen Knesebeckstr. 26, Charlottenburg ☏030/8 81 39 08. Everything for the foodie, from tortoiseshell teaspoons to Italian cookbooks. S-Bahn Savignyplatz. Mon–Fri 11am–7pm, Sat 10am–4pm.

Zauberkönig Hermannstr. 84, Neukölln ☏030/6 21 40 82. Illusions, tricks and other magicians' equipment. U-Bahn Leinestrasse. Mon–Thurs 1–6pm, Fri 10am–6pm, Sat 10am–1pm.

Directory

Addresses The street name is always written before the number and all Berlin addresses are suffixed by a five-figure postcode. Street numbers don't always run odd–even on opposite sides of the street – often they go up one side and down the other. *Strasse* (street) is commonly abbreviated to *Str.*, and often joined on to the end of the previous word. Other terms include *Weg* (path), *Ufer* (river bank), *Platz* (square) and *Allee* (avenue). Berlin apartment blocks are often built around courtyards with several entrances and staircases: the *Vorderhaus*, abbreviated as *VH* in addresses, is as the name suggests, the front building; the *Gartenhaus* (garden house) and the *Hinterhof* (*HH*; back house) are at the rear of the building. *EG* means the ground floor, *1 OG* means the first floor, etc. *Dachwohnung* means the "flat under the roof" – in other words, the top floor.

AIDS/HIV Berliner AIDS-Hilfe Meinekestr. 12, Wilmersdorf, 24hr helpline: ☏030/8 85 64 00. Free consultations. Information on all aspects of HIV and AIDS. Dispenses condoms and lubricants. U-Bahn Kurfürstendamm. Mon–Thurs 10am–6pm, Fri 10am–3pm.

Airlines Air Berlin ☏01805/73 78 00; Air France ☏01805/83 08 30; Alitalia ☏01805/07 47 47; British Airways ☏01805/26 65 22; Easyjet ☏01803/65 43 21; Iberia ☏01803/00 06 14; KLM ☏01805/25 47 50; Lufthansa ☏01803/80 38 03; Ryan Air ☏0190/17 01 00. SAS ☏01803/23 40 23.

Car rental Avis ☏01805 55 77 55, ⓦwww .avis.com; Budget ☏01805/24 43 88, ⓦwww.budget.com; Europcar ☏01805/80 00 ⓦwww.europcar.com; Hertz ☏0800/8 16 17 12; and Sixt ☏030/212 98 80 ⓦwww.e-sixt.de. A good local firm is

Robben & Wientjes, Prinzenstrasse 90–91, Kreuzberg ☏030/61 67 70 (U-Bahn Moritzplatz) and Prenzlauer Allee 96 ☏030/42 10 36 (U-Bahn Prenzlauer Allee); you can find others under "Autovermietungen" in the Yellow Pages.

Electricity The supply is 220 volts, though anything requiring 240 volts (all UK appliances) will work. American visitors, however, will need a voltage converter to run appliances. Sockets are of the two-pin variety, so a travel plug is useful.

Embassies and consulates Australia, Wallstrasse 76–78 ☏030/8 80 08 80, ⓦwww.australian-embassy.de; Canada, Friedrichstr. 95 ☏030/20 31 20, ⓦwww .kanada-info.de; Ireland, Friedrichstr. 200 ☏030/22 07 20 ⓦwww.botschaft-irland .de; New Zealand, Friedrichstr. 60 ☏030/20 62 10 ⓦwww.nzembassy.com; UK, Wilhelmstr. 70–71 ☏030/20 45 70, ⓦwww .britischebotschaft.de; US, Neustadtische Kirchstr. 4–5 ☏030/2 38 51 74, visa section, Clayallee 170 ☏030/8 32 92 33, ⓦwww.usembassy.de.

Medical emergencies For immediate medical attention, head for the 24hr emergency room of a major hospital: Charité, Schumann Str. 20–21, Mitte ☏030/2 80 20 (S-Bahn Lehrter Bahnhof); Virchow Klinikum, Augsburger Platz 1 ☏030/4 50 50 (U-Bahn Amrumer Str.). For dental emergencies get in touch with an emergency dental clinic: Zahnklinik Medeco Stresemannstr. 21 ☏030/23 09 59 60 (U- and S-Bahn Potsdamer Platz).

ID By law you need to carry proof of your identity at all times. A driver's licence or ID card is fine, but a passport is best. It's particularly essential that you carry all your documentation when driving – failure to do so may result in an on-the-spot fine.

Jaywalking This is illegal and you can be fined if caught. Even in the irreverent atmosphere of Berlin, locals stand rigidly to attention until the green signal comes on – even when there isn't a vehicle in sight. Cars are not required to stop at crossings; although walking on one should give you right of way, use your judgement and be careful.

Laundries Rosenthaler Str. 71 (7.30am–10pm); Hermannstr. 74–75 (7.30am–10pm). Other addresses are listed under "Wäschereien" in the Yellow Pages.

Left luggage There are 24-hour lockers at Zoo, Friedrichstrasse and Alexanderplatz stations; Bahnhof Zoo also has a left-luggage office.

Lost property Police lost and found department, Platz der Luftbrücke 6, Tempelhof ☎030/7 65 00 (U-Bahn Platz der Luftbrücke). For items lost on public transport, contact the BVG Fundbüro, Potsdamer Str. 180/182 Schöneberg ☎030/25 62 30 40 (U-Bahn Kleistpark).

Tipping Service is, as a rule, included in the bill. Rounding up a café, restaurant or taxi bill to the next euro or so is acceptable in most cases, though when you run up a particularly large tab you will probably want to add some more. If the service was appalling, however, there's absolutely no need to tip.

Contexts

Contexts

History

I f any city embodies the twentieth century it is Berlin. Heart of the Prussian kingdom, economic and cultural centre of the Weimar Republic, and, in the final days of Nazi Germany, the headquarters of Hitler's Third Reich, Berlin was a weather vane of European history. After the war, the world's two most powerful military systems stood face to face here, sharing the spoils of a city later to be split by that most tangible object of the East–West divide, the Berlin Wall. As the Wall fell in November 1989, Berlin was once again pushed to the forefront of world events, ushering in a period of change as frantic, confused and significant as any the city has experienced. It's this weight of history, the sense of living in a hothouse where all the dilemmas of contemporary Europe are nurtured, that gives Berlin its excitement and troubling fascination.

It was, of course, **World War II** that defined the shape of today's city. A seventh of all the buildings destroyed in Germany were in Berlin, Allied and Soviet bombing razing 92 percent of all the shops, houses and industry here. After the war, Berlin formed the stage for some of the most significant moments in the convoluted drama of the Cold War: the permanent division of the city into communist East and capitalist West, the Blockade of 1948, and, in 1961, the construction of the Berlin Wall. The city became the frontline of the Cold War, and the ideological schizophrenia of East and West is still visible in the city streets. West Berlin made a habit of tearing down its war-damaged buildings and erecting undistinguished modern ones, while East Berlin restored wherever possible, preserving some of the nineteenth-century buildings that had once made the city magnificent. Despite the current feverish construction activity in many parts of eastern Berlin, it's still easy to spot facades scarred by wartime bullets, and common to turn off a main avenue onto a street that appears to have remained unchanged for a century.

Beginnings

Archeologists reckon that people have lived around the area of modern-day Berlin for about 60,000 years. Traces of hunter-gatherer activity dating from about 8000 BC and more substantial remains of Stone Age farming settlements from 4000 BC onwards have been discovered. The Romans regarded this as barbarian territory and left no mark on the region. Although **Germanic tribes** first appeared on the scene during the fifth and sixth centuries AD, many of them left during the great migrations of later centuries, and the vacated territories were occupied by **Slavs**. Germanic ascendancy only began in the twelfth and thirteenth centuries, when Saxon feudal barons of the Mark of Brandenburg expelled the Slavs. The **Saxons** also granted municipal charters to two humble riverside towns – where the Berlin story really begins.

The twin towns

Sited on marshlands around an island (today the Museumsinsel and Fischerinsel) at the narrowest point on the River Spree, **Berlin** and **Cölln** were on a major trade route to the east, and began to prosper as municipalities. Despite many links (including a joint town hall built in 1307), they retained their separate identities throughout the fourteenth century, when both received the right to mint their own coinage and pronounce death sentences in local courts. Their admission to the powerful **Hanseatic League** of city-states in 1369 confirmed their economic and political importance. By 1391, Berlin and Cölln were virtually autonomous from the Mark of Brandenburg, which grew ever more chaotic in the early years of the fifteenth century.

Order was eventually restored by **Friedrich Hohenzollern**, burgrave of Nürnberg, whose subjugation of the province was initially welcomed by the burghers of Berlin and Cölln. However, when his son Johann attempted to treat them likewise, they forced them to withdraw to Spandau. It was only divisions within their ranks that enabled **Friedrich II**, Johann's brother, to take over the two cities. Some of the guilds offered him the keys of the gates in return for taking their part against the Berlin-Cölln magistrates. Friedrich obliged, then built a palace and instituted his own harsh rule, forbidding any further union between Berlin and Cölln.

After swiftly crushing a **rebellion** in 1448, Friedrich imposed new restrictions. To symbolize the **consolidation of Hohenzollern power**, a chain was placed around the neck of Berlin's heraldic symbol, the bear, which remained on the city's coat of arms until 1875. After the Hohenzollerns moved their residence and court here, Berlin-Cölln assumed the character of a *Residenzstadt* (royal residence) and rapidly expanded, its old wattle-and-daub dwellings replaced with more substantial stone buildings – culminating in a Renaissance Schloss finished in 1540. Yet life remained hard, for despite being involved in the Reformation, Berlin-Cölln lagged behind the great cities of western and southern Germany, and in 1576 it was ravaged by plague. The **Thirty Years' War** (1618–1648) marked a low point. After repeated plundering by Swedish troops, the twin towns had lost half their population and one-third of their buildings by the end of the war.

The Great Elector

The monumental task of postwar reconstruction fell to the Mark's new ruler, Elector Friedrich **Wilhelm of Brandenburg** (1620–1688), who was barely out of his teens. Massive fortifications were constructed, besides the residences and public buildings necessary to make Berlin-Cölln a worthy capital for an Elector. (Seven Electors – three archbishops, a margrave, duke, count and king – were entitled to elect the Holy Roman Emperor.) In recognition of his achievements, Friedrich Wilhelm came to be known as the **Great Elector**. After defeating the Swedes at the Battle of Fehrbellin in 1675, the Mark of Brandenburg was acknowledged as a force to be reckoned with, and its capital grew accordingly. Recognizing the value of a cosmopolitan population, the Elector permitted Jews and South German Catholics to move here and enjoy protection as citizens.

A later wave of immigrants affected Berlin-Cölln even more profoundly. Persecuted in France, thousands of **Protestant Huguenots** sought new homes in England and Germany. The arrival of five thousand immigrants – mostly skilled craftworkers or traders – revitalized Berlin-Cölln, whose own population was only twenty thousand. French became an almost obligatory second language, indispensable for anyone looking for social and career success. Another fillip to the city's development was the completion of the **Friedrich Wilhelm Canal**, linking the Spree and the Oder, which boosted its status as an east–west trade centre.

Carrying on from where his father had left off, Friedrich III succeeded in becoming king of Prussia to boot (and thus gained the title of Friedrich I), while Berlin continued to expand. The **Friedrichstadt and Charlottenburg quarters** and the **Zeughaus** (now the Deutsches Historisches Museum) were created during this period, and Andreas Schlüter revamped the Elector's palace. In 1709, Berlin-Cölln finally became a single city named **Berlin**. None of this came cheap, however. Both Berlin and the Mark Brandenburg were heavily in debt by the end of Friedrich's reign, to the point where he even resorted to alchemists in the hope of refilling his treasury.

Berlin under the Soldier King

The next chapter in the city's history belongs to Friedrich I's son, **Friedrich Wilhelm I** (1688–1740). Known as the **Soldier King** and generally reckoned to be the father of the Prussian state, he dealt with the financial chaos by enforcing spartan conditions on his subjects and firing most of the servants at court. State revenues were henceforth directed to building up his army, and culture took a back seat to parades (eventually he even banned the theatre). While the army marched and drilled, the populace had a draconian work ethic drubbed into them – Friedrich took to walking about Berlin and personally beating anyone he caught loafing.

Friedrich tried to introduce conscription but had to make an exception of Berlin when the city's able-bodied young men fled en masse to escape the army. Despite this, Berlin became a **garrison town** geared to maintaining the army: the Lustgarten park of the royal palace was transformed into a parade ground, and every house was expected to have space available for billeting troops. Much of modern Berlin's shape and character can be traced back to Friedrich – squares like **Pariser Platz** (the area in front of the Brandenburg Gate) began as parade grounds, and **Friedrichstrasse** was built to link the centre with Tempelhof parade ground. When Friedrich died after watching rehearsals for his own funeral (and thrashing a groom who made a mistake), few Berliners mourned.

Frederick the Great and the rise of Prussia

His son, Friedrich II – known to historians as **Frederick the Great** (1712–1786) and to his subjects as "Der alte Fritz" – enjoyed a brief honeymoon as a liberalizer, before reverting to his father's ways (see box pp.206–207). Soon Prussia was drawn into a series of wars that sent Berlin taxes through the roof, while the king withdrew to Sanssouci Palace in Potsdam, where only French was spoken, leaving the Berliners to pay for his military adventurism. Friedrich's saving grace was that he liked to think of himself as a philosopher king, and Berlin's **cultural life** consequently flourished during his reign. This was thanks in part to the work of the leading figures of the German Enlightenment, like the playwright Gotthold Ephraim Lessing and the philosopher Moses Mendelssohn, both of whom enjoyed royal patronage.

It was the **rise of Prussia** that alarmed Austria, Saxony, France and Russia into starting the **Seven Years' War** in 1756. Four years later they occupied Berlin and demanded a tribute of four million thalers, causing City President Kirchstein to faint on the spot. This was later reduced to 1.5 million when it was discovered that the city coffers were empty. Berlin was eventually relieved by Frederick, who went on to win the war (if only by default) after Russia and France fell out. Victory confirmed Prussia's power in Central Europe, but keeping the peace meant maintaining a huge standing army.

Besides direct taxation, Frederick raised money by establishing **state monopolies** in the trade of coffee, salt and tobacco. Citizens were actually required to buy set quantities of these commodities whether they wanted them or not. This was the origin of some of Berlin's most celebrated culinary delicacies: sauerkraut, *Kassler Rippchen* (salted pork ribs) and pickled gherkins were all invented by people desperate to use up their accumulated salt. Popular discontent was muffled by Frederick's **secret police** and **press censorship** – two innovations that have stuck around in one form or another ever since.

Unter den Linden came into its own during Frederick's reign, as grandiose new edifices like the **Alte Bibliothek** sprang up. Just off the great boulevard, the **Französischer Dom** was built to serve the needs of the Huguenot population, while the construction of Schloss Bellevue in the Tiergarten sparked off a new building boom, as the wealthy flocked into this newly fashionable area.

Decline and occupation

After Frederick's death Prussia went into a **decline**, culminating in the defeat of its once-invincible army by French revolutionaries at the Battle of Valmy in 1792. The decline went unchecked under Friedrich Wilhelm II (1744–1797), continuing into the Napoleonic era. As Bonaparte's empire spread across Europe, the Prussian court dithered, appeasing the French and trying to delay the inevitable invasion. Life in Berlin continued more or less as normal, but by August 1806 citizens were watching Prussian soldiers set off on the march westwards to engage the Napoleonic forces. On September 19, the king and queen left the city, followed a month later by Count von der Schulenburg, the city governor, who had assured Berliners that all was going well right up until he learned of Prussia's defeat at Jena and Auerstadt.

Five days later French troops marched through the **Brandenburg Gate** and Berlin was occupied. On October 27, 1806, Napoleon himself arrived to head a parade down Unter den Linden – greeted as a liberator by the Berliners, according to some accounts. **French occupation** was uneventful, interrupted only by a minor and unsuccessful military rebellion, and ending with the collapse of Napoleon's empire after his defeats in Russia and at the Battle of Leipzig in 1813.

The rebirth of Prussia

With the end of French rule, the Quadriga (the Goddess of Victory in her chariot) was restored to the Brandenburg Gate (see p.58), but the people of Berlin only gained the promise of a constitution for Prussia, which never materialized – a portent of later conflict. The real victor was the **Prussian state**, which acquired tracts of land along the Rhine, including the Ruhr, which contained the iron and coal deposits on which its military might was to be rebuilt.

The war was followed by an era of reaction and oppression, which did so much to stifle intellectual and cultural life in Berlin that the philosopher Wilhelm von Humboldt resigned from the university in protest at the new authoritarianism. Gradually this mellowed out into the **Biedermeier years**, in which Prussia's industrial fortunes began to rise, laying the foundation of its Great Power status. Berlin continued to grow: factories and railways and the first of the city's *Mietskaserne* or **tenement buildings** were constructed – foreshadowing what was to come with full industrialization.

Revolution and reaction

Berlin enjoyed more than thirty years of peace and stability after 1815, but it shared the revolutionary mood that swept Europe in **1848**. Influenced by events in France and the writings of Karl Marx (who lived here from 1837 to 1841), Berliners demanded a say in the running of their own affairs. King Friedrich Wilhelm IV (1795–1861) refused to agree. On March 18, citizens gathered outside his palace to present their demands. The soldiers who dispersed them accidentally fired two shots and the demonstration became a **revolution**. Barricades went up and a fourteen-hour battle raged between insurgents and loyalist troops. According to eyewitness accounts, rich and poor alike joined in the rebellion. During the fighting 183 Berliners and eighteen soldiers died.

Aghast at his subjects' anger, Friedrich Wilhelm IV ordered his troops to withdraw to Spandau, leaving the city in the hands of the revolutionaries, who failed to take advantage of the situation. A revolutionary parliament and citizens' militia were established, but rather than assaulting Spandau or taking other measures to consolidate the revolution, the new assembly concerned itself with protecting the royal palace from vandalism. No attempt was made to declare a republic or seize public buildings in what was turning out to be an unusually orderly – and ultimately doomed – revolution.

On March 21, the king appeared in public wearing the black, red and gold tricolour emblem of the revolution. Having failed to suppress it, he now proposed to join it, along with most of his ministers and princes. The king spoke at the university, promising nothing much but paying lip service to the idea of German unity, which impressed the assembled liberals. Order was fully restored; then in October, a Prussian army under General Wrangel entered Berlin and forced the **dissolution of parliament**. The Berliners either gave up the fight or followed millions of their fellow Germans into exile.

Suppression followed. Friedrich gave up the tricolour and turned to persecuting liberals, before going insane shortly afterwards. His brother Prince Wilhelm – who had led the troops against the barricades – became regent, and then king himself. **Otto von Bismarck** was appointed to the chancellorship (1862), despite the almost universal loathing he inspired among Berliners.

Meanwhile, Berlin itself continued to grow apace, turning into a cosmopolitan, modern industrial city. Its free press and revolutionary past exerted a liberal influence on Prussia's emasculated parliament, the **Reichstag**, to the irritation of Bismarck and the king (who was soon to proclaim himself emperor, or kaiser). However, Bismarck became a national hero after the Prussian victory at the **Battle of Königgrätz** (1866) had smashed Austrian military power, clearing the way for Prussia to unite – and dominate – Germany. Although militaristic nationalism caused liberalism to wither elsewhere, Berlin continued to elect liberal deputies to the Reichstag, which became the parliament of the whole nation after **German unification** in 1871.

Yet Berlin remained a maverick city. It was here that three attempts were made to kill Emperor Wilhelm I; the final one on Unter den Linden (1878) left him with thirty pieces of shrapnel in his body. While the kaiser recovered, Bismarck used the event to justify a **crackdown on socialists**, closing newspapers and persecuting trade unionists. The growth of unionism was a direct result of relentless urbanization. Between 1890 and 1900, Berlin's population doubled to two million and thousands of tenement buildings sprang up in working-class quarters like **Wedding**. These were solidly behind the Social Democratic Party (**SPD**), whose deputies were the chief dissenters within the Reichstag.

By 1890 Wilhelm II had become kaiser and "dropped the pilot" (Bismarck), but the country continued to be predominantly militaristic and authoritarian. While Berlin remained defiantly liberal, it steadily acquired the attributes of a modern capital. Now an established centre for commerce and diplomacy, it boasted electric trams, an underground railway, and all the other technical innovations of the age.

World War I and its aftermath

The arms race and dual alliances that gradually polarized Europe during the 1890s and the first decade of the twentieth century led inexorably towards **World War I**. Its outbreak in 1914 was greeted with enthusiasm by civilians everywhere – only confirmed pacifists or communists resisted the heady intoxication of patriotism. In Berlin, Kaiser Wilhelm II spoke "to all Germans" from the balcony of his palace, and shop windows across the city were festooned with national colours. Military bands played *Heil dir im Siegerkranz* ("Hail to you in the Victor's Laurel") and *Die Wacht am Rhein* ("The Watch on the Rhine') in cafés, while Berliners threw flowers to the Imperial German army or Reichswehr as it marched off to war. The political parties agreed to a truce, and even the Social Democrats voted in favour of war credits.

The General Staff's calculation that France could be knocked out before Russia fully mobilized soon proved hopelessly optimistic, and Germany found itself facing a war on two fronts – the very thing Bismarck had dreaded. As casualties mounted on the stalemated western front, and rationing and food shortages began to hit poorer civilians, **disillusionment** set in. By the summer of 1915 housewives were demonstrating in front of the Reichstag, a portent of more serious popular unrest to come. Ordinary people were beginning to see the war as an exercise staged for the benefit of the rich at the expense of the poor, who bore the brunt of the suffering. In December 1917, nineteen members of the SPD announced that they could no longer support their party's backing of the war and formed an independent socialist party known as the USPD. This party joined the "International Group" of **Karl Liebknecht** and **Rosa Luxemburg** – later known as the Spartacists – which had opposed SPD support for the war since 1915. It was this grouping that was to form the nucleus of the postwar Kommunistische Partei Deutschlands, or **KPD**. Meanwhile, fuel, food, and even beer shortages added to growing hardships on the home front.

Defeat and revolution

With their last great offensive spent, and America joining the Allied war effort, even Germany's supreme warlord, Erich von Ludendorff, recognized that **defeat** was inevitable by the autumn of 1918. Knowing the Allies would refuse to negotiate with the old absolutist system, he declared (on September 9) a democratic, **constitutional monarchy**, whose chancellor would be responsible to the Reichstag and not the kaiser. A government was formed under Prince Max von Baden, which agreed to extensive reforms. But it was too little, too late, for the bitter sailors and soldiers on the home front, where the contrast between privilege and poverty was most obvious. At the beginning of November the Kiel Garrison led a **naval mutiny** and revolutionary **Workers' and Soldiers' Soviets** mushroomed across Germany.

Caught up in this wave of unrest, Berliners took to the streets on November 8–9, where they were joined by soldiers stationed in the capital. Realizing that the game was up, **Kaiser Wilhelm II abdicated**. What Lenin described as a situation of "dual power" now existed. Almost at the same time as Philipp Scheidemann of the SPD declared a **"German Republic"** from the Reichstag's balcony, Karl Liebknecht was proclaiming a "Free Socialist Republic" from a balcony of the royal palace, less than a mile away. In the face of increasing confusion, SPD leader Friedrich Ebert took over as head of the government. A deal was struck with the army, which promised to protect the republic if Ebert would forestall the full-blooded socialist revolution demanded by the Spartacists. Ebert now became chairman of a Council of People's Delegates that ruled Berlin for nearly three months.

Between December 16 and 21, a **Congress of Workers' and Soldiers' Soviets** was held, which voted to accept a system of parliamentary democracy. However, many of the revolutionary soldiers, sailors and workers who controlled the streets favoured the establishment of Soviet-style government and refused to obey Ebert's orders. They were eventually suppressed by staunchly anti-revolutionary units of the old Imperial army, further indebting Ebert to the Prussian establishment. This itself relied heavily on the **Freikorps**: armed bands of right-wing officers and NCOs, dedicated to protecting Germany from "Bolshevism".

Things came to a head with the **Spartacist uprising** in Berlin during the first half of January 1919. This inspired lasting dread among the bourgeoisie, who applauded when the Spartacists were crushed by the militarily superior Freikorps. The torture and **murder of Liebknecht and Luxemburg** by Freikorps officers (who threw their bodies in the Landwehrkanal) was never punished once the fighting was over. This hardly augured well for the future of the **new republic**, whose National Assembly elections were held on January 19.

The Weimar Republic

The elections confirmed the SPD as the new political leaders of the country, with 38 percent of the vote; as a result, Ebert was made president, with Scheidemann as chancellor. **Weimar**, the small country town that had seen the most glorious flowering of the German Enlightenment, was chosen as the seat of government in preference to Berlin, which was tinged by its monarchic and military associations.

A **new constitution** was drawn up, hailed as the most liberal and progressive in the world. It aimed at a comprehensive system of checks and balances to ensure that power could not become too concentrated. Authority was formally vested in the people, and the state was given a quasi-federal structure to limit excessive Prussian domination. Executive authority was shared between the president (who could rule by emergency decree if necessary) and the Reich government in a highly complex arrangement. Reichstag deputies were elected by proportional representation from party lists.

While on the surface an admirable document, this constitution was hopelessly idealistic for a people so unfamiliar with democratic practice and responsibilities. No attempt was made to outlaw parties hostile to the system; this opened the way for savage attacks on the republic by extremists at both ends of the political spectrum. The use of proportional representation, without any qualifying minimum percentage of the total vote, favoured a plethora of parties promoting sectional interests. This meant that the Weimar governments were all unwieldy coalitions, whose average life was about eight months and which often pursued contradictory policies in different ministries.

Dada

World War I smashed prevailing cultural assumptions and disrupted social hierarchies. With politics in ferment, culture became another battleground. The leading exponent of the challenge to bourgeois values was the **Dada movement**, which shifted its headquarters from Zurich to Berlin in 1919. A Dada manifesto was proclaimed, followed by the First International Dada Fair (July and August), whose content aligned the movement with the forces of revolution. The right was particularly enraged by exhibits like a stuffed effigy of an army officer with a pig's head, labelled "Hanged by the Revolution", which dangled from the ceiling. All in all, it was an appropriate prelude to the new decade.

Berlin in the 1920s – the Weimar Years

The history of Berlin in the 1920s is bound up with Germany's – much of which was being dictated by the Allies. Resentment at the harsh terms imposed by the **Treaty of Versailles** led to turmoil and a wave of political violence: Matthias Erzberger, leader of the German delegation to Versailles, was among those assassinated. On March 13, 1920, Freikorps units loyal to the right-wing politician Wolfgang Kapp marched on Berlin, unopposed by the army. The government left Berlin but returned a week later, when the **Kapp putsch** collapsed. The army had withdrawn its support after protesters called for a general strike.

The early 1920s was a bad time for Berlin. War reparations to the Allies placed a crippling burden on the German economy. As the mark began to plunge in value, the government was shocked by the **assassination of Walter Rathenau**. As foreign minister, he had just signed the Treaty of Rapallo, aimed at promoting closer economic ties with the Soviet Union, since the Western powers remained intransigent. Rathenau was killed at his own house in the Grunewald by Freikorps officers. When France and Belgium occupied the Ruhr in response to alleged defaults in the reparations payments, a general strike was called across Germany in January 1923.

The combination of reparations and strikes sent the mark plummeting, causing the worst **inflation** ever known. As their savings were wiped out and literally barrowloads of paper money wasn't enough to support a family, Berliners experienced the terrors of hyperinflation. In working-class districts, street fighting between right and left flared up. Foreigners flocked in to pay bargain prices for carpets and furs that even rich Germans could no longer afford, and fortunes were made and lost by speculators. In the midst of all this, on November 8, Berliners' attention was briefly diverted to Munich, where a motley crew of right-wing ex-army officers including General Ludendorff attempted to mount a putsch. It failed, but Berliners were to hear of one of the ringleaders again – **Adolf Hitler**.

Finally, the mark was stabilized under a new chancellor, **Gustav Stresemann**, who proved to be a supremely able politician. Having come to realize that only an economically sound Germany would have any hope of meeting reparations payments, the Allies moderated their stance. Under the Dawes Plan of 1924, loans poured into Germany, particularly from America, leading to an upsurge in the economy.

Nightlife and the arts

Economic recovery affected the social life of Berlin. For many people the centre of the city had shifted from the old Regiurungsviertel (government quarter) around Friedrichstrasse and Unter den Linden, to the cafés and bars of the Kurfürstendamm. Jazz hit the **nightclubs** in a big way, like drug abuse (mainly cocaine) and all kinds of sex. There were clubs for transvestites, clubs where you could watch nude dancing, or dance naked yourself – and usually the police didn't give a damn. This was the legendary era later to be celebrated by Isherwood and others, when Berlin was briefly the most open, tolerant city in Europe, a Mecca for all those who rejected conventions and traditions.

The 1920s was also a boom time for the arts, as the Dada shockwave rippled through the decade. **George Grosz** satirized the times in savage caricatures, while **John Heartfield** used photomontage techniques to produce biting political statements. Equally striking, if less didactic, was the work of artists like **Otto Dix** and **Christian Schad**.

Producer **Max Reinhardt** continued to dominate Berlin's theatrical life, as he'd done since taking over at the Deutsches Theater in 1905. **Erwin Piscator** moved from propaganda into mainstream theatre at the Theater am Nollendorfplatz, without losing his innovative edge, and in 1928 **Bertolt Brecht**'s *Dreigroschen Oper* ("Threepenny Opera") was staged for the first time. Appropriately, Berlin also became a centre for the very newest of the arts. Between the wars the **UFA film studios** (see p.217) at Babelsberg was the biggest in Europe, producing legendary films like **Fritz Lang**'s *Metropolis*, *The Cabinet of Doctor Caligari* and *The Blue Angel* (starring Berlin-born **Marlene Dietrich**).

Middle- and lowbrow tastes were catered for by endless all-singing, all-dancing **musicals**, featuring platoons of women in various states of undress. This was also the heyday of the Berlin cabaret scene, when some of its most acidic exponents were at work.

The rise of Nazism

With inflation back under control, Germany experienced a return to relative **political stability**. The 1924 elections demonstrated increased support for centre-right and republican parties. When President Ebert died (February 28, 1925) and was succeeded by the former commander of the Imperial army, **General Field Marshal von Hindenburg**, monarchists and conservatives rejoiced. Nevertheless, it was now that the extreme right began gradually gaining ground, starting in Bavaria.

The **National Socialist German Workers' Party** (NSDAP) began as a ragbag group of misfits and fanatics, whose views were an odd mixture of extreme right and left, as the party's name suggests. It was Hitler who synthesized an ideology from existing reactionary theories, modelled the Nazis on Mussolini's *Fascisti*, and took a leaf from the Communists when it came to red flags, excessive propaganda and street fighting. For this they had the

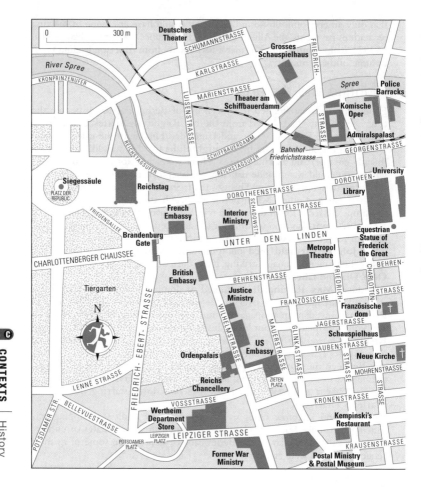

thuggish, brown-shirted **SA** (Sturmabteilung) Stormtroopers. As long as "reds" were the victims, the authorities did little or nothing to curb SA violence. The fear of street violence – foreshadowing a return to the anarchy of the postwar years – was calculated to drive the bourgeoisie towards Nazism, which promised drastic "solutions" to Germany's ills.

The Nazis made no headway in staunchly "red" Berlin until the end of 1926, when Hitler appointed **Joseph Goebbels** as *Gauleiter* (regional head) of the city's party organization. Goebbels reorganized the SA with the intention of confronting the Communists and conquering the streets of Berlin. On February 11 the following year, he rented the Pharus hall as a site for a Nazi demonstration in the predominantly Communist suburb of Wedding. A bloody brawl ensued and an **era of violence** began. Marches by the SA and the Communist Rote Frontkämpferbund (Red Fighters' Front) – often culminating in pitched battles – became a regular feature of street life in Berlin's working-class suburbs. The Nazis were here to stay.

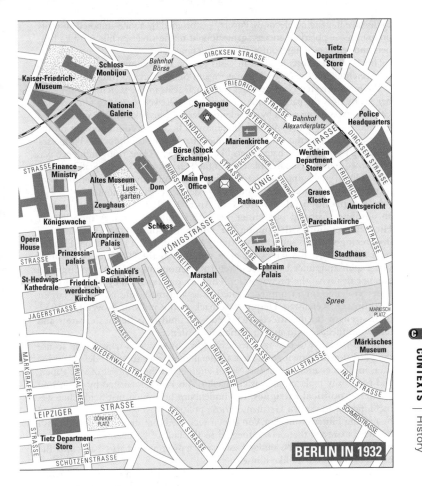

BERLIN IN 1932

Elections and unrest

In the **1928 elections** the NSDAP won 800,000 votes and gained twelve seats in the Reichstag. In May 1929 there was serious unrest in Berlin when Communist workers clashed with armed police in Wedding. Running street battles occurred and 33 civilians, many of them innocent bystanders, were killed. Fearful for their lives and property should the Communists gain ascendancy, wealthy bourgeois and the captains of finance and industry donated heavily to the Nazis.

In October 1929 Gustav Stresemann, one of Germany's few capable politicians, died. A few weeks later came the **Wall Street Crash**. All American credit ended, and international recession wiped out what was left of Germany's economic stability. By the year's end **unemployment** had reached three million, and the poverty of the immediate postwar period had returned with a vengeance. A centrist politician, Heinrich Brüning, was appointed chancellor by Hindenburg, but failed to get any legislation passed in the Reichstag and advised Hindenburg to dissolve it, pending elections. Poverty – worsened by a state-imposed austerity programme – polarized society: gangs fought in the streets, while swastika banners and red flags hung from neighbouring tenements.

The **1930 elections** resulted in gains for the Communists, and 107 seats in the Reichstag for the Nazis. There were anti-Semitic attacks throughout Berlin as the newly elected Nazi deputies took their seats in the Reichstag on October 13. By now the parliamentary system had effectively ceased to function and Germany was being ruled by presidential decree. Financial misery and disorder showed no signs of abating, and SA uniforms became a common sight on the streets of central Berlin, where Nazi thugs attacked Jewish shops and businesses, flaunting pornographic hate-sheets like *Der Stürmer*. Their rising influence was confirmed when General Schleicher of the Reichswehr General Staff began to court Hitler, envisaging the Nazis as a bulwark against the left. In Berlin – with its predominantly anti-Nazi population – despair began to mount.

At the **presidential elections** of April 10, 1932, Hindenburg gained an absolute majority, but Hitler won 13.5 million votes. A month later Hindenburg dismissed Brüning for failing to control the economy and disagreeing with his speeches, replacing him with Franz von Papen. Flanked by a cabinet that the left-wing press pilloried as the "Cabinet of Barons", von Papen announced plans for "reform", amounting to a thinly disguised attempt to revive the prewar order. The July **parliamentary elections** saw street violence on an unprecedented scale and made the Nazis the largest party in the Reichstag. Despite a setback at the polls in November 1932, their strength on the streets increased – intimidating Berlin's cabarets and left-wing theatres into muted criticism or silence.

Hitler's last steps to power were assisted by conservatives who sought to use the Nazis for their own ends. First, General Schleicher (by now defence minister, and less enamoured of the Nazis) engineered the removal of von Papen, and personally replaced him as chancellor. Von Papen retaliated by instigating a series of **political intrigues**. To Hindenburg he argued that Schleicher was incompetent to govern Germany, whose political mess could best be resolved by making Hitler chancellor. Von Papen reckoned that the Nazis would crush the left but reveal themselves unequal to the task of government; after a few months Hitler could be nudged aside and power would pass back into the hands of conservatives like himself.

Having come to an agreement with Hitler, he persuaded the virtually senile Hindenburg to appoint Hitler as chancellor and himself as vice chancellor (January 4, 1933). Knowing nothing of this, people were demanding the departure of Schleicher on the streets of Berlin. Two days after his resignation, they were horrified to see **Hitler sworn in as chancellor** on January 30. Life in Berlin would never be the same again, despite the fact that three-quarters of the city's electors had voted against the Nazis at the last elections.

The Nazi takeover

Hitler went immediately to the Reich's Chancellery to make his first public appearance as chancellor. Berlin thronged with Nazi supporters bearing torches, and the SA marched in strength through the *Regierungsviertel* to celebrate their victory. For anti-Nazis in Berlin, it was a nightmare come true.

The Nazi takeover of the state and the suppression of political opposition was spearheaded by **Hermann Göring**. As Prussian minister of the interior, he ordered the police "to make free use of their weapons wherever necessary" and built up a secret political department, soon to become notorious as the

Gestapo (Geheime Staatspolizei – "Secret State Police"). "It's not my business to do justice; it's my business to annihilate and exterminate," boasted Göring. The pretext for an all-out assault on the Nazis' opponents was provided by the **Reichstag fire** (February 28, 1933). Whether this was really caused by the Nazis themselves, or by Marius van der Lubbe, the simple-minded Dutch Communist whom they accused, is still a subject for debate. But there's no doubt that the Nazis used the Reichstag fire to their advantage.

An **emergency decree** to "protect the people and the state" was signed by Hindenburg the following day. It effectively abolished habeas corpus and provided the legal basis for a permanent state of emergency. The Nazi propaganda machine played up the Red Menace. Communist offices were raided, and the head of the Communist International, Georgi Dimitrov, was accused of instigating the Reichstag fire. In this atmosphere, the **elections of March 5** took place. The Communist vote dropped by one million, but the Nazis failed to achieve an outright majority, with 43.9 percent of the vote. Nevertheless, Hitler was poised to consolidate his grip on power.

The new Reichstag was opened in the Garrison Church in Potsdam and later transferred to a Berlin opera house. Delegates were asked to approve an **Enabling Act** that would place dictatorial powers in the hands of the predominantly Nazi cabinet. By the arrest of Communist deputies and some of the SPD, and with the support of the traditional right, Hitler was only just short of the two-thirds majority he needed to abolish the Weimar Republic quite legally. The SPD salvaged some self-respect by refusing to accede to this, but the Catholic Centrists failed to repeat their act of defiance against Bismarck, meekly supporting the Bill in return for minor concessions. It was passed by 441 votes to 84, hammering the final nails into the coffin of German parliamentary democracy.

On May 2, the Nazis clamped down on the unions, arresting leaders and sending them to **concentration camps**. In a series of subsequent moves opposition parties were effectively banned, and persecution of Nazi opponents was extended to embrace "active church members, freemasons, politically dissatisfied people . . . abortionists and homosexuals". An **exodus from Berlin** of known anti-Nazis and others with reason to fear the Nazis began. Bertolt Brecht, Kurt Weill, Lotte Lenya and Wassily Kandinsky all left the city, joining the likes of Albert Einstein and George Grosz in exile. The atmosphere of the city was changing irrevocably. The unemployed were drafted into labour battalions, set to work on the land or building autobahns.

On April 1, the SA launched an enforced **boycott of Jewish shops**, businesses and medical and legal practices in Berlin. Meanwhile, the Nazis put their own men into vital posts throughout local governments – in Berlin and the rest of Germany. This was the first stage of Gleichschaltung ("coordination"), whereby the machinery of state, and then society itself, would be Nazified. On May 11, they shocked the world by burning thousands of books that conflicted with Nazi ideology on the Opernplatz in central Berlin. After the concentration camps, the **book-burnings** (Büchverbrennung) remain one of the most potent symbols of Nazi brutality.

The Night of the Long Knives

In 1934 Nazi savagery was briefly turned inwards. Under **Ernst Röhm**, the SA had grown to 500,000 men and boasted of swallowing up the smaller Reichswehr. The SA felt cheated of the spoils of victory and muttered about a "Second Revolution". "Adolf is rotten. He's betraying all of us. He only goes around with reactionaries. . . Are we revolutionaries or aren't we?" Röhm complained. Big business, the regular army and rival Nazis like Himmler and Göring were united in their hostility towards the SA. Hitler was persuaded that Röhm and his allies were conspiring against him, and ordered a wholesale purge later known as the "**Night of the Long Knives**". On the night of June 30, the SA leaders were dragged from their boyfriends' beds in the resort of Bad Wiessee, taken to Stadelheim prison and shot in the courtyard by SS troopers; some believed this was an army coup, and died shouting "Heil Hitler!" In Berlin alone, 150 SA leaders were executed. Röhm's final words before being shot in Stadelheim prison were more appropriate: "All revolutions devour their own children."

Other victims included General Schleicher, von Papen's assistants, and the leader of the radical Nazis, Gregor Strasser. Local police and Gestapo chiefs added personal enemies to the death lists. Some of the victims had no connection with politics, like the Bavarian music critic whom the hit-squad mistook for an SA general of the same name. Aside from Hitler, Göring, and the army, the main beneficiaries of the purge were two Nazi organizations under the control of a failed chicken-farmer, **Heinrich Himmler**. His black-uniformed **SS** (Schutzstaffel – "Defence Staff"), originally Hitler's personal bodyguard, grew into the nucleus for a Nazi army. Meanwhile, the party's private intelligence service, the **SD** (Sicherheitsdienst or "Security Service"), established itself as a rival to the Gestapo and the army's Abwehr – military intelligence organization.

Following Hindenburg's death later that summer, Hitler merged the offices of president and chancellor and declared himself **Führer** of the German Reich. Defence Minister von Blomberg acceded to Hitler's request that all soldiers of the Reichswehr swear an oath of allegiance to him personally. Having assured Blomberg that the army would remain the "only bearer of arms in the nation", Hitler took the salute from the Leibstandarte Adolf Hitler regiment of the SS and the Hermann Göring Police Battalion – an indication of how he applied the policy of divide and rule even within the Führer state.

The Nazi impact on Berlin

In Berlin as in the rest of the Reich, **Nazi control** extended to all areas of life: the press and radio were orchestrated by Goebbels; children joined Nazi youth organizations; and every tenement building had Nazi-appointed wardens who doubled as Gestapo spies. It was even decreed that women should eschew make-up as an "un-German" artifice – one of the few edicts that wasn't taken seriously. Anti-Nazi criticism – even of the mildest kind – invited a visit from the Gestapo. Although Germans might avoid joining the NSDAP itself, it was difficult to escape the plethora of related organizations covering every aspect of life, from riding clubs and dog breeders to the "Reich Church" or "German League of Maidens". This was the second stage of Gleichschaltung – drawing the entire population into the Nazi net.

As the capital of the Reich, Berlin became a showcase city of banners, uniforms and parades. An image of order and dynamism, of a "new Germany" on the march, was what the Nazis tried to convey. This reached its apotheosis during the **1936 Olympics**, held at a vast purpose-built stadium in the Pichelsdorf suburb of Berlin. Hitler's expectation that the games would demonstrate Aryan racial supremacy was humiliatingly dashed when black American athlete Jesse Owens gave the greatest performance of the Olympics.

Like many previous rulers of Germany, Hitler felt uncomfortable in Berlin, probably aware that most Berliners suffered rather than supported him. He also felt the city was insufficiently grandiose for the capital of the "Thousand Year Reich", and from 1936 onwards spent much time with his favourite architect, **Albert Speer**, drawing up extensive plans for a remodelled postwar Berlin, to be called "Germania". Its main purpose would be to serve as a monument to the expected Nazi victory in the forthcoming war and as the capital of a vast empire thereafter. Hitler's millennial megalomania inspired hours of brooding on how future generations might be awed by Germania's monumental ruins – hence the need to build with the finest materials on a gigantic scale. In the meantime, he preferred to spend his time in the Berghof in Berchtesgaden.

Kristallnacht and the road to war

If the Berlin Olympics had partly glossed over the realities of Nazi brutality, Kristallnacht exposed them to the world. On the night of November 9–10, 1938, organized **attacks on Jewish shops and institutions** took place across Germany, an escalation in the Nazis' violent anti-Semitism. At least 36 Jews were murdered, and thousands injured; in Berlin Jews were beaten on the streets while passers-by looked on, and 23 of the city's 29 synagogues were destroyed. Many of the attacks were carried out by SA men in civilian clothes, to give the impression that these were spontaneous outbursts by German citizens. In the wake of Kristallnacht ("Crystal Night" – after the broken glass), new **anti-Semitic laws** were brought in, making life difficult and dangerous for German Jews, and paving the way for the greater horrors to come.

Throughout the 1930s the Nazis made **preparations for war**, expanding the army and gearing the economy for war readiness by 1940. Göring bragged of putting "guns before butter", but the real architect of the four-year plan was Hjalmar Schacht, a respected banker. It dovetailed with Hitler's foreign policy of obtaining Lebensraum ("living space") from neighbouring countries by intimidation. In 1936 the German army occupied the Rhineland (demilitarized under the terms of the Treaty of Versailles) to token protests from the League of Nations. The Anschluss ("annexation") of Austria in 1938 was likewise carried off with impunity, and a few months later Britain and France agreed to the dismemberment of Czechoslovakia at Munich.

Encouraged by their pusillanimity, Hitler made new demands on Polish territory in 1939. It's probable that he believed there would be a similar collapse of will by the Western powers, the more so since he had pulled off the spectacular coup of signing a nonaggression pact with his ultimate enemy, the Soviet Union, thus ensuring that Germany could avoid a war on two fronts. But two days after the German invasion of Poland began on September 1, Britain and France declared war in defence of their treaty obligations.

World War II

The outbreak of **World War II** was greeted without enthusiasm by Berliners, despite German victories in Poland. According to American journalist and eyewitness William Shirer (see p.333), there were few signs of patriotic fervour as the troops marched off to war through the streets of Berlin, and Hitler cancelled further parades out of pique. On October 11, there was rejoicing when a radio broadcast on the Berlin radio wavelength stated that the British government had fallen, and an immediate armistice was to be declared. Shirer noted that the Berliners showed more enthusiasm at the military parade to mark the fall of France (July 18, 1940), when German troops marched through the Brandenburg Gate for the first time since 1871. Still, he reckoned that it was the spectacle rather than martial sentiments that attracted crowds of Berliners.

Initially, Berlin suffered little from the war. Although citizens were already complaining of meagre rations, delicacies and luxury goods from occupied Europe gravitated towards the Reich's capital. What remained of the diplomatic and foreign press community, and the chic lifestyles of Nazi bigwigs, passed for high life. Open dissent seemed impossible, with Gestapo informers believed to lurk everywhere. The impact of wartime austerity was also softened by Nazi welfare organizations and a blanket of propaganda.

Air raids

Göring had publicly boasted that Germans could call him "Meyer" (a Jewish surname) if a single bomb fell on Berlin – notwithstanding which the British RAF dropped some for the first time on August 23, 1940. A further raid on the night of August 28–29 killed ten people – the first German civilian casualties. These raids had a marked demoralizing effect on Berliners, who had counted on a swift end to the war, and Hitler had to reassure the populace in a speech at the Sportpalast. Holding up a Baedeker guide to Britain, he thundered that the Luftwaffe would raze Britain's cities to the ground one by one.

However, these early **bombing raids** caused scant real damage and it wasn't until March 1, 1943 – when defeat in the Western Desert and difficulties on the eastern front had already brought home the fact that Germany was not invincible – that Berlin suffered its first heavy raid. While the RAF bombed by night, the Americans bombed by day, establishing a pattern that would reduce Berlin to ruins in relentless stages. "We can wreck Berlin from end to end if the USAAF will come in on it. It will cost us between 400 and 500 aircraft. It will cost Germany the war," the head of Bomber Command, Sir Arthur "Bomber" Harris, had written to Churchill in 1943. The first buildings to go were the Staatsoper and Alte Bibliothek on Unter den Linden. On December 22 the Kaiser-Wilhelm-Gedächtniskirche was reduced to a shell. By the year's end, daily and nightly bombardments were a feature of everyday life.

During the 363 air raids until the end of the war, 75,000 tons of high-explosive or incendiary bombs had killed between 35,000 and 50,000 people and rendered 1,500,000 Berliners homeless. Yet despite the colossal destruction that filled the streets with 100 million tons of rubble, seventy percent of the city's industrial capacity was still functioning at the war's end.

Resistance against the Nazis

Anti-Nazi resistance within Germany was less overt than in occupied Europe, but it existed throughout the war, particularly in Berlin. A group of **Communist cells** run by members of the old KPD operated a clandestine information network and organized isolated acts of resistance and sabotage. But the odds against them were overwhelming, and most groups perished. More successful was the Rote Kapelle (Red Orchestra) headed by Harold Schulze-Boysen, a prewar Bohemian aristocrat who worked in the Air Ministry on Wilhelmstrasse, with agents in most of the military offices, supplying information to the

Soviet Union. Eventually it, too, was identified and broken up by the SD and the Gestapo.

The **Kreisau Circle**, a resistance group led by Count Helmut von Moltke, and the groups around Carl Goerdeler (former mayor of Leipzig) and General Beck (ex-chief of staff) talked about overthrowing the Nazis and opening negotiations with the Western Allies, but the most effective resistance came from **within the military**. There had been attempts on Hitler's life since 1942, but it wasn't until late 1943 and early 1944 that enough high-ranking officers had become convinced that defeat was inevitable, and a wide network of conspirators was established. The one-armed Colonel von Stauffenberg was responsible for placing the bomb in Hitler's headquarters at Rastenberg in East Prussia, while Bendlerstrasse officers planned to use Fromm's Replacement Army to seize crucial points in Berlin.

On July 20, 1944, six weeks after the Allied invasion of Normandy, the coup was launched. Stauffenberg heard the bomb explode as he was leaving Rastenberg and signalled for the coup to go ahead. In fact, the **attempt to kill Hitler failed** through bad luck (see p.122), and the conspirators botched their takeover. First they failed to cut communications between Rastenberg and Berlin, and took their time seizing buildings and arresting Nazis. Goebbels succeeded in telephoning Hitler, who spoke directly to the arrest team, ordering them to obey his propaganda minister. Then Goebbels set to work contacting SS and Gestapo units, and reminding army garrisons of their oath of loyalty to the Führer. The final blow came at 9pm, when Hitler broadcast on national radio, threatening to "settle accounts the way we National Socialists are accustomed to settle them".

The ringleaders were either summarily shot, or tortured into implicating others in the basement of Gestapo headquarters on Prinz-Albrecht-Strasse. Several thousand suspects were arrested and hundreds executed. Fieldmarshal Rommel was allowed to commit suicide and receive an honourable burial, but other high-ranking conspirators went before the so-called People's Court in Berlin for a public show trial. All were sentenced to death by the Nazi judge Ronald Freisler and hanged on meat-hooks at Plötzensee Prison, their death agonies being filmed for Hitler's private delectation. Almost all of those who would have been best qualified to lead postwar Germany had thus been killed. Freisler himself was killed by an American bomb following a later show trial.

The fate of Berlin's Jews

For Berlin's Jews (and those living elsewhere in Germany) the terror began long before the war, as a noose tightened around their right to exist. Of the 160,564 Jews in Berlin at the beginning of 1933, many left in the first year of Hitler's chancellorship, when a series of laws banned them from public office, the civil service, journalism, farming, teaching, broadcasting and acting. Still more left when the so-called **Nürnberg Laws** (September 1936) effectively deprived them of German citizenship and defined apartheid-like classifications of "racial purity". Jews who could see the writing on the wall, and had money, escaped while they could (other European countries, the US and Palestine all restricted Jewish immigration); but the majority stayed put, hoping that things would improve, or simply because they couldn't afford to emigrate. After Kristallnacht, their already beleaguered position became intolerable.

Once the war began, the Nazis embarked on outright **genocide**, corralling the Jews of Europe in ghettos, branded by their yellow stars, destined for the concentration camps and eventual extermination. Emigration and murder had reduced the Jewish population of Berlin to about 6500 by 1945. Roughly 1400 of the **survivors** were "U-Boats" who lived perpetually in hiding, usually with the help of Gentile friends; the other 5100 somehow survived in precariously legal conditions, usually by being married to non-Jews, or working as grave diggers in the Weissensee Jewish Cemetery.

The fall of Berlin

Enjoy the war while you can! The peace is going to be terrible . . .

Berlin joke shortly before the fall of the city.

By autumn 1944 it was obvious to all but the most fanatical Nazis that the end was approaching fast. Even so, Hitler would brook no talk of surrender or negotiation. Teenage boys and men in their fifties were conscripted to replace the fallen millions, as Hitler placed his faith in "miracle weapons" like the V-1 and V-2, and new offensives. A wintertime counterattack in the Ardennes temporarily checked the Allies to the west, but their advance had resumed by January 1945. Meanwhile, the Red Army had launched the largest offensive ever seen on the eastern front, 180 divisions seizing East Prussia within two weeks. The distance between the Allied forces was narrowing inexorably.

On January 27, Soviet forces crossed the Oder a hundred miles from Berlin. Only Hitler now really believed there was any hope for Germany. The Nazis threw all they could at the eastern front and mobilized the Volkssturm, an ill-equipped home guard of old men, boys and cripples. Thirteen- and fourteen-year-old members of the **Hitler Youth** were briefly trained in the art of using the Panzerfaust bazooka, then sent to fight against T-34 tanks and battle-hardened infantrymen. As thousands died at the front to buy a little time for the doomed Nazi regime, life in Berlin became a nightmare. The city was choked with refugees and terrified of the approaching Russians; it was bombed day and night, and the flash of Soviet artillery could be seen on the horizon.

Behind the lines, **flying court martials** picked up soldiers and executed anyone suspected of "desertion" or "cowardice in the face of the enemy". On February 1, 1945, Berlin was declared Verteidigungsbereich (a "zone of defence") – to be defended to the last man and the last bullet. The civilian population – women, children, cripples and forced labourers – were set to work building tank traps and barricades; stretches of the U- and S-Bahn formed part of the fortifications. Goebbels trumpeted a "**fortress Berlin**", while Hitler planned the deployment of **phantom armies**, which existed on order-of-battle charts, but hardly at all in reality.

As Berlin frantically prepared to defend itself, the Russians consolidated their strength. On April 16, at 5am Moscow time, the **Soviet offensive** began with a massive bombardment lasting 25 minutes. When the artillery fell silent, 143 searchlights spaced 200m apart along the entire front were switched on to dazzle the enemy as the Russians began their advance. Three army groups totalling over 1,500,000 men moved forward under marshals Zhukov, Konev and Rokossovsky – and there was little the vastly outnumbered Germans could do to halt them. By April 20 – Hitler's 56th birthday (celebrated with tea and cakes in the *Führerbunker*) – the Red Army was on the edge of Berlin. Next day the city centre came within range of their guns, and several people queueing outside the Karstadt department store on Hermannplatz were killed by shells. On April 23, Soviet troops were in the Weissensee district, just a few miles east of the centre. The Germans were offered a chance to surrender, but declined.

Hitler's birthday party was the last time the Nazi hierarchy assembled before going – or staying – to meet their respective fates. The dictator and his mistress Eva Braun chose to remain in Berlin, and Goebbels elected to join them in the **Führerbunker** with his family. It was a dank, stuffy complex of reinforced concrete cells beneath the garden of the Reich Chancellery. Here Hitler brooded over Speer's architectural models of unbuilt victory memorials, subsisting on salads, herbal tisanes and regular injections of dubious substances by one Dr Morell. To hapless generals and faithful acolytes, he ranted about traitors and the unworthiness of the German *Volk*, declaring that the war was lost and that he would stay in the bunker to the end, after learning that General Steiner's army group had failed to stop Zhukov's advance.

The final days

By April 25, Berlin was completely **encircled by Soviet troops**, which met up with US forces advancing from the west. Over the next two days, the suburbs of Dahlem, Spandau, Neukölln and Gatow fell to the Russians, and the city's telephone system failed. On April 27 the Third Panzer Army was completely smashed; survivors fled west, leaving Berlin's northern flank virtually undefended. The obvious hopelessness of the situation didn't sway the top Nazis' fanatical **refusal to surrender**. Never mind that many of Berlin's defences existed only on paper, or that units were undermanned and poorly armed, with crippling shortages of fuel and ammunition. As the Red Army closed in, Goebbels called hysterically for "rücksichtslose Bekämpfung" – a fight without quarter – and SS execution squads worked around the clock, killing soldiers, Volkssturm guards or Hitler Youth who tried to stop fighting.

In the city the horrors mounted. The **civilian population** lived underground in cellars and air-raid shelters, scavenging for food wherever and whenever there was a momentary lull in the fighting. Engineers blasted canal locks, flooding the U-Bahn to prevent the Russians from advancing along it. Hundreds of civilians sheltering in the tunnels were drowned as a result. On April 27, the Ninth Army was destroyed attempting to break out of the Russian encirclement to the south, and unoccupied Berlin had been reduced to a strip nine and a half miles long from east to west, and three miles wide from north to south, constantly under bombardment. Next the Russians captured the Tiergarten, reducing the **last pocket of resistance** to the Regierungsviertel, where fighting focused on the Reichstag and Hitler's Chancellery, and on Potsdamer Platz, only a few hundred metres from the *Führerbunker*, by now under constant shellfire.

Hitler still hoped that one of his phantom armies would relieve Berlin, but on April 28 his optimism evaporated when he heard that Himmler had been suing for unconditional surrender to the Western Allies. In the early hours of the following day, he married Eva Braun, held a small champagne wedding reception, and dictated his will. As the day wore on, savage fighting continued around the Nazi-held enclave. At a final conference the commandant of Berlin, General Weidling, announced that the Russians were in the nearby Adlon Hotel, and that there was no hope of relief.

A breakout attempt was proposed, but Hitler declared that he was staying put. On the afternoon of April 30, after testing the cyanide on his pet German shepherd dog, **Hitler and Eva Braun committed suicide**: he with a revolver, she by poison. The bodies were taken to the Chancellery courtyard and doused with 200 litres of petrol; Hitler's followers gave the Nazi salute as the corpses burned to ashes. Meanwhile, Soviet troops were battling to gain control of the Reichstag, and at 11pm two Russian sergeants raised the red flag from its rooftop.

According to Hitler's will, Admiral Dönitz was appointed chancellor *in absentia*. In the early hours of May 1, Chief of Staff Krebs was sent out to parley with the Russians. After hasty consultation with Stalin, General Chuikov replied that only unconditional surrender was acceptable. When Krebs returned to the bunker, Goebbels rejected this and ordered the fighting to continue. That night he and his wife killed themselves, having first poisoned their children. The rest of the bunker occupants, with the exception of Krebs and General Burgdorf – Hitler's ADC, who committed suicide – now decided to try and break out. Weidling agreed not to surrender until the following dawn in order to give the fugitives time to **escape from the bunker** and through the railway tunnels towards northern Berlin. Of the 800 or so who tried, about 100 made it – the rest were either killed or captured. No one is sure about the fate of Hitler's deputy, Martin Bormann.

Capitulation and surrender

At 5am, Weidling offered the **capitulation of Berlin** to General Chuikov, who broadcast his surrender proclamation from loudspeaker vans around the city. At 3pm, firing in the city centre stopped, although sporadic, sometimes fierce, fighting continued on the outskirts, where German troops tried to break out to the west to surrender to the British or Americans rather than the Russians. Their fears were justified, for the Soviets unleashed an **orgy of rape and looting** on the capital, lasting three days. This was Stalin's reward to his troops for having fought so long and so hard.

The **official surrender of German forces** occurred at a Wehrmacht engineers' school in the Berlin suburb of Karlshorst on May 8, 1945. Wehrmacht forces in the west had already surrendered the day before, and British, French and American delegates flew in with General Keitel, High Commander of the Armed Forces, to repeat the performance for the benefit of the Russians. Berliners had already emerged from their shelters and started to clear the dead and the rubble from the streets. Now the Red Army established field kitchens.

With the final act of surrender complete, it was time to count the cost of the Battle of Berlin. It had taken the lives of 125,000 Berliners (including 6400 suicides and 22,000 heart attacks), and innumerable German soldiers from the 93 divisions destroyed by the Red Army. The Soviets themselves had suffered some 305,000 casualties in the battle, while the city itself had been left in ruins, without even basic services.

Occupation

During the immediate postwar months, civilian rations of food, fuel and medicine were cut to the bone to support the two-million-strong **Soviet occupation forces**. Survival rations were measured in ounces per day, if forthcoming at all, and civilians had to use all their wits to stay alive. The Soviet Union had taken steps towards establishing a civilian, communist-dominated administration even before the war was over. On April 30, a group of exiled German communists arrived at Küstrin airfield and were taken to Berlin, where they established a temporary headquarters in Lichtenberg. Directed by **Walter Ulbricht**, the future leader of the GDR's communist party, they set about tracking down old Berlin party members and setting up a new **municipal administration**. In each city district, they were careful to ensure that control of education and the police went to communists. This apparatus remained in place even after the arrival of the British and Americans in July.

The **western occupation sectors** had been demarcated by the Allies as far back as 1943, but the troops didn't move in until July 1–4, when fifty thousand British, American and French soldiers replaced the Red Army in the western part of the city. Here, the food situation improved marginally once American supplies began to find their way through, but public health remained a huge problem. Dysentery and TB were endemic, and there were outbreaks of typhoid and paratyphoid, all exacerbated by an acute shortage of hospital beds. British and American soldiers had endless opportunities to profit from the burgeoning **black market**: trading cigarettes, alcohol, gas, NAAFI and PX supplies for antiques, jewellery, or sexual favours. With less to offer, the Russians simply demanded "Davai chas", and took watches at gunpoint. Huge black market centres sprang up around the Brandenburg Gate and Alexanderplatz.

From July 17 to August 3 the **Potsdam conference** took place at the Cecilienhof Palace. It was to be the last great meeting of the leaders of the Big Three wartime alliance. Churchill took the opportunity to visit the ruins of the Reich's Chancellery, followed by a mob of fascinated Germans and Russians. Mid-conference he returned to Britain to hear the results of the first postwar election – and was replaced by the newly elected Labour prime minister, Clement Attlee, who could do little but watch as Truman and Stalin settled the fate of postwar Europe and Berlin.

For Germans, the worst was yet to come. Agriculture and industry had virtually collapsed, threatening acute **shortages of food and fuel** just as winter approached. In Berlin they dug mass graves and stockpiled coffins for the expected wave of deaths, and thousands of children were evacuated to the British occupation zone in the west of the country, where conditions were less severe. To everyone's surprise the winter turned out to be uncommonly mild. Christmas 1945 was celebrated after a fashion, and mothers took their children to the first postwar Weihnachtsmarkt (Christmas fair) in the Lustgarten.

Starvation and unrest

Unfortunately the respite was only temporary, for despite the good weather, food supplies remained overstretched. In March rations were reduced drastically, and the weakened civilian population fell prey to typhus, TB and other **hunger-related diseases**; the lucky ones merely suffered enteric or skin diseases. The Allies did what they could, sending government and private relief, but even by the spring of 1947 rations remained at malnutrition levels. **Crime and prostitution** soared. In Berlin alone, two thousand people were arrested every month, many of them from juvenile gangs that roamed the ruins murdering, robbing and raping. Trains were attacked at the Berlin stations, and in the countryside bandits ambushed supply convoys heading for the city. The winter of 1946–47 was one of the coldest since records began. Wolves appeared in Berlin and people froze to death aboard trains. There were rumours of cannibalism and Berlin hospitals had to treat 55,000 people for frostbite.

Meanwhile, **political developments** that were to have a lasting impact on Berlin were occurring. In March 1946, the social democratic SPD was forced into a shotgun merger with the KPD, to form the **SED** (Sozialistische Einheitspartei Deutschlands – "Socialist Unity Party of Germany"), or future **communist party** of East Germany. In the western half of the city, 71 percent of members voted against union; in East Berlin no voting was permitted, and attempts to hold ballots in the Prenzlauer Berg and Friedrichshain party offices were broken up by Russian soldiers. In October 1946, the first city-wide **free elections** since 1933 were held. The SED fared badly and the SPD triumphed, much to the annoyance of the Soviet zone authorities, who abandoned free elections after this setback.

The Berlin airlift

Already the city was becoming **divided along political lines** as the wartime alliance between the western powers (France had also been allotted an occupation zone) and the Soviet Union fell apart, ushering in a new era of conflict that would all too often focus on Berlin. The Allied Control Council met for the last time on March 20, when Marshal Sokolovsky, the Soviet military governor, protested about British and American attempts to introduce economic reform in their occupation zones.

Tension mounted over the next few months as the Allies went ahead with economic reform, while the Russians demanded the right to board Berlin-bound Allied trains, and on June 16 walked out of the four-power Kommandantura that had ultimate control over Berlin. Things came to a head with the **introduction of the D-Mark** in the western zone (June 23, 1948). On that day, the Soviets presented Berlin's mayor with an ultimatum, demanding that he accept their own Ostmark as currency for the whole city. But the city's parliament voted overwhelmingly against the Soviet-backed currency.

Everyone knew that this was asking for trouble, and trouble wasn't long in coming. On the night of June 23–24, power stations in the Soviet zone cut off electricity supplies to the western half of Berlin, and road and rail links between the western part of Germany and Berlin were severed. This was the beginning of the **Berlin blockade**, the USSR's first attempt to force the Western Allies out of Berlin. SPD politician Ernst Reuter, soon to be mayor of West Berlin, addressed a crowd at the Gesundbrunnen soccer field, promising that Berlin would "fight with everything we have".

There was now only one month's food and ten days' coal supply left in the city. The British and Americans realized that they had to support West Berlin, but were unwilling to use military force to push their way in overland. After some consideration it was decided to try to supply Berlin by air, as it was felt that the Soviets wouldn't dare risk intercepting Allied planes. However, there were serious doubts as to whether it was possible to sustain two million people by an airlift. The only previous attempt on a comparable scale – maintaining the German Sixth Army at Stalingrad – had been an utter failure. Berlin's needs were calculated at 4000 tons of supplies per day, yet the available aircraft could carry fewer than 500 tons.

Nevertheless, the **Berlin airlift** that began on June 26, 1948, soon gathered momentum. The Soviets maintained their blockade and made it plain that they regarded Germany as divided and Berlin as the capital of their half. America brought in huge C54 Skymaster transport planes to supplement the smaller C47s and Dakotas that the airlift began with. It soon became an around-the-clock precision operation. By October, planes were landing every three minutes, bringing in 4760 tons of food and fuel every day. Winter was exceptionally tough. Power cuts and severe food rationing reduced living standards to the level of the immediate postwar period. The Russians made supplies available in the eastern half of the city, but relatively few West Berliners chose to take advantage of them. At municipal elections on December 7, the SPD's **Ernst Reuter** was voted in as mayor of West Berlin, becoming a kind of human symbol of its resistance.

By the spring of 1949, planes were landing or taking off every thirty seconds and shifting 8000 tons a day. At Easter, the Allies mounted a special operation to boost morale and cock a snook at the Soviets. In just 24 hours they flew 13,000 tons of supplies into Berlin. Shortly afterwards the Soviets gave up, lifting the blockade on May 12. The first trucks and trains to reach West Berlin received a tumultuous welcome. The airlift was continued for another four months to ensure that Berlin would be supplied should the blockade be resumed at short notice. Though it cost the lives of 48 airmen and millions of dollars, the airlift thwarted Stalin's attempt to expel the Allies from West Berlin, and dealt the Soviets a resounding propaganda defeat. It also changed most Berliners' perception of the Western powers from occupiers to allies.

The birth of the two Germanys

Within six months, the political division of Germany was formalized by the creation of two rival states. First, the British, French and American zones of occupation were amalgamated to form the **Federal Republic of Germany** (May 1949); the Soviets followed suit by launching the **German Democratic Republic** on October 7. As Berlin lay deep within GDR territory, its eastern sector naturally became the official GDR capital. However, much to the disappointment of many Berliners, the Federal Republic chose Bonn as their capital. West Berlin remained under the overall control of the Allied military commandants, although it was eventually to assume the status of a Land (state) of the Federal Republic.

Although West Berlin's **economic recovery** was by no means as dramatic as that of West Germany, the city did prosper, particularly in comparison to East Berlin. The Soviets had gone in for ruthless **asset-stripping** – removing factories, rolling stock and generators to replace losses in the war-ravaged USSR – and when they eventually turned to reconstructing the GDR, the emphasis was put on heavy industrial production. West Berlin soon became an attractive destination for East Berliners, who were able to cross the **zonal border** more or less freely at this time. Many came to stay, while others worked in the city, benefiting from the purchasing power of the D-Mark. And those who did neither used the city to enjoy the entertainment and culture lacking in the more spartan East.

Political tension remained a fact of life in a city that had become an arena for superpower confrontations. The Soviets and GDR communists had not abandoned the idea of driving the Allies out of Berlin, and mounted diverse operations against them; just as the Allies ran spying and sabotage operations against East Berlin. In this cradle of **Cold War espionage**, the recruitment of former Gestapo, SD or Abwehr operatives seemed quite justifiable to all the agencies concerned. On one side were Britain's SIS (based at the Olympic Stadium) and the American CIA, which fostered the Federal Republic's own intelligence service, the Gehlen Bureau, run by a former Abwehr colonel. Opposing them were the Soviet KGB and GRU (based at Karlshorst), and the GDR's own foreign espionage service and internal security police. The public side of this rumbling underground war was a number of **incidents** in 1952. An Air France plane approaching West Berlin through the air corridor was fired upon by a Russian MiG; the East German authorities blocked streets leading from West to East Berlin and expropriated property owned by West Berliners on the outskirts of the eastern sector.

The workers' uprising

The **death of Stalin** on March 5, 1953, raised hopes that the situation in Berlin could be eased, but these were soon dashed. In the eastern sector, the communists unwittingly fuelled smouldering resentment by announcing a ten percent **rise in work norms** on June 16. For workers already hard-pressed to support their families, this demand to produce more or earn less was intolerable. The first to protest were building workers on block 40 of the prestigious Stalinallee construction project, who downed tools and marched on the city centre, joined by other workers and passers-by. At Strausberger Platz they swept aside Volkspolizei units who tried to stop them and headed, via Alexanderplatz, for Unter den Linden. From here, by now roughly eight thousand-strong, the **demonstration** marched to the House of Ministries, occupying Göring's former Air Ministry on Leipziger Strasse, where they demanded to speak with SED chief Walter Ulbricht and Prime Minister Otto Grotewohl, both of whom declined to appear.

Eventually three lesser ministers were sent out to speak to the demonstrators. Clearly alarmed at the scale of the demonstration, they promised to try and get the work norms lowered. But by now the crowd wanted more, and began calling for political freedom. After declaring a **general strike** for the next day, the protesters returned to Stalinallee, tearing down SED placards on the way. Grotewohl's announcement rescinding the new work norms later that day failed to halt the strike, news of which had been broadcast across the GDR by western radio stations. About 300,000 workers in 250 towns joined in, and by 7am a crowd of 100,000 people was marching through East Berlin towards the House of Ministries.

Ulbricht and Grotewohl feared for their lives and called for Russian help. When **Soviet tanks** appeared in Leipziger Strasse before noon, they found their route blocked by a vast crowd that refused to budge. The Soviet commandant, General Pavel Dibrova, warned by loudspeaker that martial law had been declared, and all violators would face summary punishment – but with little effect. Dibrova ordered his troops to move forward with the tanks following in close support, and it was at this point that the shooting started.

The crowd scattered as the first shots rang out, leaving youths to confront the T-34s with bricks and bottles. **Street fighting** raged throughout East Berlin for the rest of the day, and it wasn't until nightfall that the Soviets reasserted communist control. At least 267 demonstrators, 116 policemen and 18 Soviet soldiers were killed during the fighting, and it's estimated that 92 civilians (including a West Berliner just passing through) were summarily shot after the **suppression of the uprising**. The Western Allies did nothing to prevent this, nor the subsequent trials of "counter-revolutionaries" at which fourteen death sentences and innumerable prison terms were meted out – final confirmation that Berlin was divided.

Bertolt Brecht, who had returned to Berlin in 1949 and elected to live in the East, wrote an epitaph to this episode in a poem called "The Solution":

After the rising of 17 June
The secretary of the Writers' Union
Had leaflets distributed in Stalinallee
In which you could read that the people
Had lost the Government's confidence
Which it could only regain with
Redoubled efforts. Would it in that case

Not be simpler if the Government
Dissolved the people
And elected another?

Berlin was relatively quiet for the remainder of the 1950s, but important events were taking place in **West Germany** under Chancellor Konrad Adenauer. Foremost among these was the so-called **"economic miracle"**, which saw West Germany recover from the ravages of war astonishingly quickly and go on to become Europe's largest economy, which couldn't help but give a shot in the arm to the fortunes of West Berlin. On the political front, the **Hallstein doctrine** of non-recognition for the GDR reigned supreme. This was even stretched to the point of not maintaining diplomatic relations with other countries who chose to recognize the GDR. A pragmatic exception was made of the Soviet Union.

The building of the Wall

The economic disparity between East and West Germany (and their respective halves of Berlin) worsened throughout the 1950s. **Marshall Plan aid** and West German capital were transforming West Berlin into a glittering showcase for capitalism, whereas the GDR and East Berlin seemed to languish. Prospects for development in the GDR were undermined by a steady **population drain**, as mostly young and often highly skilled workers headed west for higher living standards and greater political freedom. Roughly 2,500,000 people quit the GDR during the 1950s, mostly via the open border with West Berlin, where an average of 19,000 East Germans crossed over every month. Both the GDR and Soviet governments saw this as a threat to East Germany's existence.

On November 10, 1958, Soviet leader Nikita Khrushchev demanded that the Western Allies relinquish their role in the "occupation regime in Berlin", thus facilitating the normalization of the situation in the capital of the GDR". Two weeks later, Khrushchev suggested that the Allies should withdraw and Berlin should become a free city – coupled with a broad hint that if no agreement was reached within six months, a blockade would be reimposed. The Allies rejected the ultimatum, and the Kremlin allowed the deadline to pass without incident. Tripartite **negotiations** at Geneva (May–Sept 1959) failed to produce a settlement. Meanwhile, tens of thousands of East Germans continued to cross the border into West Berlin.

By 1961 Ulbricht's regime was getting desperate, and rumours that the border might be sealed began to circulate. In mid-June Ulbricht felt compelled to assure the world that no one had "the intention of building a wall". Simultaneously, however, border controls were tightened. Yet the flood of people voting with their feet continued to rise, in what West Berlin's Springer press dubbed "mass escapes . . . of avalanche proportions". It was obvious that something was about to happen.

Shortly after midnight on August 13, 1961, East German soldiers, policemen and Workers' Militia received orders to close the border with the West. At 2am, forty thousand men went into action, stringing barbed wire across streets leading into West Berlin and closing U- and S-Bahn lines to create what their commanders called "an antifascist protection barrier". Many Berliners were rudely evicted from their homes, while others had their doors and windows blocked by bales of barbed wire and armed guards. Although the Allies reinforced patrols, they did nothing to prevent the **sealing of the border**.

C

CONTEXTS | History

Despite earlier rumours, most people in West and East Berlin were taken by surprise. Those who lived far from the border area only learned of its closure when they found all routes to West Berlin blocked. Crowds gathered and the border guards were reinforced to prevent trouble. There was little most people could do other than accept this latest development as a *fait accompli*. Others – including a few border guards – managed to take advantage of loopholes in the new barrier, and flee west. But within a few days, building workers were reinforcing the barbed wire and makeshift barricades with bricks and mortar, creating a **provisional version of the Wall**. As an additional measure, West Berliners were no longer allowed to cross the border into East Berlin.

Reaction in the West

Despite public outrage throughout West Germany and formal **diplomatic protests** from the Allies, everyone knew that to take a firmer line risked starting nuclear war. The West had to fall back on symbolic gestures: the Americans sent over General Lucius Clay, organizer of the Berlin airlift, and Vice-President Lyndon Johnson on August 18. The **separation of families** plunged morale in East Berlin to new depths and **economic problems** hit West Berlin, which was suddenly deprived of sixty thousand skilled workers who formerly commuted in from the GDR. They could only be replaced by creating special tax advantages to attract workers and businesses from the Federal Republic into West Berlin. American support for West Berlin was reaffirmed in August 1963, by President **John F. Kennedy**'s "Ich bin ein Berliner..." speech (see p.145), but for all its rhetoric and rapturous reception, the West essentially had to accept the new status quo.

From 1961 onwards the GDR strengthened its **border fortifications**, completely sealing off West Berlin from East Berlin and the East German hinterland. The Wall became an almost impenetrable barrier – in effect two walls separated by a *Sperrgebiet* (forbidden zone) dotted with watchtowers and patrolled by soldiers and dogs. Border troops had orders to shoot to kill and often did so. Yet hundreds of successful **escapes** took place before the GDR was able to refine its techniques, and thousands of people passed over, under or through the Wall by various methods, usually involving extreme danger.

Berlin in the 1960s

The **gradual reduction of political tension** that occurred after the Wall had been standing a couple of years was partly due to improved relations between the superpowers, and mostly to local efforts. Under SPD Mayor **Willy Brandt**, talks were opened between the West Berlin Senate and the GDR government, resulting in the "**Pass Agreement**" of December 1963, whereby 730,000 West Berliners were able to pay brief visits to the East at the end of the year. Three more agreements were concluded over the next couple of years until the GDR decided to use border controls as a lever for winning **diplomatic recognition** (which the Federal Republic and its Western allies refused to give under the Hallstein doctrine). Access to West Berlin via routes through GDR territory was subject to official hindrance; on one occasion, deputies were prevented from attending a plenary session of the Bundestag, held in West Berlin in April 1965. New and more stringent **passport and visa controls** were levied on all travellers from June 1968 onwards.

As the direct threat to its existence receded, West Berlin society began to fragment along generational lines. Partly because Berlin residents could legally evade West German conscription, young people formed an unusually high proportion of the population. The immediate catalyst was the wave of **student unrest** in 1967–68, when initial grievances over unreformed, badly run universities soon spread to embrace wider disaffection with West Germany's materialistic culture. As in West Germany, the APO or **extra-parliamentary opposition** emerged as a strong and vocal force in West Berlin, criticizing what many people saw as a failed attempt to build a true democracy on the ruins of Nazi Germany. Another powerful strand was anti-Americanism, fuelled by US policy in Southeast Asia, Latin America and the Middle East. Both these viewpoints tended to bewilder and enrage older Germans.

The police reacted to street demonstrations in Berlin with a ferocity that shocked even conservatives. On June 2, 1967, a student was shot by police during a protest against a state visit by the Shah of Iran. The right-wing **Springer press** (deliberately sited just near the Wall) absolved the police, pinning all the blame on "long-haired communists". When someone tried to kill student leader **Rudi Dutschke** (April 11, 1968), there were huge and violent demonstrations against the Springer press. Although the mass-protest movement fizzled out towards the end of the 1960s, a new and deadlier opposition would emerge in the 1970s – partly born from the West German establishment's violent response to what was initially a peaceful protest movement.

Ostpolitik and détente

The international scene and Berlin's place in it changed considerably around the turn of the decade. Both superpowers now hoped to thaw the Cold War and reach a *modus vivendi*, while elections in the Federal Republic brought to power a chancellor committed to rapprochement with the GDR. On February 27, 1969, US President Richard Nixon called for an easing of international tension during his visit to Berlin. Soon afterwards, **Four Power Talks** were held in the former Allied Control Council building in the American sector. Against a background of negotiations between West Germany and the Soviet Union, and proposals for a European security conference, the participants decided to set aside broader issues in an effort to fashion a workable agreement on the status of the divided city.

This resulted in the **Quadripartite Agreement** (September 3, 1971), followed in December by inter-German agreements regarding transit routes to West Berlin and travel and traffic regulations for West Berliners. These were largely due to the efforts of Chancellor Willy Brandt, whose **Ostpolitik** aimed at normalizing relations between the two Germanys. Treaties were signed with the Soviet Union and Poland in 1970, recognizing the validity of the Oder–Neisse line marking the Polish–German border. Finally, in 1972, the Federal Republic and the GDR signed a **Basic Treaty**. While stopping short of full recognition, it bound both states to respect each other's frontiers and *de facto* sovereignty.

In return for abandoning the Hallstein doctrine, West Germans were given access to friends and family across the border, which had been effectively denied to them (barring limited visits in the mid-1960s). However, the freedom to move from East to West was restricted to disabled people and senior citizens. This marked a concession by the new East German leader, **Erich Honecker**, who was regarded as a "liberal" when he succeeded Ulbricht in 1971. Aside from desiring access to West German know-how, markets and capital, Honecker had a personal reason for wanting closer ties: his own family lived in the Saarland.

The 1970s

During the 1970s Berlin assumed a new identity, breaking with the images and myths of the past. Thanks to the easing of Cold War tensions, West Berlin was no longer a frontline city, and East Berlin lost much of its intimidating atmosphere. Throughout the decade, **West Berlin** had similar problems to those of West Germany: economic upsets triggered by the quadrupling of oil prices in 1974, and a wave of terrorism directed against the establishment. In addition, West Berlin suffered from a deteriorating stock of housing and rising unemployment – both alleviated to some extent by financial help from West Germany.

East Berlin remained relatively quiet. Under Honecker, living standards improved and there was some relaxation of the tight controls of the Ulbricht days. However, most people regarded the changes as essentially trivial, and escapes continued to be attempted, although by now the Wall was formidably deadly. In 1977 a rock concert in Alexanderplatz turned into a brief explosion of street unrest, which the authorities suppressed with deliberate brutality.

The 1980s

Throughout the 1970s and early 1980s, the Quadripartite Agreement and the inter-German treaties formed the backdrop to relations between West and East Berlin. The main irritant was the **compulsory exchange** of D-Marks for Ostmarks, which the GDR raised in value from DM6.50 to DM25 in 1980, deterring significant numbers of visitors. But on the whole, a degree of stability and normality had been achieved, enabling both cities to run smoothly on a day-to-day basis, without being the focus of international tension. Even after the partial resumption of the Cold War, following the Soviet invasion of Afghanistan in 1979, Berlin remained relatively calm. The only notable event was the shooting of an American officer on an alleged spying mission in Potsdam in the spring of 1985.

As elsewhere in West Germany, Berlin witnessed a crystallization of issues and attitudes and the flowering of new radical movements. Concern about the arms race and the environment was widespread; feminism and gay rights commanded increasing support. Left-wing and Green groups formed an **Alternative Liste** to fight elections, and a left-liberal newspaper, *Tageszeitung*, was founded. Organized squatting was the radical solution to Berlin's **housing crisis**. In 1981, the new Christian Democrat administration (elected after a financial scandal forced the SPD to step down) tried to evict the squatters from about 170 apartment buildings, and police violence sparked rioting in Schöneberg. The administration compromised by allowing some of the squatters to become legitimate tenants, which had a big effect on life in West Berlin. For the first time since the late 1960s, the social divisions that had opened up showed signs of narrowing. Alternative Liste delegates were elected to the Berlin Senate for the first time in May 1981, and the same year witnessed a boom in **cultural life**, as the arts exploded into new vitality.

The **early 1980s** saw a resumption of frostiness in US–Soviet relations, which heightened concern about **nuclear weapons**. Anti-nuclear activists protested during the Berlin visit of President Ronald Reagan in June 1981. But the tension and sabre-rattling that had characterized the Cold War of the 1950s and 1960s didn't return to Berlin. In 1985 the USSR broke with its tradition of geriatric rulers when the dynamic and comparatively young **Mikhail Gorbachev** became general secretary of the Soviet Communist Party. The West was slow to appreciate the full significance of his campaigns for *glasnost* and *perestroika*, and their initial impact on Berlin was slight. The city's status – and the division of Germany into separate states – seemed assured by the Quadripartite Agreement and the Basic Treaty.

Unfortunately, ideological hostility prevented the two halves of the city from jointly celebrating Berlin's 750th anniversary in 1987. Instead, **separate anniversary celebrations** were arranged. In East Berlin, these were preceded by a massive **urban renewal project**, in both the city centre and the inner suburbs. The SED boasted that the GDR was a mature socialist state, advancing to the front rank of European nations. It saw no need for *glasnost* or *perestroika* – indeed, it regarded them with deep suspicion.

In West Berlin, the elections of spring 1989 swept the CDU administration from power, and an **SPD/Alternative Liste coalition** took over, with Walter Momper as mayor. In Kreuzberg, demonstrations against what many regarded as an Alternative Liste sell-out were put down with unwarranted force, sparking running street battles. Further violence occurred on May 1, during the now-traditional annual wrecking spree by anarchists and far-leftists espousing anti-imperialist, anticapitalist motives. For once, however, the police refrained from breaking heads, having been told to go easy by their chief.

The GDR resists perestroika

In the East there were few visible signs of change as the decade wore on, but things were happening behind the scenes. The **Protestant Church** provided a haven for several **environmental and peace organizations**, which formed a nascent opposition. But the regime seemed as intractable as ever, dismissing Gorbachev-style reforms as inappropriate to the GDR. The most memorable rebuff was delivered by SED chief ideologist Kurt Hager, who said in April 1987, "You don't need to change the wallpaper in your apartment just because your neighbour is doing his place up." Open dissent was stamped on: in January 1988, a group of protesters who unfurled banners calling for greater freedom at the official demonstration in memory of Karl Liebknecht and Rosa Luxemburg were immediately arrested and imprisoned, later being expelled from the GDR.

Fearful of the changes sweeping the Soviet Union, Hungary and Poland, the authorities banned the Soviet magazine *Sputnik* and several Russian films from the 1960s, only now released from censorship. As a further insult to their subjects, the GDR's rulers heaped honours on the odious Romanian dictator Nicolae Ceaușescu. Although Poland and Hungary had both embarked on the road to democracy, the GDR was unmoving. SED leader Erich Honecker declared that the Wall would stand for another fifty or one hundred years if necessary, to protect "our republic from robbers". East Germans could only despair.

Few believed any more the endless lies and clichés that spanned the gap between official pronouncements and reality. The SED leadership seemed totally isolated from the mood of the people. There seemed no way out except individual attempts to escape. When Chris Gueffroy was shot dead while trying to cross the border at Neukölln on February 6, 1989, no one realized that he was to be the last person killed in such an attempt.

Something had to give, and give it did in a manner so dramatic and unpredictable that it surprised the whole world.

Die Wende

1989 ranks as the most significant year in German history since 1945. In the space of twelve months a complete and unforseeable transformation (what Germans call Die Wende) occurred. German unification suddenly went from being a remote possibility to reality, forcing everyone to reassess the European order.

Once again Berlin was at the forefront of historical change, manifested in human terms by emotional scenes that caught the imagination of the world. When the Berlin Wall parted on November 9, 1989, it symbolized the end of an era: the Cold War was finally over, and a lifetime's dream had come true for most Germans – above all, those living in the East.

The beginning: exodus through Hungary

It was reform in another Eastern European country that made the incredible events of 1989 possible. On May 2, the Hungarian authorities began taking down the barbed wire along their border with Austria, creating a **hole in the Iron Curtain**. The event was televised worldwide, and thousands of East Germans saw it as a chance to get out. Aware that new visa laws making travel to Hungary more difficult would come into force in the autumn, they seized their chance during summer, when "holidays" provided a pretext.

It wasn't an easy option. Much of the barbed wire was still intact, and Hungarian troops patrolled the border. The lucky ones made it through the woods and swamps, evading soldiers who sometimes, but by no means always, turned a blind eye. In the early months, those who were caught were deported back to the GDR where jail awaited them. Later the Hungarians merely stamped the passports of those whom they intercepted, leaving it to the East German police to deal with them – if they returned home.

Wise to what was going on, the GDR authorities began trying to halt the increasing numbers of would-be escapees. Hungary-bound travellers were stopped and thoroughly searched. Anyone travelling light was deemed to be making a one-way trip and sent back. The same went for people carrying birth certificates and other important documents. Smart **escapers** began booking return tickets to destinations like Bulgaria, and travelling with baggage as if on a family holiday – only to make an unscheduled stop in Budapest.

The whole process was made slightly easier by the **illness of SED leader Erich Honecker**, which put him out of action from July 8 onwards. No one else seemed able to fill the ensuing power vacuum and enforce measures that would have enabled the state to check the draining away of its population. By August, some two hundred East Germans were crossing into Austria every night. Those who were caught could console themselves with the fact that the Hungarians no longer stamped their passports, leaving them free to try again. Many, unable to get through the border and rapidly running out of money, sought **refuge** in the West German embassy in Budapest. The situation was gradually reaching crisis point.

Mass exodus

The first **mass exodus** happened on August 19, when seven hundred East Germans surged across the border into Austria, unhindered by Hungarian border guards. They got there under the pretext of holding a frontier peace picnic near Sopron; in fact, the whole escape was prearranged by the conservative Paneuropa-Union, with the support of the reformist Magyar politician Imre Pozsgay. On August 24, others were allowed to leave after the Red Cross stamped their documents with a "Permit de Voyage". By now some six thousand people had made it across the border and their success encouraged others to make the journey from the GDR to Hungary. By the beginning of September there were over **20,000 refugees** housed in Hungarian holiday camps and the West German embassy – which was by now overflowing.

Having considered the reactions of East and West Germany, the Hungarian government opted to please the latter, and announced on September 7 that "humanitarian measures" would take place in the next few days. This was diplomatic smooth talk for **opening the border** and allowing all the East Germans to leave. When the instruction was implemented on September 10, East German refugees heard the news at 7pm. Gyula Horn, the Hungarian foreign minister, announced: "The GDR citizens staying in this country can leave with their own, in other words GDR passports, to a country that is willing to receive them." The border opened at midnight, and 300 cars crossed over within fifteen minutes. A couple of hours later the first East German car crossed the Austro-German border at Passau. For those without transport, special buses and trains were laid on. The GDR government could only condemn what it called "an organized trade in human beings", while the West German government – from whom the Magyars hoped for investment – promised it would "not forget this independent decision by Hungary".

Other East Germans had meanwhile made their way to **Prague and Warsaw**, where they took refuge in West German embassy buildings. By the last week of September there were 3500 people in the Prague embassy, while Czech police and Stasi agents tried to hold back the thousands more who hoped to gain admission. Despite strong-arm tactics, increasing numbers scaled the fence and swelled the crowd of refugees inside the embassy, where living conditions were daily growing more intolerable. Relief finally came on September 30, when **Hans-Dietrich Genscher**, West Germany's foreign minister, who had himself fled East Germany during the 1950s, appeared on the embassy balcony and announced that the refugees were to be allowed to leave. Special **trains** laid on by the GDR government were to ferry seventeen thousand refugees to West Germany via East German territory. As the trains passed through towns like Dresden, Karl-Marx-Stadt and Plauen, stations were stormed by people hoping to jump on board, and there were dozens of injuries as the police sealed off the tracks.

The October revolution

Within the GDR, morale plummeted. While people who had applied to leave and were still waiting for exit permits now despaired, thousands of others who had previously been content to make the best of things suddenly began thinking of emigration. Meanwhile, fledgling **opposition groups** like **Neues Forum** emerged, as East Germans took courage from the regime's evident disarray. People risked printing and circulating *samizdat* manifestos calling for reform and dialogue. SED leader Erich Honecker, whom West Germany's *Bild Zeitung* had already assigned to the obituary column, reappeared on the scene in time to join official celebrations marking the GDR's fortieth anniversary. Among the honoured guests were Mikhail Gorbachev, whom most East

Germans had eagerly awaited; a delegation from Beijing bearing thanks for the SED's public approval of the Tiananmen Square massacre; and Romanian dictator Nicolae Ceauşescu.

There was tension on all sides at the **anniversary celebrations** on October 7. Gorbachev stressed the need for dialogue, receptivity to new ideas and the West German viewpoint. Honecker took a contrary stance, praising the status quo in stock clichés, seemingly oblivious to growing public discontent. The vainglorious parade of weaponry and floats passed off calmly (only party loyalists were admitted to the televised zone), but side-street protests and scuffles took place along the cavalcade route. As the day wore on, these escalated into a huge demonstration, which the police and Stasi brutally suppressed. Thousands of arrests were made, and prisoners were subjected to degrading treatment and beatings. Simultaneous **demonstrations** in Dresden and Leipzig were dealt with even more harshly. But the people were growing bolder, as the regime's self-confidence diminished.

A week later, most of those arrested on October 7 were released, and sections of the press voiced oblique criticism of the party leadership's handling of the crisis. The Politbüro offered to talk with the opposition, but refused to legalize it. Monday, October 9, saw **nationwide demonstrations**, which came close to bloodshed in **Leipzig**, where 70,000 people marched through the city. Honecker ordered the local security forces to suppress the protest by any means necessary, including force of arms. City hospitals were alerted, and extra plasma was rushed in to cope with the expected casualties. But the march went ahead and Honecker's orders were never executed. Whether someone in the Politbüro countermanded them, or the local party secretary or security boss simply ignored them, remains unclear. The main point was that elements of the regime drew the line at wholesale slaughter.

Indeed, the whole Politbüro of the SED had become disenchanted with Honecker's rigidity. He was an obvious target for public hatred, and protests were gathering momentum daily. In Leipzig, now the focal point of opposition, the latest protest brought 150,000 people onto the streets. For the leadership, the strain proved too great: after eighteen years as party secretary, **Erich Honecker was suddenly replaced by Egon Krenz** on October 18. It seems that Honecker threatened to resign unless the Politbüro supported his hard line; instead, they accepted his resignation in silence, and he left the room "an old and broken man". Krenz, whom SED-watchers dubbed the "crown prince", was a 52-year-old Politbüro member with a hardline reputation of his own: it was he who had congratulated the Beijing government after it had crushed the Chinese democracy movement. Confounding expectations, however, Krenz immediately announced that the regime was ready for dialogue, although his reputation was to remain a stumbling block when it came to gaining popular trust.

The continuing exodus

Over the next week, as newspaper reports criticizing the government increased in frequency, the opposition gained ground and the exodus of GDR citizens continued. On October 27, the government declared an **amnesty** for those convicted of Republiksflucht (fleeing the country) or jailed for demonstrating, but the pressure on the streets kept rising. On November 4, East Berlin witnessed the largest **street protest** since the workers' uprising of 1953, as over one million citizens demonstrated. The vast crowd walked from the headquarters of the ADN state news agency to Alexanderplatz, where they were addressed by reformists, writers and priests. Banners calling for the demolition of the Wall were unfurled. The author Stefan Heym, a longtime critic of the regime, told the crowd: "It's as if someone's thrown open a window after years of dullness and fug, platitudes, bureaucratic arbitrariness and blindness." Author Heiner Müller added: "If the government should resign during the next week, it will be permitted to dance at demonstrations."

The authorities made hasty **concessions**. The same day, Krenz agreed to allow five thousand East Germans who were packed into the West German embassy in Prague to leave for the West. It was also announced that GDR citizens no longer required visas to visit Czechoslovakia – in effect, permitting emigration via Czechoslovakia. People swarmed across the border to exploit this loophole, and fifteen thousand of them had reached Bavaria by November 6. The same day, 500,000 citizens demonstrated in Leipzig, winning fresh concessions – the promise of thirty days' foreign travel a year – that satisfied no one.

Next, the SED tried placating people with **resignations**. The government of Prime Minister Willi Stoph quit on November 7, with the Politbüro following suit the next day. On the new executive that replaced it, Krenz and Berlin party boss Günter Schabowski were the only relics from the old order; the new prime minister, **Hans Modrow**, had acquired something of a liberal reputation during his previous job as Dresden party chief. Simultaneously, the Ministry of the Interior accepted an application from Neues Forum to be considered a legal group. Across the GDR, hardline officials were resigning in the face of ever-increasing demands from the street, and the exodus of citizens was continuing. By now, 200,000 East Germans had left the country since the beginning of 1989.

The Wall opens

The **opening of the Berlin Wall** was announced almost casually. On the evening of Thursday, November 9, Schabowski told a press conference that East German citizens were free to leave the GDR with valid exit visas, which were henceforth to be issued without delay. Journalists were puzzled: did this really mean that the Wall was effectively open? As news filtered through to the East German population, they sought confirmation by calling the TV stations, which broadcast Schabowski's announcement several times in the course of the evening. Hardly daring to believe it, citizens started heading for the nearest border crossings, with or without visas. A couple who passed through the Bornholmer Strasse crossing at 9.15pm may well have been the first to leave under the new law.

In both East and West Berlin, people flocked to the Wall. Huge crowds converged on the **Brandenburg Gate**, where an impromptu **street party** broke out. As West Berliners popped champagne corks and Germans from both sides of the Wall embraced, the Volkspolizei gave up checking documents and simply let thousands of East Germans walk through into West Berlin, from which they had been barred for 28 years. The scenes of joy and disbelief were flashed around a world taken by surprise. West German Chancellor **Helmut Kohl** had to interrupt a state visit to Warsaw and rush to West Berlin, where the international press was arriving in droves. Inside the GDR, disbelief turned to joy as people realized that the unimaginable had happened.

The opening of the Wall was a hard act to follow, but events acquired even greater momentum. On November 10, the Jannowitzbrücke U-Bahn station reopened after 28 years, making it possible for East Berliners to go to West Berlin by U-Bahn. On Saturday, November 11, **500,000 East Berliners visited**

West Berlin. There were reports of mile-long queues at checkpoints, where 2.7 million exit visas were issued during the first weekend after the opening of the Wall. West Germans – and TV-viewers around the world – gaped at the streams of Trabant cars pouring into West Berlin, where shops enjoyed a bonanza as East Germans spent their DM100 "welcome money", given to all GDR visitors by the Federal Republic. On November 12, the mayors of the two Berlins, Walter Momper and Erhard Krack, met and shook hands at the newly opened Potsdamer Platz border crossing. Just over two years earlier, Krack had spurned an invitation to the West Berlin celebrations marking the city's 750th anniversary, saying that West Berlin "does not exist for us".

Protest and further reform

Inside the GDR the pace of protest didn't slacken, although the opposition was as surprised as anyone by the rapid changes. Demonstrations continued across the country; in places like Leipzig (now known as the "hero city of the revolution") they had practically become institutionalized. Feelings were still running high against Krenz and other government figures seen as tainted by their association with the old system. Not least of the problems facing Prime Minister Modrow was the **declining value of the Ostmark**. The black market rate fell from ten to twenty Ostmarks per Deutschmark, and enforcing the official rate of 1:1 became virtually impossible. A fiscal crisis loomed on the horizon.

On the second weekend after the opening of the Wall, the GDR authorities announced that **ten million visas** had been issued since November 9 – an incredible statistic considering the whole population of the GDR was sixteen million. By now all eyes were on the Brandenburg Gate, where the Western media was massing in expectation of a grand reopening. Their hopes were dashed on November 19, when Krenz announced that the opening of the Gate was a symbolic affair in which he had no interest at the moment. Attention shifted back to events in the GDR, whose parliament, the Volkskammer, was asserting itself – particularly the hitherto "tame" parties allied to the SED.

The Volkskammer motion **ending the leading role of the SED** was passed (December 1) just as pent-up feeling against the Stasi erupted in a series of demos and sporadic attacks on its premises and members. These calmed down with a promise from the government that the dismantling of the formidable Stasi security service would begin straight away. In the first week of December, **round-table talks** between government and opposition began in an attempt to thrash out the future. After some haggling, the government agreed to one of the opposition's prime demands, pledging **free elections on May 6, 1990** – these were later brought forward to March 18.

At a special **SED conference** (December 15–17), the party decided to emulate the Hungarian Communists and repackage itself as the new, supposedly voter-friendly **PDS** – Partei des Demokratischen Sozialismus or "Democratic Socialist Party". As one of the last representatives of the old guard, Egon Krenz was consigned to political oblivion. His successor, **Gregor Gysi**, was a previously unknown lawyer who had defended a number of dissidents under the old regime. Almost immediately, Gysi and Modrow had to respond to a new initiative from **Chancellor Kohl**, who visited Dresden on December 19. Addressing a huge, enthusiastic crowd as "dear countrymen", Kohl promised that he wouldn't leave them in the lurch, and declared his ultimate goal of a **united Germany**.

Hans Modrow took Kohl's visit as an opportunity to announce the **reopening of the Brandenburg Gate**. Initially it was opened to pedestrians only, with one channel in each direction. Almost simultaneously it was announced that the **removal of visa controls and compulsory currency exchange** for West German visitors to the GDR would be implemented ahead of schedule. By the year's end there were further signs of the two Berlins drawing closer together. Numerous joint economic, industrial and cultural projects were under consideration, and East Berlin city maps began to feature S- and U-Bahn stations in West Berlin (which had previously been represented by blank spaces).

Into the 1990s

On the face of it, Berlin's future had never looked so rosy, but for many Germans in the East, the new decade began under a palpable shadow of disappointment and fear. There was a general anxiety that the change from a planned to a market economy would push up rents, close factories and wipe out the value of pensions and savings, and already the first legal claims by former owners of apartment buildings in East Berlin were being lodged. Politically, reform seemed too slow in coming, and people suspected that the apparatus of SED control had merely gone underground, biding its time. Hence the outrage in January 1990, when the government proposed establishing a new security service based on the old Stasi.

Revelations of **corruption** among the former communist leadership, and the discovery that West Germany's standard of living eclipsed anything offered by the GDR, produced massive disillusionment with the East German state. The notion of **German unification** became increasingly popular, dismaying some of the original opposition activists, who cherished hopes of a separate state, pursuing a "third way" between socialism and capitalism. Groups like Neues Forum began losing ground to parties modelled on Kohl's CDU, the social democratic SPD, and the far-right Republicans, all of which supported unification in one form or another.

When the GDR's first free elections were finally held on March 18, 1990, the result was a victory for a right-wing alliance dominated by the CDU under Lothar de Maizière. In reality this was a victory for Chancellor Helmut Kohl, the self-proclaimed champion of German unification. It was his promises of financial help and investment that had led people back to the CDU in the GDR, and it was to him that people were looking to ease the worsening economic plight.

During the two months following the election it began to seem possible that these hopes would be realized as, after a shaky start, the new government hammered out an agreement with the Federal Republic in mid-April about the introduction of the Deutschmark into the GDR, scheduled for July 1. The agreement on **economic union** was clearly a prelude to one on political union, for which a provisional date of autumn 1991 had been set. This was to be effected according to **article 23** of the Federal Republic's constitution, which made provision for any part of the GDR to request accession to West Germany. On June 17 a Volkskammer delegate called for immediate union by means of article 23; his motion was overturned but the issue of **reunification** was now firmly in the spotlight, and Kohl upped the ante by declaring 1990 the year of German unity.

However, at this stage it was the chancellor himself who was proving the biggest stumbling block en route to a united Germany. His ambiguous public stance (prompted by fear of alienating Republican support) on the inviolability of the Oder–Neisse line and other post-World War II borders was causing alarm in Poland and eliciting testy reactions from the EC countries. The advice of Foreign Minister **Hans Dietrich Genscher** finally forced Kohl to realize that he risked sacrificing German unity to party-political expediency, and to affirm German commitment to existing borders.

As planned, **currency union** was rapidly effected on **July 1**, the most enduring image being that of East Berliners thronging into city-centre banks to claim their allotment of Deutschmarks. With monetary union the GDR began to fade away rapidly; overnight, eastern produce vanished from the nation's shops, replaced by western consumer goods, and, superficially at least, it seemed as though a second "economic miracle" was about to begin. Yet for many people in the GDR, the expectation that economic reform and West German know-how would substantially improve their standards of living within a few years was tempered by fear of rent increases and factory closures during the transformation to a market economy.

The political background

For the time being, however, fears like these were overshadowed by **political developments**. It was time to address head-on the issue of reunification, and the "**two plus four**" talks between the two Germanys and the wartime Allies had established that the West would not stand in the way of the Germans – though the final approval of the Soviet Union had yet to be secured.

On July 15, Kohl met with **Mikhail Gorbachev** in the Caucasus, where they worked out a mutually acceptable series of conditions for the union of the two Germanys. It was agreed that Soviet troops would withdraw from Germany over a period of three to four years and that a united Germany would be free to decide for itself to which military alliance it would belong. An important proviso was that no foreign troops or nuclear weapons would be stationed on the territory of the former GDR.

The last obstacle in the way of unification had been removed and it was now possible to set a firm date for the event. On August 23 an all-night Volkskammer session announced that the GDR would become part of the Federal Republic on October 3, 1990, and just over a week later East and West Germany signed an 1100-page **treaty of union**. On September 12, the Allied military commanders of Berlin and the German foreign minister signed an agreement restoring full sovereignty to Germany, and a day later the Federal Republic and the Soviet Union signed a treaty of cooperation, including a nonaggression clause.

Street-level changes

The two Berlins, meanwhile, were already drawing together as the border withered away during the course of the year. Passport and customs controls for German citizens had ceased early in 1990 and, by the time of currency union, nationals of other countries, although nominally still subject to control, could cross the border unhindered. During the course of the year most of the central sections of **the Wall** had been demolished and numerous cross-border streets linked up once again.

As border controls in Berlin and elsewhere throughout the former Soviet bloc eased, Berlin became a magnet for the restless peoples of Eastern Europe. First arrivals had been the **Poles**, who set up a gigantic impromptu street market on a patch of wasteland near the Wall, much to the chagrin of Berliners, who felt the order of their city threatened by the influx of thousands of weekend street traders selling junk out of suitcases. They were followed by **Romanians**, mainly gypsies, fleeing alleged persecution at home and hoping, by taking advantage of visa-free access to what was still the GDR, to secure a place for themselves in the new Germany. Post-unification visa regulations were to put a stop to the commuting activities of the Poles, but as asylum-seekers the Romanians had the right to remain, and the sight of gypsy families begging on the streets of Berlin became commonplace.

The Stasi legacy

In East Berlin it was becoming apparent that a united German government was going to be plagued by questions arising from the immediate past of the GDR. In the run-up to reunification, activists from the GDR citizens' opposition groups occupied the former Stasi HQ in Magdalenenstrasse, demanding an end to the removal of **Stasi files** to West Germany. The protesters demanded that the files remain in the former GDR after reunification, mainly so that victims of the Stasi would have evidence of what had happened to them, enabling them to claim compensation and possibly bring their persecutors to justice. The BND (Bundesnachrichtendienst – West Germany's secret service) had other ideas, however, and was keen to get its hands on the files, presumably to dispose of potentially embarrassing revelations about the extent to which the Stasi had penetrated West German political life.

After a promise from the West German government that the files would remain in the GDR for the time being, the protest action fizzled out, and following reunification the German government discreetly removed the remaining files to Bonn.

Unification and beyond

On **October 3, 1990**, the day of **reunification**, Chancellor Kohl spoke to assembled dignitaries and massive crowds in front of the Reichstag. A conscious effort was made to rekindle the spontaneous joy and fervour that had gripped the city on the night the Wall was opened and during Berlin's first post-*Wende* new year, but for many ordinary people already experiencing the economic side-effects of the collapse of the GDR the celebrations left a bitter taste. On the sidelines anti-unification demonstrators marched through the streets, precipitating minor **clashes with the police**.

Just over a month later, on the night of November 13, the reunited Berlin experienced its first **major upheaval** when SPD mayor Walter Momper ordered the police to evict **West Berlin squatters** who had occupied a number of tenement blocks in the eastern Berlin district of Friedrichshain. The violent tactics of the police, coupled with the uncompromising stance of the radical Autonome squatters, who responded with petrol bombs and a hail of missiles from the rooftops, resulted in the fiercest **rioting** seen in the city since 1981, with dozens of police injured and over three hundred squatters arrested. Politically, the unrest resulted in the **collapse** of the fragile Red-Green SPD/Alternative Liste coalition that had governed West Berlin for the previous twenty months.

Elections and New Year problems

These events did much to ensure a **CDU victory** in the **city elections** held on **December 2** to coincide with Germany's first nationwide elections since 1933. Nationally the CDU, in coalition with the FDP (Free Democrats), triumphed easily, though in Berlin the victory was by a narrower margin. One surprise in the Berlin elections was the fact that the PDS secured 25 percent of the vote in eastern Berlin on an anti-unemployment and anti-social inequality ticket.

The immediate result of the city elections in Berlin was the replacement of SPD Mayor Momper by the **CDU's Eberhard Diepgen**, who faced the unenviable task of dealing with the united city's **mounting difficulties**: to the obvious problem of unemployment could be added a worsening housing crisis, increasing right-wing extremism, and rising crime in the eastern part of the city with its demoralized and under-equipped police force. At the start of 1991, with celebrations of the first united Christmas and New Year over, it was time for the accounting to begin in earnest. The new year brought vastly unpopular **tax increases** in the western part of Germany to pay for the spiralling **cost of unification**, which an embarrassed government was now forced to admit it had underestimated. As the year wore on and **unemployment** continued to rise, Kohl's honeymoon with the East soon came to an end. The man who had been mobbed in the former GDR only a year previously was now conspicuously reluctant to show himself there, and when he finally did, in April, he was greeted by catcalls and egg-hurlers.

Meanwhile, **ill-feeling** between easterners and westerners, which had first become apparent the previous year, continued. Western Berliners resented the tax increases and rising rents and mourned the passing of their subsidized island existence, while easterners, grappling with economic hardship, resented the fact that their poverty had reduced them to the status of second-class citizens. However, occasional strikes and dark mutterings about a long hot summer to come aside, the early part of the year passed relatively peacefully. The only major unrest in Berlin came with the outbreak of the **Gulf War** in January, which provoked large and sporadically violent **antiwar demonstrations**, recalling the early 1980s when the German peace movement had been a force to be reckoned with.

Post-unification problems

By mid-1991 the reserves of optimism topped up by currency union and unification had evaporated, particularly in the eastern part of the city, where the full force of social dislocation was felt. The loss of subsidies and tax breaks quickly had a **severe economic effect** on the previously immune West. On July 1, over 300,000 workers in subsidized, part-time work were made unemployed; at the same time, the huge **federal subsidies** that had propped up West Berlin's economy throughout the postwar years started to be scaled down to zero, removing DM8.5 million a year – around half the city's budget – from the municipal coffers. Unemployment, spiralling rents, and the wholesale flight of businesses hit the city.

Meanwhile, events at a national level were hardly encouraging. The Red Army Faction's assassination, on April 1, of **Detlev Rohwedder**, head of the Treuhandgesellschaft responsible for privatizing the ex-GDR's industry, did little to bolster hopes of imminent economic improvement. Neither was general confidence in the government's ability to deal with the situation boosted by the CDU's defeat in local elections in Kohl's local powerbase of Rheinland-Pfalz, a result seen by many as a symptom of growing disenchantment with Kohl's handling of the first months of unification.

On June 20 an unexpected Bundestag decision to **relocate the seat of government to Berlin** provided brief distraction, but by September attention was once more focused on the darker side of reunification. **Attacks on foreigners**, commonplace in the GDR even before the *Wende*, had been increasing steadily since the fall of the Wall. In September they mounted in intensity with one of the worst outbreaks taking place in the small Saxon town of **Hoyerswerda**, where a mob stormed a hostel housing asylum-seekers, necessitating the removal of the residents under police escort.

Hoyerswerda became a symbol for a wave of anti-foreigner violence that extended into western Germany, and which the government seemed unable to deal with. Rather than condemning the attacks in a forthright manner, the political establishment concentrated on calling for the reform of Germany's liberal asylum laws. Electorally this made sense – the far right was gaining ground, as shown by the Republicans gaining 10.5 percent of the vote in Baden-Württemberg's local elections in April 1992 – but many observers felt that such moral haziness only served to offer encouragement to the extremists.

But the main social pressure, one felt particularly strongly in Berlin, was the **growing distance** between West and East Germans. After forty years of separation no one expected the social gulf between them to be bridged overnight, but western anger at higher taxes to subsidize the East, and eastern resentment at what were seen as patronizing and neocolonialist western attitudes to the people of the former GDR, brought about an antipathy bordering on open hatred between the two peoples. Furthermore, it became apparent that the ever-increasing cost of reunification had pushed the German economy into recession.

By the end of 1992 the **civil war in Yugoslavia** had had its effect on the city, as Germany absorbed more Yugoslavs fleeing persecution and violence than any other European nation – again, much to the distaste of the far right, whose followers were in action elsewhere: in August a Jewish memorial was attacked in the city, and in September, neo-Nazis were convicted of beating an Angolan student to death in the town of Eberswalde-Finow, 35km northeast of Berlin. The November murders of a Berlin left-winger, three Turks (two of whom had been born in Germany), and a man mistakenly thought to be a Jew were all claimed by neo-Nazi groups.

In October 1992 the ex-mayor of the city, founder of *Ostpolitik* and international statesman **Willy Brandt** died at the age of 78: fittingly, he was given the first state funeral reunified Berlin had seen, and was buried in a small forest cemetery at the edge of the city. Meanwhile, the hunt for Erich Honecker on charges of having been responsible for the deaths of would-be escapees from East Germany had been abandoned on the grounds of his ill-health. Honecker was allowed to join his daughter in Chile at the start of 1993 and died there the following year.

Nevertheless there were other well-observed trials of GDR officials during the 1990s that brought Politbüro members, border guards, and even sports officials, accused of doping players without their knowledge, before the courts. The general feeling that the big fish had slipped through the net remained however. The trials did manage to foment debates about "victors' justice", and the legality of trying people for actions not illegal under GDR law, again highlighting the continuing role of the GDR past in the political, historical and even social life of reunified Germany.

The mid-1990s to the present

The summer of 1994 brought the **departure of the troops** of the World War II Allies, which had maintained a presence in the city since 1945. Their exit was a symbolic end to nearly fifty years of occupation and a signal that Berlin was once again in control of its own destiny.

An even more important and dramatic signal of that control, however, came with the national **government's relocation** to Berlin during the latter half of the 1990s: a tremendous task, and one carried out with usual German thoroughness. The Reichstag, seat of the parliament, was completely gutted and redesigned by British architect Sir Norman Foster, who added a glass cupola as a symbol of openness and transparent government, while ambitious buildings were erected to shelter ministries and embassies, new roads laid and U-Bahn lines constructed. In addition, the administration called for surviving Third Reich buildings to be brought into use: the Finance Ministry has moved into Göring's old Luftwaffe headquarters, and the Foreign Ministry now occupies the Central Bank building. On April 19, 1999, the Bundestag, the German parliament, met for the first time since 1933 in regular session in the Reichstag.

The **tenth anniversary** of the fall of the Wall in November of the same year brought Mikhail Gorbachev, George Bush and Helmut Kohl to the city to reminisce and congratulate each other. As they spoke inside the Adlon Hotel, a festival attracting close to 100,000 people was held at the Brandenburg Gate to mark the date. A jovial occasion, featuring music, speeches, and, of course, beer and sausages, it was altogether a rather less euphoric gathering than that which had taken place a decade earlier; time has delivered a realization of the social and economic difficulties – as well as the high cost – of reunification.

More sobering was a gathering held in the same square in front of the Gate earlier in the year, when the extreme right-wing National Partie Deutschland (National Party of Germany) held a demonstration in March. Though the whole affair was dwarfed by a counter-demonstration, it was a shock for many to see **neo-Nazis** march, in an echo of the Sturmabteilung parades of the Third Reich, in the heart of the German capital. Berlin proper is relatively untroubled by the racist violence that occurs fairly regularly in the small towns of Brandenburg, but there's no doubt that neo-Nazi parties have become better organized and brasher of late. Persistent extremism, fuelled in part by youth unemployment, continues to be a problem throughout the former East Germany, and that includes districts in eastern Berlin.

But everyone is suffering from an economy greatly weakened by the costs of pulling the two Germanys together. The whole country has been teetering on the edge of recession for years. And, though there are signs that things are picking up, real growth still seems some way off. Berlin's government is in a desperate financial situation, brought on in part by its heavy investment in development projects – many of which remain ongoing – such as the rebuilding of Lehrter Bahnhof as the city's main station and the transformation of Schönefeld airport into Berlin-Brandenburg International. And yet, when the national and local economy regains its health, the past decade of integrating and rebuilding will have put everything in place to make Berlin a great capital once again; something its position on the crossroads between eastern and western Europe requires, particularly as Poland and other Eastern European countries are absorbed into the European Union.

Books

Publishers are detailed below with the British publisher first, followed by the American publisher, where both exist. Where books are published in one of these countries only, "UK" or "US" follows the publisher's name; where the publisher is the same in the UK and US, only the publisher's name is given, and where the publisher is located elsewhere, we state the city. Books that are out of print (o/p) should be easy to track down in secondhand bookshops. "UP" means University Press. Books marked with a ⊡ symbol are particularly recommended.

History

Early and pre-World War II

Michael Farr *Berlin! Berlin!* (Kyle Cathie, US, o/p). This compressed (200-page) history of the city from its earliest origins has all the main facts and plenty of colour and character. An ideal introductory text, though by no means the deepest or fullest account.

Otto Friedrich *Before the Deluge: A Portrait of Berlin in the 1920s* (HarperPerennial, US). An engaging social history, full of tales and anecdotes, of the city when Dada and decadence reigned. An excellent history of Berlin's most engaging period.

Mary Fulbrook *A Concise History of Germany* (Cambridge UP). "Concise" is the key word for this history, whose brevity is simultaneously its strength and its weakness. Nevertheless, a useful basic history, and a clear introduction to a difficult subject.

Alex de Jong *The Weimar Chronicle* (Paddington Press, o/p; New American Library, o/p). While not the most comprehensive of accounts of the Weimar Republic, this is far and away the most lively. A couple of chapters focus on Berlin, and the book is spiced with eyewitness memoirs and a mass of engaging detail, particularly on the arts in Berlin. Worth hunting the libraries for.

Ebehard Kolb *The Weimar Republic* (Routledge, UK). The most recent study of the endlessly fascinating but fundamentally flawed state – the only previous attempt at a united and democratic German nation – that survived for just fourteen years. A bad omen?

Alexandra Ritchie *Faust's Metropolis* (HarperCollins). A thick and thorough general history of the city, beginning with the very first settlers and ending in the 1990s. Ritchie debunks a number of myths about the city – such as its supposed anti-Nazism – but her conservatism too often intrudes on the narrative.

Ronald Taylor *Berlin and Its Culture* (Yale UP). A profusely illustrated survey of the cultural movements and personalities that constituted the artistic life of the city, especially good on Weimar writing and cinematography.

Nazism and the war years

Allied Intelligence Map of Key Buildings (After The Battle, UK). This large, detailed map is an excellent resource for anyone searching for Nazi and prewar remains in the city.

Christabel Bielenberg *The Past is Myself* (Corgi, UK). Bielenberg, the niece of Lord Northcliffe, married German lawyer Peter Bielenberg in 1934 and was living with her family in Berlin at the outbreak of the war. Her autobiography (serialized for TV as *Christabel*) details her struggle to survive the Nazi period and Allied raids on the city, and to save her husband, imprisoned in Ravensbrück as a result of his friendship with members of the Kreisau resistance group.

Alan Bullock *Hitler: A Study in Tyranny* (Penguin; Konecky & Konecky). Ever since it was published, this scholarly yet highly readable tome has ranked as one of the best biographies of the failed Austrian artist and discharged army corporal whose evil genius fooled a nation and caused the deaths of millions.

George Clare *Berlin Days 1946–1947* (Papermac). "The most harrowing and yet most fascinating place on earth" is how Clare begins this account of his time spent as a British army translator. This is Berlin seen at what the Germans called the *Nullpunkt* – the zero point – when the city, its economy, buildings and society, began to rebuild almost from scratch. Packed with characters and observation, it's a captivating – if at times depressing – read.

Joachim C. Fest *The Face of the Third Reich* (Penguin; De Capo). Mainly of interest for its biographies of the men surrounding the Führer – Göring, Goebbels, Hess, Himmler, et al.

D. Fisher and A. Read *The Fall of Berlin* (Pimlico; De Capo). Superb account of the city's *Götterdämmerung*, carefully researched with a mass of anecdotal material you won't find elsewhere. An essential book for those interested in the period.

Bella Fromm *Blood and Banquets* (Carol Publishing, US, o/p). Fromm, a Jewish aristocrat living in Berlin, kept a diary from 1930 until 1938. Her job

as society reporter for the *Vossische Zeitung* gave her inside knowledge on the top figures of Berlin society, and the diaries are a chilling account of the rise of the Nazis and their persecution of Berlin's Jews.

Anton Gill *A Dance Between Flames* (Abacus; Carroll & Graf, o/p). Gill's dense but readable account of Berlin in 1920s and 1930s has lots of colour, quotation and detail but leans so heavily on a single source – *The Diary of Henry Kessler* – that you feel he should be sharing the royalties. Even so, one of the best books on the period.

Adolf Hitler *Table Talk* (Phoenix; Enigma). Hitler in his own words: Martin Bormann, one of his inner circle, recorded the dictator's pronouncements at meetings between 1941 and 1944.

Ian Kershaw *Hitler: 1889–1936 Hubris;* and *Hitler: 1937–1945 Nemesis* (W.W. Norton). The definitive biography. Using newly available documents from Soviet archives, and casting a critical eye on others (such as *Table Talk* above), Kershaw extends our understanding of the German demagogue and dictator.

Claudia Koonz *Mothers in the Fatherland* (St Martin's Press). Brilliantly perceptive study of the role of women in Nazi Germany. Includes a rare and revealing interview with the chief of Hitler's Women's Bureau, Gertrud Scholtz-Klink.

Brian Ladd *The Ghosts of Berlin: Confronting German History in the Urban Landscape* (University of Chicago Press). Much dense talk of policy issues and urban planning, but within that discussion is an excellent history of the city.

Tony Le Tissier *The Battle of Berlin* (Jonathan Cape, UK, o/p). Soldierly (the author is a retired lieutenant-colonel) shot-by-shot account of Berlin's final days. Authoritative, if a little dry. His *Berlin Then and Now*

(After the Battle, UK) is a collection of photographs of sites in the city during the war years, contrasted with the same places today. This extraordinary book is the best way to find what's left of Nazi Berlin's buildings – a startling number are barely changed – and to correct myths (such as the position of the *Führerbunker*) that have long gone unchallenged. Beg, steal or borrow a copy if you have any interest in the city's past.

Martin Middlebrook *The Berlin Raids* (Cassell). Superbly researched account of the RAF's campaign to destroy the capital of the Third Reich by mass bombing. Based on interviews with bomber crews, Luftwaffe fighter pilots and civilians who survived the raids, it's a moving, compassionate and highly exciting read.

Cornelius Ryan *The Last Battle* (Wordsworth; Touchstone). The Battle of Berlin turned into a sort of historic filmscript, with factual descriptions alongside speculated conversation. While reasonably accurate in its account of what happened, the style can be cloying.

William Shirer *The Rise and Fall of the Third Reich* (Arrow; Fawcett). The perfect complement to Bullock's book: Shirer was an American journalist stationed in Berlin during the Nazi period, and his history of the German state before and during the war has long been recognized as a classic. Notwithstanding its length and occasionally outdated perceptions, this book is full of insights and is ideal for dipping into, with the help of its exhaustive index.

Hugh Trevor-Roper *The Last Days of Hitler* (Papermac; University of Chicago Press). A brilliant reconstruction of the closing chapter of the Third Reich, set in the Bunker of the Reich's Chancellery on Potsdamer Platz. Trevor-Roper subsequently marred his reputation as the doyen of British historians by authenticating the forged Hitler Diaries, which have themselves been the subject of several books.

Marie Vassiltchikov *The Berlin Diaries* (Pimlico; Vintage). Daughter of a Russian émigré family and friend of the Bielenbergs (see p.332), Vassiltchikov's diaries provide a vivid portrait of wartime Berlin and the July 1944 bomb-plot conspirators – whose members also numbered among her friends.

Peter Wyden *Stella* (Doubleday, US). Stella Goldschlag was a young, very "Aryan"-looking Jewish woman who avoided deportation and death by working for the SS as a "catcher", hunting down Jews in hiding in wartime Berlin – including her former friends and even relatives. The author, who knew the young Stella, traces her life story and tries to untangle the morality and find some explanation for the motives behind what seem incalculably evil actions. A gripping, terrifying story.

Andreas Nachama (ed), Julius H. Schoeps and Hermann Simon *Jews in Berlin* (Henschel). Packed with source material of every kind, this well-illustrated book charts the troubled history of Berlin's Jewish community between 1244 and 2000 and is definitely worth getting hold of if you have a passing interest in the subject.

Recent history and social studies

John Ardagh *Germany and the Germans* (Penguin). Up-to-date characterization of the country and its people, taking into account its history, politics and psyche, and covering almost every aspect of national life. The section on Berlin, while brief, is packed with astute observations and illuminating facts.

Bill Buford (ed) *Granta 30: New Europe!* (Granta, US). Granta's round-up of writing on and from central Europe published in spring 1990 contains pieces by Jurek Becker on German unification, and Werner Krätschell on the opening of the Wall.

Anna Funder *Stasiland. True Stories From Behind the Berlin Wall* (Granta). Engrossing account of the experiences of those East Germans who found themselves tangled in the web of the State Security Service (Stasi) in the GDR. Nominated for the Guardian First Book Award 2003.

Norman Gelb *The Berlin Wall* (Michael Joseph, o/p; Times Books). The definitive account of the building of the Wall and its social and political aftermath – as far as 1986. Includes a wealth of information and anecdotes not to be found elsewhere.

Mark Girouard *Cities and People* (Yale UP). A well-illustrated social and architectural history of European urban development that contains knowledgeable entries on Berlin, particularly the eighteenth- and nineteenth-century periods.

Jurgen Habermas *A Berlin Republic: Writings on Germany* (University of Nebraska Press, US). A trenchant collection of essays on Germany's past and the challenges of the future by one of the country's most prominent intellectuals.

Warren Hinckle (ed) *The Fourth Reich* (Argonaut Press, US). This excellent Californian review dedicated most of an issue to the rise of neofascism and other problems confronting the new Germany. The title is a good indication of its slight tendency to alarmism, but there's so much unignorable factual material that the book is essential reading for those interested in contemporary Germany.

David E. Murphy, Serfei A. Kondrashev and George Bailey *Battleground Berlin: CIA vs KGB in the Cold War* (Yale UP). A detailed account by participants of the tense, crafty skirmishing in Berlin between the spies of the two superpowers.

Michael Simmons *The Unloved Country* (Abacus, UK, o/p). Pre-*Wende* account of the GDR by *The Guardian's* man in eastern Europe. A bit dry and dull at times, but then so was the GDR.

Hermann Waldenburg *The Berlin Wall Book* (Thames & Hudson; Abbeville). A collection of photographs of the art and graffiti the Wall inspired, with a rather self-important introduction by the photographer.

Art and architecture

Peter Adam *The Art of the Third Reich* (Harry N. Abrams Inc). Engrossing and well-written account of the officially approved state art of Nazi Germany – a subject that for many years has been ignored or deliberately made inaccessible. Includes over three hundred illustrations, many reproduced for the first time since the war.

Alan Balfour *Berlin, the Politics of Order: 1737–1989* (Rizzoli, o/p). A highly cerebral historical/ architectural deconstruction of the area around Leipziger Platz. Through quotations, structuralist commentary, allusions and reference, a huge picture of a relatively tiny strip of the city is drawn, creating a paradigm of the richness and complexity of Berlin history.

Alan Balfour (ed) *Berlin: World Cities* (Academy Editions; John Wiley). The pictorial version of the above title, this photographic essay chronicles the architectural development of the city, examining current and past projects by world-renowned figures.

Wolf-Dieter Dube *The Expressionists* (Thames & Hudson). A good general introduction to Germany's most distinctive contribution to twentieth-century art.

Peter Güttler (et al) *Berlin-Brandenburg: An Architectural Guide* (Ernst & Sohn). Brick-by-brick guide to the buildings of the city, in German and English. The definitive guide if you're interested in studying the city's architecture.

Post-War Berlin (Architecture Design Profile). A collection of scholarly essays on how the wartime legacy of destruction has been handled by the architects of the former East and West Berlin.

John Willet *The Weimar Years* (Thames & Hudson; Abbeville). Heavily visual account of art, design and culture in pre-Nazi Germany. The seemingly Dada-influenced layout is a bit of a distraction.

Michael Z. Wise *Capital Dilemma: Germany's Search for a New Architecture* (Princeton Architectural Press). An engaging discussion of the historical, political, and architectural considerations in the rebuilding of Germany's old and new capital city.

Frank Witford *Bauhaus* (Thames & Hudson). Comprehensive and well-illustrated guide to the architectural movement that flourished in Dessau and included the Berlin architect Walter Gropius (see p.124).

Berliner Festspiele & Architektenkammer Berlin *Berlin: Open City. A practical guide to Berlin's historic, modern, and newest architecture* (Architektenkammer Berlin). The best guide for architecture fans, this practical guide investigates around 600 buildings, with many photos, maps, and plans to aid navigation along ten suggested routes. The index is organized by both architect and place.

Guides and travel writing

Stephen Barber *Fragments of the European City* (Reaktion Books). Written as a series of interlocking poetic fragments, this book explores the visual transformation of the contemporary European city, focusing on Berlin. An exhilarating evocation of the intricacies and ever-changing identity of the city.

Karl Baedeker *Berlin and its Environs* (Baedeker, o/p, but widely available at secondhand bookshops). First published in 1903, the learned old Baedeker is an utterly absorbing read, describing a grand imperial city now long vanished. There's advice on medicinal brine-baths, where to buy "mourning clothes", the location of the Estonian embassy,

and beautiful fold-out maps that enable you to trace the former course of long-gone streets (see also our map on pp.300–301). An armchair treat.

John Miller and Tim Smith *Chronicles Abroad: Berlin* (Chronicle Books). A suitcase-sized anthology of fiction, reportage and impressions of the city, including pieces by Brecht, Kafka, Isherwood, E.T.A. Hoffmann and Josephine Baker.

Uwe Seidel *Berlin & Potsdam* (Peter Rump). Illustrated guide to the city that has much detail on what you can't see any more. Useful if you need more knowledge of the what-stood-where kind.

Fiction

Len Deighton *Winter: A Berlin Family 1899–1945* (HarperCollins; Ballantine). This fictional saga traces the fortunes of a Berlin family through World War I, the rise of Nazism and the collapse of the Third Reich: a convincing account of the way in which a typical upper-middle-class family weathered the wars. Better known is Deighton's *Funeral in Berlin* (HarperCollins; Acacia), a spy-thriller set in the middle of Cold War Berlin and based around the defection of an Eastern chemist, aided by hard-bitten agent Harry Palmer (as the character came to be known in the film starring Michael Caine). *Berlin Game* (HarperCollins; Ballantine) pits British SIS agent Bernard Samson (whose father appears in *Winter*) against an arch manipulator of the East Berlin secret service, and leaves you hanging for the sequels *Mexico Set* and *London Match*.

Alfred Döblin *Berlin-Alexanderplatz* (Continuum). A prominent socialist intellectual during the Weimar period, Döblin went into exile shortly after the banning (and burning) of his books in 1933. This is his weightiest and most durable achievement, an unrelenting epic of the city's proletariat.

Hugo Hamilton *Surrogate City* and *The Love Test* (Faber, UK, o/p). Hamilton has set two of his recent novels in Berlin. *Surrogate City* is a love story between an Irish woman and a Berliner and is strongly evocative of pre-*Wende* Berlin. *The Love Test* is the tale of a journalist researching the history of a woman's involvement with the Stasi and gives a realistic account of 1990s Berlin.

Robert Harris *Fatherland* (Arrow; HarperCollins). A Cold War novel with a difference: Germany has conquered Europe and the Soviet Union, and the Cold War is being fought between the Third Reich and the USA. Against this background, Berlin detective Xavier March is drawn into an intrigue involving murder and Nazi officials. All this owes much to Philip Kerr (see below) but Harris's picture of Nazi Berlin in 1964 is chillingly believable.

Lillian Hellman *Pentimento* (Little, Brown). The first volume of Hellman's memoirs contains "Julia", supposedly (it was later charged to be heavily fictionalized) the story of one of her friends caught up in the Berlin resistance. This was later made into a finely acted, if rather thinly emotional, film of the same name.

Christopher Isherwood *Goodbye to Berlin* (Minerva; W.W. Norton). Set in the decadent atmosphere of the Weimar Republic as the Nazis steadily gain power, this collection of stories brilliantly evokes the period and brings to life some classic Berlin characters. It subsequently formed the basis of the films *I Am a Camera* and the later remake *Cabaret*. See also Isherwood's *Mr Norris Changes Trains* (Minerva; New Directions), the adventures of the overweight eponymous hero in pre-Hitler Berlin and Germany.

Wladimir Kaminer *Russian Disco, Tales of Everyday Lunacy on the Streets of Berlin* (Random House). Collection of stories that are snapshots of Berlin through the eyes of a Russian immigrant from Moscow. Unusual, entertaining and well written: Kaminer has since become a somewhat minor local celebrity, DJing *Russendisko nights at Kaffee Burger* (see p.250).

Philip Kerr *Berlin Noir: March Violets The Pale Criminal* and *A German Requiem* (Penguin). Three great novels on Berlin in one omnibus edition. The first is a well-received detective thriller set in the early years of Nazi Berlin. Keen on period detail – nightclubs, the Olympic Stadium, building sites for the new autobahn – and with a terrific sense of atmosphere, the book rips along to a gripping denouement. Bernie Gunther, its detective hero, also features in the second title – a wartime Berlin crime novel. But his best work so far, *A German Requiem*, has Gunther travelling from ravaged postwar Berlin to run into ex-Nazis in Vienna.

Ian McEwan *The Innocent* (Vintage; Bantam). McEwan's novel brilliantly evokes 1950s Berlin as seen through the eyes of a post office worker caught up in early Cold War espionage – and his first sexual encounters. Flounders in its obligatory McEwan nasty final twist, but laden with a superbly researched atmosphere.

William Palmer *The Pardon of St Anne* (Vintage; Trafalger Square). The story of a morally shallow Berlin photographer whose professional involvement with the Nazis forces him – and the reader – to reassess his values.

Ulrich Plenzdorf *The New Sufferings of Young W.* (Continuum, US). A satirical reworking of Goethe's *Die Leiden des jungen Werthers* set in 1970s East Berlin. It tells the story of Edgar Wibeau, a young rebel without a cause adrift in the antiseptic GDR, and when first published it pushed against the borders of literary acceptability under the old regime with its portrayal of alienated, disaffected youth.

Holly-Jane Rahlens *Becky Bernstein Goes Berlin* (Arcade Books, US). A young Jewish girl from Queens falls in love with a German, emigrates to Berlin and discovers a new love for the city. A bouncy and funny novel full of New York wit.

Ian Walker *Zoo Station* (Abacus, o/p; Grove Atlantic o/p). Not strictly fiction but a personal recollection of time spent in Berlin in the mid-1980s. Perceptive, engaging and well informed, it is the most enjoyable account of pre-*Wende* life in the city.

Language

Language

Language

erman is not a language you can hope to master in a short time. As English was a compulsory subject in West Berlin's school curriculum, most Germans who have grown up in the West since the war have some familiarity with it, which eases communication a great deal. In the East, Russian was the language most often taught, and you won't find so many English speakers among former inhabitants of the GDR.

But wherever you are, a smattering of German will help. Also, given that the city still has leftovers of the American and British forces, who make little effort to integrate into local communities or learn German, people are particularly sensitive to presumptuous English speakers. On the other hand, most will be delighted to practise their English on you once you've stumbled through your German introduction. Of the many teach-yourself courses available, best is the BBC course, *Deutsch Direkt*. For the most useful travelling companion, look no further than the *Rough Guide to German*, a practical and easy-to-use **dictionary/phrasebook** that allows you to speak the way you would in your own language.

Pronunciation

English speakers find the complexities of German grammar hard to handle, but pronunciation isn't as daunting as it might first appear. Individual syllables are generally pronounced as they're printed – the trick is learning how to place the stresses in the notoriously lengthy German words.

Vowels and umlauts

a as in father, but can also be used as in hut
e as in day
i as in leek
o as in bottom
u as in boot

ä is a combination of a and e, sometimes pronounced like e in bet (eg Länder) and sometimes like ai in paid (eg spät)
ö is a combination of o and e, like the French *eu*
ü is a combination of u and e, like true

Vowel combinations

ai as in lie
au as in house
ie as in free

ei as in trial
eu as in oil

Consonants

Consonants are pronounced as they are written, with no silent letters. The differences from English are:

j is pronounced similar to an English y
r is given a dry throaty sound, similar to French
s is pronounced similar to, but slightly softer than, an English z

v is somewhere between f and v
w is pronounced thesame way as English v
z is pronounced ts

The German letter ß, the Scharfes S, occasionally replaces ss in a word: pronunciation is identical.

Gender

German words can be one of three genders: masculine, feminine or neuter. Each has its own ending and corresponding ending for attached adjectives. If you don't know any German grammar, it's safest to use either neuter or male forms.

Words and phrases

Basics

Yes, No	Ja, Nein	This one	Dieses
Please/ You're welcome	Bitte	That one	Jenes
		Large, Small	Gross, Klein
A more polite form of *Bitte*	Bitte schön	More, Less	Mehr, Weniger
		A little	Wenig
Thank you, Thank you very much	Danke, Danke schön	A lot	Viel
		Cheap, Expensive	Billig, Teuer
Where, When, Why?	Wo, Wann, Warum?	Good, Bad	Gut, Schlecht
How much?	Wieviel?	Hot, Cold	Heiss, Kalt
Here, There	Hier, Da	With, Without	Mit, Ohne
Now, Later	Jetzt, Später	Where is...?	Wo ist...?
All mean "open"	Geöffnet, offen, auf	How do I get to (a town)?	Wie komme ich nach...?
Both mean "closed"	Geschlossen, zu		
Earlier	Früher	How do I get to (a building, place)?	Wie komme ich zur/zumo...?
Over there	Da drüben		

Greetings and times

Goodbye	Auf Wiedersehen	Tomorrow	Morgen
Goodbye (telephone only)	Auf Wiederhören	The day before yesterday	Vorgestern
Goodbye (informal)	Tschüs	The day after tomorrow	Übermorgen
Good morning	Guten Morgen	Day	Tag
Good evening	Guten Abend	Night	Nacht
Good day	Guten Tag	Week	Woche
How are you? (polite)	Wie geht es Ihnen?	Month	Monat
How are you? (informal)	Wie geht es dir?	Year	Jahr
		Weekend	Wochenende
Leave me alone	Lass mich in Ruhe	In the morning	Am Vormittag/ Vormittags
Get lost	Hau ab		
Go away	Geh weg	In the afternoon	Am Nachmittag/ Nachmittags
Today	Heute		
Yesterday	Gestern	In the evening	Am Abend

Days, months and dates

Monday	**Montag**	August	**August**
Tuesday	**Dienstag**	September	**September**
Wednesday	**Mittwoch**	October	**Oktober**
Thursday	**Donnerstag**	November	**November**
Friday	**Freitag**	December	**Dezember**
Saturday	**Samstag**	Spring	**Frühling**
Saturday	**Sonnabend**	Summer	**Sommer**
Sunday	**Sonntag**	Autumn	**Herbst**
January	**Januar**	Winter	**Winter**
February	**Februar**	Holidays	**Ferien**
March	**März**	Bank holiday	**Feiertag**
April	**April**	Monday, the first	**Montag, der erste**
May	**Mai**	of May	**Mai**
June	**Juni**	the second of April	**Der zweite April**
July	**Juli**	the third of April	**Der dritte April**

Some signs

Women's toilets	**Damen/Frauen**	Diversion	**Umleitung**
Men's toilets	**Herren/Männer**	Attention!	**Vorsicht!**
Entrance	**Eingang**	Speed limit	**Geschwindig-**
Exit	**Ausgang**		**keitsbegrenzung**
Emergency exit	**Notausgang**	Hospital	**Krankenhaus**
Arrival	**Ankunft**	Police	**Polizei**
Departure	**Abfahrt**	No smoking	**Nicht rauchen**
Exhibition	**Ausstellung**	No entrance	**Kein Eingang**
Motorway	**Autobahn**	Prohibited	**Verboten**
Motorway entrance	**Auffahrt**	Building works	**Baustelle**
Motorway exit	**Ausfahrt**	Traffic light	**Ampel**

Numbers

1	**eins**	16	**sechszehn**
2	**zwei**	17	**siebzehn**
3	**drei**	18	**achtzehn**
4	**vier**	19	**neunzehn**
5	**fünf**	20	**zwanzig**
6	**sechs**	21	**ein-und-zwanzig**
7	**sieben**	22	**zwei-und-zwanzig**
8	**acht**	30	**dreissig**
9	**neun**	40	**vierzig**
10	**zehn**	50	**fünfzig**
11	**elf**	60	**sechzig**
12	**zwölf**	70	**siebzig**
13	**dreizehn**	80	**achtzig**
14	**vierzehn**	90	**neunzig**
15	**fünfzehn**	100	**hundert**

Questions and requests

All enquiries should be prefaced with the phrase *Entschuldigen Sie bitte* (excuse me, please). Note that *Sie* is the polite form of address to be used with everyone except close friends, though young people and students often don't bother with it. The older generation will certainly be offended if you address them with the familiar *Du*, as will all officials.

Do you speak English?	**Sprechen Sie Englisch?**	Separately or together?	**Getrennt oder Zusammen?**
I don't speak German	**Ich spreche kein Deutsch**	The menu, please	**Die Speisekarte, bitte**
Please speak more slowly	**Könnten Sie bitte langsamer sprechen**	Hello! (to get attention of waiter/waitress)	**Hallo!**
I don't understand	**Ich verstehe nicht**	Have you got something cheaper?	**Haben Sie etwas billigeres?**
I understand	**Ich verstehe**		
How do you say that in German?	**Wie sagt mann das auf Deutsch?**	Is there a room available?	**Haben Sie noch ein Zimmer frei?**
Can you tell me where... is?	**Können Sie mir bitte sagen wo...ist?**	Where are the toilets?	**Wo sind die Toiletten, bitte?**
How much does that cost?	**Wieviel kostet das?**	I'd like that one	**Ich hätte gern dieses**
		I'd like a room for two	**Ich hätte gern ein Zimmer für zwei**
When does the next train leave?	**Wann fährt der nächste Zug?**	I'd like a single room	**Ich hätte gern ein Einzelzimmer**
At what time?	**Um wieviel Uhr?**		
What time is it?	**Wieviel Uhr ist es?**	Does it have a shower, bath, toilet ...?	**Hat das Zimmer eine Dusche, ein Bad, eine Toilette ... ?**
Are these seats taken?	**Sind die Plätze noch frei?**		
The bill, please	**Die Rechnung, bitte**		

Food and drink terms

Basics

breakfast	**Frühstück**	bread	**Brot**
lunch	**Mittagessen**	bread roll	**Brötchen**
supper, dinner	**Abendessen**	butter	**Butter**
knife	**Messer**	sandwich	**Butterbrot**
fork	**Gabel**	open sandwich	**Belegtes Brot**
spoon	**Löffel**	jam	**Marmelade**
menu	**Speisekarte**	honey	**Honig**
plate	**Teller**	cheese	**Käse**
cup	**Tasse**	meat	**Fleisch**
glass	**Glas**	fish	**Fisch**
starter	**Vorspeise**	egg	**Ei**
main course	**Hauptgericht**	vegetables	**Gemüse**
dessert	**Nachspeise**	fruit	**Obst**

yoghurt	**Joghurt**	mustard	**Senf**
cream	**Sahne**	sauce	**Sosse**
sugar	**Zucker**	rice	**Reis**
pepper	**Pfeffer**	shredded pasta	**Spätzle**
salt	**Salz**	form of ravioli	**Maultaschen**
oil	**Öl**	bill	**Rechnung**
vinegar	**Essig**	tip	**Trinkgeld**

Soups and starters

soup	**Suppe**	oxtail soup	**Ochsen**
bean soup	**Bohnensuppe**		**Schwanzsuppe**
pea soup	**Erbsensuppe**	onion soup	**Zwiebelsuppe**
clear soup with	**Flädlesuppe,**	liver pâté	**Leberpastete**
pancake strips	**Pfannkuchensuppe**	smoked salmon	**Lachsbrot**
clear soup with meat	**Fleischsuppe**	on bread	
dumplings		melon and ham	**Melone mit Schinken**
thick soup in imitation	**Gulaschsuppe**	mixed green salad	**Grüner Salat**
of goulash		cucumber salad	**Gurkensalat**
chicken soup	**Hühnersuppe**	sausage and onion	**Fleischsalat**
clear soup with liver	**Leberknödelsuppe**	salad	
dumplings		chives on bread	**Schnittlauchbrot**
lentil soup	**Linsensuppe**	jellied meatloaf	**Sülze**

Meat and poultry

slices of cold	**Aufschnitt**	brains	**Hirn**
sausage		venison	**Hirsch, Reh**
chunky boiled	**Bockwurst**	chicken	**Huhn, Hähnchen**
sausage		innards	**Innereien**
grilled sausage	**Bratwurst**	cutlet in wine and	**Jägerschnitzel**
chicken	**Broiler**	mushroom sauce	
sausage served	**Currywurst**	rabbit	**Kaninchen**
with piquant sauce		smoked and pickled	**Kassler Rippen**
pigs' trotters	**Eisbein**	pork chops	
duck	**Ente**	cutlet (cheapest cut)	**Kotelett**
pheasant	**Fasan**	cabbage leaves filled	**Krautwickerl**
meatballs	**Frikadelle**	with mincemeat	
frogs' legs	**Froschschenkel**	lamb	**Lamm**
goose	**Gans**	liver	**Leber**
shredded meat,	**Geschnetzeltes**	baked meatloaf	**Leberkäse**
usually served		lungs	**Lunge**
with rice		kidneys	**Nieren**
kebab	**Gyros**	oxtail	**Ochsenschwanz**
mincemeat roast	**Hackbraten**	cutlet in cream	**Rahmschnitzel**
mincemeat	**Hackfleisch**	sauce	
mutton	**Hammelfleisch**	beef	**Rindfleisch**
hare	**Hase**	braised pickled beef	**Sauerbraten**
heart	**Herz**	pickled lungs	**Saure Lunge**

diced meat with piquant sauce	Schaschlik	thin cutlet in breadcumbs	Wiener Schnitzel
ham	Schinken	boiled pork sausage	Wienerwurst
snail	Schnecke	wild game	Wild
uncoated cutlet	Schnitzel Natur	wild boar	Wildschwein
roast pork	Schweinebraten	sausage	Wurst
pork	Schweinefleisch	cutlet in paprika sauce	Zigeunerschnitzel
bacon	Speck		
turkey	Truthahn	tongue	Zunge

Fish

eel	Aal	mussels	Muscheln
trout	Forelle	rosefish	Rotbarsch
pike	Hecht	sardines	Sardinen
herring	Hering, Matjes	haddock	Schellfisch
lobster	Hummer	plaice	Scholle
cod	Kabeljau	swordfish	Schwertfisch
carp	Karpfen	sole	Seezunge
caviar	Kaviar	scampi	Scampi
crab	Krabben	tuna	Thunfisch
salmon	Lachs	squid	Tintenfisch
mackerel	Makrele	pike-perch	Zander

Vegetables

cauliflower	Blumenkohl	green or red peppers	Paprika
beans	Bohnen	jacket potatoes	Pellkartoffeln
fried potatoes	Bratkartoffeln	mushrooms	Pilze
button mushrooms	Champignons	chips/French fries	Pommes frites
peas	Erbsen	boiled potatoes	Salzkartoffeln
green beans	Grüne Bohnen	potato cake	Reibekuchen
cucumber	Gurke	Brussels sprouts	Rosenkohl
carrots	Karotten, Möhren	beetroot	Rote Rübe
mashed potatoes	Kartoffelbrei	red cabbage	Rotkohl
creamed potatoes	Kartoffelpuree	turnip	Rübe
potato salad	Kartoffelsalat	salad	Salat
garlic	Knoblauch	pickled cabbage	Sauerkraut
potato dumpling	Knödel, Kloss	asparagus	Spargel
lettuce	Kopfsalat	tomatoes	Tomaten
leeks	Lauch	white cabbage	Weisskohl
corn on the cob	Maiskolben	onions	Zwiebeln

Fruit

pineapple	Ananas	pear	Birne
apple	Apfel	blackberries	Brombeeren
apricot	Aprikose	dates	Datteln
banana	Banane	strawberries	Erdbeeren

figs	**Feigen**	orange	**Orange**
raspberries	**Himbeeren**	grapefruit	**Pampelmuse**
redcurrants	**Johannisbeeren**	peach	**Pfirsich**
cherries	**Kirschen**	plums	**Pflaumen**
stewed fruit or	**Kompott**	raisins	**Rosinen**
fruit mousse		blackcurrants	**Schwarze Johannis**
tangerine	**Mandarine**		**beeren**
melon	**Melone**	grapes	**Trauben**
fruit salad	**Obstsalat**	lemon	**Zitrone**

Cheeses and desserts

Swiss Emmental	**Emmentaler**	shredded pancake	**Kaiserschmarrn**
cheese board	**Käseplatte**	served with	
sheep's cheese	**Schafskäse**	powdered sugar,	
cream cheese	**Weichkäse**	jam & raisins	
goat's cheese	**Ziegenkäse**	cheesecake	**Käsekuchen**
apple strudel with	**Apfelstrudel mit**	biscuit	**Keks**
fresh cream	**Sahne**	doughnut	**Pfannkuchen**
jam doughnut	**Berliner**	nuts	**Nüsse**
large yeast	**Dampfnudeln**	nut cake	**Nusskuchen**
dumplings served		fruitcake	**Obstkuchen**
hot with vanilla		chocolate	**Schokolade**
sauce		Black Forest gateau	**Schwarzwälder**
ice cream	**Eis**		**Kirschtorte**
pastries	**Gebäck**	gateau, tart	**Torte**

Common terms

in the style of	**art**	traditional German	**gut bürgerliche**
rare	**blau**	home-made	**hausgemacht**
pickled	**eingelegte**	hot	**heiss**
fresh	**frisch**	cold	**kalt**
baked	**gebacken**	cooking	**Küche**
fried, roasted	**gebraten**	skewered	**spiess**
steamed	**gedämpft**	stew, casserole	**Topf, Eintopf**
stuffed	**gefüllt**	raw meats you cook	**vom heissen Stein**
grilled	**gegrillt**	yourself on a red-hot	
cooked	**gekocht**	stone	
smoked	**geräuchert**		

Glossaries

Art and architecture

Art Deco Geometrical style of art and architecture prevalent in the 1930s.

Art Nouveau Sinuous, highly stylized form of architecture and interior design; in Germany, mostly dates from the period 1900–15, and is known as Jugendstil.

Baroque Expansive, exuberant architectural style of the seventeenth and early eighteenth centuries, characterized by ornate decoration, complex spatial arrangements and grand vistas. The term is also applied to the sumptuous style of painting from the same period.

Bauhaus Plain, functional style of architecture and design, originating in early twentieth-century Germany.

Expressionism Emotional style of painting, concentrating on line and colour, extensively practised in early twentieth-century Germany; the term is also used for related architecture of the same period.

Gothic Architectural style with an emphasis on verticality, characterized by the pointed arch, ribbed vault and flying buttress; introduced to Germany around 1235, surviving in an increasingly decorative form until well into the sixteenth century. The term is also used for paintings of this period.

Neoclassical Late eighteenth- and early nineteenth-century style of art and architecture, returning to classical models as a reaction against Baroque and Rococo excesses.

Renaissance Italian-originated movement in art and architecture, inspired by the rediscovery of classical ideals.

Rococo Highly florid, light and graceful eighteenth-century style of architecture, painting and interior design, forming the last phase of Baroque.

Romanesque Solid architectural style of the late tenth to mid-thirteenth centuries, characterized by round-headed arches and a penchant for horizontality and geometrical precision. The term is also used for paintings of this period.

Romanticism Late eighteenth- and nineteenth-century movement, particularly strong in Germany, rooted in adulation of the natural world and rediscovery of the achievements of the Middle Ages.

German terms

Altstadt Old part of a city.

Auskunft Information.

Ausländer Literally "foreigner", the word has come to be a pejorative term for any non-White non -German.

Ausstellung Exhibition.

Bäckerei Bakery.

Bahnhof Station.

Bau Building.

Berg Mountain or hill.

Berliner Schnauze Sharp and coarse Berlin wit.

Bezirk City district.

Brücke Bridge.

Burg Mountain or hill.

Bushaltestelle Bus stop.

Denkmal Memorial.

Dom Cathedral.

Dorf Village.

Einbahnstrasse One-way street.

Elector (Kurfürst) Sacred or secular prince with a vote in the elections to choose the Holy Roman Emperor. There were seven for most of the medieval period, with three more added later.

Feiertag Holiday.

Flughafen Airport.

Fluss River.

Fremdenzimmer Room for short-term let.

Gasse Alley.

Gastarbeiter "Guest worker": anyone who comes to Germany to do menial work.

Gasthaus, Gasthof Guesthouse, inn.

Gaststätte Traditional bar that also serves food.

Gemälde Painting.

Grünen, die "The Greens": political party formed from environmental and antinuclear groups.

Habsburg The most powerful family in medieval Germany, operating from a power base in Austria. They held the office of Holy Roman Emperor 1452–1806, and by marriage, war and diplomacy acquired territories all over Europe.

Hauptbahnhof Main train station.

Haupteingang Main entrance.

Hof Court, courtyard, mansion.

Insel Island.

Jagdschloss Hunting lodge.

Jugendherberge Youth hostel.

Jugendstil German version of Art Nouveau.

Junker Prussian landowning class.

Kaiser Emperor.

Kammer Room, chamber.

Kapelle Chapel.

Kaufhaus Department store.

Kino Cinema.

Kirche Church.

Kneipe Bar.

Konditorei Cake shop.

Krankenhaus Hospital.

Kunst Art.

Markt Market, market square.

Motorrad Motorbike.

Neues Forum Umbrella group for political opposition organizations within the former GDR.

Not Emergency.

Ostpolitik West German policy of détente towards the GDR.

Platz Square.

Prussia Originally an Eastern Baltic territory (now divided between Poland and the Soviet Union). It was acquired in 1525 by the Hohenzollerns, who merged it with their own possessions to form Brandenburg-Prussia (later shortened to Prussia); this took the lead in forging the unity of Germany, and was thereafter its overwhelmingly dominant province. The name was abolished after World War II because of its monarchic and military connotations.

Quittung Official receipt.

Rastplatz Picnic area.

Rathaus Town hall.

Ratskeller Cellars below the Rathaus, invariably used as a restaurant serving *burgerlich* cuisine.

Reich Empire.

Reisebüro Travel agency.

Rundgang Way round.

Sammlung Collection.

S-Bahn Commuter train network operating in and around conurbations.

Schickie Abbreviation of "Schicki-Micki": yuppie.

Schloss Castle, palace (equivalent of French chateau).

See Lake.

Staatssicherheitsdienst (STASI) The former "State Security Service" or secret police of the GDR.

Stadt Town, city.

Stammtisch Table in a pub or restaurant reserved for regular customers.

Stiftung Foundation.

Strand Beach.

Strassenbahn Tram.

Tankstelle Filling station.

Tor Gate, gateway.

Trabi Conversational shorthand for the now famous Trabant, East Germany's two-cylinder, two-stroke people's car.

Turm Tower.

U-Bahn Network of underground trains.

Verkehrsamt, Verkehrsverein Tourist office.

Viertel Quarter, district.

Volk People, folk; given mystical associations by Hitler.

Wald Forest.

Wechsel Currency exchange office.

Weimar Republic Parliamentary democracy, established in 1918, that collapsed with Hitler's assumption of power in 1933.

Wende Literally, "turning point" – the term used to describe the events of November 1989 and after.

Zeitschrift Magazine.

Zeitung Newspaper.

Zeughaus Arsenal.

Zimmer room.

Acronyms

BRD (Bundesrepublik Deutschlands) official name of former West Germany.

CDU (Christlich Demokratische Union) Christian Democratic (Conservative) Party.

DB (Deutsche Bahn) national train company.

DDR (Deutsche Demokratische Republik) official name of former East Germany.

FDJ (Freie Deutsche Jugend) East German party youth organization.

GDR (German Democratic Republic) English equivalent of DDR.

NSDAP (National SozialistiSche Deutsche Abrbeiterparte) "National Socialist German Workers' Party", the official name for the Nazis.

SED (Sozialistische Einheitspartei Deutsch-lands) "Socialist Unity Party of Germany", the official name of the East German com-munist party before December 1989.

SPD (Sozialdemokratische Partei Deutsch-lands) Social Democratic (Labour) Party.

STASI slang term for the Staatssicherheitsdi-enst, the former East German secret police.

VOPO slang for Volkspolizei, a member of the East German police force.

Rough Guides

advertiser

Algarve • Amsterdam •
Antigua & Barbuda • Athens • Barbados • Barcelona •
Bruges • Cancún & Cozumel • Costa Brava •
Edinburgh • Florence • Ibiza & Formentera •
Lisbon • London • Madrid • Mallorca • Malta & Gozo •
Marrakesh & Essaouira • New Orleans •
New York City • Paris • Prague • Rome •
San Francisco • Tenerife & La Gomera •
Venice • Washington DC

US$10.99 · CAN$15.99 · £6.99

www.roughguides.com

small print and
Index

A Rough Guide to Rough Guides

In the summer of 1981, Mark Ellingham, a recent graduate from Bristol University, was travelling round Greece and couldn't find a guidebook that really met his needs. On the one hand there were the student guides, insistent on saving every last cent, and on the other the heavyweight cultural tomes whose authors seemed to have spent more time in a research library than lounging away the afternoon at a taverna or on the beach.

In a bid to avoid getting a job, Mark and a small group of writers set about creating their own guidebook. It was a guide to Greece that aimed to combine a journalistic approach to description with a thoroughly practical approach to travellers' needs – a guide that would incorporate culture, history and contemporary insights with a critical edge, together with up-to-date, value-for-money listings. Back in London, Mark and the team finished their Rough Guide, as they called it, and talked Routledge into publishing the book.

That first *Rough Guide to Greece*, published in 1982, was a student scheme that became a publishing phenomenon. The immediate success of the book – with numerous reprints and a Thomas Cook prize shortlisting – spawned a series that rapidly covered dozens of destinations. Rough Guides had a ready market among low-budget backpackers, but soon also acquired a much broader and older readership that relished Rough Guides' wit and inquisitiveness as much as their enthusiastic, critical approach. Everyone wants value for money, but not at any price.

Rough Guides soon began supplementing the "rougher" information about hostels and low-budget listings with the kind of detail on restaurants and quality hotels that independent-minded visitors on any budget might expect, whether on business in New York or trekking in Thailand.

These days the guides – distributed worldwide by the Penguin group – offer recommendations from shoestring to luxury and cover more than 200 destinations around the globe, including almost every country in the Americas and Europe, more than half of Africa and most of Asia and Australasia. Our ever-growing team of authors and photographers is spread all over the world, particularly in Europe, the USA and Australia.

In 1994, we published the *Rough Guide to World Music* and *Rough Guide to Classical Music*; and a year later the *Rough Guide to the Internet*. All three books have become benchmark titles in their fields – which encouraged us to expand into other areas of publishing, mainly around popular culture. Rough Guides now publish:

- Travel guides to more than 200 worldwide destinations
- Dictionary phrasebooks to 22 major languages
- History guides ranging from Ireland to Islam
- Maps printed on rip-proof and waterproof Polyart™ paper
- Music guides running the gamut from Opera to Elvis
- Restaurant guides to London, New York and San Francisco
- Reference books on topics as diverse as the Weather and Shakespeare
- Sports guides from Formula 1 to Man Utd
- Pop culture books from *Lord of the Rings* to Cult TV
- World Music CDs in association with World Music Network

Visit **www.roughguides.com** to see our latest publications.

Rough Guide credits

Text editor: Alison Murchie
Layout: Jessica Subramanian
Cartography: Jasbir Sandhu
Picture editor: Mark Thomas
Proofreader: Jan Wiltshire
Editorial: **London** Martin Dunford, Kate
Berens, Geoff Howard, Claire Saunders,
Ruth Blackmore, Gavin Thomas, Polly
Thomas, Richard Lim, Clifton Wilkinson,
Sally Schafer, Karoline Densley, Andy Turner,
Ella O'Donnell, Keith Drew, Edward Aves,
Andrew Lockett, Joe Staines, Duncan Clark,
Peter Buckley, Matthew Milton, Daniel Crewe,
Nikki Birrell, Chloë Thomson; **New York**
Andrew Rosenberg, Richard Koss, Chris
Barsanti, Steven Horak, AnneLise Sorensen,
Amy Hegarty
Design & Pictures: London Simon Bracken,
Dan May, Diana Jarvis, Mark Thomas,
Jj Luck, Harriet Mills, Chloë Roberts; **Delhi**
Madhulita Mohapatra, Umesh Aggarwal,
Ajay Verma, Amit Verma

Production: Julia Bovis, Sophie Hewat,
Katherine Owers
Cartography: **London** Maxine Repath,
Ed Wright, Katie Lloyd-Jones
Delhi Manish Chandra, Rajesh Chhibber,
Jai Prakash Mishra, Ashutosh Bharti, Rajesh
Mishra, Animesh Pathak, Karobi Gogoi
Online: **New York** Jennifer Gold, Suzanne
Welles, Benjamin Ross; **Delhi** Manik
Chauhan, Narender Kumar, Shekhar Jha,
Rakesh Kumar, Lalit Sharma
Marketing & Publicity: **London** Richard
Trillo, Niki Hanmer, David Wearn, Demelza
Dallow; **New York** Geoff Colquitt, Megan
Kennedy, Milena Perez; **Delhi:** Reem Khokhar
Custom publishing and foreign rights:
Philippa Hopkins
Finance: Gary Singh
Manager India: Punita Singh
Series editor: Mark Ellingham
PA to Managing Director: Megan McIntyre
Managing Director: Kevin Fitzgerald

Publishing information

This seventh edition published July 2005 by
Rough Guides Ltd,
80 Strand, London WC2R 0RL.
345 Hudson St, 4th Floor,
New York, NY 10014, USA.
14 Local Shopping Centre, Panchsheel Park,
New Delhi 110017, India
Distributed by the Penguin Group
Penguin Books Ltd,
80 Strand, London WC2R 0RL
Penguin Putnam, Inc.
375 Hudson Street, NY 10014, USA
Penguin Group (Australia)
250 Camberwell Road, Camberwell
Victoria 3124, Australia
Penguin Books Canada Ltd,
10 Alcorn Avenue, Toronto, Ontario,
Canada M4V 1E4
Penguin Group (New Zealand)
Cnr Rosedale and Airborne Roads
Albany, Auckland, New Zealand

Typeset in Bembo and Helvetica to an original
design by Henry Iles.

Printed and bound in China

© John Gawthrop and Rough Guides

No part of this book may be reproduced in any
form without permission from the publisher except
for the quotation of brief passages in reviews.

368pp includes index
A catalogue record for this book is available from
the British Library

ISBN 1-84353-2433-5

The publishers and authors have done their
best to ensure the accuracy and currency of all
the information in **The Rough Guide to Berlin**,
however, they can accept no responsibility for
any loss, injury, or inconvenience sustained by
any traveller as a result of information or advice
contained in the guide.

3   5   7   9   8   6   4

SMALL PRINT

Help us update

We've gone to a lot of effort to ensure that the
seventh edition of **The Rough Guide to Berlin**
is accurate and up-to-date. However, things
change – places get "discovered", opening
hours are notoriously fickle, restaurants and
rooms raise prices or lower standards. If you
feel we've got it wrong or left something out,
we'd like to know, and if you can remember
the address, the price, the time, the phone
number, so much the better.

We'll credit all contributions, and send a
copy of the next edition (or any other Rough

Guide if you prefer) for the best letters.
Everyone who writes to us and isn't already a
subscriber will receive a copy of our full-colour
thrice-yearly newsletter. Please mark letters:
"Rough Guide Berlin Update" and send to:
Rough Guides, 80 Strand, London WC2R
0RL, or Rough Guides, 4th Floor, 345 Hudson
St, New York, NY 10014. Or send an email to
mail@roughguides.com

Have your questions answered and tell
others about your trip at
www.roughguides.atinfopop.com

Acknowledgements

Christian Williams thanks the people of Wedding for being the salt-of-the-earth and Anabel for a room on Berlin's most dangerous street. Also in Berlin, thanks also to Eva for her unflinching supporting of BSC Preussen and Hertha and Iris for being Marzahn's best ambassador. Thanks also to Heather, Raymond, Dave, Swetha and the Licious for providing welcome distractions and company. At Rough Guides credit goes to Kate Berens and Martin Dunford for letting me rediscover my hometown and Alison Murchie for her carefully measured editorial work. Geoff Howard also deserves a special mention for pulling everything together at the end, as does Richard Lim for sweating the details on the maps.

Readers' letters

Many thanks to all those readers who took the time to write in with helpful comments about the last edition book. These included:

Adrian Brown, Chris Clayton, Isabella De Santis, Martina Dervis, Eric Dickson, Sebastian Doering, John Everson, Mike Fisher, Hugh Giles, Lisa Godson, Sebastian Harcombe, Richard Hardy, John Harrison, Frances Harrison, Peter Herbert, Sara Humphreys, James M Hyland, Linda Jackson, Chris JJ, Peter Lowthian, Steve Moloney, Alice O'Reilly, Fiona Robb, Gavin Rodgers, Martin Rumsby, Jim Sewell, Mary Shelly, Roger Sturge, Geoff Taylor, Onno van Wilgenburg, George Walker, Clifton Wilkinson and Harvey Woolf.

Photo credits

Cover credits

Main front cover Schloss Sanssouci © Robert Harding

Small front top picture Berliner Rathaus, Rathausstrasse © Mark Thomas

Small front lower picture Botanical Gardens © Alamy

Back top picture Westphal café, Prenzlauer Berg © Alamy

Back lower picture Reichstag dome © Mark Thomas

Introduction

Street sign pointing to Unter den Linden © Picture Finders/Powerstock

Statue of Angel and Greek Warrior on the Schlossbrucke © Mark Thomas

Pergamon Museum © Doug Scott/Powerstock

Sony Center © Robert Harding Picture Library/Alamy

Kurrywurst Sausages © Bill Boch/FoodPix/Getty Images

Jewish Museum © Christian Williams

The Love Parade © Michaela Rehle/Reuters/Corbis

The Reichstag and German flag © Steven Weinberg/Getty Images

Plaque showing the route of the Berlin Wall © Jiri Rezac/Alamy

Berliner Dom © Mark Thomas

Tiergarten Park © Jorg Greuel/The Image Bank/Getty Images

The Federal Chacellery building © foybles/Alamy

Detail of the Victory Column Statue © Doug Scott/Powerstock

Waiter in Berlin café © Doug Scott/Powerstock

The Love Parade © Tom Oldham/www.everynight.co.uk

The Pergamon Museum © Doug Scott

The Olympic Stadium © Fabrizio Bensch/Reuters/Corbis

Detail of The Quadriga on The Brandenburg Gate © Doug Scott/Powerstock

Things not to miss

01 Sanssouci Palace © Christian Williams
02 The Reichstag © PCL/Alamy
03 Jewish Museum © Christian Williams
04 Tiergarten © Peter Rigaud/Network

Photographers

05 Berliner Weisse © Christian Williams
06 Berlin's clubbing scene © Walter Schmitz/Network Photographers
07 East Side Gallery © Peter W Wilson/Axiom
08 Berlinomat © Christian Williams
09 Tacheles © Diana Jarvis
10 The Pergamon Museum © Doug Scott
11 Schloss Charlottenburg © Martin Rugner/Powerstock
12 Sony Center © Robert Harding Picture Library/Alamy
13 Kaiser-Wilhelm Gedachniskirche © David Barnes/Stone/Getty Images
14 Hackescher Hofe © Atlantide S.N.C/Powerstock
15 KaDeWe Department Store © archivberlin Fotoagentur GmbH/Alamy
16 The Love Parade © Michaela Rehle/Reuters/Corbis
17 Fernsehturm © Mark Thomas
18 Kurrywurst Sausages © Bill Bock/FoodPix/Getty Images
19 Berlin Wall Memorial © Reuters/Corbis
20 People in bar © Atlantide S.N.C./Powerstock
21 Sunday Brunch © Christian Williams
22 Brandenburg Gate © Andrew Stagg/Alamy
23 Flea Market © archivberlin Fotoagentur GmbH/Alamy
24 Sachsenhausen © Christian Williams
25 Café Sibylle © Christian Williams

Black and white photos

Potsdamer Platz © Mark Thomas p.71

Alte Nationalgalerie © archivberlin Fotoagentur GmbH/Alamy p.81

Berliner Rathaus © Mark Thomas p.92

Jewish Memorial Cobbles © Christian Williams p.110

Haus der Kulturen der Welt © Pat Behnke/Alamy p.116

View along Taunzienstrasse © Christina Williams p.133

Ex Communist tower block in Karl Marx Allee © foybles/Alamy p.161

Soviet Memorial © Christian Williams p.175

Peacock on Peacock Island © Christian Williams p.196

New Palais © Joern Sackermann/Alamy p.213

Index

Map entries are in colour.

INDEX

N

O

P

Q

R

INDEX

INDEX

Piano Salon
Christophori

Martin gropious
Bauhaus

Map symbols

maps are listed in the full index using coloured text

▬▬▬▪	International boundary	ℂ	Phone office
▬ ▬ ▬	Chapter division boundary	✈	Airport (General)
▬▬▬	Motorway	✗	Airport (Domestic)
═══	Major road	(i)	Tourist office
═══	Minor road	⊠	Post office
▬▬▬	Pedestrianised road	E	Embassy
▬▬▬	Unpaved road	◉	Accommodation
▬▪▬	Railway	▣	Restaurant
▬▬▬	River	▬	Building
··········	Wall	⊞	Church
⊔	Bridge	▭	Market
✦	Place of interest	⬭	Stadium
✡	Synagogue	⊞⁺	Christian cemetery
⊙	Statue	▨	Park
Ⓤ	U-Bahn station	⠿	Beach
Ⓢ	S-Bahn station	▨	Jungle

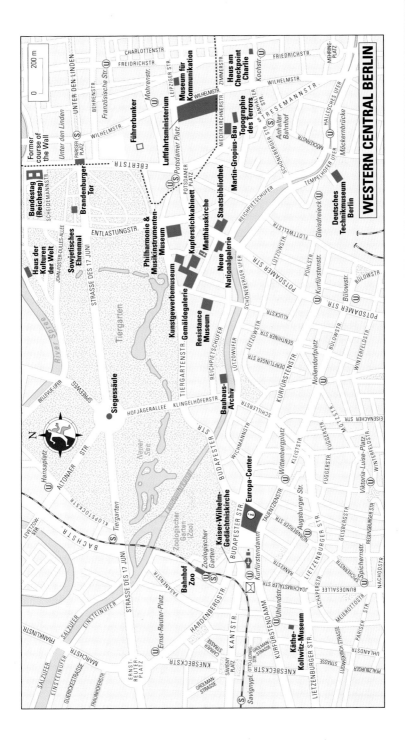

WESTERN CENTRAL BERLIN

0   200 m

Former course of the Wall

Bundestag (Reichstag)

Brandenburger Tor

Haus der Kulturen der Welt

Sowjetisches Ehrenmal

Führerbunker

Museum für Kommunikation

Haus am Checkpoint Charlie

Luftfahrtministerium

Topographie des Terrors

Martin-Gropius-Bau

Staatsbibliothek

Philharmonie & Musikinstrumenten-Museum

Kupferstichkabinett

Matthäuskirche

Kunstgewerbemuseum

Gemäldegalerie

Neue Nationalgalerie

Resistance Museum

Deutsches Technikmuseum Berlin

Bauhaus-Archiv

Siegessäule

Tiergarten

Europa-Center

Kaiser-Wilhelm-Gedächtniskirche

Bahnhof Zoo

Zoologischer Garten (Zoo)

Käthe-Kollwitz-Museum

River Spree

Unter den Linden

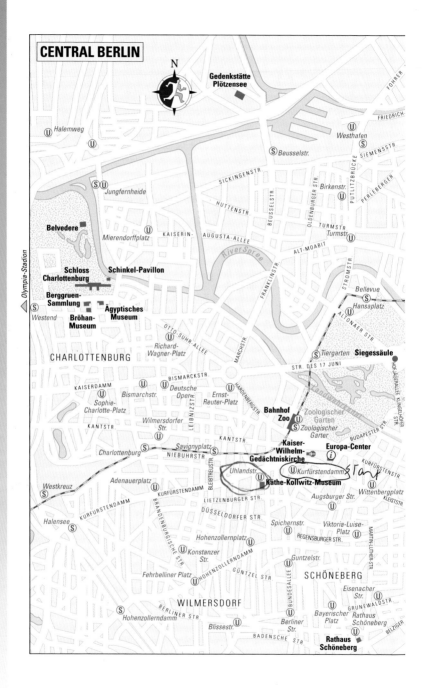

CENTRAL BERLIN

N

Gedenkstätte
Plötzensee

FÖHRER

FRIEDRICH

Ⓤ Halemweg

Ⓤ Westhafen
Ⓢ

Ⓢ Beusselstr.

SIEMENSSTR

PUTLITZBRÜCKE

PERLEBERGER

Ⓢ Ⓤ
Jungfernheide

SICKINGENSTR

Birkenstr. Ⓤ

HUTTENSTR

BEUSSELSTR

OLDENBURGER STR

Belvedere ■

Ⓤ Mierendorffplatz   KAISERIN-   AUGUSTA-ALLEE

TURMSTR
Turmstr. Ⓤ

River Spree

ALT-MOABIT

Olympia-Stadion

Schloss
Charlottenburg   Schinkel-Pavillon

FRANKLINSTR

STROMSTR

Bellevue

Ⓢ Hansaplatz

ALTONAER STR

Berggruen-
Sammlung   Ägyptisches
Westend   Bröhan-   Museum
Museum

OTTO-SUHR-ALLEE

MARCHSTR

Ⓢ Tiergarten Siegessäule ●

CHARLOTTENBURG   Richard-
Wagner-Platz

STR DES 17 JUNI

HOFJÄGERALLEE   KLINGELHÖFER STR

BISMARCKSTR.

Landwehrkanal

KAISERDAMM   Ⓤ Deutsche
Ⓤ Bismarckstr.   Oper   Ernst-
Reuter-Platz

HARDENBERGSTR

Sophie-
Charlotte-Platz   Bahnhof   Zoologischer
Zoo   Garten

KANTSTR.   Wilmersdorfer   Ⓢ Zoologischer
Str.   Garten   BUDAPESTER STR

LEIBNIZSTR

Charlottenburg Ⓢ   Savignyplatz Ⓢ   KANTSTR.   Kaiser-   Europa-Center
NIEBUHRSTR   Wilhelm-   ⓘ
Gedächtniskirche   KURFÜRSTENSTR

Uhlandstr. Ⓤ   Ⓤ Kurfürstendamm Start
BLEIBTREUSTR

Adenauerplatz Ⓤ   Käthe-Kollwitz-Museum ■   Wittenbergplatz
Ⓤ

Westkreuz   KURFÜRSTENDAMM   LIETZENBURGER STR   Augsburger Str.   KLEISTSTR
Ⓢ

BRANDENBURGISCHE STR   DÜSSELDORFER STR

Halensee   KURFÜRSTENDAMM   Spichernstr. Ⓤ   Viktoria-Luise-
Ⓢ   Platz Ⓤ

Hohenzollernplatz Ⓤ   REGENSBURGER STR

MARTIN-LUTHER-STR

Konstanzer   Ⓤ Guntzelstr.
Str. Ⓤ

Fehrbelliner Platz Ⓤ   HOHENZOLLERNDAMM   GÜNTZEL STR   SCHÖNEBERG

BUNDESALLEE

WILMERSDORF   Eisenacher
Str. Ⓤ

Ⓢ   BERLINER STR   Bayerischer   GRUNEWALDSTR
Hohenzollerndamm   Platz   Ⓤ Rathaus
Schöneberg

Blissestr.   Berliner   BELZIGER
Str.   BADENSCHE STR

Rathaus ■
Schöneberg

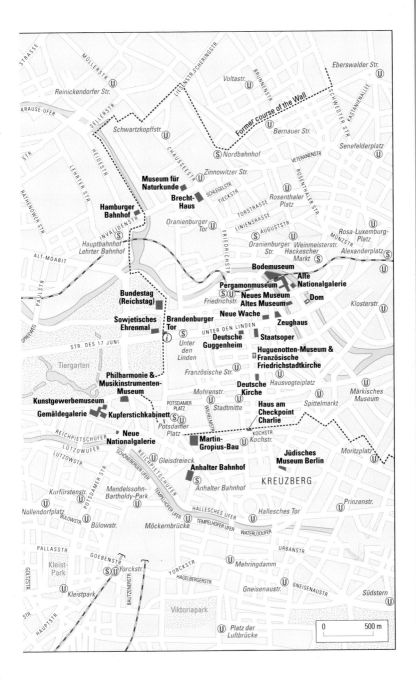

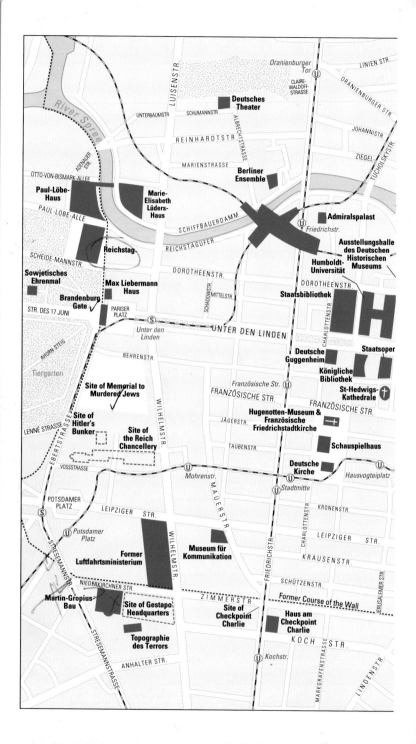

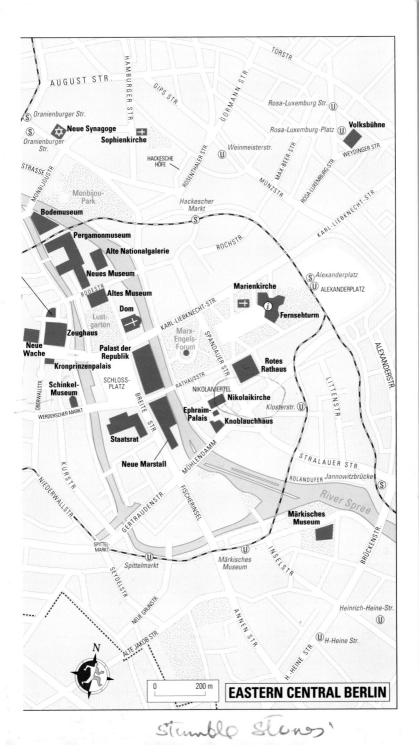

EASTERN CENTRAL BERLIN

0 — 200 m

stumble stones'

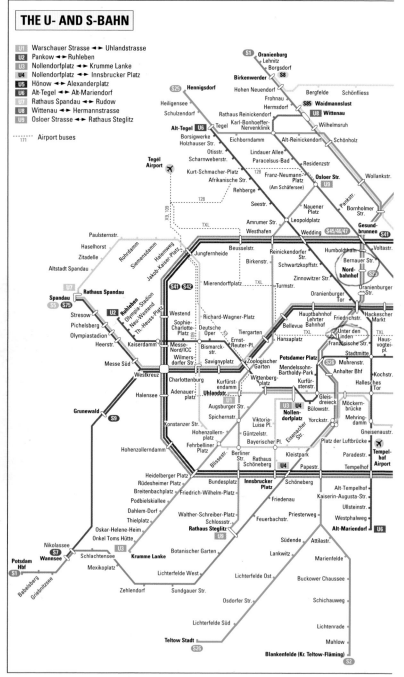

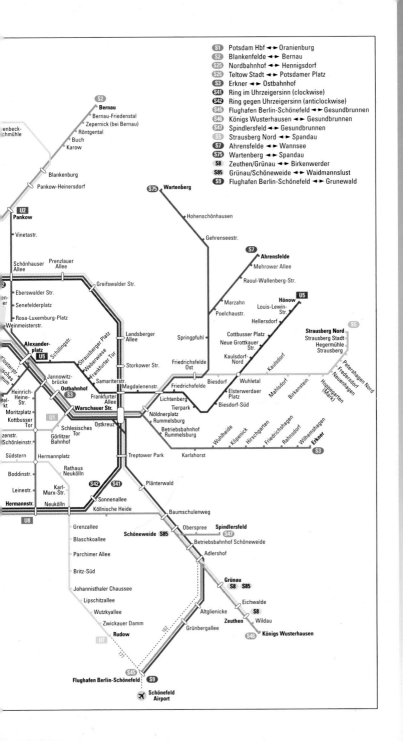

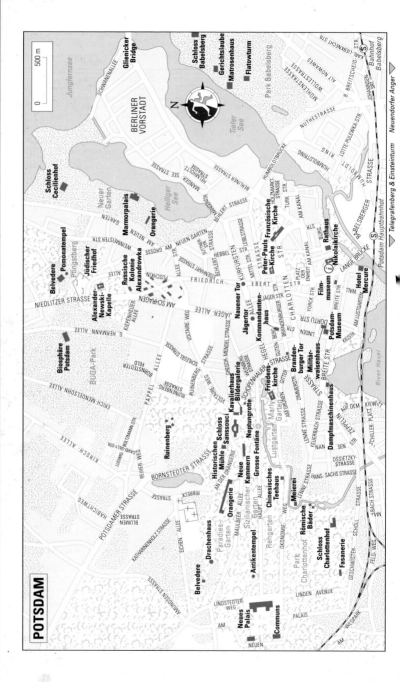

POTSDAM

0 — 500 m

Jungfernsee

Glienicker Bridge

BERLINER VORSTADT

Schloss Babelsberg
Gerichtslaube
Matrosenhaus
Flatowturm

Park Babelsberg

Tiefer See

N

SCHWANENALLEE

MÖHRENSTRASSE
WOLLESTRASSE
ALT NOWAWES

BRETSCHEID STR.
KARL-LIEBKNECHT STR.
S Bahnhof Babelsberg

JOHANNSEN STR.
WOLLSTRASSE

NUTHESTRASSE

HUMBOLDTRING
LOTTE-PULEWKA-STR.

HUMBOLDT-BRÜCKE

RING

BABELSBERGER STRASSE
S Potsdam Hauptbahnhof

BERLINER STRASSE

Schloss Cecilienhof

Neuer Garten

MANGER STRASSE
HEMLMOLTZ STRASSE
SEE STRASSE

Heiliger See

NEUEN GARTEN

Marmorpalais
Orangerie

AM NEUEN

Belvedere
Pomonatempel

Pfingstberg

Jüdischer Friedhof

WEINMEISTER STR

Russische Kolonie Alexandrowka

AM GROSSE

NEUEN GARTEN STRASSE

Peter-Pauls Kirche
Französische Kirche

HOLZMARKT STRASSE

GROSSE WEINMEISTER STRASSE

PUSCHKIN ALLEE

TÜRK STR.
AM KANAL

Rathaus
Nikolaikirche
i

Alexander-Newski-Kapelle

KIEFENHEUER ALLEE

FRIEDRICH-

EBERT

HEBBEL STR.

KURFÜRSTEN STR.

MITTEL STR.
LIEBKNECHT STR.
BEHLERT STR.

Nauener Tor

JÄGER STR.

CHARLOTTEN STR.

LINDEN STR.
DORTU STR.
BREITE STR.

EINHEIT

PLATZ DER

BURG STR.

LANGE BRÜCKE

River Havel

NIEDLITZER STRASSE

G. HERMANN ALLEE

AM SCHRAGEN

ALLEE

VOLTAIRE WEG

Jägertor

Kommandanten-haus

BRANDENBURGER STRASSE

YORCK STR.

Film-museum

Potsdam-Museum

Hotel Mercure

AM LUSTGARTEN

HALL

BREITE STR.

KIESTR.

Biosphäre Potsdam

BUGA-Park

ERICH-MENDELSOHN-ALLEE

BÖRNSTEDTER

PAPPEL ALLEE

GREGOR-MENDEL-STRASSE

RUINENBERG STRASSE

SCHLEGEL STRASSE

DREWITZER STRASSE

NUENBERG STRASSE

SCHOPENHAUER STR.

HEGEL ALLEE

GUTEN BERG STR.

ZIMMER STR.

GUTEN STR.

Bildergalerie
Kavalierhaus
Neptungrotte

Friedens-kirche

AM GRÜNEN GITTER

Marly Garten

Branden-burger Tor
Militär-waisenhaus

BRANDENBURGER STRASSE

LENNE STRASSE

FEUERBACH STRASSE

NAN

ZEPPELIN STR.

AUF DEM KIEWITT

SCHILLER PLATZ

KIRSCH- ALLEE

Ruinenberg

DAVID-GILLY-STR.

ROBERT-KOCH-STR.

REIHER- WEG

Historischen Mühle
Schloss Sanssouci

AN DER ORANGERIE

Neue Kammern

Grosse Fontäne

Lustgarten

SEN STR.

OSSIETZKY-STRASSE

HANS- SACHS STRASSE

Dampfmaschinenhaus

HABICHTWEG

POTSDAMER STRASSE

BLUMEN-STRASSE
KATHARINENHOLZ STRASSE

RIBBECK STRASSE

BORNSTEDTER STRASSE

Drachenhaus

Paradies-Garten

EICHEN ALLEE

MAULBEER ALLEE

HAUPT ALLEE

Sizilianischer Garten

Chinesisches Teehaus

Meierei

LENNE STRASSE

ÖKONOMIE WEG

Römische Bäder

GESCHWISTER-SCHOLL STRASSE

FELD- WEG

BACH STRASSE

MM

Belvedere

AMUNDSON STRASSE

Antikentempel

Rehgarten

Park Charlottenhof

Schloss Charlottenhof

Fasanerie

LINDSTEDTER WEG

AM PALAIS

LINDEN AVENUE

PALAIS

AM NEUEN

Neues Palais

Communs

NEUEN

WILDPARK

AM

▶ Telegrafenberg & Einsteinturm   Neuendorfer Anger ▶